THE JEWISH TRAVEL GUIDE 1994

Editor
STEPHEN W. MASSIL

VALLENTINE MITCHELL

First published in 1994 in Great Britain by
VALLENTINE MITCHELL & CO. LTD.
Gainsborough House, Gainsborough Road,
London E11 1RS, England

The Jewish Travel Guide is distributed in the United States
and Canada by Sepher Hermon Press Inc., Publishers and
Distributors of Better Jewish Books, 1265 46th Street,
Brooklyn, New York, N.Y. 11219. Tel. (718) 972-9010.

ISBN 0-85303-273-4
ISSN 0075-3750

Printed by KSC Printers, High Brooms Industrial Estate, Tunbridge Wells, Kent TN2 3DR

CONTENTS

IMPORTANT NOTICE

Extensive research is undertaken for every annual revision of the **Jewish Travel Guide** and every effort is made to ensure accuracy. Nevertheless, **no responsibility can be accepted for any errors or omissions,** or for kashrut and other claims by establishments listed in the Guide.

Particular attention must be drawn to the fact that many kosher establishments change hands often and suddenly, in some instances ceasing to be kosher. It is in travellers' best interests to obtain confirmation of kashrut claims before completing their arrangements.

Readers are asked kindly to draw attention to any errors or omissions.

EXPLANATION OF SYMBOLS

(K) An hotel, restaurant, caterer or other establishment under the supervision of a recognised Jewish religious authority (e.g. the London Kashrus Commission, Kedassia, the local Beth Din or rabbi). In most countries there is no central Jewish kashrut authority as in Britain.

★ An establishment which, while claiming to be strictly kosher, is not under official supervision. Such an establishment is stated to possess three essential characteristics:

(i) that the meat, and all other foods, utensils, etc., are strictly kosher;

(ii) that the separation of meat and milk in the kitchens and at table is assured;

(iii) that Shabbat and the Holy-days are observed by strict adherence to all rules including — "No smoking" — and, where possible, that religious services are held.

Establishments without a star are not kosher. They have been included because they may be of interest to readers of the *Jewish Travel Guide* for other than dietary reasons.

A figure in brackets after an establishment's name shows the number of rooms.

(V) Vegetarian establishment. A list of vegetarian organisations is given on p. 370.

ABBREVIATIONS

Accom.	Accommodation	M.	Minister
Admin.	Administrator	Mon.	Monday
Assoc.	Association	Opp.	Opposite
Av.	Avenue	Pde.	Parade
Bdway.	Broadway	Pk.	Park
Bldg(s).	Building(s)	Pl.	Place
Cl.	Close	Princ.	Principal
Cnr.	Corner	Sat.	Saturday
Cong.	Congregation	Sec.	Secretary
Cres.	Crescent	Sq.	Square
Dr.	Doctor, Drive	St.	Saint, Street
Evg(s).	Evening(s)	Str.	Straat, Strasse
Fri.	Friday	Sun.	Sunday
Gdns.	Gardens	Syn.	Synagogue
Gr.	Grove	Tel.	Telephone
Grn.	Green	Ter.	Terrace
Hd.	Headmaster/Headmistress	Thurs.	Thursday
Inf.	Information	Tues.	Tuesday
Inq.	Inquiries	Wed.	Wednesday

Festivals and Fasts in 1994 (5754-5755)

Fast of Esther	Thursday	February 24th
Purim	Friday	February 25th
First Day Pesach	Sunday	March 27th
Second Day Pesach	Monday	March 28th
Seventh Day Pesach	Saturday	April 2nd
Eighth Day Pesach	Sunday	April 3rd
Holocaust Memorial Day	Friday	April 8th
Israel Independence Day	Thursday	April 14th
Jerusalem Day	Monday	May 9th
First Day Shavuot	Monday	May 16th
Second Day Shavuot	Tuesday	May 17th
Fast of Tammuz	Sunday	June 26th
Fast of Av	Sunday	July 17th
First Day Rosh Hashanah	Tuesday	September 6th
Second Day Rosh Hashanah	Wednesday	September 7th
Fast of Gedaliah	Thursday	September 8th
Yom Kippur	Thursday	September 15th
First Day Succot	Tuesday	September 20th
Second Day Succot	Wednesday	September 21st
Shemini Atseret	Tuesday	September 27th
Simchat Torah	Wednesday	September 28th
First Day Chanucah	Monday	November 28th
Fast of Tevet	Tuesday	December 13th

Yizkor in 1994

Yizkor is recited in synagogues on the following days: Eighth day Pesach, Sunday, April 3rd; Second day Shavuot, Tuesday, May 17th; Yom Kippur, Thursday, September 15th; Shemini Atseret, Tuesday, September 27th.

Some Notable Days in 1995 (5755-5756)

First Day Pesach	Saturday	April 15th
Eighth Day Pesach (Yizkor)	Saturday	April 22nd
First Day Shavuot	Sunday	June 4th
Second Day Shavuot (Yizkor)	Monday	June 5th
First Day Rosh Hashanah (5756)	Monday	September 25th
Second Day Rosh Hashanah	Tuesday	September 26th
Yom Kippur (Yizkor)	Wednesday	October 4th
First Day Succot	Monday	October 9th
Shemini Atseret (Yizkor)	Monday	October 16th

GREAT BRITAIN

GREATER LONDON

Well over half the 300,000 (1991) Jews of Britain live in London. Numbering about 210,000, they are spread throughout the Metropolis, with the largest concentration in North-Western districts like Golders Green, Edgware and Hampstead Garden Suburb. There are also large communities in North London (Stamford Hill, Stoke Newington and Clapton) and in the East (Barkingside and Clayhall). Once it was in Stepney that the biggest part of London Jewry lived and, in spite of many changes there, Aldgate and Whitechapel should be visited, not only for the many reminders of their Jewish heyday, but also for the bustling life which is still to be seen there.

THE CITY

There are many historically interesting sites in the City, that square mile of Central London which adjoins the East End. The Bank of England, with its Underground station of the same name, is a useful starting point.

One of the numerous streets which converge on this busy hub is Poultry, leading quickly to Cheapside. The first street on the right is **Old Jewry**. Here, and in the neighbourhood, the earliest community lived before England expelled all its Jews in 1290. There were synagogues in this street and in Gresham and Coleman Sts., not far from historic **Guildhall**, which is itself a "must" for tourists.

Another synagogue stood on the site of the present National Westminster Bank at 52 Threadneedle St., which starts at the Bank of England and runs on the left of the **Royal Exchange**.

Inside the Exchange a series of murals includes one by Solomon J. Solomon, R.A., of "Charles I Demanding the Five Members", and a portrait of Nathan Mayer Rothschild, who founded the London house of the famous banking firm. There was a time when the south-east corner of the Royal Exchange was known as "Jews' Walk".

The **Rothschild headquarters** is not far away, in St. Swithin's Lane. To reach this handsome building (which has in its entrance-hall more Rothschild portraits, as well as a large tapestry of Moses striking the rock), cross carefully from the Royal Exchange to the Lord Mayor's Mansion House and then turn left into King William St.

Cornhill, which stretches eastwards from the Bank, leads to Leadenhall Street and its shipping offices and, after a short walk, to Creechurch Lane and the **Cunard building**, on the back of which is an interesting plaque. "Site of the First Synagogue after the Resettlement 1657-1701. Spanish and Portuguese Jews' Congregation" is the inscription. Here the post-Expulsion Jews whom Oliver Cromwell welcomed to England set up their house of prayer. In 1701 they built a synagogue in **Bevis Marks** (close by), modelling it on the famous Portuguese Synagogue in Amsterdam. It has been scheduled by the Royal Commission on Ancient Historical Monuments as "a building of outstanding value", and is considered one of the most beautiful pieces of synagogue architecture extant. In it are some benches from the Creechurch Lane Synagogue. Visitors wishing to see the Bevis Marks synagogue the oldest in the British Commonwealth should 'phone 071-626 1274.

London's chief Ashkenazi place of worship, the **Great Synagogue**, stood, until it was bombed during the Second World War, in Duke's Place, which adjoins Bevis Marks. The "Duke's Place Shool" (as it was called) was the country's best-known synagogue, the scene of many great occasions and a popular choice for marriages. On the wall of International House, which has replaced it, there is a plaque informing the visitor that the synagogue stood there "from 1690 and served the community continuously until it was destroyed in September, 1941".

After the Second World War and until the 1970s, the Great Synagogue was in Adler St., named after the two Chief Rabbis of that name, Rabbi Nathan Marcus Adler and his son, Rabbi Dr. Hermann Adler. Duke's Place leads to Aldgate High St. where, on the opposite side, **Jewry Street** marks another centre of the pre-Expulsion community. At the time of Richard I's coronation many Jews, escaping from rioting mobs, moved here from Old Jewry.

THE EAST END

Further eastwards, along Aldgate High St., is Middlesex St., which becomes the crowded **Petticoat Lane** every Sunday morning. The cheerful and cheeky language of the stall-holders has made "The Lane" famous throughout the world. On week-days an offshoot, Wentworth Street, continues the market.

Eastwards again, to Whitechapel, which has changed almost out of all recognition since the days before the Second World War, when it had a teeming Jewish population. Just beyond Aldgate East Underground station, three familiar spots remain Bloom's Restaurant, Whitechapel Art Gallery and Whitechapel Library.

The library's extensive Yiddish collection has been transferred to the Taylorian Library, Oxford University's modern-language library. Next comes Osborne St., leading to Brick Lane. A large and sombre building in Brick Lane (at the corner of Fournier St.) represents more than anything else the changes that have taken place in the East End over the years. The Huguenots built it as a church, the Jews turned it into a synagogue (the Machzike Hadass), and now the Bengalis, who have replaced the Jews, have converted it into a mosque.

The former synagogue in **Princelet St.** (No. 19) is being converted into a museum by the Spitalfields Trust, which is collaborating with the London Museum of Jewish Life to develop the building to show the history of the different immigrant groups which have inhabited the Spitalfields area during the past 300 years. For further information about activities at the Princelet St. Building, contact the London Museum of Jewish Life, Tel. 081-349 1143.

The Jewish Community Exhibition Centre has taken over a section of the **Spitalfields Market** for a regular display of exhibitions of Anglo-Jewish history.

Brune St., the Soup Kitchen for the Jewish Poor, was established there in 1902. It still serves the small elderly Jewish community in the area, opening on Tuesday mornings. Before Pesach, it distributes matzot and other kosher le-Pesach items. In 1991 it was taken over by Jewish Care, the largest Jewish social service organisation in Britain.

Outside **Whitechapel Underground station** and just to the right of it, opposite the London Hospital, stands a drinking fountain. It was erected in 1911 "in Loyal and Grateful Memory of Edward VII Rex et Imperator from subscriptions raised by Jewish inhabitants of East London".

Next to the former offices of the Federation of Synagogues in the former Synagogue Community Centre is the Kosher Luncheon Club. This establishment maintains a strong Jewish tradition and still caters for local as well as business people who require a wholesome dairy meal at lunchtime. This is provided in an informal atmosphere and visitors can learn from the clientele something of the former glories of the East End.

Adler Street (Whitechapel) is named after two Chief Rabbis Nathan Marcus Adler and his son Dr. Hermann Adler who served Anglo-Jewry for over 65 years.

Brady St. is the site of an old cemetery, opened for the New Synagogue in 1761 and subsequently used also by the Great Synagogue. The cemetery became full in the 1790s, and it was decided to put a four-foot thick layer of earth over part of the site, using this for further burials. This created a flat-topped mound in the centre of the cemetery. The cemetery is perhaps the only one where, because of the two layers, the headstones are placed back to back. Among those buried here are: Solomon Hirschel, who was Chief Rabbi from 1802-1842, and Nathan Meyer Rothschild (1777-1836), the banker. To view the cemetery, contact the United Synagogue Burial Society. Tel. 071-387 7891.

In **Mile End** there are three more old cemeteries: two Sephardi and one Ashkenazi. Behind 253 Mile End Rd., where the Sephardi Home for the Aged (Beth Holim) was located before moving to Wembley, is the first Resettlement cemetery, the oldest existing Anglo-Jewish cemetery, opened in 1657.

Abraham Fernandez Carvajal, regarded as the founder of the modern Anglo-Jewish community, is buried here, and also Haham David Nieto, one of the greatest of Sephardi spiritual leaders. At 329 Mile End Rd., the Nuevo Beth Chaim, opened in 1725, contains the grave of Haham Benjamin Artom. This is among the 2,000 graves remaining on the site. Some 7,500 were transferred to a site in Brentwood, Essex, during the 1970s. The earliest Ashkenazi cemetery, acquired in 1696, is in Alderney Rd., and here the founders of the Duke's Place Synagogue, Moses and Aaron Hart and others, and also the "Baal Shem of London" (the Cabbalist, Haim Samuel Falk), lie buried. In **Beaumont Gr.**, on the south side of Mile End Rd., is the Stepney B'nai B'rith Clubs and Settlement, which caters primarily for the needs of the 7,500 Jews still living in the East End.

In Commercial Rd., **Hessel Street**, another Jewish market centre, is now occupied by Bengali traders. **Henriques Street** is named after Sir Basil Henriques, a leading welfare worker and magistrate, and founder of the Bernhard Baron St. George's Jewish Settlement, who died in 1961. On the same side, three turnings along, is **Alie Street**. At the Jewish Working Men's Club here in July, 1896, Theodor Herzl addressed a meeting which was effectively the launching of the Zionist movement in Britain.

WEST CENTRAL

Chief Rabbi Hermann Adler (1891-1911) is honoured at the Central Court, the **Old Bailey** (Underground station: St. Paul's), where a mural over the entrance to Court No. 1, entitled "Homage to Justice," includes the figure of Dr. Hermann Adler. By the City Boundary High Holborn is the Royal Fusiliers City of London Regiment Memorial. The names of the 38th, 39th and 40th (Jewish Batallions) are inscribed on the monument together with all other batallions which served in the First World War. At the western edge of the City, Chancery Lane Station, Holborn, is a useful centre for several points of interest. To the east, Furnival St. has the "Jewish Chronicle" office. Northward, Gray's Inn Rd. leads to Theobald's Rd. There, at No. 22, a plaque on the wall recalls that it is the birthplace of **Benjamin Disraeli.** Further to the north is Great Russell Street, which runs along part of the south side of the British Museum. No. 77 Great Russell Street was the headquarters of the Zionist organisations from 1919 to 1964. (From then until 1980, they were at Rex House in Lower Regent Street. Since 1980, they have been in the North-West London suburb of Finchley.) Westward, in Chancery Lane, the **Public Record Office** has in its vast collection many documents of Jewish historical value, including the petitions to Cromwell.

Woburn House, in Upper Woburn Pl., near Euston Station, is British Jewry's principal communal building. The United Synagogue, the Board of Deputies of British Jews, the Anglo-Jewish Association and the Central Council for Jewish Religious Education are some of the organisations whose offices are here. Here also is the **Jewish Museum**, with a fascinating collection of old ritual articles and Anglo-Judaica. Note however, that the Museum is due to move to new premises in 1994 (see p. 18). The Chief Rabbi's offices and the court of the London Beth Din are in Adler House (Tavistock Square), which adjoins Woburn House. **B'nai B'rith-Hillel House**, the student centre, is at 1-2 Endsleigh St., close by.

This is near the University neighbourhood. In the building of University College in Gower St., the **Jewish Studies Library** houses the *Altmann, Mishcon* and *Mocatta Libraries* and the *Margulies* Yiddish Collection. And the School of Oriental and African Studies in the University precinct includes Judaica and Israelitica in its library. Hebrew printed books and manuscripts are on display in the Kings library at the British Museum in Great Russell Street.

WEST END

A permanent art collection has been accumulated by the **Ben Uri Art Society** — at 21 Dean St., Soho, above the West End Great Synagogue.

In the **Marble Arch** district, in the part of Hyde Park known as "The Dell", a Holocaust Memorial Garden was dedicated in June, 1983. The garden plot was given over by the British Government to the Board of Deputies, which commissioned Mr. Richard Seifert to design the memorial centre-piece rocks bearing a quotation from the Book of Lamentations. Also in the Marble Arch area, you will find an important associate of the United Synagogue (the recently amalgamated Western and Marble Arch Synagogues in Great Cumberland Place), as well as the West London (Reform) Synagogue (Upper Berkeley St.) and the magnificent Victorian New West End Synagogue in St. Petersburg Place, just off Bayswater Road.

The British Zionist Federation was inaugurated at the Trocadero Restaurant in **Piccadilly Circus** in January, 1899. At 175 Piccadilly was the London bureau of the Zionist Organisation, set up in August, 1917. Here, Dr. Chaim Weizmann and other Zionist leaders worked, and here, in November, 1917, the Balfour Declaration was delivered by Lord Rothschild. The **Westminster Synagogue** in Rutland Gdns., Knightsbridge, houses the Czech Memorial Scrolls Centre, where there is a permanent exhibition telling the story of the salvaging from Prague in 1964 of 1,564 Torah Scrolls confiscated by the Nazis during the Second World War, and of their restoration and the donation of many to communities throughout the world. The exhibition is open from 10a.m. to 4p.m. on Tuesdays and Thursdays, and at other times by appointment.

In **St. John's Wood** are three more interesting synagogues: the New London (Abbey Rd.) and the St. John's Wood (Grove End Rd.), where the Chief Rabbi, who lives in near-by Hamilton Terrace, generally worships. The third synagogue of great interest in St. John's Wood is the Liberal Jewish, opposite Lord's Cricket Ground recently rebuilt and renovated.

STAMFORD HILL

Of London's many synagogues, one remarkable group is the series of Chasidic "shtiblech" in Stamford Hill (and the yeshivot which are attached to some of them). **Cazenove Rd.** contains several of these, and it is here and in the vicinity that the long coats and wide hats of Chasidim and the curled sidelocks of their children are to be seen. The Lubavitch Foundation headquarters and the Yesodey Hatorah Schools are in Stamford Hill.

In this district, also, are many North African, Adeni, Indian and some Persian Jews and their synagogues.

NORTH WEST

The starting point for visiting North-West London is **Golders Green.** Jews first settled here during the First World War, and the **Golders Green Synagogue** (United) in Dunstan Rd., was opened in 1922. Walk down Golders Green Rd., from the Underground station for half a mile or so, and you will come to Broadwalk Lane on the right-hand side, where the **Lincoln Institute** is. This is the home of Ohel David, a congregation of Indian Jews, many of whom came to England when India was partitioned in 1947. Their forebears went to India from Baghdad.

On the opposite side of the road, at the end of a short turning called The Riding, is the **Golders Green Beth Hamedrash**—familiarly known as "Munk's" after its founder in the 1930s, Rabbi Dr. Eli Munk. This very Orthodox congregation, mainly of German origin, adheres to the religious principles of Rabbi Samson Raphael Hirsch. There are many other strictly Orthodox congregations in Golders Green, including Chasidic groups.

Any of the buses travelling along Golders Green Rd. away from the Underground station will take you to Bell Lane, in Hendon. A few hundred yards down on the left-hand side is Albert Rd., where you will find **Jews' College** — established in 1855 as an Institute of Higher Education and associated with London University for many years. A group of Persian Jews holds Shabbat morning services there. Its 70,000-volume library is open to the public.

Also in **Hendon** in Egerton Gardens, a turning opposite Barnet Town Hall in The Burroughs 10-15 minutes walk from Bell Lane, is **Yakar**, which provides a wide variety of adult educational and cultural programmes and has a lending library. Several minyanim are held here on Shabbat and festivals. Further information is available on 081-202 5552.

Return to Golders Green Underground station from Hendon Central, either by Underground or by bus. Once there, take a bus northwards along Finchley Rd. for two miles or so, getting off at **East End Rd.**, which is more or less opposite the bus stop.. On the right-hand side is the **Sternberg Centre**, the largest Jewish community centre in Europe. The Georgian former manor house contains **Leo Baeck College**, with its library of 18,000 books, which trains Reform & Liberal rabbis; the offices of the **Reform Synagogues of Great Britain**, and the **London Museum of Jewish Life**. In addition to permanent displays, the museum, one of London's newest, also mounts special exhibitions and runs walking tours and educational programmes. In the Centre's grounds, you will find a Holocaust memorial, as well as a biblical garden and such more mundane places as a bookshop and a dairy snack bar.

You can return to Central London by bus or Underground. (The nearest station is Finchley Central.)

Synagogues & Religious Organisations

Chief Rabbinate

Rabbi Dr Jonathan Sacks was inducted into office in September 1991 in succession to Lord Jakobovits. Inq. to the Exec. Dir., Jonathan Kestenbaum, Office of the Chief Rabbi, Adler Hse., Tavistock Sq., WC1H 9HN. Tel. 071-387 1066.

Beth Din (Court of the Chief Rabbi)
The London Beth Din is at Adler Hse., Tavistock Sq., WC1H 9HP. Tel. 071-387 5772.

United Synagogue
Executive Office: Woburn Hse., Tavistock Sq., WC1H 0EZ. Tel. 071-387 4300.
Barking & Becontree, 200 Becontree Av. Becontree, Essex, RM8 2TR.
Barnet, Eversleigh Rd., New Barnet, Herts., EN5 1NE.
Belmont, 101 Vernon Dr., Stanmore, Middx., HA7 2BW.
Borehamwood & Elstree, Croxdale Rd., Borehamwood, Herts., WD6 2QF.
Bushey, 177-189 Sparrows Herne, Bushey, Herts., WD2 1AJ.
Catford & Bromley, 6 Crantock Rd., SE6 2QS.
Central,. 36-40 Hallam Street, London, W1N 5LH
Chelsea, Smith Ter., Smith St., SW3.
Chigwell and Hainault, Limes Av., Limes Farm Estate, Chigwell, Essex.
Clayhall, Sinclair House, Wordford Bridge Rd., Ilford, Essex, IG6 1AF.
Cockfosters & N. Southgate, Old Farm Av., Southgate, N14 5QR.
Cricklewood, 131 Walm Lane, NW2 3AU.
Dollis Hill, Parkside, Dollis Hill Lane, NW2 6RE.
Ealing, 15 Grange Rd., Ealing, W5 5QN.
East London & Hackney, Brenthouse Rd., E9 6AG.
Edgware, Edgware Way, Edgware, Middx.
Edmonton & Tottenham, 41 Lansdowne Rd., N17.
Elm Park, 75 Woburn Av., Elm Park, Hornchurch, Essex, RM12 5EA.
Enfield & Winchmore Hill, 53 Wellington Rd., Bush Hill Pk., Enfield.
Epsom, Prospect Pl., East St., Epsom, Surrey.
Finchley, Kinloss Gdns., N3 3DU.
Finsbury Park, Green Lanes, N4 2NT.
Golders Green, 41 Dunstan Rd., NW11 8AE.
Hammersmith & West Kensington, 71 Brook Green, W6 7BE.
Hampstead, 1 Dennington Park Rd., NW6 1AX.
Hampstead Garden Suburb, Norrice Lea, N2 0RE.
Harold Hill, Trowbridge Rd., Harold Hill, Essex.
Hemel Hempstead, Rosetta Hse., Midland Rd., Hemel Hempstead, Herts., HD1 1RP
Hendon, Raleigh Close, NW4.
High Wycombe, 33 Hampden Rd., High Wycombe, Bucks., HP13 6SZ.
Highams Park & Chingford, 74 Marlborough Rd., E4 9AZ.
Highgate, Grimshaw Cl., North Rd., N6 4BJ.
Hounslow, 100 Staines Rd., Hounslow, Middx.
Ilford, 84 Beehive Lane, Ilford, Essex, IG1 3RT.
Kenton, Shaftesbury Av., Kenton, Middx., HA3 0RD.
Kingsbury, Woodland Cl., Kingsbury Green, NW9 8XR.
Kingston & Surbiton, 33-35 Uxbridge Rd., Kingston-upon-Thames, Surrey.
Marble Arch, See Western Marble Arch (p.)
Mill Hill, Brockenhurst Gdns. NW7 2JY.
Muswell Hill, 31 Tetherdown, N10 1ND.
New, Egerton Rd., N16 6UD
Newbury Park, 23 Wessex Close, Suffolk Rd., Newbury Park, Essex, IG3 8JU.
New West End, St. Petersburgh Pl., W2 4JT.
Palmers Green & Southgate, Brownlow Rd., N11 2BN.
Peterborough, 142 Cobden Av., Peterborough, Northants., PE1 1IL.
Pinner, 1 Cecil Park, Pinner, Middx. HA5 5HJ.
Potters Bar & District, Inq. to R. Drexler, P.O.B. 119, Potters Bar, Herts.
Richmond, Lichfield Gdns. Richmond-on Thames, Surrey, TW9 1AP.

Romford, 25 Eastern Rd., Romford, Essex.
Ruislip, Shenley Av., Ruislip Manor, Middx., HA4 6BP.
St. Albans, Oswald Rd., St. Albans, Herts.
St. John's Wood, 37-41 Grove End Rd., NW8 1AP.
South Hampstead, Eton Villas. 22 Eton Rd., NW3 4SP.
South London, 45 Leigham Court Rd., SW16 2NF.
South Tottenham, 111-113 Crowland Rd., N15 6UL.
South-West London, 104 Bolingbroke Gr., SW11 1DA.
Staines, Westbrook Rd., South St., Staines, Middx., TW18 4PR.
Stanmore & Canons Park, London Rd., Stanmore, Middx., HA7 4NS.
Sutton, 14 Cedar Rd., Sutton, Surrey, SM2 5DA.
Wanstead and Woodford, 20 Churchfields, E18 2QZ.
Watford, 16 Nascot Rd., Watford, Herts., WD1 3RE.
Welwyn Garden City, Barn Cl., Handside Lane, Welwyn Garden City, Herts., AL8 6ST.
Wembley, Forty Av., Wembley, Middx., HA9 8JW.
West Ham & Upton Park, 93-95 Earlham Gr., E7 9AN.
Willesden & Brondesbury, 143-145 Brondesbury Pk., NW2 5JL.
Woodside Park, Woodside Hall, Woodside Park Rd., N12 8RZ.

Federation of Synagogues
Headquarters: 65 Watford Way, London, NW4 3AQ. Admin: 081-202 2263. Burial: 081-202 3903. Fax. 081-203 0610.

Beth Din
Dayan Yisroel Yaacov Lichtenstein is Rosh Beth Din.
Inq. to the Clerk of the Beth Din: Ahavath Shalom (Neasden), Clifford Way, NW10.
Croydon & District, 30 Elmwood Rd., Croydon, Surrey.
East London Central, 38-40 Nelson St., E1.
Fieldgate St. Great, 41 Fieldgate St., E1.
Finchley Central, Redbourne Av., N3.
Finchley Road (Sassover), 4 Helenslea Av., London, NW11.
Great Garden St., 7 Greatorex St., E1.
Greenford Oldfield Lane, Greenford Middx.
Ilford Federation, 16 Coventry Rd., Ilford, Essex.
Leytonstone & Wanstead, 2 Fillebrook Rd., E11.
Loughton, Chigwell & District Borders Lane, Loughton, Essex, IG10 3HT.
Machzike Hadath (Spitalfields), Highfields Rd., NW11.
Notting Hill, 206-208 Kensington Park Rd., W11.
Sha'are Shomayim (Clapton), 47 Lea Bridge Rd., E5.
Shomrei Hadath, 527a Finchley Rd., NW3.
Sinai, 54 Woodstock Av., NW11.
Springfield, 202 Upper Clapton Rd., E5.
Stamford Hill Beth Hamedrash, 50 Clapton Common, E5 9AL.
Tottenham, 366 High Rd., N17.
Waltham Forest 140 Boundary Rd., E17
West End Great 21 Dean St., W1.
West Hackney, 233 Amhurst Rd., E8 2BS.
Woolwich & District, Anglesea Rd., SE8.
Yavneh, 25 Ainsworth Rd., E9 9JE.
Yeshurun, Fernhurst Gdns., Edgware, Middx., HA8 7PH.

Union of Orthodox Hebrew Congregations
Headquarters: 40 Queen Elizabeth's Walk, N16 0HH. Tel. 081-802 6226-7.
Adath Yisroel (Parent) Synagogue, 40 Queen Elizabeth's Walk, N16 0HH.
Adath Yisroel Tottenham Beth Hamedrash, 55/57 Ravensdale Rd., N16.
Ahavat Israel Synagogue D'Chasidey Viznitz, 89 Stamford Hill, N16.

Beit Knesset Chida, 147 Clapton Common, E5.
Beth Abraham Synagogue, 46 The Ridgeway, NW11.
Beth Chodosh Synagogue, 51 Queen Elizabeth's Walk, N16.
Beth Hamedrash Beis Nadvorna, 45 Darenth Rd., N16 6ES.
Beth Hamedrash D'Chasidey Belz, 99 Bethune Rd., N16.
Beth Hamedrash D'Chaddey Belz, 96 Clapton Common, E5.
Beth Hamedrash D'Chasidey Gur, 2 Lampard Grove, N16.
Beth Hamedrash D'Chasidey Ryzin, 33 Paget Rd., N16.
Beth Hamedrash D'Chasidey Sanz Klausenburg, 42 Craven Walk, N16.
Beth Hamedrash D'Chassidey Square, 22 Dunsmure Rd., N16.
Beth Hamedrash Divrei Chaim, 71 Bridge La., NW11.
Beth Hamedrash Hendon, 3 The Approach, NW4 2HU.
Beth Hamedrash Imrey Chaim D'Chasidey Vishnitz-Monsey, 121 Clapton Common, E5.
Beth Hamedrash Kehillas Yacov, 35 Highfield Av., NW1 9EV.
Beth Hamedrash Ohel Moshe, 202B Upper Clapton Rd., E5.
Beth Hamedrash Ohel Naphtoli (Bobov), 87 Egerton Rd., N16.
Beth Hamedrash of the Agudah Youth Movement, 69 Lordship Rd., N16. Also 95 Stamford Hill, N16.
Beth Hamedrash Spinke, 36 Bergholt Cres., N16 5SE.
Beth Hamedrash Torah Etz Chayim, 69 Lordship Rd., N16.
Beth Hamedrash Torah Chaim Liege, 145 Up. Clapton Rd., E5.
Beth Hamedrash Toras Chaim, 37 Craven Walk, N16 6BS.
Beth Hamedrash Vayoel Moshe, 14 Heathland Rd., N16.
Beth Hamedrash Yetiv Lev, O'Satmar, 86 Cazenove Rd., N16. Also 26 Clapton Common, E5.
Beth Israel (Trisker) Synagogue, 146 Osbaldeston Rd., N16.
Beth Shmuel Synagogue, 171 Golders Green Rd., NW11.
Beth Sholom Synagogue, 27 St. Kilda's Rd., N16.
Beth Talmud Centre, 78 Cazenove Rd., N16.
Beth Yisochor Dov Beth Hamedrash, 2-4 Highfield Av., NW11.
Birkath Yehuda (Halaser) Beth Hamedrash, 47 Moundfield Rd., N16 6DT.
Bridge Lane Beth Hamedrash, 44 Bridge Lane, NW11 0EG.
Etz Chaim Yeshiva, 83/85 Bridge Lane, NW11.
Finchley Road Synagogue, 4 Helenslea Av., NW11.
Garden Suburb Beth Hamedrash, Jacob & Alexander Gordon Hse., 5 The Bishop's Av., N2.
Hampstead Adath Yisroel Congregation (Sarah Klausner Memorial Synagogue), 10a Cranfield Gdns., NW6
Heichal Hatorah, 27 St. Kildas Rd., N16.
Hendon Adath Yisroel Synagogue, 11 Brent St., NW4 2EU.
Kehal Chasidim D'Munkatch Synagogue, 85 Cazenove Rd., N16.
Knightland Road Synagogue of the Law of Truth Talmudical College, 50 Knightland Rd., E5. Corr: 27 Warwick Grove, E5 9HX.
Lubavitch Synagogue, 107-115 Stamford Hill, N16.
Mesifta Synagogue, 82-84 Cazenove Rd., N16.
North Hendon Adath Yisroel Synagogue, Holders Hill Rd., NW4 1NA. corr.: 31 Holders Hill Crescent, NW4 1NE.
Ohel Israel (Skoler) Synagogue, 11 Brent St., NW4.
Shaare Zion, 10 Woodberry Down, N4.
Stanislowa Beth Hamedrash, 93 Lordship Park, N16
Yeshiva Horomoh Beth Hamedrash, 100 Fairholt Rd., N16 5HH.
Yeshuath Chaim Synagogue, 45 Heathland Rd., N16.
Yesodey Hatorah Synagogue, 2/4 Amhurst Pk., N16.
Zichron Shlomo Beth Hamedrash, 9 Elm Park Av., N15.

Spanish and Portuguese Jews Congregation
Bevis Marks, EC3. Inq. to 071-626-1274.
Lauderdale Rd., Maida Vale, W9.
Wembley, 46 Forty Av., Wembley, Middx.
Inq. to the Vestry Offices, 2 Ashworth Rd., W9 1JY. Tel. 071-289 2573.
Other Sephardi congs. in London include:
Aden Jews' Cong., 117 Clapton Common, E5.
Gan Eden, 140 Stamford Hill, N16.
Holland Park, St. James's Gdns., W11.
Lincoln Institute, Broadwalk Lane, NW11.
Neveh Shalom, 352-354 Preston Rd., Harrow, Middx.
Ohel David (Ilford) Cong., Newbury Pk Stn., Newbury Pk., Essex.
Sephardi Minyan, 62 Brent St., NW4.

Assembly of Masorti Synagogues
Admin. Office of Assembly of Masorti Syns., 766 Finchley Rd., NW11 7TH.
Tel. 081-201 8772. Fax. 081-201 8917.
Presiding Rabbi: Rabbi Dr. Louis Jacobs.
Edgware Masorti Syn., Brady Maccabi Centre, 4 Manor Pk. Cres., Edgware,
Middx. Office: 26 Old Rectory Gardens, Edgeware. Tel. 081-952 4987.
New Essex Masorti Cong., Prince Regent Hotel, Woodford Bridge, Essex.
Inq.: Tel. 081-524 3564.
New London Syn., 33 Abbey Rd., St. John's Wood, NW8 0AT. Tel. 071-328
1026.
New North London Syn., The Manor House, 80 East End Rd., N3 2SY. Tel.
081-346 8560.
New Whetstone Masorti Syn. Services, Oxford and St. George's 120,
Oakleigh Rd. North, N20. Inq.: Tel. 081-346 8560.
South-West London Masorti Syn. Inq.: Tel. 081-941 2984.
St. Albans Masorti Synagogue. Inq.: Tel. 0727 848778.

Independent Synagogues
Belsize Square Synagogue, 51 Belsize Square, NW3 3TP. Tel. 071-794-3949.
Golders Green Beth Hamedrash Cong., The Riding, Golders Green Rd.,
NW11 8HL. Tel. 081-455 2974. Rav: Rabbi H.I. Feldman.
Lubavitch, 107/115 Stamford Hill, N16 5RP. Tel. 081-800 0022.
Machzike Hadath, 3 Highfield Rd., NW11 9LU. Hon. Sec.: R. Shaw. Tel.
081-204 1887, M. Bitami. Tel. 081-455 0449.
Ner Yisrael Community, The Crest, off Brent St., NW4 2HY. Tel. 081-202-
6687. Rabbi A. Kimche, B.A. Tel. 081-455-7347
Persian Hebrew Congregation, East Bank, Stamford Hill, N16 5AL.
Walford Road Syn., Walford Rd., Stoke Newington, N16. Sec.: H. L. Corb.
Tel. 081-800-7839 (eves).
West End Great, 21 Dean St., W1V 6NE. Tel. 071-437 1873. Fax. 071-287
1543.
Western Marble Arch Synagogue, 32 Gt Cumberland Pl., W1H 7DJ. Tel.
071 723 7246. Sec. M. Frey.
Westminster, Rutland Gdns., Knightsbridge, SW7 1BX. Tel. 071-584 3953.

Reform Synagogues
Headquarters: The Manor House, 80 East End Rd., N3 2SY. Exec. Dir.:
Raymond M. Goldman. Tel. 081-349 4731. Mikvah on premises.
Bromley & District, 28 Highland Rd., Bromley, Kent, BR1 4AD. Tel. 081-460
5460.
Buckhurst Hill. Chairman: Frank Godson, 11A The Mall, Southgate,
London, N14. Tel. 081-886 9344
Buckhurst Hill — Services are held at Bedford House Community Centre,
Buckhurst Hill, Essex.

Edgware, 118 Stonegrove, Edgware, Middx., HA9 8AB. Tel. 081-958 9782.
Finchley, Fallowcourt Av., N12 0BE. Tel. 081-446 3244.
Hampstead. Chairman: Michael Teper, 63 Ornan Rd,, London NW3 4QD.
Tel. 071-794 8488.
Hendon, Danescroft Av., NW4 2NA. Tel. 081-203 4168.
Kol Chai — Hatch End Jewish Community, Chairman: Jon Pentel, 54
Grove Farm Park, Northwood, Middx., HA6 2BQ. Tel. 0923 825571.
Middlesex New, 39 Bessborough Rd., Harrow, Middx., HA1 3BS. Tel. 081-
864 0133.
Mill Hill, Kingsbury and District. Chairman: Michael Casale, 51 Hale
Drive, London, NW7 3EL. Tel. 081-959 8655.
Milton Keynes & District. Inf. from Chairman: Stephen Bonn, 83 Whalley
Drive, Bletchley, Milton Keynes, Bucks., MK3 6HX. Tel. 0908-649378.
North Kensington Reform Synagogue, Beit Klal Yisrael, services at 17
Chepstow Villas, London, W11. Chairman: Lesley Urbach, 32 Kingswood
Court, West End Lane, London, NW6 4SX.
North-West Surrey, Horvath Cl., Rosslyn Pk., Oatlands Dr., Weybridge,
Surrey, KT13 9QZ. Tel. 0932 55400.
North-Western, Alyth Gdns., Finchley Rd., NW11 7EN. Tel. 081-455 6763.
Radlett & Bushey, 118 Watling St., Radlett, Herts., WD7 7AA. Tel. 0923
856110.
Settlement Synagogue, 2-8 Beaumont Gr., E1. Tel. 071-790 6262.
Southgate & District, 45 High St., N14. Tel. 081-882 6828.
South-West Essex, Oaks Lane, Newbury Park, Essex, IG2 7PL. Tel. 081-559
0936.
West London Synagogue of British Jews, 33 Seymour Pl., W1N 6AT. Tel.
071-723 4404.
Wimbledon, 44-46 Worple Rd., SW19. Tel. 081-946 4836.

Liberal Synagogues
Headquarters of Union of Liberal and Progressive Syns.: 109 Whitfield St.,
W1P 5RP. Tel. 071-580 1663. Fax. 071-436 4184.
Barkingside Progressive Syn., 129 Perrymans Farm Rd., Barkingside,
Ilford, Essex.
Chiltern Progressive Syn., Friends' Meeting House, 28 Crawley Gn. Rd.,
Luton, Beds.
Ealing, Lynton Av., Drayton Gr., W13 0EB.
Finchley, 54a Hutton Gr., N12 8DR.
Harrow & Wembley Progressive Syn., 326 Preston Rd., Harrow, Middx.
Hertsmere Progressive Syn., High St., Elstree, Herts.
Kingston Liberal Syn., Rushett Rd., Long Ditton, Surbiton, Surrey.
Liberal Jewish Synagogue, 28 St John's Wood Rd., London, NW8 7HA.
North London Progressive Syn., 100 Amhurst Pk. N16 5AR.
Northwood & Pinner, Oaklands Gate, Northwood, Middx.
Settlement Synagogue, c/o Stepney Jewish Settlement, 2-8 Beaumont Gr.,
E1. (See also Reform Synagogues.)
Southgate Progressive Syn., 75 Chase Rd., N14 4QY.
South London, Prentis Rd., Streatham, SW16 1QB.
West Central, 109-113 Whitfield St., W1 5RP.
Woodford Progressive Synagogue, Marlborough Rd., George Lane, E18.

KASHRUT AUTHORITIES, etc.
Federation Kashrus Board (Federation of Synagogues), 65 Watford Way,
London NW4 3AQ. Admin: 081-202 2263 Fax. 081-203 0610. Dir. of
Kashrus: Dayan M. D. Elzas.
Kashruth Division, The London Beth Din, Adler Hse., Tavistock Sq.,

WC1H 9HP. Tel. 071-387 4300. Dir., Rabbi Jeremy Conway. Kashrut Hotline 071 383 2468.
Joint Kashrus Committee-Kedassia (Union of Orthodox Hebrew Congs.), 67 Amhurst Park, N16 5DL. Admin.: M. Kester. Tel. 081-800 6833.
London Board for Shechita, P.O.B. 579, Adastra Suite., 401-405 Nether St., N3 1YR. Tel. 081-349 9160.
Sephardi Kashrut Authority, 2 Ashworth Rd., W9 1JY. Ch.: E. H. Silas. Tel. 071-289 2573. Fax. 071-289 2709. Dir: Rabbi I. S. Abraham.

MIKVAOTH
Adath Yisroel Synagogue Mikvah, 40a Queen Elizabeth's Walk, London, N16 0HH (corner 28 Grazebrook Rd.). Tel. 081-802 2554.
Craven Walk Mikvah, 72 Lingwood Rd., N16. Tel. 081-800 8555 (day: Mrs. Dunner) 081-809 6279 (eve).
Edgware Communal Mikvah, Edgware United Synagogue grounds, Approach from 22 Warwick Ave Drive., or from Synagogue car park. Tel. 081 958 3233.
Ilford Mikvah (Fed. of Synagogues), 463 Cranbrook Road, Ilford, Essex. Tel. 081-554 8532 (even.) or Mrs. Matlin 081-554 2551 (day). All correspondence to Rabbi Livingston, 367 Cranbrook Rd., Ilford, Essex.
Kingsbury Mikveh See below: United Synagogue Mikveh.
Mikvaot (Union of Orthodox Hebrew Congs.). Central Mikvaot Board, 40 Queen Elizabeth's Walk, N16 0HH. Tel. 081-802 6226-7.
North West London Communal Mikvah, 10a Shirehall Lane, Hendon, NW4. Tel. Daytime 081-202 7692. Evenings 081-202 8517/5706.
Reform Mikvah, The Manor House, 80 East End Rd., N3 2SY. Tel. 081-349 4731.
Satmar Mikvah, 62 Filey Av., N16. Tel. 081-806 3961.
South London Mikvah, 42 St George's Rd., Wimbledon, SW19 4ED. Tel. 081-944 1581.
Stamford Hill and District Mikvah, Margaret Rd., N16. Tel. 081-806 3880; 800 5119/809 4064.
United Synagogue Mikveh, Kingsbury Green, Kingsbury, NW9 8XR. Tel. 081-204 6390.
There are also Mikvaoth in many provincial towns.

REPRESENTATIVE ORGANISATIONS
Anglo-Jewish Assoc., 5th Floor, Woburn Hse., Upper Woburn Pl., WC1H 0EP. Tel. 071-387 5937.
Assoc. of Jewish Ex-Servicemen & Women (Ajex), Ajex Hse., East Bank, N16 5RT. Gen. Sec.: Harry A. Farbey. Tel. 081-800 2844. Fax. 081-880 1117.
Assoc. of Jewish Refugees in Gt. Britain, Hannah Karminski Hse., 9 Adamson Rd., NW3 3HX. Tel. 071-483 2536.
Assoc. of Jewish Women's Orgs. in the U.K., 5th Floor, Woburn Hse., Upper Woburn Pl., WC1H 0EP. Tel. 071-387 7688.
B'nai B'rith, B'nai B'rith Hillel Hse., 1-2 Endsleigh St., WC1H 0DS. Tel. 071-387 5278. Exec. Dir.: Mark Marcus. There are more than 50 B'nai B'rith lodges in Britain & Ireland, & 24 B'nai B'rith Youth Organisation (BBYO) chapters. Further details from Tel. above.
B'nai B'rith Hillel Foundation, B'nai B'rith Hillel Hse., 1-2 Endsleigh St., WC1H 0DS. Tel. 071-388 0801. **(K)** Kosher restaurant open in term-time 12.30 p.m. to 2.00 p.m. Mon.-Thurs.; Friday night Shabbat dinners available if booked and paid in advance by Thursday 11 a.m. Students, graduates & adults from home & abroad welcomed. Closed Shabbat & festivals. Tel. 071-388 0801.
Board of Deputies of British Jews, Woburn Hse., Upper Woburn Pl., WC1H 0EP. Tel. 071-387 3952. The officially recognised representative

body of British Jewry, founded in 1760. **Central Enquiry Desk**, 071-387 4044.

Commonwealth Jewish Council, Somerset House, 37 Fortess Rd., London NW5 1AD. Tel. (071) 267 7991. Fax. (071) 267 6394.

Council of Christians & Jews, Dir. Michael Latham, M.A., Dip.Ed., F.R.S.A., 1 Dennington Pk. Rd., West End La., NW6 1AX. Tel. 071-794 8178-9. Fax. 071-431-3500.

Federation of Jewish Relief Organisations, Polish Jewish Refugee Fund, 143 Brondesbury Pk., NW2 5JL.
Tel. 081-451 3425. Sec.: Mrs. R. Gluckstein.

World Jewish Congress (United Kingdom), 79 Wimpole St., W1M 7DD. Tel. 071 935-8266. Tel. 071-491 3517. Inter alia, represents Jewish interests and rights vis-à-vis governmental and international authorities.

CULTURAL & EDUCATIONAL ORGANISATIONS, etc.

Ben Uri Art Society & Gallery, 4th Floor, 21 Dean St., W1V 6NE. Tel. 071-437 2852. Permanent collection of works by Jewish artists including Bomberg, Gertler & Epstein. Temporary exhibitions by contemporary Jewish artists and on subjects of Jewish interest. 1994 programme includes exhibitions by Alain Kleinmann, Leonard Baskin and Slade Professor Bernard Cohen. Group visits welcomed. Mon-Thurs 10-5 Sun 2-5. Closed Bank & Jew. Holidays. Curator: Julia Weiner.

British Library, Oriental & India Office Collections, 197 Blackfriars Rd., SE1 8NG. Inq. Tel. 071-928 9531, ext. 262.
The Hebrew section contains about 70,000 volumes and 13,000 manuscripts and fragments. Daily 9.30 a.m. to 4.45 p.m.: Sat, 9.30 a.m. to 12.45 p.m.

British ORT, Queen Mary and Westfield College, Kidderpore Av., NW3 7ST. Tel. 071-431 5001.

College for Higher Rabbinical Studies, Tifereth Shalom, 37 Craven Walk, London N16 6BS, Tel. 081-800-3868. Mr A. Y. Landau, Main Office, 101, Osbaldston Rd, N16 6NP.

Institute of Contemporary History and Wiener Library, 4 Devonshire St., W1N 2BH. Tel. 071-636 7247. With 50,000 books and periodicals, and over 1,000,000 press cuttings, etc., the library serves as a research institute and reference centre for 20th-century history (especially Germany), modern Jewish history and anti-semitism, minorities, refugees, fascism, etc. Mon. to Fri., 10 a.m. to 5.30 p.m.

Institute of Jewish Affairs, 79 Wimpole St., W1M 7DD. Tel. 071-935 8266. Publications, lectures, seminars on contemporary issues affecting world Jewry. Reference library available (by appointment).

Jewish Historical Society of England. Office: 33 Seymour Pl., W1H 5AP. Hon. Sec. C. M. Drukker; Admin: Mrs. J. Cannon. Tel. 071-723 4404. See also Jewish Studies Library entry.

Jewish Memorial Council, Woburn Hse., Tavistock Sq., WC1H 0EP. Tel. 071-387 3081.

Jewish Museum, 1st Floor, Woburn Hse., Tavistock Sq., WC1H 0EP. Tel. 071-388 4525. Open Sun. & Tues.-Thurs. (& Fri. in summer), 10 a.m. to 4 p.m.; Fri. & Sun. in winter, 10 a.m. to 12.45 p.m. Closed Mon., Sat. & Jewish & national holidays. Groups by previous arrangement with the Sec. Entrance £1, students with card 50p, children free. Due to move to 129 Albert St., NW1 in mid-1994 and the Museum will be closed for two months. Following this it will be open Sun.-Thurs. 10-5 throughout the year.

The Jewish Studies Library within University College London Library, Gower Street, London WC1E 6BT (Tel. 071-387 7050, Fax. 071-380 7373). In addition to materials purchased for the College's Department of Hebrew Studies it incorporates the Mocatta Library, Altmann Library, William

Margulies Yiddish Library and the Library of the Jewish Historical Society of England. Applications to use or view the collections should be made in advance in writing to the Librarian.

Jews' College, Albert Rd., NW4 2SJ. Tel. 081-203 6427. Fax. 081-203 6420. The library, which contains 80,000 volumes, 20,000 pamphlets, 700 manuscripts, and over 1000 audio and video cassettes is open as follows: Mon.-Thurs., 9 a.m. to 5 p.m.; Fri., 9 a.m. to 1 p.m.; Sun. during term-time, 9.30 a.m. to 12.30 p.m. Closed on all Jewish Holy-days, festivals & public holidays. Erev Yom Tov, closed 1 p.m.

Leo Baeck College, The Sternberg Centre for Judaism, 80 East End Rd., N3 2SY. Tel. 081-349 4525. Vegetarian Cafeteria.

London Academy of Jewish Studies (Kollel Harabbanim), 2-4 Highfield Av., NW11 9ET. Hon. Princ.: Rabbi G. Hager. Tel. 081-455 8205 (office), 081-458 1264 (students).

The London Museum of Jewish Life, The Sternberg Centre for Judaism, 80 East End Rd., London N3 2SY. (nearest tube Finchley Central). Permanent exhibition traces history of London Jewry with reconstructions of a tailoring workshop, an immigrant home and East London bakery. Also organises temporary exhibitions, guided tours, and educational programmes. Curator: Rickie Burman, MA., M.Phil, Education Officer: Ruth-Anne Lenga. Tel. 081-349 1143 & 081-346 2288. Open Mon.-Thurs., 10.30 a.m. to 5 p.m.; Sun. (except during August & Bank Holiday weekends), 10.30 a.m. to 4.30 p.m. Closed Fri., Sat, Jewish Festivals, public holidays and 25 Dec. to 4 Jan.

Lubavitch Foundation, Lubavitch Hse., 107-115 Stamford Hill, N16 5RP. Tel. 081-800 0022. Fax. 081-809 7324.

University Council — Rabbi G. Overlander. Schools Department — Rabbi A. Forta.

Small communities — Rabbi I. Sufrin. Adult Educ. — Dr T. Loewenthal.

Womens Centre — Rachel Bernstein. Hospitality — Rabbi Z. Telsner.

ORT (World Ort Union), Dir.-Gen.: J. Harmatz. ORT Administration Ltd., ORT Hse., 3 Sumpter Cl., NW3 5HR. Tel. 071-431 1333. Fax. 071-435 4784.

Yeshivat Dvar Yerushalayim of London. Princ.: Rabbi J. Freilich, Ph.C. Adult education courses, 24 Templars Av., NW11 0NS. Tel. 081-455 8631.

WELFARE ORGANISATIONS, HOSPITALS, etc.

Central British Fund for World Jewish Relief, Drayton Hse., Gordon St., WC1H 0AN. Tel. 071-387 3925. Fax. 071 383 4810.

Jewish Blind Society (incorporating Jewish Assoc. for the Physically Handicapped), see: 'Jewish Care'.

Jewish Care, Stuart Young House, 221 Golders Green Rd., London NW11 9DQ. Tel. 081-458 3282. Exec.Dir.: Melvyn Carlowe, (created by the merger of the Jewish Welfare Board and the Jewish Blind Society in January 1990).

Jewish Deaf Assoc. (Centre and Club), 90-92 Cazenove Rd., N16 6AB. Tel. 081-806 6147. Dir.: Mrs. Pat Goldring. Fax. 081-806 2251. Advisory and Resource Centre for hearing impaired people; Contact 081-806 2028.

Jewish Home & Hospital at Tottenham (formerly the Home & Hospital for Jewish Incurables), 295 High Rd., S. Tottenham, N15 4RT. Tel. 081-800 5138. General Man; Tony Shepherd, R.M.N., M.R.S.H., Cert.Ed., RNT. M.H.S.M.

Jewish Marriage Council, 23 Ravenshurst Av., NW4 4EE. Tel. 081-203 6311. Connect The Jewish Marriage Bureau. Tel. 081-203 5207.

Jewish Welfare Board, see: 'Jewish Care'.

League of Jewish Women, Voluntary Service Org., Woburn Hse., Tavistock Sq., WC1H 0EZ. Tel. 071-387 7688.

Miyad, National Jewish Crisis Helpline. Tel. 081-203 6211.

Nightingale House (The Home for Aged Jews), largest nursing/residential home for the aged in Britain and largest Jewish home in Europe, 105 Nightingale Lane, SW12 8NB. Tel. 081-673 3495. Fax. 081-675 2258. Exec. Dir.: Asher Corren. Dep.: Dir. Leon Smith.

Norwood Child Care, Norwood House, Harmony Way, NW4 2DR. Tel. & Fax: 081-203-3030.

Ravenswood Foundation, field work services, residential care and special education of mentally handicapped children and adults. Head Office: 17 Highfield Road, Golders Green, NW11 9DZ. Tel. 081-905 5557.

STUDENT & YOUTH ORGANISATIONS

Assoc. for Jewish Youth, AJY Hse., 128 East Lane, Wembley, Middx. HA0 3NL. Tel. 081-908 4747, Fax. 081-904 4323. Minicom for hard of hearing 081-904 4393. The AJY is able to give information on a wide range of Jewish youth clubs, centres, projects and movements throughout the country.

Bachad Fellowship, **Alexander Margulies Youth Centre**, Friends of Bnei Akiva, 2 Halleswelle Rd., NW11 0DJ. Chairman: Arieh L. Handler. Tel. 081-458 9370. Manchester Bnei Akiva, 72 Singleton Rd., Salford 7, Manchester; Leeds Bnei Akiva, Street Lane Gardens, Leeds 17.

Bnei Akiva, 2 Halleswelle Rd., NW11 0DJ. Tel. 081-209 1319.

Habonim-Dror, 523 Finchley Rd., NW3 7BD. Tel. 071-435 9033.

Hanoar Hatzioni, 31 Tetherdown, Muswell Hill, N10 1ND. Tel. 081-883 1022-3.

Harold Godfrey Hillel House, 25 Louisa St., E1 4NF. Tel. 071-790 9557 (office) 071-790 5426 (students).

Jewish Lads' and Girls' Brigade Inc. Headquarters: "Camperdown", 3 Beechcroft Rd., S. Woodford, E18 1LA.

Jewish Scouts and Guides. Inf. about Scouts from Peter Russell, 9 Graham Lodge, Graham Rd., NW4 3DG. Tel. 081-202 8613, and about Guides & Brownies from Mrs. N. Mitchell, 115 Francklyn Gdns., Edgware, Middx. HA8 8SB. Tel. 081-958 6440.

Jewish Student Centre, B'nai B'rith Hillel Foundation, Hillel Hse., 1-2 Endsleigh St., WC1H 0DS. Tel. 071-388 0801 Fax. 071-383 0390. Facilities include meeting rooms, common-room. **(K)** Kosher restaurant open Mon.-Thurs., 12.30 p.m. to 2.00 p.m. termtime only. Fri. night meal available if booked and paid for in advance by Thursday 11 a.m.. Students, graduates and adults from home and abroad welcome. Closed Shabbat & festivals.

Kisharon Senior Centre, 37 Moss Hall Grove, London N12. Principal: Mrs. Ch. Lehman. Centre for Education and job training including Bet Aviezer Workshop. for ages 16-24.

Maccabi Union, Gildesgame Hse., 73a Compayne Gdns., NW6 3RS. Tel. 071-328 0382. Sec. will give inf. about youth clubs in London & the provinces.

Noam (Masorti youth movement), 766 Finchley Rd., NW11 7TH. Tel. 081-201 8773; Fax. 081-201 8917.

Union of Jewish Students of UK & Eire, Hillel Hse., 1-2 Endsleigh St., WC1H 0DS. Tel. 071-387 4644, 071-380 0111. Fax. 071-383 0390.

ZIONIST ORGANISATIONS

Most of the principal London Zionist offices are now centred at Balfour Hse., 741 High Rd., N12 0BQ. Tel. 081-446 1477. They include the following: World Zionist Organisation, Zionist Federation (Tel. 081-343 9756), Jewish Agency for Israel, Joint Israel Appeal & British Aliyah Movement.

British WIZO, 107 Gloucester Pl., W1H 4BY. Tel. 071-486 2691. Fax. 071-486 7521. H. Sec: Mrs. B Harding. Chairman: Mrs. R Sotnick.

Children & Youth Aliyah Committee for Great Britain & Eire, 960 High

Rd., North Finchley N12 9YA. Exec. Dir.: Sion Mehdi. Tel. 081-446 4321. Fax. 081-343 7383.

Child Resettlement Fund Emunah, 2b Golders Green Rd., NW11 8LH. Tel. 081-458 5411. Fax. 081-458 7472. Jt. Chairman: Mrs. J. Sachs & Mrs. B. Garbacz.

Hadassah Medical Relief Assoc., 86 Gloucester Pl., W1H 3HN. Tel. 071-486 0998 & 071-224 1938.

Jewish National Fund for Israel in Great Britain & Ireland, Harold Poster Hse., Kingsbury Circle, NW9 9SP. Tel. 081-204 9911.

Mizrachi-Hapoel Hamizrachi Federation, 2b Golders Green Rd., NW11 8LH. Tel. 081-455 2243-4. Fax. 081-458 7472. Gen. Sec.: S. Kritz.

National Zionist Council, 2b Golders Green Rd., NW11 8LH. Tel. 081-455 2243-4. Fax. 081-458 7472. Gen. Sec.: Simon G. Kritz.

Poale Zion Labour Zionist Movement, c/o Hon. Sec.: Lawrie Nerva, P.O. Box 219, Wembley, Middx. HA9 8TX. Tel. 081-904 8483. Fax. 081-908 1936.

Israel Embassy,
2 Palace Green, London W8 4QB. Tel. 071-957 9500. Israeli Consulate-General, 15a Old Court Place, London W8. Nearest Underground Station: High Street, Kensington. Consular Office hours: Mon.-Thurs., 10 a.m. to 1 p.m.; Fri., 10 a.m. to 12 noon.

BOOKSELLERS
London Jewish booksellers are listed on page 374.

HOTELS, RESTAURANTS, ETC.
In the lists of hotels and restaurants the following note applies:

(K) An establishment (hotel, restaurant or caterer) under the supervision of a recognised orthodox Jewish religious authority.

LBD = London Beth Din.

FKB = Federation of Synagogues Kashrut Board.

LBS = London board of Shechita.

SKA = Sephardi Kashrut Authority.

★An establishment which, while claiming to be strictly kosher, is not under official supervision.

The **Kashrut Division** of the London Beth Din is approved by the Chief Rabbi. The Division's offices are at Adler Hse., Tavistock Sq., WC1H 9HP. Tel. 071-387 4300.

Kedassia is under the authority of the Joint Kashrus Committee of the Union of Orthodox Hebrew Congregations, Adath Yisroel Synagogues and Golders Green Beth Hamedrash. Admin.: M. J. Kester. Sec.: R. M. Hirsch, F.B.S.C., 67 Amhurst Park, N.16. Tel. 081-802 6226-7 & 081-800 6833.

The **Federation of Synagogues Kashrus Board** (FKB) Ch.: W. Ungar; Dir.: Dayan M. D. Elzas. Is under the authority of the Beth Din of the Federation of Synagogues, 65 Watford Way, NW4 3AQ. Tel. 081-202-2263.

The **Sephardi Kashrut Authority** is under the supervision of the joint Ecclesiastical Authorities of the Spanish & Portuguese Jews' Congregation. 2 Ashworth Rd., W9 1JY. Tel. 071-289 2573. Dir.: Rabbi I. S. Abraham.

HOTELS
★ **Mrs. Abramsky,** 26 Highfield Av., NW11 9ET. Tel. 081-455 7136. Bed & Breakfast. Other meals by arrangement.

★ **Andrews Hotel,** 12 Westbourne St., W2 2TZ. Tel. 071-723 4514, Fax. 071-706 4143; (office), 071-723 5365 (guests) (Hebrew spoken).

(K) Croft Court Hotel (LBD) (20), 44-46 Ravenscroft Av., Golders Green, NW11 8AY. Tel. 081-458 3331. Fax. 081-455 9175.

(K) Eshel Hotel, Stamford Hill, N16. Tel. 081-800 1445.

(K) Golders Green Hotel (FKB), 147-149 Golders Green Rd., NW11 9BN. Tel. 081-458 7127-9.

★ **Hampstead House** Residential Hotel, 12 Lyndhurst Gdns., NW3 5NR. Tel. 071-794 6036. B. Newton.

★ **Mrs. Herskine**, 67 West Way, Edgware, Middx., HA8 9LA. Tel. 081-958 4409.

★ **Kacenberg's (Guest House)**, 1 Alba Gdns., NW11 9NS. Tel. 081-455 9238 or 3780. Bed & breakfast. Shabbat meals.

(K) Kadimah Hotel (LBD) (21), 146 Clapton Common, E5 9AB. Tel. 081-800 5960/1716. Fax. 081 800 6237.

(K) (Ked.). Menorah Hotel & Caterers, 54-54a Clapton Common, E5. Tel. 081-806 4925 (reception) & 6340 (guests).

★ **Pension Strom** (8), 22 Rookwood Rd. N16 6SS. Tel. 081-800 1151. Bed & breakfast. Other meals to order.

★ **Mrs. H. Shaer** (Guest House), 3 Elm Cl., NW4 2PH. Tel. 081-202 0642. Bed & breakfast. Other meals by arrangement.

★ **Woodstock Guest House**, 68 Woodstock Av., NW11 9RJ. Tel. 081-209 0637 (bookings) & 081-455 4120 (guests).

Brookland Guest House, 220 Golders Green Rd., NW11 9AT. Tel. 081-455 6678.

Buckland Hotel, 6 Buckland Cres., NW3 5DX. Tel. 071-722 5574. Bed & breakfast (16).

Carmel Guest House, 137 North End Rd., NW11. Tel. 081-455 0891.

Central Hotel (40), 35 Hoop Lane, NW11 8BS. Tel. 081-458 5636. Fax. 081-455 4792.

The Churchill Inter-Continental (450), Portman Sq., W1A 4ZX. Tel. 071-486 5800. Fax. 071-486 1255.

Clive Hotel at Hampstead, Primrose Hill Rd., NW3 3NA. Tel. 071-586 2233 (96).
Cumberland Hotel (907), Marble Arch, W1A 4RF. Tel. 071-262 1234.
Hendon Hall Hotel, Ashley La., off Parson St., NW4 1HF. Tel. 081-203 3341. Fax. 081-203-9709.
London Regents Park Hilton, 18 Lodge Rd., NW8 7JT. Tel. 071-722 7722.
London Hilton on Park Lane (446), 22 Park Lane, W1A 2HH. Tel. 071-493 8000.
SAS Portman Hotel, 22 Portman Sq., W1H 9FL. Tel. 071-486 5844. Fax. 071-935 0537.

RESTAURANTS
(K) Aviv (FKB), 87 High St., Edgware, Middx. Tel. 081-952 2484.
(K) Bloom's World-Famous Kosher Restaurants (LBD), 90 Whitechapel High St., E1 7RA. Tel. 071-247 6835 (nearest Underground station, Aldgate East), & 130 Golders Green Rd., NW11 8HB. Tel. 081-455 1338. Free delivery service. Fax. 081-552 3123. Fully air-conditioned.
(K) Le Buffet (SKA), 8-9 Sentinel Sq., NW4 2EL. Tel. 081-202 2112.
(K) Curzon Plaza Coffee Lounge (FKB), 56 Curzon St., W1Y 7PF. Tel. 071-499 4121.
(K) DD's Kosher Sandwich Bar (LBD), 41 Greville St., EC1. Tel. 071-242 5487.
(K) Deli at West London Synagogue, 33 Seymour Place, W1. Tel. 071-723 4404.
(K) Hillel Restaurant (LBD) B'nai B'rith-Hillel Foundation, Hillel Hse., 1-2 Endsleigh St., WC1H 0DS. Tel. 071-388 0801. Mon. - Thurs., 12.30 to 2 p.m. Fri. night Sabbath meal available if booked in advance by Thursday 11 a.m. Closed July/August.

(K) Kaifeng (LBD), Kosher Oriental Restaurant, 51 Church Road, Hendon, NW4 4DU. Tel. 081-203 7888.

(K) Kosher Luncheon Club (FKB), Morris Kasler Hall, Gt. Garden St. Syn., Greatorex St., E1 5NF. Tel. 071-247 0039. Dairy meals only. Open Sun. & Mon.-Fri., 12 noon to 3 p.m.

(K) Marcus's (LBD), 5 Hallswelle Pde., Finchley Rd., NW11 0DL. Tel. 081-458 4670.

★ **Morry's Milk Bar Restaurant**, 4 Windus Rd., N16.

(K) New Connaught Rooms (SKA), Great Queen St., WC2B 5DA. Tel. 071-405 7811.

The Nosherie, 12-13 Greville St., EC1. Tel. 071-242 1591.

(K) Old Jaffa (SKA), 27 Finchley Lane, NW4. Tel. 081-203 0750.

Pizza Pitta, 119 Golders Green Rd., NW11 8HR. Tel. 081-455 8921.

(K) La Princière, 4 Hallswelle Pde., Finchley Rd., NW11. Tel. 081-458 9090.

Rabin's Salt Beef Bar, 28 Gt. Windmill St., W1. Tel. 071-434 9913.

(K) Rendezvous (LBD), Lincoln Gate, 152 Golders Green Rd., NW11. Tel. 081-455 9001. Fish, Dairy, Pasta. Open Sun.-Thurs., 11 a.m. to 11 p.m.; Fri., 11 a.m. to 1.30 p.m. (winter), 3 p.m. (summer); Sat., one hour after Motzei Shabbat to midnight. Winter only.

(K) Reubens (SKA), 20a Baker St., W1. Tel. 071-935 5945.

(K) Sami's Restaurant, 85 Brent St., NW4. Tel. 081-202 9247.

(K) Savyon, 2 The Burroughs, NW4. Tel. 081-202 6403.

(K) Solly's Restaurant (LBD), 148a Golders Green Rd., London NW11. Tel. 081-455 0004.

Stars Restaurant, 11 Soho Sq., W1V 5DB. Tel. 071-437 6525 & 9535.

(K) The White House Kosher Restaurant (LBD), 10 Bell Lane, London NW4. Tel. 081-203 2427.

(K) Zizi's (SKA), 1023 Finchley Rd., NW11. Tel. 081-201 8777.

FISH RESTAURANTS

★ **Grahame's Sea Fare Restaurant**, 38 Poland St., W1V 3DA. Tel. 071-437 3788 & 0975. Fax. 071-294 1808.

Café Fish & Café Fish Wine Bar, 39 Panton St., SW1. Tel. 071-930 3999.

Redford's Fish Restaurant, 313 Hale La., Edgware, Middx. Tel. 081-958 2229.

Rudland & Stubbs, Green Hill Rents, Cowcross St., EC1. Tel: 071-253 0148.

Sea Shell, 49 Lisson Gr., NW1 6UH. Tel. 071-723 8703 & 071-724 1063; 424-426 Kingsland Rd., E8. Tel. 071-254 6152.

VEGETARIAN RESTAURANTS

Barrow House, 45 Barrow Rd, SW16 5PE. Tel. 081-677-1925. B&B.

Bet Teva (Jewish Vegetarian & Natural Health Society), 853-5 Finchley Rd., NW11 8LX. Tel. 081-455 0692.

Bibacq Vegetarian Restaurant, 2 Gillespie Rd, Highbury N5 1LN. Tel. 071-704-0088.

Blah Blah Blah, 78 Goldhawk Rd, Shepherds Bush, W12. Tel. 081-746-1337.

Cherry Orchard, 241 Globe Rd, Bethnal Green E2 0JD. Tel. 081-980-6678.

Cordon Vert, 136 Merton Rd, Wimbledon SW19 1EH. Tel. 081-543-9174.

Cranks Restaurants, 37 Marshall St., W1V 1LL. Tel. 071-437 9431; 9 Tottenham St., W1P 9PB. Tel. 071-631 3912.

Diwana Bhel Poori House, 121 Drummond St, NW1 2HL; 50 Westbourne Grove, W2 5SH. Tel. 071-387-5556.

Food for Thought, 31 Neal St., Covent Garden, WC2H 9PK. Tel. 071-836-0239.

Futures, 8 Botolph Alley, EC3 8DR. Tel. 071-623-4529.

Greenhouse, 16 Chenies St, WC1E 7EX. Tel. 071-637-8083.
Indian Veg Bhal Poori House, 92 Chapel Market, Islington, N1 9EX. Tel. 071-837-4607.
Mandeer, 21 Hanway Place, off Tottenham Court Rd, W1P 9DG. Tel. 071-323-0660.
Millward's Restaurant, 97 Stoke Newington Church St, N16. Tel. 071-254-1025.
Mrs. Poynter's, 102 Arthur Rd, Wimbledon Park, SW19 7DT. Tel. 081-946-0902, B&B.
Rani, 3 Long Lane, N3 2PR. Tel. 081-349 2636.
Raw Deal, 65 Yale St., W1H 1PQ. Tel. 071-262 4841.
Sabras, 263 High Rd, Willesden Green, NW10 2RX. Tel. 081-459-0340.
Seasons Vegetarian Restaurant, Harcourt St, W1. Tel. 071-402-5925.
Shan Vegetarian Restaurant, 200 Shaftesbury Av., WC2H 8JL. Tel. 071-240-3348.
Spices, 30 Stoke Newington Church St, N16 0LU. Tel. 071-254-0528.
Surya Indian Vegetarian Restaurant, 59 Fortune Green Rd, NW6 1DR. Tel. 071-435-7486.
Veganomics, 314 Lewisham Rd, SE13 7PA. Tel. 081-852-7978.
Wilkins Natural Foods, 61 Marsham St, SW1P 3DP. Tel. 071-222-4038.
Windmill Wholefood Restaurant, 486 Fulham Rd, SW6 5NH. Tel. 071-385-1570.
Yours Naturally, 45 Shelton St, Covent Garden, WC2E 9MJ. Tel. 071-497-0079.
ZZZ's Cafe, 238 Gray's Inn Rd, WC1. Tel. 071-278-5391.

DELICATESSEN, ETC.

Kosher World, 46 Vivian Av., NW4. Tel. 081-203 8108.

Kosher World, Market Pl., Falloden Way, NW11. Tel. 081-201 8057.

(K) Patisserie Delice (FKB), 225 Golder Green Rd. NW11 9PN. Tel. 081-455 8195.

Pelter Stores, 82 Edgware Way, Edgware, Middx. Tel. 081-958 6910.

BUTCHERS

(K) N. Goldberg (LBS), Claybury Broadway, Redbridge, Ilford, Essex. Tel. 081-551 2828.

(K) Louis Mann (LBS), 23 Edgwarebury Lane, Edgware, Middx. Tel. 081-958 3789.

(K) Mehadrin Meats (LBS), 25a Belfast Rd., N16. Tel. 081 806 7686/3002.

(K) Menachem's (LBS), Russell Pde., Golders Green Rd., NW11. Tel. 081-201 8629/8630.

(K) Ivor Silverman (LBS), 4 Canons Corner, Stanmore, Middx. Tel. 081-958 8682/2692. Fax. 081-958 1725.

CATERERS AND FUNCTIONS

(K) E. G. M. Ltd. (FKB), 74 High Rd., Chigwell, Essex, IG7 6PX. Tel. 081-501 3200.

(K) Grosvenor Rooms Ltd (FKB), 92 Walm Lane, NW2 4QY. Tel. 081-451 0066.

(K) Mrs. E. Kamhi (SKA), 26 Ravenscroft Av., Wembley, Middx. Tel. 081 904 2161.

(K) Nadine Abensur (SKA) vegetarian. Tel. 081-883 3799.

(K) Kenneth Arfin Banqueting (Selfridges Hotel) (FKB). Tel. 0202 765910.

(K) The Langham Hilton Hotel (SKA), 1 Portland Place, W1N 3AA. Tel. 071-636 1100. Fax. 071-323 2340.

(K) Park Lane Hotel (FKB), Piccadilly, W1Y 8BX. Tel. 071-499 6321.

(K) The Prince Regent Hotel (SKA), Manor Rd., Woodford Bridge, Essex, IG8 8AG. Tel. 081-505 9966. Fax. 081-506 0807.

(K) Philip Small (FKB), Unit 3, The Harp Business Centre, Apsley Way, NW2 7LW. Tel. 081-208 3000.

(K) The Savoy Hotel (SKA), PO Box 189, Strand, London. Tel. 071-836 4343. Fax. 071-872 8894.

(K) Sharett (Caterers) (SKA), 17 London Rd., Stanmore, Middx. Tel. 081 905 4081. Fax. 081-958 1422.

REGIONS

ALDERSHOT (Hants.)

Inq. to Senior Jewish Chaplain H.M. Forces, Rev. M. Weisman, Woburn Hse., Upper Woburn Pl., London, WC1H 0EP. Tel. 071-387 3081.

BASILDON (Essex)

Syn: "Whiteway", Basildon Rd., Laindon. (Affiliated to Southend Hebrew Cong.). Inq.: M. Kochmann, 3 Furlongs, SS16 4BW. Tel. 0268 524947.

BIRMINGHAM (W. Midlands)

This Jewish com. is one of the oldest in the Provinces, dating from 1730, if not earlier. Birmingham was a centre from which Jewish pedlars covered the surrounding country week by week, returning to their homes for the Sabbath.

The first synagogue of which there is any record was in The Froggery in 1780. But there was a Jewish cemetery in the same neighbourhood in 1730, and Moses Aaron is said to have been born in Birmingham in 1718. The synagogue of 1780 was extended in 1791, 1809 and 1827. A new and larger synagogue, popularly known as "Singers Hill", was opened in 1856.

Representative Organisations

B'nai B'rith Joint Lodge. Jt. Sec.: Frank & Herta Linden, 7 Westbourne Gdns., Edgbaston B15 3TJ. Tel. 021-454 5042.
Representative Council of Birmingham & Midland Jewry. Sec.: L. Jacobs, 37 Wellington Rd., B15 2ES. Tel. 021-236 1801 (office), 021-440 4142 (home).

Synagogues & Religious Organisations

Birmingham Hebrew Congregation, Singers Hill, Ellis St., B1 1HL. Tel. 021-643 0884. Min.: Rev. L. L. Tann, B.A.
Central, 133 Pershore Rd., B5 7PA. Min.: Rabbi M. Singer, B.A. Sec.: Paul Hartheimer. Tel. 021-440 4044.
New, 11 Park Rd., B13 8AB. Min.: Rabbi R. Goodman. Tel. 021-449 3544.
Park Rd. Assembly Hall, B13 8AB. Tel. 021-449 3435.
Progressive, 4 Sheepcote St., B16 8AA. Tel. 021-643 5640.
Shechita Board, Singers Hill, Ellis St., B1 1HL. Sec.: R. Singer.

Cultural & Educational Organisations

Cultural Society. Hon. Sec.: Mrs. V. I. Harris, 11 Viceroy Cl., B5 7UR. Tel. 021-440 4788. Publishes "Birmingham Jewish Recorder" (monthly).
International Jewish Genealogical Resources. Co-Directors: Dr. A. P. Joseph & Mrs. Judith Joseph. Same address & Tel. as Jewish Historical Society.
Jewish Historical Society, Birmingham Branch. Ch.: Dr. A. P. Joseph, 25 Westbourne Rd., B15 3TX. Tel. 021-454 0408.
Lubavitch Centre, 95 Willows Rd., B12 9QF. Tel. 021-440 6673. Dir.: Rabbi S. Arkush. Mikva on premises. Inq.: Mrs. Arkush. Tel. 021-440 5853.
Reference Library. Syn. Offices, Singers Hill, Ellis St., B1 1HL. Tel. 021-643 0884.

Welfare Organisations, Hospitals, etc.

Birmingham Jewish Housing Assoc. Ltd. Same address & Tel. as Birmingham Jewish Welfare Board.
Birmingham Jewish Welfare Board, 1 Rake Way, B15 1EG. Tel. 021-643 2835. Home for Aged. Stirchley House, River Brook Drive, Stirchley, Birmingham B30 2SH. Tel. 021-458 5000. Inq. to Birmingham Jewish

Welfare Board, 1 Rake Way, B15 1EG. Tel. 021-643 2835. The Joseph & Doris Cohen Day Centre is also at this address.
Jewish Blind Society. Sec.: David Winroope, 179 Lordswood Rd., Harborne, B17 9BP. Tel. 021-427 1766 (home), 021-552 1645 (office).

Student & Youth Organisations
Birmingham Jewish Youth Trust, Youth Office, c/o Youth Centre, King David School, Alcester Rd., B13 8EY. Tel. 021-442 4459.
Birmingham Union of Jewish Students, c/o Hillel House. Address as below. Tel. 021-454 5684 & 021-455 8116.
Hillel House Students' Hostel, 26 Somerset Rd., Edgbaston, B15 2QD. Tel. 021-454 5684. Further inf.: Frank Linden. Tel. 021-454 5042. Mrs. Ruth Jacobs. Tel. 021-440 4142. Chaplain: Rabbi Fishel Cohen. Tel. 021-440 1359.
Youth Centre, 19 Sandhurst Rd., Moseley, B13 8EU. Tel. 021-442 4459.

Zionist Organisations
Israel Information Centre, Singers Hill, Blucher St., B1 1QL. Dir.: W. Schott. Tel. 021-643 2688.
J.I.A., J.N.F. and WIZO, address as Israel Information Centre above.
Zionist Council. Same address as J.I.A. Tel. 021-454 5050. Ch.: Walter Schott.

Miscellaneous Organisations
Council of Christians & Jews. Hon. Sec.: Mrs. L. F. Gompertz, 325 Pershore Rd., B5 7RY. Tel. 021-472 0117.
Friendly Circle (Social and Cultural Group for the Over-40s). Hon. Sec.: Mrs. G. Jacobs, 44 Pitmaston Ct., Goodby Rd., B13 8RL. Tel. 021-449 0084.
Jewish Graduates' Assoc. Sec.: S. Rose, 40 Lordswood Sq., B17. Tel. 021-427 9259.

Bookseller
Lubavitch Bookshop, 95 Willows Rd., B12 9QF. Tel. 021-440 6673.

Butchers & Delicatessen
(K) A. Gee, 75 Pershore Rd., B5 7NX. Tel. 021-440 2160.
(K) Jaremon, Unit 4, 214 Alcester Rd., B13 8EZ. Tel. 021-442 2144.

Caterers
(K) B'tayavon, 20 Hampton Ct., George Rd., Edgbaston, B15 1PU. Tel. 021-456 2172.
(K) Golda, 125 Salisbury Rd., B13. Tel. 021-449 2261 & 440 1925.

Restaurant
(V) **Zebedees**, 190 Alum Rock Rd, Saltley, B8 1NJ. Tel. 021-327-1187.

BLACKPOOL (Lancs.)

Synagogues & Religious Organisations
United Hebrew Cong. (Orthodox), Synagogue Chambers, Leamington Rd., FY1 4HD. Tel. 0253 28164. Daily services 7.45 a.m. and 7 p.m. (7.30 p.m. in summer). Min.: Rev. David Braunold. Hon. Sec.: Mr. M. Savage, 1 North Park Drive, Blackpool F73 8LP; Tel. 0253 396761. Ch., Ladies' Guild: Mrs. Cynthia Lefton, 98 W. Park Dr., FY3 9HU. Tel. 0253 63584.
Reform Jewish Cong., 40 Raikes Pde., FY1 4EX. Tel. 0253 23687. Chairman: Leon Tax, 110 Worcester Rd., FY3 9SZ. Tel. 0253 761763.

Miscellaneous Organisations
Blackpool, St. Annes & District Ajex. Inq. to N. Futter, 7 Kingscote Dr., FY3 8HB. Tel. 0253 32510.

Blackpool & Fylde Jewish Welfare Soc. Hon. Treas.: N. L. Marcuson, 184 High Cross Rd., Poulton-le-Fylde, FY6 8DA. Tel. 0253 883026. President: Gene Kay, 15 Crestway, Blackpool. Tel. 0253 392513.
Council of Christians and Jews. Hon. Sec.: Mrs. Gene Kay, 15 Crestway, Newton Dr., FY3 8PA. Tel. 0253 392513.
League of Jewish Women. Hon. Sec. of Fylde group: Mrs. Lilian Cohen, 3 Antrim Rd., FY2 9UR. Tel. 0253 53102.
St. Annes and Fylde Jewish Literary Society. Hon. Sec.: Mrs. Gene Kay, 15 Crestway, Newton Dr., Blackpool FY3 8PA. Tel. 0253 392513.

Delicatessen
Lytham Delicatessen, 53 Warton St., Lytham St. Annes. Tel. 0253 735861.

BOGNOR REGIS (W. Sussex)

Ch. & Hon. Sec. of Cong.: J. S. Jacobs, "Elm Lodge", Sylvan Way, PO21 2RS. Tel. 0243 823006.

BOURNEMOUTH (Dorset)

The Bournemouth Hebrew Congregation was established in 1905, when the Jewish population numbered fewer than 20 families. Today the town's permanent Jewish residents number 3,500 out of a total population of some 151,000. During the season and at the Holy-days and festivals, however, there are many more Jews than this in Bournemouth, for it is an extremely popular resort, with its Jewish hotels, guest houses and other holiday accom.

Synagogues
Bournemouth Hebrew Cong. (Orthodox), Synagogue Chambers, Wootton Gdns., BH1 1PW. Tel. 0202 557433. Min.: Rabbi S. Harris. Mikva on premises.
Bournemouth Reform Syn., 53 Christchurch Rd., BH1 3PN. Tel. 0202 557736. Min.: Rabbi D. M. B. Soetendorp. Tel. 0202 514788.

Representative Organisations
Bournemouth Jewish Representative Council. Ch.: Mrs. A. Filer. Hon. Sec. Mrs. T. Lurie, 59 Fitzharris Avenue, BH9 1BY. Tel. 0202 523550.
Council of Christian & Jews, 108 Avon Rd., BH8 8SF. Sec.: Mrs. R. Falkenberg, 8 Wimbledon Hall, Derby Rd, Bournemouth. Tel. 0202 552286.

Welfare Organisations
Braemar Royal, Grand Av., Southbourne, BH6 3SY. Tel. 0202 423246.
Home for Aged. Hannah Levy Hse., 15 Poole Rd., BH2 5QR. Tel. 0202 765361.
Holiday Home for Physically Handicapped, **(K)** "Carlton Dene", 21 Stourwood Av., Southbourne, BH6 3PW. Administered by Jewish Care. Inq. Tel. 081-458 3282.

Miscellaneous Organisations
Friendship Club. Inf. from Sec.: Mr. S. Mazin, 3 Garden House, Meyrick Rd., Bournemouth BH1 3E.

Hotels, etc.
★ **Grove House Hotel**, 61 Grove Rd., BH1 3AT. Tel. 0202 554161.
(K) New Ambassador Hotel (LBD) (112, all with bathroom en suite), E. Cliff, BH1 3DP. Tel. 0202 55453.
(K) Normandie Hotel (71) (Ked), Manor Rd., E. Overcliff Dr., BH1 3HL. Tel. 0202 552246.
Anglo Swiss Hotel, Gervis Rd., BH1 3EQ. Tel. 0202 554794.

Cliffeside Hotel (64), E. Overcliff Dr., BH1 3AQ. Tel. 0202 555724.
Cumberland Hotel, E. Overcliff Dr., BH1 3AF. Tel. 0202 290722.
Durley Dean Hotel, Westcliff Rd., BH2 5HE. Tel. 0202 557711 [N].
Durlston Court Hotel, Gervis Rd., BH1 3DD. Tel. 0202 291488.
East Cliff Court Hotel (70), E. Overcliff Dr., BH1 3AN. Mr. & Mrs. P. Proctor. Tel. 0202 554545.
Norfolk Royale Hotel, Richmond Hill, BH2 6EN. Tel. 0202 551521.
Queens Hotel, Meyrick Rd. Tel. 0202 554415. (115 rooms).
Royal Bath Hotel, Bath Rd., BH1 2EW. Tel. 0202 555555.
Taurus Park Hotel, 16 Knyreton Rd., BH1 3QN. Tel. 0202 557369.

Kosher Meat, etc.
(K) Bournemouth Kosher Butchers, 224 Holdenhurst Rd., BH8 8AX. Tel. 0202 554524. Lic. by Bournemouth Hebrew Congregation & National Council of Shechita Boards.
(K) Louise's Deli (Ked), 164 Old Christchurch Rd., BH1 1NU. Tel. 0202 295979.

Restaurant
(V) Henry's Wholefood Restaurant, 6 Lansdowne Rd., BH1 1SD, Tel. 0202-297887. Closed Sunday and Monday eves, Winter.

BRADFORD (W. Yorks.)

The Jewish com. although only about 130 to 140 years old, has exercised much influence on the city's staple industry: wool. Jews of German birth developed the export trade of wool yarns and fabrics. The Syn. of British and Foreign Jews, "Reform" in character (later called the Reform Syn. and

still later the Bradford Syn.), was built in 1880 in Bowland St. An Orthodox syn. came into being in 1886, in Snowden St. Today's syn. in Springhurst Rd., Shipley, was built in 1970.

Synagogues
Bradford Hebrew Cong. (Orthodox), Springhurst Rd., Shipley, BD18 3DN. Services: 10 a.m. monthly on Shabbat Mevarchim, High Holy-days & certain festivals. Hon. Sec.: Mrs. I. Goodman. Pres.: A. A. Waxman.
Bradford Syn. (Reform) Bowland St., Manningham Lane, BD1 3BW (Reform). Tel. 0274 544420. Services: Fri., 6 p.m.; Sat., 11 a.m.; Festivals, 6 p.m. & 11 a.m.

Representative Organisation
B'nai B'rith West Riding, Shalom Lodge, Bradford. Hon. Sec.: Mrs. A. Fabian, 26 Thorndale Rise, Poplars Farm, Kings Rd., BD2 1NU.
W.I.Z.O. Bradford. C/o Bfd Hebrew Congregation, Springhurst Rd., Shipley, BD18 3DN.

BRIGHTON & HOVE (E. Sussex)
The first known Jewish resident of Brighton lived there in 1767. The earliest synagogue was founded in Jew St. in 1789. Henry Solomon, vice-president of the congregation, was the first Chief Constable of the town. He was murdered in 1844 by an insane youth. His brother-in-law, Levi Emanuel Cohen, founded the "Brighton Guardian" and was twice elected president of the Newspaper Society of Gt. Britain. Other 19th-century notables living in Brighton and Hove included Sir Isaac Lyon Goldsmid and numerous members of the Sassoon family. The town's Jewish population is now about 12,000.

Synagogues
Brighton & Hove Hebrew Cong.: Middle St. Syn., 66 Middle St., Brighton, BN1 1AL. Min.: Rabbi Leonard Book. W. Hove Syn., 29 New Church Rd., Hove, BN3 4AD. Hon. Sec.: B. J. Goldberg. Tel. 0273 27785. Jun. M. Rabbi M. Shaw.
Hove Hebrew Cong., 79 Holland Rd., Hove, BN3 1JN (Orthodox). Tel. 0273 732035. Min.: Rabbi Michael Dick. Sec.: S. Farrell.
New (Reform), Palmeira Av., Hove, BN3 3GE. Tel. 0273 735343. Min.: Rabbi J. Collick. Sec.: Lana Kaye. Tel. 0273 735343.
Progressive Syn., 6 Lansdowne Rd., Hove, BN3 1FF. Ch.: Mrs. S. Walker. Tel. 0273 737223 9.30 a.m. to 1 p.m.
There is a mikva in the Prince Regent swimming pool complex, Church St., BN1 1YA. For further inf., Tel. 0273 21919.

Representative Organisation
Jewish Representative Council. Ch.: Dr. H. Sless. Tel. 0273 735632. Sec.: Mrs. D. Levinson, 55 Langdale Gdns., BN3 4HL.

Welfare Organisations
Brighton & Hove Jewish Welfare Board. Inq.: Mrs. J. Markham, Tel. 0273 722523.
Brighton & Hove Jewish Home for the Aged, 20 Burlington St., Brighton, BN2 1AU. Tel. 0273 688226-7.

Miscellaneous Organisations
Brighton & Hove Jewish Centre & Friendship Clubs, Ralli Hall, 81 Denmark Villas, Hove, BN3 3TH. Administrator:- Norina Duke. Tel. (0273) 202254.

Brighton & Hove Joint Kashrus Committee. Hon. Sec.: H. Breger, 5 The Paddock, The Droveway, Hove. Tel. 0273 506574.
(K) Hillel House, 18 Harrington Rd., Brighton, BN1 6RE. Tel. 0273 503450. Closed during summer vacation. Further inf. from Mrs. H. Sless. Tel. 0273 735632. Fri. evg. meals available.
Lubavitch Chabad Hse., 15 The Upper Dr., Hove BN3 6GR. Tel. 0273 21919. Dir.: Rabbi P. Efune. (Torah Academy)

Hotel
Norfolk Resort Hotel (120), 149 Kings Rd., Brighton BN1 2PP. Tel. 0273 738201.

Butchers and Poulterers
(K) Shoshana's, 8 Manor Parade, Hove St., BN3 2DF. Tel. 0273-725751.
(K) H. Lewis (Butchers) Ltd., 37 Preston St., Brighton, BN1 2HP. Tel. 0273 27318.

Delicatessen
★ Cantor's of Hove, 20 Richardson Rd., Hove, BN3 5BB. Tel. 0273 723669.

Caterer
(K) Glassman's Catering, 1 Shirley Dr., Hove BN3 6NQ. Tel. 0273 565343. Under supervision of Brighton & Hove Kashrus Com.

Restaurants
(V) Rozanne Mendick, 14 Chatsworth Rd., BN1 5DB, Tel. 0273-556584. B&B.
(V) Slims Health Food Restaurant, 92 Churchill Sq., BN1 2EP. Tel. 0273 24582.

BRISTOL (Avon)
Bristol was one of the principal Jewish centres of medieval England. The rich Jew of Bristol, whose teeth were extracted one by one until he surrendered his fortune to King John, is a famous historical figure. Even after the Expulsion from England (1290) there were occasional Jewish residents or visitors. The medieval mikvah in Jacobs Wells Rd. is the oldest in Europe and dates from the 12th century. A community of Marranos lived here for 15 years during the Tudor period. The present community was founded before 1754, and a synagogue was opened in 1786. The present one dates from 1871, and incorporates fittings from the earlier building.

Synagogues
9 Park Row, BS1 5LP. Minister: Rabbi Hillel Simon. Tel. 0272-255160. Enq. to: Mrs. Y. Saunders. Tel. 0225 859082. Occasional Fri. night services, in summer, 7.30 p.m. Sat., 9.45 a.m. Kosher delicatessen, alternate Sundays 10 a.m.
Bristol Progressive Syn. (Bristol & West Progressive Jewish Cong.), 43 Bannerman Rd., Easton, BS5 0RR. Tel. 0272 541937. Min.: Rabbi F. Berry. Tel. 0272 563025. Inq. Tel. 0225 318908.
Hillel House. Tel. 0272 737177. See below for address.

Miscellaneous Organisations
Bristol Jewish Liaison Com. Sec.: Henry Harris, Hazel Crest, 88 Gloucester Rd., Rudgeway, BS12 2QN. Tel. (evgs. only) 0454-419877.
Bristol University & Polytechnic Jewish & Israel Society. Inq. to Jewish Soc. Ch., c/o Hillel Hse.
Hillel Hse.: 8 Alma Vale Rd., Clifton, BS8 2HY. Contact Mrs. A Holt, Pound House, Old Charfield GL12 8LJ. Tel. 0454 261208.

Jewish Women's Guild. Hon. Sec.: Mrs. E. Elman, 6 Trelawney Rd., Cotham, Bristol BS6 6EA. Tel. 0272 735646.

Restaurants

(V) Cherries, 122 St Michael's Hill, BS2 8BU. Tel. 0272-293675.

(V) Greenleaf Vegetarian/Vegan Cafe, 82 Colston St. (basement). Tel. 0272 2911369.

(V) McCreadies, 26 Broad St., Nr St Johns Gate, BS1 2HG. Tel. 0272-265580.

(V) Millwards Vegetarian Restaurant, 40 Alfred Place, Kingsdown, BS2 8HD, Tel. 0272-245026.

BROMLEY (Greater London)

Reform Syn., 28 Highland Rd., BR1 4AD Kent. Tel. 081-460 5460. Min.: Rabbi S. Rothschild.

BUCKHURST HILL (Essex)

Buckhurst Hill Reform Syn. Services, P.O.B. 14, Loughton, Essex IG10 1QW. Tel. 081-508 3428.

CAMBRIDGE (Cambs.)

Syn/Student Centre, 3 Thompson's Lane, CB5 8AQ. Daily, morn & eve services during term time. Sat. morning during vacations, other services by arrangement). Inq.: R.R.Domb, Cambridge Traditional Cong. Tel. 0223 68346; or 0223 354783.

There is a **(K)** kosher canteen during term time serving lunch most weekdays and on Sat., and supper on Fri.

Beth Shalom Reform Syn.: Inf. from Jonathan Harris, 86 Union Lane, CB1 1QB. Tel. 0223 67175.

Cambridge Jewish Residents' Assoc. welcomes visitors to all activities. Inq. to Ch.: Mrs. E. Shepherd. Tel. 0223-246751.

CANTERBURY (Kent)

Canterbury Jewish Com. Ch.: Irving Morris. Hon. Sec.; Mrs. R. Morris, 26 Meadow Rd., Sturry, CT2 0JF. Tel. 0227 711455.

Restaurant

(V) Teapot Mother Earth, 34 St Peter's St., CT16 1BK. Tel. 0227 463175.

CHELMSFORD (Essex)

The cong. holds regular services, Hebrew classes and a lively social and cultural programme. Tel. (0245) 266150.

CHELTENHAM

The congregation was established in 1824 and the present synagogue opened in 1829. However after two generations, the congregation declined, until the synagogue was closed in 1903. Refugees from Central Europe and evacuated children and others from Jewish centres in England formed a new community, and in 1939 the old synagogue was reopened.

Syn.: St. James's Sq. Inq.: H. Bazar, Kynance, 22 Sydenham Rd., GL52 6EA. Tel. 0242 525032.

Restaurant

(V) The Barleycorn, 317 High St. GL50 3HN, Tel. 0242 241070.

CHESTER (Ches.)

Inq. to Mrs. A. Mayorcas, 5 Lache Lane, CH4 7LP. Tel. 0244 675240.

Restaurant
(V) Abbey Green Restaurant, 2a Abbey Green, Off Northgate St., CH1
2JH. Tel. 0244 313251. 12-2.30, Mon-Sat; 6.30-10, Tues-Sat.

CHIGWELL (Essex)

Syn: Limes Av., Limes Farm Estate, Chigwell.
Com. inq.: E. G. Levy, 76 The Lowe.
Abridge Golf & Country Club: Epping La., Abridge, Stapleford Tawney
(near Chigwell), RM4 1ST. Tel. 040 28 396.

COLCHESTER (Essex)

Colchester and District Jewish Community, the Synagogue, Fennings
Chase, Priory St. CO1 2QB. Services held Friday evening and on all
Festivals. The Community has many families with young children and
there is a Cheder every Sunday morning. The community has close links
with the University of Essex at Colchester which is a popular choice for
Israeli students wishing to study for a law degree. For information about
services, Cheder and social events please contact: the Hon. Sec. Mrs. N. B.
Stevenson. Tel. 0206 45992.

COVENTRY (W. Midlands)

There were Jews in Coventry in 1775, if not earlier. Today's Jewish
population is about 50 families. The present synagogue was consecrated in
1870.
Syn.: Barras Lane, CV1 3BW. Tel. 0203 220168.
Coventry, Leamington and District Fed. of Women Zionists (WIZO). Hon.
Sec.: Mrs. M. P. Benjamin, 290 Valley Rd, Lillington, Leamington Spa, CV32
7UE, Warwickshire. Tel. 0926 337600.

CRAWLEY (W. Sussex)

Progressive Cong.: Inf. from Hon. Sec.: Lynda Bloom, 44 Brighton Rd.,
Southgate. Tel. Crawley 34294.

CROYDON (Greater London)

Syn.: 30 Elmwood Rd., Croydon, CR0 2SG. Inq. to the Sec. Tel. 01-684 4726.

Restaurant
(V) Hockney's, 98 High St. CR0 1ND, Tel. 081-688 2899.

DARLINGTON (Durham)

Darlington Hebrew Congregation, 13 Bloomfield Rd., Darlington, Co
Durham. Chairman: Martin Finn, 17 Thornbury Rise, Darlington, Co
Durham DL3 9NF. Tel. 0325 467902.

EASTBOURNE (E. Sussex)

Syn.: 22 Susans Rd., BN21 3TJ. Hon. Sec.: Mrs. M. Mindell, "Woodthorpe",
Forest Pl., Waldron, Heathfield, TN21 0TG. Tel. (0435) 866928.

EPPING (Essex)

★ Gaynes Park, Coopersale, nr. Epping CM16 7RJ. Tel. 0378 76021/72566. Weekend seminar & conference centre.

EPSOM (Surrey)

Syn.: Prospect Pl., East St. Inq. to H. L. Lehmann, Cranmere, Woodcote Rd., KT18 7QS. Tel. 0372 721150.

EXETER (Devon)

In pre-Expulsion times Exeter was an important Jewish centre. The synagogue was built in 1763, while the cemetery in Magdalen Road dates from 1757.
Syn.: Synagogue Pl., Mary Arches St., EX4 3BA. Tel. 0392 51529. Services, fortnightly Fri./Sat. and High Holydays.

Restaurants
(V) **Brambles**, 31 New Bridge St., EX4 3AH. Tel. 0932 74168.
(V) **Herbies**, 15 North St., EX4 3QS. Tel. 0392 58473.

GATESHEAD (Tyne & Wear)

Syn.: 180 Bewick Rd., NE8 1UF. Tel. 091-4770111. Min.: Rabbi B. Rakow, 138 Whitehall Rd., NE8 1TP. Tel. 091-4773012. Hon. Sec.: M. Guttentag, 205 Dryden Rd. Tel. 091-4773871.
Mikva, 180 Bewick Rd., NE8 1UF. Appointments: Tel. 091-4773552.

Educational Organisations, Schools, etc.
Beis Hatalmud, 1 Ashgrove Ter., NE8. Tel. 091-4784352. Princ.: Rabbi S. Steinhouse.
Beth Midrash Lemoroth (women teachers' training college), 50 Bewick Rd., NE8. Tel. 091-4772620. Princ.: Rabbi M. Miller.
Gateshead Jewish Boarding School, 37 Gladstone Ter., NE8 4HE. Tel. 091-4771431. Princ.: Rabbi R. Kohn.
Institute for Higher Rabbinical Studies-Kolel, 22 Claremont Pl., NE8 1TL. Sec.: S. Ehrentreu. Tel. 091-4772189.
Jewish High School for Girls, 6 Gladstone Ter., NE8 4DY. Principal: Rabbi D. Bowden. Tel. 091-4773471.
Jewish Primary School, 18-20 Gladstone Ter., NE8 4EA. Principal: Rabbi S. Wagschal. Tel. 091-4772154.
Jewish Teachers' Training College, 50 Bewick Rd., NE8 4DQ. Tel. 091-4772620. P. Rabbi M. Miller.
Kindergarten, Alexander Rd. Tel. 091-4783723.
Sunderland Talmudical College, Prince Consort Rd., NE8. Princ.: Rabbi S. Zahn. Tel. 091-4900195.
Yeshiva, 88 Windermere St., NE8 1UB. Tel. 091-4772616 & 091-4785210.
Yeshiva L'Zeirim Tiferes Yaacov, 36-38 Gladstone Ter., NE8 4EF. Principal: Rabbi E. Jaffe. Tel. 091-477 1317.

Bookseller
J. Lehmann, 20 Cambridge Ter., NE8 1RP. Tel. 091-490 1692.

Baker, Confectioner & Grocer
(K) Stenhouse, 215 Coatsworth Rd., NE8 1SR. Tel. 091-4772001.

Butcher
(K) K. L. Kosher Butcher, 83 Rodsley Av., NE8. Tel. 091-4773109.

Caterer

Mrs. J. Rose, 14 Limetree Gdns., and Mrs. J. Poznanski, 9 Ashgrove Ter. Tel. 091-477 2880.

GREENFORD (Greater London)

Syn.: 39-45 Oldfield Lane South, UB6 9LB. Inq. to Hon. Sec.: R. A. Hyams.

GRIMSBY (S. Humberside)

Syn.: Sir Moses Montefiore Synagogue, Heneage Rd., DN32 9DZ. Services: Fri., 7 p.m. Sabbath, Services: First Saturday in month. 9.30 a.m. Hon. Sec.: M. M. Lewis, 18 Crescent St., DN31 2HB. Tel. 0472 342579.

GUILDFORD (Surrey)

Guildford & District Syn., York Rd., GU1 4DR. Inq. to Hon. Sec., Mrs. H. Gould, Lynwood, Hillier Rd., GU1 2JG. Tel. 0483 576470.

HARLOW (Essex)

Syn.: Harbert's Rd., CM19 4DT. Constituent of Reform Synagogues of Great Britain. Services: Fri., 8.15 p.m. Ch: Ian. Jackson 34 Greenhills, Harlow, Essex CM20 3SX. Tel. 0279 416138.

HAROLD HILL (Greater London)

Syn.: Trowbridge Rd. Inq. to Miss D. Meid, 4 Portmadoc Hse., Broseley Rd., RM3 9BT. Tel. Ingrebourne 48904.

HARROGATE (N. Yorks)

Syn.: St. Mary's Walk, HG2 0LW. Services: Fri., 7 p.m. in summer; Sabbath, 9.30 a.m. Hon. Sec.: P. E. Morris, Crimple Lodge, Fulwith Mill La., HG2 8HJ. Tel. 0423 871713.
Harrogate Zionist Group (WIZO). Inq. to Mrs. A. Marks, 15 Swan Court, HG1 2AQ. Tel. 0423 526580.

Restaurant

(V) **Amadeus**, 115 Franklin Rd., HG1 5EN, Tel. 0423-5-5151.

HASTINGS (E. Sussex)

Includes Bexhill, Battle, Rye & St. Leonards. Inq. about Hastings District Jewish Soc. to Mrs. Ilse Éton, 6 Gilbert Rd., St. Leonards-on-Sea, East Sussex, TN38 0RH. Tel. 0424 436551. Meetings, 7 p.m. on first Fri. of every month at Hugh Smith Hall, 45 Eversley Rd., Bexhill.
(V) Vegetarian Boarding House: Merryfield, 3 St. Matthews Gardens, St. Leonards, TN38 0TS. Tel: 0424 424953.

HEMEL HEMPSTEAD (Herts.)

Syn.: Morton Hse., Midland Rd., HD1 1RP. Hon. Sec.: Harry Nathan. Tel. 0923 32007.
Lady Sarah Cohen Com. Centre, Midland Rd., HD1 1OR.

HIGH WYCOMBE (Bucks.)

Hebrew Cong. Inq. to Mrs. R. Weiss, 33 Hampden Rd., HP13 6SZ. Tel. 0494 529821.

HIGHAMS PARK (Greater London)

Highams Park and Chingford Syn., Marlborough Rd., E4 9AZ. Min.: Rev. M. J. Broder, M.A. Sec.: Mrs. S. R. Benjamin, 77 Royston Av., Chingford, E4 9DE. Tel. 081-527 4750.

HORNCHURCH (Greater London)

Syn.: Elm Park (Affiliated) Syn., Woburn Av., Elm Pk., Hornchurch, Essex. Hon. Sec.: H. Gaynor. Tel. 0708 442079.
Hilton National Hotel (140), on the A127 at Hornchurch, RM11 3UJ. Tel. 04023 46789.

HULL (Humberside)

In Hull, as in other English port towns, a Jewish community was formed earlier than in inland areas. The exact date is unknown, but is thought by some to be the early 1700s. Certainly, there were enough Jews in Hull to buy a former Roman Catholic chapel, damaged in the Gordon Riots of 1780, and turn it into a syn. Previously, services had been held in a substantial private house in the High St. A cemetery is believed to have been acquired in the late 1700s.
Hull was then the principal port of entry from northern Europe, and most of the Jewish immigrants came through it. In 1851 the Jewish community numbered about 200. Today it numbers some 350 families. Both the Old Hebrew Synagogue in Osborne St., and the Central Synagogue in Cogan St., were destroyed in air raids during the Second World War. On the Osborne Street site a new synagogue was consecrated in September, 1955, and a new synagogue hall was opened in 1956.
At present, both Orthodox congs. share the Linnaeus St. site & will continue to do so until a new syn. is built in the Western suburbs, where most of the com. now live.

Synagogues & Religious Organisations

Western Synagogue, Linnaeus St., HU10 6DF (est. 1902). Hon. Sec.: E. Pearlman, 277 Beverley Rd., Kirkella, HU10 7AQ. Tel. 0482 653398.
Western Syn. Board of Shechita. Hon. Ch.: Dr. C. Rosen. Tel. 0482 20869.
Reform Synagogue. Great Gutter Lane, Willerby, HU10 7JT. Chairman: Ron Stone. Tel. 0482 651337.

Representative & Welfare Orgs.

Board of Guardians, 135 Woodland Dr., Anlaby, HU10 7HS. Hon. Sec.: S. Pearlman. Tel. 0482 650192.
Board of Guardians Flatlets for Aged. 335 Anlaby Rd. Sec.: Mrs. F. Flasher. Tel. 0482 651616.
Jewish Representative Council. Pres.: S. Pearlman. Hon. Sec.: B. Donn, 4 Drydales, Kirkella, Hull. HU10 7JU. Tel. 0482 658902.

Student & Youth Organisations

Hillel Hse., 18 Auckland Av., HU6 7SG. Tel. 0482 48196. Inq. to I. Dysch, 1000 Anlaby High Rd., HU4 6AT. Tel. 0482 54947.
Provincial Hillel Foundation. Co-ordinator: Jack Lennard, 771 Anlaby High Rd., Hull, HU4 6DJ. Tel. 0482 53981 or 26848. Fax. 0482-568756.
University and Colleges Jewish Students' Society. Inf. from Hon. Sec., c/o Hillel Hse. Address above.

LANCASTER (Lancs.)

Lancaster University Jewish Society, Interfaith Chaplaincy Centre,

University of Lancaster, LA1 4YW. Tel. 0524 65201, Ext. 4071. Visitors welcome.

Restaurant
(V) Fairview, 32 Hornby Rd, Caton, LA2 9QS. Tel. 0524-770118. B&B.

LEEDS (W. Yorks.)

The Leeds Jewish community is the second largest in the Provinces, and numbers about 12,000. The community dates only from 1804, although a few Jews are known to have lived there in the previous half-century. Until 1846 the community worshipped in a small room. The first synagogue building was erected in 1860, when there were about 60 Jewish families.

Synagogues & Religious Organisations
Beth Hamedrash Hagadol Syn., 399 Street Lane, LS17 6HQ. Min.: Rabbi Y. Shemaria. Exec. Officer: Mrs. M. Wilson. Tel. 0532 692181.
Chassidishe, c/o Talmud Torah, 2 Sandhill La., LS17 6AQ. All inq. to M. Kent, Flat 8, Sandhill Lawns, Sandhill La., LS17 6TT.
New Central Vilna Synagogues. Etz Chaim, 411 Harrogate Rd., LS17 7TT. Mins.: Rabbi Y. Angyalfi, Rev. G. Harris & Rev. A. Gilbert. Sec.: Tel. 0532 662214. Office 584 Harrogate Rd., Leeds LS17 8DP.
Shomrei Hadass, 368 Harrogate Rd., LS17 6QB. Independent Orthodox cong. Min.: Dayan Y. Refson. Tel. 0532 681461. Mikva at rear of premises.
Sinai (Reform), Roman Av., off Street Lane, LS8 2AN. Tel. 0532 665256. Services, Fri., 8 p.m., Sat., 10.30 a.m. Min.: Rabbi Walter Rothschild.
United Hebrew Cong., Shadwell La. Syn., 151 Shadwell La., LS17 8DW. Min.: Rabbi I. Goodhart. Sec.: M. S. Samuel. Tel. 0532 696141.
Beth Din, 7A Stainburn Parade, LS17 6NA. Tel. 0532 696902. Inf. about kosher food & accom. from the Registrar, Rev. A. Gilbert, B.A.

Representative Organisations
Leeds Jewish Representative Council, Shadwell La. Syn., 151 Shadwell La., LS17 8DW. President: Mrs. Toni Port. Inf. from Exec. Officer: Barry Abis, JP. Tel. 0532 697520.
B'nai B'rith Men's Lodge. Hon. Pres.: Barry Abis. Tel. 0532 685847.
B'nai Brith Women's Lodge. Pres.: Mrs. Marilyn Sefton. Tel. 0532 665899.

Cultural and Educational Organisations
Jewish Education Board (Talmud Torah), 2 Sandhill Lane, LS17 6AQ. Tel. 0532 683390.
Jewish Library, Porton Collection, Central Library, Municipal Bldgs., LS1 3AB.
Jewish Resources Centre, (Makor), 411 Harrogate Rd., LS17 7TT. Tel. 0532 680899.

Welfare Organisations, Hospitals, etc.
Home for Aged Jews, Donisthorpe Hall, Shadwell Lane, LS17 6AW. Admin.: S. Stone. Tel. 0532 684248.
Hospital meals & Visitation. Non-residents of Leeds who may be admitted to one of the city's hospitals should contact the Exec. Officer, Leeds Jewish Representative Council. Tel. 0532 697520.
Leeds Jewish Blind Society, 311 Stonegate Rd., LS17 6YW. Tel. 0532 684211.
Leeds Jewish Welfare Board, 311 Stonegate Rd., LS17 6AS. Tel. 0532 684211. Chief Exec.: Sheila Saunders.

Student and Youth Organisations
Bnei Akiva, "Bayit", Street Lane Gdns., Street Lane, LS17. Tel. 0532 692324.

Jewish Lads' & Girls' Brigade. Commanding Officer: S. Wane, 3 Elmhurst Gdns., LS17 8GB. Tel. 0532 667490.
Jewish Scouts: 15th Northvale Scout Group (7th Central Leeds). Group Scout Leader: D. Kingsley, 3 Nunroyd Gr., LS17 6PW. Tel. 0532 680303; 16th Northvale Scout Group & 61st Jewish Guides, Fir Tree Lane, LS17. Inq. to Group Scout Leader: Melvyn Sumroy, 63 Primley Pk. Cres., LS17. Tel. 0532 687453; 2nd Moortown (Sinai) Jewish Brownies & Guides, Sinai Com. Centre, Roman Av., Street La., LS8 2AN. Leader: Cathryn Firth, 19 Kingswood Grove, Leed, LS8 2BY. Tel. 0532 666151
Jewish Students' Assoc. Inq. to Warden, Hillel Hse., 2 Springfield Mount, LS2 9NE. Tel. 0532 433211. Male & female students may apply for residence at Hillel Hse., where **(K)** meals are provided, by writing to Dr. R. D. Pollard, Dept. of Electronic Engineering, University of Leeds LS2 9JT. Chaplaincy: 17 Queens Rd., LS6 1NY. Tel. 789597/671805.

Zionist Organisations
All information about Zionist orgs. and activities in Leeds can be obtained from the Area Director, Leeds Zionist Council, 411a Harrogate Rd., LS17 7TT. Tel. 0532 668419.

Club
Moor Allerton Golf Club Ltd., Wike Coal Rd., LS17 9NH. Exec. Vice President Jay J. Harris. Tel. 0532 661154-5 (members), 0532 665209 (professional).

Newspapers
Jewish Gazette, 1 Shaftesbury Av., LS8 1DR. Tel. 0532 666000.
Jewish Telegraph, 4A Roman View, LS8 2LW. Tel. 0532 695044.

Kosher Bakery
(K) Chalutz Bakery, 378 Harrogate Rd., LS17. Tel. 0532 691350.

Kosher Butchers & Delicatessen
(K) Fisher's, 391 Harrogate Rd., LS17 6DJ. Tel. 0532 686944.
(K) Gourmet Foods, 584 Sandhill Pde., Harrogate Rd., LS17 8DP. Tel. 0532 652726.
(K) Myers Kosherie, 410 Harrogate Rd., LS17 6PY. Tel. 682943.

Hotels, Restaurants, etc.
Beegee's Guest House, 18 Moor Allerton Dr., Moortown, LS17 6RZ. Tel. (0532) 666221. Fax (0532) 753300. Props.: Mr. & Mrs. B. Gibbs.
(K) Donisthorpe Restaurant, Shadwell Lane, LS17 6AW. Tel. 684248.
(V) Greenwoods, 5 Longfield Dr., Rodley, LS13 1JX. Tel. 0532 579639. B&B.
(V) Hansa's, 72 North St., LS2 7PN. Tel. 0532-444408.

LEICESTER (Leics.)

There have been Jewish coms. in Leicester since the Middle Ages, but the first record of a "Jews' synagogue" dates from 1861 in the Leicester Directory. The present synagogue was built in 1897 and consecrated by Chief Rabbi Dr. Hermann Adler.
Syn. & Com. Centre: Highfield St., LE2 0NQ. Min.: Rabbi Chaim Ingram. Hon. Sec.: G. J. Louis, 4 Lyndhurst Ct., London Rd., LE2 2AP. Tel. 0533 700997.
Mikva: Synagogue bldg., Highfield St.
Progressive Jewish Cong. Tel. 0533 832927. Services, Fri. and festivals. Religion school.
Ajex. Ch.: B. Besbrode, 50 Arden Way, Market Harborough. Tel. 0858 466480.

B'nai B'rith. Leicester Unity Lodge. Pres.: Joe Markham, 74 Wakerley Rd., LE5 6AQ. Tel. 0533 737620.

Bookshop: Com. Centre, Highfield St., LE5 6AQ. Inq.: J. Markham, address & Tel. as above.

Hillette. Inq.: Monty Simmons, 125 Carisbrooke Rd., LE2 3PG. Tel. 0533 706600.

Jewish Library: Com. Hall, Highfield St., LE2 0NQ.

Maccabi Assoc., Leicester Communal Hall, Highfield St., LE2 0NQ. Tel. 0533 540477.

WIZO. Ch.: Mrs. Helen Naftalin, 15 Knighton Grange Rd. Tel. 0533 703358.

Leicester Aviv. Ch.: Mrs. Beverley Levy, 37 Southernhay Rd. Tel. 0533 701218.

Kosher meat, poultry & delicatessen are obtainable from the kosher department of L. A. Cant (Butchers) Ltd., 75 Uppingham Rd., LE5 3TB, supervised by Rev. M. Fine.

Vegetarian Restaurants. The Chaat Hse., 108 Belgrave Rd., LE4 5AT. Tel. 0533 660513; **The Good Earth**, 19 Free Lane, LE1 1JX. Tel. 0533 626260; **Blossoms**, 17b Cank St., LE1 5GX. Tel. 0533 539535.

Bread and Roses, 70 High St., LE1 5YP, Tel. 0533-532448. 10-4, Tues-Sat.

Richard's Place, 157 Wanlip Lane, Birstall, LE4 4GL, Tel. 0533-673107. B&B. All year.

Sharmilee, 71 Belgrave Rd., LE4 6AS, Tel. 0533-610503. 12-2.30, 6-9, Tues-Thurs; 12-9, Fri-Sun.

LIVERPOOL (Merseyside)

There is evidence of an organised community before 1750. It is believed to have been composed of Sephardi Jews and to have had some connection with the West Indies or with Dublin, but some authorities believe that they were in the main German Jews.

This small community, which was known to John Wesley, the religious reformer, declined at first, but was reinforced, probably in about 1770, by a new wave of settlers, mostly from Europe. The largely Ashkenazi Jews were to some degree intending emigrants for America and the West Indies, who changed their minds and stayed in Liverpool.

By 1807 the community had a building of some size in Seel St., the parent of the present synagogue in Princes Road, one of the handsomest in the country. It celebrated its centenary in 1974.

Synagogues & Religious Organisations

Allerton, cnr. Mather & Booker Avs., L18 9TB. Tel. 051-427 6848. M.: Rabbi M. Barron M.A., Rev. S. Cohen; Sec: A. Benjamin.

Childwall Hebrew Cong., Dunbabin Rd., L15 6XL. Mikva in syn. precinct. Tel. 051-722 2079. M.: Rabbi M. L. Cofnas. Admin.: J. Abrahams.

Greenbank Drive Hebrew Cong., Greenbank Dr., L17 1AN. Tel. 051-733 1417. M., Sec. & Registrar: Rev. H. M. Chait.

Old Hebrew Cong., Princes Rd., L8 1TG. Tel. 051-709 3431. M.: Rev. H. Caplan.

Ullet Rd., Hebrew Cong., 101 Ullet Rd., L17.

Liverpool Progressive Syn., 28 Church Rd. N., L15 6TF. Tel. 051-733 5871. M.: Rev. N. Zalud.

Liverpool Kashrut Commission (incorporating Liverpool Shechita Board) c/o Liverpool Jewish Youth and Community Centre, Harold House, Dunbabin Rd., Liverpool L15 6XL. Hon Sec.: Rodney Berman. Tel. 051-733 2292/3.

Rav to the Bd: Rabbi R. Margulies. Tel. 061-7731045; Hon. Sec.: Rodney Berman. Tel. 051 421 0055.

Representative Organisation

Merseyside Jewish Representative Council, 433 Smithdown Rd., Liverpool L15 3JL. Tel. 051-733 2292. Hon. Sec.: Mrs. D. B. Salamon .

Welfare Organisations, Hospitals, etc.

Home for Aged Jews, Stapely North, Mossley Hill Rd., L18 8BR. Tel. 051-724 3260. Hospital wing, Tel. 051-724 4548.

Merseyside Jewish Welfare Council, Shifrin House, 433 Smithdown Rd., Liverpool, L15 3JL. Tel. 051-733 2292-3.

Student & Youth Organisations

Hillel House, 12 Greenbank Drive, L17 1AW Tel. 051-735 0793. Annexe, 16 Borrowdale Rd., L15 3LE. For Hillel House self-catering accom. for students, contact Mrs. C. Lewis. Tel. 051-722 5021.

Jewish Students' Society, Inq. to Sec., c/o Guild of Undergraduates, 2 Bedford St. N., L7 7BD or Hillel Hse. As above.

Jewish Youth and Community Centre, Harold Hse., Dunbabin Rd., L15 6XL. Tel. 051-722 5671. Bnei Akiva; Harold Hse. Youth Club; Haroldeans Football Club; H.Q. of J.L.B.; Shifrin Drama & Music Centre; Tennis Club; Kindergarten; Resource Centre. Tel. 051-722 3514; JIA office: 051 722 8707; J.N.F. office: 051 722 8025. Liverpool Jewish Telegraph office: 051 722 3999. There is a (K) restaurant at the Centre, open Sun., Tues. & Thurs., 6.30 to 11 p.m. Licenced Bar. Out-of-town visitors welcome. Also take-away service. Tel. 051-722 5825/5671. Many other facilities available.

Student accom. Liverpool University's halls of residence contain more than 2,000 single bedrooms. These are available during vacations for conferences, student groups, tourists, etc. No kosher catering facilities available, however. Also available, self-catering flats. Inq. to: Conference Office, Liverpool University, P.O. Box 147, L69 3BX. Tel. 051-794 6440.

Zionist Organisations

These are concentrated at the Zionist Offices, Harold Hse., Dunbabin Rd., L15 6XL. Tel. 051-722 8707.

Sports

Lee Park Golf Club, Liverpool, L27 3YA. Sec.: Mrs. D. Barr. Tel. 051-487 3882.

Sir George Bean Memorial Sports & Tennis Centre, c/o Harold Hse., Dunbabin Rd., L15 6XL. Tel. 051-722-8736.

Books, etc.

A Jewish book and gift centre operates at the Jewish Youth and Community Centre, Dunbabin Rd., L15 6XL on Sun. from 11 a.m. to 1 p.m. Tel. 051-722-5661.

Liverpool Jewish Resource Centre, Harold Hse., Dunbabin Rd., L15 6XL. Large range of audio-visual and printed materials for sale or hire. Tel. 051-722 3514. Mon.-Thurs., 2.30 p.m. to 5.30 p.m.; Sun., 11 a.m. to 1 p.m. Answerphone.

Newspapers

Jewish Gazette, 14 Bristol Rd., L15. Tel. 051-733 3625.

Jewish Telegraph, Harold Hse., address above. Tel. 051-722 3999 & 3444.

Caterers

(K) M & E Stoops Catering, 23 Montclair Dr., 18. Tel. 051-722 7459.

(K) Elaine Marco, 20 Beauclair Dr., L15 6XG. Tel. 051-722 1536.

(K) Celia Clyne, 54 Chapeltown St., Manchester M1. Tel. 061-273 8888.

Restaurant
(K) **Marcos**, Harold House, Dunbabin Rd., L15 6XL. Tel. 051-722 5825.
(V) **Munchies Eating House**, Myrtle Parade. Tel. 051-709-7896.

LONDON AIRPORT (Heathrow) (Greater London)

A Jewish chaplain is on call at the airport. Chaplaincy Office, TW6 1JH. Tel. 0784 50498.

Heathrow Penta Hotel (636), Bath Rd., Hounslow, TW6 2AQ. Tel. 081-897 6363.

The Edwardian International Hotel (459). Tel. 081-759 6311.

LOUGHTON (Essex)

Syn.: Borders Lane, IG10 1TE. Tel. 081-508 0303. Services: Fri. evg., 8 p.m.; Sat. morn., 9.30 a.m. Min.: Rev. J. D. Lorraine, 93 The Lindens, Loughton, Essex. Tel. 081-508 0270.

LUTON (Beds.)

Syn.: 116 Bury Park Rd., LU1 1HE. Tel. 0582 25032. Hon. Sec.: D. Bailey, P.O. Box 215, LU1 1HW. Services: Fri. night & Sabbath morn. Office open Sun., 9.30 a.m. to 12.30 p.m.

Friendship Club: Adj. the syn. Open Sun. afternoons, 2-4.30 p.m. Ch.: S. Gonshor. Tel. 0582 26761.

Hebrew Parent-Teachers' Assoc. Inq. to Syn.

Judean Youth Club, PO Box 215, LU1 1HW. Ch., Exec. Com.: Mrs. B. Felson. Tel. 0582 22939.

MAIDENHEAD (Berks.)

Maidenhead is a growing Jewish area. The syn. (membership, 550 families) covers Berks. and Bucks area.

Syn. (Constituent of Reform Synagogues of Gt. Britain): 9 Boyn Hill Av., SL6 4ET. Services, Fri., 8.30 p.m., Sat., 10.30 a.m. Inq.: Rabbi Dr. Jonathan Romain. Tel. 0628 71058.

MANCHESTER (Greater Manchester)

The Manchester Jewish community is the second largest in the United Kingdom, numbering about 35,000.

There was no organised community until 1780. A cemetery was acquired in 1794. The present Great Synagogue claims with justice to be the direct descendant of this earliest community.

The leaders of Manchester Jewry in those early days had without exception come from the neighbouring relatively important Jewish community of Liverpool. After the Continental revolutions of 1848, the arrival of "liberal" Jews began. One of them, a Hungarian rabbi and soldier of the Revolution, Solomon Schiller-Szinessy, became minister of a Reform synagogue established in 1856.

In 1871 a small Sephardi group from North Africa and the Levant drew together and formed a congregation, which extended to fill two handsome synagogues, one in Cheetham Hill Rd., and the other in W. Didsbury. However, the Cheetham Hill Rd. congregation has now moved to Salford, and its former house of worship has been turned into a Jewish museum.

Synagogues & Religious Organisations

Adass Yeshurun, Cheltenham Cres., Salford, M7 0FE. Min.: Dayan G. Krausz. Sec.: S. Gluckstadt. Tel. 061-792 1233.

Adath Yisroel Nusach Ari, Upper Park Rd., Salford, M7 0HL. Sec.: Rev. S. Simon. Tel. 061-740 3905.

Bury Hebrew Cong., Sunnybank Rd., Bury, BL9 8EP. Min.: Rabbi B. Singer. Admin.: Mrs. M. Wilson. Tel. 061-796 5062.

Central & North Manchester (incorporating Hightown Central and Beth Jacob), Leicester Rd., Salford, M7 0HH. Min.: Rabbi J. Rubinstein. Sec.: M. Green. Tel. 061-740 4830.

Cheetham Hebrew Cong., 453-5 Cheetham Hill Rd., M8 7PA. Tel. 061-740 7788. Min. Rabbi Yakov Abenson. Sec.: J. E. Freeman.

Cheshire Reform Cong., Menorah Synagogue, Altrincham Rd., M22 4NZ. Min.: Rabbi Dr. M. Hilton. Tel. 061-428 7746.

Congregation of Spanish and Portuguese Jews, 18 Moor La., Kersal, Salford, M7 0WX. Hon. Sec.: P. R. Pereira. Tel. 061-766 7246.

Hale & District Hebrew Cong., Shay La., Hale Barns, Ches., WA15 8PA. Min.: Rabbi Joel Portnoy. Hon. Sec.: A. Wiseberg. Tel. 061-980 8846.

Heaton Park Hebrew Cong., Ashdown, Middleton Rd., M8 6JX. Min.: Rev. L. Olsberg. Admin.: Cecil Ashe. Tel. 061-740 4766.

Higher Crumpsall & Higher Broughton, Bury Old Rd., Salford M8 6EX. Tel. 061-740 1210. Min.: Rabbi Arnold Saunders B.A.. Sec.: Mrs. E. Somers. Tel. 061-740 8155.

Higher Prestwich, 445 Bury Old Rd., Prestwich, M25 5TY. Min.: Rev. H. Hillman. Sec.: Vacant. Tel. 061-773 4800.

Hillock Hebrew Cong., Ribble Dr., Whitefield. Sec.: M. Freedman. Tel. 061-766 5986.

Holy Law South Broughton Cong., Bury Old Rd., Prestwich, M25 8EX. Morn. and evg. services daily. M.: Rabbi Yossi Chazan. Admin.: S. Wilner. Tel. 061-740 1634.

Hulme Hebrew Cong. Services held at Hillel Hse., Greenheys La., M15 6LR. Hon. Sec.: Malcolm Edis. Tel. 061-740 6818.

Kahal Chassidim, 62 Singleton Rd., M7 0LU. Sec.: B. Lewis. Tel. 061-798 8205.

Machzikei Hadass, Syn. & Com. Office: 17 Northumberland St., Salford, M7 0FE. Org. Sec.: A. Vogel. Tel. 061-792 1313.

Manchester Great & New Synagogue, Stenecourt, Holden Rd., M7 0NL. Min.: Rev. Gabriel Brodie. Tel. 061-792 8399.

Manchester Reform Synagogue, Jackson's Row, M2 5WD. Tel. 061-834 0415 & 0514. Min.: Rabbi Dr. Reuven Silverman. Sec.: N. J. Franks.

North Salford, Vine St., Salford, M7 0NX. Min.: Rabbi L. W. Rabinowitz. Hon. Sec.: D. Rose. Tel. 061-792 8638.

Ohel Torah, 132 Leicester Rd., Salford, M7 0EA. Sec.: P. Koppenheim, 5 Granville Av., Salford, M7 0HB. Tel. 061-740 6678.

Prestwich Hebrew Cong., Bury New Rd., M25 8WN. M.: Rabbi Mordechai Ginsbury. Sec.: A. Frankel. Tel. 061-773 1978.

Sale & District Hebrew Cong., 14 Hesketh Rd., Sale, M33 5AA. Tel. 061-973 2172. Min.: Rabbi Gershon Overlander. Hon. Sec.: M. J. Coppel. Tel. 061-973 4054.

Sedgley Park (Shomrei Hadass), Park View Rd., Prestwich, M25 5FA. Sec.: G. R. Marks. Tel. 061-773 6092.

Sha'are Sedek Syn. & Talmud Torah, Old Lansdowne Rd., W. Didsbury, M20 8NZ. Tel. 061-445 5731. Min.: Rabbi S. Ellituv. Tel. 061-434 6903.

Sha'arei Shalom (Reform), Elms St., Whitefield, M25 6GQ. Gen. Sec.: Henry Abrahams, 25 Hillingdon Rd., Whitefield M25 7QQ.

South Manchester, Wilbraham Rd., Fallowfield, M14 6JS. Min.: Rabbi Y. R. Rubin. Admin.: S. L. Rydz. Tel. 061-224 1366.

United Synagogue, Meade Hill Rd., M8 6LS. Tel. 061-740 9586. Min.: Rabbi I. W. Freedman. Pres.: S. Huller.
Whitefield Hebrew Cong., Park Lane, Whitefield, M25 7PB. Tel. 061-766 3732. Min.: Rabbi Jonathan Guttentag, B.A. Admin.: Mrs. P. M. Deach.
Withington Cong. of Spanish & Portuguese Jews, 8 Queenston Rd., W. Didsbury, M20 8WZ. Min.: Rabbi M. Van den Bergh. Tel. 061-445 1943.
Yeshurun Hebrew Cong., Coniston Rd., Gatley, Cheshire, SK8 4AP. Min.: Dr. Alan Unterman. Admin.: Mrs. N. Shepherd. Tel. 061-428 8242.
Beth Din & Shechita Board Offices, 435 Cheetham Hill Rd., M8 7PF. Tel. 061-740 9711. Rosh Beth Din: Dayan G. Krausz. Administrator: J. Brodie.
Mikvaot: Com. Mikva (under the authority of the Manchester Beth Din), Broom Holme, Tetlow Lane, Salford, M7 0BU. Tel. 061-792 3970 during opening times; Manchester & District Mikva (under the authority of Machzikei Hadass), Sedgley Pk. Rd., Prestwich. Tel. 061-773 1537 & 7403. Whitefield Hebrew Congregation Mikva, Park Lane, Whitefield M25 7PB. Tel. 061-766 3732.

Representative Organisations
Jewish Representative Council of Greater Manchester & Region, Jewish Cultural Centre, Bury Old Rd., M8 6FY. Tel. 061-720 8721. Affiliated to the Council are 140 syns. and orgs. Pres.: Mrs. Rita Rosemarine.

Cultural & Educational Organisations
Central Library, St. Peter's Sq., M2 5PD. Large collection of Jewish books for reference and loan, including books in Hebrew. Tel. 061-234 1983/1984. Contact the Social Sciences Library..
Jewish Cultural Centre, Bury Old Rd., M8 6FY. Tel. 061-795 4000. Syn.; student accom.; short-term accom.; library.
Manchester Jewish Museum, 190 Cheetham Hill Rd., M8 8LW. Tel. 061-834 9879 & 061-832 7353. Mon.-Thurs., 10.30 a.m. to 4 p.m. Sundays, 10.30 a.m. to 5 p.m. Admission charge. Exhibitions, Heritage trails, Demonstration & Talks. Calendar of events available on request. Educational visits for schools and adult groups *must* be booked in advance.
Manchester Central Board for Hebrew Education & Talmud Torah, Emanuel Raffles Hse., 57 Leicester Rd., Salford M7 0DA. Tel. 061-708 9200.

Welfare Organisations, Hospitals, etc.
Brookvale Homes for the Mentally Handicapped. Simister Lane, Prestwich, M25 5SF. Director of Services Mrs. L. Richmond,. Tel. 061-653 1767. Short term care available.
Manchester Jewish Blind Society, Nicky Alliance Day Centre, Middleton Rd., M8 6JY. Tel. 061-740 0111.
Manchester Jewish Social Services, 12 Holland Rd., Higher Crumpsall, M8 6NP. Tel. 061-795 0024. Pres. William Kintish.
Outreach, Manchester Jews' Benevolent Society, League of Jewish Women, Heathlands, Home for the Aged. Morris Feinmann Home for the Aged.

Student & Youth Organisations
Bnei Akiva (North of England), c/o Holy Law South Broughton Synagogue, Bury Old Rd., M25. Tel. 061-740 1621.
Habonim-Dror, Moadon Habonim, 11 Upper Park Rd., Salford, M7 0HY. Tel. 061-795 9447. Fax. 061 740 1981.
Hillel House, Greenheys La., M15 6LR. Tel. 061-226 1139 (Warden). **(K)** Meals (under Manchester Beth Din). Inq. about accom. to Accom. Officer.
Jewish Scouts & Guides. 401st Manchester Scout Group and 5th Cheetham Guides & Brownies, H.Q., Willow Hill Rd., Crumpsall, Manchester 8. Tel. 061 792 3431. Group Scout Leader: Howard Balkind, 16 Vine St., Kersal, Salford, M7 0PG.

Lubavitch Community & Youth Centre, Lubavitch Hse., 62 Singleton Rd., Salford, M7 0LU. Tel. 061-740 9514.

University & Polytechnic Jewish Societies. Sec.: Hillel Hse., Greenheys La., M15 6LR.

Zionist Organisations

Kibbutz Representatives: 11 Upper Pk. Rd., Salford M7 0HY. Tel. 061-795 9447. Fax. 061 740 1981.

Zionist Central Council of Greater Manchester, Joseph Mamlock Hse., 142 Bury Old Rd., M8 6HD. Tel. 061-740 1825 (also the offices of the Joint Israel Appeal, Jewish National Fund (Tel. for both 061-740 1825), Jewish Agency Aliya Dept. Tel. 061-740 2864, and Women's Zionist Council (Wizo and Emunah). Tel. 061-740 3367).

Sport

Whitefield Golf Club, Higher Lane, Whitefield, M25 7EZ. Sec.: Mrs. R. L. Vidler. Tel. 061-766 2904.

Dunham Golf Forest and Country Club, Oldfield Lane, Attrincham, Cheshire WA4 4TY. Tel. 061-928 2605.

Newspapers

Jewish Chronicle (Northern Office), 27 Bury Old Rd., Prestwich, M25 8EY. Tel. 061-740 5171.

Jewish Gazette, 27 Bury Old Rd., Prestwich, M25 8EY. Tel. 061-740 5171 and 061-682 3657.

Jewish Telegraph, Telegraph Hse., 11 Park Hill, Bury Old Rd., Prestwich, M25 8HH. Tel. 061-740 9321.

Booksellers

J. Goldberg, 11 Parkside Av., Salford, M7 0HB. Tel. 061-740 0732.

B. Horowitz, 20 King Edward Bldgs., Bury Old Rd., M8. Tel. 061-740 5897, & 2 Kings Rd., Prestwich, M25. Tel. 061-773 4956.

Hyman's, Wilmslow Rd., Cheadle, Cheshire.

Jewish Book Centre (Terence Noyek), 25 Ashbourne Gr., Salford, M7 0DB. Tel. 061-792 1253.

Hotel

(K) Fulda's Hotel and Restaurant (15), 84 Bury Old Rd., M8 6HE. Tel. 061-740 4551 & 061-740 4748. Fax. 061 740 4551

Restaurants

(K) Broadway Kosher Diner, 7-9 Kings Rd., Prestwich, M25 8LE. Tel. 061-773 2909. Under Manchester Beth Din.

Captain Restaurant, 85 Rochdale Rd. Tel. 061-839 7198.

★ **Lapidus**, 21 Bury Old Rd., Prestwich, M25 8EQ. Tel. 061-740 3095.

The Nose, 6 Lapwing Lane, West Didsbury. Tel. 061-445 3653.

(V) Pie in the Sky, 160b Wellington Rd., Withington, M20 9UH. Tel. 061-4452772.

Terrace Restaurant, Jewish Cultural Centre, Bury Old Road, M86 6FY.

(V) The Greenhouse, 331 Western St., Rusholme, M14 4AN. Tel. 061-2240730.

Caterers

(K) Celia Clyne Catering Ltd., 54 Chapeltown St., Manchester. M1 2NN.

(K) I & M Kosher Banqueting Caterers, 54 Brookland Rd., Prestwich, Manchester M25 8ED. Tel. 061-740 8624.

(K) Renee Hodari, 36 Brooklawn Dr., Withington, M20 9GZ.

(K) Simon's Catering, 105 Leicester Rd., Salford, 7.

Sheila Mendelson Catering, 81-87 Silverdale Rd., Gatley, Cheshire, SK8 4QR.

Delicatessen
(K) Deli King, Kings Rd., Prestwich, M25 8LQ. Tel. 061-798 7370.

MARGATE (Kent)

Syn.: Godwin Rd., Cliftonville, CT9 2HA. Sec.: D. Kaye, 43 Eastchurch Rd., Cliftonville, CT9 3HY. Tel. 0843 223219.
B'nai B'rith, Thanet Montefiore Unity Lodge. Pres.: Mr. Joe M. Klein, 153 Botany Rd., Broadstairs, Kent, CT10 3TX. Tel. 0843-62878.

MIDDLESBROUGH (Cleveland)

Syn.: Park Rd. S., TS5 6LE. Sec.: Lionel Simons. Tel. 0642 819034 (for details of services). J. Bloom. Tel. 0642-781363.

Restaurant
(V) Filberts, 47 Borough Rd., TS1 4AF. Tel. 0642-245455.

MILTON KEYNES

Milton Keynes & District Reform Synagogue, Services at Tinkers Bridge Meeting Place, Milton Keynes. Chairman: Mr. Stephen Bonn, 83 Whalley Drive, Bletchley, MK3 6HX. Tel. 0908 649378.

NEWCASTLE UPON TYNE (Tyne & Wear)

The community was established before 1831, when a cemetery was acquired. (Jews have lived in Newcastle since 1775). There are about 1,200 Jews in the city today.

Synagogues & Religious Organisations
United Hebrew Congregation. Syn., Graham Park Rd., Gosforth, NE3 4BH. Daily morn. & evg. services throughout the year. Mikva on premises. Min.: Rabbi M. M. Baddiel, 22 Moor Rd. N., Gosforth, NE3 1AD. Tel. 091 2855147. Sec.: Mrs. P. Ashton, Lionel Jacobson Hse., address below. Tel. 091 2840959.
Lionel Jacobson Hse., Graham Park Rd., Gosforth, NE3 4BH. Full communal facilities available inc. Kashrus Com., Hebrew Classes & Jewish Welfare Soc.
Newcastle Reform Syn. Services at The Croft, off Kenton Rd., Gosforth, NE3 4RF. Tel. 091 2848621. Min.: Rabbi Moshe Yehuday. Tel. 091 285 2593.

Representative Organisation
Representative Council of North-East Jewry, Lionel Jacobson Hse., address above. Pres.: Geoffrey Lurie. Hon. Sec.: Mr. V. Gallant. Tel. 091 2857533. Publishes fortnightly "The North-East Jewish Recorder".

Miscellaneous
Bnei Akiva, Inf.: Ms A Rosen, 16 Moor Crescent, Gosforth.
Hillel Hse., 29-31 Hawthorn Rd., Gosforth. (K) Student meals available Fri. nights. Further inf. from G. Lurie, 32 St. Mary's Pl., NE1 7PS. Tel. 091 2610577 or 2857928.
Bridge Club, c/o Mr. A. Deane. Tel. 091-281 1992.
Newcastle Jewish Leisure Group, c/o Mr. W. Sharman. Tel. 091-285 4133.
Newcastle Maccabi –
Badminton, c/o Mr. B. Lewis. Tel. 091-285 5501
Junior Maccabi, c/o Mr. H. White. Tel. 091-285 2054.

Table Tennis, c/o Mr. H. Ross. Tel. 091-285 4043.
Tennis, c/o Mr. P. Mickler. Tel. 091-285 5195.
North-East Jewish Youth Study Group. Inf. from D. Ross, 56 Southwood
Gardens, Kenton, NE3 4LT. Tel. 091 2854043.

Kosher Meat, Poultry & Groceries
(K) Zelda's Delicatessen, Unit 7 Kenton Park Shopping Centre NE3 4RU.
Tel. 091-2130013. Under Newcastle Kashrus Committee.

Restaurants
(V) Old School House, Kirkwhelpington, NE19 2RT. Tel. 0830-40226. B&B.
(V) The Red Herring, 3 Studley Terrace, Fenham, NE4 5AH. Tel. 091-
2723484.

NORTHAMPTON (Northants.)
Syn.: Overstone Rd. Sec.: A. Moss. Tel. 0604 646658. Services: Fri. night.

NORWICH (Norfolk)
The present community was founded in 1813, Jews having been resident in
Norwich during the Middle Ages, and connected with the woollen and
worsted trade, for which the city was at that time famous. A resettlement
of Jews is believed to have been completed by the middle of the eighteenth
century. A syn. was built in 1848 and destroyed in an air raid in 1942. A
temporary syn. opened in 1948. A new syn. was consecrated by the Chief
Rabbi in 1969. The congregation serves a large area, having members in
Ipswich, Gt. Yarmouth, Lowestoft and Cromer.
Syn.: 3a Earlham Rd., Norwich, NR2 3RA. Hon. Sec.: J. Griffiths, 23 Varvel
Av., Sprowston, Norwich, NR7 8PH.
Israel and Social Society, 3a Earlham Rd., Norwich. P.: Jennifer Salman;
Hon Sec.: Maureen Leveton.
Progressive Jewish Community of East Anglia. Information from Hon.
Sec.: Beverley Simmonds. Tel. 05088 666.

Restaurants
(V) Eat Naturally, 11 Wensum St., NR3 1LA. Tel. 0603-660838.
(V) The Treehouse, 16 Dove St., NR2 1DE. Tel. 0603 625560.

NOTTINGHAM (Notts.)
Syn.: Shakespeare St., NG1 4FQ. Sec.: Tel. 0602 472004. For times of
services, telephone Syn. Sec. Min: 0602 624691.
Nottingham Progressive Jewish Cong. Syn.: Lloyd St., Sherwood,
Nottingham, NG5 4BP. Chairman: R. Sylvester. Tel. 0602 307628.
★ Jewish Rest Home. Miriam Kaplowitch Hse., 470 Mansfield Rd., NG5
2EL. Tel. 0602 622038 (Matron & Administrator), 0602 624274 (residents).
Jewish Welfare Board. Ch.: Dr. M. Caplan. Hon. Sec.: Peter Seymour, 115
Selby Rd., West Bridgford, NG2 7BB. Tel. 0602-452895.
Jewish Women's Benevolent Society. Ch.: Mrs. D. Christie, 8 Croft Rd.,
Edwalton, NG12 4BW. Tel. 0602 231105. Hon. Sec.: Mrs. H. Markson. Tel.
0602 231177.
Students: Jewish & Israel Soc., University of Nottingham, University Pk.,
NG7 2RD.

Restaurants
(V) Krisha Restaurant, 144 Alfreton Rd., Redford, NG7 3NS. Tel. 0602-
708608.

(V) Maxine's Salad Table, 56 Upper Parliament St., NG1 2AG. Tel. 0602-473622.

(V) Rita's Cafe, 15 Goosegate, Hockley, NG1 1FE. Tel. 0602-481115.

(V) The Vegetarian Pot, 375 Alfreton Rd., Redford, NG7 5LT. Tel. 0602-703333.

OXFORD (Oxon.)

There was an important medieval com., and the present one dates from 1842. The Oxford Syn. and Jewish Centre, opened in 1974, serves both the city & the university. It is available for all forms of Jewish worship.

The Syn. and Jewish Centre is at 21 Richmond Rd., OX1 2JL. For inf. about services, Tel. 0865 53042. Pres. of Cong.: L. Wollenberg, 131 Eynsham Rd., Oxon, OX2 9BY; Tel. 0865-862704. Hon. Treas.: A. Curtis, 257 Woodstock Rd., OX2 7AE. Tel. 0865 515107.

(K) A kosher meals service operates during term time. Inq. to 0865 53042.

Organisations

Menorah Society, Hon. Sec.: Mrs. B. Grant, 6 Woodlands Cl., Headington, OX3 7RY. Tel. 0865 62156.

For Jewish Youth activities, Hannah Faust, 21 Richmond Rd., Oxford, OX1 2JL. Tel. 0865 863210.

Women's Zionist Org. Helena Harper, 48 Hutchcomb Rd., Botley, Oxford. Tel. 0865 248992.

PETERBOROUGH (Cambs.)

Syn.: 142 Cobden Av., PE1 1YL. Inq. to C. Conn, 22 Edinburgh Av., Werrington. Tel. 0733 571282.

PLYMOUTH (Devon.)

The cong. was founded in 1752 and a syn. erected ten years later. This is now the oldest Ashkenazi syn. building in England still used for its original purpose. It is a scheduled historical monument. In 1815 Plymouth was one of the four most important provincial centres in Anglo-Jewry.

Syn.: Catherine St., PL1 2AD. Sec.: Miss Reva Joseph. Tel. 0752 661626. Services: Fri., 6 p.m. Sat., 9.30 a.m.

Cong. offers free use of minister's modern flat as holiday accom. in return for conducting Orthodox Fri. evg. & Sabbath morn. services. Inq.: Reva Joseph, c/o Syn.

A Jewish collection of fiction & non-fiction books, mainly lending copies, has been integrated into the stock of the Plymouth Central Library, Drake Circus, PL4 8AL. It is known as the Holcenberg Collection.

Restaurant

(V) Plymouth Arts Centre Vegetarian Restaurant, 38 Looe St., PL4 0EB. Tel. 0752 660060.

PORTSMOUTH & SOUTHSEA (Hants.)

The Portsmouth com. was founded in 1746. Its first syn. was in Oyster Row, but the cong. removed to a building in White's Row, which it continued to occupy for almost two centuries. A new building was erected in 1936. The cemetery is in a street which was once known as Jews' Lane. It is the oldest in the Provinces still used for the interment of Jews.

Syn.: The Thicket, Southsea, PO5 2AA. Tel. 0705 821494. Min.: Rev. A. Dee.

PRESTON (Lancs.)

Inf. from Hon. Sec. of com.: Dr. C. E. Nelson, 31 Avondale Rd., Southport, Merseyside.

RAMSGATE (Kent)

Syn.: Montefiore Endowment, Hereson Rd. Communications to Spanish & Portuguese Synagogue, 2 Ashworth Rd., London, W9 1JY. Tel. 01-289 2573. Visitors wishing to see the Montefiore Mausoleum and Synagogue should apply to A. G. G. Da Costa, 33 Luton Av., Broadstairs. Tel. 0843 62507.
Thanet and District Reform Synagogue, 293A Margate Rd., Ramsgate, Kent, CT12 6TA. Tel. 0843-851164. Services: Fri. 8.00pm, Sat. 11.00am.

READING (Berks.)

The community began in 1886 with the settlement of a number of tailors from London. The synagogue was opened in 1900, and has been in continuous use ever since. This flourishes today as the centre of the Reading Hebrew Congregation, which has a growing membership of 160 families, and is the only Orthodox congregation in Berkshire. The Sir Hermann Gollancz Hall next to the synagogue is the venue of many social groups.
Synagogue, Goldsmid Rd., Reading, RG1 7YB. Tel. 0734 571018. Hon. Sec.: Mrs. Louise. Creme, Maisonette 2, 52 Russell St., RG1 7XH. Tel. 0734 571710.
Ladies Guild. Mrs. V. Stein, 343 Peppard Rd., Emmer Green, Reading. Tel. 0734 472711.
Mothers and Toddlers/Babies. Mrs. Carol Kay, 33 Monks Way, Reading. Tel. 0734 575069.
University Jewish Society, c/o Reading Hillel House, 82 Basingstoke Rd., Reading. Tel. 0734 873282.
Cheder. c/o the Synagogue. Tel. 0734 571018.
Thames Valley Progressive Jewish Community, 6 Church St., Reading. Chairman: Ms D. Edelman. Tel. 0734 867769/500551.
WIZO. Mrs. P. Kay, 17 Southcote Rd., Reading. Tel. 0734 573680.
(K) Food shop – kosher meat and provisions – Mrs. C. Kay. Tel. 0734 575069.
Judaica shop – Mrs. P Kay. Tel. 0734 573680.
Youth Centre – HaNoar Hatzioni. Enq. to Secretary. Tel. 0734 571710.

ROCHESTER (Kent)

Syn.: Magnus Memorial Synagogue, High St., Rochester, ME1 1TE. (Listed Building, known as The Chatham Memorial Synagogue.) Inq.: H. Halpern, Boley Hill Hse., Boley Hill, Rochester, Kent, ME1 1TE. Tel. 0634 842405.

ROMFORD (Greater London)

Syn.: 25 Eastern Rd. Inq.: H. Lexton, 11 Mulberry Cl., Gidea Pk.

RUISLIP (Greater London)

Syn.: Shenley Av., Ruislip Manor, HA4 6BP. Min.: Rev. D. Wolfson. Tel. 0895 632934. Inq. The Synagogue, Shenley Avenue, Ruislip Manor, Middx., HA4 6BT. Tel. 0895 622059.

ST. ALBANS (Herts.)

Syn.: Oswald Rd., AL1 3AQ. Tel. 56 54872. Services, Fri. 8 p.m.

St. Alban's Masorti Syn. Inq. Sec: S. Gess, 38 Battlefield Rd., Tel. 0727 848778.

ST. ANNES-ON-SEA (Lancs.)

Syn.: Orchard Rd., FY8 1PJ. Tel. 0253 721831. Services 7.30 a.m. and 8 p.m.
Min.: President.: P. Davidson. Tel. 0253 723920.
Hon. Sec.: M. Brody. Tel. 0253 734722.
Ladies' Guild. Ch.: Mrs. S. Naftel, 39 Curzon Rd. Tel. 0253 729383.
St. Annes and Fylde Jewish Literary Society & Friendship Club. Hon. Sec.: Mrs. Gene Kay, 15 Crestway, Newton Dr., Blackpool, FY3 8PA. Tel. 0253 392513.

Delicatessen

Safeway Food Store, St. Andrew's Rd., North St.; The Lytham Delicatessen, 53 Warton St., FY8 2JE. Tel. 0253 735861.

SHEFFIELD (S. Yorks.)

The earliest records of the Sheffield cong. date from 1837, although it had already been in existence for some time before then.

Synagogues

Sheffield Jewish Congregation and Centre, Wilson Rd., S11 8RN. Jt. Hon. Sec.: Mrs. J. Flowers, Mrs. M. Shaw. Tel. 0742 362217.
Sheffield & District Reform Jewish Cong. Services alternate Fri. evgs. Chairman: Howard Saffer, 60 Muskoka Drive, Bents Green, S11 7RJ. Tel. 0742 308433. Further inf.: Tel. 0742 308433 or 360970.
Jewish Centre, 127 Psalter Lane, S11 8UX. Tel. 0742 552296.
Communal inq. to S. Burchhardt, 7 Ranelagh Dr., S11 9HE. Tel. 0742 368187.

SOLIHULL (W. Midlands)

Syn.: Solihull & District Hebrew Cong., 3 Monastery Dr., St. Bernard's Rd., B91 3HN. Min.: Rabbi H. Rader. Services Fri. evg., Sat., 9.45 a.m., Sun., 9 a.m. Hon. Sec.: P. D. Fiddler. Tel. 021-707 5199.
Jewish Social and Cultural Soc. Hon. Sec.: Mrs. P. Singer, 7 Nebsworth Cl., Solihull, B90 3NS. Tel. 021-744 6912.
Shirley Golf Course Ltd., Stratford Rd., Monkspath, Shirley, B90 4EU. Tel. 021-744 6001. Sec.: A. J. Phillips.
Shirley Park Sports Club, Stratford Rd., Monkspath, Shirley, B90 4EW. Chairman: R. Gold. Tel. 021-745 6190.

SOUTH SHIELDS (Tyne & Wear)

Syn.: 25 Beach Rd., NE33 2QA. Services 6pm. Friday & on High Holy-days & festivals.

SOUTHAMPTON (Hants.)

Syn.: Mordaunt Rd., The Inner Av., SO2 0GP. Services, Sat. morn., 10 a.m.
Southampton & District Jewish Soc. Hon. Sec.: c/o Hillel Hse., address below.
Residential accom. for students (8 rooms) is available at Hillel House, 5 Brookvale Rd., Portswood, SO2 1QN.
The Hartley library at the University of Southampton houses both the Parkes Library and the Anglo-Jewish Archives.

SOUTHEND & WESTCLIFF (Essex)

Jews began settling in the Southend area in the late 19th century, mainly from the East End of London. The first temporary syn. was built in Station Rd., Westcliff, in 1906. Six years later, the present syn. was erected in Alexandra Rd., and has been in continuous use ever since.

In 1928, a breakaway group built its own syn. in Ceylon Rd., but later reunited with the Alexandra Rd. cong. When a new syn. was built in Finchley Rd., Westcliff, in 1968, the Ceylon Rd. building was turned into a youth centre. The Southend and Westcliff area's Jewish population is about 5,500.

Synagogues & Religious Organisations

Southend and Westcliff Hebrew Cong. Syn., Finchley Rd., Westcliff, SS0 8AD. Min.: Rabbi Michael Harris. Also at 99 Alexandra Rd., Southend. Syn. office: Finchley Rd., Westcliff, SS0 8AD. Sec.: Mrs. R. Silver. Tel. 0702 344900.

Southend Reform Syn., 851 London Rd., Westcliff. Tel. 0702 75809. Services: Fri., 7.30 p.m. Sabbath, 10.30 a.m. Hon Sec.: Mrs. A. Klass, 22 Crowstone Av., Westcliff, SS0 8HU. Tel. 0702 338460.

Jewish Cemetery: Sutton Rd. (entrance Stock Rd.), Southend. Inq.: Tel. 0702 344900.

Representative Organisation

Southend & District Jewish Representative Council. Sec.: D. Baum, 12 Marine Av., Leigh-on-Sea, SS9 2JE. Tel. 0702 470644 (PR).

Clubs, Organisations, etc.

Aid Society (Welfare Board). Chairman: H. Kanutin Esq., 96 Willingale Way, Thorpe Bay, Essex.

Ajex. Sec.: J. Barcan, 22 Second Av., Westcliff, SS0 8HY. Tel. 0702 343192.

AJEX Club. Ch. H. Eichen Esq., 53 Hamlet Court Rd., Westcliff-on-Sea, Essex.

B'nai B'rith Unity Lodge. Chairman: M. Bloch, 43 Finchley Rd. West, Westcliff. Tel. 0702 341134. Women's Sec.: Mrs. E. Ross, 29 Albion Rd., Westcliff. Tel. 0702 347718. BBYO Ch.: David Cregor, 162 Lifstan Way, Thorpe Bay. Tel. 0702 68334.

Day Centre, Victoria Oppenheim Hse., 1 Cobham Rd., Westcliff, SS0 8EG. Tel. 0702 334655. Organiser: Mrs. Christine Carter.

Emunah, Chairman: Mrs. L. Sober, Emunah, 16 Crosby Rd., Westcliff-on-Sea, Essex.

Friends of Ravenswood. Chairman: J. Freeman Esq., 111 Hampton Gds., Southend-on-Sea, Essex.

Invicta Tennis Club, Crosby Rd., Westcliff, SS0 8LB. Hon. Captain: M. King, 16 Galton Rd., Westcliff, SS0 8LE. Tel. 0702 341604.

J.I.A., Chairman: S. Salt Esq., 157 Chalkwell Av., Westcliff-on-Sea, Essex.

J.L.G.B. Chairman: A. Kalms Esq., 6 Leitrim Av., Thorpe Bay, Essex.

Kosher Meals on Wheels. Sec.: Mrs. B. Franks, 90 Chalkwell Av., Westcliff-on-Sea, Essex.

Ladies Guild (Orthodox) Sec.: Mrs. G. Jay, 15 Seymour Rd., Westcliff-on-Sea, Essex.

Ladies Guild (Reform) Chairman: Mrs. R. Brenner, 12 The Drive, Westcliff-on-Sea, Essex.

Myers Communal Hall, Finchley Rd., Westcliff, SS0 8AD. Tel. 0702 345152.

Peruaders. Chairman: M. Franks Esq., 90 Chalkwell Av., Westcliff-on-Sea, Essex.

Raymond House for the Aged, 7-9 Clifton Ter., Southend. Tel. 0702 340054 (residents), 0702 352956 (matron).

Shalom Club. Chairman: G. Kalms Esq., Flat 14, Tower Court, Westcliff Parade, Westcliff-on-Sea, Essex.
Southend Jewish Youth Centre, 38-40 Ceylon Rd., Westcliff, SS0 7HS. Tel. 0702 346545. Sec.: David Jay.
Thursday Friendship Club. Sec.: Mrs. M. Davis, 9 Britannia Rd., Westcliff.
Weizmann Society. Pres.: Mrs. Frankie King, 16 Galton Rd., Westcliff, SS0 8LE. Tel. 0702 341604.
Women's Zionist Society. Hon. Sec.: Mrs. J. Barnett, 22 Kings Rd., Westcliff, SS0 8LL. Tel. 0702 340731.
Young Marrieds Cultural & Social Group. Secs.: L. & F. Herlitz, 10 Cliff Rd., Leigh-on-Sea, SS9 1HJ. Tel. 0702 715676.
Youth Centre. 38 Ceylon Rd., Westcliff. Tel. 0702 346545.
Zionist Society. Chairman: I. Burns, 6 Chadwick Rd., Westcliff. SS0 8LS. Tel. 0702 341776.

Bookseller
Dorothy Young, 21 Colchester Rd., Southend, SS2 6HW. Tel. 0702 331218 for appointment. Religious articles, Israeli giftware, etc., also stocked.

Hotels & Restaurants
★ **Archery's Hotel,** 27 Grosvenor Rd., Westcliff. Janice & Glen Archery. Tel. 0702 353323 or 334001.
★ **Embassy Hotel** (53), 35-41 Grosvenor Rd., Westcliff, SS0 8EP. Tel. 0702 335803 (reservations) & 341175 (visitors). Mark & Mildred Friedlander.
★ **Redstone's Hotel** (38), Pembury Rd., Westcliff, SS0 8DS. Mrs. H. Redstone & family. Tel. 0702 348441.

Butchers & Delicatessen
(K) Bite Me Bakery
(K) Bite Me Butchers
(K) Bite Me Delicatessen, Hamlet Court Rd., Westcliff. Tel. 0702 433685. Licensed by Southend & Westcliff Kashrus Commission.

Caterers
(K) De Metz Caterers, 28 St. Vincent's Rd., Westcliff, SS0 7PR. Tel. 0702 352847.
(K) Norma Ansell, 100 Chalkwell Av., Westcliff. Tel. 0702 76370.
(K) Turansky Caterers, 17 Leasway, Westcliff. Tel. 0702 78332. Licensed by Southend & Westcliff Kashrus Commission.

SOUTHPORT (Merseyside)

Synagogues
Southport Hebrew Cong., Arnside Rd., PR9 0QX. Tel. 0704 532964. Min.: Rabbi Mair Rogosnitzky. Tel. 0704 537606. Sec.: Mrs. Maureen Cohen. Tel. 0704 540247. Services twice daily, week-days and Sabbath. Mikva on premises.
New (Reform), Portland St., PR8 1LR. Tel. 0704 535950. Min.: Rabbi Amanda Golby. Tel. 0704 66235.

Representative Organisations
Council of Christians and Jews. Hon. Sec.: Mrs. M. Roche, 4 Bells Cl., Lydiate, Merseyside. Tel. 051-531 9551.
Jewish Representative Council. Pres.: Dr. Cyril Nelson, 31 Avondale Rd., PR9 0NH. Tel. 0704-538276.

Social & Welfare Organisations
Friendship Club. Ch.: Mrs. C. Cowan, 23 Warren St., Westcliffe Rd.

Homes

Jewish Convalescent & Aged Home, 81 Albert Rd., PR9 9LN. Tel. 0704 531975 (office), 0704 530207 (visitors).

(K) Sharon Rest Home, 111 Leyland Rd., PR9 0JL. Tel. 0704 531386 (office), 530170 residents. Mr. & Mrs. A. Sawitz. (Manchester Beth Din.)

(K) Southport Nursing & Care Home, 126 Leyland Rd., PR9 0JL. Tel. 0704 531386 (office), 543898 (Matron), 544116 (residents). (Manchester Beth Din.)

Meat & Delicatessen

Kosher Counter at Tesco, Town Lane, Kew, Southport.

STAINES (Surrey)

Includes Slough and Windsor.

Syn.: Westbrook Rd., South St., TW18 4PR. Hon. Sec.: P. D. Fellman. Tel. 0784 254604.

STOKE ON TRENT (Staffs.)

Syn.: Birch Ter., Hanley, ST1 3JN. Tel. 0782 616417.

SUNDERLAND (Tyne & Wear)

Communal Rav: Rabbi S. Zahn, 11 The Oaks E., SR2 8EX. Tel. 091 5650224.

Synagogues

Sunderland Hebrew Cong., Ryhope Rd., SR2 7EQ. Incorporating Sunderland Beth Hamedrash. Services twice daily. Sec.: T. Jackson. Tel. 091 5658093.

Mikva: Contact Mrs. Zahn, Tel. 091-5650224.

Education

Centre for Advanced Rabbinics (Kolel), 2 The Oaks W., SR2 8HZ. Tel. 091 5671108.

Welfare

North-East Joel Intract Memorial Home for Aged Jews, 6 Gray Rd., SR2 8JB. Administrator: Rachel Z. Lewis, B.A. (Hons.). Tel. 091 5144816 (office), 5656574 (residents).

Butcher & Delicatessen

(K) S.K. Butchers, 14 Briery Vale Rd., SR2 7HE. Tel. 091 5676341.

SUTTON & DISTRICT (Surrey)

(Covering Banstead, Belmont, Carshalton, Carshalton Beeches, Cheam, Croydon, Epsom, Hackbridge, Kingswood, Mitcham, Morden, Sutton, Wallington, Worcester Pk.)

Syn.: 14 Cedar Rd., Sutton, SM2 5DA. Hon. Sec.: Mr. L. Goodblar. Tel. 081-337 8600.

SWINDON

Swindon Jewish Community. Chairman: Mr. Martin Vandervelde, 4 Lakeside, Swindon, Wilts OM3 1QE.

TORQUAY (South Devon)

(Covering also Brixham & Paignton.)

Syn.: Old Town Hall, Abbey Rd., Torquay, TQ1 1BB. Hon. Sec.: Anne

Salter. Tel. 0803 607724. Services, first Sabbath of every month & festivals, 10.30 a.m. Inq. to Ernest Freed, "Son Bou", 7 Broadstone Park Rd., Livermead, TQ2 6TY.

Restaurant
(V) **Brookesby Hall Hotel** (14), Hesketh Rd., Meadfoot Beach, PR1 2LN. Tel. 0803 292194. B&B.

WALLINGFORD (Oxon.)

Carmel College, Mongewell Pk., Wallingford, Oxon., OX10 8BT. Tel. 0491 837505. Boarding school for boys & girls, 11-18. Founder, the late Rabbi Kopul Rosen. Hd.: Philip Skelker, M.A. (Oxon.). Day Prep School for boys & girls, 3-11.
(K) Kosher meals available in term time (except on Shabbat), provided Bursar is telephoned in advance.

WATFORD (Herts.)

(Covering also Carpenders Pk., Croxley Gn., Garston, King's Langley & Rickmansworth.)
Syn.: 16 Nascot Rd., WD1 3RE. M. Rabbi: A. Blackman. Tel. 0923 222755. Sec.: Mrs. C. Silverman. Tel. Watford 32168.

WELWYN GARDEN CITY (Herts.)

(Affiliated to United Synagogue. Covering also Hatfield, Harpenden, Hertford, Letchworth, St. Albans & Stevenage.)
Syn. (with Ladies' Guild): Handside Lane, AL8 6SP. Hon. Sec.: Mrs. Hirschfield, 3 Newton Cl., Harpenden, Herts., AL5 1SQ. Tel. 05827 62829.

WHITLEY BAY (Tyne & Wear)

Syn.: 2 Oxford St. Services Rosh Hashana & Yom Kippur. Visitors welcome. Free seats. Hon. Sec.: M. A. Sonn, 2 Grasmere Cres., NE26 3TB. Tel. 0670 367053 (day), 091-2521367 (night).

WOLVERHAMPTON (W. Midlands)

Syn.: Fryer St., WV1 1HT (est. over 150 years ago). Membership 24 families. (Services, Fri. evg. & some Sabbath morns.) Sec.: H. Kronheim, 94 Wergs Rd., Tettenhall, WV6 8TH.
Please write to the Sec. for times of Friday evening service.

WORTHING (W. Sussex)

Lyons Hotel (10), 5 Windsor Rd., BN11 2LU. Tel. 0903 210265.

YORK

There is a memorial stone at Clifford's Tower, York Castle, marking the massacre of the city's Jewish community in 1190. Jews returned to York in later years, continuing to live in the city until the expulsion of 1290. There is a small community living in York today.
Contact: A. Burton, Tel. 0532-436786.

Restaurants
(V) 10 Melbourne St., Fishergate, YO1 5AQ. Tel. 0904-620082. B&B.
(V) **Mrs. Moore's**, 21 Park Gr., YO3 1LG. Tel. 0904-644790. B&B.
(V) **The Vegetarian Cafe**, Gillygate Whole Food Bakery, Miller's Yard, Gillygate YO3 7EB. Tel. 0904-610676.

CHANNEL ISLANDS

ALDERNEY

On the Corblets Rd. at Longy, there is a memorial to the victims of the Nazis during their occupation of the Channel Islands during the Second World War. It bears plaques in English, French, Hebrew and Russian.

JERSEY

There is a syn. in Route des Genets, St. Brelade. Services every Sab. morn. at 10.30 a.m. and on festivals. Hon. Sec.: Stephen Regal, c/o The Synagogue. Information: Mrs. D. Bloom, 3 Batisse de la Mielle, St. Brelade, Jersey. Tel. 0534 71644. Visiting Min.: Rev. M. Weisman, c/o Woburn Hse., Upper Woburn Pl., London, WC1 0EP. Tel. 071-387 3081. H. 081-459 4372. Mr. Weisman is also the visiting Min. for Guernsey.

A limited selection of kosher meat & poultry is available to order from Merricks Butchers 1/3 Cheapside, St Helier. Tel. 27766.

Restaurant

(V) Argilston Guesthouse, Mont Nicolle, St. Brelade. Tel. 0534-44027. 12-2, 7.30-9.30. Feb-Dec.

ISLE OF MAN

There are more than 70 Jews on the island.

DOUGLAS

Hon. Ch. of Hebrew Cong.: J. Beech, "Hilldene", 7 Links View, Onchan. Tel. 0624 24214. Visiting Min.: Rev. M. Weisman, c/o Woburn Hse., Upper Woburn Pl., London WC1 0EP. Tel. 01-387 3081/081-459 4372.

WALES

CARDIFF (S. Glamorgan)

Jews settled in Cardiff about the year 1787. The present community was founded in 1840.

Synagogues & Religious Organisations

Cardiff United Synagogue (Orthodox), Brandreth Rd., Penylan. Sec.: Mrs. S. C. Glavin. Tel. 0222 473728/491795.
Cardiff New Synagogue (constituent of the Reform Synagogues of Great Britain), Moira Ter., CF2 1EJ, opp. Howard Gdns. Sec.: Mrs. I. Pollock, 27 Millwood, Lisvane, CF4 5TL. Tel. 0222 750852.
Mikva, Wales Empire Pool Bldg., Wood St., CF1 1PP. Tel. 0222 382296.

Representative Organisation

Cardiff Jewish Representative Council. Sec.: Mrs. Judy Cotsen, 71 Cyncoed Rd., Cardiff CF2 6AB. Tel. 0222 484999.

Welfare Organisations

Penylan House, Jewish Retirement & Nursing Home, Penylan Rd., CF2 5YG. Tel. 0222 485327.
Cardiff Jewish Helpline. Hon. Sec.: Mrs. A. Schwartz, 5 Woodvale Av., Cyncoed, CF2 6SP. Tel. 0222 753361.

Student & Youth Organisations, etc.

Cardiff Jewish Students' Assoc.: Hillel Hse. Address below.
Hillel Hse. 17 Howard Gdns., Roath, CF2 1EF. Tel. 0222 481227. Self-catering accomm. Inq. to G. Rapport, 189 Cyncoed Rd., CF2 6AJ.
Jewish Students' Society, Inq. to Ch., c/o Hillel Hse., Address above. Inq. about student accom. to the Dir., Hillel Hse.
Cardiff Maccabi: Jamie Cotsen. Tel. 0222-484999.

Restaurant

(V) Munchies Wholefood Co-op, 60 Crwys Rd, Cathays, CF2 4NN. Tel. 0222-399677.

LLANDUDNO (Gwynedd)

Syn.: 28 Church Walks, LL30 2HL. Hon. Sec.: B. Hyman, 9 Glyn Isaf, Llandudno Junction. Tel. 0492 572549. No resident minister, but visiting ministers during summer months.

SWANSEA (W. Glamorgan)

Syn.: Ffynone. All correspondence to Hon. Sec.: J. Arron, 17 Ffynone Drive, Swansea, SA1 6DB. Tel. 0792 473333.
Dr. N. H. Saunders (95 Cherry Gr., Sketty, Swansea, SA2 8AX. Tel. 0792 202106) and Dr. L. Mars (70 Gabalfa Rd., Sketty, Swansea, SA2 8NE. Tel. 0792 205263), are willing to help and advise students coming to University College.

Restaurant

(V) Chris's Kitchen, The Market, SA1 3PE. Tel. 0792-643455. 8.30-5.30, Mon-Sat.

SCOTLAND

ABERDEEN (Grampian)

Syn.: 74 Dee St., AB1 2DS. Tel. 0224 582135. Inq. to Sec.: Tel. 0467 42726, or caretaker. Two-bedroomed flat available for long stay students.

Restaurant

(V) Jaws Wholefood Cafe, 5 West North St., AB1 3AT. Tel. 0224-645676. 10-3, Mon-Sat; 10-9 Thur-Fri.

DUNDEE (Tayside)

Syn.: St. Mary Pl., DD1 5RB. Inq. to Harold Gillis, 49 Meadowside, DD1 1EQ. Tel. 0382 23557.
Jewish Students' Society: c/o Sec., Students' Union, Dundee University.

EDINBURGH (Lothian)

The Town Council and Burgess Roll minutes of 1691 and 1717 record applications by Jews for permission to live and trade in Edinburgh. Local directories of the eighteenth century contain Jewish names.
There is some reason to believe that there was an organised Jewish com. in 1780 (but no cemetery) and in 1817 it removed to Richmond Court, where there was also for a time a rival cong. In 1795 the Town Council sold a plot of ground on the Calton Hill to Herman Lyon, a Jewish dentist, to provide a burial place for himself and his family. In 1816, a syn. was opened and a cemetery acquired. There is a Jewish cemetery dating from the middle of

the nineteenth century at Sciennes Hse. Pl., E9 (behind the police station in Causewayside). In 1932, two smaller congs. merged to form a single large one with a 1,000-seat synagogue. Major alterations were carried out in 1980, creating a complex of syns., halls & classrooms within the existing shell.

Syn.: 4 Salisbury Rd., EH16 5AB. Tel. 031-667 3144. Daily services 6.30 p.m.; Sat., 10 a.m.; Sun., 9 a.m. Min.: Rabbi S. Shapira, 67 Newington Rd. Tel. 031-667 9360. Hon. Sec.: Dr. Ian Leifer, 2 Observatory Green, EH9 3HL. Tel. 031-668-2910

Guest Houses
Craigewan (10), 48 Minto St., EH9 2BR. Tel. 031-667 2615. Bed & breakfast. Prop.: Mrs. Jaye Levey. Opp. Syn.

Roselea, 11 Mayfield Rd. Tel. 031-667 6115. Bed & breakfast. Jewish guests welcome. Ten mins. from Syn.

Kosher Products
(K) Kosher bread & bakery products under the supervision of the Edinburgh Hebrew Cong. obtainable from William Innes Wood, 84 E. Crosscauseway, EH8 9HQ. Tel. 031-667 1406.

Kosher Meat
Kosher Meat:- Regular deliveries from suppliers in Glasgow and Manchester. Further information from Hon. Sec. of Synagogue.

Restaurants
(V) Black Bo's, Blackfriars St. Tel. 557-6136.

(V) Henderson's 94 Hanover St., EH2 1DR. Tel. 031-225 2131.

(V) Kalpna Restaurant, 2 St. Patrick Sq., EH8 9EZ. Tel. 031-667-9890.

(V) Lachana, 3 Bristo Pl., EH1 1EY. Tel. 031-225-46717.

(V) Pierre Lapin, West Nicholson St. Tel. 668-4332.

GLASGOW (Strathclyde)

In point of age Glasgow is one of the junior Jewish centres in Britain, the first synagogue having been opened in 1823. A second was established in the 1840s, but the two afterwards amalgamated. Very little information is available about the earlier history of the Glasgow community.

The present synagogue in Garnethill was erected in 1879. A second synagogue was opened in 1904. From then the Jewish population grew considerably as a consequence of the arrival of refugees from Russian persecution, and more synagogues were established.

Synagogues & Religious Organisations
Garnethill, 127 Hill St., G3 6UB. Tel. 041-332 4151. Min.: Aharon Sondry. Pres.: A. Freedman. Tel. 041-638 9876. Sec.: Mrs. V. Livingston. Tel. 041-339 7572.

Giffnock & Newlands, Maryville Av., Giffnock, G46 7NE. Min.: Rabbi Phillip T. Greenberg. Sec.: Mrs. G. Gardner. Tel. 041-638 6600.

Glasgow New Synagogue (Reform), 147 Ayr Rd., Newton Mearns, G77 6RE. Tel. 041-639 4083. Admin: D. Kraven. Tel. 041-639 1838.

Langside, 125 Niddrie Rd., G42 8QA. Tel. 041-423 4062. Min.: Rabbi Michael Rosin, M.A., 93 Holeburn Rd., G43. Tel. 041-637 5171. Hon. Sec.: N. Barnes. Tel. 041-637 7313.

Netherlee-Clarkston, Clarkston Rd. at Randolph Dr., G76 8AN. Sec.: Mrs. V. R. Mann. Tel. 041-644 3611. Services: Week-days, 7.30 a.m.; Fri. evg., at sunset; Sat., 10 a.m. and 1 hour before nightfall.

Newton Mearns, Beech Av., G77 5AP. Min.: Rabbi Y. Black. Tel. 041-639 2442. Sec.: H. Smullen. Tel. 041-639 2620.

Queens Park, Falloch Rd., G42 9QX. Min.: Rabbi M. Fletcher. Hon. Sec.: Mrs. J. Slater. Tel. 041-632 1743.
Beth Din.: Falloch Rd., G42 9QX. Tel. 041-649 3704. Rav of Beth Din: Rabbi M. Rosin, M.A. Tel. 041-637-5171.
Mikva: Giffnock & Newlands Syn. Inq. to Mrs. Bennarroch. Tel. 041-649 3740.

Representative Organisation
Glasgow Jewish Representative Council, 49 Coplaw St., G42 7JE. Tel. 041-423 8917.

Welfare Organisations
Glasgow Jewish Welfare Board, 49 Coplaw St., G42 7JE. Tel. 041-423 8916.
Newark Lodge, 41-43 Newark Dr., G41 4QA. Tel. 041-423 8941. Nursing home for the elderly.

Student & Youth Organisations
Glasgow Jewish Students' Society. Hon. Sec.: Miss C. Livingstone. Tel. 041-639 6767.
Habonim-Dror Youth Centre, 6 Sinclair Dr., G42 9QE. Tel. 041-632 9017.
Jewish Lads' & Girls' Brigade. Youth organisation providing uniformed as well as sports and social activities. Commanding Officer: B/Captain Pamela Livingston, 90 Beechwood Av., Clarkston, G76 7XG. Tel. 041-639 7194.
Maccabi & Youth Centre, May Ter., Giffnock, G46 6LD. Tel. 041-638 6177.
Northern Region Chaplaincy Board. Chairman: H. Kaplan, 1/L 11 Millwood St., G41 3JY. Tel. 01-649 4526.

Zionist Organisations
WIZO. Sec.: Mrs. F. Warrens. Tel. 041-639 4386.
Zionist Centre, Abraham Links Hse., 43 Queen Sq., G41 2BD. Zionist Central Council. Tel. 041-620 2194; J.N.F. Tel. 041-423 4089; J. I. A. Tel. 041-423 8785; Jewish Agency (Immigration Dept.) & World Zionist Org. Tel. 041-423 7379.

Clubs, etc.
Bonnyton Golf Club, Eaglesham, G76 0QA. Tel. 035 53 2781. Hon. Sec.: H. J. Beach.
Jewish Senior Citizens' Club. Inf. from: Mrs. B. Mann. Tel. 041-644 3611.

Bookseller
J. & E. Levingstone, 47 & 55 Sinclair Dr., G42 9PT. Tel. 041-649 2962. Religious requisites also stocked.

Hotel
Guest House (Bed and Breakfast), 26 St. Clair Av., Giffnock, G46 7QE. (Kosher but not supervised) Tel. 041-638 3924.

Restaurants
(K) Freed's, 49 Coplaw St., G42 7JE. Tel. 041-423 8911. With sanction of Glasgow Beth Din. Open Sun.-Thurs., 12.30 p.m. to 2.30 p.m. & 5.30 p.m. to 8 p.m.
The Inn Place, Maccabi Youth Centre, May Terrace, Giffnock, G46. Tel. 041-620 3233.
(V) The Third Eye Centre, 350 Sauchiehall St., G2 3JD. Tel. 041-332-7521. 10am-late, Tues.-Sat.; 12-5 Sun.

Kosher Food
(K) Seymour's Kitchen Deli & Bakery (Kosher), 200 Fenwick Rd., Giffnock, G46. Tel. 041-638 8267 & 632 2313.

★ Kosher (Glasgow) Food Shop Ltd., 2 Burnfield Rd., Giffnock, G46 7QB. Tel. 041-638 4383.
★ Michael Morrison & Son, 52 Sinclair Dr., G42 9PY. Tel. 041-632 6091 & 0998.

ST. ANDREW'S (Fifeshire)

Jewish Students' Soc., c/o Sec., Students' Union, St. Andrew's University, KY16 9UY.

NORTHERN IRELAND

Vegetarian Society of Ulster, 66 Ravenhill Gdns, Belfast BT6 8QG. Tel: 0232 457888.

BELFAST

There were Jews living in Belfast in the year 1652, but the present community was founded in 1869.
Syn.: 49 Somerton Rd., BT15 3LH. Tel. 0232 777974. Services: Sat., Sun., Mon., & Thurs am; no minister at present. Mikva on premises.
Pres. of Hebrew Cong.: Harold Smith, 36A Myrtlefield Pk., BT9 6NF. Tel. 0232 682317. Sec.: Mrs. N. Simon, 42 Glandore Av. Tel. 779491.
Hebrew School, Wolfson Centre, 49 Somerton Rd., BT15 3LH. Tel. 0232 777974.
WIZO. Co-Ch.: Rose Moss, Nadia Lantin. Hon. Sec.: Margaret Black. Tel. 662859.
(K) Kosher meals can be obtained at the Jewish Com. Centre, 49 Somerton Rd., BT15 3LH. Tel. 777974. By arrangement.
Delicatessen: Levey's (J. Glackin), 493 Antrim Rd., BT15 3BP. Tel. 0232 777462.

TRAVEL ABROAD
TRAVEL AGENTS SPECIALISING IN TRAVEL TO ISRAEL

Note: A full list of members (£20.00) can be obtained from the Assoc. of British Travel Agents, 55-57 Newman St., W1P 4AH. Tel. 071-637 2444.

Gee Travel Service/UK/Ltd. 12 Stamford Hill, N16 6XZ. Tel. 081 806 3434 Open Sundays. After hours 081 800 1082. 24 hour airport ticketing service.

Goodmos Tours, Dunstan Hse., 14a St. Cross St., EC1N 8XA. Tel. 071-430 2230. Fax. 071-405 5049. Telex 21676.

Longwood Holidays, 182 Longwood Gdns., Ilford, Essex, IG5 0EW. Tel. 081-551 4494. Open Sun., 10 a.m. to 2 p.m.

Magic of Israel, 47 Shepherds Bush Green, W12 8PS. Tel. 081-743-9000.

Peltours Ltd., Sovereign Hse., 11-19 Ballards La., N3 1UX. Tel. 081-346 9144. Telex 24542 PELTOUR G. Fax. 081-343 0579; 240 Station Rd., Edgware, Middx., HA8 7AU. Tel. 081-958 1144. Fax. 081 958 5515.

Sabra Travel Ltd., 9 Edgwarebury Lane, Edgware, Middx., HA8 8LH. Tel. 081-958 3244-7.

Travelink Group Ltd., 3 Caxton Walk, Phoenix St., off Charing Cross Rd., WC2H 8PW. Tel. 071-379 5959. Fax. 071-379 5222.

Goodmos Tours, 23 Leicester Rd., Salford, M7 0AS. Tel. 061-792 7333.

Peltours Ltd., 27-29 Church St., Manchester, M4 1QA. Tel. 061-834 3721. Telex 667893 PELTOUR G. Fax. 061-832 9343.

KOSHER FOOD ON FLIGHTS

El Al (Israel Airlines), 185 Regent St., W1R 8EU. Tel. 071-437 9255, & 231-232 Royal Exchange, Manchester, M2 7FF. Tel. 061-832 4208.

El Al, the Israeli national airline, maintains its own fully equipped **(K)** kosher kitchens at London Heathrow airport.

The kitchens, which are under the direct supervision of the London Federation of Synagogues, have a Mashgiach (supervisor) on duty on a permanent basis. They supply every El Al flight out of London and also supply kosher meals to most other airlines, including British Airways. El Al also supplies glatt kosher, vegetarian and a range of dietetic meals.

Orthodox Jewish passengers on airlines other than El Al should see that their kosher food boxes are sealed with the official Federation Commission label. No previous notice of the desire for kosher food is needed by El Al. Swissair supplies passengers with kosher food on request. Pan American supplies supervised kosher food prepared by kosher caterers in the various cities served, if 24 hours' notice is given. American Airlines Inc. and Delta Air Lines Inc. supply kosher food if the request for it is made at time of ticket reservation. Other American companies supply food supervised by the New York rabbinical authorities. South African Airways appreciate 24 hours' notice. Lufthansa has a kosher kitchen and supplies kosher food on European and intercontinental flights on which meals are served. Prior notification 24 hours before departure is necessary. Passengers with other airlines should inform them well in advance if kosher food is required.

(K) Kedassia meals supplied by Hermolis & Co. Ltd., 26a Abbey Manufacturing Estate, Mount Pleasant, Alperton, Middx., HA0 1OA, are available on request on most flights from the majority of British airports. Passengers should confirm with their airline that they require this facility, which is free..

KLM Royal Dutch Airlines have a kosher kitchen at Schiphol Airport, Amsterdam, Swissair have one at Zurich, and there is also one at Orly airport, Paris.

Packed kosher meals are obtainable at Dublin Airport, under the aegis of Aer Lingus and also on any Aer Lingus flights from Britain on which there is full meals service. They should be requested at the time of booking, or 48 hours before departure.

KOSHER FOOD ON SHIPS

Most shipping lines provide packaged kosher food on request. Intending passengers requiring this should obtain written confirmation well in advance.

TRAVEL GUIDES

The following selection of travel guides may be of interest to readers:

Israel:
Culture shock!: Israel, by Dick Winter. London: Kuperard, 1992 (A guide to etiquette and customs series).
Essential Jerusalem, Greer Fay Cashman. London: Automobile Association, 1991.
The heart of Jerusalem, by Arlynn Nellhan. London: John Muir Publication 1988.
The Holy Land: the indispensable archaeological guide for travellers, 3rd ed., Jerome Murphy O'Connor, Oxford: OUP, 1992.
Israel tourist and accommodation guide, 1993-94: B&B in Israel. Gedera: B B. Gilon Ltd., 1992.
Jerusalem, Kay Prag. London: A & C Black, 1989. (The Blue Guide).
Jerusalem, written by Norman Atkins. APA Publications, 1988.
Jewish Israel: a guide for Jews to the land of their fathers. London: Namlock Ltd., 1988.
Kibbutz volunteer, by John Bedford; revised by Victoria Pybus. Oxford: Vacation Work, 1990.
Lets go: the Budget guide to Israel and Egypt, by Lorraine Shang-Huei Chang. London: Pan Books, 1992.
The museums of Israel, by Nitza Rosovsky and Joy Ungerlieder-Mayerson. New York: Harry N. Abrams, 1989.

Jewish travel guides to other countries:
Guide to Jewish Europe — Western Europe, 8th edition. Brooklyn: Israelowitz Publishing, 1993.
Guide to Jewish Italy, by Annie Sacerdoti in collaboration with Luca Fiorentino; translated by Richard F. de Lossa. Brooklyn: Israelowitz Publishing, 1989.
Guide to kosher eating and accommodation in North America, by Judith Korey Charles and Lila Teich Gold. Cold Spring, N.Y.: Nightingale Resources, 1991.

Jewish heritage travel: a guide to Central and Eastern Europe, by Ruth Gruber. New York: Wylie, 1992.
Jewish sites and synagogues in Greece, by Nicholas P. Stavroulakis and Timothy J. DeVinney. Athens: Talos Press, 1992.
Oscar Israelowitz's Guide to Jewish Canada and USA — Vol. I: Eastern Provinces. Brooklyn: Israelowitz Publishing, 1990.
Oscar Israelowitz's Guide to Jewish New York City. Brooklyn: Israelowitz Publishing, 1990.
A travel guide to Jewish Europe, by Ben G. Frank. Gretna: Pelican Publishing Co., 1992.

ISRAEL
(Total population 4,600,000. Jews 3,755,000; others 845,000).
Intending visitors to Israel should get in touch as early as possible with the
nearest Israel Government Tourist Office, which will supply literature and
detailed information about hotels, tours, and so on.

Israel Government Tourist Offices
The tourist offices listed below supply all relevant literature and
information, but **do not make bookings.**

Austria   Offizielles Israelisches Verrkehrsbuero, Rossauer Lande 41/12,
A-1090 Wein. Tel. 0043-1-3108174. Fax. 0043-1-3103917.
Canada   Israel Government Tourist Office, 180 Bloor Street West, Suite 700,
Toronto, Ontario M5S 2V6. Tel. 001-416-964-3784. Fax. 001-416-961-3962.
Germany   Staatliches Israelisches Verkehrsbureau, Bettinastr. 62 7th Floor,
6000 **Frankfurt**/Main 1. Tel. 0049-69-752084. Fax. 0049-69-746249.
Staatliches Israelisches Verkehrsbureau, Kurfuerstendamm 202, 100 **Berlin**
15. Tel. 0049-30-8819685/8836759. Fax. 0049-30-8824093. Staatliches
Israelisches Verkehrsbureau, Stollbergstr. 6, **Muenchen.** Tel. 0049-89-
2289568. Fax. 0049-89-2289569.
France   Office National Israelien de Tourisme, 14 rue de la Paix, Paris
75002. Tel. 0033-1-4261-0197/4261-0367. Fax. 0033-1-49270946.
Holland   Israelisch Nationaal Verkeersbureau, Wijde Kapelsteeg 2 (hoek
Rokin), 1012 NS Amsterdam. Tel. 0031-20-6249642/6249325. Fax. 0031-20-
6242751.
Hungary   Israeli Nagykovetsege Ykovetseg, 1026 Budapest 11, Fullank
U.8. Tel. 1767-896/7.
Italy   Uffizio Nazionale Israeliano del Turismo, Via Podgora 12/b, Milan
20122. Tel. 0039-55187152. Fax. 0039-2-55187062.
Japan   Israel Government Tourist Office, Kojimachi Sanbancho Mansion
#406, 9-1 Sanbancho, Chiyoda-Ku, Tokyo 102. Tel. 0081-3-32389081/2. Fax.
0081-3-32389677.
South Africa   Israel Government Tourist Office, 5th Floor, Nedbank
Gardens, 33 Bath Ave., Rosebank, P.O. Box 52560, Saxonwold 2132,
Johannesburg. Tel. 0027-11-7881700. Fax. 0027-11-4473104.
Spain   Oficina Nacional Israeli de Turismo, Gran via 69, Ofic 801, 28013
Madrid. Tel. 559-7903. Fax. 542-6511.
Sweden   Israeliska Statens Turistbyra, Sveavagen 28-30, 4 tr., Box 7554,
10393 Stockholm 7. Tel. 0046-21 33 86/7. Fax. 0046-8-217814.
Switzerland   Offizielles Israelisches Verkehrsbureau, Lintheschergasse
12, 8021 Zurich. Tel. 0041-211-2344/5. Fax. 0041-1-2122036.
United Kingdom   Israel Government Tourist Office, 18 Great
Marlborough St., London W1V 1AF. Tel. 0044-71-434-3651. Fax. 0044-71-
4370527.
U.S.A.   Israel Government Tourist Office, 19th Floor, 350 Fifth Ave., New
York, **New York** 10118. Tel. 001-212-5600738/5600600. Fax. 001-212-6294368.
Israel Government Tourist Office, 5 South Wabash Av., **Chicago,** Illinois
60603. Tel. 001-312-7824306. Fax. 312-782 1243. Israel Government Tourist
Office, 6380 Wilshire Boulevard #1700, **Los Angeles,** California 90048. Tel.
001-213-6587462/6587240. Israel Government Tourist Office, 12700 Park
Central Drive, **Dallas,** TX, 75251. Tel. 001-214-991-9098/7. Fax. 001-214-392-
3521. Israel Government Tourist Office, 420 Lincoln Road Suite 745, **Miami
Beach,** FLa 33139. Tel. 001-305-673-6862-3. Fax. 001-305-6734486. Israel
Government Tourist Office, 1100 Spring St., NW Suite 440, **Atlanta,** Ga.
30309. Tel. 001-404-875-9924. Fax. 001-404-875-9926.
The Ministry of Tourism publishes a "Best of Israel Guide" detailing shops
participating in the VAT refund scheme and recommended restaurants.
Available 6 Wilson St., Tel Aviv. Fax. (03)-562339.

HOW TO GET THERE

You can travel by sea or air, or a combination of both. Air France, Air Sinai, Alitalia, Austrian Airlines, British Airways, Cyprus Airways, El Al Israel Airlines, Iberia Airlines of Spain, KLM, Lufthansa, Olympic Airways, Pan American Airways, Sabena, SAS, South African Airways.

Swissair, Tarom Romanian Airlines and T.W.A. maintain regular services to Israel.

If you are flying to South Africa by El Al, or to the Far East or Australia by British Airways, Air France, Alitalia (from Rome) or T.W.A., you can break your journey in Israel at no extra cost.

There are scheduled and charter flights to Israel from a number of European countries, including Britain, as well as from the United States.

There are no direct sea passenger services between Israel and Britain, but there are regular services between Israel and Greece and/or Italy. Many cruise liners also call at Israeli ports.

Student Travel to Israel

Throughout the long summer vacation student flights to Israel are operated by ISSTA (Israel Students' Tourist Association), in conjunction with various other national student travel bureaux. In London these are operated by the National Union of Students Travel Dept., 3 Endsleigh St., WC1. Tel. 071-387 2184. ISSTA has offices in Haifa (28 Nordau St. Tel. (04) 660411), Jerusalem (5 Eliashar St. Tel. (02) 225258) and Tel Aviv (109 Ben-Yehuda St. Tel. (03) 247164-5). WST Charters, Priory Hse., 6 Wright's La., W8 6TA. Tel. 071-938 4362, also specialises in Israel holidays for students and young people.

Individual arrangements for working on a kibbutz for a minimum period of one month can be made for any time of the year, except July and August, through Hechalutz b'Anglia, the Jewish Agency, 741 High Rd., Finchley, N12 0BQ. Tel. 01-446 1477. Details of other kibbutz schemes are available from Kibbutz Representatives, 523 Finchley Rd., London, NW3 7BD. Tel. 01-794 5692. Airlines and most shipping lines offer reductions to students.

Passports and Visas

Applications for British passports should be made to any of the five Passport Offices in London, Liverpool, Newport (Gwent), Peterborough and Glasgow.

Those holding a British visitors passport (obtainable from a post office and valid for one year) will be allowed in provided they also carry with them a full passport that has expired within the past five years.

Holders of valid U.K. passports do not need a transit or visitor's visa for entry into Israel.

The passports of U.K. subjects must conform with the following conditions: (a) Place of residence must be stated in the passport as being in the United Kingdom, Northern Ireland, the Channel Islands or the Isle of Man; (b) national status should appear in the passport as "British citizen".

Other countries whose nationals do not require a transit or visitor's visa to Israel are: Austria, Bahamas, Barbados, Belgium, Bolivia, Colombia, Costa Rica, Denmark, Dominican Republic, Dutch Antilles, Ecuador, El Salvador, Fiji, Finland, France, Greece, Guatemala, Haiti, Holland, Hong Kong, Iceland, Jamaica, Japan, Lesotho, Liechtenstein, Luxembourg, Maldive Islands, Mauritius, Mexico, Norway, Paraguay, Philippines, Surinam, Swaziland, Sweden, Switzerland, Trinidad and Tobago.

Citizens of the following countries receive a visa **free of charge at the place of entry**: Argentina, Australia, Brazil, Canada, Central African Republic, Chile, Germany (if born after January 1, 1928), Italy, New Zealand, San

Marino, South Africa, Spain, United States of America, Uruguay. Citizens of the Republic of Ireland also receive a visa at the place of entry, **but are required to pay the requisite fee**.

Citizens of the following countries receive a visa free of charge, but must apply for it **before departure** to any Israel diplomatic or Consular mission: Cyprus, Germany (if born before January 1, 1928), Yugoslavia. (Until further notice, Israel is represented in Yugoslavia by the Belgian Embassy.)

Citizens of the following countries receive a visa on application to the nearest diplomatic or Consular mission and **must pay the prescribed fee:** Bermuda, Botswana, Burma, Cambodia, Cameroon, Chad, (People's Republic of) Congo, Dahomey, Egypt, Equatorial Guinea, Ethiopia, Gabon, Gambia, Ghana, Guinea, Guyana, Honduras, India, Ivory Coast, Kenya, (South) Korea, Laos, Liberia, Madagascar, Malawi, Mali, Malta, Nepal, Nicaragua, Niger, Nigeria, Panama, Peru, Portugal, Romania, Rwanda, Senegal, Sierra Leone, Singapore, Spain, Thailand, Togo, Turkey, Tanzania, Upper Volta, Venezuela, Vietnam, Zaire and Zambia.

Citizens of countries not listed above must apply for a visa to the nearest Israel diplomatic or Consular mission and pay the requisite fee. Israel visas, when necessary, can be obtained at all Israel Consulates. In London application should be made in person or by post to the Consulate of Israel, 2 Palace Green, London, W8 5QB. Office hours, Mon. to Thurs., 10 a.m. to 12.30 p.m.; Fri., 10 a.m. to 12 noon. Inquiries to Visa Section. Tel. 01-937 8050.

A visitor's visa is valid for a stay of three months from the date of arrival.

Health Regulations

There are no vaccination requirements for tourists entering Israel.

However, vaccination against smallpox is required by some countries from travellers returning from abroad, so it is advisable for visitors to check the health regulations of their own country and, if vaccination is required, to obtain it before departure. Tourists already in Israel wishing to obtain vaccination against smallpox, cholera and yellow fever can do so at any Ministry of Health district or sub-district office.

Customs & Currency Regulations

The red-green dual-channel customs clearance system operates at Ben-Gurion airport, Lod. Tourists bringing any articles expressly specified in lists 1A and 1B below may leave the airport by the green channel after collecting their luggage. Tourists bringing in articles not mentioned in the lists, even if they are exempt from duty and intended for re-export, must take the red channel.

1A. Every tourist aged 17 or over may bring into Israel the following free of duty, provided they are for personal use and are brought in on the ship or aircraft on which the tourist arrives: Eau de cologne or perfume not exceeding 0.44 pint [¼] litre); wine up to 3.55 pints (2 litres); other alcoholic beverages not exceeding 1.77 pints (1 litre); tobacco or cigars not exceeding 250 grammes, or 250 cigarettes; gifts up to approximately [$150 in value c.i.f. (including assorted foodstuffs not exceeding 6.6 lb. or 3 kg. in weight, but excluding typewriters, cameras, movie cameras, tape recorders and TV sets); clothing and footwear.

1B. The following items may also be brought in free of duty and the green channel taken, provided that they are appreciably used and are to be re-exported on departure: one pair of binoculars, cameras (1 still and 1 cine less than 16 mm.), tape recorder, typewriter, sports and camping equipment, radio, portable musical instruments, perambulator, bicycle, 10 plates or rolls of film for still cameras and 10 reels of cine film, 750 yards of recording tape or 2 cassettes, portable record player, personal jewellery in reasonable quantities.

The following items are subject to deposits, and tourists bringing in any of them should take the red channel: Hand-held and operated professional tools and instruments for personal use up to [1,650 in value c.i.f., rowing-, sailing-, or motor-boat, scuba-diving equipment (portable and used), reasonable quantity of used records, portable used T.V. set, TV & video cameras. The deposits are refundable when the items are re-exported on departure.

Certain additional items are liable for flat-rate duty and, in some cases, V.A.T.

Import duties and taxes are payable in full on such items as refrigerators, radiograms, washing machines and electric ovens and cookers.

Tourists may bring into Israel any amount of foreign currency, which need not be declared upon entry. Foreign currency can be exchanged only at banks.

There is no restriction on the amount of Israeli currency which can be brought into the country by tourists, but they are allowed to take out no more than 500 Shekels.

During each visit, tourists over 18 may reconvert into foreign currency Shekels up to a maximum of the equivalent of [5,000. The maximum for tourists under 18 is the equivalent of [2,000.

Tourists leaving Israel may change Shekels in their possession up to a maximum of the equivalent of 50. Tourists are permitted to pay for all services and purchases in freely exchangeable currencies, including Canadian and United States dollars, South African rands, pounds sterling, Australian dollars, Swiss and French francs, Danish and Swedish kroner, Norwegian kronor, Dutch florins, German marks, Belgian francs, Italian lire, Austrian schillings and Japanese yen.

However, where payment in foreign currency is not acceptable, payment must be made in Israeli currency. In all cases, change may be given in Israeli currency.

Rates of Exchange
The Israeli currency unit is the Shekel. There are coins and notes of various denominations. Rates of exchange are subject to fluctuation and vary from bank to bank.

Free Trade Zone
Elat has been a free trade zone since 1985. Details of how this benefits tourists can be obtained from all Israel Government Tourist Offices.

Cars
Provided his foreign car registration is valid and he is in possession of a valid driving licence, a tourist may import his vehicle into Israel free of duty and taxes for a maximum period of one year, against a personal undertaking to re-export it when he leaves Israel or within a year, whichever is the shorter period. No customs document or deposit of duty is required. Once the vehicle has been re-exported, it (or a replacement) cannot be re-imported for at least three months, during which time the tourist concerned must have been outside Israel.

A valid International Driving Licence is recognised and preferred, although a valid national driving licence is also accepted, provided it has been issued by a country maintaining diplomatic relations with Israel and recognising an Israeli driving licence.

Further information with regard to licences, as well as other information and legal and technical advice, are available free of charge to visiting

motorists from the Automobile & Touring Club of Israel (MEMSI), whose offices are at the following addresses:
Head Office: 19 Derech Petach Tikva, Tel Aviv. Telegraphic address: Actail, Tel Aviv. Tel. (03) 622961. Address for correspondence: P.O.B. 36144, Tel Aviv. Office hours: Sun. to Thurs., 9 a.m.-3.30 p.m.; Fri. & eve of Holy-days and festivals, 9 a.m.-12 noon.
Beersheba: Beit Uniko. Tel. (057) 36264.
Eilat: c/o Yaela Office, New Commercial Centre. Tel. (07) 372166.
Haifa: 7 Shmaryahu Levin St. Tel. (04) 674343.
Jerusalem: 31 King George St. Tel. (02) 244828. Office hours: Sun. to Thurs., 8 a.m.-3.30 p.m. Fri. & eve of holidays, 8 a.m.-1 p.m.
Netanya: c/o Shartours, 6 Shmuel Hanatziv St. Tel. (053) 31343-4.
Tiberias: c/o Shahak, 23 Yohanan Ben-Zakai St. Tel. (067) 90715.
The Automobile & Touring Club of Israel is affiliated to the Fédération Internationale de l'Automobile and to the Alliance Internationale de Tourisme.
Third-party (Act) insurance is compulsory in Israel in respect of bodily injury to all third parties. Further information is available from Act Pool Insurance, 70 lbn Gvirol St., P.O.B. 2622, Tel Aviv. Tel. 268146-8. Office hours: Sun. to Thurs., 8 a.m. to 1 p.m. Fri. & eve of holidays, 8 a.m. to 11 a.m.

Green Card
The following countries have so far signed Green Card agreements with Israel:
Austria, Belgium, Britain, Bulgaria, Denmark, Finland, France, Greece, Holland, Iceland, Irish Republic, Italy, Luxembourg, Norway, Portugal, Romania, Spain, Sweden, Switzerland, Turkey, West Germany and Yugoslavia.
Tourists wishing to bring their cars to Israel may acquire a Green Card from insurance companies in any of the above countries.
If "Israel" and the national identification letters, "IL", do not appear on the Green Card, it must be accompanied by an endorsement certifying that it is valid for Israel.
Without "Israel" and "IL" on the Green Card or endorsement, the card cannot be used in Israel, and insurance cover will have to be taken out at the port of arrival.
For further details concerning car insurance, consult your local Israel Government Tourist Office or travel agent **before leaving for your visit.**

Traffic Regulations
Traffic travels on the right and overtakes on the left. Drivers coming from the right have priority, unless indicated otherwise on the road signs, which are international.
Distances on road signs are always given in kilometres (1 km. is equal to 0.621 miles).
The speed limit is 50 km. (approx. 31 miles) per hour in built-up areas; 80-90 km. (approx. 50-56 miles) per hour on open roads.
All vehicles in Israel (including those of visiting motorists) must be equipped with striped reflective strips. For private cars these strips must be 2" deep x 18" wide (5 cm. x 45cm.), and affixed to both the left and right-hand sides of the rear bumper.
All motor-cycle and scooter riders, as well as pillion passengers, must wear safety helmets.
It is compulsory for drivers and front-seat passengers to wear safety belts on all journeys. Back-seat passengers must wear seat belts in post 1986 vehicles.

Climate

With a long Mediterranean coastline, Israel's climate is similar to that of the French and Italian Rivieras. It may also be compared to that of Florida and southern California. Winters are mild and summers warm.

There are differences not only in temperature, but also in rainfall between the northern and southern regions of the country, as well as between the hills and valleys. The rainless summer lasts from April to October.

The winter season, November to March, is characterised by bright sunshine with occasional rain. During this period, Tiberias on the Sea of Galilee, Sdom on the Dead Sea and Eilat on the Red Sea, are all absolutely ideal for winter holidays.

Airport Tax

All passengers departing by air must pay an airport tax. This is equivalent to approximately £10.

Some General Information

Electrical Equipment: Israel's electrical current is 220 volts, A.C., single phase, 50 cycles. Your dealer will advise you further.

Emergencies: Fire, Tel. 102; Medical and first aid, Tel. 101 (Magen David Adom); Police, Tel. 100. Note that the foregoing applies to Haifa, Jerusalem and Tel Aviv only.

Medical Equipment: Wheelchairs, oxygen cylinders and many other items are available on temporary loan free of charge from the Yad Sarah Organisation for the Free Loan of Medical Equipment in Haifa (4a Mapu St., Ahuza. Tel. (04) 245286), Jerusalem (49 Haneviim St. Tel. (02) 244242 or 244047), Tel Aviv (14a Ruppin St. Tel. (03) 238974) and many other places.

Photographic Hints: Take along an adequate supply of cine film, since it is not readily available. Colour roll film, however, is obtainable.

No colour cine film can be processed in Israel, but you can develop your Kodachrome colour roll film. Keep your film well protected against heat and direct sunlight. The light, both direct and reflected, is much stronger in Israel than in most countries of Europe and North America.

Tourists leaving Israel at Ben-Gurion airport are advised to ensure that their cameras are empty of film, in order to facilitate the checking of cameras before boarding.

Radio. You can hear the news in English four times a day on Israel Radio at 576, 1170, and 1458 kHz: 7 a.m.; 1p.m.; 5 p.m.; 8 p.m. BBC. World Service at 1322 kHz.; 1400, 1700 and 2015 G.M.T. Voice of America at 1260 kHz: 5 to 6 a.m. and 8 to 9 a.m. 5 p.m. 5.30 p.m. 11 p.m.

It must be emphasised that only selected, albeit wide-ranging, information can be given here. Full details are available from Israel Government Tourist Offices and travel agents.

Average Temperature (Celsius)

	Jerusalem	Tel Aviv	Haifa	Tiberias	Eilat
January	12	15	14	17	17
March	16	18	17	17	22
May	22	22	21	26	29
July	23	24	25	30	35
September	23	26	26	30	32
November	16	19	19	21	21

Rainy Days

	Jerusalem	Tel Aviv	Haifa	Tiberias	Eilat
January	12	14	15	12	1
March	8	8	9	5	2
May	2	1	1	1	0
July	0	0	0	0	0
September	0	1	1	0	0
November	7	8	5	5	1

THE THREE MAIN CITIES

HAIFA

This city of sea and mountain is built on three levels, each with its distinctive and highly special character. Mount Carmel (Har Hacarmel), the top level, which offers some magnificent views, is mostly residential and recreational; Hadar Hacarmel, the central level, is also residential, but it also contains the city's main commercial district. The third level, the lowest, contains the port area, Israel's largest, and another business district. Over recent years the beach front to the south of the port has been attractively refurbished.

Like Jerusalem and Tel Aviv, Haifa has a university, and it is also the home of the Technion — Israel's Institute of Technology. The city's theatre and symphony orchestra are well-known, and its array of unusual museums are worth a visit. They include the National Maritime Museum, the Grain Museum, the Mané Katz Museum and the Illegal Immigration Museum.

In addition to being Israel's premier port and a major industrial centre, Haifa is also a tourist resort, with miles of bathing beaches and acres of woodland parks and well-tended gardens. It is also the scene of international flower shows, folklore festivals, conventions and other events.

JERUSALEM

Despite her present-day accessibility, Jerusalem is a secret city. Your tourist coach or taxi will show you her face. But to find her heart, you must take to your feet, climbing her hills, strolling her streets and lanes, and pushing on beyond the seemingly closed gates which enclose a myriad life styles.

To sense the mystery of Jerusalem, start with Mount Scopus just before dawn. Watch the red ball of a new day's sun ascend the mists from behind the Mountains of Moab and set afire the Judean Desert which laps at the city's skirts. Near sunset, look down again from near the same vantage point on the city itself, when the light catches the gold of the Dome of the Rock, scattering its rays across Jerusalem's many hills.

Now, with a new clarity, you catch the poignant imagery of Jerusalem's contemporary poet-laureate, Yehuda Amihai, when he speaks of a "port city on the shores of eternity."

But Jerusalem is also a city of people, a collection of villages separated by faith and custom. Enter the Old City by Jaffa Gate and turn right on to Armenian Patriarchate Road, where you will find the Cathedral of St. James. Walk through the side gate and you are in a unique, hidden village community homes, shops, schools, playgrounds, churches, all are contained within the ancient and massive compound, where the gates close at 8.30 p.m., after which time no one may enter or leave.

The language here is Armenian. The children learn it in school, the people talk it in the streets and there is a fine printing press preparing Armenian Bibles and other literature for distribution to a community which, like the Jews, is scattered throughout the world.

By contrast, spend a Friday morning in Mea Shearim, the walled city of ultra-Orthodoxy, where the ghetto way of life is maintained with fierce pride and where still live Jewish communities which deny the existence of the Jewish State and speak only Yiddish, Hebrew being retained as the holy language of prayer and study.

Friday all is abustle. A bescarfed housewife hurries to the slaughterer with a live chicken. Youngsters, their earlocks bouncing like coiled springs, scamper out of school in a babble of Yiddish (although, increasingly, their language of conversation is Hebrew). Men, young and old, their eyes averted from the passing tourists, hurry to the mikva, for here males as well as females take the ritual cleansing bath.

But also in Jerusalem, you must touch history, not the spurious history of this tomb or that stone, but the reality, say, of such as Hezekiah's Tunnel, hewn by the Judean king's workmen through the rock of Jerusalem nearly 2,700 years ago so that water would be available in the city in time of war.

The tunnel, still a conduit for water through which intrepid Jerusalem explorers frequently wade the 600 yards of its winding course, starts close by the spring of Gihon in the Kidron Valley, on the edge of the ancient City of King David, south-west of the Old City, with its excavations.

As it has since the beginning of recorded time, the spring still gushes its waters at regular intervals throughout the day, and Arabs from the adjoining village of Silwan come there regularly with pots, jugs and, an accommodation with the twentieth century, jerricans, to take their water from its flow.

Near by is the "Archaeological Garden" being created from the manifold finds in the two decades of excavation in the area adjoining the Temple Mount.

Jerusalem is also a city of today, and you feel this nowhere better than in one of the city's newer suburbs. Take a bus or taxi to Denmark Square in Bet Hakerem and ask to be put down outside the huge supermarket there. Sit awhile among the stone seats and sculptures in the square, watching the continuous parade of young mothers and children, and sprightly oldsters out for a stroll. You will find that you do not sit alone for long.

Jerusalem now has pavement cafés in the part of Ben-Yehuda Street which is closed to traffic. There are also many stalls selling a variety of foods to be enjoyed as one strolls, and they are well patronised. When night falls, which it does quite early as compared with the slow dusk of the West, it seems that most of the inhabitants have gone to bed.

Many have, because the day's early start, despite the traditional afternoon siesta, dampens any inclination for late nights. But there is a night-life of sorts.

Also, Israel being an immigrant country, there is an enormous variety of national and ethnic food available in numerous restaurants. These offer everything from kosher Chinese to kosher Argentine.

The Israel Philharmonic Orchestra provides frequent concerts at Binyanei Ha'Ooma, and tickets can be bought for performances by the fast-rising Israel Radio Symphony Orchestra, whose headquarters is in the superb Jerusalem Theatre (which also boasts a fine kosher dairy restaurant and bar, with entertainment from 10 p.m. into the small hours).

There are a couple of discotheques, but since these are apt to come and go, it is best to ask your taxi-driver what is in vogue. If you know some Hebrew, the leading companies from Tel Aviv perform one-night stands at both the Jerusalem Theatre and Bet Ha'am.

If your next stop is Tel Aviv, rent a car from one of the hire-it-here, leave-it-there agencies and drive yourself down. Don't take the main highway out of Jerusalem. Instead, travel one of the least known but most beautiful roads in the whole of Israel, the one that leaves Jerusalem by way of the magnificent village of Ein Karem (which contains, incidentally, a fine gallery of modern Israeli art and prints, run by a brother and sister from England, as well as a music centre specialising in excellent concerts of solo and small-group music) and cuts through the hills and forests, via Eshtaol, to bring you out on the old Jerusalem-Tel Aviv road.

TEL AVIV

While Jerusalem is introvert, Tel Aviv is extrovert. It wears its noisy heart on its sleeve, and all you need do is to move with the crowds, pausing only for refreshment and to watch the passing scene from a Dizengoff Street café table.

The central sea-front has had to adapt, so as not to be over-shadowed by the huge new hotels which have gone up along the length of Hayarkon Street. But if you walk past the Dan Hotel in the direction of Jaffa, you can see the fine, recently laid-out sea-front parks and yachting marinas which have transformed this once dingy end of the city into a first-class resort area.

Tel Aviv, say the Tel Avivians, has everything, which is true since Beth Hatefutsoth, the Nahum Goldmann Museum of the Diaspora, has been built and an art museum added to the city's offerings of theatre, music and cinema. It also has something else, which can bring a few hours' relief to sore-pressed parents — an amusement park in the Exhibition Grounds on the northern outskirts of the city.

If you want to see Tel Aviv at its most colourful, an hour or two during the morning at the Carmel Market will provide sufficient boisterous clamour until the evening, when the Yemenite quarter, with its narrow streets and exotic restaurants, can offer another glimpse of a little-known face of Israel's largest city.

Thanks are due to Geoffrey D. Paul, lately the Editor of the "Jewish Chronicle", and who was formerly the paper's correspondent in Israel, for writing the introduction to the three main cities.

HOTELS AND MOTELS

The Ministry of Tourism abolished the hotel star grading system in 1992 for a two year period. Instead, hotels are to be classified as a "Listed Hotel" according to minimum requirements covering the business licence, security and fire facilities. Regulations stipulate that prices should be quoted in Shekels and US Dollars.

All hotels in the following list are recommended by the Israel Ministry of Tourism. Most are members of the Israel Hotel Association, Head Office, 29 Hamered St., P.O.B. 50066, Tel Aviv, 68125. Tel. (03) 650131.

Kashrut

Hotels marked **(K)** are kosher, which in Israel means under official rabbinical supervision.

Hotel Rates

Rates vary slightly from resort to resort according to season.

AKKO (ACRE)

(K) Argaman Motel, Sea Shore. Tel. (04) 916691-7.
(K) Palm Beach Club Hotel, Sea Shore. Tel. (04) 815815.

ARAD

(K) Arad, 6 Hapalmach St. Tel. (057) 957040.
(K) Margoa, Mo'av St. Tel. (057) 957014.
(K) Nof Arad, Moav St. Tel. (057) 975056-8.

ASHDOD

(K) Miami, 12 Nordau St. Tel. (08) 522085.

ASHKELON

(K) Samson's Gardens, 38 Hatamar St., Afridar. Tel. (051) 36641, 34666 and 711039.

(K) Shulamit Gardens, 11 Hatayassim St., Afridar Beach. Tel. (051) 711261.

BAT YAM

Armon Yam, 95-96 Ben-Gurion Av. Tel. (03) 5522424.
Bat Yam, Ben-Gurion Av. Tel. (03) 864373 & 871646.
Sarita, 127 Ben-Gurion Av. Tel. (03) 5529183.

BEERSHEBA

(K) Arava, 37 Ha'histadrut St. Tel. (057) 78792.
(K) Aviv, 40 Mordei Hagetaot St. Tel. (057) 78059.
(K) Desert Inn. Tel. (057) 424922.
(K) Hanegev, 26 Ha'atzmaut St. Tel. (057) 77026.

BETHLEHEM

Bethlehem Star, Al-Baten St. Tel. (02) 743249.
Paradise, Manger St. Tel. (02) 744542.

CAESAREA

(K) Dan Caesarea Golf Hotel. Tel. (06) 362266-8.

DEAD SEA

(K) Ein Bokek, 86930 Ein Bokek. Tel. (057) 584331-4.
(K) Galei Zohar, Ein Bokek. Tel. (057) 584311-4.
(K) Hod, Ein Bokek. Tel. (057) 584644.
(K) Lot, Ein Bokek. Tel. (057) 584321-4.
(K) Moriah Gardens, Mobile Post Dead Sea. Tel. (057) 584351.
(K) Moriah Plaza Dead Sea Spa Hotel, Mobile Post Dead Sea. Tel. (057) 584221.
(K) Nirvana on the Dead Sea, Ein Bokek. Tel. (057) 584626.
(K) Tsell Harim, Ein Bakek. Tel. (057) 584121-2.

EILAT

Adi, Tzofit, P.O.B. 4100. Tel. (07) 376151-4.
(K) Americana Eilat, PO Box 27, North Beach. Tel. (07) 333777.
(K) Caesar, North Beach. Tel. (07) 333111.
(K) Caravan Sun Club, Coral Beach. Tel. (07) 373145-7.
(K) Carlton Coral Sea, Coral Beach. Tel. (07) 333555.
Club In, Coral Beach. Tel. (07) 334555.
(K) Dalia, North Beach. Tel. (07) 334004.
(K) Edomit, New Tourist Center. Tel. (07) 379511.
(K) Etzion, Hatmarim St. Tel. (07) 374131.
(K) Galei Eilat, North Shore. Tel. (07) 334222.
(K) King Solomon's Palace, North Beach. Tel. (07) 334111.
(K) Lagoona, North Beach. Tel. (07) 333666.
(K) Marina Club all suite hotel, North Beach. Tel. (07) 334191.
(K) Moriah Plaza Eilat, North Beach. Tel. (07) 332111.
(K) Neptune, North Beach. Tel. (07) 334333.
(K) Queen of Sheba, North Beach. Tel. (07) 334121.
(K) Red Rock, North Beach, 88102 P.O.B. 306. Tel. (07) 373171.
(K) Shulamit Gardens, North Beach. Tel. (07) 333999.
(K) Sport, North Beach. Tel. (07) 333333.
La Coquille N.L. all suite hotel. Tel. (07) 370031.
(K) Paradise N.L., North Beach, 88000. Tel. (07) 335050.
(K) Red Sea Sport N.L., Coral Beach. Tel. (07) 373145-7.
Riviera Apartment Hotel N.L. Tel. (07) 333944.
(K) Sonesta Suites N.L., Harava Rd. Tel. (07) 376222.

GALILEE

(K) Ayelet Hashahar Kibbutz Guest House, Upper Galilee, 12200. Tel. (06) 932611.
Kalanit, 10, Nesiei Israel Blvd., Karmiel. Tel. (04) 983878.
Sea View, Rosh Pina. Tel. (06) 937013.
Vered Hagalil, Guest Farm, M.P. Korazin. Tel. (06) 935785.
(K) Kfar Hittim N.L., DN. Galil Tachton. Tel. (06) 795921.
(K) Rakefet N.L., Gush Segev, Western Galilee. Tel. (04) 800403.

HAIFA

Beth-Shalom Carmel, 110 Hanassi St. Tel. (04) 337481-2.
(K) Dan Carmel, 87 Hanassi Av. Tel. (04) 386211.
(K) Dan Panorama, 107 Hanassi Av. Tel. (04) 352222.
(K) Dvir, 124 Yefe Nof St. Tel. (04) 389131-7.
Marom, 51 Hapalmach St. Tel. (04) 254355.
(K) Nesher, 53 Herzl St. Tel. (04) 640644.
(K) Nof, 101 Hanassi Av. Tel. (04) 354311.
(K) Shulamit, 15 Kiryat Sefer St. Tel. (04) 342811.
Talpiot, 61 Herzl St. Tel. (04) 673753.
(K) Yaarot Hacarmel, Mt. Carmel. Tel. (04) 229144-9.
Haifa Tower N.L., 63 Herzl St. Tel. (04) 661863.

HERZLIA

(K) Dan Accadia, Herzlia on Sea. Tel. (052) 556677.
Eshel Inn, Herzlia on Sea. Tel. (052) 570208.
(K) The Daniel Hotel & Spa, Herzlia on Sea. Tel. (052) 544444.
(K) The Sharon, Herzlia on Sea. Tel. (052) 575777.
(K) Tadmor, 38 Basel St. Tel. (052) 572321

JERUSALEM

Alcazar, 6 Almutanabi St. Tel. (02) 281111, 288800 and 288628.
American Colony, Nablus Rd. Tel. (02) 285171.
(K) Ariel, 31 Hebron Rd. Tel (02) 719222.
Az-Zahra, 13 Az-Zahra St. Tel. (02) 282447.
(K) Caesar, 208 Jaffa Rd. Tel. (02) 382156.
Capitol, 17 Salah Eddin St. Tel. (02) 282561-2.
(K) Central, 6 Pines St. Tel. (02) 384111.
Christmas, 1 All Ibn Abi Taleb St. Tel. (02) 282588.
Commodore, Samuel ben Adiya St. Tel. (02) 284845.
Gloria, Jaffa Gate. Tel. (02) 282431-2.
Holyland Hotel, P.O. Box 2461, 91023. Tel. (02) 437777
Holyland East, 6 Rashid St. Tel. (02) 284841-2.
(K) Hyatt Regency Jerusalem, 32 Lehi St. Tel. (02) 821333.
(K) Jerusalem Gate, 43 Yirmiyahu St. Tel. (02) 383101.
(K) Jerusalem Hilton, Givat Ram. Tel. (02) 536151.
Jerusalem Meridian, 5 Ali Ibn Abi Taleb St. Tel. (02) 285212-4.
Jerusalem N.L., Nablus Rd. Tel. (02) 283282.
Jerusalem Panorama, Hill of Gethsemane. Tel. (02) 284886-7.
(K) Jerusalem Renaissance, 6 Wolfson St. Tel. (02) 511524.
(K) Jerusalem Tower, 23 Hillel St. Tel. (02) 252161.
(K) King David, 23 King David St. Tel. (02) 221111.
(K) Kings, 60 King George St. Tel. (02) 247133.
(K) King Solomon, 32 King David St. Tel. (02) 241433.
(K) Knesset Tower, 4 Wolfson St. Tel. (02) 511111.
(K) Laromme, 3 Jabotinsky St. Tel. (02) 697777.
Lawrence, 18 Salah Eddin St. Tel. (02) 282585.
Lev Yerushalayim N.L., 18 King George St. Tel. (02) 250333.

61

Metropole, 6 Salah Eddin St. Tel. (02) 282507.
(K) Moriah Plaza Jerusalem, 39 Keren Hayesod St. Tel. (02) 232232.
Mount of Olives, Mount of Olives Rd. Tel. (02) 284877-8.
Mount Scopus, 10 Sheikh Jarrah. Tel. (02) 828891-2.
(K) Mount Zion, 17 Hebron Rd. Tel. (02) 724222.
National Palace, 4 Az-Zahara St. Tel. (02) 273273.
New Imperial, Jaffa Gate, Old City, P.O.B. 14085. Tel. (02) 272400.
New Metropole, 8 Salah-el-din St. Tel. (02) 283846.
New Regent, 20 Azzahra St. Tel. (02) 284540 & 272825.
Palace, Mount of Olives Rd. Tel. (02) 271126-8.
(K) Palatin, 4 Agripas St. Tel. (02) 231141.
Pilgrims Inn, Al Rashid St. Tel. (02) 284883 & 283337.
Pilgrims Palace, Sultan Sulaiman St. Tel. (02) 283337 & 283338.
(K) Reich, 1 Hagai St., Bet Hakerem. Tel. (02) 523121.
Ritz, 8 Ibn Khaldoun St. Tel. (02) 273233.
Rivoli, 3 Salah Eddin St. Tel. (02) 284871.
(K) Ron, 44 Jaffa Rd. Tel. (02) 253471.
Seven Arches, Mt. of Olives. Tel. (02) 894455.
(K) Sheraton Jerusalem Plaza, 47 King George St. Tel. (02) 259111.
(K) Sonesta Jerusalem, 2 Wolfson St. Tel. (02) 528221.
St. George International, Salah Eddin St. Tel. (02) 282571-5.
Strand, 4 Ibn Jubeir St. Tel. (02) 280279.
Tirat Bat Sheva, 43 King George St., Tel. (02) 232121.
Victoria, P.O.B. 20606. Tel. (02) 286220.
(K) Windmill, 3 Mendele St. Tel. (02) 663111.
Y.M.C.A. 26 King David St. Tel. (02) 227111.
Y.M.C.A. Aelia Capitolina, 29 Nablus Rd. Tel. (02) 282375-6.
Y.W.C.A., Wadi Joz. Tel. (02) 282593.
(K) Zion, 4 Luntz St. Tel. (02) 232367.
(K) Zion, 10 Dorot Rishonim. Tel. (02) 259511.
(K) Zohar, 47 Leib Jaffe St. Tel. (02) 717557.

Kibbutz Hotels
Kibbutz Hotels Office: 90 Ben-Yehuda St., P.O.B. 3193, Tel Aviv 61031. Tel. (03) 246161.
(K) Ayelet Hashahar, Upper Galilee, 12200. Tel. (06) 932611.
(K) Ein Gedi, Kibbutz Ein-Gedi. Tel. (057) 584757-8.
Ein Gedi Camping Village, Mobile Post Dead Sea. Tel. (057) 584342-3.
Ein Gev, Kibbutz Ein-Gev. Tel. (06) 758027-8.
(K) Gesher Haziv, Western Galilee. Tel. (04) 825715.
Hafetz Hayim, Hafetz Haim. Tel. (08) 593888.
(K) Hagoshrim, Upper Galilee. Tel. (06) 956231.
Ha'on Camping Village, Sea of Galilee. Tel. (06) 757555-6.
(K) Kfar Blum, Upper Galilee. Tel. (06) 943666.
(K) Kfar Giladi, Upper Galilee. Tel. (06) 941414-5.
(K) Kiriat Anavim, Judea Hills. Tel. (02) 348999.
(K) Lavi, Lower Galilee. Tel. (06) 799450.
(K) Ma'ale Hachamisha, Judea Hills. Tel. (02) 342591.
Ma'Agan Camping Village, Sea of Galilee. Tel. (06) 753753.
Metzoki Dragot N.L. Tel. (02) 964501.
(K) Mitzpeh Rachel, M.P. North Judea 90900. Tel. (02) 702555.
Nahsholim, (Hof Dor) M.P. Hof Carmel. Tel. (06) 399533.
Neve Ilan, Judea Hills. Tel. (02) 341241.
Nir Etzion, Carmel Beach Mobile Post. Tel. (04) 842541-3.
Nof Ginosar, Kibbutz Ginosar. Tel. (06) 792161.
Shefayim, Kibbutz Shefayim. Tel. (052) 547234-5.
Shoresh, Judea Hills. Tel. (02) 341171-5.

Ye'Elim, M.P. Hevel Eilot. Tel. (07) 374362.

METULA
(K) Arazim. Tel. (06) 944143-5.
(K) Hamavri. Tel. (06) 940150.
(K) Sheleg Halevanon, P.O.B. 13. Tel. (06) 944015-7.

NAHARIYA
(K) Astar, 27 Gaaton Blvd. Tel. (04) 923431.
(K) Beit Hava, Shavei Zion. Tel. (04) 820391.
(K) Carlton, 23 Ha'gaaton Blvd. Tel. (04) 922211.
(K) Eden N.L., Meyasdim St. Tel. (04) 923246-7.
Erna House, 29 Jabotinsky St. Tel. (04) 920170.
(K) Frank, 4 Haaliya St. Tel. (04) 920278.
(K) Kalman, 27 Jabotinsky St. Tel. (04) 920355 926539.
Nes Ammim Guest House, Mobile Post Ashrat. Tel. (04) 825522.
(K) Panorama, 6 Hamaapilim St. Tel. (04) 920555.
(K) Rosenblatt, 59 Weizmann St. Tel. (04) 920069.

NAZARETH
Nazareth, 6th Paulus St. Tel. (06) 577777.

NETANYA
(K) Blue Bay, 37 Hamelachim St. Tel. (053) 623322.
(K) Gal Yam, 46 Dizengoff St. Tel. (053) 625033.
(K) Galei Hasharon, 42 Ussishkin St. Tel. (053) 341946.
(K) Galei Zans, 6 Ha'melachim St. Tel. (053) 621777.
(K) Galil, 18 Nice Blvd. Tel. (053) 624455.
(K) Ginot Yam, 9 David Hamelech St. Tel. (053) 341007.
(K) Goldar, 1 Usishkin St. Tel. (053) 338188.
(K) Grand Yahalom, 15 Gad Makhnes St. Tel. (053) 624888.
(K) Green Beach, P.O.B. 230. Tel. (053) 54166.
(K) Jeremy N.L., 11 Gad Machnes St. Tel. (053) 622651.
(K) King Koresh, 6 Harav Kook St. Tel. (053) 613555.
(K) King Solomon, 18 Hamaapilim St. Tel. (053) 338444.
La Promenade all suite hotel N.L., 6 Gad Machness St. Tel. (053) 626450.
(K) Margoa (new), 9 Gad Makhnes St. Tel. (053) 624434.
(K) Maxim, 8 King David St. Tel. (053) 621062.
(K) Metropol Grand, 17 Gad Makhnes St. Tel. (053) 624777.
(K) Palace N.L., 33 Gad Machnes St. Tel. (053) 620222.
(K) Park, 7 David Hamelech St. Tel. (053) 623344.
(K) Residence, 18 Gad Machnes St. Tel. (053) 623777.
The Seasons Hotel, Nice Blvd. Tel. (053) 618555.
(K) Topaz, 25 King David St. Tel. (053) 624555.

REHOVOT
Margoa, 11 Moskowitz St. Tel. (08) 451303.

TEL AVIV AREA
(K) Adiv, 5 Mendele St. Tel. (03) 229141.
(K) Ambassador, 56 Herbert Samuel. Tel. (03) 5103993.
(K) Ami, 152 Hayarkon St. Tel. (03) 5249141-5.
(K) Armon Hayarkon, 268 Hayarkon St. Tel. (03) 455271-3.
Astor, 105 Hayarkon St. Tel. (03) 223141.
(K) Avia, B. G. International Airport Area. Tel. (03) 5360221.
Aviv, 88 Hayarkos St. Tel. (03) 51027845, 655486.
(K) Basel, 156 Hayarkon St. Tel. (03) 244161.

(K) Bell, 12 Allenby St. Tel. (03) 5177011.
Best Western Regency Suites all suite hotel, 80 Hayarkon St. Tel. (03) 663266.
(K) Carlton Tel Aviv, Eliezer Peri St. Tel. (03) 5201818.
(K) City, 9 Mapu St. Tel. (03) 5246253.
Country Club, Namir Rd., Gelilot. Tel. (03) 669066.
(K) Dan Panorama, 10 Y. Kaufman St.. Tel. (03) 5190190.
(K) Dan Tel Aviv, 99 Hayarkon St. Tel. (03) 5241111.
(K) Deborah, 87 Ben-Yehuda St. Tel. (03) 5448282.
(K) Diplomat , 145 Hayarkon St. Tel. (03) 294422.
Dizengoff Square, 2 Zamanhof St. Tel. (03) 296181-4
Dizengoff Square Hostel, 11 Dizengoff Sq., Tel. (03) 522-5184 Fax. (03) 522-5181.
(K) Florida, 164 Hayarkon St. Tel. (03) 5242184.
(K) Grand Beach, 250 Hayarkon St. Tel. (03) 5466555.
Hagalil N.L., 54-56 Allenby St. Tel. (03) 655036.
Havakook Exclusive Apartment Hotel, 7 Havakook St. Tel. (03) 440011.
Imperial, 66 Hayarkon St. Tel. (03) 657002 & 657672.
Kfar Maccabiah, Ramat Gan, POB 919. Tel. (03) 715715.
(K) Maxim, 86 Hayarkon St. Tel. (03) 5173721-5.
Melonit Savoy Apartment Hotel, 5 Geula St. Tel. (03) 5102939.
Miami, 8 Allenby St. Tel. (03) 5103868.
(K) Monopol N.l. on the promenade, 4 Allenby St. Tel. (03) 655906.
(K) Moriah Plaza Tel Aviv, 155 Hayarkon St. Tel. (03) 5271515.
Moss, 6 Ness Ziona St. Tel. (03) 5171655.
Nes Ziona N.L., 10 Ness-Ziona St. Tel. (03) 5103404.
(K) Ora N.L., 35 Ben Yehuda St. Tel. (03) 650941.
(K) Ramada Continental, 121 Hayarkon St. Tel. (03) 5272626.
(K) Ramat Aviv, 151 Derech Namir. Tel. (03) 6990777.
(K) Shalom, 216 Hayarkon St. Tel. (03) 5243277.
(K) Sheraton Tel Aviv, 115 Hayarkon St. Tel. (03) 5286222.
(K) Sinai, 11-16 Trumpeldor St. Tel. (03) 652621.
(K) Tal, 287 Hayarkon St. Tel. (03) 5442281.
Tamar, 8 Gnessin St. Tel. (03) 5286997.
(K) Tel Aviv Hilton, Independence Park. Tel. (03) 5202222.
(K) Tayelet N.L. On the promenade, 6 Allenby St. Tel. (03) 5105845.
(K) Wagshal, 13 Meltzer St., Bnei, Brak. Tel. (03) 784536, 785052.
(K) Wiznitz, 16 Damesek Eliezer St., Bnei-Brak. Tel. (03) 777141-3.
(K) Yamit Towers, 79 Hayarkon St. Tel. (03) 5171111.

TIBERIAS

(K) Ariston, 19 Herzl Blvd. Tel. (06) 790244.
(K) Astoria, 13 Ohel Ya'akov St. Tel. (06) 722351-2.
Beit Berger N.L., 25 Nieberg St. Tel. (06) 720850.
(K) Caesar, Tel. (06) 732333.
Club Hotel Tiberias, Ahad Ha'am St. Tel. (06) 791888
(K) Daphna, Ussiskin St. Tel. (06) 792261-4.
Eden, 4 Ohel Ya'akor. Tel. (06)-790070.
(K) Eshel, Tabur Haaretz St. Tel. (06) 90562.
(K) Gai Beach, Derech Hamerchatzaot Tel. (06) 790790.
(K) Galei Kinnereth, 1 Eliezer Kaplan St. Tel. (06) 792331.
(K) Galilee, Elhadef St. P.O.B. 616.Tel. (06) 791166-8.
(K) Ganei Hamat, Habanim St. nr. Hot Springs. Tel. (06) 792890.
Ganei Menora, P.O.B. 99. Tel. (06) 792770.
(K) Golan, 14 Achad Ha'am St. Tel. (06) 791901-4.
(K) Hawai, P.O.B. 366 Migdal. Tel. (06) 790202, 720549, 720568.
(K) Jordan River, Habanim St. Tel. (06) 721111.

(K) Kinar, N.E. Sea of Galilee. Tel. (06) 732670.
Kolton Inn N.L., 2 Ohel Ya'acov. Tel. (06) 791641-2.
(K) Moriah Plaza Tiberias, Habanim St. Tel. (06) 792233.
(K) Quiet Beach, Gdud Barak St. Tel. (06) 790125.
(K) Ramot-Resort Hotel, Sea of Galilee. Tel. (06) 732636.
Ron Beach, Gdud Barak St. Tel. (06) 791350.
Sara, 7 Saidel St. (06) 720826.
The Sea of Galilee Club N.L., P.O.B. 400, Migdal. Tel. (06) 724824.
(K) Tzameret Inn, Plus 2000 St. Tel. (06) 794951.
(K) Washington, 13 Seidel St. Tel. (06) 791861-3.

ZEFAT

(K) David, Mr. Canaan. Tel. (06) 920062.
(K) Nof Hagalil, Mt. Canaan. Tel. (06) 921595.
(K) Pisgah, Mr. Canaan. Tel. (06) 920105.
(K) Rimon Inn, Artists Colony, Tel. (06) 920665-6.
(K) Ron, Hativat Yiftah St. Tel. (06) 972590.
Ruckenstein, Mt. Canaan. Tel. (06) 920060.

ZICHRON YA'ACOV

(K) Barons' Heights & Terraces N.L., P.O.B. 332. Tel. (06) 396111.

HOLIDAY VILLAGES

Holiday villages are all situated on or near the sea-shore and offer water and other sports, as well as entertainment.

ACHZIV

Club Méditerranée. Members only. Tel. (04) 923291.

ASHKELON

Club Ashkelon. Tel. (051) 36733-6.

BIKAT BET KEREM

(K) Manof Recreation Village. Tel. (04) 914583 & 914592.

CAESAREA

Hofshonit. Tel. (06) 362927.

CARMEL COAST

Nachsholim, Dor Beach. Tel. (06) 399533.

DEAD SEA

Ein Gedi. Tel. (057) 84757; Metsokei Dragot. Tel. (02) 228114.

EILAT

Blue Sky Caravan Holiday Village, North Beach. Tel. (059) 73953-4.
Club In Labroke Villa Resort, Coral Beach. Tel. (059) 79577.
Des Coraux Holiday Village. Open to
Club Méditerranée members only. Tel. (059) 73977.
Marina Club, North Beach. Tel. (059) 76036.
Sun Bay Holiday Village, North Beach. Tel. (059) 73105-6.
Ye'elim. Tel. (059) 74362.

EIN GEV

Holiday Village, Sea of Galilee. Tel. (06) 758027-8.

HADERA
Nueiba. Mediterranean Holiday Village, Miramar Beach, S. Hedera. Tel. (053) 96397.

HAON
(K) Kibbutz Haon, Jordan Valley. Tel. (06) 757555-6.

JERUSALEM
(K) Youth Recreation Centre Holiday Village, Yefei Nof. Jerusalem Forest. Tel. (02) 416060.

KORAZIM
(K) Amnon Bay Recreation Centre. Tel. (06) 934431.
Vered Hagalil Guest Farm. Tel. (06) 935785.

MAAGAN
Maagan Vacation Centre, Sea of Galilee. Tel. (06) 753753.

NETANYA
(K) Green Beach Holiday Village. Tel. (053) 44166 & 52422.

RAMAT GAN
(K) Kfar Hamaccabiah, Bernstein St. Tel. (03) 715715.

YOUTH HOSTELS
There are 33 Youth Hostels in Israel for students, youth groups and young adults. They are supervised by the Israel Youth Hostels Association (a member of the International Youth Hostels Association).
Most offer the standard hostel facilities: dormitories, dining-room, self-service kitchen, etc. Some are air-conditioned. Every hostel has a resident warden.
The Israel Youth Hostels Association offices are at 3 Dorot Harishonim St. P.O.B. 1075, Jerusalem, 91009. Tel. (02) 222706, 227439, 221648 or 243520.
In the following list of hostels, the number of beds is shown in brackets after the name of the hostel.

GALILEE
Karei Deshe (Tabgha): Yoram (191). Tel. (06) 720601. 11 miles north of Tiberias.
Poria: Taiber (144). Tel. (06) 750050. 2½ miles south of Tiberias.
Rosh Pina: Hovevei Hateva (104). Tel. (06) 937086. 16 miles north of Tiberias.
Safed: Bet Benyamin (116). Tel. (06) 931086 or 973514. In southern part of town.
Tel Hai (156). Tel. (06) 940043. 38 miles north of Tiberias.
Tiberias: Yosef Meyouhas (248). Tel. (06) 721775 or 790350. Hayarden St., cnr. Alhadif St.

GOLAN HEIGHTS
Hispin (100). Tel. (06) 763305 or 763461. 17 miles east of Tabgha, near Ramat Magshimim.

HAIFA, CARMEL & WESTERN GALILEE
Akko (Acre) (125). Tel. (04) 911982. Old City, near lighthouse.
Haifa: Carmel (280). Tel. (04) 531944 or 532516. At southern approaches to city.

Maayan Harod: Hankin (150). Tel. (06) 581660. 7 miles east of Afula.
Naharia: Kalman (50). Tel. (04) 920355. 27 Jabotinsky St., a short walk from
Central Bus Station.
Ramat Yohanan: Yehuda Hatzair (180). Tel. (04) 442976. 11 miles north-east
of Haifa.
Sulam Tzor: Yad Leyad (300). Tel. (04) 823345. 4 miles north of Naharia.

JERUSALEM

Bar-Giora (250). Tel. (02) 911073. 15 miles south-west of Jerusalem.
Bayit Vegan: Louise Waterman-Wise (300). 8 Hapisgah St. Tel. (02) 423366
or 420990.
Bet Bernstein (80). 1 Keren Hayesod St. Tel. (02) 228286.
Bet Meir: Ramot Shapira (150). Tel. (02) 342691 or 343793. 12½ miles west of
Jerusalem.
Bet Shmuel (240). 13 King David St. Tel. (02) 203466 or 203467.
Ein Karem (97). Tel. (02) 416282. 10 mins. from Louise Waterman-Wise
Hostel in Bayit Vegan.
Jerusalem Forest (98). Tel. (02) 416060.
Kfar Etzion (273). Tel. (02) 935133 or 935233. 14 miles south of Jerusalem.
Groups only.
Kiryat Anavim: Haezrahi (100). Tel. (02) 342770. 7½ miles west of Jerusalem.
Moreshet Yahadut (75). Tel. (02) 288611. Old City. Groups only.

NEGEV

Arad: Bet Blau-Weiss (150). Tel. (057) 957150. Centre of town.
Beersheba: Bet Yatziv (270). Tel. (057) 77444 or 71490. 79 Ha'atzmaut St.
Ein Gedi: Bet Sara (206). Tel. (057) 84165. 1½ miles north of Kibbutz Ein
Gedi, on Dead Sea.
Eilat (240). Tel. (059) 72358.
Masada: Isaac H. Taylor (150). Tel. (057) 84349. 28 miles from Arad.
Mitzpeh Ramon: Bet Noam (164). Tel. (057) 88443 or 88074.

TEL AVIV AREA

Kfar Vitkin: Emek Hefer (220). Tel. (053) 666032. 25 miles north of Tel Aviv.
Petach Tikva: Yad Labanim (147). Tel. (03) 926666. Yahalom St. 7½ miles
north-east of Tel Aviv.
Tel Aviv (300). Tel. (03) 455042 or 5460719. 32 Bnei Dan St.

WESTERN NEGEV

Hevel Katif: Hadarom (220). Tel. (051) 47596 or 47597.

For more detailed information, apply either to the Israel Youth Hostels
Association or to the nearest Israel Government Tourist Office.

CAMPING

There are camping sites at Achziv and Lehmann, in Western Galilee; Tal, in
Upper Galilee; Kibbutz Ein Gev, Kibbutz Haon, and Maagan, all on the Sea
of Galilee; Kfar Hittim, 1½ miles west of Tiberias; Harod, south of Nazareth;
Kibbutz Neve Yam, south of Haifa, on the coast, and Moshav Dor, south of
Neve Yam, also on the coast; Ashkelon; Ramat Rachel, 1½ miles from the
centre of Jerusalem, and Mevo Betar, 9 miles south-west of Jerusalem; Bet
Zayit, in the Judean Hills; Neve Zohar and Ein Gedi, north of Sdom; Elat
on the Red Sea; Ye'elim, nr. Yotvata, in the southern Negev, about 12 miles
north of Elat.
All the above sites, which belong to the Israel Camping Union, P.O.B. 53,
Naharia, Tel. (04) 925392 (London representative: Project 67, 36 Great
Russell St., WC1B 3PP. Tel. 01-636 1262), are easily accessible. They all have

hot showers, toilets, drinking water, electricity, and a small restaurant or facilities for buying provisions. All except Tal, Haon, Kfar Hittim, Moshav Dor and Harod (which are open from April-October) are open all year round. There is also a camping village at Ein Gedi, on the Dead Sea. Tel. 84342-3. Open all year round.

SOME RECOMMENDED RESTAURANTS & CAFES

Kosher restaurants under rabbinical supervision display a kashrut certificate. They are indicated here by the symbol **(K)**.

AFULA

(K) La Cabania, Ha'atzmaut Sqr. Tel. (06) 591638.
Mifgash Mizra, Kibbutz Mizra. Tel. (06) 599622.
(K) San Remo, 4 Ha'atzmaut St. Tel. (06) 522458.
Ta Tung, 81 Habanim St. Tel. (06) 590509.

AKKO (ACRE)

Amirei Hagalil, Akko-Safed Rd. nr. Moshav Amirim. Tel. (06) 989120.
Audeh Brothers, Han el Franji. Tel. (04) 912013.
Babushka, Derech Ha'Arava. Tel. (04) 917870.
Monte Carlo, Salah A'din St. Tel. (04) 916173.
Nanking, Dlr. El Asad. Tel.: (04) 984662.
(K) Palm Beach. Tel. (04) 912891.
Ptolemais. Tel. (04) 916112.

ARAD

(K) Bulgaria, 112 Kesen Kayemet St. Tel. (057) 38504.
Café Ugit (Coffee Shop), 6 Eliezer Ben-Yair St. Tel. (057) 958311.
Galit, Commercial Centre. Tel. (057) 950793.
(K) Hahavaya, 32 Hapalmach St. Tel. (057) 952186.
Rachel, Commercial Centre. Tel. (057) 959219.
Marcel, Commercial Centre. Tel. (057) 957685.
Tokio (Coffee Shop), Commercial Centre.

ASHKELON

Furama, 24 Ort St., Afridar Centre. Tel. (051) 38497.
(K) Rachel, 29/7 Chen St., Industrial Centre. Tel. (057) 959219.
Riko (K without supervision), 51 Ben-Yehuda St. Tel. (051) 24592.
Shanghai, New Tourist Centre. Tel. (051) 75306.

BAT YAM

Aouva, 11 Jerusalem St.
Bourger San, 1 Barshaoul St.
Dovdou, 48 Hertzl St.
Makor Hafalaffel, 45 Rothschild.
Mediterranean Tower, 2 Hayam St.
Miznon Hamana, 3 Anevim.
Tsaad Temani, 85 Balfour.
Tsipora, 5 Bar Shaoul

BEERSHEBA

Bar Sheva, 32 Kfar Darom St. Tel. (057) 77191.
Beersheba Chinese Restaurant, 79 Histadrut St. Tel. (057) 75375.
(K) Beit Halimon (Cafeteria), 18 Histadrut St. Tel. (057) 71095.
(K) Ceparis, 1 Herzl St. Tel. (057) 32392.
(K) Chin Shin, 100 Herzl St. Tel. (057) 70983.

Jade Palace, 79 Histadrut St. Tel. (057) 75375.
Montana Milk Bar, 1 Pekua St. Tel. (057) 76373.
Oholei Keidar, Tel Sheba. Tel. (057) 690104.
Le Bistrot, 55 Hahistadrut St. Tel. (057) 35258.
(K) Palm Trees Garden, 17 Hapoalim St. Tel. (057) 85997.
Skateland Meeting, 2 Hagefen St. Tel. (057) 35186.

BENYAMINA
Em Derakhim. Tel. 8092.

B'NEI BERAK
(K) Chapanash, 6 Jabotinsky St.

CAESAREA
Charley's, Old City. Tel. (06) 363050.
Harbour Citadel, Old Caesarea. Tel. (06) 361988.
(K) Caesarean (Self-service), Paz petrol station. Tel. (06) 334609.

DIMONA
Kafria Paz, Industrial Centre. Tel. (057) 59392.

EILAT
(K) Arizona, on main road to Tel Aviv. Tel. (059) 72710.
Au Bistro, Eilot St. Tel. (059) 74333.
Barakuda, Coral Beach.
(K) Bar-B-Que, Hatemarim Blvd. Tel. (059) 73634 & 75793.
Beber, 14 Ye'elim Av. Tel. (059) 72504.
(K) Café Royal, King Solomon's Palace Hotel, North Beach. Tel. (059) 76111.
Capriccio Milk Bar, 133 Hatemarim Blvd. Tel. (059) 76100.
China Town Express, New Tourist Centre. Tel. (059) 73551.
(K) Chinese Restaurant, Shulamit Gardens Hotel, North Beach. Tel. (059) 77515.
Casablan, Delek petrol station, Arava Rd. Tel. (059) 76070.
(K) Dolphin Buffet, New Tourist Centre.
Eddie's Hideaway, 68 Almogim St. Tel. (059) 71137.
Edom Tower, New Tourist Centre. Tel. (059) 76060.
(K) Egged, Central Bus Station. Tel. (059) 75161.
El Gaucho, Ha'abrava Rd. Tel. (059) 31549.
(K) El Morocco, New Tourist Centre. Tel. (059) 71296.
Fisherman's Boat, 1 Hativat Yerushalayim St. Tel. (059) 71339.
Fish's Net, New Industrial Area. Tel. (059) 78856.
(K) Golden Lagoon, New Lagoona Hotel, North Beach. Tel. (059) 72176.
(K) Hakerem, Elot St. cnr. Hatemarim Blvd. Tel. (059) 74577.
(K) Halleluyah, Bldg. 9, New Tourist Centre. Tel. (059) 75752.
Holiday Inn, Paz petrol station, near airport. Tel. (059) 72500.
Jackson's Tavern, Angelica Beach. Tel. (059) 763334.
Jade Garden, 1 Arava Rd. Tel. (059) 72500.
La Bodega, 259 Chorev St. Tel. (059) 72560.
La Boheme, Coral Beach. Tel. (059) 74222.
La Coquille, North Beach. Tel. (059) 73461.
La Tour Eiffel, 1 Commercial Centre. Tel. (059) 71404.
Little Italy, 1 Hativat Golani St. Tel. (059) 4468.
Lotus, next to Caesar Hotel. Tel. (059) 76161.
Luxembourg Chez Henry, Ye'elim Av. Tel. (059) 72504.
Mac David, New Tourist Centre.
Mandy's, Coral Beach. Tel. (059) 72238.

(K) Marhaba, Aviya-Sonesta Hotel, Taba Beach. Tel. (059) 76191.
(K) Marrakesh, New Tourist Centre. Tel. (059) 76246.
Me and Me, North Beach. Tel. (059) 71786.
(K) Metamei Teman, Hatemarim Blvd.
Mini Golf. Tel. (059) 74402.
Moulin Rouge, Richter Centre, Hatemarim Blvd. Tel. (059) 73887.
(K) Neve Elat, Hatemarim Blvd.
Neviot, North Shore. Tel. (059) 971081.
(K) Off the Wharf, King Solomon's Palace Hotel, North Beach. Tel. (059) 79111.
(K) Panorama, New Commercial Centre. Tel. (059) 71965.
Pat Bar (K dairy), Elot St. nr. Yerushalayim Hashlema St. Tel. (059) 72853.
Pundak Haarava, New Tourist Centre. Tel. (059) 73908.
Rhapsody in White, North Shore Marina. Tel. (059) 74697.
Rimini, New Tourist Centre. Tel. (059) 76060.
Sea Rose, Coral Beach. Tel. (059) 72437.
Shanghai, New Tourist Centre. Tel. (059) 75306.
Shrimp House, Hatemarim Blvd. Tel. (059) 72758.
Targa, Shalom Centre. Tel. (059) 71619.
Teddy's Pub, Ophira Park. Tel. (059) 73949.
The Last Refuge, Coral Beach. Tel. (059) 72437.
The Tavern, New Tourist Centre.
Yoske, New Tourist Centre. Tel. (059) 72719.
There are three **(K)** tour boats at the marina: Pirate, Tel. (059) 76549; Sea Bird, Tel. (059) 76549; Orionia, Tel. (059) 72902.

EIN HATZEVA

(K) Pundak Ein Hatzeva, Arava Rd. Tel. (057) 81407.

EIN HOD

Ein Hod (K without supervision), Artists' Village. Tel. (06) 794209.

EIN YAHAV

Ein Yahav Oasis Restaurant. Tel. (057) 81119.

GAN HAIR

Tai-Chi, 91 Ibn Gvirol St. Tel. (03) 5449212.

GOLAN HEIGHTS

(K) Hamat Gader. Tel. (06) 751039.

GUSH ETZION

(K) Moshav Elazar Restaurant. Tel. (02) 741191.

HAIFA AREA

Abed, Paris Sq. Tel. (04) 663723.
Allenby, 43 Allenby Rd. Tel. (04) 529928.
Baigel Nash, 135 Hanassi Blvd. Tel. (04) 385293.
Ba-Li, 3 Hanevim St. Tel. (04) 645242.
(K) Bankers' Tavern, 2 Habankim St. Tel. (04) 528439 (lunch only. Closed Sat.)
Beitenu, 29 Jerusalem St. Tel. (04) 668059. (Self-service).
Belinches House, 35 Haneviim St. Tel. (04) 672751.
(K) Ben Ezra, 71 Hazayit St. Tel. (04) 842273.
Benni, 23 Hechalutz St. Tel. (04) 660395.
Bizcocho, 6 Herzlia St. Tel. (04) 667348.
Boustan Ha'emek, Kiryat Haroshet, Tivon. Tel. (04) 934837.

Bucharest, Haifa Bay Industrial Zone. Tel. (04) 722227.
Café Carmel, 125 Hanassi Blvd. Tel. (04) 381082.
Café Gallery Ritz, 6 Haim St. Tel. (04) 662520.
Café Kapulsky, Panorama Centre. Tel. (04) 373029.
Chinese House, Hagana Blvd., Paz petrol station next to Central Bus Station. Tel. (04) 538642.
(K) Chinese Restaurant of Nof, Nof Hotel, 101 Hanassi Blvd. Tel. (04) 38873.
Chin Lung, 126 Hanassi Blvd. Tel. (04) 381308.
Dalia, 22 Ben-Gurion Blvd. Tel. (04) 522157.
Diab, 6 Herzlia St. Tel. (04) 660342.
Dolphin, 3 Bat Galim Blvd. Tel. (04) 523837.
(K) Egged, Central Bus Station. Tel. (04) 515221. (Self-service.)
Einat, 178 Hahistadrut St. Tel. (04) 727249.
El Soloh, 2 Eliahu Hanavi St. Tel. (04) 661998.
Finjan, 4 Mahanayim St. Tel. (04) 382862.
(K) Gan Rimon, 10 Habroshim St. Tel. (04) 381392. (Lunch only.)
Gat, 4 Aharon St. Tel. (04) 662075.
Ha'ahim, 66 Derech Ha'atzmaut.
(K) Ha'atzmaut, 63 Derech Ha'atzmaut. Tel. (04) 523829.
Hahalom, Stella Maris Centre, Tchernichovsky St. Tel. (04) 334321.
Hakadarim, Carmel Beach. Tel. (04) 512018.
Hakotev, 23 Kibbutz Galuyot St. Tel. (04) 643409.
(K) Hamber Burger, 61 Herzl St. Tel. (04) 666739.
Hamizrach, 4 Haneviim St. Tel. (04) 642093.
Hatahana, 119 Hanassi Blvd.
Hippotame, 116 Hanassi Av. Tel. (04) 374366.
Home Sandwich, 28 Derech Yafo. Tel. (04) 642223.
Hoummous, 27 Haneviim St. Tel. (04) 667265.
Iskandar, 3 Hazionut Blvd. Tel. (04) 524407.
Karol, 33 Haneviim St. Tel. (04) 644810.
Kefir, 9 Bialik St. Tel. (04) 668077.
La Chaumière, 40 Ben-Gurion Blvd. Tel. (04) 538563.
La Trattoria, 119 Hanassi Blvd. Tel. (04) 379020.
Leon & Yoji, 31 Haneviim St. Tel. (04) 538073.
Long Sueng, 140 Acco Rd., Kiryat Bialik. Tel. (04) 718941.
(K) Mac David, 131 Hanassi Blvd. & 1 Balfour St. Tel. (04) 383684.
Makom Aher, 131 Hanassi Blvd. Tel. (04) 82391.
Matamim, 24 Herzl St. Tel. (04) 665172.
Mayflower, Stella Maris Centre, Tchernichovsky St. Tel. (04) 521295.
Me and Me, 17 Ben-Gurion Blvd. Tel. (04) 522093.
Mifgash Istamboul, 31 I. L. Peretz St.
Milk Bar-Restaurant, Hamashbir Lazarchan Bldg., 1 Yona St. Tel. (04) 660936. (Lunch only.)
(K) Milky Pinky (Milk Bar), 28 Haneviim St. Tel. (04) 664166.
Mirabelle, Stella Maris Centre, 35 Tchernichovsky St. Tel. (04) 330799.
Misadag, 20 Pinhas Margolin St. Tel. (04) 524441.
Mishu, 46 Derech Yafo. Tel. (04) 535839.
Mizlalat Habasar, 3 Hechalutz St. Tel. (04) 538628.
Naim, 6 Eliahu Hanavi St. Tel. (04) 640309.
Natkei Dagim, Sonol petrol station, Akko-Haifa Rd. Tel. (04) 914120.
Neptune, 19 Pinhas Margolin St., Tel. (04) 535205.
Nof Yam, 1 Liberia St. Tel. (04) 254594.
Nosh, 34 Gilboa St. Tel. (04) 221926.
Pagoda, 1 Bat Galim Blvd. Tel. (04) 524585.
Panorama, 120 Yefeh Nof St. Tel. (04) 382979.
Pancake, 186 Jaffa St. Tel. (04) 538 642.

(K) Paznon, Hof Carmel. Tel. (04) 538181.
Peer, 130 Hanassi Blvd. Tel. (04) 382333.
Peer Amram Brothers, 1 Athlit St. Tel.
(04) 665707.
Pizza Italiano, 119 Hanassi Blvd. Tel. (04) 381336.
Popolo, Ruppin Rd., nr. Paz petrol station. Tel. (04) 252654.
Prego, 23 Nordau Mall. Tel. (04) 671570.
Pundak Hacarmel, Daliat el Carmel. Tel. (04) 223537.
Pundak Hagolan, 29 Haneviim St. Tel. (04) 661444.
Quick Bar, 15 Nordau St. Tel. (04) 644826. (Lunch only.)
(K) Restaurant Hamidrachov, 10 Nordau St. Tel. (04) 662050.
Rimini-Hadar, 20 Haneviim St. Tel. (04) 640201.
Rimon, 37 Derech Ha'atzmaut. Tel. (04) 667412.
Ritz (Coffee Shop), 6 Haim St. Tel. (04) 662520.
(K) Rondo, Dan Carmel Hotel, 87 Hanassi Blvd. Tel. (04) 386211.
Rothschild Centre, 142 Hanassi Blvd. Tel. (04) 387877.
Saleh Brothers, 5 Hameginim St. Tel. (04) 640763.
Sandis, Shavei Zion. Tel. (04) 923338.
Seaview, 2 Liberia St. Tel. (04) 254594.
Sea Waves, 99 Yefe Nof St. Tel. (04) 386602.
Senior Sandwich, 33 Derech Yafo. Tel. (04) 514059.
Shikmona, 3 Nahum Dovrin St. Tel. (04) 666253. (Lunch only. Closed Sat.)
Shmulik & Dany, 7 Habankim St. Tel. (04) 514411. (Lunch only. Closed Sat.)
Sin Sin, 28 Derech Yafo. Tel. (04) 642223.
Star, 19 Hameginim St. Tel. (04) 640666.
Taiwan, 59 Ben-Gurion Blvd. Tel. (04) 532082.
Taiwan Hakrayot, 5 Ha'atzmaut St. Tel. (04) 728625.
Tchernichovsky, 2 Edmond Fleg St. Tel. (04) 529483.
(K) Technion, Neve Shaanan. Tel. (04) 233011. (Self-service, lunch only.)
Tenuvah Shelanu, 17 Bialik St. Tel. (04) 645618.
The Bank, 119 Hanassi Blvd., Tel. (04) 389623.
(K) The Chinese Restaurant of Nof, Nof Hotel, 101 Hanassi Blvd. Tel. (04) 388731.
The Fifth, Haneviim Tower. Tel. (04) 671191.
The Pie House, 2 Trumpeldor Blvd. Tel. (04) 229900.
(K) The Second Floor, 119 Hanassi Blvd. Tel. (04) 382020.
1001, 3 Daniel St. Tel. (04) 663704.
(K) Tsemed Hemed, Herbert Samuel Sq. Tel. (04) 242205.
Um, 10 Hazionut Blvd. Tel. (04) 531046.
Voila, 21a Nordau Mall. Tel. (04) 664529.
Zimchonia, 30 Herzl St.
Zvi, 3 Hameginim St., Paris Square.

HAMAT GADER
(K) Hamat Gader Restaurant, Golan Heights. Tel. (06) 751039.

HAMEI MAZOR
Ein Gedi Restaurant. Tel. (057) 84544.

HERZLIA
Baigel Nash, De Shalit Sq. Tel. (09) 570233.
Henry VIII, nr. Sharon Hotel. Tel. (09) 938586.
Indonesian Dining Room, 4 Keren Hayesod St., Herzlia Pituach.
(K) La Cabana, 60 Medinat Hayehudim St., Tel. (09) 55037.
Safari Steak House, Keren Hayesod St., Herzlia Pituach. Tel. (09) 77404.
Seagull, Kikar Hazionut, nr. Daniel Tower Hotel. Tel. (09) 930263.

Zevulun Beach Restaurant, between Daniel Tower Hotel & Sharon Hotel, Herzlia Pituach. Tel. (09) 930046.

JAFFA
Acropolis, Caliph Bldg. Tel. (03) 838397.
Alhambra, 30 Jerusalem Blvd. Tel. (03) 834453.
Baiuca, 103 Yehuda Hayamit St. Tel. (03) 827289.
Christian Rest, 330 Jerusalem Blvd. Tel. (03) 834453.
(K) Emerald, 4 Pasteur St. Tel. (03) 829595.
Hanemala, 44 Hatekuma St. Tel. (03) 829175.
Il Patio, 48 Shaarei Nikanor St. (entrance 56 Yefet St.). Tel. (03) 838051.
Jeanette, 4 Retzif Aliya Shniya, Old Jaffa. Tel. (03) 825575.
La Luca, 101 Yefet St. Tel. (03) 867803.
Le Castel, 14 Kikar Kedumim, Old Jaffa. Tel. (03) 836507.
M. & K. Lipski, 45 Yefet St. Tel. (03) 828456.
Mandarin, 14 Kikar Kedumim, Old Jaffa. Tel. (03) 829460.
Saigon House, 17 Yehuda Hayamit St. Tel. (03) 824606.
Taj Mahal (K without supervision), 12 Kikar Kedumim, Old Jaffa. Tel. (03) 821002.
Toutoune, 1 Mazal Dagim St. Tel. (03) 820693.
Via Maris, 6 Kikar Kedumim, Old Jaffa. Tel. (03) 828451 & 868407.
Yamit, 16 Kikar Kedumim, Old Jaffa. Tel. (03) 825353.

JERUSALEM
(K) Abu Tor, 5 Ein Rogel St., Abu Tor. Tel. (02) 718088.
(K) Agam, 121 Agrippas St. Tel. (02) 222445.
Alla Gondola, 14 King George St. Tel. 225944.
(K) Alno (Coffee Shop), 15 Ben-Yehuda St. Tel. (02) 223821.
Alpin (K, Vegetarian), 25 King George St. Tel. (02) 226626.
(K) Alumah, 8 Yavetz St. Tel. (02) 225014.
(K) Ashafit, Jerusalem Theatre. Tel. (02) 630078.
Atara, 7 Ben-Yehuda St. Tel. (02) 225008.
(K) Au Sahara, 17 Jaffa Rd. Tel. (02) 233239.
(K) Backstage, Jerusalem Theatre, 20 Marcus St. Tel. (02) 669351.
(K) Bagel Nash (Coffee Shop), 14 Ben-Yehuda St. Tel. (02) 225027.
(K) Bangkok 15 Hebron Rd. Tel. (02) 713077.
(K) Beit Maskit (Dairy & Fish), 12 Harav Kook St. Tel. (02) 227941.
Beit Ot Hamutzar, 12 Derech Hebron. Tel. (02) 66778.
(K) Besograyim, 45 Ussishkin St. Tel. (02) 245353.
Bet Ha'Ella, Ella Junction, near Bet Shemesh. Tel. (02) 911098.
Bet Maskit Garden, 12 Harav Kook St. Tel. (02) 227941.
Bistro, Bet Agron, 37 Hillel St.
(K) Burger Ranch, 18 Shlomzion Hamalka St., Tel. (02) 222392, & 3 Lunz St. Tel. (02) 225935.
(K) Cactus, 36 Keren Hayesod St. Tel. (02) 667719.
(K) Café Center, Centre 1, Jaffa Rd. Tel. (02) 383507-8.
(K) Café Finzi, 11a Ben-Yehuda St. Tel. (02) 243436.
(K) Café Ha'uga, 2 Hasoreg St. Tel. (02) 244491.
(K) Café Max, 23 Ben-Yehuda St. Tel. (02) 233722.
(K) Café Navah, 44 Jaffa Rd. Tel. (02) 222861.
Cannibal Pub Restaurant, 21 Chutzot Hayotzer Arts Centre, nr. Jaffa Gate. Tel. (02) 272276.
(K) Casa della Pasta, 7 King George St. Tel. (02) 244228.
Cavalier, 1 Ben-Sira St. Tel. (02) 242945.
(K) Charlie Chan, 2 Lunz St. Tel. (02) 242464.
Chez Simon, 15 Shammai St. Tel. (02) 225602.
Chin Chen, Paz Station, Golomb St., Ramat Danya. Tel. (02) 421600.

(K) Chung Ching, 122 Herzl Blvd., Bet Hakerem. Tel. (02) 525152.
Chung Hwa, 1 Zangwill St., Kiryat Hayovel. Tel. (02) 422746.
(K) Citadel (Cafeteria), 14 Hativat Yerushalayim St. opp. David's Citadel. Tel. (02) 288887.
The Clock, 7 Rivlin St. Tel. (02) 247501.
(K) Csardas, 11 Shlomzion Hamalka St. Tel. (02) 243186.
(K) Dagim Beni, 1 Mesilat Yesharim St. Tel. (02) 222403.
Da-La Thien, 34 Dereah Beit Lahem St. Tel. (03) 717521.
Dallas, 9 Az-Zahara St. Tel. (02) 284439.
(K) Daglicataesse, 6 Ibn Shaprut St. Tel. 632657.
Danielle, 3 Horkenos St. Tel. (02) 227904.
(K) The Derby, 2 Ben-Yehuda St. Tel. (02) 244454.
Domino, 6 Hillel St. Tel. (02) 245515.
(K) Eema, 189 Agrippas St. Tel. (02) 246860.
El Aelat, 77 Khan El-Zeit St., Old City. Tel. (02) 283435.
Elat Hayam, 3 Ben-Sira St. Tel. (02) 246122.
(K) El Gaucho, 22 Rivlin St. Tel. (02) 226665.
(K) El Marrakesh, 4 King David St. Tel. (02) 227577.
(K) Europa, 42 Jaffa Rd., at Zion Sq. Tel. (02) 228953.
(K) Feferberg's, 53 Jaffa Rd. Tel. (02) 224841.
Fink's, 2 Histadrut St./King George St. Tel. (02) 234523.
(K) Fish Shlomo, 27 Salmon St. Tel. (02) 231631.
(K) Fonte Bella, 8 Rabbi Akiva St. Tel. (02) 248408.
(K) Four Seasons, 54 Haneviim St. Tel. (02) 222195.
Gabi's Restaurant, 21 King George St. Tel. (02) 222922.
(K) Goldschmidt, 3 Dorot Harishonim St. Tel. (02) 221830.
Goliath, 28 King David St.
Goulash Inn, Ein Kerem. Tel. (02) 419214.
Gourmet Pasta, Ben-Sira St. Tel. (02) 251132.
(K) Habostan, 68 Jaffa Rd. Tel. (02) 231675.
(K) Hahoma, 128 Hayehudim St., Jewish Quarter. Tel. (02) 271332.
(K) Hakerem, 21 King George St. Tel. (02) 222922.
(K) Hama'alot, 3 Hama'alot St. Tel. (02) 234235.
Harp of David, Mt. Zion nr. Zion Gate. Tel. (02) 716597.
Hassan Afendi, 3 Rashid St., E. Jerusalem. Tel. (02) 283599.
(K) Ha'uga, 2 Hasoreg St. Tel. (02) 244491.
(K) Heppner's Deli, 4 Lunz St. Tel. (02) 221703.
Himo Coffee Shop, Damascus Gate. Tel. (02) 271351.
(K) Ima, 189 Agrippas St. Tel. (02) 246860.
Israel Museum Cafeteria, Israel Museum.
Jans, Jerusalem Theatre Plaza, Chopin St.
(K) Jerusalem, 7 Hyrcanos St. Tel. (02) 222757.
(K) Jerusalem Skylight, Eilon Tower Hotel, 34 Ben-Yehuda St. Tel. (02) 233281.
Jerusalem Star, 32 El Wad St. Tel. (02) 287175.
Jozi's Courtyard, 38 Emek Refaim St., German Colony. Tel. (02) 664323.
Judean Lion, 24 Rav Haggan St. Tel. (02) 242963.
Kamin, 4 Rabbi Akiva St. Tel. (02) 234819.
Krazy Kangaroo, 1 Shimon Bet, Shetach St. Tel. (02) 245565.
Kapulski, Klal Centre, 97 Jaffa Rd. Tel. (02) 225057.
Katy, 16 Rivlin St. Tel. (02) 226746.
Kfir, Salah A'Din St.
La Belle, 18 Rivlin St. Tel. 240807.
La Carreta, 21 Hativat Yerushalayim St. Tel. (02) 272276.
(K) La Fondue, 37 Hillel St. Tel. (02) 224352.
La Gondola, 14 King George St. Tel. (02) 225944.
(K) La Pasta, 16 Rivlin St. Tel. (02) 227687.

La Scala, 31 Jaffa Rd. Tel. (02) 228065.
(K) Lee, 33 Hillel St. Tel. (02) 225955.
Leviathan, 11 Rashid St. Tel. (02) 283655.
Lev Yerushalayim, 31 Hillel St. Tel. (02) 225911.
Liber, 10 Ben Yehida St. Tel. (02) 222007.
Lieber (K, Vegetarian), 10 Ben-Yehuda St. Tel. (02) 222007.
(K) Little Jerusalem, 59 Hanevi'im St. Tel. (02) 244377.
(K) Little Mama Mia (Self-service Dairy), 9 Dorot Rishonim St. Tel. (02) 232368.
(K) Mac David, 16 King George St.
Magdalena, 22 Shlomo Hamelech St. Tel. (02) 224710.
(K) Mama Mia (Dairy), 18 Rabbi Akiva St. Tel. (02) 248080.
Mandarin, 2 Shlomzion Hamalka St. Tel. (02) 222890.
(K) Marcel's Stage, 20 Marcus St. Tel. (02) 30078.
Marhaba, 14 Shlomzion Hamalka St. Tel. (02) 226278.
(K) Marina, President Hotel, 3 Ahad Ha'am St. Tel. (02) 31273.
(K) Mei Naftoah, 11 Lifta Tachtit. Tel. (02) 521374.
Mercaz, 26 Bezalel St. Tel. (02) 226835.
(K) Michael's, 13 Maayan St., Ein Kerem. Tel. (02) 431840.
(K) Min Hamuchan, 19 Keren Kayemet St. Tel. (02) 639845.
Misadonet (K but not under rabbinical supervision), 74 Bethlehem Rd. Tel. (02) 719903.
Mishkenot Haro'im, E. Talpiot. Tel. (02) 717666.
Mishkenot Shaananim, Yemin Moshe. Tel. (02) 233424.
(K) Monitin, 220 Jaffa Rd. Tel. (02) 380761.
Morriss Place, 27 Jaffa Rd. Tel. (02) 250534.
Moses Snack Bar, Omar el Katab Sq. Tel. (02) 280975.
Motza Inn, Motza Junction. Tel. (02) 531713.
(K) Navah (Coffee Shop), 44 Jaffa Rd. Tel. (02) 222861.
(K) Norman's, 9 Yoel Salomon St.
Ocean (Fish & Sea Food), 7 Rivlin St. Tel. (02) 247501.
(K) Of Course!, Zionist Confederation Hse., Emile Botta St. Tel. (02) 245206.
(K) Off the Square (Dairy), 6 Yoel Salamon St. Tel. (02) 242549; (Meat) **(K)**, 17 Yoel Salamon St. Tel. (02) 227719. (Dairy/Mediterranean) 51 Derech Beit Lehem. Tel. (02) 715118. (Dairy) 102 Herzl Bld. Tel. (02) 438297.
(K) Original Pie Shop, 4 Nachlat Shiva St.
(K) Palmachi, 13 Shammai St. Tel. (02) 234784.
Petra, 11 El Rashid St. Tel. (02) 283655.
Philadelphia, 9 Az-Zahra St. Tel. (02) 289770.
Phoenix, 36 Ben-Yehuda St. Tel. (02) 245363.
(K) Pinat Hahumous, 14 Ben-Yehuda St. Tel. (02) 225027.
(K) Pizzeria Papi, 9 Ben-Hillel St. Tel. (02) 223914 & 234 Jaffa Rd. Tel. (02) 535881.
(K) Pizzeria Rimini, 43 Jaffa Rd., Tel. (02) 225534, 15 King George St. Tel. (02) 226505, & 7 Paran St., Ramat Eshkol.
(K) Pizzeria Trevi, 8 Leib Yaffe St. Tel. (02) 724136.
(K) Poire et Pomme, The Khan Theatre, 2 Remez Sq. Tel. (02) 719602.
(K) Primus (Dairy & Fish), 3 Yavetz St. Tel. (02) 246565.
Prince Milk Bar (K, dairy products), 52 King George St. Tel. (02) 228531.
(K) Rimon, 41 Lunz St. Tel. (02) 222772.
(K) Rondo, 41 King George St. Tel. (02) 242874.
Rudi's, 64 Emek Refaim St. Tel. (02) 663210.
(K) Savion Hut (Fish & Dairy), 12 Gaza St. Tel. (02) 632813.
Sea Dolphin, 11 Rashid St. Tel. (02) 282788.
Select, 71 Armenian Orthodox Patriarchate St. Tel. (02) 283325.
Sheh Lee, Paz Station. Tel. (02) 437930.
(K) Shemesh, 21 Ben-Yehuda St. Tel. (02) 222418.

(K) Shipodei Hagefen, 74 Agrippas St. Tel. (02) 222 367.
(K) Shteisel, 11 Malchei Israel St. Tel. (02) 245775.
(K) Sinai Café, 6 Ben-Yehuda St. Tel. (02) 222627.
(K) Sova, 3 Histadrut St. Tel. (02) 222266.
Summer at Ze Ze, 11 Bezalel St. Tel. (02) 231761.
Taj (K but not under rabbinical supervision), 27 Jaffa Rd. Tel. (02) 241515.
Tavern, 14 Rivlin St. Tel. (02) 224500.
(K) Tavlin, 16 Yoel Salamon St. Tel. (02) 243847.
(K) Tchung Tching, 122 Herzl Blvd. Tel. (02) 528152.
(K) Ten Li Chow, 8 Ramban St. Tel. (02) 665956.
Thai Ki House, 9 Shammai St. Tel. (02) 228956.
(K) The Sixth Place, 12 Helron Rd. Tel. (02) 716857.
(K) Villa B., 104 Shderot Herzl. Tel. (02) 439002.
Wooden Horse, 3 Rivlin St. Tel. (02) 224831.
(K) Yemenite Step, 12 Yoel Salamon St. Tel. (02) 240477.
Yesh Veyesh, 48 Emek Refaim St., German Colony. Tel. (02) 630098.
(K) Yo-si Peking, 5 Shimon Ben-Shetach St. Tel. 226893.
(K) Zeze (Dairy), 11 Bezalel St. Tel. (02) 231761.
Tel. (04) 668596.

KATZRIN

Golan Heights Winery, Industrial Zone. Tel. (06) 962011.
(K) Lev Hagolan, 30 Dror St. Tel. (06) 9616643.
(K) Orcha, Commercial Centre. Tel. (06) 961440.

KFAR SABA

San Chen, 44 Jerusalem St. Tel. (09) 953311.
Ta Tung, 40 Tel Hai St. Tel. (09) 448692.
Taipeh, 40 Tel Chai St. Tel. (09) 448692.

KFAR SHMARYAHU

Hasilon, Commercial Centre. Tel. (09) 72209.
Taste of Sze Chuan, Commercial Centre. Tel. (09) 70448.

KFAR TOURAN

Nimir. Tel. (06) 784258.

KIBBUTZ BEIT HA'EMEK

Beit Ha'emek Restaurant. Tel. (04) 960411/962682.

KIBBUTZ DOVRAT

Pundak Dovrat. Tel. (06) 599520.

KIBBUTZ EIN GEDI

(K) Pundak Ein Gedi. Tel. (057) 84761.

KIBBUTZ EIN GEV

Seafood Restaurant. Tel. (06) 751166.

KIBBUTZ GONEN

Kibbutz Gonen Restaurant (K without supervision). Tel. (06) 744958.

KIBBUTZ HAON

Holiday Village Restaurant. Tel. (06) 757555.

KIBBUTZ HARDOF

Eruach Kafri. Tel. (04) 965655.

KIBBUTZ RAMAT RACHEL
Mitzpeh Rachel. Tel. 717621.

KIRYAT SHMONA
Hagong Restaurant, Tsahal Sq. Tel. (04) 9568.
Sin Galil, Commercial Centre. Tel. (04) 951238.

KIRYAT TIVON
Boustan Haemek, Kiryat Haroshet. Tel. (04) 934837.

KIBBUTZ YAD MORDECHAI
Yad Mordechai. Tel. (051) 20568.

KIBBUTZ YOTVATA
Dairy restaurant. Tel. (057) 74138.

METULLA
Bagoren. Tel. (06) 944126.
Hahakura. Tel. (067 943300.

MITZPE RAMON
(K) Tzukit. Tel. (057) 88019.

MOSHAV ANIRIM (NR)
Amirie Hagalil, Acco-Safed Rd. Tel. (06) 989120.

MOSHAVA KINNERET
Shaldag Restaurant.

MOSHAV MAVKIM
Hei Daroma. Tel. (051) 29511.

MOSHAV SHORESH
Shoresh Restaurant. Tel. (02) 528030 & 533479.

NAHARIA
(K) Café Tsafon, 10 Gaaton Blvd. Tel. (04) 922567.
Chinese Inn, 28 Gaaton Blvd. Tel. (04) 923709.
Donau, 32 Gaaton Blvd. Tel. (04) 928699.
El Gaucho, 31 Gaaton Blvd. Tel. (04) 920027.
Maxims, 43 Weizman St. Tel. (04) 921088.
Singapore, 17 Jabotinsky St. Tel. (04) 923426.

NAZARETH
Abu Diab Mahroum (Coffee Shop), Casanova St. Tel. (06) 576022.
Abu Nassar, Casanova St., next to Government Tourist Office. Tel. (06) 555889 & 554171.
Astoria, 1 Casa Nova St., Nazareth Centre. Tel. (06) 577965.
El Amal, Paul VI St., Tel. (06) 565109.
El Juneineh, Kikar Hama'ayan. Tel. (06) 554022.
Fahoum, 6 Paulus St. Tel. (06) 554144.
(K) Hamerkaz, 1 Casanova St. Tel. (06) 556905.
Holyland Inn, Paul VI St. Tel. (06) 575415.
(K) Iberia, Rassco Centre, Nazareth Elite. Tel. (06) 556314.
Israel Restaurant, Paul VI St. Tel. (06) 554114.
(K) Nof Nazareth, 23 Hacarmel St., Nazareth Elite. Tel. (06) 554366.
Omar El Khayam, Nazareth-Afula Rd. Tel. (06) 576610.

Reneh's Well, Nazareth-Tiberias Rd. Tel. (06) 555514.
St. Joseph's Restaurant, Kfar Yafia. Tel. (06) 555637.
Riviera (Tabar's), 4 & 114 Paul VI St. Tel. (06) 554963.
Yafe Nof, 15/1022 Tiberias St. Tel. (06) 556384.

NETANYA

American Dream, 10 Herzl St.
(K) Bagel Nash, 10 Ha'atzmaut Sq. Tel. (09) 616920.
Baguette Nosh, 10 Herzl St. Tel. (09) 323651.
Baiza, 5 Herzl St.
Brooklyn, 12 Herzl St.
Buffet, 5 Herzl St.
Casa Mia, 10 Herzl St. Tel. (09) 347228.
Chung Shing. 10 Herzl St. Tel. (09) 332304.
Diamond, 7 Zobotinsky St. Tel. (09) 619052.
Dugit, 8 Ha'atzmaut Sq.
Elysee, 7 Ha'atzmaut Sq.
Exodus, 1 Herzl St.
Falafel, 3 Ha'atzmaut Sq.
Faragino, 4 Herzl St.
Gambo, 5 Ha'atzmaut Sq.
Gilda, 8 Herzl St.
Golden Beer, 6 Herzl St.
Ha'atzmaut, 33 Dizengoff St.
(K) Hagozal, 95 Herzl St. Tel. (09) 335301.
Hametzuda, 4 Ha'atzmaut Sq.
Hanassi, 5 Herzl St.
La Françoise, 2 Ussishkin St.
Lev Hapri, 7 Ha'atzmaut Sq.
(K) MacDavid, 7a Ha'atzmaut Sq. Tel. (09) 618711.
Miami, 2 Herzl St.
Mifgash Hapri, 2 Ussishkin St.
Mifgash Hawai, 5 Ha'atzmaut Sq.
(K) Milky Way, 6 Herzl St. Tel. (09) 324638.
Neori, 10 Ha'atzmaut Sq.
On One Foot, 3 Herzl St.
Pancake, 7 Ha'atzmaut Sq.
Papa, 13 Ha'atzmaut Sq.
Pizzeria, 7 Herzl St.
Pub Beer, 15 Herzl St.
Pundak Hayam, 1 Harav Kook St. Tel. (09) 341222.
Renaissance, 9 Ha'atzmaut St. Tel. (09) 29653.
Rimini, 3 Herzl St.
Sammy Borikas, 2 Herzl St.
Select Canton, 2 Gad Makhnes St. Tel. (09) 23400.
Shuf Pulet, 10 Ha'atzmaut Sq.
Tahiti, 7 Ha'atzmaut Sq.
Taipei, 7 Ha'atzmaut Sq.
Thai Garden (Glatt K), 5 Ha'atzmaut Sq. Tel. (09) 333342.
Tivoli, 5 Ha'atzmaut Sq.
Topaz, 10 Ha'atzmaut Sq.
Ugati, 1 Herzl St.
(K) Zli-Esh, 6 Shaar Hagai St. Tel. (09) 324295.

PEKI'IN

Peki'in Meeting. Tel. (04) 978650.

RAANANA

(K) Dana, 198 Achuza Tel. (09) 901452.
(K) Lady D, 158 Achuza Tel. (09)-916517.
(K) Pica Aduma, 87 Achuza Tel. (09) 910508.
(K) Limosa 5 Eliazar Jaffe Tel. (09) 903407.

RAMAT GAN

Apropo, Canion Ayalon. Tel. (03) 799088.

RAMAT HAGOLEN

Banyas (Glatt K), Banyas Site. Tel. (06) 323365.

RAMAT HASHARON

Papillon, 33 Bialik St. Tel. (03) 471347.
Szechuan Gardens, 50 Habanim St. Tel. (03) 482491.
The Golden Duck, Herzliya Rd. Tel. (03) 491873.

REHOVOT

(K) Rehovot Chinese Restuarant, 202 Herzl St. Tel. (08) 471616.
Yellow Chinese, Paz petrol station, Ramle Passage. Tel. (08) 226408.

RISHON-LE-ZION

(K) Gan Dror Yaacov Affendi Inn, 12 Tarmav St. Tel. (03) 942416.
Sini Speed, 68 Herzl St. Tel (03) 942160.
Sunflower, 44 Jabotinsky St. Tel. (03) 992026.

ROSH PINA

Main Rd. Tel. (06) 936250.

SAFED

Hamifgash, 75 Jerusalem St. Tel. (06) 730510.
Meyer Pizzeria, 77 Jerusalem St. Tel. (06) 930428.
Misouyan, 59 Jerusalem St. Tel. (06) 930428.
Pinati, 81 Jerusalem St. Tel. (06) 930855.
Pub-Restaurant Hakikar, Kikar Hameginim. Tel. (06) 930910.
The Place, 70 Jerusalem St. Tel. (06) 970394.

SAVYON

Canton House, 23 Hashikma St. Tel. (03) 754509.

TEL AVIV

Alhambra Chez Christian, 30 Jerusalem Blvd. Tel. (03) 834453.
(K) Ambassador Grill Room, Diplomat Hotel, 45 Hayarkon St. Tel. (03) 294422.
America House, 35 Shaul Hamelech Blvd. Tel. (03) 268933.
Ankara, 192 Ben-Yehuda St. Tel. (03) 287784.
Apropo, 4 Tarsat Blvd., Tel. 281289.
(K) Asia House, 4 Weizmann St. Tel. (03) 210717.
Asia House Chinese, 4 Weizmann St. Tel. (03) 218216.
Baba, 1 Yeshayahu St.
Babai at the Port, Shed 1, Jaffa Port Gate.
Babushka, 20 Yirmiyahu St.
(K) Bagel Nash, 72 Ibn Gvirol St. Tel. (03) 261348; 38 Tagore St., Neveh Avivim. Tel. (03) 424687; Dizengoff Centre, Bridge Floor. Tel. (03) 285420.
Baiuca, 103 Yehuda Hayamit St. Tel. (03) 827289.
Balkan Corner, Rokach Blvd., Maccabi Tsafon Tennis Courts. Tel. (03) 417440.

Banana, 334 Dizengoff St. Tel. (03) 457491.
Batia, 197 Dizengoff St. Tel. (03) 211335.
Bucharest, 52 Chen Blvd. Tel. (03) 262922.
Budapest, 9 Hayarden St. Tel. (03) 58412.
Butterflies (Glatt Kosher), 94 Dizengoff Circle. Tel. (03) 246332.
Burger Ranch, 21 Ben-Yehuda St. Tel. (03) 657365.
Café Ben-Yehuda (Coffee Shop), 120 Ben-Yehuda St. Tel. (03) 229573.
Café de Paris, 17 Trumpeldor St. Tel. (03) 285803.
Capriccio, 288 Hayarkon St. Tel. (03) 451151-2.
Capri, 107 Dizengoff St. Tel. (03) 220602.
Cartier, 2 Shaul Hamelech Blvd. Tel. (03) 259843.
Casa Mia, 38 Shlomo Hamelech St. Tel. (03) 239856.
Casba, 32 Yirmiyahu St. Tel. (03) 449101.
Cherry, 166 Dizengoff St. Tel. (03) 248612.
(K) China Palace, 102 Hayarkon St. Tel. (03) 224455.
China Town Express, 93 Dizengoff St. Tel. (03) 221681.
China Village, 199 Herzlia Rd., Ramat Hasharon. Tel. (03) 491873.
Chin Chin, 42 Frishman St. Tel. (03) 451282.
Chopsticks, 23 Achimeir St. Tel. (03) 451891.
(K) Dag Bareshet, 196 Dizengoff St. Tel. (03) 232919.
(K) Dagim Beni, 192 Ben-Yehuda. Tel. (03) 237784.
Danis, 54 Yirmiyahu St. Tel. (03) 447984.
(K) Delicatesse, 53 Shenkin St. Tel. (03) 201651.
Dolphin, 16 Shalom Aleichem St. Tel. 280937 & 282600.
Dolphin Stern, 189 Dizengoff, St. Tel. (03) 232425.
Drugstore, 206 Dizengoff St. Tel. (03) 234304.
Edris, 14 lbn Gvirol St.
El Gaucho, 90 Hayarkon St. Tel. (03) 220166 & 2 Shaul Hamelech Blvd. Tel. (03) 250079.
El Sombrero, 50 Dizengoff St.
(K) Fish'n Chips, 196 Dizengoff St. Tel. (03) 232919.
Fontainebleau, 193 Dizengoff St. Tel. (03) 232386.
Galgalim, 80 Herbert Samuel Blvd.
(K) Galit, 3 Wingate St., Yad Eliahu, 67611. Tel. (03) 338032.
(K) Gamliel (Pninat Hakerem), 47 Hakovshim St. Tel. (03) 658779.
(K) Gan Oranim, Rokach Blvd. Tel. (03) 422171.
Gimmel Kan, 19 Ahimeir St. Tel. (03) 5413744.
Golden Dragon, 262 Ben-Yehuda St. Tel. (03) 455070.
Gondola, 57 Pinsker St. Tel. (03) 283788.
(K) Habikta, Shalom Tower.
(K) Ha Blintzes Ha Hungari, 94 Dizengoff Circle.
(K) Hamakom, 1 Lilienblum St. Tel (03) 5101823.
(K) Ha Pinna, 317 Hayarkon St. Tel. (03) 443864.
Happy Casserole, 342 Dizengoff St. Tel. (03) 442360 & 723885.
Hasilonit, 14 Frishman St. Tel. (03) 231534.
Hasinit Bedizengoff, 110 Dizengoff St. Tel. (03) 237766.
Hatafrit, 13 Yefet St., Jaffa. Tel. (03) 828012.
(K) Herli, 114 Yehuda Halevy St. Tel. (03) 282059.
(K) Holyland, 49 Bograshov St. Tel. (03) 287382.
Hong Kong House, 6 Mendele St. Tel. (03) 247300.
Imperia, behind Carlton Hotel. Tel. (03) 292310.
Itzhak Dana, 30 Ibn-Gvirol St. Tel. (03) 267567.
Jacky's Lebanese Restaurant, 52 Chen Blvd. Tel. (03) 262922.
Kasbah, 32 Yirmiyahu St. Tel. (03) 442617.
Keton, 145 Dizengoff St. Tel. (03) 233679.
(K) King Donald Ben-Yehuda, 59 Ben Yehuda St. Tel (03) 246752.
(K) Kum Kum, Sheraton Hotel, Hayarkon St. Tel. (03) 286222.

La Barchetta, 326 Dizengoff St. Tel. (03) 448405.
La Beaujolais, 33 Yirmiyahu St. Tel. (03) 449722.
La Club, 288 Hayarkon St. Tel. (03) 451282-3.
La Couronne, 22 Pinsker St. Tel. (03) 299966.
Le Versailles, 37 Geulah St. Tel. (03) 655552.
Long Sang, 113 Allenby St. Tel. (03) 663769.
(K) Lool, 39 Ben-Yehuda St. cnr. Bograshov.
Lotus, 12 Kehilat Venezia St. Tel. (03) 494203.
Mac David, cnr. Dizengoff & Frishman Sts.
Macao, 7 Yirmiahu St. Tel. (03) 5464311.
M.A. Gallery Club, 270 Hayarkon St. Tel. (03) 449806.
Maganda, 26 Rabbi Meir St., Kerem Hatemanim. Tel. (03) 659990.
Mama Mia, 17 Yirmiyahu St. Tel. (03) 447850.
Mandy's Little Old Tel Aviv, 300 Hayarkon St. Tel. (03) 450109.
Manfred's Piano Pub, 7 Yirmiahu St. Tel. (03) 5464273.
(K) Marina Chinese, Marina Hotel, Namir Sq. Tel. (03) 282244.
Mash, 275 Dizengoff St. Tel. (03) 451007.
Me and Me, the Pizzeria, 293 Dizengoff St. Tel. (03) 443427.
Mendele, 5 Mendele St. (Self-service). Tel. (03) 229141.
Mr. Wong, 104 Dizengoff St. Tel. (03) 246049.
Mon Jardin, 186 Ben-Yehuda St. Tel. (03) 231792.
(K) My Zedeh's Place, Namir Sq. Tel. (03) 287933.
(K) Naknikiot, 4 Dizengoff Circle. Tel. (03) 280939.
(K) Natalie Blintzes, Dizengoff Centre. Tel. (03) 289252.
(K) New York, 164 Dizengoff St. Tel. (03) 225966.
Non-Stop, 315 Hayarkon St. Tel. (03) 457115.
Olympia, 41 Carlebach St. Tel. (03) 283312.
Osteria Ristorante, 44 Ben-Yehuda St. (cnr. Bograshov St.).
Pagoda, 267 Dizengoff St. Tel. (03) 5463807.
Palet, 3 Yordei Hasira St. Tel. (03) 5463498.
Panorama (Vegetarian, K), Astor Hotel, 105 Hayarkon St. Tel. (03) 238913.
(K) Passage to India, 1 Yordei Hasira St. Tel. (03) 441438.
Pattaya, 54 Yirmiyahu St. Tel. (03) 447984.
Peking Restaurant, 265 Dizengoff St. Tel. (03) 453423.
Piltz Café (Coffee Shop), 81 Hayarkon St. Tel. (03) 652778.
Pirozki, 265 Dizengoff St. Tel. (03) 457599.
(K) Pizza Pino, 169 Ben Yehuda St. Tel. (03) 239582.
Pizza Tango, 249 Dizengoff St. Tel. (03) 442794.
Pizzeria Rimini, 93 Dizengoff St. Tel. (03) 221681.
Plintzi, 17 Yirmiyahu St. Tel. (03) 443617.
(K) Pninat Hakerem, 47 Hakovshim St. Tel. (03) 658779.
(K) Princess of the Nile, 18 Hatsorfim St. Tel. (03) 814266.
Pundag Restaurant, 8 Frishman St. Tel. (03) 222948.
Ramada Continental, 21 Hayarkon St. Tel. (03) 29644.
Rami's Cellar, 41 Frishman St. Tel. (03) 222191.
Ricci-The Pier, 78 Herbert Samuel Blvd. Tel. (03) 281308.
(K) Rickshaw Kosher, 163 Ben-Yehuda St. Tel. (03) 227813.
Rishon Cellar, 11 Allenby Rd. Tel. (03) 55834.
Ron, 86 Herbert Samuel Sq. Tel. (03) 53530.
Rondo, Namir Sq. Tel. (03) 287704.
Safari Steakhouse, Namir Sq. Tel. (03) 283125.
Scala-Taste of Szechuan, 10 Marmorek St. Tel. (03) 227424.
Selina Vietnam, 52 Chen Blvd. Tel. (03) 210618.
Shaldag, 256 Ben-Yehuda St. Tel. (03) 445465.
Shanghai Garden, Gate 1, Dizengoff Centre. Tel. (03) 289673.
(K) Shaul's Inn, 11 Elyashiv St., Kerem Hatemanim. Tel. (03) 653303.
Shelley, 50 Dizengoff St. Dizengoff Centre. Tel. (03) 290369.

Shipudei Hatikva, 37 Etzel St. Tel. (03) 378014.
(K) Shmulik Cohen, 146 Herzl St. Tel. (03) 810222.
(K) Shoshana & Uri's Hungarian Blintzes, 35 Yirmiyahu St. Tel. (03) 450674.
(K) Sinima, 65 Dizengoff St. Dizengoff Centre. Tel. (03) 200484.
Singing Bamboo, 317 Hayarkon St. Tel. (03) 451282.
Sophie, 115 Ben Gurion St. Tel. (03) 5524600.
Stagecoach, 216 Hayarkon St. Tel. (03) 241703.
Stern Restaurant, 189 Dizengoff St. Tel. (03) 232425.
Suki Yaki, 302 Dizengoff St. Tel. (03) 443687.
Tandoori, 2 Zamenhof St. Tel. (03) 296185.
Taste of Honey, 14 Frishman St.
Ten Li Chow (Glatt Kosher), 3 Yordei Hasira St. Tel. (03) 456852.
The Chinese Restaurant, 326 Dizengoff St. Tel. (03) 440325.
The Corner, 317 Hayarkon St. Tel. (03) 443864.
The Cream Cheese House, 13 Arlosoroff St. Tel. (03) 230048.
The Promenade, 80 Herbert Samuel Esplanade. Tel. (03) 656992.
The Red Chinese Restaurant, 326 Dizengoff St. Tel. (03) 440325.
Tip Top (Glatt Kosher), 4 Mikveh Israel St. Tel. (03) 613244.
Triana, 12 Carlebach St. Tel. (03) 264949.
Tripoli, 27 Raziel St., Jaffa. Tel. (03) 830831.
Tsameret Aviv, 43 Brodetsky St. Tel. (03) 410678. (Vegetarian).
Tuxedo Ltd., 2 Kaufman St. Tel. (03) 664303.
(K) Twelve Tribes, Sheraton Hotel, Hayarkon St. Tel. (03) 286222.
Vietnam Restaurant, 52 Chen Blvd. Tel. (03) 210638.
Vittorio, 106 Hayarkon St. Tel. (03) 240909.
White Gallery, 4 Habimah Sq. Tel. (03) 201730.
White Hall Steak House, 6 Mendele St. Tel. (03) 249282.
Yin Yang, 64 Rothschild St. Tel. (03) 621833.
Yonathan, 29 Levinsky St. Tel. (03) 826390.
Yo-si Peking (Glatt K), 16 Oppenheimer St. Tel. (03) 421888.
(K) Zion Exclusive, 28 Peduim St. Tel. (03) 658714.

TIBERIAS

Abu Shkara, Hagalil St. Tel. (06) 792103.
Avi's Restaurant, Hakishon St. Tel. (06) 791797.
Bistrotal, Habanim St. Tel. (06) 790941.
Blue Beach, Gedud Barak St. Tel. (06) 720105.
Café-Hayam-Ely, Hatayelet St. Tel. (06) 722089.
Crimson Flower, 32 Habanim St. Tel. (06) 790221.
Donna Grazia, Donna Grazia St. Tel. (06) 722308.
Gai Beach, Hamerchazaot Rd. Tel. (06) 720257.
(K) Gan Esther, Hadishon St. Tel. (06) 729946.
(K) Hamat Gader Restaurant, Tel. (06) 751049.
Habikta, Kaplan St. opp. Gai Beach. Tel. (06) 791222.
Karamba, Old Promenade. Tel. (06) 791546.
King's Garden, Sonol petrol station, Alhadef St. Tel. (06) 720461.
Laguna, 2 Habanim Mall. Tel. (06) 722321.
(K) Lido Kinneret, Gdud Barak St. Tel. (06) 721538.
Nof Kinneret, Hayarkon St. Tel. (06) 720773.
Pagoda, Lido Beach. Tel. (06) 792353.
Panorama, Hagalil St. Tel. (06) 790441.
Pinary, Donna Grazia St. Tel. (06) 790242.
(K) Quiet Beach, Gedud Barak St. Tel. (06) 790125.
Ron Beach, Gedud Barak St. Tel. (06) 721418.
(K) Sironit Beach, Hamerchazaot Rd. Tel. (06) 721449.
The House, Gdud Barak St. Tel. (06) 792353.

Tiberias Hot Springs, nr. Hamat Tiberias. Tel. (06) 791967.
Tiberius, Donna Grazia St. Tel. (06) 792477.
Tuv-Ta'am, Ohel Yaakov-Kiryat Shmuel. Tel. (06) 721693.
(K) Zion, 28 Peduim St. Tel. 658714

TIBERIAS-ROSH PINA ROAD
Vered Hagalil. Tel. (06) 737085.

YAVNEH
Chon Lee, 1 Haegoz St. Tel. (08) 436831.

TOURIST INFORMATION OFFICES
The offices listed below are operated by the Ministry of Tourism, 24 King
George St., Jerusalem. Tel. (02) 237311.
[Tourist coordinators for the Administered Territories: Allenby Bridge.
Fax. (02) 942294. Jerusalem Fax. (02) 240571.]
Akko: Eljazar St. Tel. 04-911764.
Allenby Bridge: Near Jericho. Tel. (02) 941038.
Arad: 28 Eliezer Ben Yair St. Tel. 057-954409.
Ashdod: 4 Haim Moshe Shapira St. Tel. (08) 550672.
Ashkelon: Commercial Centre, Afridar. Tel. (07) 32412.
Bat Yam: 43 Sderot Ben Gurion. Tel. (03) 5072777.
Beersheba: 6a Ben-Zvi St. (opp. Central Bus Station). Tel. (057) 236001-3.
Bethlehem: Manger Sq. Tel. (02) 741581/3.
Eilat: Mercaz Amiel, Hakhan. Tel. (07) 334353.
Haifa Port: Shed 12. Tel. (04) 663988. (Open only on arrival of ships.)
Haifa Town: 20 Herzl St. Tel. (04) 666521/2.
Jerusalem: 24 King George St. (Head Office). Tel. (02) 754888; Jaffa Gate.
Tel. (02) 282295-6.
Lod: Ben-Gurion airport. Tel. (03) 9711485.
Naharia: Egged Bus Station, Gaaton Blvd. Tel. (04) 879800.
Nazareth: Casanova St. Tel. (06) 573003/570555.
Netanya: Ha'atzmaut Sq. Tel. (09) 827286.
Rafiah, Rafiah Terminal, Ashkelon. Tel. (07) 734080.
Safed: 50 Jerusalem St. Tel. (06) 920633/920961.
Tel Aviv: 5 Shalom Aleichem St. Tel. 03-660259/61.
Tiberias: Rehor Habanim. Tel. (06) 720992.

Tours
Regular scheduled tours, using air-conditioned coaches, are operated by
Egged and other companies on week-days to all parts of the country,
starting from Jerusalem, Tel Aviv and Haifa. Egged's intercity toll – free
information number is 177022 5555.
Among the most important sites visited are the Western Wall; the Old City
of Jerusalem; Mount Scopus; the Mount of Olives; Rachel's Tomb in
Bethlehem; the Tomb of the Patriarchs (Cave of Machpela) in Hebron;
Jericho, and the Dead Sea. Tours starting in Jerusalem also visit Beersheba,
Masada, Sdom, Ein Gedi and Galilee.
From Tel Aviv, regular tours go south to the Dead Sea and Elat, and north
to Galilee and the Golan Heights as far as Banias.
From Haifa, regular tours go north to Galilee, and south to all places
visited by tours from Jerusalem and Tel Aviv.
Air tours, operated by Arkia, Israel's internal airline (Sde Dov airport, Tel
Aviv. Tel. (03) 424266), cover all of Israel.
In addition a number of smaller companies operate flights and tours to all
parts of the country on a charter basis.

It is now possible to fly to Cairo from Israel, as well as to enter Egypt by land. Full details are available from all Government Tourist Information Offices in Israel and Israel Government Tourist Offices abroad.
Information about coach and air tours inside Israel is available from all Government Tourist Information Offices in Israel.

Transport in Israel
Buses are the most popular means of transport, both for urban and inter-urban journeys.
The Israel Railway runs from Naharia in the north to Beersheba in the south, and fares are lower than on the buses. All passenger trains have a buffet car.
Taxis are quick and convenient. All urban taxis have meters, which drivers must use.
Certain taxi companies operate a "Sherut" service in and between the main cities on weekdays, and some independent taxi owners operate similar services seven days a week. Individual seats are sold at fixed prices, with up to seven people sharing a taxi. In some cities and towns, "Sherut" taxis follow the main bus routes, charging slightly higher fares than the buses.
Self-drive cars and motor-cycles can also be hired.

Some Interesting Visits
There are guided tours of the Knesset (Parliament) on Sun. and Thurs. between 8.30"a.m. and 2.30"p.m. Further inf. from Knesset P.R. Dept. Tel. (02) 554111.
On Saturday mornings at 10"a.m. the Jerusalem municipality organises a free walking tour to various points of interest. Details from Tourist Information Offices.
The Quartercentre in the Jewish Quarter contains a memorial site for the fighters of the War of Independence in 1948, an exhibition of photographs taken during the conquest of the quarter in 1948, and a sight and sound presentation about the quarter.
A visit to Hechal Shlomo, the Supreme Religious Centre in King George St., Jerusalem, is a "must". This magnificent building houses the Chief Rabbinate, the Central Rabbinical Library and the Supreme Rabbinical Court, as well as a museum. Adjoining it is the outstanding Great Synagogue, inaugurated in August, 1982, which is dedicated to the memory of the six million victims of the Holocaust and all who fell in the founding and defence of the State of Israel. Services, Fri. evg. & Sat. morn. Visits are by appointment only. Further inf. Tel. (02) 635212.
The Holyland Hotel model of ancient Jerusalem at the time of the Second Temple is worth seeing.
Bayit Lepletot Girls' Town is worth a visit. Inf. from 1 Beharan St., nr. Strauss St., Jerusalem. Tel. (02) 227986 or 228581.
Visitors are welcome at the Mother & Baby Convalescent Home, 22 Hapisga St., Bayit Vegan, Jerusalem. Tel. (02) 22581 or 284056.
Free tours of the Jewish Quarter and free accom. in the American P'eylim Student Union hostel in the quarter, at 10 Shoarim St., Tel. (02) 532131, as well as Shabbat hospitality with either a Chasidic family in Mea Shearim or a modern Orthodox family in the Jewish Quarter, are offered to Jewish students by Jeffrey Seidel. Jewish students are also offered free acccom. at the Jerusalem Jewish Youth Centre in the quarter, at 9 Shonei Halachot St. Tel. (02) 285623.
On Friday nights local youth groups entertain visitors with songs and dances of Israel at Z.O.A. House in Tel Aviv.
Israel Nature Trails, the touring section of the Society for the Protection of Nature in Israel, offers guided tours on set dates throughout the year. All

start in Tel Aviv and most can be joined in Jerusalem. Full inf. from the Society, 13 Helen Hamalka St., P.O. Box 930, Jerusalem. Tel. (02) 249567.
Every Wednesday at 9.30 a.m. there is a free walking tour of Jaffa, organised by the Tel Aviv-Yafo Tourism Assoc. The tour, which takes about 2½ hours, starts in Clock Square near Yefet St., in the centre of Jaffa.
The Zoological Centre in Ramat Gan (Tel. (03) 744991 & 762586) combines a safari park and a conventional zoo.
Thursday is market day in Beersheba. Beduin come into the town from all parts of the Negev and hold a market.
In Haifa, there is an Oneg Shabbat at the Dan Carmel Hotel every Friday night at 9 p.m.
On Sundays, Mondays, Tuesdays, Thursdays and Saturdays at 9.30 a.m., there are guided tours of Mount Carmel, Druse villages, Kibbutz Bet Oren and Ein Hod artists' colony. On Wednesdays at 9.30 a.m., there are guided tours of the Bahai shrine and gardens, Druse villages, Muchraka, the Moslem village of Kababir, the Carmelite monastery and Elijah's Cave. For bookings and further inf., Tel. (04) 674342.
There is a first-class, modern golf course at Caesarea, with its ancient ruins, situated on the Mediterranean. Caesarea Golf & Country Club Ltd., Or Akiva. Tel. (063) 88174.

Culture & the Arts
Music: The Israel Philharmonic Orchestra gives subscription concerts and special concerts throughout the year, both in the main cities and towns and smaller centres. There are also a number of chamber music ensembles, choirs and music-lovers' associations. In Jerusalem there is a Spring Festival of the performing arts in April and May.
Theatre: The Habimah, Ohel and Chamber Theatre companies have their headquarters in Tel Aviv, but frequently tour other towns and rural centres. There is also a Haifa Theatre.
Art: There are several permanent and many special art exhibitions in the three main cities and in quite a number of smaller centres such as Safed and Ein Hod, which have attracted artists' colonies.
See: The museums of Israel, by Nitra Rosovsky and Joy Ungerleider — Mayerson. New York: Harry N. Abrams, 1989.

Museums and Exhibitions
Haifa: Edible Oil Museum, Shemen Factory, 2 Tovim St. Tel. (04) 670491; Haifa Museum includes Museums of Ancient Art, Modern Art, Music & Ethnology, 26 Shabetai Levy St. Tel. (04) 523255; Reuben & Edith Hecht Museum, Haifa University. Tel. (04) 240577; Israel Railways Museum, Haifa Railway Station (East); National Maritime Museum, 198 Allenby Rd.; Moshe Shtekelis Museum of Pre-History, 124 Hatishbi St., entrance from Gan Ha'em; Tikotin Museum of Japanese Art, 89 Hanassi Blvd., Mount Carmel; Mané Katz Museum, 89 Panorama Rd.; Museum of Clandestine Immigration & Naval Museum, 204 Allenby Rd.; Bet Pinchas Biological Institute, 124 Hatishbi St., includes Nature Museum; Dagon Grain Museum, Plumer Sq.; Technoda, National Museum of Science and Technology, opp. 15 Balfour St. Tel. (04) 671372.
Jerusalem: Ammunition Hill Memorial & Museum, Ramat Eshkol. Tel. (02) 828442; Bible Lands Museum, 25 Granot St. Tel. (02)-611066. Herzl Museum, Herzl Blvd., Mount Herzl; Israel Museum, Hakirya, includes Bezalel National Museum, Samuel Bronfman Biblical & Archaeological Museum, Shrine of the Book, & the Rockefeller Museum in East Jerusalem; L.A. Mayer Memorial Institute of Islamic Art, 2 Hapalmach St.; Museum of the History of Jerusalem, Tower of David, Jaffa Gate. Tel. (02) 283273; Museum of Musical Instruments, Rubin Academy of Music, 7 Smolenskin

St.; Museum of Natural History, 6 Mohilever St.; Nahon Museum of Italian Jewish Art, 22 Hillel St., 94581. Tel. (02) 241610. Old Yishuv Court Museum, 6 Or Hachayim St., Jewish Quarter, Old City; Shocken Institute, 6 Balfour St.; Sir Isaac & Lady Wolfson Museum, Hechal Shlomo, 58 King George St.; S.Y. Agnon's House, 16 Klausner St., Talpiot; Siebenberg House Archaeological Museum, 6 Hagittit St., Jewish Quarter. Tel. (02) 282341; Tourjeman Post Museum, 1 Hel Hahandassa St. Tel. 281278; Yad Vashem, Martyrs' & Heroes' Remembrance Authority, Har Hazikaron; Yad Vashem Art Museum, same address.

Tel Aviv: Bet Bialik, 22 Bialik St.; Bet Eliahu-Bet Hahagana, 23 Rothschild Blvd.; Goldmann Museum of the Diaspora (Beth Hatefutsoth), Klausner St., Ramat Aviv; Haaretz Museum includes eight smaller museums at Ramat Aviv, as well as the Israel Theatre Museum, 17 Ben-Gurion Blvd., Antiquities Museum, 10 Mifratz Shlomo St., & Tel Aviv History Museum, 27 Bialik St.; Independence Hall Museum and Bet Hatanach, 16 Rothschild Blvd.; Jabotinsky Institute, 38 King George St.; Tel Aviv Museum, 27-29 Shaul Hamelech Blvd., includes Helena Rubinstein Pavilion, 7 Tarsat St.

Other Museums: Akko Municipal Museum, Old City; Kibbutz Ashdot Yaakov; Avihail, Bet Hagedudim (History of Jewish Brigade); Kibbutz Ayelet Hashahar; Beersheba, Negev Museum, Ha'atzmaut St., cnr. of Herzl St. & Man in the Desert Museum, 5 miles north-east of the city; Bet Shean Museum, 1 Dalet St.; Kibbutz Dan, Bet Ussishkin; Kibbutz Degania Alef, Bet Gordon; Dimona Municipal Museum; Kibbutz Ein Harod, Bet Sturman & Art Institute; Elat, Museum of Modern Art, Hativat Hanegev St.; Hadera, Khan Museum, 74 Hagiborim St.; Kibbutz Hanita, Tower & Stockade Period Museum; Kibbutz Hazorea, Wilfrid Israel House of Oriental Art; Kibbutz Kfar Etzion, Gush Etzion Museum; Kibbutz Kfar Giladi, Bet Hashomer; Katzrin (Golan Heights), Golan Archaeological Museum; Kibbutz Kfar Menachem; Kibbutz Lohamei Hagetaot, Ghetto Fighters', Holocaust & Resistance Museum; Kibbutz Maabarot; Kibbutz Maayan Baruch; Midreshet Ruppin; Naharia Municipal Museum, Hagaaton Blvd.; Netanya Museum of Biology & Archaeology; Neve Zohar (Dead Sea area), Bet Hayotser; Kibbutz Nir David; Kibbutz Palmachim; Petach Tikva, Bet Yad Labanim, 30 Arlosorov St.; Ramat Gan, Bet Emmanuel Museum, 18 Chibat Zion St., & Pierre Gildesgame Maccabi Museum, Kfar Hamaccabiah; Safed, Bet Hameiri Institute (History & Heritage of Safed); Safed, Israel Bible Museum; Safed, Museum of Printing Art, Artists' Colony; Tel Hai; Tiberias; Tiberias Hot Springs Lehmann Museum, Hammat Tiberias National Park; Kibbutz Yad Mordechai; Kibbutz Yifat; Zichron Yaakov, Nili Museum & Aaronson House, 40 Hameyasdim St.

Nature Reserves

The National Parks and Nature Reserves Law was passed in 1963 and established a Nature Reserves Authority. There are some 300 nature reserves in Israel although not all have attained official recognition. The recognised reserves occupy 741,000 acres. Visitors to reserves must adhere to a strict code of behaviour. Advance reservation and entrance fees are required at most of the reserves.
The following are the major reserves:
Metulla: Nahal Ayoun (HaTanur) Reserve; Tel. 011-972-6-951519;
Tel Dan: Tel. 011-972-6-951579;
Nahal Hermon (Banias) Reserve. Tel. 011-972-6-950272;
Huleh Reserve. Tel. 011-972-6-937069;
Gamla. Tel. 011-972-6-762040;
Ein Afeq. Tel. 011-972-4-704992;
Nahal Mearot. Tel. 011-972-4-841750;
Soreq Caves. Tel. 011-972-2-911117;

Ein Gedi Reserve. Tel. 011-972-57-84285;
Arad Visitors' Centre. Tel. 011-972-57-954409;
Ramon Crater. Tel. 011-972 -57-88691;
Yotvata Hai Bar Visitors' Center. Tel. 011-972-59-76018;
Coral Beach Reserve. Tel. 011-972-59-76829.

Shopping, Bank & Office Hours

Shops and offices are open from Sun. to Thurs. inclusive, from 8a.m. to
1p.m. and from 4p.m. to 7p.m. Shopping hours on Fri. are from 8.30"a.m.
to 2p.m. In Haifa, most shops are closed on Tues. afternoons. Banks are
open Sun., Tues., and Thurs. from 8.30 a.m. to 12.30 p.m. Branches of most
banks are also open from 4 to 6p.m. On Mon. & Wed., they open from 8.30
a.m. to 12.30 p.m. only. On Fri. and the eve of Holy-days and festivals, they
open at 8.30a.m. and close at 12 noon. Government offices are generally
open to the public Sun. to Thurs. inclusive from 8a.m. to 1p.m.

Useful Addresses

HAIFA

Syns.: Central, 60 Herzl St.; Eliahu Hanavi, 16 Sinai Blvd., Mount Carmel;
Hechal Netanel (Sephardi), 43 Herzl St.; Moriah (Conservative), 7 Horeb
St., Mount Carmel; Mount Carmel Central, 10 Sea Rd., Mount Carmel; Or
Hadash Progressive Cong., Bet Rothschild, 142 Hanassi Blvd., Central
Carmel.
Fri. evening services are also held at the Dan Carmel Hotel, Hanassi Blvd.

Central Bus Station: 2 Hagana Blvd. For bus inf. Tel. (04) 549121/131.
Railway Station: near Central Bus Station. Tel. (04) 564564.
Technion, Israel Institute of Technology: Campus, Neve Shaanan. Guided
tours. Visitors' Centre. Tel. (04) 320664
University of Haifa: Mount Carmel. Tel. (04) 240097. Guided tours.
Main Post Office: 19 Palyam Blvd. Tel. (04) 640892. Hadar Post Office &
Philatelic Service: 22 Haneviim St.
Municipal Information Offices: Municipality Bldg. Tel. (04) 645359; Central
Bus Station, 2 Hagana Blvd. Tel. (04) 512208; 23 Haneviim St. Tel. (04)
663056; 119 Hanassi Blvd. Tel. (04) 383683.
Haifa Tourism Development Assoc.: 10 Ahad Ha'am St. Tel. (04) 671645-7.
Voluntary Tourist Service also at this address.
Municipal Theatre: 50 Pevsner St. Tel. (04) 670956.
"What's on in Haifa" 24-hour telephone service: Tel. (04) 640840.
Consulates: Austria, 12 Allenby Rd. Tel. (04) 522498; Belgium &
Luxembourg, 104 Derech Ha'atzmaut. Tel. (04) 533261; Costa Rica, 9
Disraeli St. Tel. (04) 241157; Denmark, 53 Derech Ha'atzmaut. Tel. (04)
645428; Finland, 7 Hayovel St. Tel. (04) 338585; France, 37 Hagefen St. Tel.
(04) 526281; Germany, 35 Hameginim Blvd. Tel. (04) 534112; Greece, 59
Derech Ha'atzmaut. Tel. (04) 522098; Guatemala, 43 Derech Ha'atzmaut.
Tel. (04) 643232; Holland, 11 Givat Downes St. Tel. (04) 241962; Honduras,
37 Liberia St. Tel. (04) 255318; Ivory Coast, 55 Hanamal St. Tel. (04) 670456;
Madagascar, 31 Derech Ha'atzmaut. Tel. (04) 645386; Norway, 20 Hanamal
St. Tel. (04) 670141; Panama, 5 Baerwald St. Tel. (04) 665265; Peru, 62
Sweden St. Tel. (04) 253304; Spain, 3 Anilewitz St. Tel. (04) 510228; Sweden
(also representing Liberia & Hungary), 2 Khayat Sq. Tel. (04) 643162;
U.S.A., 37 Derech Ha'atzmaut. Tel. (04) 672176; Uruguay, 67 Moriah St. Tel.
(04) 245165.

JERUSALEM

There are 450 synagogues in Jerusalem. The following are the most representative and easily accessible: Yeshurun, 44 King George St. (Ashkenazi). Great adjoining Hechal Shlomo, 60 King George St. Italian Synagogue, 29 Hillel St. (Italian rite). Baba Tamah Synagogue, 5 David St. (Bokharan). Emet V'Emuna, Narkis St., Gan Rehavia. Har El (Progressive), 16 Shmuel Hanagid St. Hebrew Union College (Reform), 13 King David St. Metivta Hagedola (Ashkenazi upstairs, Sephardi downstairs), 31 Jabotinsky St. Midrash Porat Yosef, Geula St., Mount Zion (Ashkenazi and Sephardi). President, 22 Ussishkin St., Rehavia.

To place messages at the Western Wall use Fax. (02) 61222.

Embassies: Cost Rica, Clal Centre, 97 Jaffa Rd., 7th Floor, Room 714. Tel. (02) 244418; El Salvador, 16 Kovshei Katamon St. Tel. (02) 633575; Ivory Coast, 4 Elroy St., German Colony. Tel. (02) 632296.

Centre for Guiding of the City, 17 Jaffa Rd. Tel. (02) 241379 or 232251.

General Post Office, 23 Jaffa Rd.

Hebrew University. Tel. (02) 585111.

Ministry of Tourism, 24 King George St. Tel. (02) 237311.

NETANYA

There are more than 200 syns. & places of worship here. The following cater to English-speakers:

Cong. Agudat Achim, 45 Jabotinsky St.

New Syn. of Netanya, 7 MacDonald St.

Young Israel of N. Netanya, cnr. Shlomo Hamelech & Yehuda Hanassi Sts.

Netanya Assoc. for Tourism, 15 Herzl St. Tel. (09) 30583.

Ohel Shem Civic Auditorium, Cultural Centre, 4 Raziel St. Tel. (09) 336688.

RAANANA

Syn.: Great, 103 Achuza; Cons, 8 Borochov. Mikva Herzl St.

RAMAT GAN

Bar-Ilan University. Tel. (03) 718111. Guided tours daily.

TEL AVIV

Synagogues

Bilu, 122 Rothschild Blvd.

Great, 314 Dizengoff St.

Ihud Shivat Zion, 86 Ben-Yehuda St. (Central European rite).

Kedem (Progressive), 20 Carlebach St.

Main Synagogue, 110 Allenby Rd. (Ashkenazi).

Ohel Mis'ad, 5 Shadal St. (Sephardi).

Tiferet Zvi, Hermann Hacohen St.

Automobile Club & Touring Association, 19 Petach Tikva Rd. Tel. (03) 622961.

Hadassah Club for Overseas Visitors, 80 Hayarkon St. Tel. (03) 56039.

Israel Office of Zionist Federation of Gt. Britain & Ireland, 76 lbn Gvirol St. Tel. (03) 240142.

Magen David Adom Central Headquarters, 60 Giborei Israel St. Tel. (03) 336222.

Ministry of Tourism (Tel Aviv & Central Region). Tel. (03) 223268 & 231263.

Moadon Haoleh, Club for English-Speaking Immigrants and Tourists, 109 Hayarkon St. Tel. (03) 236102.

Tel Aviv-Yafo Assoc. for Tourism, City Hall, Malchei Israel Sq., Tel. (03) 232581.

Tel Aviv Municipality, City Hall, Malchei Yisrael Sq. Tel. (03) 243311.

Tel Aviv University, Ramat Aviv. Tel. (03) 416111.

Z.O.A. (Zionist Organisation of America) House & Tourist Club, 1 Daniel Frisch St. Tel. (03) 259341.

Embassies

Argentina: 112 Hayarkon St., 2nd Floor. Tel. (03) 293411; Australia: 185 Hayarkon St. Tel. (03) 243152; Austria, 11 Herman Cohen St. Tel. (03) 246186; Belgium, 266 Hayarkon St. Tel. (03) 454164-6; Bolivia, 85 Ben-Gurion Blvd. Tel. (03) 230868; Brazil, 14 Heh Be'Iyar St., Hamedina Sq., 5th Floor. Tel. (03) 219292-4; Britain, 192 Hayarkon St. Tel. (03) 249171-8; Burma, 19 Yona St., Ramat Gan. Tel. (03) 783151; Canada, 220 Hayarkon St. Tel. (03) 228122-5; Chile, 54 Pincus St., 11th Floor. Tel. (03) 440414-5; Colombia, 52 Pincus St., 6th Floor. Tel. (03) 449616; Denmark, 23 Bnei Moshe St. Tel. (03) 440405-6; Dominican Republic, 32 Zamenhof St., Herzlia B. Tel. (052) 72422; Ecuador, Asia Hse., Room 231, 4 Weizmann St. Tel. (03) 258764; Egypt, 54 Basel St. Tel. (03) 224151; Finland, Bet Eliahu, 8th Floor, 2 Ibn Gvirol St. Tel. (03) 250527-8; France, 112 Herbert Samuel Blvd., Tel. (03) 245371-3; Germany, 16 Soutine St. Tel. (03) 243111-5; Greece (Diplomatic Representation), 35 King Saul Blvd. Tel. (03) 259704; Guatemala, 1 Bernstein Cohen St., Flat 10, Ramat Hasharon. Tel. (03) 490456; Haiti, Asia Hse., Room 230, 4 Weizmann St. Tel. (03) 252084; Holland, Asia Hse, 4 Weizmann St. Tel. (03) 257337-9; Italy, Asia Hse., 4 Weizmann St. Tel. (03) 264223-5; Japan, Asia Hse., 4 Weizmann St. Tel. (03) 257292-4; Liberia, 119 Rothschild Blvd. Tel. 247507; Mexico, 14 Heh Be'Iyar St., Hamedina Sq. Tel. (03) 210266; Norway, 10 Heh Be'Iyar St., Hamedina Sq. Tel. (03) 295207-8; Panama, 28 Heh Be'Iyar St., Hamedina Sq. Tel. (03) 253158; Peru, 52 Pincus St., 8th Floor. Tel. (03) 454065; Philippines Republic, 12 Heh Be'Iyar St., 4th floor, Hamedina Sq. Tel. (03) 258143; Poland (Interest Section), 2 Isaac Ramba St., Ramat Gan. Tel. (03) 7520555. Romania, 24 Adam Hacohen St. Tel. (03) 247379; South Africa, 2 Kaplan St., 9th Floor. Tel. (03) 256147; Sweden, Asia Hse., 4 Weizmann St. Tel. (03) 258111. Switzerland, 228 Hayarkon St. Tel. (03) 244121-2; Turkey (Legation), 34 Amos St. Tel. (03) 454155-6; United States, 71 Hayarkon St. Tel. (03) 654338; Uruguay, 52 Pincus St., 2nd Floor. Tel. (03) 440411; Venezuela, 2 Kaufman St. Tel. (03) 656287; Zaire, 1 Rachel St. Tel. 222002.

UNITED STATES OF AMERICA

Though there had been individual Jewish settlers before 1654 in the territory which is now the United States, it was not until that year that Jewish immigrants arrived in a group at New Amsterdam – 23 of them, who probably came from Brazil by way of Cuba and Jamaica. The story of the growth of Jewry in the U.S.A. is the story of successive waves of immigration resulting from persecution in Russia, Germany and other countries. Today the Jewish population has grown to 5,950,000, of whom some 2,500,000 live in Greater New York.

National Organisations
Unless otherwise stated, the addresses given are all in New York.

Representative Organisations
American Jewish Committee: 165 E. 56th St., 10022. Tel. (212) 751-4000. Offices in Boston, Philadelphia, Dallas, Chicago, Cleveland, Newark, St. Louis, Los Angeles, San Francisco, Seattle, Miami, Washington and Cincinnati. European H.Q.: 41 Av. Paul Doumer, 75016 Paris.
American Jewish Congress: Stephen Wise Congress House, 15 E. 84th St., 10028. Tel. (212) 879-4500.
Anti-Defamation League of B'nai B'rith: 823 United Nations Plaza, 10017. Tel. (212) 490-2525.
B'nai B'rith International, Headquarters: 1640 Rhode Island Av. N.W., Washington, D.C., 20036. Tel. (202) 857-6600.
Conference of Presidents of Major American Jewish Organisations: 515 Park Av., 10022. Tel. (212) 752-1616.
Council of Jewish Federations, 730 Broadway, 10003. Tel. (212) 475-5000.
Jewish War Veterans of the U.S.A.: 1811 "R" St. N.W., Washington, D.C. 20009. Tel. (202) 265-6280.
National Conference on Soviet Jewry: 10 E. 40th St., Suite 907, 10016. Tel. (212) 679-6122.
National Council of Jewish Women: 15 E. 26th St., 10019. Tel. (212) 532-1740.
National Jewish Community Relations Advisory Council: 443 Park Av. S., 11th Floor, 10016. Tel. (212) 684-6950.
North American Jewish Students' Network: 15 E. 26th St.
World Jewish Congress: 501 Madison Av., 17th Floor, 10022. Tel. (212) 755-5770.

Cultural & Scientific Organisations
American Academy for Jewish Research: 3080 Broadway, 10027.
American Jewish Historical Society: 1 Thornton Rd., Waltham, Mass., 02154. Tel. (617) 891-8110. Fax (617) 899-9208.
Assoc. of Orthodox Jewish Scientists: 1373 Coney Island Av., 11219. Tel. (718) 338-8592.
Histadruth Ivrith of America: 1841 Broadway, 10023. Tel. (212) 581-5151.
Jewish Book Council: 15 E. 26th St., 10010. Tel. (212) 532-4949.
Jewish Information & Referral Service: 130 E. 59th St., 10022. Tel. (212) 753-2288.
Jewish Museum: 1109 Fifth Av., 10028.
Jewish Publication Society of America: 1930 Chestnut St., Philadelphia, Pa., 19103. Tel. (215) 564-5925. (New York: 60 E. 42nd St., 10017.)

*Many thanks are due to "Jewish Chronicle" correspondents and numerous voluntary helpers throughout the United States for their valuable assistance and suggestions.

Memorial Foundation for Jewish Culture: 15 E. 26th St., 10010. Tel. (212) 679-4074.
Yivo Institute for Jewish Research: 1048 Fifth Av., 10028. Tel. (212) 535-6700.

Overseas Aid Organisations
American Jewish Joint Distribution Committee: 711 Third Av., 10017.
American Ort Federation: 817 Broadway, 10003. Tel. (212) 677-4400.
United Hias Service: 200 Park Av. S., 10003. Tel. (212) 674-6800.
United Jewish Appeal: National Office, 1290 Av. of the Americas, 10104. Tel. (212) 757-1500.

Religious, Educational, Etc Organisations
Agudath Israel World Org.: 84 William St., 10273. Tel. (212) 791-1807. The org. will provide free of charge a list of people in most major US cities who can provide reliable inf. about local kashrut.
American Assoc. of Rabbis: 350 5th Av., Suite 3308, 10001. Tel. (212) 244-3350.
American Fed. of Jewish Fighters, Camp Inmates & Nazi Victims: 823 United Nations Plaza, 10017. Tel. (212) 697-5670.
American Sephardi Fed.: 8 W. 40th St., Suite 1203, 10018. Tel. (212) 730-1210.
B'nai B'rith Hillel Foundations: 1640 Rhode Island Av. N.W., Washington, D.C., 20036. Tel. (202) 857-6600.
Central Conference of American Rabbis (Reform): 21 E. 40th St., 10016. Tel. (212) 684-4990.
Central Sephardic Jewish Community of America: 8 W. 70th St., 10023. Tel. (212) 787-2850.
Council for Jewish Education: 114 Fifth Av., 10011. Tel. (212) 575-5656.
Federation of Reconstructionist Congregations & Havurot, 270 W. 89th St., 10024. Tel. (212) 496-2960.
Jewish Ministers' Cantors' Assoc.: 3 W. 16th St., 10011. Tel. (212) 675-6601.
Lubavitch Movement: 770 Eastern Parkway, Brooklyn, 11213. Tel. (718) 493 9250.
National Council of Young Israel: 3 W. 16th St., 10003. Tel. (212) 929-1525.
National Jewish Committee on Scouting: 1325 Walnut Hill La., Irving, Texas, 75062. Tel. (214) 659-2059.
National Jewish Girl Scout Committee: 327 Lexington Av., 10016. Tel. (212) 686-8670.
Rabbinical Alliance of America (Igud Harabonim) (Orthodox): 156 Fifth Av., Suite 807, 10010. Tel. (212) 242-6420.
Rabbinical Assembly (Conservative): 3080 Broadway, 10027. Tel. (212) 678-8060.
Rabbinical Council of America (Orthodox): 275 7th Av., 10001. Tel. (212) 807-7888.
Synagogue Council of America: 327 Lexington Av., 10016. Tel. (212) 686-8670.
Union of American Hebrew Congregations (Reform): 838 Fifth Av., 10021. Tel. (212) 249-0100.
Union of Orthodox Jewish Congregations of America: 333 Seventh Ave., 10001. Tel. (212) 563-4000.
Union of Orthodox Rabbis of the U.S. and Canada: 235 E. Broadway Av., 10002. Tel. (212) 964-6337.
Union of Sephardic Congregations: 8 W. 70th St., 10023. Tel. (212) 873 0300.
United Synagogue of America (Conservative): 155 Fifth Av., 10010. Tel. (212) 533-7800.

World Council of Synagogues (Convervative): 155 Fifth Av., 10010. Tel. (212) 533-7800.
World Union for Progressive Judaism: 838 Fifth Av., 10021. Tel. (212) 249-0100.
World Union of Jewish Students: 15 E. 26th St., 10010.

Welfare Organisations
Baron de Hirsch Fund: 386 Park Av. S., 10016. Tel. (212) 532-7088.
City of Hope National Medical Centre & Beckman Research Institute: 208 W. 8th St., Los Angeles, 90014. Tel. (213) 626-4611. (New York Office: 250 W. 57th St., 10019.)
Jewish Braille Institute of America: 110 E. 30th St., 10016. Tel. (212) 889-2525.
Jewish Welfare Board: 15 E. 26th St., 10010. Tel. (212) 532-4949.

Zionist Organisations
America-Israel Friendship League: 134 E. 39th St., 10016. Tel. (212) 679-4822.
America-Israel Cultural Foundation: 485 Madison Av., 10022. Tel. (212) 751-2700.
American Israel Public Affairs Committee: 444 N. Capitol St. N.W., Suite 412, Washington, D.C., 20001.
American Red Magen David for Israel: 888 7th Av., 10019. Tel. (212) 757-1627.
American Zionist Federation: 515 Park Av., 10022.
Emuna Women of America: 370 7th Av., 10001. Tel. (212) 564-9045.
Hadassah (Woman's Zionist Org. of America): 50 W. 58th St., 10019. Tel. (212) 355-7900.
Jewish National Fund of America: 42 E. 69th St., 10021. Tel. (212) 879-9300.
Religious Zionists of America: 25 W. 26th St., 10010. Tel. (212) 889-5260.
State of Israel Bonds Org.: 215 Park Av. S., 10003. (212) 677-9650.
United Israel Appeal: 515 Park Av., 10022. Tel. (212) 688-0800.
World Confederation of United Zionists: 30E. 60th St., 10022. Tel. (212) 371-1452.
World Zionist Organisation – American Section: 515 Park Av., 10022. Tel. (212) 752-0600.
Zionist Org. of America: 4 E. 34th St., 10016. Tel. (212) 481-1500.
Israel Consulate-General: 800 Second Av., 10017.

Local Synagogues and Organisations
NOTES: The letter (O) after the name of a syn. means that the practice is Orthodox (akin to the Minhag of the United Synagogue in Britain). (C) stands for Conservative (corresponding roughly to the ritual of the W. London Syn. of British Jews). (R) stands for Reform (the form of worship is similar to that of the Liberal Jewish movement in Britain).
There is no unified Jewish ecclesiastical control in America. A Chief Rabbinate, such as Anglo-Jewry has, is unknown.
Kashrut: There is little official supervision of kashrut, so the standard of observance at kosher hotels and restaurants is by no means uniform. Travellers should always check with a local rabbi or religious organisation.
It should be pointed out here that space limitations and other difficulties make it impossible to list every synagogue in the U.S.A., and in many cases the choice is unavoidably an arbitrary one. However, we should be glad to receive details from users of the Guide of any omissions they consider to be particularly glaring.
The Jewish Community Councils and similar bodies in the larger centres

generally publish an annual directory of local Jewish organisations which are invaluable.

ALABAMA

BIRMINGHAM

Syn.: Knesseth Israel (O), 3225 Montevallo Rd., 35223; Beth-El (C), 2179 Highland Av., 35205; Emanu-El (R), 2100 Highland Av., 35205.
Mikva: 3225 Montevallo Rd., 35213 and 2179 Highland Av., 35255.
Birmingham Jewish Fed., 3966 Montclair Rd., 35213. Tel. (205) 879 0416.
Com. Centre: 3960 Montclair Rd., 35213. The Hess Library is at the same address.
Delicatessen: Browdy's, 2607 Cahaba Rd., 35223.
Visitors requiring information about kashrut, temporary accommodation, etc., should contact Rabbi Reuven Tradburks, of Knesseth Israel.

HUNTSVILLE

Syn.: Etz Chayim (C), 7705 Bailey Cove Rd. S.E., 35802.

MOBILE

Syn.: Ahavas Chesed (C), 1717 Dauphin, 36604. Tel. (205) 476-6010; Spring Hill Av. Temple (R), 1769 Spring Hill Av., 36607.

MONTGOMERY

Syn.: Etz Ahayem (Sephardi, O), 725 Augusta Rd., 36111; Agudath Israel (C) 3525 Cloverdale Rd., 36111. Mikva attached; Beth Or (R), 2246 Narrow Lane, 36106.
Jewish Fed., P.O. Box 20058, 36120. Tel. (205) 277-5820.
There is a Jewish chapel at Maxwell Air Force base. The Jewish chaplain can be contacted at Bldg. 833, Chaplain's School, at the base.

ALASKA

ANCHORAGE

Syn.: Beth Sholom (R), 7525 E. Northern Lights Blvd., 99504. Tel. (907) 338-1836. This is the only synagogue in Alaska and it has the only Jewish pre-school in the state.
There is also an Orthodox minyan called Cong. Shomerei Ohr. Inf. from 1026 E26th, 99508.

ARIZONA

MESA

Syn.: Beth Sholom Cong. (C), 316 Le Seuer St., 85204. Tel. (602) 964-1981.

PHOENIX

Syn.: Chabad-Lubavitch Centre (O), 2110 E, Lincoln Dr. Pheonix, 85020.Tel./ (602) 944-2753; Cong. Beth Joseph (O), 515 E. Bethany Home Rd., 85012. Tel. (602) 277-7479; Cong. Beth El (C), 1118 W. Glendale, Phoenix 85021. Tel. (944 3359) (944-2464); Temple Beth Ami (R), 4545 N. 36th St., No. 211, 85018. Tel. (602) 956-0805; Temple Beth Israel (R), 3310 N. 10th Av., 85013, whose building also houses a Judaica Museum. Tel. (602) 264 4428. Temple Chai (R), 4645 E. Marilyn Av., 85032. Tel. (602) 971-1234.

Congregation Shaarei Tzedek (O); P: Marty Miller, 7608 N. 18th Avenue, Phoenix 85021 (944-1133).

Temple Kol ami (R), 10210 N. 32nd St. 204 85028 Tel. (602) 788 0939.

Jewish Fed. of Greater Phoenix, 32 W. Coolidge Av., 85013. Tel. (602) 274-1800.

Phoenix Jewish Community Center, 1718 W. Maryland Av., Phx. 85015. Tel. (602) 249-1832

Tri-Cities Jewish Community Center 1965 E. Hermosa Temp, AZ 85282 Tel. (602) 897-0588.

Restaurants & Delis: Segal's New Place, 4818 N. 7th St., 85015. Tel. (602) 285-1515; Valley Kosher, 1331 E. Northern Av., 85015. Tel. (602) 371-0999; Visitors requiring information about kashrut should contact Rabbi David Rebibo, Phoenix Hebrew Academy, 515 E. Bethany Home Rd., 85012. Tel. (602) 277-7479.

SCOTTSDALE

Syn.: Ahavat Torah (C), 6815 E. Cactus St., 85254. Tel. (602) 991 5645; Beth Emeth of Scottsdale (C), 5406 E. Virginia Av., 85254. Tel. (602) 947-4604; Har Zion (C), 5929 E. Lincoln Dr., 85253. Tel. (602) 991-0720. Temple Solel, (R), 6805 E. MacDonald Dr., 85253. Tel. (602) 991-7414. Beth Joshua Congregation (C), 6230 E. Shea Blvd. Scottsdale 85254 (991-5404).

SOLOMONSVILLE

The town was founded by Isador E. Solomon, a friend of the Indians, in 1876.

Beth Sholom of Mesa (C), 316 LeSeuer St., Mesa 85204 (964-1981).

Har Zion - Conservative, 5929 E. Lincoln Drive, Paradise Valley 85253 (991-0720).

SUN CITY & SUN CITY WEST

Syn.: Beth Emeth of Sun City (C), 13702 Meeker Blvd., Sun City West, 85373. Tel. (602) 584-1953; Beth Shalom of Sun City (R), 12202 101st Av., Sun City, 85351. Tel. (602) 977-3240.

TEMPE

Syn.: Chabad-Lubavitch Centre (O), 23 W. 9th St., 85281. Tel. (602) 966-5163; Temple Emanuel (R), 5801 S. Rural Rd., 85283. Tel. (602) 838-1414. Tri-City Jewish Com. Centre, 1965 E. Hermosa Dr., 85282. Tel. (602) 897-0588.

TUCSON

Syn.: Cong. Chofetz Chayim (O), 5150 E. 5th St., 85711; Young Israel (O), 2442 E. 4th St., 85719; Anshei Israel (C), 5550 E. 5th St., 85711; Cong. Bet Shalom (C), 3881 E. River Rd., 85718; Temple Emanuel (R), 225 N. County Club Rd., 85716.

Jewish Fed. of Southern Arizona, 3822 E. River Rd., 85718. Tel. (602) 577-9393.

Kosher Meat and Delicatessen: Feig's Kosher Foods, 5071 E. 5th St., 85711.

ARKANSAS

EL DORADO

Syn.: Beth Israel (R), 1130 E. Main St.

HELENA
Syn.: Temple Beth-El (R), 406 Perry St., 72342. Founded 1875.

HOT SPRINGS
Syn.: House of Israel (R), 300 Quapaw St., 71901.
Hot Springs is known for its curative waters. The Leo Levi Memorial Hospital (for joint disorders, such as arthritis) was founded by B'nai B'rith, as was the adjacent Levi Towers, a senior citizen housing project.

LITTLE ROCK
Syn.: Agudath Achim (O), 7901 W. 5th St., 72205. Mikva & Hebrew School on premises. The only Orthodox syn. in the State of Arkansas open all year round; B'nai Israel (R), 3700 Rodney Parham Rd., 72212., open all year.
Jewish Fed. of Arkansas, 2821 Kavanaugh, Garden Level., 72205. Tel. (501) 663-3571.
Kosher Bakery: André's, 11121 Rodney Parham Rd., 72212. Under supervision of Rabbi Seymour Weller, of Agudath Achim.

CALIFORNIA
As the general population of California continues to increase – it now stands at 30,000,000 – the Jewish community has grown to 915,000.
Places of worship abound, from Eureka in the north to San Diego in the south, just a few miles from the Mexican border, but the major part of the community lives and prospers in the Los Angeles metropolitan area. There is an increasing number of truly kosher restaurants and, in addition, "kosher-style" delicatessens are everywhere. The hungry traveller should bear in mind that English-style "salt beef" is "corned beef" in the United States, but most popular European dishes are readily available.

ALAMEDA
Syn.: Temple Israel (R), 3183 Mecartney Rd., 94501.

ALHAMBRA
Syn.: Temple Beth Torah (C), 225 S. Atlantic Blvd., 91801. Tel. (818) 284-0296.

ANAHEIM
Syn: Temple Beth Emet (C), 1770 W. Cerritos Av., 92804. Tel. (714) 772-4720.

ARCADIA
Syn.: Temple Shaarei Tikvah (C), 550 S. 2nd Av., 91006. Tel. (818) 445-0810.

ARLETA
Syn.: Temple Beth Solomon of the Deaf (R), 13580 Osborne St., 91331. Tel. (818) 899-2202 or 896-6721.

BAKERSFIELD
Syn.: B'nai Jacob (C), 600 17th St., 93301; Temple Beth El (R), 2906 Loma Linda Dr., 93305.

BERKELEY
Syn.: Beth Israel (O), 1630 Bancroft Way, 94703; Chabad Hse. (O), Chabad Hse., 2643 College Av., 94704; Temple Beth El (R), 2301 Vine St., 94708.
Netivot Shalom (C) has services on Sat. morning at the Berkeley-Richmond Jewish Community Center at 1414 Walnut St.

Hillel Foundation, 2736 Bancroft Way, 94704. Tel. (510) 845-7793. Traditional egalitarian services on Fri. evening.
Judah L. Magnes Museum – Jewish Museum of the West, 2911 Russell St., 94705, is the largest institution of its kind West of New York. It includes the Western Jewish History Centre & Rabbi Morris Goldstein Library.
Lehrhaus Judaica, 2736 Bancroft Way, 94704.
(See also under Oakland.)

BEVERLY HILLS

Note: Beverly Hills, Hollywood and Los Angeles are contiguous communities and in many cases have overlapping bodies.
Syns.: Beth Jacob (O), 9030 Olympic Blvd., 90211; Young Israel of Beverly Hills (O), 8701 W. Pico Blvd., 90211; Temple Emanuel (R), 8944 Burton Way, 90211.

BURLINGAME

Syn.: Peninsula Temple Sholom (R), 1655 Sebastian Dr. 94010.

CARMEL

Cong. Beth Israel (R), 5716 Carmel Valley Rd., 93923. Tel. (408) 624-2015.

CASTRO VALLEY

Syn.: Shir Ami (R), 4529 Malabar Av., 94546. Tel. (415) 537-1787.

COSTA MESA

Syn.: Temple Sharon (C), PO Box 11788 617 West Hamilton, 92627. Tel. (714) 631 3262.

DALY CITY

Syn.: B'nai Israel (C), 1575 Annie St., 94015. Tel. (415) 756-5430.

DAVIS

Syn.: Davis Jewish Fellowship (R), 1821 Oak Av., 95616.

DOWNEY

Syn.: Temple Ner Tamid (R), 10629 Lakewood Blvd., Downey 90241. Rabbi R. Ettleston, Tel. (310) 861-9276.

EUREKA

Syn.: Beth El (R), Hodgson & T Sts., 95501. Tel. (707) 444 2846.

FREMONT

Syn.: Temple Beth Torah (R), 42000 Paseo Padre Pkwy., 94539. Tel. (415) 656-7141.

FRESNO

Syn.: Beth Jacob (C), 406 W. Shields Av., 93705; Temple Beth Israel (R), 6622 N. Maroa Av., 93704. This syn. has its own etrog tree, planted from a sprig brought to the United States from the Holy Land.
Com. Centre and Jewish Fed. Office: 5094 N. West Av., 93711.
Chabad House (orthodox) 6735 N. ILA, 93711.

GARDENA

Syn.: Southwest Temple Beth Torah (C), 14725 S. Gramercy Pl., 90249.

GARDEN GROVE

Jewish Fed. of Orange County, 12181 Buaro St., 92640. Tel. (714) 560-6636.

HOLLYWOOD

Syn.: Young Israel of Los Angeles (O), 660 N. Spaulding Av., 90036; Hollywood Temple Beth El (C), 137 N. Crescent Heights Blvd., Los Angeles 90046; Temple Israel (R), 7300 Hollywood Blvd., Los Angeles 90046.
Kosher Information Bureau, 12732 Chandler Blvd., No. Hollywood, CA 91607. (818) 762-3197.

LAFAYETTE

Syn.: Temple Isaiah (R), 3800 Mt. Diablo Blvd., 94549. Tel. (415) 283-8575.

LAKEWOOD

Syn.: Beth Zion-Sinai (C), 6440 Del Amo Blvd., 90713. Tel. (213) 429-0715.

LONG BEACH AREA

Syn: Cong. Lubavitch (O), 3981 Atlantic Av., 90807; Beth Shalom (C), 3635 Elm Av., 90807; Cong. Shalom of Leisure World (C), 1661 Golden Rain Rd., Northwood Clubhouse No. 3, Seal Beach 90740; Adat Chaverim (C) P.O. Box 662, Los Alamitos 90720; Temple Beth Zion Sinai (C), 6440 Del Amo Blvd., 90713; Temple Israel (R), 338 E. 3rd St., 90812.; Temple Beth David (R) 6100 Hefley St., Westminster.
Young Israel (O), 4134 Atlantic, 90807.
Mikva: 3847 Atlantic Av., 90807.
Jewish Fed. of Greater Long Beach & W. Orange County, 3801 E. Willow St., 90815. Tel. (310) 426-7601.
Newspaper: Jewish Fed. News, 3801 E. Willow St., 90815.
Fairfax Kosher Meat Market, 11196 Los Alamitos Blvd., Los Alamitos 90720 (310) 594-4609.

LOS ALAMITOS

Fairfax Kosher Market & Bakery, 1196-98 Los Alamitos Blvd. Tel. (213) 594-4600.

LOS ALTOS HILLS

Syn.: Congregation Beth Am (R), 26790 Arastradero Rd., 94022. Tel. (415) 493-4661.

LOS ANGELES

Los Angeles is America's, and the world's second largest Jewish metropolis, with a Jewish population of 600,000.
Fairfax Av. and Beverly Blvd. together form the crossroads of traditional Jewish life while a growing Orthodox enclave centres around Pico and Robertson Blvds. Fairfax Av. is lined with Jewish book and gift shops, delicatessens and restaurants, and all kinds of small stores.
The most complete selection of books of Jewish interest can probably be found at J. Roth, 9020 W. Olympic Blvd., 90211. Tel. (213) 276 9414. The owners encourage browsing.
The Skirball Museum of Hebrew Union College has an outstanding collection of Jewish ceremonial art and archaeological artifacts, a photographic record of destroyed Jewish landmarks in Europe and changing exhibitions.
The Jewish Studies Collection at the University of California, Los Angeles (UCLA), is the largest of its kind in the western United States, with 180,000 volumes of Judaica and Hebraica. Other major libraries are at the Jewish Community Building, University of Judaism, University of Southern California (USC) and the Frances-Henry Library of the Hebrew Union

College. The Wiesenthal Centre is a major repository of Holocaust literature.

There are three Jewish weeklies: the "B'nai B'rith Messenger", the "Heritage-Southwest Jewish Press," and the "Jewish Journal" all published on Fri. "Jewish News" appears monthly. Others include: Jewish calendar magazine, Yisrael Shelanu, Jewish news and Israel today.

Syn.: B'nai David Congregation (O), 8906 W. Pico Blvd., 90035; Breed St. Shule (O), 247 N. Breed St., 90033. This syn. is of historical interest; Chabad House (O), 741 Gayley Av., W. Los Angeles, 90025; Etz Chaim (O), 8018 W. 3rd St.; Etz Jacob (O), 7659 Beverly Blvd., 90036; Kahal Joseph (Sephardi, O), 10505 Santa Monica Blvd. 90025; Magen David (Sephardi, O), 7454 Melrose Av., 90046; Mogen David (O), 9717 W. Pico Blvd., 90035; Ohel David (O), 7967 Beverly Blvd., Ohev Shalom (O), 525 S.Fairfax Av., 90036; Temple Tifereth Israel (Sephardi, O), 10500 Wilshire Blvd., 90024; Young Israel of Hancock Pk. (O), 140 S. La Brea Blvd., 90036; Adat Shalom (C), 3030 Westwood Blvd., 90034; Beth Am (C), 1039 S. La Cienega Blvd., 90035; Sinai Temple (C), 10400 Wilshire Blvd., 90024; Leo Baeck Temple (R), 1300 N. Sepulveda Blvd., 90049; Stephen S. Wise Temple (R), 15500 Stephen S. Wise Dr., Bel Air, 90024; Temple Akiba (R), 5249 S. Sepulveda Blvd., Culver City 90230. Temple Isaiah (R), 10345 W. Pico Blvd., 90064; University Syn. (R), 11960 Sunset Blvd., 90049; Wilshire Blvd. Temple (R), 3663 Wilshire Blvd., 90010; Kehillath Israel (Reconstructionist), 16019 Sunset Blvd., Pacific Palisades, 90272. Beth Chayim Chadishim (R), 6000 W. Pico Blvd, 90035.

Los Angeles Mikva; 9548 W. Pico Blvd., 90035.

Jewish Fed.-Council of Greater Los Angeles, 6505 Wilshire Blvd., 90048.

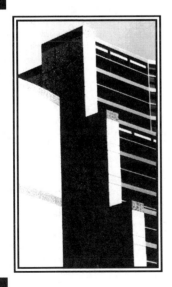

At same address: Bd. of Rabbis of Southern California. Exec. P.: Rabbi Paul Dubin. Tel. (213) 852-1234.

Com. Bldgs.: Los Angeles Jewish Com. Bldg., 650 Wilshire Blvd., 90048; West Side Com. Centre, 5870 W. Olympic Blvd., 90036. This address also houses the Jewish Centres Assoc. of Los Angeles; and includes a 'hands-on' museum for children. Hollywood-Los Feliz Centre, 1110 Bates Av., 90029; Bay Cities Centre, 2601 Santa Monica Blvd., Santa Monica, 90404; South Bay Centre, 22401 Palos Verdes Blvd., Torrance 90505; Valley Cities Centre, 13164 Burbank Av., Van Nuys, 91401; W.V.J.C.C., 22622 Van Owen, West Hills.

There is a statue of the American Jewish pioneer, Haym Salomon, in the W. Wilshire Recreation Centre.

Institutions of Learning: Hebrew Union College (R), 3077 University Av., 90007; Kollel Bais Avrohom (O), 7466 Beverly Blvd.; Yeshiva Gedolah of Los Angeles (O), 5822 W. 3rd St.; Yeshivah Ohr Elchanon Chabad (O), 808 N. Alta Vista Blvd.; University of Judaism (C), 15600 Mulholland Dr., 90024; Yeshiva University of Los Angeles (O), 9760 W. Pico Blvd., 90035. The Simon Wiesenthal Centre, Tel. (213) 553-9036, is on Yeshiva University campus.

Cedars-Sinai Medical Centre, 8700 Beverly Blvd., 90048.

Israel Consulate & Govt. Tourist Office: 6380 Wilshire Blvd., 90048.

Kosher Information Bureau: (818) 762-3197; Fax (818) 980-6908; and **Kashrut Authorities:** Rabbinical Council of California, Att: Rabbi A. Union, 1122 S. Robertson Blvd., Los Angeles, CA 90035. (310) 271-4160; Bureau of Jewish Education, 6505 Wilshire Blvd., Suite #710, Los Angeles, CA 90048. (213) 852-7702; Board of Rabbis, 6505 Wilshire Blvd., Suite #511, Los Angeles, CA 90048. (213) 852-7710; Rabbi Bukspan, 6407 Orange St., Los Angeles, CA 90048. (213) 653-5083.

Note: The RCC is undergoing an upgrading of enforcement of kosher standards. They now claim that all their non-deli meat restaurants use glatt kosher meat exclusively. All restaurants labeled "Mahadrin" have permanent, on-site kosher supervision. All information supplied and updated as a community service by Rabbi Aaron Simkin (818) 368-8881.

Hotels with ability to do kosher affairs — must request kosher supervision. Bel Air Hotel, West Los Angeles (RCC); Radisson Bel Air Summit, LA, (213) 476-6571 (RCC); Beverly Grand, LA, (213) 939-1653 (RCC); Beverly Hilton, Beverley Hills, (213) 274-7777; Beverly Wilshire, Beverly Hills, (213) 275-4282 (RCC); Century Plaza, Century City, (213) 277-2000 (RCC); Four Seasons, LA (RCC) (213); Hyatt (Airport), Inglewood, (231) 670-9000 (RCC); La Bel Age, LA, (213) 854-1111 (RCC); Marriott-Century City, (213) 277-2777 (RCC); Marriott-Woodland Hills, (818) 887-4800 (RCC); Ramada-Airport, (213) 337-2800 (RCC); Sheraton Grand, LA (213) 617-1133 (RCC);

Universal City Hilton, (Formerly Registry Hotel), Universal City, (213) 617-0666 (RCC); Valley Hilton, (818) 981-4500 (RCC); Westin Boneventure, LA (213) 624-1000 (RCC).

Kosher Restaurants & Delicatessens: Pico Kosher Deli, 8826 W. Pico Blvd., LA, (213) 273-9381 (RCC); Ole's, 7912 Beverly Blvd., LA (213) 937-7162; Serravalle, 8837 W. Pico Blvd., LA, (213) 550-8372; Simone, 8706 W. Pico Blvd., LA, (213) 657-5552 (RCC-Mehadrin); Beverly/Fairfax & Downtown; East Side Kosher, 7231 Beverly Blvd., LA, (213) 936-1653; Beverly Grand Hotel, 7359 Beverly Blvd., LA, (213) 939-1653; Cellar Cafe, 6505 Wilshire Blvd., LA, (213) 852-1234 (RCC); Dizingoff Restaurant, 8107 Beverly Blvd., LA, (213) 651-4465 (RCC); Elite Cuisine, 7119 Beverly Blvd., LA, (213) 930-1303 (RCC); Fairfax Kosher Pizza, 453 N. Fairfax Av., LA, (213) 653-7200; Fish Grill, 7226 Beverly Blvd., LA, (213) 937-7162; Grill Express, 501 N. Fairfax Av., LA, (213) 655-0649; Judy's, 129 N. Labrea Av., LA, (213) 934-7667 (RCC-Mehadrin); Pizza World, 365 S. Fairfax Av., LA, (213) 653-2896; Perfect Pita, 415 N. Fairfax Av., LA, (213) 651-5330.

Pico Robinson Area *(Los Angeles):* The Fishing Well, 8975 W. Pico Blvd., LA (213) 859-9429 (RCC); I'm a Deli, 8930 W. Pico Blvd., LA, (213) 274-3452; Kosher Kolonel, 9301 W. Pico Blvd., LA, (213) 858-0111; Kosher Pizza Nosh, 8644 W. Pico Blvd., LA, (213) 276-8708; Micheline's, 8965 W. Pico Blvd., LA, (213) 274-6534 (RCC-Mehadrin); The Milky Way, 9108 W. Pico Blvd., LA, (213) 859-0004; Nagila Pizza, 9216 W. PIco Blvd., LA, (213) 550-7735; Pat's, 923 W. Pico Blvd., LA, (213) 205-8705; PIzza Mayven, 140 N. Labrea Av., LA, (213) 847-0353; Shimon's Restaurant, 914 S. Hill St., LA, (213) 627-6535 (RCC); Simon's La Glatt, 446 N. Fairfax Av., LA, (213) 658-7730 (RCC-Mahadrin); Tami's Fish House, 553 B, Fairfax Av., LA, (213) 655-7953.

Note. See also Beverly Hills, Hollywood, San Fernando Valley and Venice (Cal.).

MODESTO

Syn.: Congregation Beth Shalom (C), 1705 Sherwood Av., 95350. Tel. (209) 522-5613. Mailing address: P.O.B. 4082, 95352.

NAPA

Syn.: Cong. Beth Sholom (unaffiliated), 1455 Elm St., 94559. Tel. (707) 253-7305.

OAKLAND

Syn.: Temple Israel (R), 3183 Mecartney, Alameda 94501; Beth El (R), 2301 Vine, Berkeley 94708; Beth Israel (O), 1630 Bancroft, Berkeley 94704; Netivot Shalom (C), PO Box 12761, Berkeley 94701; Kehilla (Renewal), PO Box 3063, Berkeley, 94703; Aquarian Minyan (JR), c/o Goldfarb, 2020 Essex, Berkeley 94703; Chabad (O), 2643 College Av., Berkeley 94704; Shir Ami (R), 4529 Malabar Av., Castro Valley 94546; Beth Torah (R), 42000 Paseo Padre Parkway, Fremont 94538; Beth Emek (R), PO Box 722, Livermore 94550; Beth Abraham (C), 327 MacArthur Blvd., Oakland 94610; Beth Jacob (O) 3778 Park Blvd., Oakland 94610; Temple Sinai (R), 2808 Summit, Oakland 94609; Beth Sholom (C), 642 Dolores, San Leandro 94577; Temple Isaiah (R), 3800 Mt Diablo Blvd., Lafayette 94549; Beth Chaim (I), PO Box 23632, Pleasant Hill 94523; Beth Hillel (R), 801 Park Central, Richmond 94803; B'nai Shalom (C), 74 Eckley Lane, Walnut Creek 94596; Beth Am Minyan (C), c/o Ben-Eliezer, 2720 Oak Rd., #130, Walnut Creek 94596; B'nai Tikvah (R), 25 Hillcroft Way, Walnut Creek 94596; B'nai Israel of Rossmoor (I), c/o Fred Rau, 2601 Ptarmigan #3, Walnut Creek 94595. Mikva: Beth Jacob, address as above.

Jewish Com. Centers: Berkeley/Richmond JCC, 1414 Walnut St., Berkeley 94709; Contra Costa JCC, 2071 Tice Valley Blvd., Walnut Creek 94595; Oakland/Piedmont JCC, 3245 Sheffield Av., Oakland 94602.
Jewish Fed. of the Greater East Bay: 401 Grand Av., #500, Oakland 94610.
Museum: Judah L. Magnes Memorial Museum, 2911 Russell St., Berkeley 94705.
Kosher Delicatessen: Oakland Kosher Foods, 3256 Grand Av., Oakland 94610; Holy Land Restaurant, 677 Rand Av., Oakland 94610.

PALM DESERT

Syn.: Temple Sinai (R), 43-435 Monterey Av., 92260. Tel. (619) 568-9699.

PALM SPRINGS

Syn.: Temple Isaiah & Jewish Com Centre (C), 332 W. Alejo Rd., 92262. Desert Syn. (O), 1068 N. Palm Canyon Dr., Ca. 92262. Tel. (619) 327-4848.
Jewish Fed. of Palm Springs Desert Area, 611 S. Palm Canyon Dr., 92264. Tel. (619) 325-7281.

PALO ALTO

Syn.: Cong. Chabad (O), 3070 Louis Rd., 94308. Tel. (415) 429 8444. Palo Alto Orthodox Minyan (O), 453 Sherman Av., 94306. Tel. (415) 326-5001; Kol Emeth (C), 4175 Manuela Av., 94306. Tel. (415) 948-7498.
The Albert L. Schultz Com. Centre is at 655 Arastradero Rd., 94306. Tel. (415) 493 9400.

PASADENA

Syn.: Jewish Temple & Center (C): 1434 N. Altadena Dr., 91107. Rabbi Gilbert Kollin. Tel. (818) 798 1161.

POMONA

Syn.: Temple Beth Israel (R), 3033 N. Towne Av., 91767. Tel. (714) 626-1277.

RICHMOND

Syn.: Temple Beth Hillel (R), 801 Park Central, 94803.

ROHNERT PARK

Syn.: Sonama County Syn. Centre (Reconstructionist), 4627 Snyder La., 94928. Tel. (707) 664-8622.

SACRAMENTO

Syn.: Knesset Israel Torah Centre (O), 1024 Morse Av., 95864. Tel. (916) 481-1159; Mosaic Law (C), 2300 Sierra Blvd., 95825 Tel. (916) 488-1122.; Beth Shalom (R), 4/46 El Camino Av., 95608 Tel. (916) 485-4478. B'nai Israel (R), 3600 Riverside Blvd., 95818. Tel (916) 446-4861. Sunrise Jewish Congregation, P.O. Box 405, 95610. Tel. (916) 965-8322. Congregation Bet Haverim-Davis 1821 Oak Av., 95616, Tel. (916) 758-0842.
Com. Centre: Same address & Tel. as Jewish Fed. below.
Jewish Fed. of Sacramento, 2351 Wyda Way, 95825. Tel. (916) 486-0906.
Restaurant: (K) Sarah's Catering & Fine Foods, 2319 El Camino Av., 95821. Tel. (916) 971-9500.

SALINAS

Syn.: Temple Beth El (R), 1212 S. Riker St., 93901. Tel. (408) 424-9151.

SAN BERNARDINO

Syn.: Emanu-El (R), 3512 N. "E" St., 92405. Tel. 886-4818.

The city's central library is named in honour of Rabbi Norman F. Feldheym, who was the rabbi of Temple Emanu-El from 1937 to 1971.
The "Home of Eternity" cemetery, at 8th St. & Sierra Way, presented by the Mormons, is one of the oldest Jewish cemeteries in the western U.S.A. Here lies buried Wolf Cohn, believed for many years to have been the first Jew to be scalped by the Red Indians. He was in fact shot dead in 1862 by a drunken man described by a contemporary San Bernardino newspaper as "a noted desperado."

SAN DIEGO AREA

Syn.: Beth Jacob Cong. (O), 4855 College Av., 92115. Tel. (619) 287-9890; Beth Torah Cong. (O), 5080 Bonita Rd., Suite F, Bonita, Ca. 91902. Tel. (619) 472-2144; Chabad Hse. (O), 6115 Montezuma Rd., 92115. Tel. (619) 265-7700; Chabad of La Jolla/University City (O), 3232 Governor Dr., Suites B & R, 92122. Tel. (619) 455-1670; Chabad of Rancho Bernardo (O), 16934 Espola Rd., Poway, 92064. Tel. (619) 451-0455; Cong. Adat Yeshurun (O), 8950 Villa La Jolla Dr., Suite 1224, La Jolla, 92037. Tel. (619) 535-1196; Young Israel of San Diego (O), P.O. Box 202134, Ca. 92120. Tel. (619) 226-5762. Cong. Adat Ami (C), 1233 Camino del Rio St., Suite 275, 92108. Tel. (619) 260 0626; Cong. Beth Am (C), 525 Stevens Av., Solana Beach, 92075. Tel. (619) 481-8454; Cong. Beth El (C), 8660 Gilman Dr., La Jolla, 92037. Tel. (619) 452-1734; Cong. Beth Tefilah (C), 4967 69th St., 92115. Tel. (619) 463-0391; Cong. Ner Tamid (C) 16981 Via Tazon, Suite G. 92127. Tel. (619) 592 9141; Temple Beth Sholom (C), 208 Madrona St., Chula Vista, 91910. Tel. (619) 420-6040; Temple Judea (C), 1930 Sunset Dr., Vista, 92083. Tel. (619) 724-8318; Tifereth Israel (C), 6660 Cowles Mountain Blvd., 92119. Tel. (619) 697-6001; Cong. Beth Israel (R), 2512 3rd Av., 92103. Tel. (619) 239-0149; Cong. Etz Chaim (R), PO Box 1138 Ramona 92065. Tel. (619) 789 7393; Temple Adat Shalom (R), 15905 Pomerado Rd., Poway, 92064. Tel. (619) 451-1200; Temple Emanu-El (R), 6299 Capri Dr., 92120. Tel. (619) 286-2555; Temple Solel (R), 552 S. El Camino Real, Encinitas, 92024. Tel. (619) 436-0654; Cong. Dor Hadash (Reconstructionist), 5790 Miramar Rd., Suite 208, 92121. Tel. (619) 587-1270.
Com. Centres: Lawrence Family Jewish Com. Ctr., Central Office, 4201 Eastgate Mall, La Jolla, 92037. Tel. (619) 457-3161; 4126 Executive Dr., La Jolla, 92037. Tel. (619) 457-3030; 552 S. El Camino Real, Encinitas, 92024 (North County branch). Tel. (619) 944-0640. East County Ctr., 4079 54th St. 92105 Tel. (619) 583-3300.
Homes for Aged, 4075 54th St., 92105. Tel. (619) 582 5168; 211 Saxony Rd., Encinitas 92024. Tel. (619) 632 0091.
Jewish Campus Centres, 5742 Montezuma Rd., 92115. Tel. (619) 583-6080).
United Jewish Fed. of San Diego County, 4797 Mercury St., 92111. Tel. (619) 571-3444.
Balboa Park, the largest public park in San Diego, includes the House of Pacific Relations, which comprises 30 cottages for various ethnic groups. These include the Cottage of Israel, which mounts exhibitions throughout the year, portraying the history & traditions of the Jewish people, & of biblical and modern Israel. Open Sun. 1.30 p.m. to 4.30 p.m., except on Holy-days & major festivals.
Newspapers: "Heritage", 3443 Camino Del Rio S., Suite 315, 92108. Tel. (619) 282-7177; "San Diego Jewish Times", 2592 Fletcher Pkwy., El Cajon, 92020. Tel. (619) 463-5515.
Restaurants, etc.: Blumer's Bakery Jewish Delicatessen, 5379 El Cajon Blvd. (at 54th St.), 92115. Tel. (619) 582-2791; City Delicatessen, 6th Av. & University Av., 92103. Tel. (619) 295-2747; Croce's Restaurant-Jazz Bar, 802 5th Av. (at "F" St.), 92101. Tel. (619) 233-4355; D.Z. Akin's Deli, 6930

Alvarado Rd., 92120. Tel. (619) 265-0218; Lang's Loaf (Milchik shop/restaurant), 6165 El Cajon Blvd., 92041. Tel. (619) 286-7306; L'Chaim Vegetarian Cafe, 134 W. Douglas St. (in alley), El Cajon, 92020. Tel. (619) 442-1331; Mavin's New York Scene, 824 Camino del Rio N., 92108. Tel. (619) 299-0620; Pittluck Cafe, Jewish Com. Centre, 4126 Executive Dr., La Jolla, 92037. Tel. (619) 457-3030; Western Kosher, 7739 Fay Av., La Jolla, 92037. Tel. (619) 454-6328.
Butcher & Delicatessen: Kosher Connection, 7520 El Cajon Blvd, 92041. Tel. (619) 460-7887.

SAN FERNANDO VALLEY

The Adat Ari El Synagogue is at 5540 Laurel Canyon Blvd., N. Hollywood, 91607. In the David Familian Chapel at the syn. are eleven beautiful stained-glass windows, designed by Mischa Kallis, depicting significant dates in the religious calendar.
Other synagogues in the Valley (which is about 12 miles from Hollywood) include Chabad Hse. (O), 4917 Hayvenhurst, Encino, 91346; Shaarey Zedek (O), 12800 Chandler Blvd., N. Hollywood, 91607; Beth Ami (C), 18449 Kittridge St., Reseda, 91335; Cong. Beth Kodesh (C), 7401 Shoup Av., Canoga Park; Beth Meier Cong. (C), 11725 Moorpark, Studio City; Ner Maarev Temple (C), 5180 Yarmouth Av., Encino, 91316; Temple Aliyah (C), 24400 Aliyah Way, Woodland Hills, 91367; Temple B'nai Hayim (C), 4302 Van Nuys Blvd., Sherman Oaks; Temple Emanu-El (C), 1302 N. Glenoaks Av., Burbank, 91504; Temple Ramat Zion (C), 17655 Devonshire Av., Northridge; Valley Beth Shalom (C), 15739 Ventura Blvd., Encino, 91316; Beth Emet (R), 320 E. Magnolia Blvd., Burbank, 91502; Temple Ahavat Shalom (R), 11261 Chimineas Av., Northridge; Temple Judea (R), 5429 Lindley Av., Tarzana. Shir Chadash (R) 17000 Ventura Blvd., Encino.
Mikva: Teichman Mikvah Soc., 12800 Chandler Blvd., N. Hollywood, 91607. Tel. (818) 506-0996.
Aish Hatorah College of Jewish Studies, 6348 Whitsett Av., N. Hollywood, 91607.
Emek Hebrew Academy, 12753 Chandler Blvd., N. Hollywood, 91607. The Kashrus Information Bureau, Rabbinic Administrator, Rabbi Eliezer Eidlitz, is also at the above address. Tel. (818) 762-3197.
Jewish Community Centers: North Valley Center, 16601 Rinaldi St., Granada Hills, 91344; Valley Cities Center, 13164 Burbank Blvd., Van Nuys, 91401; West Valley Center, 22622 Vanowen St., West Hills, 91307.
All the restaurants & delicatessens listed below are under rabbinical supervision.
Kosher Restaurants: (K) Carvel's Ice Cream, 25948 McBean Parkway, Valencia (805) 259-1450 (KOF-K); (K) Drexler's Kosher Restaurant, 12519 1/2 Burbank Blvd., N. Hollywood, (818) 761-6405; (K) Flora Falafel, 12450 Burbank Blvd., No. Hollywood, (818) 766-6567 (RCC); (K) Golan, 6353 Woodman Av., Van Nuys, (818) 989-5423 (RCC-Mehadrin); (K) Hadar, 12514 Burbank Blvd., N. Hollywood, (818) 762-1155; (K) La Pizza, 12515 Burbank Blvd., N. Hollywood, (818) 760-8190; (K) Shalom, 21036 Victory Blvd., Woodland Hills, (818) 887-9593; (K) Sharon's Kosher Restaurant, 18608 1/2 Ventura Blvd., Tarzana; (K) Sportsman's Lodge, Sherman Oaks, (818) 984-0202; (K) Tiberias, 18046 Ventura Blvd., Encino, (818) 343-3705.

SAN FRANCISCO

Syn.: Adath Israel (O), 1851 Noriega St., 94122. Tel. 564-5665; Anshey Sfard (O), 1500 Clement St., 94118. Tel. 752-4979; Chabad House (O), 11 Tillman Pl., 94108. Tel. 956-8644; Chevra Thilim (O), 751 25th Av., 94121. Tel. 752-2866; Keneseth Israel (O), Suite 203 655 Sutter Street, 94102. Tel. 771-3420.

Magain David (Sephardi, O), 351 4th Av., 94118. Tel. 752-9095; Torat Emeth (O), 768 27th Av., 94121. Tel. 386-1830; Beth Sholom (C), 14th Av. & Clement St., 94118. Tel. 221-8736; B'nai Emunah (C), 3595 Taraval St. 94116 Tel. 664-7373; Ner Tamid (C), 1250 Quintara St., 94116. Tel. 661-3383; Beth Israel-Judea (C-R), 625 Brotherhood Way, 94132. Tel. 586-8833; Richmond Torah Center (Chabad), 2044 Clement St., 94121. Tel. 386-8123. Young Israel (O), 1806-A Noriega St., 94122. Tel. 752-7333. Sha'ar Zahav (R), 220 Danvers St.;94114 Tel. 861-6932. Sherith Israel (R), 2266 California St., 94118. Tel. 346-1720; Emanu-El (R), Arguello Blvd. & Lake St., 94118. Tel. 751-2535.
Mikva, 3355 Sacramento St., 94118. Tel. 921-4070.
Board of Rabbis of Northern California, 121 Steuart St., Suite 403, 94105. Tel. 788-3630
Bureau of Jewish Education & Jewish Com. Library, 639 14th Av., 94118. Tel. 751-6983
Hillel Foundation, 33 Banbury St., 94132. Tel. 334 4440
Holocaust Library & Research Centre, 601 14th Av., 94118. Tel. 751-6040
Jewish Home for Aged, 302 Silver Av., 94112.
Mt. Zion Hospital, 1600 Divisadero St., 94115.
Jewish Com. Fed. of San Francisco, the Peninsula, Marin & Sonoma Counties, 121 Steuart St., 94105. Tel. (415) 777-0411.
Marin Jewish Community Center, 200 N. San Pedro Road, San Rafael, 94903. Tel. 479-2000.
Albert L. Schultz Jewish Community Center, 655 Arastradero Road, Palo Alto, 94306. Tel. 493-9400.
Jewish Com. Museum; same address as Jewish Com. Fed. Tel. 543-8880
Jewish Com. Information & Referral, same address as Jewish Com. Fed. Tel. (415) 777-4545.
San Francisco Jewish Com. Center: 3200 California St., 94118. Tel. 346-6040
Brotherhood Way Com. Centre, 655 Brotherhood Way, 94132. Tel. 334-7474
Peninsula Com. Centre, 2440 Carlmont Dr., Belmont, 94002. Tel. 591-4438.
Jewish Family & Children's Service Agency, 1600 Scott St., 94115 Tel. 564-8860.
Kosher Delicatessen, Meat & Poultry:
Tel Aviv Strictly Kosher Meats, 1301 Noriega St., cnr. 20th Av. Tel. 661-7588. Under supervision of Orthodox Rabbinical Council. Kosher meals are available at the Kosher Nutrition Kitchen, Montefiore Senior Center, 3200 California Av., and through Gourmet Kosher Meals, cooked and prepared in the kitchens of Cong. Adath Israei (o), 1851 Noriega St., 94122. Further inf. about Kosher meals etc. from Board of Rabbis of Northern California.
Kosher Meat Israel & Cohen Kosher Meats, 5621 Geary Blvd., 94121, Tel. 752-3064.
Jacob Kosher Meats, 2435 Noriega St., 94122. Tel. 564-7482.
Tel Aviv Kosher Meats 1301 Noriega St., 94122 Tel. 661-7588.
Natan's Kosher Grill, 420 Geary (at Mason), 94108. Tel. 776-2683. Under Rabbinic supervision of Cong. Thilim.
Lotus Garden, 532 Grant Av., 94108. Tel. (415) 397-0130.

SAN JOSE

Syn.: Am Echad (O), 1537a Meridian Av., 95125; Sinai (Trad.), 1532 Willowbrae Av., 95125; Beth Sholom (R), 4849 Pearl Av., 95136; Cong. Shir Hadash (R), 16555 Shannon Rd., Los Gatos, 95030; Temple Emanu-El (R), 1010 University Av., 95126.
Com. Centre, 14855 Oka Rd., Los Gatos, 95030. Tel. (408) 358-3636.
Jewish Fed. of Greater San Jose, 14855 Oka Rd., Los Gatos 95030. Tel. (408) 358-3033.

Kosher Delicatessen: Willow Glen Kosher Deli, 1185 Lincoln Av., 95125. Tel. (408) 297-6604. Under Rabinical supervision.

SAN RAFAEL

Syns.: Cong. Kol Shofar (C), 215 Blackfield Dr., 94920; Rodef Sholom (R), 170 N. San Pedro Rd., 94903.
Marin Jewish Com. Centre: 30 N. San Pedro Rd., 94903.

SANTA BARBARA

Syn.: Young Israel of Santa Barbara (O), 1826C Cliff Dr., 93109. Tel. (805) 966-4565. Cong. B'nai B'rith (R), 900 San Antonio Creek Rd., 93111.

SANTA MONICA

Syn.: Chabad Hse. (O), 1428 17th St., 90404; Beth Sholom (R), 1827 California Av., 90403.

SANTA ROSA

Syn.: Com. Centre, Beth Ami (C), 4676 Mayette Av., 95405. Tel. (707) 545-4334. Dairy kitchen on premises; ; Shomrei Torah (R), Services at United Methodist Church, 1717 Yulupa Av., 95405. Tel. (707) 578-5519.

SARATOGA

Syn.: Cong. Beth David (C), 19700 Prospect Rd. at Scully, 95070-3352. Tel. (408) 257-3333.

STOCKTON

Stockton is one of the oldest communities west of the Mississippi River, founded in the days of the California Gold Rush. Temple Israel was founded as Congregation Ryhim Ahoovim in 1850 and erected its first building in 1855.
Syn, Temple Israel (R), 5105 N. El Dorado St., 95207.

SUNNYVALE

School: S. Peninsula Hebrew Day School, 1030 Astoria Dr., 94087. Kashrut & com. inf. from the Principal, Rabbi Yitchak Young.

THOUSAND OAKS

Syn.: Temple Etz Chaim (C), 1080 E. Janss Rd., 91360. Hebrew School on premises. Kosher catering. Inf. from Rabbi Shimon Paskow. Tel. (805) 497-6891. Synagogue contains unique artistic Aron Kodesh & Holocaust memorial.

TUSTIN

Syn.: Cong. B'nai Israel (C), 655 S. "B" St., 92680. Tel. 730-9693.
Jewish Fed. of Orange County, 1385 Warner Av., Suite A, 92680. Tel. (714) 259-0655.

VALLEJO

Syn.; Cong. B'nai Israel (unaffiliated, 1256 Nebraska St., 94590 Tel. (707) 642-6526

VENICE

Syn.: Pacific Jewish Centre Syn. (O), 505 Ocean Front Walk, 90291. Tel. (213) 392-8749; Pacific Jewish Centre (O), 720 Rose Av., 90291. Tel. (213) 392-8749. The centre has a mikva and an elementary day school with summer camp facilities for visitors. It also offers a full range of kosher food, bakery products and meat, as well as accom.; Mishkon Tephilo (C), 206 Main St., 90291.

VENTURA

Syn.: Ventura County Jewish Council-Temple Beth Torah (R), 7620 Foothill Rd., 93004. Tel. (805) 647-4181.

WALNUT CREEK

Syn.: Cong. B'nai Shalom (C), 74 Eckley Lane, 94596; Cong. B'nai Tikvah (R), 25 Hillcroft Way, 94596.
Contra Costa Jewish Com. Centre (C), 2071 Tice Valley Blvd., 94596.

WHITTIER

Syn.: Beth Shalom Syn. Centre (C), 14564 E. Hawes St., 90604. Tel. (213) 914-8744.

COLORADO

COLORADO SPRINGS

Syn.: Chabad Hse. (O), 3465 Nonchalant Circle, 80909. Tel. 596-7330; Temple Shalom (C-R), 1523 E. Monument St., 80909. Reform services are held on Fri. evg. & Conservative services on Sat. morn. Tel. 634-5311. There is a Jewish chapel at the U.S. Air Force Academy.

DENVER

Syn.: Bais Medrash Kehillas Yaakov (O), 295 S. Locust St., 80224. Tel. 377-1220; Beth Joseph (O), 825 Ivanhoe, 80220; B.M.H. Cong. (O), 560 S. Monaco Pkwy., 80222; E. Denver Syn. (O), 198 S. Holly, 80222. Tel. 322-7943; Hebrew Educational Alliance (O), 1555 Stuart St., 80204; Zera Abraham (O), 1560 Winona Ct., 80204; Zera Israel (O), 3934 W. 14th Av. at Perry, 80204. Tel. 571-0166; Beth Shalom (C), 2280 E. Noble Pl., Littleton, 80121. Tel. 794-6643; Rodef Shalom (C), 450 S. Kearney, 80222; Southeast Syn. (C), P.O. Box 5071, Englewood, 80155; Cong. Temple Emanuel (R), 51 Grape St., 80220; Temple Micah (R), 2600 Leyden St., 80207; Temple Sinai (R), 8050 E. Dartmouth Av., 80231; Colorado Jewish Reconstructionist Fed. (Rec.), 6445 E. Ohio, 80224. Tel. 388-4441; B'nai Torah (Unaffiliated), P.O. Box 5488, Arvada 80005; Zera Abraham Congregation, 1560 Winona Ct., Denver, CO 80204. Tel. (303) 825-7517.

Com. Orgs.: Allied Jewish Fed. of Colorado, 300 S. Dahlia St., 80222. Tel. (303) 321-3399. Com. Centre, 4800 E. Alameda Av., 80222 (the Com. Centre also operates a kosher children's camp); Jewish Family & Children's Service, 1335 S. Colorado Blvd., Building C-800, Denver, CO 80222. Tel. (303) 759-4890; Rose Medical Centre, 4567 E. 9th Av., 80220.

Newspaper: Jewish News, 1275 Sherman St., 80203. Tel. (303) 861-2234. Fax (303) 832-6942.

Kosher Delicatessen: B & J's Utica Grocery & Deli, 4500 W. Colfax Av., 80204. Shomer Shabbat; Steinberg's Kosher Grocery, 4017 W. Colfax Av., 80204. Tel. (303) 534-0314. Glatt kosher. Under supervision of Denver Vaad Hakashrus.

Kosher Restaurants: East-Side Kosher Deli, Inc., 5475 Leetsdale Dr., Denver, 80222. Tel. (303) 322-9862; Mediterranian Cafe, 2817 E. 3rd Av., Denver, CO 80206. Tel. (303) 399-2940.

For inf. about kashrut, visitors should contact Rabbi Nathaniel Lauer, 1470 Utica St., 80204. Tel. (303) 825-4938 (home); (303) 893-1333 (business).

LITTLETON
Syn.: Beth Shalom (C), 2280 E. Noble Pl., 80121.

PUEBLO
Syn.: United Hebrew Cong. (C), 106 W. 15th St., 81003; Temple Emanuel (R), 1325 Grand Av., 81003.

CONNECTICUT

BRANFORD
Jewish Centre, Svea Av., 06405.

BRIDGEPORT
Syn.: Agudas Achim (O), 85 Arlington St. 06606; Ahavath Achim (O), 1571 Stratfield Rd., Fairfield, 06432; Bikur Cholim (O), Park & Capitol Avs., 06604; Shaare Torah Adath Israel (O), 3050 Main St., 06606; B'nai Torah (C), 5700 Main St., Trumbull, 06611; Cong. Beth El (C), 1200 Fairfield Woods Rd., Fairfield, 06430; Rodeph Sholom (C), 2385 Park Av., 06604; Temple B'nai Israel (R), 2710 Park Av., 06604; Cong. Shirei Shalom (Reconstructionist), P.O. Box 372, Monroe, 06468.
Mikveh Israel, 1326 Stratfield Rd., Fairfield, 06432.
Com. Centre: 4200 Park Av., 06604.
Jewish Fed. of Greater Bridgeport, 4200 Park Av., 06604. Tel. (203) 372-6504.
Delicatessen: Moishe's Kosher Delicatessen & Bakery, 2081 Black Rock Turnpike, Fairfield, 06430.

DANBURY
Syn.: Cong. B'nai Israel (C), 193 Clapboard Ridge Rd., Danbury 068111. Tel. (203) 792-6161; United Jewish Center (R), 141 Deer Hill Av., Danbury 06810. Tel. (203) 748-3355.
The Jewish Fed. 39 Mill Plain Rd., Suite 4, Danbury 06811. Tel. (203) 792-6353. Fax (203) 748-5099.

DERBY
Syn.: Beth Israel Syn. Centre (C), 300 Elizabeth St., 06418.

HAMDEN
Syn.: Beth Sholom (C), 1809 Whitney Av., 06514; Temple Mishkan Israel (R), 785 Ridge Rd., 06514.
Kosher Restaurant & Delicatessen: Abel's, 2100 Dixwell Av., 06514. Under rabbinical supervision.

HARTFORD
Syn.: Agudas Achim (O), 1244 N. Main St., W. Hartford, 06117; Beth David (O), 20 Dover Rd., W. Hartford, 06119; Chabad House of Greater Hartford (O), 798 Farmington Av., W. Hartford, 06119; Teferes Israel (O), 27 Brown St., Bloomfield, 06002; United Synagogue of Greater Hartford, (O), 840 N. Main St., W. Hartford, 06117; Young Israel of Hartford (O), 1137 Troutbrook Dr., W. Hartford, 06119; Young Israel of West Hartford (O), 2240 Albany Av., W. Hartford, 06117; Beth El (C), 2626 Albany Av., W. Hartford 06117; Beth Tefilah (C), 465 Oak St., E. Hartford, 06118; B'nai Sholom (C), 26 Church St., Newington, 06111; Temple Emanuel (C), 160 Mohegan Dr., W. Hartford, 06117; Beth Israel (R), 701 Farmington Av., W. Hartford, 06119; Temple Sinai (R), 41 W. Hartford Rd., Newington, 06011.
Mikva: 61 N. Main St., W. Hartford, 06119.

Greater Hartford Jewish Fed., 333 Bloomfield Av., W. Hartford, 06117. Tel. (203) 232 4483.
Com. Centre: 335 Bloomfield Av., W. Hartford, 06117.
Hebrew Academy, 53 Gabb Rd., Bloomfield, 06002.
Bookshop: Israel Gift Shop/Hebrew Book Store, 262 S. Whitney St., 06105. Tel. (203) 232-3984.
For kosher meal & Shabbat arrangements, contact Chabad Hse. above.

MANCHESTER

Syn.: Temple Beth Sholom (C), 400 Middle Turnpike E., 06040.

MERIDEN

Syn.: B'nai Abraham (C), 127 E. Main St., 06450.

MIDDLETOWN

Syn.: Adath Israel (C), 48 Church St., 06457.

NEW BRITAIN

Syn.: Tephereth Israel (O), 76 Winter St., 06051; B'nai Israel (C), 265 W. Main St., 06051.

NEW HAVEN

Syn.: Beth-Hamedrosh Westville (O), 74 West Prospect St., 06515; Bikur Cholim Sheveth Achim (O), 278 Winthrop Av., 06511; Cong. Beth Israel (O), 232 Orchard St.; Young Israel of New Haven (O), 292 Norton St., 06511; Beth-El Keser Israel (C), 85 Harrison St., 06515.
Mikva: 86 Hubinger St. Tel. (203) 387-2184.
Com. Center, 360 Amity Rd., Woodbridge Ct. 06525. Tel. (203) 387-2522.
Jewish Fed. of New Haven, 360 Amity Rd., Woodbridge Ct. 06525. Tel. (203) 387-2424.
Jewish Historical Society of New Haven, 1 Long Wharf, New Haven, 06511. Tel. (203) 787-3183.
Yale University has a large collection of Judaica, housed in the Sterling Memorial Library. Tel. (203) 432-2798.
Kosher Snacks and Delicatessen: M & T Kosher Delicatessen, 1150 Whalley Av., 06515; Zackey's, 1304 Whalley Av., 06515.
Kosher meals available at Young Israel House, Yale University, 305 Crown St., if ordered in advance. Tel. (203) 432-1890.

NEW LONDON

Syn.: Ahavath Chesed (O), 590 Montauk Av., 06320; Cong. Beth El (C), 660 Ocean Av., 06320.

NORWALK

Syn.: Beth Israel (O), 40 King St., 06851; Beth El (C), 109 E. Av., 06851. This synagogue contains a number of religious frescoes painted by Raymond Katz; Temple Shalom (R), Richards Av., 06850.
Jewish Fed. of Greater Norwalk: Shorehaven Rd., E. Norwalk, 06855. Tel. (203) 853-3440.

NORWICH

Syn.: Brothers of Joseph (O), Broad & Washington Avs., 06360. Mikva attached; Beth Jacob (C), 400 New London Turnpike, 06360.

ORANGE

Syn.: Or Shalom (C), 205 Old Grassy Hill Rd., 06477; Temple Emanuel (R), 150 Derby Av., 06477.

STAMFORD

Syn.: Agudath Shalom (O), 301 Strawberry Hill Av., 06902; Young Israel of Stamford (O), 69 Oaklawn Av., 06905; Beth El (C), 350 Roxbury Rd., 06902; Temple Sinai (R), 434 Lakeside Dr., 06903.
United Jewish Fed., 1035 Newfield Av., 06905. Tel. (203) 322-6935.
Kosher Delicatessen: Nosherye, JCC Bldg., 1035 Newfield Av., 06905.

WALLINGFORD

Syn.: Beth Israel Cong. (C), 22 N. Orchard St.

WATERBURY

Syn.: Beth El (C), 359 Cooke St., 06710; Temple Israel (R), 100 Williamson Dr., 06710.
Jewish Fed. of Waterbury, 1020 Country Club Rd., 06708. Tel. (203) 758-2441.

WEST HAVEN

Syn.: Sinai (C), 426 Washington Av, 06517.

WESTPORT

Syn.: Temple Israel (R), 14 Coleytown Rd., 06880.

WILLIMANTIC

Syn.: B'nai Israel (C), 327 Jackson St., 06226.

WOODBRIDGE

Syn.: B'nai Jacob (C), 75 Rimmon Rd., 06525. Tel. 389 2111.

DELAWARE

DOVER

Syn.: Cong. Beth Sholom of Dover, P.O. Box 223, Dover, DE 19903.

NEWARK

Syn.: Temple Beth El, 101 Possum Pk. Rd., Newark De19711.

WILMINGTON

Syn.: Adas Kodesh Shel Emeth (O), Washington Blvd. & Torah Dr., 19802; Beth Shalom (C), 18th St. and Baynard Blvd., 19802; Beth Emeth (R), 300 W. Lea Blvd., 19802.
Jewish Com Center, 101 Garden of Eden Road. Wilmington, DE 19803 Tel. (302) 478-6200.

DISTRICT OF COLUMBIA

WASHINGTON

Syn.: Beth Sholom (O), 13th St. & Eastern Av. N.W., 20012; Kesher Israel (O), 2801 "N" St. N.W., 20007. Tel. 333-4808; Ohev Sholom Talmud Torah (O), 1600 Jonquil St. N.W., 20012; Adas Israel (C), 2850 Quebec St. N.W., 20008; Tifereth Israel (C), 7701 16th St. N.W., 20012; Temple Micah (R), 600 "M" St. S.W., 20024; Temple Sinai (R), 3100 Military Rd. N.W., 20015; Washington Hebrew Cong. (R), 3935 Macomb St. N.W., 20016.
Rabbinical Council of Greater Washington, 7826 Eastern Av. N.W., 20012 will provide inf. about kashrut.
For details of the Eruv in Georgetown area, call 338-ERUV.

Communal & Cultural Organisations

Jewish Com. Council of Greater Washington, 1522 "K" St. N.W., 20005. Tel. (202) 347-4628. Fax (202) 737-3257. Publishes a Directory of Jewish Organisations in Greater Washington.

American Israel Public Affairs Committee, Suite 412, 500 N. Capitol St. N.W., 20001.

A memorial to Oscar S. Straus, the first Jew to serve in the U.S. Cabinet, is in front of the Commerce Dept. Bldg., 1st St. & Constitution Av.

The Samuel Gomperts Memorial, corner 10th St. & Massachusetts Av. of the American Federation of Labour. He was English-born.

George Washington University B'nai B'rith Hillel Foundation, 2300 "H" St., 20037. Tel. (202) 296-8873. The building also houses a strictly kosher restaurant under the supervision of the Rabbinical Council of Greater Washington: Garden of Eat'n.

Hirshhorn Museum & Sculpture garden, Independence Av. & 8th St. S.W. Joseph Hirshhorn, a Jewish immigrant from Latvia, donated his collection of modern art to the American people. The museum contains more than 4,000 paintings and 2,000 pieces of sculpture.

Jewish Historical Society of Greater Washington, 701 3rd St. N.W., 20001-2624. Tel. (202) 789-0900. Maintains the Lillian & Albert Small Jewish Museum, 3rd & "G" Sts. N.W., 20008. Housed in Washington's oldest synagogue building, Adas Israel, built 1876.

Jewish War Veterans, USA National Memorial 1811 R. St. N.W, 20009. Tel. (202) 265-6280.

The Library of Congress has a large collection of Judaica.

The Natural History Building of the Smithsonian Institute, 10th & Constitution Avs. N.W., 20001, contains a collection of Jewish ritual articles.

The National Portrait Gallery, "F" St. between 7th & 8th Sts., houses more than 100,000 portraits, including Albert Einstein, Mrs. Golda Meir and George Gershwin.

The National Archives, Pennsylvania Av. at 8th St. N.W., contain historical Jewish documents.

The Isaac Polack Building, 2109 Pennsylvania Av. N.W., built in 1796, was the home of the first Jew to settle in Washington.

In the John F. Kennedy Centre, 2700 "F" St. N.W., is an Israeli lounge donated by the people of Israel.

B'nai B'rith Museum, Klutznick Exhibit Hall, 1640 Rhode Island Av. N.W., 20036. There is a bookshop on the premises.

United States Holocaust Memorial Museum. Details from 2000L Street NW, #717, DC 20036-4907. Tel. (202) 822-6464.

Newspaper: "The Jewish Week", 1910 "K" St. N.W., 20006.

Israel Embassy, 3514 International Dr. N.W., 20008.

Restaurants:
Hunan Deli, 2300 "H" St., NW: Wednesday Evening Dinner, Lunch Mon-Friday 202-833-1018.

Hunan Garden, 7081 Brookfield Plaza, Springfield Va 703-451-1960.

Hunan Gourmet, 350 Fortune Terrace (7 Locks Plaza), Potomac Md 301-424-0192.

Nuthouse, 11419 Georgia Av., Wheaton Md. 20901. Tel. (301) 942-5900.

Royal Dragon 4840 Boiling Brook, Parkway Rockville Md 301-468-1922.

Wooden Shoe Bakery, Silver Springs. 301-942-9330.

Shalom Meat Market, 2307 University Blvd West, Silver Spring. MD 301-946-6500.

Shaul & Hershel Meat Market, Silver Spring. 301-949-8477 (Delivers to G W Hillel every Wednesday).
Katz Supermarket, 4860 Boiling Brook Parkway, Rockville Md 301-468-0400.
Wasseman & Lemberger, 610 Reistertown Rd., Baltimore, MD 301-486-4191 (Will Deliver to DC on Monday).
Nut House Pizza 301-942-5900.
Posins Bakery & Deli, 5756 Georgia Av., NW 202-726-4424. Bakery is under Conservative Hashgacha.
Potomac Wines and Spirits, 3057 M St., NW WDC (202) 333-2847.
St James Preffered Residence, 950 24th St NW WDC 202-457-0500 (Gives discount to Kesher Israel Guests).
Note: The Greater Washington area includes a number of locations in Maryland and Virginia. See notes at the end of the entries for those States.

FLORIDA
It started with three Sephardic Jews from Louisiana who established businesses in Pensacola in 1763. By 1896 Jewish settlers arrived in the Miami area. The United States entry into WWII dramatically changed Florida. Tourist facilities were converted to accommodate troops. The post war population including the Jewish population, exploded. From fewer than 25,000 Jews in 1940 it grew to a present state population of over 740,000.

BELLE GLADE
Syn.: Temple Beth Sholom (C), 224 N.W. Av. "G", 33430. Tel. 996-3886.

BOCA RATON
Syn.: Boca Raton Syn. (O). 7900 Monyoya Circle 33433 Tel. 394-5732; Congregation Beth Ami (C), 1401 NW 4th Av 33432 Tel. 347-0031; B'nai Torah Congregation (C), S.W.18th St., 33433. Tel. 392-8566.Congregation B'nai Israel (R) 2200 Yamato Rd., 33431. Tel. 241-8118.Young Israel of Boca Raton (O), Las Brisas Clubhouse, Montoya Circle, 22070 Las Brisas Circle FL 33433. Tel. 407-391-3235;
South Palm Beach County Jewish Fed., The Richard and Carole Siemens Jewish Campus of the South Palm Beach County, Jewish Fed., 9901 Donna Klein Blvd., Boca Raton, FL 33428-1788. Tel. (407) 852-3100; Adolph and Rose Levis Jewish Community C., 9801 Donna Klein Blvd., Boca Raton, FL 33428. Tel. (407) 852-3200; Donna Klein Jewish Academy, 9701 Donna Klein Blvd., Boca Raton, FL 33428. Tel. (407) 852-3300; Ruth Rales Jewish Family Service, 21300 Ruth & Baron Coleman Blvd., Boca Raton, FL 33428. Tel. (407) 852-3333; Jewish Association of Res. Care, 9901 Donna Klein Blvd., Boca Raton, FL 33428-1788. Tel. (407) 852-3174.

CAPE CORAL
Syn.: Temple Beth El (R), 2721 Del Prado Blvd., P.O.B. 972, 33904.

CLEARWATER
Syn.: Young Israel of Clearwater (O), 1323 Pierce St., 34616; Beth Shalom (C), 1325 S. Belcher Rd., 34624. Tel. (813) 531-1418; B'nai Israel (R), 1685 S. Belcher Rd., 34624. Tel. (813) 531-5829; Temple Ahavat Shalom (R), 1575 Curlew Rd., Palm Harbor, 34683. Tel. (813) 785-8811.
Golda Meir Center, 302 S. Jupiter Av., 34615. Tel. (813) 461-0222.
Jewish Fed. of Pinellas County, 301 S. Jupiter Av., 34615. Tel. (813) 446-1033.
Kent Jewish Com. Center, 1955 Virginia St., 34623. Tel. (813) 736-1494.

Gulf Coast Jewish Family Service 11401 5 Belcher Rd., Largo 34643. Tel. (813) 541-7441.

DAYTONA BEACH

Syn.: Temple Beth Shalom (R), Wellington Dr., Palm Coast, 3235. Tel. (904) 445-3006; Temple Israel (C), 1400 S. Peninsula Dr., 32018. Tel. (904) 252-3097; Temple Beth El (R), 579 N. Nova Rd., Ormond Beach, 3274. Tel. (904) 677-2484.

Jewish Fed. of Volusia & Flagler Counties, 533 Seabreeze Blvd., Suite 300, 32118. Tel. (904) 255-6260.

DELRAY BEACH

Syn; Anshei Emuna (O), 16189 Carter Rd., 33445. Tel. 499-9229; Temple Anshei Shalom of W. Delray (C), Oriole Jewish Centre, 7099 W. Atlantic Av., 33446. Tel. 495-1300; Temple Emeth (C), 5780 W. Atlantic Av., 33446. Tel. 498-3536; Temple Sinai (R), 2475 W. Atlantic Av., 33445. Tel. 276-6161.

Restaurant: **(K) Mandarin,** 5046 West Atlantic Av., FL 33 484 (Pines Plaza) Tel. (407) 496-6278.

FORT LAUDERDALE AREA

Syn.: Chabad Lubavitch Community Syn. (O), 9791 W. Sample Rd., Coral Springs, 33065. Tel. (305) 344-4855; Cong. Migdal David (O), 8575 W. McNab Rd., Tamarac, 33321. Tel. (305) 726-3583; Syn. of Inverrary Chabad (O), 4561 N. University Dr., Lauderhill, 33351. Tel. (305) 748-1777; Temple Ohel B'nai Raphael (O), 4351 W. Oakland Pk. Blvd., Lauderdale Lakes, 33313. Tel. (305) 733-7684; Young Israel of Deerfield Beach (O), 1880 W. Hillsboro Blvd., Deerfield Beach, 33441. Tel. (305) 421-1367; Young Israel of Hollywood-Fort Lauderdale (O), 3291 Stirling Rd., 33312. Tel. (305) 966-7877; Beth Ahm (C), 9730 Stirling Rd., Hollywood, 33024. Tel. (305) 431-5100; Beth Am (C), 7205 Royal Palm Blvd., Margate, 33063. Tel. (305) 974-8650; Beth Israel (C), 7100 W. Oakland Pk. Blvd., Sunrise, 33313. Tel. (305) 742-4040; Beth Israel of Deerfield Beach (C), 200 S. Century Blvd., Deerfield Beach, 33441. Tel. (305) 421-7060; B'nai Moshe (C), 1434 S.E. 3rd St., Pompano Beach, 33060. Tel. (305) 942-5380; Cong. Beth Hillel of Margate (C), 7640 Margate Blvd., Margate, 33063. Tel. (305) 974-3090; Cong. Beth Tefilah (C), 6435 W. Commercial Blvd., Tamarac, 33319. Tel. (305) 722-7607; Conservative Syn. of Coconut Creek (C), Lyons Plaza, 1447 Lyons Rd., Coconut Creek, 33063. Tel. (305) 975-4666; Hebrew Cong. of Lauderhill (C), 2048 N.W. 49th Av., Lauderhill, 33313. Tel. (305) 733-9560; Tamarac Jewish Centre (C), 9101 N.W. 57th St., Tamarac, 33321. Tel. (305) 721-7660; Temple Sha'aray Tzedek (C), 4099 Pine Island Rd., Sunrise 33321. Tel. (305) 741-0295; Temple Sholom (C), 132 S.E. 11th Av., Pompano Beach, 33060. Tel. (305) 942-6410; Temple Bat Yam (R), 5151 N.E. 14th Ter., 33334. Tel. (305) 928-0410; Temple Bet Chavarim, 10444 W. Atlantic Blvd., Coral Springs, FL 33071. Tel. 475-8045; Temple Bet Tikvah (R) 3000 N. University Dr., Sunrise, FL 33322. Tel. (305) 741-8088; Temple Beth Orr (R), 2151 Riverside Dr., Coral Springs, 33065. Tel. (305) 753-3232; Temple B'nai Shalom of Deerfield Beach (R), Menorah Chapels, 2305 W. Hillsboro Blvd., Deerfield Beach, 33441. Tel. (305) 426-532; Temple Emanu-El (R), 3245 W. Oakland Pk. Blvd., Lauderdale Lakes, 33311. Tel. (305) 731-2310; Temple Kol Ami (R), 8200 Peters Rd., Plantation, 33324. Tel. (305) 472-1988; Ramat Shalom (Reconstructionist), 11301 W. Broward Blvd., Plantation 33325. Tel. (305) 472-3600. Young Israel of Hollywood (O), 3291 Stirling Rd. Tel. (305) 966-7877.

Jewish Fed. of Greater Fort Lauderdale, 8358 W. Oakland Pk. Blvd., 33321. Tel. (305) 748-8400.

Kosher Restaurants: **East Side Kosher Restaurant & Deli,** 6846 W. Atlantic

Blvd., Margate, 33063; David Shai King, 5599 N. University Dr., Lauderhill, 33321. Tel. (305) 572-6522; Kosher Cafe (Victor), 5485 N. University Dr., Lauderhill, 33321. Tel. (305) 572-6522.

FORT PIERCE

Syn.: Temple Beth-El (R), 4600 Oleander Av., 34982. Tel. (407) 461-7428.

HOLLYWOOD & VICINITY

Syn.: B'nai Aviv (C), 200 Bonaventure Blvd., Weston; B'nai Sephardim (Seph), 3670 Stirling Rd., Ft. Lauderdale; Century Pines Jewish Center (C), 13400 S.W. 10 St., Pembroke Pines; Chabad Ocean Syn. (O), 4000 S. Ocean Dr., Hallandale; Chabad of Southwest Broward (L), 11251 Taft St., Pembroke Pines; Congregation Ahavat Shalom (O), 315 Madison St., Hollywood; Cong. Levi Yitzchok-Lubavitch (L), 1295 E. Hallandale Beach Blvd., Hallandale; Hallandale Jewish Center (C), 416 N.E. 8 Av., Hallandale; Hollywood Community Syn. (L), 4441-51 Sheridan St., Hollywood; Temple Adath Or (New Age), 11450 S.W. 16 St., Davie; Temple Beth Ahm Israel (C), 9730 Stirling Rd., Hollywood; Temple Beth El (R), 1351 S. 14 Av., Hollywood; Temple Beth Emet (R), 10801 Pembroke Rd., Pembroke Pines; Temple Beth Shalom (C), 1400 N. 46 Av., Hollywood; Temple Judea of Carriage Hills (C), 6734 Stirling Rd., Hollywood; Temple Sinai (C), 1201 Johnson St., Hollywood; Temple Solel (R), 5100 Sheridan St., Hollywood; Young Israel of Hollywood/Ft. Lauderdale (O), 3291 Stirling Rd., Ft. Lauderdale; Young Israel of Pembroke Pines (O), 13400 S.W. 10 St., Pembroke Pines.

Jewish Fed. of South Broward 2719 Hollywood Blvd., Hollywood, FL 33020. Tel. (305) 921-8810.

David Posnack Jewish Community Center, 5850 S. Pine Island Rd., Davie, FL 33328. Tel. (305) 434-0499.

Jewish Family Service of Broward County, 6100 Hollywood Blvd., Suite 410, Hollywood, FL 33024. Tel. (305) 966-0956.

Joseph Meyerhoff Senior Center, 3081 Taft St., Hollywood, FL 33021. Tel. (305) 966-9805.

South Broward Central Agency for Jewish Education, 3081 Taft St., Hollywood, FL33021. Tel. (305) 964-9040.

Newspaper: The Jewish Community Advocate of South Broward, 2719 Hollywood Blvd., Hollywood, FL 33020. Tel. (305) 922-8603.

Restaurants: Pita Plus, 5650 Stirling Rd., Hollywood, FL 33021. Tel. (305) 985-8028; Jerusalem Pizza II, 5650 Stirling Rd., Hollywood, FL 33021. Tel. (305) 964-6811.

JACKSONVILLE

Syn.: Etz Chaim (O), 10167 San Jose Blvd., 32257. Mikva on premises. Tel. (904) 262-3565; Beth Shalom (C), 4072 Sunbeam Rd., 32257. Tel. (904) 268-0404; Jewish Center (C), 3662 Crown Point Rd., 32257. Tel. (904) 292-1000; Cong. Ahavath Chesed (R), 8727 San Jose Blvd, 32217. Tel. (904) 733-7078.

Jacksonville Jewish Fed., 8505 San Jose Blvd., 32217. Tel. (904) 448-5000.

Jewish Community Alliance, 8505 San Jose Blvd., 32217. Tel. (904) 730-2100.

Jewish Family & Community Services, 3601 Cardinal Point Dr., 32257. Tel. (904) 448-1933.

River Garden Hebrew Home for Aged, 11401 Old St. Augustine Rd., 32258. Tel. (904) 260-1818.

Kosher Nutrition Centre, 5846 Mt. Carmel Terr., 32216. Tel. (904) 737-9075.

KEY WEST

Syn.: Cong. B'nai Zion (C), 750 United St., 33040-3251. Rabbi. Louis Dimpson. Tel. (305) 294-3437.

LAKELAND

Syn.: Temple Emanuel (C), 600 Lake Hollingsworth Dr., 33803. Tel. (813) 682-8616.

MIAMI, MIAMI BEACH & VICINITY

South-Eastern Florida, often called the state's Gold Coast, is the only tropical area in the United States, and is visited yearly by millions of tourists, winter as well as summer. Comprising three counties – Dade, Broward & Palm Beach – with several dozen cities, it is actually a megalopolis with 695,000 Jews, the second largest concentration of Jews in the United States after Metropolitan New York. The best known cities in this area are Miami & Miami Beach, in Dade County, whose population of 1,823,000 includes 200,000 Jews. The center of Jewish population in South Florida is shifting northly and is now near Oakland Park Boulevard in Broward County (Fort Lauderdale) with 29% (202,000) of the Jewish population living in Dade County (Miami), 41% (284,000) in Broward County (Hollywood/Fort Lauderdale), and 30% (209,000) in Palm Beach. Currently South Florida is the second largest Jewish community in the United States. Syns. are listed below according to where they are situated. Other institutions are listed after the syns.

Other Gold Coast communities include Boca Raton, Fort Lauderdale, Hallandale, Hollywood, Miramar, Pompano Beach and West Palm Beach.

North Dade County

Syn.: Agudath Achim (O), 19255 N.E. 3rd Av., Miami, 33179; B'nai Sephardim (O), 17495 N.E. 6th Av., N. Miami Beach, 33162; Cong. Ahavas Yisroel-Chabad (O), 21001 Biscayne Blvd., N. Miami Beach, 33180; Sephardic Jewish Centre (O), 17100 N.E. 6th Av., N. Miami Beach, 33162; Shaaray Tefilah (O), 971 N.E. 172nd St., N. Miami Beach, 33162; Young Israel of Greater Miami (O), 990 N.E. 171st St., N. Miami Beach, 33162; Young Israel of Sky Lake (O), 1850 N.E. 183rd St., N. Miami Beach, 33179; Aventura-Turnberry Jewish Center-Beth Jacob, 20400 NE 30th Av., Aventura, 33180; Beth Moshe (C), 2225 N.E. 121st St., N. Miami, 33181; Beth Torah Adath Yeshurun (C), 1051 N. Miami Beach Blvd., N. Miami Beach, 33162; Temple Tifereth Jacob (C), 951 E. 4th Av., Hialeah, 33010; Temple Israel of Greater Miami (R), 137 N.E. 19th St., Miami, 33101; Temple Sinai of N. Dade (R), 18801 N.E. 22nd Av., N. Miami Beach, 33180.

South Dade County

Syn.: Ahavat Shalom (O), 985 S.W. 67th Av., Miami, 33144; B'nai Israel & Greater Miami Youth Syn. (O), 16260 S.W. 288th St., Naranja, 33033; Young Israel of Kendall (O), 7880 S.W. 112th St., 33156; Anshe Emes (C), 2533 S.W. 19th Av., Miami, 33133; Beth David (C), 2625 S.W. 3rd Av., Miami, 33129; Bet Shirah (C), 7500 S.W. 120th St., Miami, 33156; Homestead Jewish Centre (C), 183 N.E. 8th St., Homestead, 33030; Temple Beth Tov (C), 6438 S.W. 8th St., Miami, 33144; Temple Samu-El Or Olom (C), 9353 S.W. 152nd Av., Miami, 33196; Temple Zamora (C), 44 Zamora Av., Coral Gables, 33134; Temple Zion Israelite Centre (C), 8000 Miller Rd., Miami, 33155; Bet Breira (R), 9400 S.W. 87th Av., Miami, 33176; Beth Am (R), 5950 N. Kendall Dr., 33156; Temple Judea (R), 5500 Granada Blvd., Coral Gables, 33146; Temple Shir Ami (R), 7205 SW 125 Av., Miami, 33183; Temple Beth Or (Rec.), 11715 S.W. 87th Av., Miami, 33173; Havurah of S. Florida (non-denominational), 9315 SW 61st Court, Miami, 33156.

Miami Beach

Syn.: Agudath Israel Hebrew Inst. (O), 7801 Carlyle Av., 33141; Beth Israel (O), 770 W. 40th St., 33140; Beth Jacob (O), 311 Washington Av., 33139; Beth

Tfilah (O), 935 Euclid Av., 33139; Beth Yoseph Chaim (O), 843 Meridian Av., 33139; Hebrew Academy (O), 2400 Pine Tree Dr., 33140; Kneseth Israel (O), 1415 Euclid Av., 33139; Lubavitch Cong. (O), 1120 Collins Av., 33139; Mogen David (O), 9348 Harding Av., 33154; Ohev Shalom (O), 7055 Bonita Dr., 33141; Ohr Hachaim (O), 317 47th St., 33140; Shul of Bal Harbour (O), 9445 Harding Av., 33154; Temple Moses (O), 1200 Normandy Dr., 33141; W. Av. Jewish Centre (O), 1140 Alton Rd., 33139; Young Israel of Sunny Isles (O), 17395 N. Bay Rd., 33160; Beth Raphael (C), 1545 Jefferson Av., 33139. This syn. is dedicated to the six million martyrs of the Holocaust. On an outside marble wall, a large six-light menorah burns every night in their memory. Six hundred names, representing each city, have been inscribed on the marble. There is also a notable **Holocaust Memorial** at Dade Av., and Meridian Av.; B'nai Zion Temple (C), 200 178th St., 33160; Cuban Hebrew Cong.-Temple Beth Shmuel (C), 1700 Michigan Av., 33139; Temple Beth El of North Bay Village (C), 7800 Hispanola Av., 33141; Pavilion Hebrew Study Group (C), 5601 Collins Av., 33140; Temple Emanu-El (C), 1701 Washington Av., 33139; Temple Menorah (C), 620 75th St., 33141; Temple Ner-Tamid (C), 7902 Carlyle Av., 33141; Temple Beth Sholom (R), 4144 Chase Av., 33140. Has a beautiful landscaped Biblical Garden containing plants of the Bible, and a year-round art gallery.

Institutions, Organisations & Services
American Jewish Committee: 3000 Biscayne Blvd., 33137.
American Jewish Congress: 420 Lincoln Rd., Suite 601, Miami Beach 33139.
Anti-Defamation League: 150 S.E. Second Av., 33132.
B'nai B'rith: 3107 W. Hallandale Beach Blvd., Suite 105, Hallandale, 33009, Miami. Tel. (305) 667-5964.
Central Agency for Jewish Education: 4200 Biscayne Blvd., 33137. There are about 25 Jewish afternoon & week-end schools in the Greater Miami area.
Florida Hillel Council (serving students at all colleges in Florida), University of Miami, 1100 Stanford Dr., 33146.
Greater Miami Jewish Federation, 4200 Biscayne Blvd., 33137. Tel. (305) 576-4000.
Hadassah: 4200 Biscayne Blvd., Miami, 33137 & 300 71 St., Miami Beach, 33140.
Jewish Community Centres: N. Dade, 18900 N.E. 25th Av., N. Miami Beach, 33180; S. Dade, 11155 S.W. 112 Av., Miami, 33176; Miami Beach Branch, 4221 Pine Tree Dr., Miami Beach, 33140; Senior Adult Centre, 610 Espanola Way, Miami Beach, 33139.
Jewish Family Service: 1790 S.W. 27th Av., 33145.
Jewish Home for Aged: 151 N.E. 52nd St., 33137.
Jewish Library of Greater Miami: 3950 Biscayne Blvd., 33137.
Jewish National Fund: 420 Lincoln Rd., Miami Beach, 33139.
Jewish Vocational Service: 735 N.E. 125th St., 33161.
Mikva: Daughters of Israel (R), 151 Michigan Av., 33139.
Mount Sinai Hospital: 4300 Alton Rd., Miami Beach, 33140.
Museums: Temple Emanu-El, 1701 Washington Av., Miami Beach, 33139; Temple Israel, 137 N.E. 19th St., Miami, 33132.
National Council of Jewish Women: 12944 W. Dixie Highway, N. Miami, 33161.
Women's American ORT: 2101 Hallandale Beach Blvd., 33009.
Most national Jewish orgs. have branches in the Greater Miami area.

Kosher Hotels
Caribbean Hotel, 3737 Collins Av., 33140, and Crown Hotel, 4041 Collins Av., 33140, are under the supervision of the Union of Orthodox Jewish Congregations of America.

The following hotels are under local kashrut supervision: Casablanca Hotel, 6345 Collins Av., 33141; Royal Palm Hotel, 1545 Collins Av., 33139; Saxony, 3201 Collins Av., 33140; Sans Souci Hotel, 31st St., & Collins Av., 33140; Shore Club, 1901 Collins Av., 33139; Tarleton, 2469 Collins Av., 33139.

Some of the above hotels are open all year round. The others close for varying lengths of time between the end of Pesach and November 20.

Some other leading Miami hotels are: Alexander, 5225 Collins Av., 33140; Carriage House, 5401 Collins Av., 33140; Doral, 4833 Collins Av., 33140; Eden Roc, 4525 Collins Av., 33140; Fontainebleau-Hilton, 4441 Collins Av., 33140; Harbor House Hotel Apartments, 10275 Collins Av., 33154; Marco Polo, 19201 Collins Av., 33160; Sea View, 9909 Collins Av., 33154; Shawnee Miami Beach Resort, 4343 Collins Av., 33140; Sheraton Bal Harbor, 9701 Collins Av., 33154.

Kosher Restaurants
The following restaurants are under local kashrut supervision: Bagel Factory, 1427 Alton Rd., Miami Beach, 33139. Embassy 41, 534 41st St., Miami Beach, 33140; Embassy Peking Tower Suite, 4101 Pine Tree Dr., Miami Beach, 33140; Guisseppe Goldberg's Glatt Kosher Italian Ristorante, Sans Souci Resort Hotel, 31st St. & Collins Av., 33140; Hamifgash Israeli Restaurant, 17044 W. Dixie Highway, N. Miami Beach, 33160; Jerusalem Peking, 4299 Collins Av., Miami Beach, 33140; Jerusalem Pizza, 761 N. E. 167th St., N. Miami Beach, 33162; Ozzie's Dairy Snack Shop, 1901 Collins Av., Miami Beach, 33139; Pita Plus, 20103 Biscayne Blvd., N. Miami Beach, 33180; Pub Hzrif, 240 Sunny Isles Blvd., N. Miami Beach, 33160; Royal Hungarian, 3425 Collins Av., Miami Beach, 33140; Sarah's Kosher Pizza & Dairy Cafeteria, 2214 NE 123 St., N. Miami and 1127 NE 163 St., N. Miami Beach; Shalom, Haifa, 1330 NE 163 St., N. Miami Beach, 33162; Shalom Terrace Restaurant, 16690 Collins Av., N. Miami Beach, 33162; South Beach Pita, 1448 Washington Av., Miami Beach, 33139; Zigi's Yogurt Shop, 744 41st St., Miami Beach, 33141.

Visitors requiring further information about kosher meals & Shabbat accom. should contact Dr. Jerry Berman, 1250 N. E. 172 St., N. Miami Beach, 33162. Tel. (305) 651-3531.

A printed booklet 'South Florida guide to kosher living', listing all kosher hotels, restaurants, bakeries, butchers, bookstores, nursing homes, etc. in Dade, Broward and Palm Beach Counties is available from: Information and Referral Service, Greater Miami Jewish Federation, 4200 Biscayne Blvd., Miami, FL 33137. Tel. (305) 576-4000.

ORLANDO

Syn.: Chabad Hse. (O), 1035 E. Semoran Blvd., Summit Plaza, Casselberry, 32707. Tel. (407) 332-7906; Cong. Beth Shalom (C), 13th & Center Sts., Leesburg, 32748. Tel. (904) 742-0238 or 787-3946; Cong. Ohev Shalom (C), 5015 Goddard Av., 32804. Tel. (407) 298-4650; Kissimmee Jewish Community (C), 713 Wood La. E., Kissimmee, 32758. Tel. (813) 427-0059; Temple Israel (C), 4917 Eli St., 32804. Tel. (407) 647-3055; Williamsburg Jewish Cong. (C), 5121 Gateway Av., 32821. Tel. (407) 351-1745; Cong. of Liberal Judaism (R), 928 Malone Dr., 32810. Tel. (407) 645-0444; Cong. Shalom (R), 6349 Oak Meadow Bend, 32801. Tel. (407) 351-9491.

Jewish Fed. of Greater Orlando, 851 N. Maitland Av., Maitland FL 32751, P.O.B. 1508, Maitland FL 32794-1508 Tel. (407) 645-5933.

Kosher Restaurants: Palm Terrace, Hyatt Orlando, 6375 W. Space Coast Pkwy., Kissimmee, 32741. Tel. (407) 396-1234.

Kosher Meat & Delicatessen: Amira's, 1351 E. Altamonte Dr., Altamonte Springs, 32701. Tel. (407) 767-7577.

Delicatessen, Meat: Superior, 677 N. Orlando Av., Maitland, 32751. Tel. (305) 645-1704.

(K) 172 Oxford Rd., Fern Park, FL. 32730. Tel. (407) 834-4335.

Kosher meals can be obtained at a number of the restaurants in Disney World. Inf. from Disney World.

PALM CITY

Syn.: Treasure Coast Jewish Center-Cong. Beth Abraham (C), 3998 S.W. Leighton Farms Av., 34990. Tel. 287-8833.

PENSACOLA

Syn.: B'nai Israel (C), 1829 N. 9th Av., 32503; Beth El (R), 800 N. Palafox St., 32501.

PORT ST. LUCIE

Syn.: Cong. Beth Israel (R), P.O. Box 7146, Fl. 34935. Tel. (407) 879-1879.

ROCKLEDGE

Jewish Federation of Brevard, 108A Barton Av., 32955. Tel. (407) 636-1824.

ST. AUGUSTINE

Syn.: First Sons of Israel (O), 161 Cordova St., 32084.

ST. PETERSBURG

Syn.: Beth Chai (C); Beth Shalom (C), 1844 54th St. S., 33707; B'nai Israel (C), 301 59th St. N., 33710; Beth-El (R), 400 Pasadena Av. S., 33707. Tel. (813) 347-6136.

J. Com. Center: 5001 Duhme Rd., Madeira Beach, 33708. Tel. (813) 392-3424.

Menorah Center, 250 58th St. N., 33710.

Jo-El's Specialty Foods, 2619 23rd Av. N., 33713. Tel. 321-3847. Under rabbinical supervision.

SARASOTA

Syn.: Beth Sholom (C), 1050 S. Tuttle Av., 34237. Tel. (813) 955-8121; Chabad Lubavitch of Sarasota & Manatee Counties, 7119 S. Tamiami Tr., Suite L, 34231. Tel. (813) 925-0770; Temple Emanu-El (R), 151 S. McIntosh Rd., 34232. Tel. (813) 371-2788; Temple Beth El, 2209 – 75th St. W. Bradenton 34209. Tel. (813) 792-0870; Temple Beth El/North Port (C), P.O. Box 7195, North Port 34287. Tel. (813) 426-1108 or 426-4854; Temple Beth Israel (R), 567 Bay Isles Rd., Longboat Key, 34228. Tel. (813) 383-3428; Venice Jewish Community Center, P.O. Box 62, Venice 34284. Tel. (813) 484-2022.

Sarasota-Manatee Jewish Fed., 580 S. McIntosh Rd., 34232. Tel. (813) 371-4546.

SURFSIDE

Syn.: The Shul, 9540 Collins Av., 33154. Tel. (305) 868 1411. The Shul of Bal Harbor, Bay Harbor & Surfside.

TAMPA

Syn.: Bais Tefilah (O), 3418 Handy Rd., 33618. Tel. (813) 968 8372. Orthodox pre-school on premises. Hebrew Academy (O), 14908 Penington Rd., 33624. Tel. (813) 963-0706; Young Israel of Tampa (O), 3721 W. Tacon St., 33629. Tel. (813) 832-3018; Kol Ami (C), 3919 Moran Rd., 33618. Tel. (813) 962-6338; Rodeph Sholom (C), 2711 Bayshore Blvd., 33629. Tel. (813) 837-1911; Temple David (C), 2001 Swann Av., 33606. Tel. (813) 254-1771; Schaarai Zedek (R), 3303 Swann Av., 33609. Tel. (813) 254-1771.

VERO BEACH

Syn.: Temple Beth Shalom (R), 365 43rd Av., 32968. Tel. (407) 569-4700.

WEST PALM BEACH & VICINITY

Syns.: Chabad House, (O) 5335, N. Military Trail, W. Palm Beach, Fl 33407. Tel. (407) 640-8111. Aitz Chaim (O), 2518 N. Haverhill Rd., W. Palm Beach 33417. Tel. (407) 686-5055; Boynton Beach Jewish Centre-Beth Kodesh (C), 501 N.E. 26th Av., Boynton Beach, 33435. Tel. (407) 586-9428; Cong. Anshei Sholom (C), 5348 Grove St., W. Palm Beach, 33417. Tel. (407) 684-3212; Golden Lakes Temple (C), 1470 Golden Lakes Blvd., W. Palm Beach, 33411. Tel. (407) 689-9430; Beth Tikvah; Lake Worth Jewish Centre (C), 4550 Jog Rd., Lake Worth, 33463. Tel. (407) 967-3600; Temple Beth David (C), 4657 Hood Rd., Palm Beach Gardens, 33418. Tel. (407) 694-2350; Temple Beth El (C), 2815 N. Flagler Dr., W. Palm Beach, 33407. Tel. (407) 833-0339; Temple Beth Sholom (C), 224 N.W. Avenue 'G' Belle Glade, 33430. Tel. (407) 996-3886; Temple Beth Zion (C), 129 Sparrow Dr., Royal Palm Beach, 33411. Tel. (407) 798-8888; Temple B'nai Jacob (C), 2177 S. Congress Av., W. Palm Beach, 33406. Tel. (407) 433-5957; Temple Emanu-El (C), 190 N. County Rd., Palm Beach, 33480. Tel. (407) 832-0804; Temple Torah (C), 9776D, S. Military Trail, Boynton Beach, 33436. Tel. (407) 369-1112; Reform Temple of Boynton Beach (R), P.O. Box 3791 Boynton Beach, 33424. Tel. (407) 738-5068; Temple Beth Am (R), 759 Parkway St., Jupiter 33458. Tel. (407) 747-1109; Temple Beth Torah (R), 900 Big Blue Trace, W. Palm Beach, 33414. Tel. (407) 793-2700; Temple Israel (R), 1901 N. Flagler Dr., W. Palm Beach, 33407. Tel. (407) 833-8421; Temple Judea (R), 100 Chillingworth Dr., W. Palm Beach, 33401. Tel. (407) 471-1526.

Jewish Com. Centre of the Palm Beaches, 3151 N. Military Trail, 33409. Tel. (407) 689-7700.

Jewish Federation of Palm Beach County, 4601 Community Dr., W. Palm Beach, FL 33417. Tel. (407) (407) 478-0700.

Jewish Family & Children's Service, 4605 Community Dr., W. Palm Beach, FL 33417. Tel. (407) (407) 684-1991.

Commission for Jewish Education, 4603 Community Dr., W. Palm Beach, FL 33417. Tel. (407) 640-0700.

Jewish Com. Day School of Palm Beach County, 5801 Parker Av., 33405. Tel. (407) 585-2227.

GEORGIA

ATHENS

Syn.: Cong. Children of Israel (R), Dudley Dr., 30606. Tel. (404) 549-4192.

ATLANTA

Syn.: Anshe S'fard (O), 1324 Northland Av., 30306. Tel. (404) 325-8318; Beth Jacob (O), 1855 La Vista Rd., 30329. Tel. (404) 633-0551. Mikva on premises; Beth Tefillah (Observant), 5065 Highpoint Rd., 30342. Tel. (404) 843-2464; B'nai Torah (Traditional), 700 Mt. Vernon Highway, 30328. Tel. (404) 257-0537. Mikva on premises; Cong. Or Ve Shalom (Traditional, Sephardi), 1681 N. Druid Hills Rd., 30319. Tel. (404) 633-1737; Shearith Israel (Traditional), 1180 University Dr., 30306. Tel. (404) 873-1743; Ahavath Achim (C), 600 Peachtree Battle Av., 30327. Tel. (404) 355-5222; Beth Shalom (C), 5303 Winters Chapel Rd., 30360 Tel. (404) 399-5300; Etz Chaim (C), 1190 Indian Hills Pkwy., Marietta, 30067. Tel. (404) 973-0137; Beth David (R), 1885 McGee Rd., Snellville, 30278. Tel. (404) 978-3916; Beth Tikvah (R), PO Box 1425, Roswell, 30077. Tel. (404) 642-0434; B'nai Israel

(R), PO Box 383, Riverdale, 30274. Tel. (404) 471-3586; Kehillat Chaim Cong. (R), 10200 Woodstock Rd., Roswell, 30075. Tel. (404) 641-8630; Temple Emanu-El (R), 1580 Spalding Dr., Dunwoody, 30338. Tel. (404) 395-1340; Kol Emeth (R), 2509 Post Oak Tritt, Marietta, 30066. Tel. (404) 973-3533; Temple Sinai (R), 5645 Dupree Dr., 30327. Tel. (404) 252-3073; The Temple (R), 1589 Peachtree Rd. N.W., 30367. Tel. (404) 873-1731. (The sanctuary is designed along the lines of the Biblical Temple.) Ner Hamizrach (Iranian) (service held at Beth Jacob Syn.) Tel. (404 636-2473; Chabad Centre, 5060 Highpoint Rd., 30342. Tel. (404) 843-2464.

Com. Centre: 1745 Peachtree Rd., 30309. Tel. (404) 875-7881. Zaban branch, 5342 Tilly Mill Rd., Dunwoody, 30338. Tel. (404) 396-3250. 2509 Post Oak Tritt, Marietta 30062. Tel. (404) 971-8901.

Jewish Fed., 1753 Peachtree Rd., 30309. Tel. (404) 873-1661.

Zachor Holocaust Centre, 1745 Peachtree Rd., 30309. Tel. (404) 873-1661.

Emory Hillel House, 1531 Clifton Rd., 30329. Tel. (404) 634-6664; Hillel Atlanta (Federation), Drawer 'A', Emory University, 30322. Tel. (404) 727-6490.

Israel Consulate; 1100 Spring St., Suite 440, 30309. Tel. (404) 875-7851.

Kosher Restaurant & Meat: Arthur's, 2166 Briarcliff Rd., 30329. Tel. (404) 634-6881; Quality Kosher, 2161 Briarcliff Rd., 30329. Tel. (404) 636-1114.

Visitors requiring kosher & Shomer Shabbat bed & breakfast accom. should contact Bed & Breakfast Atlanta, 1801 Piedmont Av. (Suite 208), 30324. Tel. (404) 875-0525. Fax (404) 875-9672.

AUGUSTA

Syn.: Adas Yeshuron (O), 935 Johns Rd., Walton Way, 30904.

Jewish Fed., P.O.B. 3251, Sibley Rd., 30904. Tel. (404) 736-1818.

Delicatessen: Strauss, 965 Broad St., 30902; Sunshine Bakery, 1209 Broad St., 30902; Parti-Pal, Daniel Village, 30904.

COLUMBUS

Syn.: Shearith Israel (C), 2550 Wynnton Rd., 31906; Temple Israel (R), 1617 Wildwood Av., 31906.

MACON

Syn.: Sherah Israel (C), 1st & Plum Sts., 31201; Beth Israel (R), 892 Cherry St., 31201.

Delicatessen: Yellins, 566 Cotten St., 31201.

SAVANNAH

Syn.: B'nai B'rith Jacob (O), 5444 Abercorn St., 31405; Agudath Achim (C), 9 Lee Blvd., 31405; Mickve Israel (R), Bull & Gordon Sts., 31401. (This is the oldest synagogue in Georgia, having been founded before 1790.)

Jewish Fed., 5111 Abercorn St., 31405. Tel. (912) 355-8111. The Com. Centre is in the same building.

One of the oldest Jewish cemeteries in North America is to be found in Savannah.

Delicatessen: Allan Gottlieb's Delicatessen, 5500 Abercorn Expressway, 31405. Strictly kosher.

Visitors requiring inf. about kashrut, temporary accommodation, etc., should contact Rabbi Avigdor Slatus, 5444 Abercorn St., 31405.

HAWAII

HILO
Syn.: Temple Beth Aloha (unaffiliated), P.O.B. 1538, 96720. Tel. (808) 969-4153.

HONOLULU
Syn.: Chabad of Hawai (O), 4851 Kahala Av. Tel. (808) 735-8161; Cong. Sof Ma'arav (C), 2500 Pali Highway, 96817. Tel. (808) 373-1331 or 923-5726; Temple Emanu-El (R & Trad.), 2550 Pali Highway, 96817. Tel. (808) 595-7521.
Jewish Fed. of Hawaii, 677 Ala Moana, Suite 803, 96813. Tel. (808) 531-4634.
Kosher food available at Foodland Supermarket Beretania, cnr. Kalakana; and, 'Down to Earth' on King's St. nr. University Av.
Bed & Breakfast, 3242 Kaohinani Dr., 96817. Tel. (808) 595-7533. Fax (808) 595-2030. Contact Mary Lee Bridges.

KONA
Syn.: Kona Beth Shalom (R), Kailua-Kona. Tel. 322-9144.

MAUI
Syn.: Maui Cong. Tel. (808) 669-7695.

PEARL HARBOR
There are combined military-civilian congs. in Pearl Harbor, on the island of Guam and on Kwajalein Atoll. Details from the Jewish Chaplain at Pearl Harbor, c/o Aloha Jewish Chapel (Military), Makalapa Gate. Tel. 471-0050.

WAIKIKI
Syn.: Chabad, Park Plaza, 1956 Ala Moana Blvd. Tel. 734-0457.

IDAHO

BOISE
Syn.: Ahavath-Beth Israel (C), 1102 State St., 83702.

ILLINOIS

CHAMPAIGN-URBANA
Syn.: Sinai Temple (R), 3104 Windsor Rd., Champaign, 61821. Tel. (217) 352-8140.
Champaign-Urbana Jewish Fed., 503 E. John St., Champaign, 61820. Tel. (217) 367-9872.

CHICAGO
Note. This entry also includes Evanston, Glencoe, Skokie, Wilmette, Highland Park, and Lincolnwood. They are all part of Greater Chicago, which has a Jewish population of some 250,000.
Syn.: Adas B'nai Israel (O), 6200 N. Kimball Av., 60659; Adas Yeschurun (O), 2949 W. Touhy Av., 60645; Anshe Mizrach (O), 627 W. Patterson Av., 60613; Anshe Motele (O), 6520 N. California Av., 60645; Anshe Sholom B'nai Israel (O), 540 W. Melrose Av., 60657; Beth Itzchok of West Rogers Park (O), 6716 N. Whipple St., 60645; Beth Sholom Ahavas Achim (O), 5665 N. Jersey St., 60659; Bnei Ruven (O), 6350 N. Whipple St., 60659; Chabad Hse. (O), 2014 Orrington Av., Evanston, 60201; Chesed L'Avrohom Nachlas David (O), 6342 N. Troy St., 60659; Chevro Kadiso Machzikai Hadas (O), 2040 W. Devon Av.; Cong. Yehuda Moshe (O), 4721 W. Touhy

Av., Lincolnwood, 60646; Persian/Iran Hebrew Cong. (O), 3820 Main St., Skokie, 60076; Sephardic Congregation (O), 1819 W. Howard St., Evanston, 60202; Kehilath Jacob Beth Samuel (O), 3701 W. Devon Av., 60659; Lev Someach (O), 5555 N. Bernard St., 60625; Mishne Ugmoro (O), 6045 N. California Av., 60659; Or Torah, (O), 3738 W. Dempster St., Skokie, 60076; Poalie Zedek West Rogers Park (O), 2801 W. Albion St., 60645; Shaarei Torah Anshei Maariv (O), 2756 W. Morse Av., 60645; Warsaw Bikur Cholim (O), 3541 W. Peterson Av., 60659; A.G. Beth Israel (Traditional), 3635 W. Devon Av., 60659; Agudas Achim-Bickur Cholim (Trad.) 8927 S. Houston Av., 60617; Agudath Jacob (Traditional), 633 Howard St., Evanston, 60202; Beth Sholom of Rogers Park (Traditional), 1233 W. Pratt Blvd., 60626; B'nai Shalom (Traditional), 701 Aptakisic Rd., Buffalo Grove, 60090; Chicago Loop Syn. (Traditional), 16 S. Clark St., 60603; Ezras Israel (Traditional), 7001 N. California Av., 60645; K. I. N. S. of West Rogers Park (Traditional), 2800 W. North Shore Av., 60645; Lake Shore Drive Syn. (Traditional), 70 E. Elm St., 60611; Lawn Manor-Beth Jacob (Traditional), 6601 S. Kedzie St., 60629; Lincolnwood Jewish Cong. (Traditional), 7117 N. Crawford Av., Lincolnwood, 60646; Mikro Kodesh Anshe Tiktin (Traditional), 2832 W. Foster Av., 60625; Or Chodash (Traditional), 2356 Hassel Rd., Hoffman Estates, 60195; Skokie Central Traditional Cong. (Traditional), 4040 Main St., Skokie, 60076; Skokie Valley Traditional Syn. (Traditional), 8825 E. Prairie Rd., Skokie, 60076. (Traditional syns. use the Orthodox prayer book, but there is no mechitza, and men and women sit together at services.) Agudas Achim N. Shore Cong. (C), 5029 N. Kenmore Av., 60640; Am Echad (C), 160 Westwood Dr., Park Forest, 60466; Am Yisrael (C), 4 Happ Rd., Northfield, 60093; Anshe Emet (C), 3760 N. Pine Gr., 60613; Beth Hillel Cong. of Wilmette (C), 3220 Big Tree Lane, Wilmette, 60091; Beth Judea of Buffalo Grove (C), P.O. Box 62, Buffalo Grove, 60092; Beth Shalom Cong. of Northbrook (C), 3433 Walters Av., Northbrook, 60062; B'nai Emunah (C), 9131 Niles Centre Rd., Skokie, 60076; B'nai Israel Cong. of Proviso (C), 10216 Kitchener St., Westchester, 60153; B'nai Jacob Cong. of West Rogers Park (C), 6200 N. Artesian St., 60659; B'nai Tikvah (C), 795 Wilmot Rd., Deerfield, 60015; B'nai Zion (C), 6759 N. Greenview Av., 60626; Central Syn. of the South Side Hebrew Cong. (C), 30 E. Cedar St., 60611; Cong. Mishpaha-Our Family (C), Congregation Hse., 760 Checker Dr., Buffalo Grove, 60090; Etz Chaim Cong. of DuPage County (C), 1710 S. Highland Av., Lombard, 60148; Ezra-Habonim (C), 2620 W. Touhy Av., 60645; Ezra Habonim (C), 2095 Landwehr Rd., Northbrook; Kol Emeth (C), 5130 W. Touhy Av., Skokie, 60077; Maine Township Jewish Cong. (C), 8809 Ballard Rd., Des Plaines, 60016; Mikdosh El Hagro Hebrew Centre (C), 303 Dodge St., Evanston, 60202; Moriah Cong. (C), 200 Hyacinth St., Deerfield, 60015; Ner Tamid Cong. of North Town (C), 2754 W. Rosemont Av., 60659; North Sheridan Hebrew Cong. Adath Israel (C), 6301 N. Sheridan Rd., 60660; North Suburban Syn. Beth El (C), 1175 Sheridan Rd., Highland Park, 60035; Northwest Suburban Jewish Cong. (C), 7800 W. Lyons Rd., Morton Grove, 60053; Rodfei Zedek (C), 5200 S. Hyde Pk. Blvd., 60615; Shaare Tikvah (C), 5800 N. Kimball Av., 60659; West Suburban Temple Har-Zion (C), 1040 N. Harlem Av., River Forest, 60305; Am Chai (R), 504 Iverson St., Schaumburg, 60172; Am Shalom (R), 614 Sheridan Rd., Glencoe, 60022; Anshe Shalom (R), 20820 Western Av., Olympia Fields, 60461; Beth El (R), 3050 W. Touhy Av., 60645; Beth El (R), 3610 Dundee Rd., Northbrook; Beth Emet (R), 1224 Dempster St., Evanston, 60202; Beth Israel (R), 3601 Dempster, Skokie, 60076; Beth Sholom (R), 1 Dogwood Av., Park Forest, 60466; Beth Tikvah (R), 300 Hillcrest Blvd., Hoffman Estates, 60172; B'nai Jehoshua Beth Elohim (R), 901 Milwaukee Av., Glenview, 60025; B'nai Torah (R), 2789 Oak St., Highland Park, 60035; B'nai Yehuda (R), 1424 W. 183rd St., Homewood, 60430; Chicago Sinai

Cong. (R), 5350 S. Shore Dr., 60615; Emanuel Cong. (R), 5959 N. Sheridan Rd., 60660; K.A.M. Isaiah Israel Cong. (R), 1100 Hyde Pk. Blvd., 60615; Kol Ami (R), 845 N. Michigan Av., 60611; Lakeside Cong. for Reform Judaism (R), 1221 County Line Rd., Highland Park, 60035; North Shore Cong. Israel (R), 1185 Sheridan Rd., Glencoe, 60022; Oak Park Temple (R), 1235 N. Harlem Av., Oak Park, 60302; Or Shalom (R), 21 Hawthorne Pkwy., Vernon Hills, 60061; Solel Cong. (R), 1301 Clavey Rd., Highland Park, 60035; Temple Jeremiah (R), 937 Happ Rd., Northfield, 60093; Temple Judea Mizpah (R), 8610 Niles Center Rd., Skokie, 60076; Temple Menorah (R), 2800 W. Sherwin St., 60645; Temple Shalom (R), 3480 N. Lake Shore Dr., 60657; Jewish Reconstructionist Cong. (Reconstructionist), 303 Dodge, Evanston, 60202; Niles Township Jewish Cong. (C-Reconstructionist), 4500 Dempster St., Skokie, 60076; Beth Or (Humanist-Reconstructionist), 2075 Deerfield Rd., Deerfield, 60015; Bene Shalom of the Hebrew Assoc. of the Deaf (Independent), 4435 Oakton St., Skokie, 60076; Etz Chaim Cong. of Des Plaines, 335 Bellaire Av., Des Plaines, 60016.

Organisations
B'nai B'rith Council: 9933 N. Lawler St., Skokie, 60076.
Chicago Board of Rabbis (Orthodox, Conservative, Reform, Rec.): 1 S. Franklin St., 60606.
Chicago Mikva Assoc.: 3110 W. Touhy Av., 60645.
Chicago Rabbinical Council (Orthodox): 3525 W. Peterson Av., 60659. Inf. about kashrut and allied matters may be obtained from the Council; also Dinei Tora and Religious Divorces (Gittin).
The Ark, 6450 N. California, 60645, is a privately-run Orthodox org. providing free legal, medical and welfare advice.
Jewish Fed. of Metropolitan Chicago, 1 S. Franklin St., 60606. Tel. (312) 346-6700.
Jewish United Fund of Metropolitan Chicago, 1 S. Franklin St., 60606. Tel. (312) 346-6700.
Com. Centres: Florence G. Heller Centre, 524 W. Melrose Av., 60657; Bernard Horwich Centre, 3003 W. Touhy Av., 60645; Hyde Park Centre, 1100 E. Hyde Park Blvd., 60615; Mayer Kaplan Centre, 5050 W. Church St., Skokie, 60076; North Suburban Centre, 633 Skokie Hwy. #407, Northbrook, 60062; Northwest Suburban Centre, 1250 Radcliffe Rd., Buffalo Gr., 60090; Anita M. Stone Centre, 3400 W. 196th St., Flossmoor, 60422; Russian Jewish Cultural Centre, 3003 W. Touhy Av., 60645.
Hebrew Theological College-Jewish University of America, 7135 N. Carpenter Rd., Skokie, 60076.
Spertus College of Judaica, 618 S. Michigan Av., 60605. The Maurice Spertus Museum of Judaica and the Asher Library are housed at the College. Tel. 922-9012. Fax 922-6406.
Yeshivot: Brisk Yeshiva, 2961 W. Peterson Av., 60659; Telshe Yeshiva (Rabbinical College of Telshe-Chicago Inc.), 3535 W. Foster Av., 60625.
Hebrew Theological College, 7135 Carpenter Rd., Skokie, IL 60077.
Israel Consulate, 111 E. Wacker Dr., 60601.
Booksellers: Chicago Hebrew Book Store, 2942 W. Devon Av., 60645; Hamakor Judaica, 4150 Dempster, Skokie; Rosenblum, 2906 W. Devon Av., 60659; Spertus College Museum Store, 618 S. Michigan Av., 60605.
Kosher Restaurants & Carryouts: Slice of Life (Dairy), 4120 W. Dempster Av., Skokie, 60076; Dunkin' Donuts (Dairy), 3132 W. Devon Av., 60659; Newspapers: The Sentinel, 175 W. Jackson, 1927, 60604; JUF News, 1 Ben Gurion Way; Falafel King (Glatt), 4507 W. Oakton St., Skokie, 60076; Jerusalem Café, 3014 W. Devon Av., 60659; Kosher Gourmet (Glatt), 3553 W. Dempster Av., Skokie, 60076; Kosher Karry (Glatt), 2828 W. Devon Av., 60659; Take-away only La Misada, Hyatt Regency, Glatt 151 E. Wacker Dr.,

Tel. 312/565-1234; Dog-On-It (Glatt) 2748 W. Devon 60659; North Shore Deli (Glatt); Tel Aviv Kosher Pizza & Dairy Restaurant, 6349 N. California Av., 60659; Adis, 2700 W. Pratt, 60645; Kosher City, 3353 Dempster Av., Skokie, 60076; North Shore Deli, 2915 W. Touhy Av., 60645.
Kosher Meat & Delicatessen: Hungarian Kosher Foods, 4020 Oakton St., Skokie, 60076; Kosher Zion Sausage Co., 5511 N. Kedzie Av., 60625; Miller's Meat Market, 2725 W. Devon Av., 60659; New York Kosher Sausage Corp., 2900 W. Devon Av., 60659; Romanian Kosher Sausage Co., 7200 N. Clark St., 60626; Selig's Kosher Delicatessen, 209 Skokie Valley Rd., Crossroads Shopping Centre, Highland Park, 60035; Tel Aviv Kosher Deli & Supermarket, 4956 W. Dempster Av., 60077; Wally's Milk Pail & Deli, 3320 W. Devon (Glatt available) Lincolnwood, IL 60645.

DECATUR

Syn.: B'nai Abraham (R), 1326 West Eldorado St. 62521.

JOLIET

Syn.: 250 N. Midland Av. at Campbell St., 60435.

PEORIA

Syn.: Agudas Achim (O), 3616 N. Sheridan Av., 61604. Tel. (309) 688-4800; Anshai Emeth (R), 5614 N. University St., 61614. Tel. (309) 691-3323.
Jewish Fed., Town Hall Bldg., Junction City 5901 N. Prospect Rd., Peoria, IL 61614. Tel. (309) 689-0063.
Bradley University Hillel, 1410 W. Fredonia, Peoria, IL 61606. Tel. (309) 676-0682.

ROCK ISLAND

Syn.: Tri-City Jewish Centre (C), 2715 30th St., 61201. See also Davenport, Iowa.
Jewish Fed. of the Quad Cities, 224 18th St., Suite 303, 61201.

ROCKFORD

Syn.: Ohave Sholom (C), 3730 Guildford Rd., 61107; Temple Beth El (R), 1203 Comanche Dr., 61107. Tel. (815) 398-5020.
Jewish Fed., 1500 Parkview Av., 61107. Tel. (815) 399-5497.

SPRINGFIELD

Syn.: Temple Israel (C), 1140 West Governor St., 62704; B'rith Sholom (R), 1004 S. 4th St., 62703.
Jewish Fed., 730 E. Vine St., Room 212, 62703. Tel. (217) 528-3446.

INDIANA

EAST CHICAGO

Syn.: B'nai Israel (O), 3517 Hemlock St., 46312; Beth Sholom (C), 4508 Baring Av., 46312.

EVANSVILLE

Syn.: Adath Israel (C), 3600 E. Washington Av., 47715; Washington Av. Tempe (R), 100 Washington Av., 47713.

FORT WAYNE

Syn.: B'nai Jacob (C), 2340 S. Fairfield Av., 46807; Achduth Vesholom (R), 5200 Old Mill Rd., 46807.
Jewish Fed.: 227 E. Washington Blvd., 46802. Tel. (219) 422-8566.

GARY

Syn.: Temple Israel (R), 601 N. Montgomery St., 46403. Tel. (219) 938-5232.

HAMMOND

Syn.: Beth Israel (C), 7105 Hohman Av., 46324; Temple Beth-El (R), 6947 Hohman Av., 46324.

INDIANAPOLIS

Syn.: B'nai Torah (O), 6510 Hoover Rd., 46260; Etz Chaim (Sephardi, O), 760 W. 64th St., 46260; Shaarey Tefillah Cong. (C), 5879 Central Av., 46220; Beth-El Zedeck (C), 600 W. 70th St., 46260; Indianapolis Hebrew Cong. (R), 6501 N. Meridian St., 46260.
Anglo-Jewish visitors are invited to get in touch with the Exec. Vice-Pres., Jewish Fed. of Greater Indianapolis, 615 N. Alabama St., 46204. Tel. (317) 637-2473.
Bureau of Jewish Education, 6711 Hoover Rd., 46260.
Hooverwood Home for Aged, 7001 Hoover Rd., 46260.
Jewish Com. Centre, 6701 Hoover Rd., 46260.
Jewish Com. Relations Council, 1100 W. 42nd St., 46208.
Jewish Family & Children's Services, 9002 N. Meridian 46260.

LAFAYETTE

Syn.: Sons of Abraham (O), 661 N. 7th St., 47906; Temple Israel (R), 620 Cumberland St., 47901. Kosher frankfurters & salamis are available at the Jewel Food Store, which will also order kosher frozen foods on request. The store also stocks Pesach goods.

MICHIGAN CITY

Syn.: Sinai Temple (R), 2800 S. Franklin St., 46360. Tel. (219) 874-4477.

MUNCIE

Syn.: Temple Beth El (R), 525 W. Jackson St., (cnr. Council St.), 47305. Tel. (317) 288-4662.

NORTH WEST INDIANA

Jewish Fed. of North West Indiana, 2939 Jewett St., Highland 46322. Tel. (219) 972-2251.

SOUTH BEND

Syn.: Hebrew Orthodox Cong. (O), 3207 S. High St., 46614; Sinai (C), 1102 E. Lasalle St., 46617; Beth-El (R), 305 W. Madison St., 46601; B'nai Yisrael (Reconstructionist), 420 S. William St., 46625.
Jewish Fed. of St. Joseph Valley, 105 Jefferson Centre, Suite 804, 46601. Tel. (219) 233-1164. Fax. 219-288-4103.
Visitors requiring information about kashrut, temporary accommodation, etc., should contact Rabbi Y. Gettinger, at the Hebrew Orthodox Cong., address above, Tel. (219) 291-4239 or 291-6100, or Michael Lerman, Tel. 1-800 348-2529. For mikva appointments, Tel. (219) 291-6240.

TERRE HAUTE

Syn.: United Hebrew Cong. (R), 540 S. 6th St., 47807.
Kosher Meat & Sandwiches: 410 W. Western Av., 47807.

VALPARAISO

Syn: Temple Israel (c), P.O. Box 2051, 46383.

WHITING

Syn.: B'nai Judah (O), 116th St. & Davis Av., 46394.

IOWA

CEDAR RAPIDS

Syn.: Temple Judah, 3221 Lindsay La. S.E., 52403.Tel. (319) 362-1261.

DAVENPORT

Syn.: Temple Emanuel (R), 12th St. and Mississippi Av., 52803. Davenport is part of the Rock Island, Illinois, area, which is divided by the Mississippi River. See Rock Island entry.

DES MOINES

Syn.: Beth El Jacob (O), 954 Cummins Pkwy., 50312; Tifereth Israel (C), 924 Polk Blvd., 50312; B'nai Jeshurun (R), 51st & Grand, 50312.
Bureau for Jewish Education: 924 Polk Blvd., 50312.
Iowa Jewish Senior Life Centre, 900 Polk Blvd., 50312.
Jewish Fed. of Greater Des Moines, 910 Polk Blvd., 50312. Tel. (515) 277-6321. Also at this address: Jewish Community Relations Com. & Jewish Family Services.
Kosher Food: Pickle Barrel, 1241 6th Av., 50314; The Nosh, 800 First St., W. Des Moines, 50265.

DUBUQUE

Syn.: Beth El, 475 W. Locust St., 52001.

FORT DODGE

Syn.: Beth El (C), 501 N. 12th St., 50501. Tel. (515) 573-8925 (office), (515) 955-6013 (home).

IOWA CITY

Syn.: Agudas Achim (C & R), 602 E. Washington St., 52240.

SIOUX CITY

Syn.: United Orthodox (O), 14th & Nebraska Sts., 51105; Shaare Zion (C), 1522 Douglas St., 51105; Mt. Sinai (R), 815 38th St., 51105.
Jewish Fed.: 525 14th St., 51105. Tel. (712) 258-0618.
Kosher Meat & Food: Sam's Food Market, 1911 Grandview, 51104.

KANSAS

OVERLAND PARK

Syn.: Young Israel (O), 8716 Woodward, 66212; Kehilath Israel (Traditional. Generally Orthodox ritual, but mixed seating), 10501 Conser Av., 66212.
Day School: Hyman Brand Hebrew Academy of Greater Kansas City, 5801 W. 115th St, Suite 102.
Central Agency for Jewish Education, 5801 W. 115th St., Suite 104, 66211.
Weekly newspaper: "Kansas City Jewish Chronicle", 7375 W. 107th St., 66204.

PRAIRIE VILLAGE

Syn.: Ohev Sholom (C), 5311 W. 75th St., 66208.
Butcher: Jacobsons Strictly Kosher Foods, 5200 W95th St., Prairie Village, Ka 66207.

Note: The institutions and organisations in Overland Park and Prairie Village form part of the community of Metropolitan Kansas City, Missouri (which see).

TOPEKA

Syn.: Beth Sholom (R), 4200 Munson St., 66604.
Topeka Lawrence Jewish Fed., 4200 Munson Av., 66604.

WICHITA

Syn.: Hebrew (O), 1850 N. Woodlawn Av., 67208; Temple Emanu-El (R), 7011 E. Central St., 67206.
Grocers: Dillon's, 21st St. & Rock Rd., & 13th St. & Woodlawn St.; Foodbarn Woodlawn & Central Sts., 67208; Ketteman's Bakery, 2607 E. Douglas.

KENTUCKY

LEXINGTON

Syn.: Lexington Havurah (C), P.O.B. 54958, 40551; Ohavay Zion (C), 2048 Edgewater Ct., 40502; Adath Israel (R), 124 N. Ashland Av., 40502.
Central Kentucky Jewish Fed., 340 Romany Rd., Ky 40502. Tel. (606) 268-0672/0775.

LOUISVILLE

Syn.: Anshei Sfard (O), 3700 Dutchman's Lane, 40205. Mikva attached; Keneseth Israel (T), 2531 Taylorsville Rd., 40205; Adath Jeshurun (C), 2401 Woodbourne Av., 40205; Temple Shalom (R), 4615 Lowe Rd., 40205; The Temple (R), 5101 Brownsboro Rd., 40241.
The Com. Centre is at 3600 Dutchman's Lane, 40205.
Eliahu Academy, 3595 Dutchmans Lane, 40205.
Hillel, Ecumenical Centre, University of Louisville, 40292. Contains the Banks-Kaplan Jewish Affairs Library.
Jewish Com. Fed., 3630 Dutchman's Lane, 40205.
Jewish Family & Vocational Service, 3640 Dutchman's La., 40205.
Jewish Hospital, 217 E. Chestnut St., 40202.
Jewish Educational Assoc., 3600 Dutchman's Lane, 40205.
Shalom Tower, 3650 Dutchman's Lane, 40205.

PADUCAH

Syn.: Temple Israel (R), 330 Joe Clifton Dr., 42001.

LOUISIANA

ALEXANDRIA

Syn.: B'nai Israel (C), 1907 Vance St., 71301; Gemiluth Chassodim (R), 2021 Turner St., 71301.
Jewish Welfare Fed., 2815 Hill St., 71301.
Library: Meyer Kaplan Memorial Library (Judaica), c/o B'nai Israel.
Kosher food: By arrangement, from Dr. and Mrs. B. Kaplan, 100 Park Place, 71301. Tel. (318) 445 9367.

BATON ROUGE

Syn.: B'nai Israel (R), 3354 Kleinert Av., 70806; Beth Shalom Syn. (R), 9111 Jefferson Highway, 70809.

Jewish Fed. of Greater Baton Rouge, P.O.B. 80827, 70898. Tel. (504) 291-5895.

LAFAYETTE

Syn.: Temple Rodef Sholom (R), 603 Lee Av., 70501.
There is a very fine Judaica library at the University of Southwestern Louisiana.

NEW ORLEANS

Syn.: Anshe Sfard (O), 2230 Carondelet St., 70130; Beth Israel (O), 7000 Canal Blvd., 70124. There is a mikva attached to this syn.; Chabad Hse. (O), 7037 Freret St., 70118; Chevra Thilim (C), 4429 S. Claiborne Av., 70125; Young Israel of Metairie Syn. (O), 4141 W. Esplanade Av., Metairie, 70002. Rabbi Yossi Nemes. Tel. (504) 887-6997; Tikvat Shalom (C), 3737 W. Esplanade Av., Metairie, 70002; Gates of Prayer (R), 4000 W. Esplanade Av., Metairie, 70002; Temple Sinai (R), 6227 St. Charles Av., 70118; Touro (R), 1501 General Pershing Av., 70115 (the oldest in the Mississippi Valley). Jewish Com. Centre, 5342 St. Charles Av., 70115.
Jewish Fed. of Greater New Orleans, 1539 Jackson Av., 70130. Tel. (504) 525-0673.
Visitors wishing Glatt kosher b&b in New Orleans should contact Dr. & Mrs. Saul Kahn, 4000 Clifford Dr., Metairie, 70002. Tel. (504) 831-2230 or 833-1352. Fax 834-6563 We keep glatt kosher. "Having guests from all over the world enriches our lives."
Grocery Kosher Cajun Deli and Grocery, 3520 N. Hullen St., Metairie, 70002. Tel. (504) 888 2010.

SHREVEPORT

Syn.: Agudath Achim (C), 9401 Village Green Dr., 71115. Tel. (318) 797-6401; B'nai Zion (R), 245 Southfield Rd., 71105.
Jewish Fed., 2032 Line Av., 71104. Tel. (318) 221-4129.

MAINE

AUBURN

Syn.: Cong. Beth Abraham (C), Main St. & Laurel Av., 04210. Tel. (207) 783-1302; Temple Shalom (C), 74 Bradman St., 04210. See also Lewiston, below.

BANGOR

Syn.: Beth Abraham (O), 145 York St., 04401; Cong. Beth Israel (C), 144 York St., 04401.
(K) The Bagel Shop, 1 Main St., Bangor, Maine 04451. Tel. (207) 947-1654.

LEWISTON

Lewiston-Auburn Jewish Fed., 74 Bradman St., 04210. Tel. (207) 786-4201.

OLD ORCHARD BEACH

Syn.: Beth Israel (O), 49 E. Grand Av., 04064. Daily minyan, May 28 to Yom Kippur. Shabbat & Yomtov minyan all year round.
For kashrut inf. contact: Eber Weinstein, 187 E. Grand Av., 04064. Tel. (207) 934-2460; Albert Mosseri, Beach Camera Co., 24 Old Orchard St., 04064, or Harold Goodkovski. Tel. (207) 934-4210.

PORTLAND

Syn.: Etz Chaim (O), 267 Congress St., 04101; Shaare Tphiloh (O), 76 Noyes

St., 04103; Mikva & Levey Day School on premises; Beth El (C), 400 Deering Av., 04103; Cong. Bet Ha'am (R), 111 Wescott St., 04106.

Jewish Com. Centre, 57 Ashmont St., 04103. Tel. (207) 772-1959.

Jewish Fed.-Com. Council of Southern Maine, 57 Ashmont St., 04103. Tel. (207) 773-7254.

(K) Abraham's House of Coffee, 548 Congress St., Portland, Maine 04101. 207 -TRY-ABES.

MARYLAND

ANNAPOLIS

Syn.: Kneseth Israel (O), 1125 Spa Rd., 21403; Cong. Kolami (C), 1909 Hidden Meadow La., 21401; Temple Beth Sholom (R), 1461 Baltimore-Annapolis Blvd., Arnold, 21012.

There is now a Jewish Chapel at the US Naval Academy, and midshipmen usually worship there.

BALTIMORE

The city's Jewish community, numbering some 93,000, is one of the most cohesive and dynamic in the whole of the United States.

There are at least 50 syns in the Baltimore metropolitan area, but only the most important are listed below.

Syn.: Agudath Israel (O), 6202 Park Heights Av., 21215; Beth Jacob (O), 5713 Park Heights Av., 21215; Beth Tfiloh (O), 3300 Old Court Rd., 21208; Shomrei Emunah (O), 6221 Greenspring Av., 21209; Suburban Orthodox (O), 7504 Seven Mile Lane, 21208; Beth El (C), 8101 Park Heights Av., 21208; Beth Israel (C), 9411 Liberty Rd., Randallstown, 21133; Chizuk Amuno (C), 8100 Stevenson Rd., 21208; Baltimore Hebrew Cong. (R), 7401 Park Heights Av., 21208; Har Sinai (R), 6300 Park Heights Av., 21215; Oheb Shalom (R), 7310 Park Heights Av., 21208.

Only one Jewish historical institution in the United States includes two historic syns. (Lloyd St. & B'nai Israel), a museum and a research centre – the Jewish Heritage Centre, at 15 Lloyd St., 21202 (Tel. 732-6400), which is run by the Jewish Historical Society of Maryland. The Lloyd St. Syn., built in 1845, is the third oldest syn. building in the US. B'nai Israel, built in 1876, is the oldest syn. in continuous use in Baltimore.

At Gay and Water Sts. is the community's Holocaust Memorial, maintained by the Baltimore Jewish Council.

Mikva of Baltimore, Inc., 3207 Clarks Lane, Baltimore, MD 21225. Tel. 664-5834.

Associated Jewish Community Fed. of Baltimore, 101 W. Mount Royal Av., 21201. Tel. (301) 727-4828.

Jewish Com. Centres: 5700 Park Heights Av., 21215. Tel. 542-4900; 3506 Gwynnbrook Av., Owings Mills, 21117. Tel. 356-5200.

Baltimore Hebrew University, 5800 Park Heights Av., 21215. Tel. 578-6900.

Baltimore Jewish Council, 101 W. Mount Royal Av., 21201. Tel. 235-9006.

Board of Jewish Education, 5800 Park Heights Av., 21215. Tel. 578-6943.

Meyerhoff Library, 5800 Park Heights Av., 21215. Tel. 578-6936.

Ner Israel Rabbinical College, Mount Wilson Lane, 21208 (Tel. 484-7200), claims to be the largest yeshiva campus anywhere.

Jewish Historical Society of Maryland: 5800 Park Heights Av., 21215.

Sinai Hospital: Greenspring & Belvedere Avs., 21202. Tel. 578-5678.

Kosher Restaurants: Chapps Kosher Chinese, Pomona Sq. Shopping Centre, 1700 Reisterstown Rd., 21208; Kosher Bite, 6309 Reisterstown Rd., 21215; Royal Restaurant, 7006 Reisterstown Rd., 21208; Tov Pizza, 6313

Reisterstown Rd., 21208. The Charles Street Eatery, 305 N. Charles St., Baltimore, MD 21201.

Kosher Delicatessens and Take out; Knish Shop, 508 Reisterstown Rd., 21208; Liebes, 607 Reisterstown Rd., Pikesville, MD 21208. Tel. 653-1977; Danielle's, 401 Reisterstown Rd., 21208.

Kosher Supermarkets: Shapiro's Food Mart, 1504 Reisterstown Rd., 21208; Seven Mile Market, 4000 Seven Mile La., 21208. D & L Kosher Mart, 708-710 Reistertown Rd., Balitmore, MD 21208. Tel. 484-2545.

Bakeries: Goldman's Kosher Bakery 6848 Reisterstown Rd., 21208; Pariser's Kosher Bakery, 6711 Reisterstown Rd., 21208; Schmell & Azman Kosher Bakery, 104 Reisterstown Rd., Pikesville, 21208.

For all kashrut inf., contact: Orthodox Jewish Council Vaad Hakashrut, 11 Warren Rd., Baltimore, MD 21208. Tel. 484-4110.

Jewish Info. Service is open from 10.00 am to 2 pm daily at 5750 Park Heights Av., 21215. Tel. (301) 466-4636. For help about almost anything.

Baltimore is the home town of the late Henrietta Szold. There is a street named after her.

BETHESDA

Syns.: Beth El of Montgomery County (C), 8215 Old Georgetown Rd., 20814; Bethesda Jewish Cong. (unaffiliated), 6601 Bradley Blvd., 20817.

United Jewish Appeal-Fed. of Greater Washington, 7900 Wisconsin Av., 20814. Tel. (301) 652-6480.

BOWIE

Syn.: Nevey Shalom (C), 12218 Torah Lane, 20715 (changed from Trinity Lane after a petition to the city government); Temple Solel (R), 2901 Mitchelville Rd., 20716. Tel. 249-2424.

CHEVY CHASE

Syn.: Ohr Kodesh (C), 8402 Freyman Dr., 20815. Tel. 589-3880. Temple Shalom (R), 8401 Grubb Rd., 20815. Tel. 587-2273..

CUMBERLAND

Syn.: Beth Jacob (C), 11 Columbia St., 21502; B'Er Chayim (R), 107 Union St., 21502.

Kosher Dairy Restaurant, Delicatessen & Bakery: The Bagel Shop, 1 Main St., 04401. Tel. (207) 947-1654. Also take out. Closed Sats. Under rabbinical supervision.

GAITHERSBURG

Syn.: Gaithersburg Hebrew Cong. (C), 9915 Apple Ridge Rd., 20879. Tel. 869-7699.

GREENBELT

Syn.: Mishkan Torah (C), Westway and Ridge Rd., 20770. Tel. 474-4223.

HAGERSTOWN

Syn.: B'nai Abraham (R), 53 E. Baltimore St., 21740. Tel. 733-5039.

HYATSVILLE

Beth Torah Cong. (C), 6700 Adelphi Rd., 20782. Tel. 927-5525.

KENSINGTON

Syn.: Temple Emanuel (R), 10101 Connecticut Av., 20895. Tel. 942-2000.

School: Silver Spring Hebrew Day Institute, 10101 Connecticut Av., 20895.

LAUREL

Syn.: Oseh Shalom (Reconstructionist), 8604 Briarwood Dr., 20708. Tel. 498-5151.

LEXINGTON PARK

Syn.: Beth Israel (C), Bunker Hill Dr., 20650. Tel. 862-2021.

OLNEY

Syn.: B'nai Shalom (C), 18401 Burtfield Dr., 20832. Tel. 774-0879.

POCOMOKE

Syn.: Temple Israel (C), 3rd St., 21851.

POTOMAC

Syn.: Beth Sholom of Potomac (O), 11825 Seven Locks Rd., 20854. Tel. 279-7010; Har Shalom (C), 11510 Falls Rd., 20854. Tel. 299-7087.
Restaurant: **(K)** Hunan Gourmet, 350 Fortune Terrace. Tel. 424-0191.

ROCKVILLE

Syn.: Beth Tikvah (C), 2200 Baltimore Rd., 20853; B'nai Israel (C), 6301 Montrose Rd., 20852; Temple Beth Ami (R), 800 Hurley Av., 20850. Tel. 340-6818.
Jewish Com. Centre of Greater Washington & Hebrew Home, 6125 Montrose Rd., 20852.
Kosher Restaurant: Moshe Dragon Glatt Kosher Chinese Restaurant, 4840 Boiling Brook Pkwy. Tel. 468-1922. Under Supervision of Rabbinical Council of Washington.

SALISBURY

Syn.: Beth Israel (C), Camden Av. & Wicomico St., 21801.

SILVER SPRING & WHEATON

Syn.: Ezras Israel (O), 1100 E. West Highway, 20832. Tel. 829-6105; Ohavei Zedek (O), 8055 13th St., 20910; Silver Spring Jewish Centre (O), 1401 Arcola Av., 20901. Tel. 649-4425. Mikva on premises; South-East Hebrew Cong. (O), 10900 Lockwood Dr., 20901; Woodside Syn. Ahavas Torah (O), 9001 Georgia Av., 20910; Young Israel Shomrai Emunah (O), 1132 Arcola Av., 20902; Har Tzeon-Agudath Achim (C), 1840 University Blvd. W., 20902; Shaare Tefila (C), 11120 Lockwood Dr., 20901; Temple Israel (C), 420 University Blvd. E., 20901. Tel. 439-3600.
Mikva: 8901 Georgia Av., 20907.
Orthodox Rabbinical Assoc., 1401 Arcola Av., 20902.
The Hebrew Sheltering Society has premises where people visiting the Washington area who are unable to afford a hotel can stay for up to three nights. This "guest house" is at 11524 Daffodil La., 20902. In addition, if space is available, people wishing to stay within walking distance of a syn. on Shabbat or Yom Tov can be accommodated. (The Silver Spring Jewish Centre is only one short block away.) For further inf., Tel. 649-3141, 649-4425 or 649-2799 (Rabbi Herzel Kranz).
Bookshops: Lisbon's Hebrew Book Store & Giftshop, 2305 University Blvd. W., Wheaton, 20902; The Jewish Bookstore, 11250 Georgia Av., 20902.
Kosher Dairy Restaurants: The Nut House, 11419 Georgia Av., Wheaton, 20902. Tel. 942-5900; Under the supervision of the Rabbinical Council of Greater Washington.
Bakeries: Virtuoso, 11203A Lockwood Av., 50901. Tel. 593-6034; The Wooden Shoe Pastry Shop, 11301 Georgia Av., 20902.
Meat & Delicatessen: Shalom, 2307 University Blvd., 20902.

TEMPLE HILLS

Syn.: Shaare Tikva (C), 5405 Old Temple Hills Rd., 20748. Tel. 894-4303.
Note: Bethesda, Bowie, Chevy Chase, Gaithersburg, Greenbelt, Hyattsville, Kensington, Laurel, Lexington Park, Olney, Potomac, Rockville, Silver Spring & Wheaton and Temple Hills are all part of Greater Washington, D.C.

MASSACHUSETTS

ACTON

Syn.: Beth Elohim (Independent), 10 Hennessey Dr., 07120. Tel. (508) 263-3061.

ANDOVER

Temple Emanuel (R), 7 Haggett's Pond Rd., 01810. Tel. (508) 470-1356.

ATHOL

Syn.: Temple Israel (Independent), 107 Walnut St., 01331. Tel. (508) 249-9481.

ATTLEBORO

Syn.: Agudas Achim Cong. (C), Kelly & Toner Blvds., 02703. Tel. (508) 222-2243.

AYER

Syn.: Cong. Anshey Sholom (Independent), Cambridge St., 01432. Tel. (508) 772-0896.

BELMONT

Syn.: Beth El Temple Centre (R), 2 Concord Av., 02178. Tel. (617) 484-6668.

BEVERLY

Syn.: B'nai Abraham (C), 200 E. Lothrop St., 01915. Tel. (508) 927-3211; Cong. Ohev Shalom (Independent), 3 Beckford St., 01915. Tel. (508) 922-2495.

BOSTON AREA (Greater Boston)

Greater Boston includes some 69 cities and towns in the contiguous area. Its Jewish population is now concentrated in Brookline, Newton and Sharon (which see), and not in Boston proper.
Syn.: Chabad House (O), 491 Commonwealth Av., 02215. Tel. (617) 523-0453; The Boston Synagogue at Charles River Park (O), 55 Martha Rd., 02114. Tel. (617) 523-0453; Cong. Kadimah-Toras Moshe (O), 113 Washington St., Brighton, 02135. Tel. (617) 254-1333; Lubavitch Shul of Brighton (O), 239 Chestnut Hill Av., Brighton, 02135. Tel. (617) 782-8340; Hillel B'nai Torah (C), 120 Corey St., W. Roxbury, 02132. Tel. (617) 323-0486; Temple B'nai Moshe (C), 1845 Commonwealth Av., Brighton, 02135. Tel. (617) 254-3620; Temple Israel (R), Plymouth St. & Longwood Av., 02115. Tel. (617) 566-3960.
For inf. about the many syns.and kosher restaurants in other parts of the Greater Boston area, contact the Syn. Council of Massachusetts, 1320 Centre St., Newton Centre, 02159. Tel. (617) 244 6506.
Vaad Harabonim of Massachusetts, 177 Tremont St., 02111. Tel. (617) 426-2139. The Kashruth Commission, which is at the same address, provides inf. about kosher restaurants, accom. and products. Also at 177 Tremont St. are the Rabbinical Council of New England & the Rabbinical Court.

Mikva: Daughters of Israel, 101 Washington St., Brighton, 02135.
Combined Jewish Philanthropies of Greater Boston 1, Lincoln Plaza, 02111. Tel. (617) 330-9500.
Jewish Com. Relations Council of Greater Boston, 1 Lincoln Plaza, Suite 308, 02111. Tel. (617) 330-9600, represents 34 community organisations in the area.
Brandeis University in Waltham, Massachusetts, est. 1948, Tel. (617) 8918110, is the second university in the U.S.A. under Jewish auspices. It is a secular institution. The American Jewish Historical Society library on the Brandeis campus contains the largest collection of American Hebraica in the world.
The Public Library has a number of Sargent paintings of the Prophets and many other items of Jewish interest, as well as one of the largest collections of Anglo-Judaica in the country. Boston University has a library containing many items of Jewish interest.
Restaurant: Milk St. Café, 50 Milk St. Tel. (617)-542-FOOD. Dairy foods only. Under rabbinical supervision; The Park at Post Office Sq. Tel. (617)-350-PARK; Longwood Galleria, 350 Londwood Av. Tel. (617)-350-739-CAFE.
Rabbinically supervised kosher meals are available (by previous arrangement) at the Hillel Foundation, Boston University. Tel. (617) 266-3882.

BRAINTREE

Syn.: Temple Bnai Shalom (C), 41 Storrs Av., 02184. Tel. (617) 843-3687.

BROCKTON

Syn.: Agudath Achim (O), 144 Belmont Av., 02401. Tel. (508) 583-0717; Beth Emunah (C), Pearl & Torrey Sts., 02401. Tel. (508) 583-5810; Temple Israel (R), 184 W. Elm St., 02401. Tel. (508) 587-4130.
The Jewish Com. Centre is in Stoughton, which see.

BROOKLINE

Syn.: Beth David (O), 64 Corey Rd., 02146. Tel. (617) 232-2349; Beth Pinchas (Bostoner Rebbe) (O), 1710 Beacon St., 02146. Tel. (617) 734-5100; Chai Odom (O), 77 Englewood Av., 02146. Tel. (617) 734-5359; Young Israel of Brookline (O), 62 Green St., 02146. Tel. (617) 734-0276; Beth Zion (C), 1566 Beacon St., 02146. Tel. (617) 566-8171; Kehillath Israel (C), 384 Harvard St., 02146. Tel. (617) 277-9155; Ohabei Shalom (R), 1187 Beacon St., 02146. Tel. (617) 277-6610; Temple Sinai (R), Charles St. & Sewall Av., Coolidge Cnr., 02146. Tel. (617) 277-5888; Sfardic Cong. of New England, 151 Salisbury Rd., Tel. (617) 964-1526.
New England Hebrew Academy, 9 Prestcott St., 02146.
Yeshiva: Maimonides, Philbrick Rd. at Boylston St., 02146.
The Hebrew College at 43 Hawes St., 02146, Tel. (617) 232-8710, is the only institution of higher Jewish learning in the six New England States. Its library contains more than 85,000 volumes of Hebraica & Judaica, manuscripts, etc. It has a kosher cafeteria.
Kosher Restaurants: Café Shalom, 404a Harvard St., 02146. Dairy & vegetarian only; Rubin's, 500 Harvard St., 02146. Tel. (617) 566-8761 or 731-8787. All the foregoing are under the supervision of the Vaad Harabonim. Haim's Glatt Kosher Deli, 1657 Beacon St., 02146. Tel. (617) 734-8625; Rami's, 324 Harvard St. Tel. (617) 738-3577; Ruth's Kitchen, 401 Harvard St. Tel. (617) 734-9810.
Harvard St. is the Jewish commercial centre, with art & bookshops, as well as many kosher butcher's shops & bakeries.

BURLINGTON

Syn.: Temple Shalom Emeth (R), 14-16 Lexington St., 01803. Tel. (617) 272-2351.

CAMBRIDGE

Syn.: Temple Beth Shalom of Cambridge (C), 8 Tremont St., 02139. Tel. (617) 864-6388; Cong. Kahal B'raira (Independent), 9 William St., 02139. Tel. (617) 868-8627.
Kosher meals are obtainable (by previous arrangement) at Hillel Hse., Harvard University, 74 Mt. Auburn St., 02138; Hillel Hse., Massachusetts Institute of Technology, 312 Memorial Dr., 02139; all the foregoing are under rabbinical supervision.

CANTON

Syn.: Beth Abraham (C), 1301 Washington St., 02021. Tel. (617) 828-5250; Temple Beth David of the South Shore (R), 256 Randolph St., 02021. Tel. (617) 828-2275.

CHELMSFORD

Syn.: Cong. Shalom (R), Richardson Rd., 01863. Tel. (508) 251-8091.

CHELSEA

Syn.: Agudas Shalom (O), 145 Walnut St., 02150. Tel. (617) 884-8668; Cong. Ahavas Achim Anshe Sfard (O), 57 Cou1e Zion (O), 76 Orange St., 02150. Tel. (617) 884-0498; Shomrei Linas Hazedek (O), 140 Shurtleff St., 02150. Tel. (617) 884-9443; Temple Emmanuel (Independent), Carey Av. & Tudor St., 02150. Tel. (617) 884-9699.

CHESTNUT HILL

Syn.: Cong. Lubavitvch (O), 100 Woodcliff Rd., 02167. Tel. (617) 469-9007; Temple Emeth (C), 194 Grove St., 02167. Tel. (617) 469-9400; Mishkan Tefila (C), 300 Hammond Pond Pkwy., 02167. Tel. (617) 332-7770. This is the oldest Conservative cong. in New England.

CLINTON

Syn.: Shaarei Zedeck, (Independent), Water St., 01510.

DOVER

Syn.: B'nai Jacob (T), PO Box 66, 7 Donnelly Dr., 02030. Tel. (508) 785-0990.

EAST FALMOUTH

Syn.: Falmouth Jewish Cong. (R), 37 Hatchville Rd., 02536. Tel. (508) 540-0602.

EASTON

Syn.: Temple Chayai Shalom (Traditional), 9 Mechanic St., 02356. Tel. (508) 238-4896.

EVERETT

Syn.: Tifereth Israel (Traditional), 34 Malden St., 02149. Tel. (617) 387-0200.

FALL RIVER

Syn.: Adas Israel (O), 1647 Robeson St., 02720. Tel. (508) 674-9761; Beth El (C), 385 High St., 02720. Tel. (508) 674-3529.
Fall River Jewish Com. Council, Room 327, 56 N. Main St., 02720.

FITCHBURG

Syn.: Agudas Achim (Independent), 40 Boutelle St., 01420. Tel. (508) 342-7704.

FRAMINGHAM

Syn.: Chabad Hse. (O), 74 Joseph Rd., 01701. Tel. (508) 877-8888; Beth Sholom (C), Pamela Rd., 01701. Tel. (508) 877-2540; Beth Am (R), 300 Pleasant St., 01701. Tel. (508) 872-8300.
Greater Framingham Jewish Fed., 76 Salem End Rd., 01701. Tel. (617) 879-3301.

GLOUCESTER

Syn.: Ahavath Achim (C), 86 Middle St., 01930. Tel. (508) 281-0739.

GREENFIELD

Syn.: Temple Israel (C), 27 Pierce St., 01301. Tel. (413) 773-5884. Rabbi Louis A. Reiser.

HAVERHILL

Syn.: Anshe Sholom (O), 427 Main St., 01830. Tel. (508) 372-2276; Temple Emanu-El (R), 514 Main St., 01830. Tel. (508) 373-3861.

HINGHAM

Syn.: Cong. Sha'aray Shalom (R), 1112 Main St., 02043. Tel. (617) 749-8103.

HOLBROOK

Syn.: Temple Beth Sholom (C), 95 Plymouth St., 02343. Tel. (617) 767-4922.

HOLLISTON

Temple Beth Torah (C), 2162 Washington St., 01746. Tel. (508) 429-6268.

HOLYOKE

Syn.: Rodphey Sholom (O), 1800 Northampton St., 01040. Tel. (413) 534-5262; Sons of Zion (C), 378 Maple St., 01040.Tel. (413) 534-3369.

HULL

Syn.: Temple Beth Sholom (C), 600 Nantasket Av., 02045. Tel. (617) 925-0091. Temple Israel of Nantasket (C), 3 Hadassah Way, 02045. Tel. (617) 332-7978.

HYANNIS

Syn.: Cape Cod Syn. (R), 145 Winter St., 02601. Tel. (508) 775-2988.

HYDE PARK

Syn.: Temple Adas Hadrath Israel, 28 Arlington St., 02136. Tel. (617) 364-2661; Georgetowne Syn. (Independent), 412 Georgetowne Dr., 02136. Tel. (617) 361-3780.

LAWRENCE

Syn.: Ansha Shalum (O), 411 Hampshire St., 01841. Tel. (508) 683-4544; Cong. Tifereth Anshai Sfard & Sons of Israel (C), 492 Lowell St., 01841. Tel. (508) 686-0391.
Jewish Com. Council of Greater Lawrence, 580 Haverhill St., 01841. Tel. (617) 686-4157.

LEOMINSTER

Syn.: Cong. Agudat Achim (C), 268 Washington St., 01453. Tel. (508) 534-6121.

LEXINGTON

Syn.: Chabad Centre (O), 9 Burlington St., 02173. Tel. (617) 863-8656; Temple Emunah (C), 9, Piper Rd., 02173. Tel. (617) 861-0300; Temple Isaiah (R), 55 Lincoln St., 02173. Tel. (617) 862-7160.

LOWELL

Syn.: Cong. Montefiore (O), 460 Westford St., 01851. Tel. (508) 459-9400; Temple Beth El (C), 105 Princeton Blvd., 01851. Tel. (508) 453-7744; Temple Emanuel of Merrimack Valley (R), 101 W. Forest St., 01851. Tel. (508) 454-1372.

LYNN

Syn.: Ahabat Shalom (O), 151 Ocean St., 01902. (Houses the Eliot Feuerstein Library). Tel. (617) 593 9255; Anshai Sfard (O), 150 S. Common St., 01905. Tel. (617) 599-7131; Chevra Tehilim (O), 12 Breed St., 01902. Tel. (617) 598-2964.
North Shore Jewish Historical Society, 31 Exchange St., 01901.

MALDEN

Syn.: Beth Israel (O), 10 Dexter St., 02148. Tel. (617) 322-5686; Young Israel (O), 45 Holyoke St., 02148. Tel. (617) 322-5686; Ezrath Israel (C), 245 Bryant St., 02148. Tel. (617) 322-7205; Tifereth Israel (R), 539 Salem St., 02148. Tel. (617) 322-2794; Cong. Agudas Achim (Traditional), 160 Harvard St., 02148. Tel. (617) 322-9380.

MARBLEHEAD

Syn.: Orthodox Cong. of the North Shore (O), 17 Seaview Av., 01945. Tel. (617) 631-4925; Temple Sinai (C), 1 Community Rd., 01945. Tel. (617) 631-2244; Temple Emanu-El (R), 393 Atlantic Av., 01945. Tel. (617) 631-9300.
N. Shore Com. Centre, 4 Community Rd., 01945. Houses the Eli & Bessie Cohen Library.
Jewish Fed. of the North Shore, 4 Community Rd., 01945. Tel. (617) 598-1810.

MARLBORO

Syn.: Temple Emanuel (C), 150 Berlin Rd., 01752. Tel. (508) 485-7565 or (508) 562-5105.

MEDFORD

Syn.: Temple Shalom (C), 475 Winthrop St., 02155. Tel. (617) 396-3262.

MELROSE

Syn.: Temple Beth Shalom (R), 21 E. Foster St., 02176. Tel. (617) 665-4520.

MILFORD

Syn.: Beth Shalom (C), 49 Pine St., 01757. Tel. (508) 473-1590.

MILLIS

Syn.: Cong. Ael Chunon (O), 334 Village St., 02054. Tel. (508) 376-5984.

MILTON

Syn.: B'nai Jacob (O), 100 Blue Hill Pkwy., 02187. Tel. (617) 698-0698; Temple Shalom (C), 180 Blue Hill Av., 02186. Tel. (617) 698-3394.

NATICK

Syn.: Chabad Lubavitch Centre (O), 2 East Mill St., 01760. Tel. (508) 650-1499; Temple Israel (C), 145 Hartford St., 01760.

NEEDHAM

Syn.: Temple Aliyah (C), 1664 Central Av., 02192. Tel. (617) 444-8522; Temple Beth Shalom (R), Highland & Webster Sts., Needham Heights, 02194. Tel. (617) 777-0077.

NEW BEDFORD

Syn.: Ahavath Achim (O), 385 County St., 02740. Tel. (508) 994-1760; Tifereth Israel (C), 145 Brownell Av., 02740. Tel. (508) 997-3171.
Jewish Fed. of Greater New Bedford, 467 Hawthorn St., N. Dartmouth, 02747. Tel. (508) 997-7471.

NEWBURYPORT

Syn.: Cong. Ahavas Achim, Washington & Olive Sts., 09150. Tel. (508) 462-2461.

NEWTON

Syn.: Cong. Agudas Achim-Anshe Sfard (O), 168 Adams St., 02160. Tel. (617) 244-7353; Cong. Beth El-Atereth Israel (O), 561 Ward St., 02159. Tel. (617) 244-7233; Cong. Shaarei Tefillah (O), 35 Morseland Av., 02159. Tel. (617) 527-7637; Mishkan Tefila (C), the oldest Conservative cong. in New England, is "located in two cities which overlap" – Newton & Chestnut Hill, Mass., which see; Temple Emanuel (C), 385 Ward St., 02159 Tel. (617) 332-5770; Temple Reyim (C), 1860 Washington St., 02166. Tel. (617) 527-2410; Beth Avodah (R), 45 Puddingstone La., 02159. Tel. (617) 527-0045; Temple Shalom (R), 175 Temple St., 02165. Tel. (617) 332-9550; Shir Hadash (Rec.), 1320 Centre St., 02159. Tel. (617) 965-6862; Dorshei Tzedek (Rec.), 67 Chester St., 02161. Tel. (617) 965-0330.
Syn. Council of Massachusetts, 1320 Centre St., Newton Centre, 02159. Tel. (617) 244-6506.
Jewish Com. Centre of Greater Boston, 333 Nahanton St., 02159. Tel. (617) 965 7410. Snack bar supervised by Orthodox Rabbinical Council of Massachusetts. (K) Café Bigalle, 333 Nahanton St. Tel. 965-8513.

NORTH ADAMS

Syn.: Cong. Beth Israel (Independent), 265 Church St., 01247. Tel. (413) 663-5830.

NORTHAMPTON

Syn.: B'nai Israel (C), 253 Prospect St., 01060. Tel. (413) 584-3593.
Hillel Foundation, Smith College, Elm St. & Round Hill Rd., 01060. Tel. (413) 584-2700.

NORWOOD

Syn.: Temple Shaare Tefilah (C), 556 Nichols St., 02062. Tel. (617) 762-8670.

ONSET

Syn.: Beth Israel (O), cnr. of Onset Av. & Locust St., 02558. Services three times daily from last Sat. in June to Labour Day. Services are also held on the High Holy-days. Further inf. from Burt Parker, Tel. (508) 295 9185.
Bridge View Hotel, 12 S. Water St., 02558, welcomes Jewish guests. Self-catering flatlets available. Kosher meat and other products supplied. Tel. (508) 295-9820. Self-catering flatlets also available at Bay View Motel, 181 Onset Av., 02558. Tel. (508) 295-5937. Flatlets also available at Sgarzi Apts.,

Onset Avenue 155-157-159 Onset, Ma 02558 (508) 295-4736. Rooms available also at the Onset Point Inn, Onset Ma., 02558., breakfast included

PEABODY

Syn.: Temple Ner Tamid (C), 368 Lowell St., 01960. Tel. (508) 532-1293; Beth Shalom (R), 489 Lowell St., 01960. Tel. (508) 535-2100; Cong. Sons of Israel (Traditional), Park & Spring Sts., 01960. Tel. (508) 531-7576; Cong. Tifereth Israel (Independent), Pierpont St., 01960. Tel. (508) 531-8135.

PITTSFIELD

Syn.: Ahavath Sholom Cong. (O), 177 Robbins Av., 01201. Tel. (413) 442-6609; Knesset Israel (C), 16 Colt Rd., 01201. Tel. (413) 445-4872; Anshe Amunim (R), 26 Broad St., 01201. Tel. (413) 442-5910.
Ahavath Sholom Synagogue (C), North St., Great Barrington, MAS 01230. Tel. (413) 528-4155.
Beth Israel Synagogue, 265 Church St., North Adams, MA 01247. Tel. (413) 528-4155 (C).
Hevreh (C), Box 912, Great Barrington, MA 01230. Tel. (413) 298-3394.
Jewish Fed. of the Berkshires, 235 East St., 01201. Tel. (413) 442-4360.

PLYMOUTH

Syn.: Cong. Beth Jacob (R), 8 Pleasant St., 02361. Tel. (508) 746-1575.
Holocaust Memorial Monument, at Beth Jacob Cemetery, 1km west of Plymouth Center.

QUINCY

Syn.: Adas Shalom (C), 435 Adams St., 02169. Tel. (617) 471-1818; Temple Beth El (C), 1001 Hancock St., 02169. Tel. (617) 479-4309; Beth Israel (Independent), 33 Grafton St., 02169. Tel. (617) 472-6796.

RANDOLPH

Syn.: Young Israel – Kehillath Jacob of Mattapan & Randolph (O), 374 N. Main St., 02368. Tel. (617) 986 6461; Temple Beth Am (C), 871 N. Main St., 02368. Tel. (617) 963-0440.
Bookshop: Davidson's Hebrew Book Store, 1106 N. Main St., 02368.

REVERE

Syn.: Ahavas Achim Anshei Sfard (O), 89 Walnut Av., 02151. Tel. (617) 289-1026; Tifereth Israel (O), 43 Nahant Av., 02151. Tel. (617) 284-9255; B'nai Israel (Independent), 1 Wave Av., 02151. Tel. (617) 284-8388.
Com. Centre, Shirley Av., 02151.
Kosher Meat & Take-Away, Myer's Kosher Kitchen, 168 Shirley Av., 02151.

SALEM

Syn.: Temple Shalom (C), 287 Lafayette St., 01970. Tel. (508) 741-4880.

SHARON

Syn.: Chabad Centre (O), 101 Worcester Rd., 02067. Tel. (617) 784-8167; Young Israel of Sharon (O), 9 Dunbar St., 02067. Tel. (617) 784-6112. Mikva on premises, operated by Mikveh Org. of the S. Shore, Chevrat Nashim; Adath Sharon (C), 18 Harding St., 02067. Tel. (617) 784-2517; Temple Israel (C), 125 Pond St., 02067. Tel. (617) 784-3986; Temple Sinai (R), 100 Ames St., 02067. Tel. (617) 784-6081.
Restaurant: **(K)** King David, 384 South Main St., 02067. Tel. (617) 784-8899.

SOMERVILLE

Syn.: B'nai Brith of Somerville (Independent), 201 Central St., 02145. Tel. (617) 625-0333.

SPRINGFIELD & LONGMEADOW

Syn.: Beth Israel (O), 1280 Williams St., Longmeadow, 01106. Tel. (413) 567-3210; Cong. Kodimoh (O), 124 Sumner Av., 01108, the largest Orthodox cong. in New England. Tel. (413) 781-0171; Kesser Israel (O), 19 Oakland St., 01108. Tel. (413) 732-8492; Lubavitcher Yeshiva Syn. (O), 1148 Converse St., Longmeadow, 01106. Tel. (413) 567-8665; B'nai Jacob (C), 2 Eunice Dr., Longmeadow, 01106. Tel. (413) 567-3163; Temple Beth El (C), 979 Dickinson St., 01108. Tel. (413) 733-4149; Temple Sinai (R), 1100 Dickinson St., 01108. Tel. (413) 736-3619.

Mikveh Assoc., 1138 Converse St., Longmeadow, 01106.

Jewish Fed. of Greater Springfield, 1160 Dickinson St., 01108. Tel. (413) 737-4313. The Com. Centre is at the same address.

Kosher Meat: Abe's Kosher Meat Market, 907 Sumner Av., Springfield MA 01108.

STONEHAM

Syn.: Temple Judea (C), 188 Franklin St., 02180. Tel. (617) 665-5752.

STOUGHTON

Syn.: Cong. Ahavath Torah (C), 1179 Central St., 02072. Tel. (617) 344-8733. Striar Jewish Com. Centre on the Fireman Campus, 445 Central St., 02072. Tel. (617) 341-2016.

(K) Café Bigalle, JCC Campus. Tel. 341-2016.

SUDBURY

Syn.: Cong. Beth El (R), Hudson Rd., 01776. Tel. (508) 443-9622; Cong. B'nai Torah (Independent), Woodside Rd., 01776. Tel. (508) 443-2082.

SWAMPSCOTT

Syn.: Beth El (C), 55 Atlantic Av., 01907. Tel. (617) 599-8005; Temple Israel (C), 837 Humphrey St., 01907. Tel. (617) 595-6635.

Kosher Bakery: Newman's, 252 Humphrey St., 01907.

VINEYARD HAVEN

Syn.: Martha's Vineyard Hebrew Centre, Center St., 02568. Tel. (508) 693-0745.

WAKEFIELD

Syn: Temple Emmanuel (C), 120 Chestnut St., 01880. Tel. (617) 245-1886.

WALTHAM

Syn.: Beth Israel (C), 25 Harvard St., 02154. Tel. (617) 894-5146.

American Jewish Historical Society, 1 Thornton Rd., 02154. Tel. (617) 891-8110. Fax (617) 899-9208.

WAYLAND

Syn.: Temple Shir Tikva (R), 141 Boston Post Rd., 01778. Tel. (508) 358-5312.

WELLESLEY HILLS

Syn.: Beth Elohim (R), 10 Bethel Rd., Wellesley Hills, 02181. Tel. (617) 235-8419.

WESTBORO

Syn.: B'nai Shalom (R), 117 E. Main St., 01581. Tel. (508) 366-7191.

WESTWOOD

Syn.: Beth David, 40 Pond St., 02090. Tel. (617) 769-5270.

WINTHROP

Syn.: Tifereth Abraham (O), 283 Shirley St., 02152. Tel. (617) 846-5063; Tifereth Israel (O), 93 Veterans' Rd., 02152. Tel. (617) 846-1390.

WORCESTER

Syn.: Cong. Beth Judah Young Israel of Worcester (O), 889 Pleasant St., 01602. Tel. (508) 754-3681; Shaarai Torah East (O), 32 Providence St., 01604. Tel. (508) 756-3276; Shaarai Torah West (O), 835 Pleasant St., 01602. Tel. (508) 791-0013; Yeshiva Syn. Chabad, Tifereth Israel, Sons of Jacob (O), 22 Newton Av., 01602. Tel. (508) 752-0904; Beth Israel (C), Jamesbury Dr., 01609. Tel. (508) 756-6204; Temple Emanuel (R), 280 May St., 01602. Tel. (508) 755-2519; Temple Sinai (R), 661 Salisbury St., 01609. Tel. (508) 755-2519.
Mikva, Huntley St., 01602. Tel. (508) 755-1257.
Com. Centre, 633 Salisbury St., 01609. Tel. (508) 756-7109.
Jewish Fed., 633 Salisbury St., 01609. Tel. (617) 756-1543.
Jewish Home for Aged, 629 Salisbury St., 01609. Tel. (508) 798-8653.
For inf. about kashrut, temporary accom., etc. visitors should contact Rabbi Reuven Fischer, 69 S. Flagg St., 01602, Ch., Agudath Israel of America Hachnosas Orchim Committee, or Rabbi Hershel Fogelman, 22 Newton Av., Tel. (617) 752-5791.
Kosher food is available on a daily basis at the "kosher kitchen" of Clark University, Main St., 01610.

MICHIGAN

ANN ARBOR

Syn.: B'nai B'rith Hillel Foundation (O,C,R), 1429 Hill St., 48104; Chabad House (O), 715 Hill St., 48104. Mikva on premises; The Orthodox Minyan (O), 1429 Hill St., 48104; Beth Israel Cong. (C), 2000 Washtenaw St., 48104; The Conservative Minyan, (C), 1429 Hill St., 48104; Temple Beth Emeth (R), 2309 Packard St., 48104; The Reform Havurah (R), 1429 Hill St., 48104.
B'nai B'rith Hillel Foundation, University of Michigan. Office: 1429 Hill St., 48104.
Com. Centre, 2935 Birch Hollow Dr., 48108.
Hebrew Day School of Ann Arbor, 2935 Birch Hollow Dr., 48108.
Jewish Com. Assoc./UJA, 2939 Birch Hollow Dr., 48108.

BENTON HARBOR (St. Joseph)

Syn.: Temple B'nai Shalom (C), 2050 Broadway, 49022.

DETROIT

Syn.: Bais Chabad of Farmington Hills (O), 32000 Middlebelt Rd., Farmington Hills, 48018; Bais Chabad of W. Bloomfield (O), 5595 W. Maple Rd., W. Bloomfield, 48322; Beth Jacob-Mogain Abraham (O), 15751 W. Lincoln Dr., Southfield, 48076; Beth Tefilo Emanuel Tikvah (O), 24225 Greenfield Rd., Southfield, 48075; B'nai Israel-Beth Yehuda (O), 15400 W. Ten Mile Road, Oak Park, 48237; B'nai Jacob (O), 15230 Lincoln Rd., Oak Park, 48237; B'nai Zion (O), 15250 W. Nine Mile Rd., Oak Park, 48237; Dovid Ben Nuchim (O), 14800 W. Lincoln Rd., Oak Park, 48237; Mishkan Israel, Nusach H'Ari, Lubavitch Centre (O), 14000 W. Nine Mile Rd., Oak Park, 48237; Shaarey Shomayim (O), 15100 W. Ten Mile Rd., Oak Park, 48237; Shomrey Emunah (O), 25451 Southfield Rd., Southfield, 48075; Shomrey Emunah Ohel Moed (O), 6191 Farmington Rd., W. Bloomfield, 48322; Young Israel of Greenfield (O), 15140 W. Ten Mile Rd., Oak Park, 48237; Young Israel of Oak Woods (O), 24061 Coolidge Av., Oak Park,

48237; Young Israel of Southfield (O), 27705 Lahser Rd., Southfield, 48034; B'nai David Cong. (Traditional), 24350 Southfield Rd., Southfield, 48075; Adat Shalom (C), 29901 Middlebelt Rd., Farmington Hills, 48018; Beth Abraham Hillel Moses (C), 5075 W. Maple Rd., W. Bloomfield, 48322; Beth Achim (C), 21100 W. Twelve Mile Rd., Southfield, 48076; Beth Isaac (C), 2730 Edsel Dr., Trenton, 48143; Beth Shalom (C), 14601 W. Lincoln Rd., Oak Park, 48237; B'nai Israel (C), 4200 Walnut Lake Rd., W. Bloomfield, 48033; B'nai Moshe (C), 6800 Drake Rd., W. B. 48322Downtown Synagogue (C), 1457 Griswold, 48226; Livonia Jewish Cong. (C), 31840 W. Seven Mile Rd., Livonia, 48152; Shaarey Zedek (C), 27375 Bell Rd., Southfield, 48034; Cong. Shir Tikvah, 3633 W. Big Beaver Rd., Troy, 48084. Tel. (313) 643-6520; Temple Beth El (R), 7400 Telegraph Rd., Birmingham, 48010; Temple Beth Jacob (R), 79 Elizabeth Lake Rd., Pontiac, 48053; Temple Emanu-El (R), 14450 W. Ten Mile Rd., Oak Park, 48237; Temple Israel (R), 5725 Walnut Lake Rd., W. Bloomfield, 48033; Temple Kol Ami (R), 5085 Walnut Lake Rd., W. Bloomfield, 48033; Temple Shir Shalom (R), 5642 Maple Rd., W. Bloomfield, 48322. Tel. (313) 737-8700; The Birmingham Temple (Humanistic), 28611 Twelve Mile Rd., Farmington Hills, 48018; T'chiyah Cong. (Unaffiliated), 1404 Nicolet Pl., 48207.
Council of Orthodox Rabbis of Detroit (Vaad Harabonim): 17071 W. Ten Mile Rd., Southfield, 48075. Tel. 559-5005/06.

Organisations
(K) B'nai B'rith Hillel Foundations, Wayne State University, 667 Charles Grosberg Religious Centre, 48202. Hot lunch, sandwiches, salads, soups served during academic year (Sept.—April).
Jewish Com. Council of Metropolitan Detroit: recently relocated.
Com. Centre: 6600 W. Maple Rd., W. Bloomfield, 48033. Kosher restaurant. Centre branch: 15110 W. Ten Mile Rd., Oak Park, 48237.
Holocaust Memorial Centre, 6602 W. Maple Rd., W. Bloomfield. Tel. (313) 661-0840. Founder-Dir.: Rabbi Charles H. Rosenzveig.
Homes for Aged: 26051 Lahser Rd., Southfield, Maple, W. B. 48034. Borman Hall, 19100 W. Seven Mile Rd., 48219; Fleischman Residence, 6710 W. Maple, West Bloomfield, 48322.
Machon L'Torah (The Jewish Network of Michigan) W. 10 Mile Rd. 48237.
Sinai Hospital, 6767 W. Outer Dr., 48235.
Kosher Restaurants: Mertz's Cafe Katon, 23055 Coolidge Rd., Oak Park, 48237. Tel. (313) 547-3581; Sarah's Glatt Kosher Deli, 15600 W. Ten Mile Rd., Southfield, 48075. Tel. (313) 443-2425; Sperber's Kosher Karry-Out, 25250 W. Ten Mile Rd., Oak Park, 48237. Tel. (313) 443-2425.
For inf. about kosher food contact the Council of Orthodox Rabbis at the address above.

EAST LANSING
Syn.: Shaarey Zedek (C & R), 1924 Coolidge Rd., 48823.
B'nai B'rith Hillel Foundation, Michigan State University. Office: 402 Linden St., 48823. Guest room. Kosher meals available during academic year.

FLINT
Syn.: Cong. Beth Israel (C), 5240 Calkins Rd., 48532; Temple Beth El (R), 501 S. Ballenger Highway, 48532.
Flint Jewish Fed., 619 Wallenberg St., 48502. Tel. (313) 767-5922.
Jewish Social Services, 619 Wallenberg St., 48502. Tel. (313) 767-5922.
Chabad House, 5385 Calkins, Flint, MI 48532. Tel. (313) 230-0770.

GRAND RAPIDS

Syn.: Chabad Hse. of Western Michigan (O), 2615 Michigan St. N.E., 49506;
Cong. Ahavas Israel (C), 2727 Michigan St. N.E., 49506; Temple Emanuel
(R), 1715 E. Fulton St., 49503.
Jewish Com. Fund of Grand Rapids, 2609 Berwyck St. S.E., 49506. Tel. (616)
956-9365.

JACKSON

Syn.: Temple Beth Israel (R), 801 W. Michigan Av., 49202.

KALAMAZOO

Syn. Cong. of Moses (C), 2501 Stadium Dr., 49008.

LANSING

Syn.: Kehillat Israel (C), 2014 Forest Rd., 48910.

SAGINAW

Syn.: Temple B'nai Israel (C), 1424 S. Washington Av., 48601; Cong. Beth El
(R), c/o Leo A. Kahan, 100 S. Washington Av., 48607.

SOUTH HAVEN

Syn.: First Hebrew Cong. (O), 249 Broadway, 49090.

MINNESOTA

DULUTH

Syn.: Adas Israel (O), 302 E. 3rd St., 55802; Temple Israel (C-R), 1602 E. 2nd
St., 55812.   Jewish Fed. & Com. Council, 1602 E. 2nd St., 55812. Tel. (218)
724-8857.

MINNEAPOLIS

Syn.: Gemilus Chesed (O), 28th St. & Rhode Island Av., 55426; Kenesseth
Israel (O), 4330 W. 28th St., 55416. Mikva on premises; Adath Jeshurun (C),
34th St. & Dupont Av. S., 55408; Beth El (C), 5224 W. 26th St., 55416; B'nai
Emet (C), 3115 Ottawa Av. S., 55416; Bet Shalom (R), 201 9th Av. N.,
Hopkins, 55343; Temple Israel (R), 24th St. & Emerson Av. S., 55405.
Jewish Com. Center of Greater Minneapolis: 4330 Cedar Lake Rd. S., 55416.

ROCHESTER

Among other services, the Lubavitch Bais Chaya Moussia Hospitality
Centre, 730 2nd St. S.W., 55902, Tel. (507) 288-7500, provides Shabbat
dinners, hospital visitations, Judaica lending library.
Mikvah under construction.

ST. PAUL

Syn.: Adath Israel (O), 2337 Edgcumbe Rd., 55116; Beth Jacob (C), Highway
110 & Hunter La., 55118; Temple of Aaron (C), 616 S. Mississippi River
Blvd., 55116. Temple Mount Zion (R), 1300 Summit Av., 55105.
Com. Centre: 1375 St. Paul Av., 55116.
United Jewish Fund & Council: 790 S. Cleveland Av., Suite 201, 55116. Tel.
(612) 690-1707.
Kosher Restaurant: L'chaim, 655 Snelling Av., 55116.

MISSISSIPPI

GREENVILLE
Syn.: Hebrew Union Cong. (R), 504 Main St., 38701.

GREENWOOD
Syn.: Ahavath Rayim (O), Market & George Sts., P.O. Box 1235, 38930. Tel. 453-7537.
Delicatessen: Old Tyme Deli, Interstate 55 North at Northside Dr.

NATCHEZ
Syn.: B'nai Israel (R), Washington & S. Commerce Sts., P.O.B. 2081, 39120 (oldest synagogue in Mississippi).

TUPELO
Syn.: B'nai Israel (C), Marshall & Hamlin Sts., 38801.

MISSOURI

KANSAS CITY
(N.B. Please consult also, under Kansas, Overland Park and Prairie Village, since Kansas City spans both Missouri and Kansas. The syn. Kehilath Israel in Overland Park is the largest Traditional Cong. Syn, in the U.S.A.)
Syn.: Beth Israel Abraham & Voliner (O), 8310 Holmes Rd., 64131; Chabad Hse. 6201 Indian Creek Drive, Overland Park, Kansas 66207; Ohev Sholom (Traditional. Generally Orthodox ritual, but mixed seating), 5311 W. 75th St., Prairie Village, Kansas, 66208; Beth Shalom (C), 9400 Wornall Rd., 64114; B'nai Jehudah (R), 712 E. 69th St., 64131; New Reform Temple (R), 7100 Main St., 64114. Beth Torah (R), 9401 Nall, Suite 200, Shawvee Mission, Kansas 66207 .
Com. Centre: 5801 W. 115th St., Suite 101, Overland Park, Kansas 66211; Jewish Fed. of Greater Kansas City, 5801 W. 115th St., Suite 201, Overland Park, Kansas, 66211. The Jewish Com. Foundation, (Suite 202) & Jewish Family & Children Services, (Suite 103), are also at the foregoing address; Jewish Vocational Service, 1608 Baltimore Av. Kansas City, MO 64108; Menorah Medical Centre, 4949 Rockhill Rd. Kansas City, MO 64110; Shalom Geriatric Centre, 7801 Holmes Av., Kansas City, MO 64131.
The Harry S. Truman Library, 24 Highway & Delaware, Independence, Mo., 64050, contains the silver Ark & Torah scroll presented to ex-President Harry Truman by Israel's first President, Dr. Chaim Weizmann.
Restaurant **(K)** Sensations, 1148 W. 103 St., 64114.
Weekly newspaper: "Kansas City Jewish Chronicle", 7375 W. 107th St., Overland Park, Kansas, 66204.

ST. LOUIS
Syn.: Agudas Israel (O), 8202 Delmar Blvd., 63124; Bais Abraham (O), 6910 Delmar Blvd., 63130; Beth Hamedrosh Hagodol (O), 1227 North & South Rd., 63130; Chesed Shel Emeth (O), 700 North & South Rd., 63130; Nusach Hari B'nai Zion (O), 8630 Olive Blvd., 63132; Tpheris Israel Chevra Kadisha (O), 14550 Ladue Rd., Chesterfield, 63017; Young Israel (O), 7800 Groby Rd., 63130; B'nai Amoona (C), 324 S. Mason Rd., 63141; B'rith Sholom Kneseth Israel (C), 1107 Linden St., 63117; Shaare Zedek (C), 829 N. Hanley Rd., 63130; B'nai El (R), 11411 Highway 40, 63131; Shaare Emeth (R), 11645 Ladue Rd., 63141; Temple Emanuel (R), 12166 Conway Rd., 63141; Temple

Israel (R), 10675 Ladue Rd., 63141; Traditional Cong., 12437 Ladue Rd., 63141.
Mikva: 4 Millstone Campus, 63146. Tel. (314) 569-2770.
Com. Centre: 2 Millstone Campus Dr., 63146. Tel. (314) 432-5700.
Jewish Fed.: 12 Millstone Campus Dr., 63146. Tel. (314) 432-0020. The Brodsky Jewish Com. Library is also at this address.
The Vaad Hoeir (United Orthodox Jewish Community of St. Louis), 4 Millstone Campus, 63141, Tel. (314) 569-2770, is the recognised Orthodox religious authority for the city. Any inquiries concerning kashrut, etc., should be addressed to the Executive Director.
The following establishments are under the supervision of the Vaad Hoeir and are strictly kosher:
Hotels & Banquet Facilities: Adam's Mark Hotel, 4th & Chestnut. Tel. 241-7400; Airport Marriott Hotel, I-70 at Airport, Tel. 423-9700; Frontenac — The Grand Hotel, 1335 S. Lindbergh. Tel. 993-1100; Hyatt Regency, 1 St. Louis Union Station. Tel. 241-6664; The Ritz Carlton, One Ritz Carlton Dr., Tel. 863-6300.
Caterers: Simon Kohn's Kosher Meat & Deli, 10424 Old Olive. Tel. 569-0727; Lazy Suzan Imaginative Catering, 110 Millwell Dr., Tel. 291-6050; Sol's Kosher Meat Market, 8627 Olive. Tel. 993-9977; Thomas W. Klein Catering, 5823 Dewey. Tel. 351-5555; Top of the 230, 230 S. Bemiston. Tel. 863-2333; Galler's Kosher Meat Market, 8502 Olive. Tel. 993-4535.
Bakeries: Petrofsky's Bakery, 7649 Delmar. Tel. 725-1802; Pratzel's Bakery, 727 N. New Ballas. Tel. 567-9197, 928 N. McKnight. Tel. 991-0708; Schnucks Nancy Ann Bakery, Olive & Mason. Tel. 434-7323, Olive & Spoede. Tel. 567-3838, Overland Plaza. Tel. 426-3800; Mister Donut, 7758 Olive. Tel. 863-8005. Dining: The Hangar (twice monthly), Airport Marriott Hotel. Tel. 423-9700; NoBull Cafe, 10477 Old Olive. Tel. 991-9533; Diamant's, 618 North & South Rd. Tel. 712-9624; Simon Kohn's, 10424 Old Olive. Tel. 569-0727; Sol's, 8627 Olive. Tel. 993-9977; The Jewish Hospital, 216 S. Kingshighway. Tel. 454-7150. Butchers: Diamant's Kosher Meat Market, 618 North & South Rd., Tel. 721-9624. S. Kohn's, 10424 Old Olive St. Rd., Tel. 569-0727; Galler's, 8502 Olive. Tel. 993-4535; Sol's, 8627 Olive. Tel. 993-9977.
The Jewish Tercentenary monument and flagpole are in Forest Park.

MONTANA

BILLINGS

Syn.: Cong. Beth Aaron, 1148 N. Broadway, Billings, 59101. Tel. (406) 248-6412.

GREAT FALLS

Syn.: Aitz Chaim (R), P.O.B. 6192, Great Falls, 59406. Tel. (406) 542-9521.

MISSOULA

Syn.: New Missoula Jewish Community, P.O.B. 7581, Missoula, MT 58907. Tel. (406) 543-3356.

NEBRASKA

LINCOLN

Syn.: Tifereth Israel (C), 3219 Sheridan Blvd., 68502; South St. Temple B'nai Jeshurun (R), 20th & South Sts, 68502.

OMAHA

Syn.: Beth Israel (O), 1502 N. 52nd St. 68104; Beth El (C), 14506 California St., Omaha 68154, Temple Israel (R), 7023 Cass St., 68132.
Com. Mikva: 323 S. 132nd St., 68154.
Jewish Fed. of Omaha, 333 S. 132nd St., 68154. Tel. (402) 334-8200.
Friedel Jewish Academy, 12604 Pacific St., 68154.
Rose Blumkin Jewish Home for Aged, 323 S. 132nd St., 68154.

NEVADA

LAS VEGAS

For additional info. call: Mrs. Beverly Eisen, Community Relations Dir. (702) 732-0556.
Syn.: Cong. Shaarei Tefilla (O), 1331 S. Maryland Pkwy., 89104. Tel. (702) 384-3565; Temple Beth Sholom (C), 1600 E. Oakey Blvd., 89104. Tel. (702) 384-5070; Temple Emanu-El (C), 4925 So. Torrey Pines Dr., Tel. (702) 363-8722; Cong. Ner Tamid (R), 2761 E. Emerson Av., 89105. Tel. (702) 733-6292; Temple Beth Am (R), 4765 Brussels Av., 89121 (702) 456-7014; Chabad of Southern Nev. (0) 1805 Ivanhoe Wy. 89102. Fax. 732-3228; Or-Bamidbar (O) Sefardic 2959 E. Emerson Av., 89121. Tel. (702) 361-1175; Bet Knesset Bamidbar of Sun City (C), 8813 Marble Dr., 89134. Tel. (702) 254-5973; Adat Ari El (R), 2800 W. Sahara, Bldg. 4-B, 89102. Tel. (702) 221-6064.
Jewish Fed., 1030 E. Twain Av., 89109. Tel. (702) 732-0556.
Kosher Food: Jerusalem Kosher Restaurant & Deli, 1305 Vegas Valley, 89109. Tel. (702) 791-3668.

RENO

Syn.; Temple Emanu-El (C), 1031 Manzanita La. at Lakeside Dr., 89509. Tel. (702) 825-5600.

NEW HAMPSHIRE

BETHLEHEM

Syn.: Machzikei Hadas (O), Lewis Hill Rd, 03574 (summer only); Bethlehem Hebrew Cong. (C), Strawberry Hill, 03574.
Kosher Hotels: Arlington (summer only); Pinewood Motel.

MANCHESTER

Syn.: Temple Israel (C), 678 Pine St., 03104 Adath Yeshurun (R), 152 Prospect St., 03104.
Jewish Fed. of Greater Manchester, 698 Beech St., 03104. Tel. (603) 627-7679.

NEW JERSEY

ABERDEEN

Syn.: Bet Tefilah (O), 479 Lloyd Rd., Matawan, 07747. Tel. 583-6262.
Day School: Bayshore Hebrew Academy, 479 Lloyd Rd., Mattawan, 07747. Tel. 583-1229.

ATLANTIC CITY

Syn.: Rodef Shalom (O), 3833 Atlantic Av., 08401; Beth El (C), 500 N. Jerome Av., Margate, 08402; Beth Judah (C), 6725 Ventnor Av., Ventnor, 08406; Chelsea Hebrew Cong. (C), 4001 Atlantic Av., 08401; Community Syn. (C), Maryland & Pacific Avs., 08401; Beth Israel (R), 2501 Shore Rd.,

Northfield, 08225; Temple Emeth Shalom (R), 8501 Ventnor Av., Margate, 08402.
Fed. of Jewish Agencies of Atlantic County, 5321 Atlantic Av., Ventnor, 08406. Tel. (609) 822-1722.

BAYONNE

Syn.: Ohab Sholom (O), 1016-1022 Av. "C", 07002; Ohav Zedek (O), 912 Av. "C", 07002; Uptown Syn. (O), 49th St. & Av. "C", 07002; Temple Emanuel (C), 735 Kennedy Blvd., 07002; Temple Beth Am (R), 111 Av. "B", 07002.
Jewish Com. Centre, 1050 Kennedy Blvd., 07002. Tel. (201) 436-6900.

BELMAR

Syn.: Sons of Israel Cong. (O), P.O.B. 298, 07719.
Hotel: New Irvington, 112 12th Av., 07719.

BRADLEY BEACH

Syn.: Cong. Agudath Achim (O), 301 McCabe Av., 07720.

BRIDGETON

Syn.: Cong. Beth Abraham (C), 330 Fayette St., 08302.
Jewish Fed. of Cumberland County. See entry for Vineland, New Jersey.

BURLINGTON

Syn.: B'nai Israel (C), 212 High St., 08016.

CARMEL

Syn.: Temple Beth Hillel, 08332.

CARTERET

Com. Centre, 44 Noe St., 07008.

CHERRY HILL

Syn.: Sons of Israel (O), 720 Cooper Landing Rd., 08002. Mikva on premises; Beth El (C), 2901 W. Chapel Av., 08002; Beth Jacob-Beth Israel (C), 850 Evesham Rd., 08003; Temple Emanuel (R), Cooper River Parkway at Donahue, 08002.
Com. Centre: 2395 W. Marlton Pike, 08002.
Jewish Fed. of Southern New Jersey, 2393 W. Marlton Pike, 08002. Tel. (609) 665-6100.
Newspaper: "The Jewish Community Voice", 2393 W. Marlton Pike, 08002.
Kosher Bakery: Pastry Palace, State Highway 70, 08034. Tel. 429-3606.
Kosher Meat: Cherry Hill Kosher Market, 907 W. Marlton Pike, 08002.

CINNAMINSON

Syn.: Temple Sinai (C), New Albany Rd. & Route 130, 08077.

CLARK

Syn.: Temple Beth O'r (C), 111 Valley Rd., 07066. Tel. 381-8403.

CLIFTON

Syn.: Clifton Jewish Centre (C), 18 Delaware St., 07011; Beth Sholom (R), 733 Passaic Av., 07012.
Jewish Fed. of Greater Clifton-Passaic, 199 Scoles Av., 07012. Tel. (201) 777-7031.
Jewish Family Services, 199 Scoles Av., 07012. Tel. (201) 777-7638
YM-YWHA, 199 Scoles Av., 07012. Tel. (201) 779-2980.

Newspaper: "Jewish Com. News", 199 Scoles Av., 07012.

COLONIA

Syn.: Ohev Shalom (C), 220 Temple Way, 07067. Tel. (908) 388 7222.

CRABURY

Syn.: Jewish Cong. of Concordia, c/o Club House, 08512. Tel. (609) 655 8136.

CRANFORD

Syn.: Temple Beth El (C), 338 Walnut Av., 07016. Contact Rabbi Hoffberg for kosher hospitality. Tel. (201) 276-9231
Solomon Schechter Day School of Essex & Union, 721 Orange Av., 07016. Tel. 272-3400.

EAST BRUNSWICK

Syn.: Young Israel of E. Brunswick (O), 193 Dunham Corner Rd., 08816. Tel. (908) 254-1860; E. Brunswick Jewish Centre (C), 511 Ryders La., 08816. Tel. (908) 257-7070; Temple B'nai Shalom (R), Old Stage Rd. & Fern Rd., 08816. Tel. (908) 251-4300.
Jewish Family Service of Southern Middlesex, 517 Ryders La., 08816. Tel. (908). 257-4100.
Butcher: East Brunswick Kosher Meats, 1020, State Highway 18, 08816. Tel. (908) 257-0007.

EDISON

Syn.: Beth El (C), 91 Jefferson Blvd., 08817. Ohr Torah (O), 2 Harrison St., 08817. Tel. (908) 572-0526; or 572-7181; ; Temple Emanu-El. Tel. (908) 549-4442. (R), 100 James St., 08820. Chabad House (O), 8 Sicard St., New Brunswick, NJ 08901. Tel. (908) 828-9191.
Jewish Family Service of Northern Middlesex, 10 Franklin Av., 08837. Tel. (908) 738-5225.
Jewish Fed. of Greater Middlesex County, 100 Metroplex Dr. (Suite 101), 08817. Tel. (908) 985-1234. Fax (908) 985-3295.
Jewish Com. Centre of Middlesex County, 1775 Oak Tree Rd., 08820.
Butcher.: Edison Kosher Meats, State Highway 27, and Evergreen Rd., Tel. (201) 549-3707.

ELIZABETH

Syn.: Adath Israel (O), 1391 North Av., 07208; Adath Jeshurun (O), 200 Murray St. Tel. 355-6723; Bais Yitzchok Chevrah Thilim (O), 153 Bellevue St., 07202. Tel. 354-4789; Cong. Bris Avrohom (O), 555 Westminster Av., 07208. Tel. 289-0770; Elmora Hebrew Centre (O), 420 West End Av., 07202. Tel. 353-1740; Jewish Educational Centre (O), 330 Elmora Av., 07208; Jewish Education Centre (Adath Israel) (O), 1391 North Av., 07208; B'nai Israel (C), 1005 E. Jersey St., 07208; Temple Beth El of Elizabeth (R), 737 N. Broad St., 07208. Tel. 354-3021.
Inf. about kosher food, temporary accom., etc. can be obtained from Rabbi Elazar Teitz, 35 North Av., 07208.

ENGLEWOOD

Syn.: Ahavath Torah (O), 240 Broad Av., 07631; Shomrei Emunah (O), 273 Van Nostrand Av., 07631; Temple Emanu-El (C), 147 Tenafly Rd., 07631.
Kosher Bakery: Gourmet Gallery, 10 S. Dean St., 07631.
Kosher Butcher: Greenspan's, 93 W. Palisade Av., 07631.

FAIR LAWN

Syn.: Ahavat Achim (O), 18-19 Saddle River Rd., 07410; Cong. United Brotherhood (O), 8-09 Plaza Rd., 07410; Shomrei Torah (O), 19-19 Morlot Av., 07410; Beth Sholom (C), 40-25 Fair Lawn Av., 07410; B'nai Israel (C), Pine Av. & 30th St., 07410; Fair Lawn Jewish Centre (C), 10-10 Norma Av., 07410; Temple Avoda (R), 10-10 Plaza Rd. 07410.
Restaurants: Kosher Nosh Deli Restaurant, 894 Prospect Av., Glen Rock, 07140. Tel. (201) 445-1186. Plaza Pizza, 14-20 Plaza Rd., 07410. Tel. (201) 796-3113. Dairy only. Under rabbinical supervision.
Sandwiches, etc.: River Road Hot Bagels, 13-38 River Rd., 07410. Tel. (201) 791-5646. Under rabbinical supervision.
Kosher Groceries, Meat, etc. Ben-David International Foods Emporium, 24-28 Fair Lawn Av., 07410. Tel. (201) 794-7740; Harold's Kosher Meat Market, 19-11 Fair Lawn Av., 07410. Tel. (201) 796-0003; New Royal Bake Shop, 19-09 Fair Lawn Av., 07410. Tel. (201) 796-6565; Petak Bros. Kosher Deli, 19-03 Fair Lawn Av., 07410. Tel. (201) 797-5010.
Meat Restaurant: Fair Lawn Glatt Kosher Deli & Israeli Restaurant, 14-20 Plaza Rd., Fair Lawn, N.J. 07410 Tel. (201) 703-0088.
Sandwiches: Hot Bagels, 6-07 Saddle River Rd., Fair Lawn, N. J. 07410. Tel. (201) 796-9625.
Please note that in both stores, only the bagels are Kosher under Rabbinical Supervision.

FREEHOLD

Syn.: Agudath Achim (O), Broad & Stokes Sts., 07728.

HACKENSACK

Syn.: Temple Beth El (C), 280 Summit Av., 07601.
Jewish Fed. of Com. Services of Bergen County, 170 State St., 07601.

HADDON HEIGHTS

Syn.: Beth Sholom (C), Green St. at White Horse Pike, 08035.

HIGHLAND PARK

Syn.: Cong. Ahavas Achim (O), PO Box 4242. Tel. (201) 247-0532; Cong. Etz Ahaim (O, Sephardi), 230 Dennison St., 08904. Tel. (201) 247-3839; Cong. Ohav Emeth (O), 415 Raritan Av., 08904. Tel. (201) 247-3038; Highland Park Conservative Temple & Centre (C), 201 S. 3rd Av. 08904. Tel. (201) 545-6482.
Park Mikva, 112 S. 1st Av., 08904.
Y.M.-Y.W.H.A. of Raritan Valley, 2 S. Adelaide Av., 08904. Tel. 249-2221.
Bookshop: Highland Park Sefarim & Judaica, 227 Raritan Av.
Kosher Restaurant: Jerusalem Pizza, 231 Raritan Av., 08904.
Also under rabbinical supervision: B & E Kosher Meat Market, 76 Raritan Av., Tel. (201) 846-3444; Berkley Bakery, 405 Raritan Av., 08904; Dan's Deli & Meat Market, 515 Raritan Av., 08904; Jerusalem Meating Place, 231 Raritan Av., 08904.

HILLSIDE

Syn.: Cong. Sinai Torath Chaim (O), 1531 Maple Av., 07205. Tel. 923-9500.
Temple Shomrei Torah (C), 910 Salem Av., 07205. Tel. 289-0770.

HOBOKEN

Syn.: United Synagogue of Hoboken (C), 830 Hudson St. & 115 Park Av., 07030.
Freehold: Congregation Agudath Achim (O), Freehold Jewish Center, Broad & Stokes St., Freehold, New Jersey 07728.

JAMES BURG

Syn.: Rossmoor Jewish Cong. Rossmoor Meeting Room, 08831. Tel. (609) 655-0439.

JERSEY CITY

Syn.: Agudath Shalom (O), 2456 Kennedy Blvd., cnr. Gifford Av., 07304; Mount Sinai (O), 128 Sherman Av., 07307; Mount Zion (O), 233 Webster Av., 07307; Rogosin Yeshiva Synagogue (O), 25 Cottage St., 07306; Sons of Israel (O), 294 Grove St., 07302; B'nai Jacob (C), 176 W. Side Av., 07305; Temple Beth-El (R), 71 Bentley Av., 07304.

LAKEWOOD

Syn.: Lakewood Yeshiva (O), Private Way & 6th St., 08701; Sons of Israel (O), Madison Av. & 6th St., 08701; Ahavat Shalom (C), Forest Av. & 11th St., 08701; Beth Am (R), Madison Av. & Carey St., 08701.
Ocean County Jewish Fed., 301 Madison Av., 08701. Tel. (201) 363-0530.
Hotel: Capitol Hotel (Kosher).
Restaurant: Kosher Experience, Kennedy Blvd., 08701. Closed on Sabbath & all Holy-days & festivals. Under supervision of manager, Rabbi Chumsky.
Delicatessen: R. & S. Kosher, 416 Clifton Av., 08701. Closed on Sabbath & all Holy-days & festivals. Meat only. Under supervision of Vaad Hakashruth of Lakewood.

LINDEN

Syn.: Cong. Anshe Chesed (O), 100 Orchard Ter. at St. George Av., 07036. Tel. 486-8616. Mekor Chayim Suburban Jewish Centre (C), Deerfield Rd. & Academy Ter., 07036. Tel. 925-2283.

LIVINGSTON

Syn.: Synagogue of the Suburban Torah Center, 85 W. Mt. Pleasant Av., Livingston, New Jersey 07039. Tel. (201) 994-0122/2620.
Restaurants: (K) Metro Glatt/Delancey St., 515 S. Livingston Av., Livingston, New Jersey 07029. Tel. (201) 992-9189; **(K)** Jerusalem Restaurant & Pizzeria (Dairy), 16 East Mt. Pleasant Av., Livingston, New Jersey 07039. Tel. (201) 533-1424; **(K)** Super Duper Bagels, 498 S. Livingston Av., Livingston, New Jersey 07039. Tel. (201) 533-1703.

METUCHEN

Syn.: Neve Shalom (C), 250 Grove Av., 08840. Tel. 548 2238.

MILLVILLE

Syn.: Beth Hillel (C), 3rd Av. & Oak St., 08332.
Jewish Fed. of Cumberland County. See entry for Vineland, New Jersey.

MORRISTOWN

Syn.: Cong. Ahavath Yisrael (O), 9 Cutler St., 07960. Tel. (201) 267-4184. The syn. operates a kosher food buying service for the community, dealing only in strictly kosher products. Further inf. from Baila Mandel, Tel. (201) 267-4184; Rabbinical College of America (O), 226 Sussex Av., 07960; Morristown Jewish Center (C), 177 Speedwell Av., 07960. Tel. (201) 538-9292; Temple B'nai Or (R), Overlook Rd., 07960.

MOUNT FREEDOM

Syn.: Mount Freedom Jewish Centre (O), 1209 Sussex Turnpike, 07970.

NEW BRUNSWICK

Syn: Chabad Hse. Friends of Lubavitch (O), 8 Sicard St., 08901. Tel. (201) 828-9191; Anshe Emeth Memorial Temple (R), 222 Livingston Av., 08901. Tel. (201) 545-6484; Cong. Poile Zedek (unaffiliated), 145 Neilson St., 08901. Tel. (201) 545-6123.

B'nai B'rith Hillel Foundation, Rutgers University, Clifton Av. & Ryders La., 08903. Tel. (201) 545-2407.

NEWARK & DISTRICT (Essex, Morris, Sussex, Warren and parts of Union and Hudson Counties)

Syn.: Agudath Israel (O), 1125 Stuyvesant Av., Irvington, 07111; Ahavas Achim B'nai Israel (C), 706 Nye Av., Irvington, 07111; Ahavas Sholom (O), 145 Broadway, 07104; Ahavath Zion (O), 421 Boyden Av., Maplewood, 07040; Ahawas Achim B'nai Jacob and David (O), 700 Pleasant Valley Way, W. Orange, 07052; Anshe Lubowitz (O), 74 Mill Rd., Irvington, 07111; Beth Ephraim-B'nai Zion (O), 520 Prospect St., Maplewood, 07040; Cong. Ahavat Torah (O), 1180 Route 46, Colony Plaza, Parsippany, 07054; Chabad Center of North West N.J. (O), 23-25 Pawnee Av., Rockaway, 07866; Cong. Israel of Springfield (O), 339 Mountain Av., Springfield, 07081; Federation Plaza (O), 750 Northfield Av., W. Orange, 07052; Daughters of Israel Geriatric Centre (O), 1155 Pleasant Valley Way, W. Orange, 07052; Hillside Jewish Centre (O), 1538 Summit Av., Hillside, 07205; Lev Israel (O), 1548 Summit Av., Hillside, 07205; Mount Sinai Cong. (O), 250 Mt. Vernon Pl., Newark, 07106; Sinai Torath Chaim (O), 1531 Maple Av., Hillside, 07205; Suburban Torah Centre (O), 85 W. Mount Pleasant Av., Livingston, 07039; Young Israel (O), 1 Henderson Dr., W. Caldwell, 07006; Young Israel of W. Orange (O), 567-569 Pleasant Valley Way, W. Orange, 07052; Adat Israel Cong. (C), 200 Overlook Rd., Boonton, 07005; Adath Shalom (C), 18 Thompson Av., Dover, 07801; Agudath Israel (C), 20 Academy Rd., Caldwell, 07006; Ahavath Achim (C), 122-139 Academy St., Belleville, 07109; Ahavath Achim B'nai Israel (C), 706 Nye Av., Irvington, 07111; Beth Ahm (C), 60 Temple Drive, Springfield, 07081; Beth El (C), 222 Irvington Av., S. Orange, 07079; Beth Shalom (C), 193 E. Mount Pleasant Av., Livingston, 07039; B'nai Abraham (C), 300 E. Northfield Rd., Livingston, 07039; B'nai Israel (C), 160 Millburn Av., Millburn, 07041; B'nai Israel (C), 192 Center St., Nutley, 07110; B'nai Israel of Kearny & North Arlington (C), 780 Kearny Av., Kearny, 07032; Cong. Beth Ahm of W. Essex (C), Box 329, 56 Grove Av., Verona, 07044; Jewish Centre of Sussex County (C), 13 Washington St., Box 334, Newton, 07860; B'nai Shalom Jewish Centre of W. Orange (C), 300 Pleasant Valley Way, W. Orange, 07052; Jewish Com. Centre of Summit (C), 67 Kent Pl. Blvd., Summit, 07901; Lake Hiawatha Jewish Centre (C), 140 Lincoln Av., Lake Hiawatha, 07034; Oheb Shalom-Beth Torah (C), 170-180 Scotland Rd., S. Orange, 07079; Pine Brook Jewish Centre (C), 174 Changebridge Rd., Montville, 07045; Shomrei Emunah (C), 67 Park St., Montclair, 07042; Suburban Jewish Centre of Morris County (C), 165 Ridgedale Av., Florham Park, 07932; Temple Ner Tamid (C&R), 936 Broad St., Bloomfield, 07003; Temple Hatikvah (C), Pleasant Hill Rd., Flanders, 07836; White Meadow Temple (C), White Meadow Rd., Rockaway, 07866; B'nai Jeshurun (R), 1025 S. Orange Av., Short Hills, 07078; Shaarey Shalom (R), 78 S. Springfield Av., Springfield, 07081; Sharey Tefilo-Israel (R), 432 Scotland Rd., S. Orange, 07079; Temple Beth Ahm (R), 879 S. Beverwick Rd., Parsippany, 07054; Temple Emanu-El of W. Essex (R), 264 W. Northfield Rd., Livingston, 07039; Temple Shalom of Sussex County (R), Oak St., Franklin; Temple Shalom (R), 215 S. Hillside Av., Succasunna, 07876; Temple Sholom of W. Essex (R), 760 Pompton Av., Cedar Grove, 07009; Temple Sinai (R),

208 Summit Av., Summit, 07901; B'nai Keshet (Rec.), Church St. and Trinity Place, Montclair, 07042.

Organisations

Beth Israel Medical Center: 201 Lyons Av., 07112.

Mikvaot: Mikvah of Essex County, 717 Pleasant Valley Way, West Orange 07052; Sarah Esther Rosenhaus Mikvah Institute, 93 Lake Rd., Morristown, 07960.

United Jewish Fed. of Metrowest, 901 Route 10, Whippany, NJ 07981. Tel. (201) 884-4800; Fax (201) 884-7361.

Newspaper: "The Metrowest Jewish News," 901 Route 10, Whippany, NJ 07981. Tel. (201) 887-3900; is published weekly. It is owned by the United Jewish Fed. of Metrowest.

Booksellers: Rabbi L. Sky, Hebrew Book Store, 1923 Springfield Av., Maplewood 07040. Tel. (201) 763-4244-5.

Restaurants: Arlington Kosher Deli, Restaurant & Caterers, Arlington Shopping Center, 744 Route 46W, Parsippany, NJ 07054. Tel. (201) 335-9400; David's Deco-Tessen, 555 Passaic Av., West Caldwell, NJ 07006. Tel. (201) 808-3354. Fax (201) 808-5806; (K) Gourmet Galaxy, 659 Eagle Rock Av., West Orange, NJ 07052. Tel. (201) 736-0060; (K) Jerusalem West, 16 E. Mt. Pleasant Av., Livingston, NJ 07039. Tel. (201) 533-1424; (K) Metro Glatt/Delancey Street, 515 Livingston Av., Livingston, NJ 07039. Tel. (201) 992-9189. Fax (201) 992-6430 (for take-out); Pleasantdale Kosher Meat, 470 Pleasant Valley Way, West Orange, NJ 07052. Tel. (201) 731-3216; (K) Reuben's Deli Delite, 500 Pleasant Valley Way, West Orange, NJ 07052. Tel. (201) 731-6351; Zayda's Super Value, Meat Market & Deli, 309 Irvington Av., South Orange, NJ 07079. Tel. (201) 762-1812.

NORTH BRUNSWICK

Syn.: Cong. B'nai Tikvah (C), 1001 Finnegins Lane 08902. Tel. (201) 297-0696.

PARLIN

Syn.: Ohav Shalom (C), 3018 Bordertown Av., 08859. Tel. (201) 727-4334.

PASSAIC

Syn.: Adas Israel (O), 565 Broadway, 07055; Bais Torah U'Tfila (O), Collegiate School, Kent Court, 07055; T: Fereth Israel (O), 180 Passaic Av., 07055; Young Israel of Passaic-Clifton (O), 200 Brook Av., 07055; Ahavas Israel (Traditional), 181 Van Houten Av., 07055; Temple Emanuel (C), 181 Lafayette Av., 07055.

Beth Israel Hospital: 70 Parker Av., 07055. Kosher restaurant on premises.

Hillel Academy, 565 Broadway, 07055.

Jewish Fed. of Greater Clifton-Passaic. See entry for Clifton, New Jersey.

School: Yeshiva Ktana of Passaic, 252 High St., 07055. Tel. (201) 916-0666.

Yeshiva: Talmudic Research Centre, 35 Ascension St., 07055.

Rituarium: Mikvah Yisroel, 242 High St., 07055.

Kosher Restaurant: Jerusalem II Pizza of Passaic, 224 Brook Av., 07055.

Kosher Meat: Brook Kosher, 222 Brook Av., 07055.

Food: B&Y Kosher Korner Inc., 200 Main Av., 07055. Tel. (201) 777-1120.

PATERSON

Syn.: Community Syn. (C), 660 14th Av., 07504; Temple Emanuel (C), 151 E. 33rd St., 07514.

PERTH AMBOY
Syn.: Shaarey Tefiloh (O), 15 Market St., 08861. Tel. 826-2977; Beth Mordechai (C), 224 High St., 08861. Tel. 442-2431.
Y.M.H.A., 316 Madison Av., 08861. Tel. 442-0365.

PISCATAWAY
Syn.: Cong. B'nai Shalom (R), 25 Netherwood Av., 08854. Tel. (908) 885-9444.

PLAINFIELD
Syn.: United Orthodox Synagogue (O), 526 W. 7th St., 07060; Beth El (C), 225 E. 7th St., 07060. Tel. (201) 755-0043; Temple Sholom (R), 815 W. 7th St., 07063. Tel. (201) 756-6447.

PRINCETON
Syn.: Jewish Centre (C), 457 Nassau St., 08540.

RAHWAY
Syn.: Temple Beth Torah (C), 1389 Bryant St., 07065. Tel. 576-8432.

RIVER EDGE
Syn.: Temple Sholom (R), 385 Howland Av., 07661.
United Jewish Community of Bergen County, 111 Kinderkamack Rd., 07661. Tel. (201) 488-6800.

RUMSON
Syn.: Cong. B'nai Israel (C), Hance & Ridge Rds., 07760. Tel. 842-1800.

SCOTCH PLAINS
Syn.: Temple Israel Fanwood (C), 1920 Cliffwood St., 07076. Tel. 889-1830.
Jewish Com. Centre of Central New Jersey, 1391 Martine Av., 07076. Tel. 889-1830.

SOMERSET
Syn.: Temple Beth El (C) 1495 Amwell Rd., 08873. Tel. (201) 873-2325.

SOUTH RIVER
Syn.: Cong. Anshe Emeth (Trad.), 88 Main St., 08882. Tel. (201) 257-4190.

SPOTSWOOD
Syn.: Monroe Township Jewish Centre (R), 11 Cornell Av., 08884. Tel. (201) 251-1119.

TEANECK
Syn.: Bnai Yeshurun (O), 641 W. Englewood Av., 07666. Tel. (201) 836-8916; Cong. Beth Aaron (O), 950 Queen Anne Rd., 07666; Roemer Syn. (O), Whittier School, W. Englewood Av., 07666; Beth Sholom (C), Rugby Rd. & Rutland Av., 07666; Jewish Centre of Teaneck (C), 70 Sterling Place, 07666; Beth Am (R), 510 Claremont Av., 07666; Rinat Yisrael (O), 389 W. Englewood Av., 07666; Temple Emeth (R), 1666 Windsor Rd., 07666.
Mikveh: 1726 Windsor Rd., 07666. Tel. (201) 837-8220.
Kosher Foods: Glatt Express, 1400 Queen Anne Rd., 07666. Tel. (201) 837-8110.; Hot Bagels, 513 Cedar La., 07666. Tel. (201) 836-9705.; Maadan, 446 Cedar La., 0766. Tel. (201) 692-0192.
Restaurants: Noah's Ark, 482 Cedar La., 07666. Tel. 692-1200; Hunan Teaneck, 515 Cedar La., 07666. Tel. (201) 692-0099; Jerusalem Pizza (Dairy), 496 Cedar La., 07666. Tel. (201) 836-2120 or 836-2165; Grill Express, 540

Cedar La., 07666. Tel. 836-4115. Santoro's, 439 Cedar La., 07666. Tel. 836-9505
All the foregoing are under orthodox rabbinical supervision.
Bakery: Butterflake, 448 Cedar Lane. Tel. (201) 836-3516.
Bookstore: Zoldan's Judaica Center, 406 Cedar Lane. Tel. (201) 907-0034.

TRENTON

Syn.: People of Truth (Anshe Emes) (O), 1201 W. State St., 08618; Workers of Truth (O), 832 W. State St., 08618. Tel. (609) 396-2231; Adath Israel (C), 1958 Lawrenceville Rd, Lawrenceville, N. J. 08648; Ahavath Israel (C), 1130 Lower Ferry Rd., 08618; Cong. Brothers of Israel (C), 499 Greenwood Av., 08618; Har Sinai (R), 491 Bellevue Av., 08618. Tel. (609) 392 7143.
Jewish Fed. of Mercer & Bucks Counties, 999 Lower Ferry Rd., 08628. Tel. (609) 883-5000.

UNION

Syn: Beth Shalom (C), 2046 Vauxhall Rd., 07083; Temple Israel (C), 2372 Morris Av., 07083. Tel. (201) 686-2120.
Jewish Fed. of Central New Jersey, Green La., 07083. Tel. (201) 351-5060.
YM-YWHA of Union County, Green La., 07083. Tel. (201) 289-8112.

VINELAND

More than 1,000 families were settled in the Vineland area after being liberated from Nazi concentration camps in Europe. Some 60 years earlier, the area was the site of many farm settlements founded at the end of the last century with aid from Baron de Hirsch.
Syn: Ahavas Achim (O), 618 Plum St., 08360; Sons of Jacob (O), 321 Grape St., 08360; Beth Israel (C), 1015 E. Park Av., 08360.
Jewish Fed. of Cumberland County, 629 Wood St., Suite 202-204, 08360. Tel. (609) 696-4445. Also serves the Bridgeton & Cumberland County areas.

WARREN

Syn.: Mountain Jewish Com. Centre (R), 104 Mt. Horeb Rd., 07060. Tel. 356-8777.
Jewish Fed. of Central New Jersey, Suburban Services Office, 117 Stirling Rd. 07060. Tel. 580 1122.

WAYNE

Syn.: Shomrei Torah (C), 30 Hinchman Av., 07470; Temple Beth Tikvah (R), 950 Preakness Av., 07470.
Jewish Fed. of N. Jersey, 1 Pike Dr., 07470. Tel. (201) 595-0555.
YM-YWHA, 1 Pike Dr., 07470.

WEST NEW YORK

Syn.: Congregation Shaare Zedek (O); 5308 Palisade Av., 07093.

WESTFIELD

Syn.: Temple Emanu-El (R), 756 E. Broad St., 07090. Tel. 232-6770.

WILLINGBORO

Syn.: Beth Torah (C), Beverley-Rancocas Rd., 08046; Temple Emanu-El (R), John F. Kennedy Way, 08046.

WOODBRIDGE

Syn.: Adath Israel (C), 424 Amboy Av., 07095. Tel. 634-9601.

NEW MEXICO

ALBUQUERQUE

Syn.: B'nai Israel (C), 4401 Indian School Rd. N.E., 87110. Tel. (505) 266-0155; Cong. Albert (R), 3800 Louisiana Av. N.E., 87110. Tel. (505) 883-1818; Nahalat Shalom (R), 295 La Plata N.W. Albuquerque, 87107. Tel. (505) 344-6773.
Jewish Fed. of Greater Albuquerque: 8205 Spain N.E., 87111.
Visitors requiring kosher meals should contact The JFGA, Tel. (505) 821-3214.

LAS CRUCES

Syn.: Temple Beth El,Parker Rd. at Melendres, Las Cruces.

LOS ALAMOS

Syn.: Jewish Centre, 2400 Canyon Rd., 87544. Tel. (505) 662-2440.

RIO RANCHO

Syn.: Rio Rancho Jewish Center, 2009 Grande Blvd., Rio Rancho, 87124. Tel. (505) 892-8511.

SANTA FE

Syn.: Pardes Yisroel (O). Tel. (505) 986-2091; 205 E. Barcelona Rd., 98501. for inf. about home hospitality, Shabbos, Mikva, Kosher catering, Tel. 986-2091. Rabbi Weinbaum, 983-8065; Temple Beth Shalom (C) & (R), 205 E. Barcelona Rd., 87501. Tel. (505) 982-1376. (R) & (C) also held here. Rabbi Bentley, 983-7446.
Kosher Food: Kaunes Food Town, Wild Oats, Market Place.

NEW YORK STATE

Work on revising the sections on New York State and New York City is in progress.
New York City may be a world metropolis, but the other places in New York State – these are America.
Indeed, New York State, which stretches from New York City to the Canadian border, possesses within its 50,000 square miles a superb array of natural features.
Apart from New York City and its suburbs, with its 2 1/2 million Jews (probably 90 per cent of the Jewish population of New York State), numerous up-state cities and towns, like Buffalo, Rochester, Binghamton, Syracuse, Utica, Schenectady and many more, have flourishing Jewish communities. At least 25 of them have communities numbering several thousand or more. Actually, the Dutch first colonised New York, which was then known as New Amsterdam, and they ruled it until, September, 1664, when four British warships took possession of the Dutch colony for King Charles II who made a present of it to his brother, James, Duke of York, and it was hastily renamed and became the Province of New York.
The first group of Jews had reached New Amsterdam from Recife in 1654, and some of them made their way northwards soon afterwards, including Asser Levy, who began dealing in real estate up in Albany, now the state capital. He also traded up and down the Hudson River, as did Jacob de Lucena in 1678, who reached as far north as Kingston. By 1760, Jews had settled on Long Island, which today has a Jewish population of some 450,000 and about 150 synagogues. Jews came to Westchester a century later, in 1860, and Westchester County now boasts a Jewish population of

more than 135,000. In Newburgh, Jewish merchants set up a trading post in 1777, but it was not until 1848 that a Jewish community was established there.

The first Jewish community in the State outside New York City is no longer in existence. It was in the lush hills of Ulster County, now in the centre of the Catskills resort area, and was founded by twelve families and called Sholom. The oldest existing com. above New York City is Albany, where Congregation Beth El (now merged into Beth Emeth) was founded in 1838.

It was in Albany that Benjamin N. Cardozo served as Chief Justice of the State before becoming an Associate Justice of the U.S. Supreme Court. The law school at Yeshiva University in New York City is named after him. The late Herbert H. Lehman presided over the State as Governor from 1933 to 1942, and his brother, Irving, was Chief Judge from 1939 to 1942.

The State Capitol building had as co-architect Leopold Eidlitz. In the cornerstone are a prayer and a mezuza from the Albany Jewish community.

To the south and south-west of Albany is the famous Catskills resort area. Covering two counties, and known as the "Borscht Belt" or "Circuit", it is about two hours from New York City by car, bus or door-to-door limousine service. From Memorial Day (the last weekend in May) to Labour Day (the last weekend in September), tens of thousands flock to the Catskills for their holidays, to fill scores of hotels ranging from the luxurious to the simple, and clusters of rented cottages known as bungalows or retreats (which used also to be known as "kuchaleins" – meaning, roughly: "Do your own cooking"), many owned by Orthodox groups, including Chasidim belonging to the various sects.

On a summer's day in the Catskills, it is a common occurrence to see groups of bearded young men with side-curls, dressed in black hats and long black coats, walking along the edge of a country road and hoping to catch a ride into the nearest town or hamlet.

Some of the bigger hotels now remain open throughout the year, offering golf on some of the finest courses in the land, indoor and outdoor bathing pools, and skiing when there is snow (and in some places, which have "snow machines," even when there is no snow).

All the larger Jewish hotels and many of the smaller ones have special services for Passover and the High Holy-days, presenting the finest chazanim and choirs obtainable.

Entertainment is the key word as far as the Catskills are concerned. No star is too big or expensive for the larger hotels, and some of the most famous American Jewish entertainers – people like the late Danny Kaye and Jerry Lewis – got their first break in the Catskills.

All this had its beginnings in a Jewish relief project during the first great wave of East European immigration in the last two decades of the past century, when Jewish agencies made it possible for newcomers to leave the East Side of New York City and start small farms in the area. Some became successful farmers, others – most of the others – had to take in boarders to make a living. Boarding houses became small hotels and small hotels large ones.

The Concord (Kiamesha Lake, 12751) is the best-known hotel. It is under rabbinical supervision and has excellent kosher cuisine, a fine golf course, indoor and outdoor bathing pools, ice-skating rinks, tennis courts and all other facilities designed to keep people happy. The Concord has an increasing number of non-Jewish guests year by year, who enjoy the food and opulence and do not mind not being allowed to smoke in the public rooms on the Sabbath.

Another popular top hotel under rabbinical supervision is the glatt kosher Homowack Hotel in Spring Glen, 12483, which also has complete holiday and recreational facilities. Two additional glatt kosher hotels are the Lake House Hotel in Woodridge, 12789, and Gibber's Hotel at Kiamesha Lake, 12751.

Some of the many other top hotels which list themselves as kosher and are popular with Jewish visitors are: Brown's, at Loch Sheldrake, 12759, the favourite of Jerry Lewis, who was a page boy there; the Pines at South Fallsburg, 12779; Kutsher's, at Monticello, 12701, and Tamarack Lodge, at Greenfield Park, 12435.

On the periphery of the Catskills are two villages founded by Chasidim – New Square at Spring Valley, a misspelling by a county official of "Skvir" from which this sect stems, and Monsey, two miles away. They are worth a visit. Both New Square and Monsey are, of course, run on strictly Orthodox lines, so all commercial activities and traffic cease before Shabbat comes in on Friday afternoon or evening.

There is an International Synagogue at Kennedy Airport in New York, with a museum which includes contributions from every Jewish community in the world.

ALBANY

Syn.: Beth Abraham-Jacob, 380 Whitehall Rd., 12208. Tel. (518) 489-5819 or (518) 489-5179 (O); Shomray Torah (O), 463 New Scotland Av., 12208; Chabad-Lubavitch Centre of the Capital District (O), 122 S. Main Av., 12208. Tel. (518) 482-5781; Daughters of Sarah Nursing Home (Traditional & R), Washington Av. Extension, 12208. Tel. (518) 456-7831; Traditional service, Sat. 9.15 a.m. Reform service, Fri. 3 p.m.; Ohav Shalom (C), New Krumkill Rd., 12208. Tel. (518) 489-4706; Temple Israel (C), 600 New Scotland Av., 12208. Tel. (518) 438-7858; Beth Emeth (R), 100 Academy Rd., 12208. Tel. (518) 436-9761. (At this 160-year-old congregation, Rabbi Isaac Mayer Wise, founder of American Reform Judaism, served when he first arrived in the United States); B'nai Sholom (R), 420 Whitehall Rd., 12208. Tel. (518) 482-5283.

Mikva: Bnos Israel of the Capital District, 190 Elm St., 12202.

Com. Centre, 340 Whitehall Rd., 12208. Tel. (518) 438-6651.

Jewish Family Services, 930 Madison Av., 12208. Tel. (518) 482-8856.

Shabbos House, State University of New York, 67 Fuller Rd. Tel. (518) 438-4227.

Restaurants: Dahlia Vegetarian & Dairy Restaurant, 858 Madison Av. between Ontario & Partridge Sts., 12203. Tel. (518) 482-0931. Under supervision of Vaad Hakashruth.

Price Chopper Market, 1892 Central Av., 12205. Tel. (518) 456-2970. Full service kosher department. Under supervision of Vaad Hakashruth.

AMSTERDAM

Syn.: Cong. Sons of Israel (C), 355 Guy Pk. Av., 12010. Tel. (518) 842-8691.

BEACON

Hebrew Alliance: 55 Fishkill Av., 12508.

BINGHAMTON

Syn.: Beth David (O), 39 Riverside Dr., 13905; Temple Israel (C), Deerfield Pl. Vestal, 13850; Temple Concord (R), 9 Riverside Dr., 13905; Temple Beth El (Reconstructionist), 117 Jefferson Av., Endicott, 13760.

Com. Centre: 500 Clubhouse Rd., 13903.

Jewish Fed. of Broome County, 500 Clubhouse Rd., Vestal 13850. Tel. (607) 724-2332.

The Jewish Fed. publishes the weekly "Reporter", Tel. (607) 724-2360, at the same address.

BUFFALO

Syn.: B'nai Shalom (O), 1675 N. Forest Rd.; Amherst Syn. (O), 504 Frankhauser Rd., 14421; Beth Abraham (O), 1073 Elmwood Av., 14222; Chabad Hse. (O), 3292 Main St., 14214 & 2501 N. Forest Rd., 14068; Saranac Syn. (O), 85 Saranac Av., 14216; Young Israel of Greater Buffalo (O), 105 Maple Rd., Williamsville, 14221; Kehilat Shalom (Traditional), 700 Sweet Home Rd., 14226; Beth El (C), 2360 Eggert Rd., 14223; Hillel Foundation (C), 40 Capen Blvd., 14214; Shaarey Zedek (C), 621 Getzville Rd., 14226; Beth Am (R), 4660 Sheridan Dr., 14221; Beth Shalom (R), Union & Center Sts., Hamburg; Beth Zion (R), 805 Delaware Av., 14209; Cong. Havurah (R), 6320 Main St.; Temple Sinai (Reconstructionist), 50 Alberta Dr., 14226.
Mikva: 1248 Kenmore Av., 14216.
Jewish Centre of Greater Buffalo: 787 Delaware Av., 14209 & 2640 N. Forest Rd., Getzville, 14068. Tel. (716) 688-4033 & 886-3145.
Jewish Fed. of Greater Buffalo: 787 Delaware Av., 14209. Tel. (716) 886-7750.

CLIFTON PARK

Syn.: Beth Shalom (C), Clifton Pk. Center Rd., 12065. Tel. 371-0608.

DELMAR

Delmar Chabad Centre (O), 109 Elsmere Av., 12054. Tel. 439-8280; Reconstructionist Havurah of the Capital District (Rec.), 98 Meadowland St., 12054. Tel. 439-5870.

ELLENVILLE

Syn.: Ezrath Israel (O), Rabbi Eisner Sq., 12428. Tel. (914) 647-4450. Min.: Rabbi Moshe Frank. Mikva, same address.

ELMIRA

Syn.: Shomray Hadath (O), Cobbles Pk., 14905; B'nai Israel (R), Water & Guinnip Sts., 14905.
Com. Centre & Jewish Young Men's & Women's Assoc.: 115 E. Church St., 14901.

FALLSBURG & SOUTH FALLSBURG

Kosher Hotel: The Pines, S. Fallsburg, 12779.

FLEISCHMANNS

(K) Glatt Kosher Hotel: Oppenheimer's Regis, 12430. Tel. (914) 254-5080. Under supervision of Rabbinate of K'hal Adas Jeshurun, New York City.

GENEVA

Syn.: Temple Beth El (C), 755 South Main St. Tel. (315) 789 2945.

GILBOA

Catskill Mountain "Dude Ranch Vacations" Near: Howe Caverns, Cooperstown, Catskill Game Farm. Golden Acres Farm & Ranch. 1-800-252-7787, 1-800-847-2251 Rabbinical Supervision, Services.

GLENS FALLS

Syn.: Shaarey Tefila (C), 68 Bay St., 12801. Tel. 792-4945; Temple Beth El (R), 3 Marion Av., 12801. Tel. 792-4364.

GLOVERSVILLE

Syn.: Knesseth Israel (C), 34 E. Fulton St., 12078. Tel. 725-0649.
Com. Centre: 28 E. Fulton St., 12078.

GREENFIELD PARK

Kosher Hotel: Tamarack Lodge, 12435.

HAVERSTRAW

Syn.: Cong. Sons of Jacob (O), 37 Clove Av., 10927.

HUDSON

Syn.: Anshe Emeth (C), 240 Jolsen Blvd., 12534. Tel. 828-9040.
The Rose Kline Memorial Judaica Collection is housed in the library of the
Daughters of the American Revolution.

HYDE PARK

There are many items of Jewish interest in the Franklin D. Roosevelt
Memorial Library.

ITHACA

Syn.: Temple Beth El (C), 402 N. Tioga St., 14850.

KIAMESHA LAKE

Kosher Hotel: Concord, 12751. Tel. (914) 794-4000. Fax (914) 794-7471.

LAKE PLACID

Syn.: 30 Saranac Av. (Traditional), 12946. Tel. 523-3876.

LATHAM

United Jewish Fed. of Northeastern New York, 800 New Loudon Rd.,
12110. Tel. 783-7800.
United Jewish Federation of Northeastern New York, 800 New Loudon
Rd., (Latham Circle Mall on Rt. 9) Tel. (518) 783-7800.

LOCH SHELDRAKE

Kosher Hotel: Brown's, 12759.

LONG ISLAND
Synagogues
Orthodox

Cong. Ahavat Yisrael, 1742 Union Av., Hewlett, 11557. Tel. (516) 295-2282;
Cong. Beth Sholom, 390 Broadway, Lawrence, 11559. Tel. (516) 569-3600;
Cong. Beth Sholom, Sunrise Jewish Centre, 550 Rockaway Av., Valley
Stream 11581. Tel. (516) 825-2822; Cong. Etz Chaim, Tel. (516) 543-1441;
Cong. Lubavitch, 65 Valleywood Rd., Commack, 11725. Tel. (516) 543-1307;
Cong. Ohav Sholom, 145 S. Merrick Av., Merrick, 11566. Tel. (516) 378-
1988; Cong. Ohr Torah, 410 Hungry Harbor Rd., N. Woodmere, 11581;
Cong. Shaare Zedek, New South & Old Country Rd., Hicksville., 11801;
Cong. Shaar Hashamayin, 3309; Skillman Av., Oceanside, 11572. Tel. (516)
764-6888 Coram Jewish Centre, 981 Old Town Rd., Coram, 11727. Tel. (516)
698-3939; E. Nassau Hebrew Cong., 310 A.S. Oyster Bay Rd., Syosset,
11791. Tel. (516) 921-1800; Elmont Jewish Centre, 500 Elmont Rd., Elmont,
11003. Tel. (516) 488-1616 (near the Beth David Cemetery); Great Neck
Syn., 26 Old Mill Rd., 11023; Jewish Centre of Atlantic Beach, 11509; Lido
Beach Syn., Lido Blvd., & Fairway Rd., Lido Beach, 11561. Tel. (516) 889-
9650; Lubavitch of the E. End, 6 Hyde La., Coram, 11727. Tel. (516) 698-
9428; Plainview Syn., 255 Manetto Hill Rd., 11803. Tel. (516) 433-6590;
Roslyn Syn., 270 Garden St., Roslyn Heights, 11577. Tel. (516) 484-9138;
Shaaray Tefila, 25 Central Av., Lawrence, 11559. Tel. (516) 239-2444;
Temple Beth El of Long Beach, 570 W. Walnut St., Long Beach, 11561;

Temple Israel, 305 Riverside Blvd., Long Beach, 11561. Tel. (516) 432-1410; Young Israel of E. Northport, 547 Larkfield Rd., E. Northport, 11731. Tel. (516) 368-5880; Young Israel of Great Neck, 236 Middle Neck Rd., Great Neck, 11023. Tel. (516) 829-6040; Young Israel of Lawrence-Cedarhurst, 28 Columbia Av., Cedarhurst, 11516. Tel. (516) 569-0163; Young Israel of Long Beach, 158 Long Beach Blvd., Long Beach, 11561; Young Israel of New Hyde Park, 264-15 77th Av., New Hyde Park, 11040. Tel. (718) 343-0496; Young Israel of N. Bellmore, 2428 Hamilton Av., N. Bellmore, 11710. Tel. (516) 826-0048); Young Israel of N. Woodmere, 785 Golf Dr., N. Woodmere, 11581. Tel. (516) 7911-5099; Young Israel of Oceanside, Oceanside Rd., and Waukena Av., Oceanside, 11572. Tel. (516) 764-1099; Young Israel of Patchogue, 45 Oak St., Patchogue, 11771. Tel. (516) 475-1882; Young Israel of Plainview, 132 Southern Parkway, Plainview, 11803. Tel. (516) 433-4811; Young Israel of W. Hempstead, 630 Hempstead Av., W. Hempstead, 11552. Tel. (516) 481-7291; Young Israel of Woodmere, 859 Peninsula Blvd., Woodmere, 11598. Tel. (516) 295-0150.

Conservative
Baldwin Jewish Centre, 885 E. Seaman Av., Baldwin, 11510; Bellmore Jewish Centre, 2250 S. Center Av., Bellmore, 11710; Bethpage Jewish Com. Centre 600 Broadway, Bethpage, 11714; Beth Sholom of Amityville & the Massapequas 79 County Line Rd., Amityville, 11701. Tel. (516) 264-2891; Commack Jewish Centre, 83 Shirley Ct., Commack, 11725. Tel. (516) 543-3311; Cong. Beth David 188 Vincent Av., Lynbrook, 11563. Tel. (516) 599-9464; Cong. Beth El, 99 Jerusalem Av., Massapequa, 11758; Cong. Beth Emeth of Hewlett, 36 Franklin Av., Hewlett, 11557. Tel. (516) 374-9220; Cong. Beth Israel, 141 Hilton Av., Hempstead, 11550. Tel. (516) 489-1818; Cong. Beth Sholom 441 Deer Park Av., Babylon, 11702. Tel. (516) 587-5650; Cong. Beth Sholom 700 E. Park Av., Long Beach, 11561; Cong. Beth Sholom, 261 Willis Av., Mineola, 11501; Cong. B'nai Israel, 91 N. Bayview Av., Freeport, 11520; Cong. Sons of Israel, 111 Irving Pl., Woodmere, 11598; Cong. Tree of Life, Jewish Com. Centre of Alden Ter., 502 N. Central Av., Valley Stream, 11580. Tel. (516) 825-2090; Dix Hills Jewish Centre, Vanderbilt Pkwy. & DeForest Rd., Dix Hills, 11746. Tel. (516) 499-6644; E. Meadow Jewish Centre 1400 Prospect Av., E. Meadow, 11554; E. Northport Jewish Centre, 328 Elwood Rd., E. Northport, 11731. Tel. (516) 368-6474; Franklin Square Jewish Centre, Pacific Av. & Lloyd St., Franklin Square, 11010; Hewlett E. Rockaway Jewish Centre, 295 Main St., E. Rockaway, 11518; Hicksville Jewish Centre, Jerusalem Av., & Magley Dr., Hicksville, 11801; Huntington Jewish Centre 510 Park Av., Huntington, 11743. Tel. (516) 427-1089; Israel Jewish Centre, 3235 Hempstead Turnpike, Levittown, 11756; Jericho Jewish Centre, N. Broadway, Jericho, 11753; Jewish Centre of Bay Shore, 34 N. Clinton Av., Bay Shore, 11706. Tel. (516) 665-1140; Jewish Centre of Island Park, 191 Long Beach Rd., Island Park, 11558. Tel. (516) 432-6706; Jewish Centre of the Moriches, Main St., Center Moriches, 11934. Tel. (516) 878-0388; Jewish Centre of Ocean Harbor, 3159 Royal Av., Oceanside, 11572. Tel. (516) 536-6481; Jewish Com. Centre of W. Hempstead, 711 Dogwood Av., W. Hempstead, 11552; Kings Park Jewish Centre, Route 25A, Kings Park, 11754. Tel. (516) 269-1133; Lake Success Jewish Centre, 354 Lakeville Rd., Lake Success. Tel. (516) 466-0569; Lindenhurst Hebrew Cong., N. 4th Av. at West & John Sts., Lindenhurst, 11757. Tel. (516) 226-2022; Malverne Jewish Centre, 1 Norwood Av., Malverne, 11565. Tel. (516) 593-6364; Manetto Hill Jewish Centre, 244 Manetto Hill Rd., Plainview, 11803. Tel. (516) 935-545; Merrick Jewish Centre, 225 Fox Blvd., Merrick, 11566. Tel. (516) 378-9600; Midway Jewish Centre, 330 S. Oyster Bay Rd., Syosset, 11791; N. Shore Jewish Centre, Norwood Av. at Old Town Rd., Port Jefferson Station, 11776. Tel. (516) 928-

3737; Old Westbury Hebrew Cong., 21 Old Westbury Rd., Old Westbury, 11568; Oyster Bay Jewish Centre, Marion St., Oyster Bay, 11771. Tel. (516) 922-6650; Plainview Jewish Centre, 95 Floral Dr., Plainview, 11803; Seaford Jewish Centre, 2343 Seamans Neck Rd., Seaford, 11783. Tel. (516) 785-4570; Sephardic Temple, Branch Blvd., Cedarhurst, 11516. Tel. (516) 295-4614; Shelter Rock Jewish Com. Centre, Shelter Rock & Searingtown Rd., Roslyn, 11576; S. Baldwin Jewish Centre, 2959 Grand Av., Baldwin, 11510; S. Huntington Jewish Centre, 2600 New York Av., Melville, 11747. Tel. (516) 421-3224; Suburban Park Jewish Centre, 400 Old Westbury Rd., E. Meadow, 11554; Suffolk Jewish Centre, 330 Central Av., Deer Park, 11729. Tel. (516) 667-7695; Temple Beth Am, 28 6th Av., Brentwood, 11717. Tel. (516) 273-2525; Temple Beth Chai, 870 Town Line Rd., Hauppauge, 11748. Tel. (516) 724-5807; Temple Beth El, Locust Av., & Broadway, Cedarhurst, 11516. Tel. (516) 569-2700; Temple Beth El, 1373 Bellmore Rd., N. Bellmore, 11710; Temple Beth El of Patchogue, 45 Oak St., Patchogue, 11771. Tel. (516) 475-1182; Temple Beth Israel, Temple Dr., Port Washington, 11050; Temple Beth Sholom, Roslyn Rd., Roslyn, 11577; Temple Beth Torah, 243 Cantiague Rd., Westbury, 11590; Temple B'nai Sholom, 100 Hempstead Av., Rockville Center, 11570; Temple Gates of Zion, 322 N. Corona Av., Valley Stream, 11580; Temple Israel, 108 Old Mill Rd., Great Neck, 11023; Temple Israel, 490 Northville Turnpike, Riverhead, 11901. Tel. (516) 727-3191; Temple Israel S. Merrick, 2655 Clubhouse Rd., Merrick, 11566.

Reform

B'nai Israel Temple, 67 Oakdale-Bohemia Rd., Oakdale, 11769. Tel. (516) 563-1660; Central Syn. of Nassau County, 430 DeMott Av., Rockville Centre, 11570; Com. Reform Temple, 712 The Plain Rd., Westbury, 11590; Com. Syn., 150 Middle Neck Rd., Port Washington, 11050. Tel. (516) 883-3144; Cong. B'nai Shalom, Mastic Beach Hebrew Centre, Neighbourhood Rd., cnr. Hemlock Dr., Mastic Beach 11951. Tel. (516) 281-8282; Garden City Jewish Centre, 168 Nassau Blvd., Garden City, 11530; Jewish Centre of the Hamptons, 44 Woods Lane, E. Hampton, 11937. Tel. (516) 324-9632; Nassau Com. Temple, 240 Hempstead Av., W. Hempstead, 11552; N. Country Reform Temple, Crescent Beach Rd., Glen Cove, 11542; New Hyde Park Jewish Com. Centre, 100 Lakeville Rd., New Hyde Park, 11040; N. Shore Syn., 83 Muttontown Rd., Syosset, 11791. Tel. (516) 921-2282; Oceanside Jewish Centre, 2860 Brower Av., Oceanside, 11572. Tel. (516) 536-6112; Shaarei Shalom E. Bay Reform Temple, 2569 Merrick Rd., Bellmore, 11710. Tel. (516) 781-5599; Sinai Reform Temple, 39 Brentwood Rd., Bay Shore, 11706. Tel. (516) 665-5755; Suburban Temple, 2900 Jerusalem Av., Wantagh, 11793; Temple Adas Israel, Elizabeth St. & Atlantic Av., Sag Harbor, 11963. Tel. (516) 725-0904; Temple Avodah, 3050 Oceanside Rd., Oceanside, 11572; Temple Beth Am, Kirkwood & Merrick Avs., Merrick, 11566; Temple Beth David, 100 Hauppauge Rd., Commack, 11725. Tel. (516) 499-0915; Temple Beth El, 5 Old Mill Rd., Great Neck, 11021; Temple Beth El, 660 Park Av., Huntington, 11743. Tel. (516) 421-5835; Temple Beth Elohim, 926 Round Swamp Rd., Old Bethpage, 11804; Temple Beth Torah, 35 Bagatelle Rd., Dix Hills, 11746. Tel. (516) 643-1200; Temple B'nai Israel, Elmont Rd. & Bayliss Av., Elmont, 11003; Temple Emanuel, 123 Merrick Av., E. Meadow, 11554. Tel. (516) 794-8911; Temple Emanuel, 150 Hicks La., Great Neck, 11024; Temple Emanuel, Saperstein Plaza, Lynbrook, 11563; Temple Emanuel, 3315 Hillside Av., New Hyde Park, 11040; Temple Emanuel of Long Beach, 455 Neptune Blvd., Long Beach, 11561; Temple Hillel, 1000 Rosedale Rd., N. Woodmere, 11581; Temple Isaiah, 1404 Stony Brook Rd., Stony Brook, 11790. Tel. (516) 751-8518; Temple Israel, 140 Central Av., Lawrence, 11559; Temple Judea, Jerusalem & Central Avs., Massapequa, 11758; Inwood Jewish Com. Centre, Bayswater Blvd. & Elm Rd., Inwood, 11696. Tel. (516)

239-8647; Temple Judea of Manhasset, 333 Searingtown Rd., Manhasset, 11030. Tel. (516) 621-8049; Temple Or Elohim, 18 Tobie La., Jericho, 11753; Temple Sinai, 425 Roslyn Rd., Roslyn Heights, 11577; Temple Sinai, 270 Clocks Blvd., Massapequa, 11758. Tel. (516) 795-5015; Temple Sinai of Long Island, 131 Washington Av., Lawrence, 11559. Tel. (516) 569-0267; Tifereth Israel Cong. 519 4th St., Greenport, 11944. Tel. (516) 477-2062; Union Reform Temple, 475 N. Brookside Av., Freeport, 11520.

Other
Bachurei Chemed Cong., 210 Edward Blvd., Long Beach, 11561. Tel. (516) 431-3434; Cong. Beth Torah (Traditional), 26 Ronkonkoma Blvd., Centereach, 11720. Tel. (516) 736-0505; Cong. Darchei Noam, cnr. Skillman & Waukena Avs., 11572. Tel. (516) 536-8487; Cong. Kehillath Shalom (Reconstructionist), 58 Goose Hill Rd., Cold Spring Harbour, 11724. Tel. (516) 367-4589; Cong. Lev Torah, Uniondale Jewish Centre, 760 Jerusalem Av., Uniondale, 11553. Tel. (516) 485-4492; Farmingdale Jewish Centre, 425 Fulton St., Farmingdale, 11735. Tel. (516) 694-2343; Inwood Jewish Com. Centre, Bayswater Blvd. & Elm Rd., Inwood, 11696. Tel. (516) 239-8647; Lake Grove Jewish Centre (C Modern) 821 Hawkins Av., Lake Grove, 11755. Tel. (516) 585-0521; N. Shore Sephardic Syn., 26 Old Mill Rd., Great Neck, 11023. Tel. (516) 482-1655; Reconstructionist Syn. of N.S. (Reconstructionist), Willow St. & Burnham Av., Roslyn. Tel. (516) 621-5540; Sephardic Cong. of Long Beach, 161 Lafayette Blvd., Long Beach, 11561. Tel. (516) 432-9224; Temple Beth Sholom (C-Liberal), Edgewood Av., & River Rd., Smithtown, 11787. Tel. (516) 724-0424; Temple Shalom (C-Traditional), Sayville Jewish Com. Centre, 225 Greeley Av., Sayville, 11782. Tel. (516) 567-3207; Temple Zion, 62 Maryland Av., Long Beach, 11561. Tel. (516) 432-5657; Tifereth Israel Cong., 519 4th St., Greenport, 11944. Tel. (516) 477-2062.

Organisations
Mikvaot: 26 Old Mill Rd., Great Neck, 11023. Tel. (516) 487-2726; Sharf Manor, 274 W. Broadway, Long Beach, 11561. Tel. (516) 431-7758; 3397 Park Av., Oceanside, 11572. Tel. (516) 766-3242; 775 Hempstead Av., W. Hempstead, 11552. Tel. (516) 489-9358; Peninsula Blvd., Hewlett, 11557. Tel. (516) 569-5514.
Rabbinical Orgs.: Long Island Board of Rabbis (O, C & R), 330 Central Av., Deer Park, 11729. Tel. (516) 667-7695; Long Island Commission of Rabbis (O), 1300 Jericho Turnpike, New Hyde Park, 11040. Tel. (718) 343-5993.
Conference of Jewish Orgs. of Nassau County, North Shore Atrium, 6900 Jericho Turnpike, Syosset 364-4477, 11791. Tel. 516-3644477.
Suffolk Jewish Communal Planning Council, 74 Hauppauge Rd., Commack, 11725. Tel. (516) 462-5826.
Newspapers: "Long Island Jewish Week", 98 Cutter Mill Rd., Great Neck, 11020. Tel. (516) 773-3679; "Long Island Jewish World", 115 Middle Neck Rd., Great Neck, 11021. Tel. (516) 829-400.
Bookshop: Theodore S. Cinnamon, 420 Jerusalem Av., Hicksville, 11801. Tel. (516) 935-7480.
Kosher Restaurants: Ben's, 933 Atlantic Av., Baldwin. Tel. (516) 868-2072; 140 Wheatley Plaza, Greenvale. Tel. (516) 621-3340; 135 Alexander Av., Lake Grove. Tel. (516) 979-8770. All under rabbinical supervision; Hunki's Kosher Pizza & Felafel, 338 Hempstead Av., W. Hempstead. Tel. (516) 538-6655; Jacob's Ladder (Glatt), 83 Spruce St., Cedarhurst. Tel. (516) 569-3373; King David, 550 Central Av., Cedarhurst. Tel. (516) 569-2920; Pastrami 'N Friends, 110A Commack Rd., Commack, 11725. Tel. (516) 499-9537.
For all kashrut information, contact the Long Island Commission of Rabbis, address above.

MIDDLETOWN
Com. Centre: 13 Linden Av., 10940.

MONROE
Syn.: Cong. Eitz Chaim (C), County Route, 105. Tel. (914) 783-7424.; Monroe Temple of Liberal Judaism (R), 314 N. Main St., 10950.

MONSEY
See New York State and Spring Valley & Monsey entries.

MONTICELLO
Syn.: Tifereth Israel (O), Landfield Av., 12701; Temple Sholom (R), Port Jervis & Dillon Rds., 12701. (Daily services).
Kosher Hotel: Kutsher's Country Club, 12701. (Daily Services).

MOUNT VERNON
Syn.: Brothers of Israel (O), 116 Crary Av., 10550; Fleetwood (O), 11 E. Broad St., 10552.
Y.M.H.A. & Y.W.H.A.: 30 Oakley Av., 10550.

NASSAU
Syn.: Route 20, Albany St. Tel. 477-6691.
Jewish Fed. of Greater Orange County, 360 Powell Av., 12550. Tel. (914) 562-7860.

NEW CITY
Syn.: New City Jewish Centre (C), Old Schoolhouse Rd., 10956; Temple Beth Sholom (R), 228 New Hempstead Rd., 10956.

NEW ROCHELLE
Syn.: Anshe Shalom (O), 50 North Av., 10804; Young Israel (O), 1228 North Av., 10804; Bethel (C), Northfield Rd.; Temple Israel (R), 1000 Pine Brook Blvd., 10804.

NEW SQUARE
See note on New York State.

NEW YORK CITY
"Shtetl on the Hudson" is what some call this towering Manhattan Island. Some "shtetl", you might say.
There are more Jews here than in any other city in the world and more than in any country except Israel, Russia, and the rest of the U.S. itself. Nobody knows the true Jewish population figures in the U.S.A. Best estimates say that 1.1 million Jews live in New York City's five boroughs, and 750,000 or so in its immediate suburbs.
The headquarters of practically every national Jewish organisation in the United States is located in New York City, otherwise known as the unofficial capital of Jewish America.
It is probably the only city in the world where Yiddish words have entered the everyday vocabulary of its non-Jewish residents – kibbitz, gannef, kosher ("that deal doesn't smell kosher to me"), shlemiel, shlepp ("I shlepped my feet off looking for a job"), shnook, megilla ("he spouted a whole megilla at me") and, of course, goy.
This city, the largest urban Jewish community in history, opens its arms to the Jewish traveller, who will have no problem whatsoever in finding a minyan at practically any hour; eating in a kosher restaurant; attending a

Jewish lecture; going to play with or about Jews; or browsing in a Jewish bookstore.

There are streets named after David Ben-Gurion, the Prophet Isaiah, Natan Sharansky, Golda Meir, Richard Tucker and Jacob H. Schiff. A huge modern convention centre commemorates the name of the late Senator Jacob K. Javits, and the late Solomon R. Guggenheim has given his name to a magnificent museum. Such commemorative buildings abound throughout the city.

As for food, there is kosher Chinese, kosher Moroccan, kosher Italian, kosher Romanian. It's all here, and easy to find.

There are many Jewish neighbourhoods: the Lower East Side, Borough Park, Williamsburg, and even what they now call the "Fourth City of Israel", which is Forest Hills in the borough of Queens, because so many Israelis live there. There is also Riverdale, as well as the Upper West Side and, in its own affluent way, the Upper East Side.

But Jews do not live only in Jewish neighbourhoods; they live everywhere in the Greater New York region, including Nassau, Suffolk, Rockland and Westchester counties – the greatest concentration of Jews in one metropolitan area in the world.

For over 300 years, Jews have emigrated to New York from their countries of origin. They still do. Hungarian Jews came here after the Hungarian Revolution. Cuban Jews arrived here after Castro took over. Egyptian, Syrian, Russian, and Iranian Jews have settled here. And there are probably several hundred thousand former Israelis who live, work, study and raise families in the New York area. They help keep alive a number of home-grown Hebrew newspapers, as well as ones flown in daily from the Jewish State. They also keep the Israeli felafel restaurants churning out countless orders.

It all began one day early in September, 1654, when 23 Sephardi and Ashkenazi Jews aboard the French privateer, "St. Catherine", docked in New York harbour after a tortuous journey from Recife, Brazil. The story is well-known: "Governor" Stuyvesant tried to keep them out; the Jews protested to the Dutch West Indies Company, and it overruled him and allowed the Jews to settle. They have been coming ever since, first in trickles and then a deluge between 1880 and 1924, when more than two million Jews reached the shores of the land they called "the goldene medineh".

About one third of all American Jews live in and around New York City. One supposes this is because New York City is still the financial, commercial, intellectual and art capital of the United States. Perhaps it is also because this is "where the action is."

Jews feel at home here. Their impact and contributions are meaningful.

The minute you land in N.Y.C., whether by train, boat, bus, car, or airline, you will feel the vibrancy of a great, throbbing metropolis which is constantly on the go. One thing is for certain: despite the hectic pace here, Jews will take time out to greet you. After all, they have been doing it for each layer of Jewish immigrants, as well as for thousands of visitors. As the sign says: "Welcome!"

The Central Synagogue (Reform) at 652 Lexington Av., 10022, is the city's oldest Jewish house of worship on an original site, and has been designated an official "Landmark of New York." It is a fine example of Moorish-style architecture, and seats 1,300 people. B'nai Jeshurun (Conservative) over which Rabbi Dr. Israel Goldstein presided for more than 40 years, is at 270 W. 89th St., 10024, and is the oldest Ashkenazi congregation in New York (1825). On the roof of the Wall St. Synagogue (Orthodox) at 47 Beekman St., 10038, is a replica of the first synagogue in America. The synagogue operates a kosher luncheon club to which Stock

Exchange brokers and insurance company executives belong. Services are held four times daily, seven days a week.

Nearest to the United Nations is the Sutton Place Synagogue (Conservative) at 225 E. 51st St., 10022. A very popular Orthodox synagogue particularly with the young, stylish, upscale set is the Lincoln Square Synagogue, 200 Amsterdam Av., 10023. It houses a remarkable singles scene. Also to be mentioned is the congregation Kehilath Jacob on W. 79th Street in Manhattan which is presided over by the famous Rabbi Schlomo Carlebach, the singing Rabbi.

Among Ashkenazi synagogues where visitors may say Kaddish are the Millinery Centre Synagogue, 1025 Av. of the Americas (near 38th St.), 10018; B'nai Jeshurun, 270 W. 89th St., 10024; (now the home pulpit of the controversial Rabbi Marshall Meyer, a brave crusading Rabbi of the left from Argentina, the Jewish Centre, 131 W. 86th St., 10024); Sutton Place Synagogue, 225 E. 51st St., 10022; Park East Synagogue, 16 E. 67th St., 10021, and the Fifth Av. Synagogue, 5 E. 62nd St., 10021.

The Synagogue of the Society for the Advancement of Judaism at 15 W. 86th St., 10024, belongs to the Reconstructionist Foundation established by the late Rabbi Dr. Mordecai M. Kaplan. Women as well as men are called to the Torah. Worth noting are murals depicting the rebirth of Israel.

The Ethiopian Hebrew Congregation, 1 W. 123rd St., 10027, in Harlem, is one of several synagogues in which Black Jews worship.

Also worth a visit is Cong. Kehilath Jeshurun (Orthodox), at 125 E. 85th St.

Synagogues

There are several thousand Orthodox, Conservative, Reform, Reconstructionist and traditional synagogues, chavurot and shtiblech in the city, but only a few can be listed here, for obvious reasons.

Complete lists of synagogues in New York City – and throughout the country, for that matter – are available from the following national organisations, whose addresses appear at the beginning of the United States section: Union of Orthodox Jewish Congregations of America; National Council of Young Israel (Orthodox); United Synagogue of America (Conservative); Union of American Hebrew Congregations (Reform); Federation of Reconstructionist Congregations & Havurot.

Below is a selection of what N.Y.C. has to offer.

First, Shearith Israel (the Spanish and Portuguese Synagogue), Central Park W. and 70th St., 10023, one of the oldest congregations in America, stemming from the 23 refugees from the Inquisition in Brazil who landed in New Amsterdam in 1654. The present building has religious appurtenances dating to the early days of the congregation, and its small chapel is a gem of the colonial period.

The impressive Temple Emanu-El (Reform), the city's (and the world's) largest Jewish house of worship, is on Fifth Av. and 65th St., 10021. Dating from 1929, the building can seat more than 2,000 people. The congregation itself was founded in 1848. The beautiful Fifth Av. Synagogue (Orthodox) at 5 E. 62nd St., 10021, was, until early in 1967, presided over by Rabbi Dr. I. Jakobovits, now Chief Rabbi of Britain and the Commonwealth.

At 163 E. 67th St. is the Park East Synagogue, which is presided over by the father-and-son team of Rabbis Arthur & Marc Schneier. Founded in 1890, it has been designated an historic landmark. The Stephen Wise Free Synagogue (Reform) is at 30 W. 68th St., 10023. Its religious decorations were designed by a Jewish artist, A. Raymond Katz.

The most modern synagogue is the windowless Reform Temple Shaaray Tefila at 250 E. 79th St., 10021. The largest German Jewish congregations are Kahal Adath Jeshurun Synagogue (Orthodox) at 90 Bennett Av., 10033, in the Washington Heights section, and Habonim Congregation at 44 W. 66th St., 10023.

Among the synagogues most worth visiting is the Park Av. Synagogue (Conservative) at 50 E. 87th St., 10128, where the spiritual leader is Rabbi David H. Lincoln. The rabbi emeritus is Rabbi Judah Nadich. Ansche Chesed, at 251 W. 100th St. and West End Av., 10025, is where B'nai B'rith was founded more than a century ago.

Libraries and Museums

The Jewish Museum, under the auspices of the Theological Seminary of America, at Fifth Av. and 92nd St., 10028, is one of the outstanding museums in the city and a "must" not only for Jews, but for all interested in art. The permanent display consists of one of the finest collections of Jewish ritual and ceremonial art in the world, along with notable paintings and sculptures.

The Yivo Institute for Jewish Research, 1048 Fifth Av., 10028, has the largest collection of original documents on Jewish life extant, along with some 300,000 volumes, and thousands of photographs, music sheets, gramophone records, etc. Visitors welcome. The Jewish Division of the New York Public Library, Fifth Av. at 42nd St., 10017, has 125,000 volumes of Judaica and Hebraica, along with extensive microfilm and bound files of Jewish publications, one of the finest collections in existence. The Zionist Archives and Library of Keren Hayesod are located at the Jewish Agency Building, 515 Park Av. at 60th St., 10022. Some notable collections are to be found there. The murals at the entrance of the building are by the well-known Israeli artist, Perlo.

In 1973, Yeshiva University opened a museum at its main centre in Amsterdam Av. at 185th St., 10033. The museum's salient feature is a permanent display of scale-model synagogues.

The library of the Jewish Theological Seminary of America, housing what is believed to be the greatest collection of Judaica and Hebraica in the world, is in the Seminary building at 3080 Broadway at 122nd St., 10027. Rare manuscripts, including a work in the hand of Maimonides, as well as Cairo Geniza fragments, may be seen on application to the librarian. Other libraries of note: the New York University Library of Judaica and Hebraica has a stunning collection of priceless items; the Butler Library of Columbia University, Broadway at 116th St., 10027, has some 6,000 Hebrew books and pamphlets, plus 1,000 manuscripts and a Hebrew psalter printed at Cambridge University in 1685 and used by Samuel Johnson at the graduation of the first candidates for bachelor's degrees at King's College; the Levi Yitzhak Library is at 305 Kingston Av., Brooklyn, 11213.

The House of Living Judaism, the centre of the Reform movement in the U.S.A., at 5th Av. and 65th St., frequently shows paintings and ritual objects. The twelve marble pillars symbolising the Twelve Tribes, in the lobby, the sculptures and the paintings, make a visit to this fine building well worth while.

The Leo Baeck Institute, 129 E. 73rd St., 10021, has vast collections of books, manuscripts, letters and photographs of German Jewish authors, scientists, rabbis & communal leaders, as well as an art collection of the Jews of Germany.

The Chasidic Art Institute is at 375 Kingston Av., Brooklyn.

Institutes of Learning

Yeshiva University, with its main centre at 500 W. 185th St., 10033, is America's oldest and largest university under Jewish auspices, and celebrated its centenary in 1985. It has an enrolment of 7,000 male and female students.

At the main centre are the undergraduate schools for men – Yeshiva College, Isaac Bruer College of Hebraic Studies, and the James Striar School of General Jewish Studies; four graduate schools – the Mazer School of Talmudic Studies, the Bernard Revel Graduate School, the Wurzweiler School of Social Work and the Harry Fischel School for Higher Jewish Studies. The mid-town centre, 245 Lexington Av. (at 35th St.), 10016, houses the undergraduate schools for women – Stern College for Women, the Teachers' Institute for Women and the School for Jewish Graduate Education. At 2540 Amsterdam Av., 10033, is the Rabbi Isaac Elchanan Theological Seminary. At the Brookdale Centre, 55 Fifth Av. (at 12th St.), 10003, is the Benjamin N. Cardozo School of Law.

The Bronx Centre, at Eastchester Rd. & Morris Pk. Av., 10461, is the home of the Albert Einstein College of Medicine, the Sue Golding Graduate Division of Medical Sciences, the Belfer Institute for Advanced Biomedical Studies, the Camp David Institute for International Health and the Ferkauf Graduate School of Psychology.

Kosher meals may be obtained at the cafeterias of the main, mid-town and Bronx centres.

The Jewish Theological Seminary of America (Conservative), 3080 Broadway at 122nd St., 10027, stands in the academic centre of Morningside Heights, neighbour to the Union Theological Seminary and Columbia University. The seminary, dedicated to Sabato Morais, its founder, and Solomon Schechter, under whose guidance it became one of the great Jewish institutions of the world, is well worth the trip up town for its library. Its cafeteria is open for luncheon and dinner, and there are services in its synagogues daily, open to all. The buildings house all the various components of the Conservative movement in America, as well as the World Council of Synagogues.

Hebrew Union College-Jewish Institute of Religion (Reform), New York branch, is at 1 W. 4th St., 10012. The main seminary is in Cincinnati, Ohio. Open to the public are ancient manuscripts and books, as well as the collection of personal letters, speeches, articles and other writings in the hand of Rabbi Dr. Stephen S. Wise.

Touro College, 30 W. 44th St., has courses in Jewish studies, in addition to undergraduate and graduate curricula.

In the Williamsburg and other sections of Brooklyn are grouped many Chasidic institutions including the Lubavitch movement's headquarters at 770 Eastern Parkway, 11211, where the Rebbe, Rabbi Menachem Mendel Schneerson, conducts his world-wide activities.

The Satmarer Synagogue at 152 Rodney St., 11211, has a regular Saturday attendance of some 4,000.

Special Points of Interest

On a plaque on the Statue of Liberty, the focal point of New York harbour, was the poem "The New Colossus" – "Give me your tired, your poor, your huddled masses yearning to breathe free . . ." by the Jewish poetess, Emma Lazarus. The plaque is now in the museum at the base of this huge statue. In Battery Park, near where the ferry to the Statue of Liberty takes on its passengers, is a plaque commemorating the spot where the first 23 Jews landed in 1654.

Also in Battery Park are the remains of "Castle Garden," the first entry place of the wave of Jewish immigration beginning in the 1880s. It was replaced by Ellis Island, now abandoned, which can be seen from the Park. The Lower East Side, the cradle of the American Jewish community, which once had a Jewish population of more than 11/2 million, is no longer wholly Jewish, as it once was when Jews came there in the stream of mass immigration from Eastern Europe between 1881 and the beginning of the

First World War. Now their tenements are for the most part peopled by other groups of immigrants like Hispanics and Asians, as well as by Blacks, who have created a diverse area of small shops, push carts and open markets. In addition, an effort is under way to bring affluent young adults into the neighbourhood. The Lower East Side is increasingly favoured as a good place to live by employees of the large financial institutions in nearby Wall Street.

However, there is still enough to see to make a "Jewish tour" of the section worthwhile, especially on a Thursday afternoon, for Jews from all over the city still come to the Lower East Side then to lay in their week's supply of fresh meat, live carp, black bread and chalot.

Sunday morning is also a good time to take a walk along Essex, Delancey, E. Broadway, Canal and Hester Sts. There are dozens of stores, large and small, stacked with Jewish books in various languages, as well as yarmulkas, talitot, tefilin, prayer books and other Jewish articles, religious as well as general. Stavsky's, at 147 Essex St., 10002, is typical of these stores, and also sells records and tapes.

For browsers, the J. Levine Co. "department store" of Jewish items, 5 W. 30th St., 10001 between Broadway & 5th Av. is well worth a visit Levine's, into its fourth generation, also has a mid-town store at 5 W 30th St 1001, between Broadway and 5th Av. Zelig Blumenthal, 13 Essex St., 10002, has a wide variety of religious items.

Side by side with the bookstores and the stores selling religious items are delis; kosher restaurants old-fashioned luncheonettes – and old synogogues like Beth Hamidrash Hagodol, on Norfolk St., still in the building it acquired in 1888, & the Eldridge St. Synagogue, a National Historic Landmark. Also worth seeing are the Bialystoker Synagogue, 7 Willett St., and the First Roumanian American Congregation at 89 Rivington St.

Stop in at Shapiro's Wine Company at 124 Rivington St., which has been in business since 1899. Call (212) 475-7383 for free tours.

When you reach 39 Essex St., say "Shalom" to Leibel Bistritsky, who has a wonderful kosher food and provision store, and even holds a daily minyan.

Of course, many old-time institutions are gone or have moved. The "Jewish Forward" building used to be located at 175 East Broadway. This famous newspaper has moved to 45 East 33rd Street, and its former location is now a church. Another important Yiddish newspaper is the "Algemeiner Journal", 404 Park Avenue S.

Another colourful shopping area is Orchard Street, New York City's Petticoat Lane, with dozens of outdoor stalls and racks. Most of the owners are Jewish, but they employ many Hispanic salesmen, who hawk their wares in Spanish.

In the neighbourhood is the Henry Street Settlement, founded by the Jewish pioneer in social work, Lilian Wald, and along 2nd Av. are what is left of the Jewish theatres. Also in the neighbourhood, in Chatham Sq., is what remains of the first Jewish cemetery in America. For a tour, call the sexton or clerk of Shearith Israel. Another old cemetery is on 21st St., near Avenue of the Americas. The Educational Alliance, the settlement-house that did so much to Americanise the many thousands of Jewish immigrants at the turn of the century, is at East Broadway and Jefferson St. The area is dotted with yeshivas and synagogues too numerous to mention individually.

Williamsburg, which had become the centre of Chasidic life in America, if not in the world, is now beginning to lose some rebbes and their flocks, as they move away into suburban areas where they can lead their cloistered lives undisturbed by the world around them. One such village is New

Square. A trip into Williamsburg is recommended. There, along Bedford Av., one can see the kaftaned sect going about its business. The area is crowded with synagogues and shtiblech.

Boro Park, also in Brooklyn, is almost totally inhabited by Chasidic Jews. On Sundays one can see husbands escorting their wives and children along the streets. The shops are open, of course, and sell all kinds of Chinese, Hungarian, Turkish and Greek kosher food.

Crown Heights, another part of Brooklyn, is the "spill-over" from Williamsburg, and a fair number of Chasidic sects are now to be found there.

One of the most colourful sights is the diamond centre on 47th St., 10036, between 5th Avenue & Avenue of the Americas (6th Av.). Many Chasidim are in the diamond business, and they can be seen trading with each other in what amounts to an open-air market. Deals are sealed with a handshake and the words "Mazzel brocha," a "contract" binding throughout the world.

Three-quarters of the diamonds entering the United States pass through this single block.

The Jewish Conciliation Board at 225 Broadway, 10007, is presided over by a rabbi, a judge and a businessman. Disputes arising over synagogue matters are among the cases heard.

For entertainment, and art, there is the Y.M.H.A. & Y.W.H.A. at 92nd St. and Lexington Av., which has a kosher cafeteria. The 92nd St. Y. is one of the premier venues in New York (perhaps the nation) in a wide range of cultural fields including poetry. Indeed, the 'Y's poetry centre is one of the nation's most prestigious forums for poets' reading. The various Jewish lecture series attract many of the most important figures of the day. Some

of its cultural activities are suspended during the summer, but call (212) 427-6000 to see what is on. The Jewish Theatre for Children puts on plays at 154 W. 93rd St. on Sunday afternoons from November until March.

The Abraham Goodman House-Hebrew Arts School, 129 W. 67th St., 10023, has an art gallery and houses the Merkin concert hall, which puts on many Jewish music programmes. The school also organises walking tours.

Productions are also staged by the Jewish Repertory Theatre, at the Midtown YMHA, 344 E. 14th St. Tel. (212) 505-2667 or 674-7200 for further information.

BOROUGH SYNAGOGUES

There are literally thousands of synagogues in the five boroughs of New York and suburbs. The following list contains a few of the more representative ones.

MANHATTAN

Orthodox

Beth Hillel of Washington Heights, 571 W. 182nd St., 10033.
Emunath Israel, 236 W. 23rd St., 10011.
Fifth Avenue, 5 E. 62nd St., 10021.
First Rumanian American (East Side), 89 Rivington St., 10002.
Fur Centre, 230 W. 29th St., 10001.
Garment Centre, 205 W. 40th St., 10018.
Jewish Centre, 131 W. 86th St., 10024.
Kahal Adath Jeshurun, 90 Bennet Av., 10033.
Kehillath Jacob (Carlebach Shul), 305 W. 79th St., 10024.
Kehilath Jeshurun (and Remaz School), 125 E. 85th St., 10028.
Lincoln Square, Lincoln Sq. at 69th St., 10023.
Ohab Zedek, 118 W. 95th St., 10025.
Park E. Syn., 163 E. 67th St., 10021. Tel. (212) 737-6900.
Radio City, 30 W. 47th St., 10036.
Ramath Orah, 550 W. 110th St., 10025.
Shearith Israel (Sephardi), Central Park W. & 70th St., 10023.
Wall Street, 47 Beekman St., 10038.
West Side Institutional Synagogue, 122 W. 76th St., 10023.
Young Israel of West Side, 210 W. 91st St., 10024.

Conservative

B'nai Jeshurun, 270 W. 89th St., 10024.
Little Syn., 27 E. 20th St., 10003.
Millinery Centre, 1025 Av. of the Americas, nr. 38th St., 10018.
Park Avenue, 50 E. 87th St., 10028.
Shaare Zedek, 212 W. 93rd St., 10025.
Sutton Place, 225 E. 51st St., 10022.
Temple Ansche Chesed, W. End Av. & 100th St., 10025.

Reform

Central, 123 E. 55th St., 10022.
East End, 398 2nd Av., 10010.
Metropolitan, 10 Park Av., 10016.
Rodeph Sholom, 7 W. 83rd St., 10024.
Shaaray Tefila, 270 E. 79th St., 10021.
Stephen Wise Free Synagogue, 30 W. 68th St., 10023.
Temple Emanu-El, 5th Av. at 65th St., 10021.
Temple Israel, 112 E. 75th St., 10021.

Reconstructionist
Society for the Advancement of Judaism, 15 W. 86th St., 10024.

THE BRONX

Orthodox
Concourse Centre, 2315 Grand Concourse, 10468.
Kingsbridge Heights Jewish Centre, 124 Eames Pl., 10468.
Riverdale Jewish Centre, 237th St. & Independence Av., 10471.

Conservative
Jacob H. Schiff, 2510 Valentine Av., 10458.
Conservative Synagogue of Riverdale, 250th St. & Henry Hudson Parkway, 10471.
Pelham Parkway, 900 Pelham Parkway S.

Reform
Riverdale Temple, 246th St. & Independence Av., 10471.

BROOKLYN

Orthodox
Agudath Israel of Boro Park, 4511 14th Av., 11219.
Ahi Ezer, 1885 Ocean Parkway, 11223.
Beth-El of Boro Park, 4802 15th Av., 11219.
Beth Medrash Hagadol of Boro Park (of the Infants' Home of Brooklyn), 1358 56th St., 11219.
Cong. Ahaba ve Ahva of Ocean Parkway (Egyptian), 1801 Ocean Parkway, 11223. Tel. (718) 998-0283.
Kingsway Jewish Centre, 2902 Kings Highway, 11229.
Prospect Park, 1604 Av. "R" & E. 16th St.
Shromrei Emunah, 5202 14th Av., 11219.
United Lubavitcher, 770 Eastern Parkway, 11213.
Young Israel of Flatbush, Coney Island Av. & Avenue I, 11230.

Conservative
Beth-El, Manhattan Beach, 111 West End Av., 11235.
Brooklyn Jewish Centre, 667 Eastern Parkway, 11213.
East Midwood Jewish Centre, 1625 Ocean Av., 11230.
Flatbush and Shaare Torah Jewish Centre (Cong. Ahavath Achim), Church Av. & Ocean Parkway, 11218.
Temple Emanuel of Boro Park, 1364 49th St., 11201.

Reform
Beth Elohim, 8th Av. & Garfield Pl., 11215.
Progressive Syn., 1395 Ocean Av., 11230.
Union Temple of Brooklyn, 17 Eastern Parkway, 11238.

QUEENS

The Borough of Queens is a wide area of suburban coms., all with their own congs. A call to the Union of Orthodox Jewish Congs., the United Syn. of America (Conservative), or the Union of American Hebrew Congs. (Reform) will elicit the name and location of the synagogue of your choice.

Orthodox
Beth El, 30-85 35th St., Astoria, 11102.
Kneseth Israel, 728 Empire Av. (cnr. Sage St.), Far Rockaway, 11691.
Queens Jewish Centre, 66-05 108th St., Forest Hills, 11375.

Shaaray Tefila, 1295 Central Av., Far Rockaway, 1691.
Tifereth Israel, 88th & 32nd Ave., Jackson Heights, 11369. (Nr. La Guardia).
Young Israel of Kew Gardens Hills, 150-05 70th Rd., Flushing, 11367.

Conservative
Forest Hills Jewish Centre, 106-06 Queens Blvd., 11375.
Gates of Prayer, 38-20 Parsons Blvd., 11354.
Hillcrest Jewish Centre, 183-02 Union Turnpike, Flushing, 11366.
Hollis Hills Jewish Centre, 210-10 Union Turnpike, 11364.
Jackson Heights Jewish Centre, 34-25 82nd St., 11372.
Jewish Centre, 182-69 Wexford Ter., Jamaica, 11432.
Rego Park Jewish Centre, 97-30 Queens Blvd., 11374.

Reform
Free Synagogue, 41-60 Kissena Blvd., Flushing, 11355.
Temple Isaiah, 75-24 Grand Central Parkway, Forest Hills, 11375.
Temple Israel, 188-15 McLaughlin Av., Jamaica, 11423.

STATEN ISLAND
Orthodox
Agudath Achim Anshe Chesed, 641 Delafield Av., 10310.
Young Israel of Staten Island (O), 835 Forest Hill Rd.

Conservative
B'nai Israel, 45 Twombly Av., 10306.
Temple Emanu-El, 984 Post Av., 10302.

Reform
Temple Israel, 315 Forest Av., 10310.

Restaurants, Hotels, Etc.
There is a kashrut law in New York State which makes it a punishable fraud to advertise or sell non-kosher food as kosher. The law is administered by the Kosher Law Enforcement Section of the State Department of Agriculture under the supervision of Rabbi Shulem Rubin, a respected Orthodox rabbi.

There are heavy penalties on "a person who, with intent to defraud, sells or exposes for sale in any hotel, restaurant or other places where food products are sold . . . food or food products . . . and falsely represents the same to be kosher . . . or as having been prepared under . . . the Orthodox Hebrew religious requirements . . . or sells or exposes for sale in the same place of business both kosher and non-kosher . . . food or food products . . . and who fails to indicate on his window signs and all display advertising in block letters at least four inches in height 'Kosher and non-kosher food sold here'," etc.

The Union of Orthodox Jewish Congregations issues "The Kosher Directory" listing kosher food products supervised and recommended by them and bearing their U-in-a-circle insignia. The directory, for which a charge is made, is available from the UOJC at 45 W. 36th St., New York City, N.Y., 10018. Other reliable kashrut insignia include the Circle K trademark of Organised Kashrus Laboratories, P.O. Box 218, Brooklyn. Tel. 851-6428.

The Crown Palace Hotel, in Brooklyn at 570-600 Crown St., is glatt kosher.

It should be noted at this point that packaged kosher food, cooked and uncooked, is available in most supermarkets, so one need not go hungry, even if there is no restaurant near by, although Manhattan has enough kosher restaurants to eat in for months, and a good variety too.

You can get kosher Won-Ton soup, couscous, hot pastrami and corned (salt) beef sandwiches, gefilte fish, felafel, hummus, tehina and much, much more.

Other kosher places (in Manhattan unless otherwise stated) include:

Berso (glatt kosher), 64-20 108th St., Forest Hills, Queens. Tel. (718) 275-9793.

Cafeteria (glatt kosher), Crown Palace Hotel, 570-600 Crown St., Brooklyn, 11213.

Chaap-a-Nosh (glatt kosher), 1424 Elm Av., Brooklyn. Tel. (718) 627-0072.

Chez David, 494 Amsterdam Av. Tel. 874-4974.

David's Harp, 150 W. 46th St., (6th & Bdng); Tel. (212) 463-9893.

Deli Kasbah, 251 W. 85th St. Tel. (212) 496-1500.

Eden Terrace, 475 Park Av. S. at 32nd St. Tel. 545-0455.

Edna's Restaurant & Deli (glatt kosher), 125 Church Av., Brooklyn, 11202.

Empire Kosher Restaurant, 100-19 Queens Blvd., Forest Hills. Tel. (718) 997-7315.

Galil Restaurant, (glatt kosher), 1252 Lexington Av. Tel. (212) 439-9886.

Highway Kosher Steak House, 910 Kings Highway, Brooklyn.

Jewish Theological Seminary of America cafeteria, 3080 Broadway at 122nd St., 10027. Tel. (212) 678-8000.

Kosher Delight (glatt kosher), 1359 Broadway (37th St.). Tel. (212) 563-3366; 4600 13th Av. (cnr. 48th St.), Boro Park. Tel. (718) 435-8500; 1223 Av. "J" (E. 13th St.), Flatbush. Tel. (718) 377-6873.

La Kasbah (glatt kosher), 70 W. 71st St. Tel. (212) 769-1690.

Levana Restaurant (glatt kosher), 141 W. 69th St. Tel. (212) 877-8457.

Lou G. Siegel's (glatt kosher), 209 W. 38th St., 10018. Tel. 921-4433.

Madras Palace, 104 Lexington Av. Tel. (212) 532-3314.

Magen David, (glatt kosher), 866 Av. of Americas between 30th & 31st Sts. Tel. (212) 686-8319.

Moishe's Delicatessen & Restaurant, (glatt kosher), 157 Dreiser Loop Shopping Centre, No. 1 Co-op City, The Bronx. Tel. (212) 671-3608.

Mr. Broadway, 1372 Broadway. Tel. 921-2152.

Ratner's, 138 Delancy St., 10002.

Second Avenue Delicatessen-Restaurant, 156 2nd Av., cnr. 10th St. Tel. (212) 677-0606.

Shang-Chai (glatt kosher), 2189 Flatbush Av., Brooklyn, 11234. Tel. (212) 377-6100.

Trastavere Restorante (glatt kosher), 155 E. 84th St. Tel. (718) 744-0210.

Yeshiva University: Main centre, 500 W. 185th St., 10033; Mid-town centre, 245 Lexington Av. at 35th St., 10016; Bronx centre, Eastchester Rd. & Morris Pk. Av., 10461.

Yun-Kee (glatt kosher), 1424 Elm Av., cnr. E. 15th St. & Av. "M", Brooklyn. Tel. (718) 627-0072.

Dairy Restaurants

Diamond, 4 W. 47th St., 10036, in the diamond centre. Tel. (212) 719-2694, 398-1668.

Famous Dairy Restaurant, 222 W. 72nd St., 10023. Tel. (212) 595-8487.

Great American Health Bar, 35 W. 48th St. & 35 W. 57th St.

Greener Pastures Restaurant, 117 E. 60th St., 10022. Tel. (212) 832-2312.

Levy's Kosher Pizza, 330 7th Av. Tel. 594-4613.

Steinberg's, 21 Essex St., 10002.

The following, although not listed as kosher, may have a special interest for Jewish tourists because of their menus, atmosphere or clientele:

Aroh, 152-45 Melbourne Av., 11367.

Carnegie Deli, 854 7th Av., 10019. Tel. (212) 757-2245. Very popular with entertainment & Broadway people.
Cumaga Luncheonette, 1426 Cumaga Av., 11691.
Deli City, 433 7th Av.
Deli King, 2845 Richmond Av., 10314.
Feenjon Café, 117 McDougal St., 10012, in Greenwich Village. Israeli and general Middle East entertainment.
Irene & Magda Dairy Restaurant, 99-13 Queens Blvd., 11374.
Jasa, 27-35 Crescent St., 11102.
Knish-Knosh, 101-02 Queens Blvd., 11375.
Orange Bowl, Staten Island Mall, 10314.
Stage Delicatessen, 834 7th Av., 10019. Popular with television & entertainment people.
The Stuffed Bagel, 107-04 70th Rd., 11375.

NEWBURGH

This is the nearest Jewish com. to West Point, the United States Military Academy, which is worth a visit.
Syns.: Agudas Israel (O), 290 North St., 12550; Temple Beth Jacob, Gidney & Fullerton Avs., 12550.

NIAGARA FALLS

Syns.: Beth Israel (C), College & Madison Avs., 14305. Tel. (716) 285-9894; Beth El (R), 720 Ashland Av., 14301. Tel. (716) 282-2717.
Jewish Fed. of Niagara Falls, c/o Beth Israel above. Tel. (716) 284-4575.

ORANGEBURG

Syn.: Orangetown Jewish Centre (C), Independence Av., 10962.

PEEKSKILL

Syn.: First Hebrew Cong., 1821 E. Main St., 10566. Tel. (914) 739-0500.

PORT CHESTER

Syn.: Kneses Tifereth Israel (C), 575 King St., 10573. Tel. (914) 939 1004.

POUGHKEEPSIE

Syn.: Shomre Israel (O), 18 Park Av., 12603; Temple Beth El (C), 130 Grand Av., 12603; Vassar Temple (R), 140 Hooker Av., 12601.
Jewish Community Center of Dutchess County 110. Grand Av., 12603. Tel. (914) 471-0430.

ROCHESTER

Syn.: Beth Hakneses Hachodosh (O), 19 N. St. Regis Dr., 14618; Beth Sholom (O), 1161 Monroe Av., 14618; B'nai Israel-Ahavas Achim (O), 692 Joseph Av., 14621; Light of Israel (O), 206 Norton St.; Talmudical Institute of Upstate New York (O), 759 Park Av.; Beth Hamedrash-Beth Israel (C), 1369 East Av., 14610; Temple Beth Am (C), 3249 E. Henrietta Rd., Henrietta, 14467; Temple Beth David (C), 3200 St. Paul Blvd., 14617; Temple Beth El (C), 139 S. Winton Rd., 14610; B'rith Kodesh (R), 2131 Elmwood Av., 14618; Temple Emanu-El (R), 2956 St. Paul Blvd., 14617; Temple Sinai (R), 363 Penfield Rd., 14625. Temple b'rith Kodesh (R), 2131 Elmwood Av., 14618; Etz. Chaim Synagogue (R), P.O. Box 522, Pittsford, 14534.
Jewish Com. Centre of Greater Rochester, 1200 Edgewood Av., 14618. Tel. (716) 461-2000.
Jewish Com. Fed., 441 E. Av., 14607. Tel. (716) 461-0490.

Jewish Newspaper: "Jewish Ledger," 2525 Brighton-Henrietta Town Line Rd., 14623.
(K) Kosher Delicatessen: Brownstein's Deli and Bakery, 1862 Monroe Av., 14618; Fox's Kosher Restaurant and Delicatessen, 3450 Winton Place, 14623; (K) Jewish Home of Rochester Cafeteria, 2021 S. Winton Rd., 14618.

SARATOGA SPRINGS

Syn.: Shaarei Tefilah Orthodox Minyon (O), 11 Spring St., 12866. Tel. (518) 584-2234. Shaare Tfille (C), 260 Broadway, 12866. Tel. 584-2370; Temple Sinai (R), 509 Broadway, 12866. Tel. 584-8730.

SCARSDALE

Syn.: Magen David Sephardic Cong., 1225 Weaver St., 10583. Tel. (914) 636-4304.

SCHENECTADY

Syn.: Beth Israel (O), 2195 Eastern Parkway, 12309. Tel. (518) 377-3700; Gates of Heaven (R), 852 Ashmore Av., 12309. Tel. (518) 374-8173; Agudat Achim (C), 2117 Union St., 12309. Tel. (518) 393-9211.
Com. Centre.: 2565 Balltown Rd., 12309. Tel. 377-8803.
Jewish Family Services, 246 Union St., 12305. Tel. 372-3716.

SPRING GLEN

Kosher Hotel: Davidman's Homowack Hotel, 12483 Tel. (914) 647-6800. Glatt kosher. Under the supervision of the Union of Orthodox Jewish Congregations. Fax. 914-647-4908; Toll Free number from US and Canada 800-243-4567.e
Syn.: Beth Israel (O), Main St., Monsey, 10952; Beth Rochel (O), 210 Maple Av., Monsey, 10952; B'nai Jeshurun (O), Park Lane, Monsey, 10952; Community Syn. (O), W. Maple Av., Monsey, 10952; Kehilath Israel (O), Old Nyack Turnpike,Spring Valley, 10977; Yeshiva Wiznitz (O), Phyllis Ter., Monsey, 10952; Young Israel (O), 23 N. Union Rd., Spring Valley, 10977; Com. Centre (C), 250 N. Main St., Spring Valley, 10977; Monsey Jewish Centre (C), 101 Route 306, Monsey, 10952; Ramat Shalom (C), Lomond Av., Spring Valley, 10977; Shaare Tfiloh (C), 972 S. Main St., Spring Valley, 10977; Temple Beth El (R), 415 Viola Rd., Spring Valley, 10977.
Mendel & Sarah Zuber, 32 Blauvelt Rd., Monsey, 10952, write: "Anyone wishing to spend a Shabbat or Yomtov with us is more than welcome. We are Lubavitch Chasidim, glatt kosher". Tel. (914) 425-6213.
Kosher Hotel: Gartner's Inn, Hungry Hollow Rd., Spring Valley, 10977. Tel. 356-0875.

Kosher Restaurants & Delicatessen: Heshey's Kosher Pizza, 33½ Maple Av., 10977; GPG Deli, Main St., 10977; Crest Hill Deli, 279 Main St., 10977; K & G Deli, 31 S. Central Av., 10977. All in Spring Valley. Mehadrin Restaurant, 82 Route 59, Monsey, 10952.

New Square, the village of the Skvirer Chasidim, is near by.

SYRACUSE

Syn.: Young Israel (O), 4313 E. Genesee St., Dewitt, 13214. Mikva attached; Temple Beth El (Modern Orth.), 3528 E. Genesee St., 12306; Adath Yeshurun (C), 450 Kimber Rd., 13224; Beth Sholom (C), 5205 Jamesville Rd., Dewitt, 13214; Ner Tamid (R), 5061 W. Taft Rd., N. Syracuse; Society of Concord (R), 910 Madison St., 13210.

Com. Centre: 5655 Thompson Rd., Dewitt, 13214.

TROY

Syn.: Beth Tephila (O), 82 River St., 12180. Tel. 272-3182; Troy Chabad Centre (O), 2306 15th St., 12180. Mikva on premises. Tel. (518) 274-5572; Temple Beth El (C), 411 Hoosick St., 12180. Tel. 272-6113; Berith Sholom (R), 167 3rd St., 12180. Tel. 272-8872.

Com. Centre: 2500 21st St., 12180.

UTICA

Syn.: Cong. Zvi Jacob (O), 112 Memorial Pkwy., 13501; Temple Beth El (C), 1607 Genesee St., 13501; Temple Emanu-El (C), 2710 Genesee St., 13502.

Com. Centre, 2310 Oneida St., 13501.

Jewish Fed., 2310 Oneida St., 13501. Tel. (315) 733-2343.

WEST POINT

Site of the U.S. Military Academy, most of it on land originally owned by Eleazer Levy, a New York businessman. There are some points of Jewish interest in the area.

WHITE PLAINS

Syn.: Hebrew Institute of White Plains (O), 20 Greenridge Av., 10605; Temple Israel (C), Old Mamaroneck Rd. at Miles Av., 10605; Bet Am Shalom (Rec.), 295 Soundview Av., 10606.

Jewish Comm. Center (R), 252 Soundview Av.; Young Israel, 2 Gedney Way. Tel. (914) 683-YIWP.

WOODBOURNE

Kosher Hotel: Chalet Vim, 12788. Glatt kosher.

WOODRIDGE

Kosher Hotel: The Lake House Hotel, 12789. Tel. (914) 434-7800 or (212) 740-8686. Glatt kosher. Cholov Yisroel products only. Open Pesach to Succot.

YONKERS

Syn.: Rosh Pinah (O), Riverdale Av., 10705; Sons of Israel (O), 105 Radford Av., 10705; Agudas Achim (C), 21 Hudson St., 10701; Lincoln Park Centre (C), 323 Central Park Av., 10704; Temple Emanu-El (R), 306 Rumsey Rd., 10705.

Com. Centre: 122 South Broadway, 10701.

NORTH CAROLINA

ASHEVILLE

Syn.: Cong. Beth Israel (C), 229 Murdoch Av., 28804; Beth Ha-Tephila (R), 43 N. Liberty St., 28801.

CHARLOTTE

Syn.: Chabad Hse. (O), 6500 Newhall Rd., 28205. Mikva on premises. Temple Israel (C), 1014 Dilworth Rd., 28203; Temple Beth El (R), 1727 Providence Rd., 28207.
Jewish Fed., 5007 Providence Rd., 28226. Tel. (704) 366-5007. Other orgs. at the same address include the Com. Centre, the Hebrew Academy & Social Services.

DURHAM

Syn: Beth El (C), Watts St., 27701; Judea (R), 2115 Cornwallis Rd., 27705. An (O) kehilla has taken over the smaller sanctuary at Beth-El. It also has a mikva & nursery school. Inf. about Beth El from Leon Dworsky, 1100 Leon St., Apt. 28, 27705, & about Judea from Rabbi John Friedman. Tel. (919) 489-7062.
Durham-Chapel Hill Jewish Fed. & Com. Council, 205 Mt. Bolus Rd., Chapel Hill, 27514. Tel. (919) 967-6916.
The B'nai B'rith Hillel House at Chapel Hill serves kosher meals by previous arrangement.

FAYETTEVILLE

Syn.: Beth Israel Cong. (C), 2204 Morganton Rd., 28303. Tel. (919) 484-6462.

FORT BRAGG

U.S. Army Jewish Chapel, adjoining Chaplain's Activities Centre. Rabbi's duty Tel. (919) 396-7574.

GREENSBORO

Syn.: Beth David (C), 804 Winview Dr., 27410; Temple Emanuel (R), 713 N. Greene St., 27401.
Jewish Fed., 713a N. Greene St., 27401.

HENDERSONVILLE

Syn.: Agudas Israel Cong., (C), 328 N. King St., P.O.B. 668, 28793.

RALEIGH

Syn.: Cong. Sha'arei Israel (O), 7400 Falls of the Neuse Rd., 27615. Tel. (919) 847-8986. Mikva, pre-school & primary school on premises. Distributor of kosher meat & poultry; Beth Meyer Syn. (C), 504 Newton Rd., 27615. Tel. (919) 848-1420; Temple Beth Or (R), 5315 Creedmoor Rd., 27612. Pre-school. Tel. (919) 781-4895.
Restaurant: Bagels, Etc., 3209 Gresham Lake Rd., 27615. Tel. (919) 872-0818.

WILMINGTON

Syn.: B'nai Israel (C), 2601 Chestnut St. 28401.

WINSTON-SALEM

Syn.: Beth Jacob (C), 1833 Academy St., 27101; Temple Emanuel (R), 201 Oakwood Dr., 27103. Tel. 722-6640.
Jewish Com. Council, P.O.B. 15441, 27113. Tel. (919) 725-9091.

Blumenthal Jewish Home for the Aging, 7870 Fair Oaks Dr., Clemmons, 27012. Kosher meals available for visitors. Tel. 766-6401.

NORTH DAKOTA

FARGO

Syn.: Fargo Hebrew Cong., (O), 901 S. 9th St., 58103; Temple Beth El (R), 809 11th Av. S., 58103.

OHIO

AKRON

Syn.: Revere Rd. (O), Revere Av. & Smith Rd., 44320; Beth El (C), 464 S. Hawkins Av., 44320; Temple Israel (R), 133 Merriman Rd., 44303.
Com. Centre, 750 White Pond Dr., 44320.
Jerome Lippman Jewish Com. Day School, 750 White Pond Dr., 44320.
Jewish Com. Fed., 750 White Pond Dr., 44320. Tel. (216) 867-7850.

CANTON

Syn.: Agudas Achim (O), 2508 Market St. N., 44704; Shaaray Torah (C), 423 30th St. N.W., 44709; Temple Israel (R), 333 25th St. N.W., 44709.
Com. Centre, 2631 Harvard Av., N.W. 44709. Tel. (216) 453-0132.
Jewish Com. Fed., 2631 Harvard Av. N.W., 44709. Tel. (216) 452-6444.

CINCINNATI

Syn.: Chabad Hse. (O), 1636 Summit Rd., 45237; Golf Manor Syn. (O), 6442 Stover Av., 45237; Kehelath B'nai Israel (O), 1546 Kenova Av., 45237. Mikva on premises. Tel. 821-6679; Kneseth Israel (O), 1515 Section Rd., 45237; New Hope Cong. (O), 1625 Crest Hill, 45237; N. Avondale Syn. (O), 3870 Reading Rd., 45229; Ohav Sholom Cong. (O), 1834 Section Rd., 45237; Orthodox Jewish Home for Aged (O), 1171 Towne St., 45216; Roselawn Syn. (O), 7600 Reading Rd., 45237; Adath Israel (C), 3201 E. Galbraith Rd., 45236; B'nai Tzedek (C), 1580 Summit Rd., 45237; Downtown Syn. (C), 36 E. 4th St., 7th Floor, 45202; Northern Hills Syn. (C), 715 Fleming Rd., 45231; Sephardic Beth Sholom Cong. (C), P.O. Box 37431, 45222; Hebrew Union College Chapel (R), 3101 Clifton Av., 45220; Isaac M. Wise Temple (R), 8329 Ridge Rd., 45236; Plum St. Temple (R), 8th & Plum Sts., 45202; Rockdale Temple (R), 8501 Ridge Rd., 45236; Temple Sholom (R), 3100 Longmeadow, 45236; Valley Temple (R), 145 Springfield Pike, 45215; Beth Adam Cincinnati Cong. for Humanistic Judaism, 1720 Section Rd., Apt. 107, 45237.
Com. Centre: 1580 Summit Rd., 45237.
Com. Fed.: 1811 Losantiville, Suite 320, 45237.
Hillel Jewish Students' Centre, 2615 Clifton Av., 45220.
Homes for Aged: Glen Manor, 6969 Glenmeadow Dr., 45237; Orthodox Home, 1171 Towne St., 45216.
Jewish Com. Relations Council, 105 W. 4th St., 45202.
Jewish Hospital, 3200 Burnet Av., 45229.
Details of schools, afternoon Hebrew schools, etc. are available from: Bureau of Jewish Education, 1580 Summit Rd., 45237.
The Hebrew Union College-Jewish Institute of Religion, at 3101 Clifton Av., 45220, is the oldest and largest Jewish theological seminary in America for training Reform rabbis. Its library is one of the largest Jewish libraries in the world. It also has a gallery of art and artifacts, housing a collection of

Jewish objets d'art, religious and ceremonial appurtenances, rare books and manuscripts.

The University of Cincinnati has a Department of Judaic Studies.

The Chestnut St. Cemetery, Chestnut St. & Central Av., is the oldest Jewish cemetery west of the Alleghany Mountains. It was founded in 1821.

Newspaper: "American Israelite", 906 Main St., 45202. Oldest Anglo-Jewish weekly in the United States.

Kosher Bakery: Golf Maron, 2200 Losantiville Av. (All parve. Closed Sat.)

Kosher Food: Bilkers, 7648 Reading Rd., 45237; Hot Bagels Factory, 7617 Reading Rd., 45237 & 477 E. Kemper Rd., 45246. Also available at Com. Centre & Jewish Hospital (addresses above).

Kosher Meat: Toron's Meat, 1436 Section Rd., 45237; Pilder's Kosher Foods, 7601 Reading Rd., 45237.

CLEVELAND

Syn.: Ahavath Israel (O), 1726 S. Taylor Rd. Tel. 371-3665-90; Beth El (O), 15808 Chagrin Blvd., 44120. Tel. 991-6044; Chabad House of Cleveland (O), 4481 University Pkwy., 4418; Green Road Syn., (O), 2437 Green Road Syn., 44122; Beth Hamidrosh Hagodol-Heights Jewish Center (O), 14270 Cedar Rd., 44121. Tel. 382-1958; City of Refuge (O), 2004 S. Green Rd. Tel. 691-0770; Kehillat Yaakov-Warrensville Center Syn. (O), 1508 Warrensville Center Rd., 44121; K'Hal Yereim, 1771 S. Taylor Rd. Tel. 321-9554. Tel. 382-6566; Menorah Park, 27100 Cedar Rd. Tel. 831-6500; Sinai Syn. (O), 3246 De Sota Av., 44118; Oheb Zedek-Taylor Rd. (O), 1970 S. Taylor Road Syn., 44118; Oheb Zedek-Taylor Rd. (Beachwood Branch) (O), Cleveland Hebrew Schools Building, Fairmount Blvd. and Richmond Rd. Tel. 321-4875; Rinat Israel (O), 2308 Warrensville Center Rd. Tel. 932-7664; Torah U'Tefilah (O), 1861 S. Taylor Road Syn., 44118; Young Israel of Cleveland (O), 14141 Cedar Rd., 44121; Young Israel of Beechwood (O) 2120 S. Green Rd., 44121. Zemach Zedek (O), 1922 Lee Rd., 44118; Zichron Chaim (O), 2203 S. Green Rd., 44122 Tel. 291-5000; Agudath B'nai Israel (C), Meister Rd. at Plle Av., Lorain. Tel. 1-282-3307; Oer Chodesh Anshe Sfard (O), 3466 Washington Blvd., 44118; Beth Am Community Temple (C), 3557 Washington Blvd., Cleveland Heights, 44118; Bethaynu (C), 27900 Gates Mills Blvd., 44124; B'Nai Abraham (C), 530 Gulf Rd., Elyria. Tel. 1-366-1171; B'nai Jeshurun-Temple on the Heights (C), 27501 Fairmount Blvd., Tel. 831-6555; Cong. Shaarey Tikvah (C), 26811 Fairmount Blvd, 44124; Park Synagogue-Anshe Emeth Beth Tefilo Cong. (C), 3300 Mayfield Rd. (Park Synagogue East, Shaker Blvd. at Brainard Circle). Tel. 371-2244; Am Shalom of Lake County (R), 7599 Center St. Tel. 1-255-1544; Anshe Chesed-Fairmount Temple (R), 23737 Fairmount Blvd.Tel. 464-1330; Beth Israel-The West Temple (R), 14308 Triskett Rd., 44111; Beth Shalom (R), On the Green, Hudson, Ohio. Tel. 1-650-0133; Chevrei Tikva (R), (Outreach to Gay/Lesbian), P.O. Box 18120, Cleveland 44118:0120. Tel. 932-551; Suburban Temple (R), 22401 Chagrin Blvd., 44122; Temple Emanu El (R), 2200 S. Green Rd., 44121; Temple Israel (R), 1732 Lander Rd., 44124; Ner Tamid of Euclid (R), Lake Shore Blvd. at E. 250th St. Tel. 261-2280; The Temple-Tifereth Israel (R), University Circle at Silver Pk. Tel. 791-7755. (Branch: 26000 Shaker Blvd. Tel. 831-3233).

Mikvaot: 1774 Lee Rd., 44118; Lubavitch, 2479 S. Green Rd.

Cleveland Hillel Foundation, 11291 Euclid Av., 44106.

Bureau of Jewish Education, 2030 S. Taylor Rd., 44118.

Jewish Com. Centers: 3505 Mayfield Rd., 44118; 26001 S. Woodland Rd., 44122.

Jewish Com. Fed. of Cleveland, 1750 Euclid Av., 44115. Tel. (216) 566-9200.

All inf. about Cleveland Com. from Jewish Community Federation, 1750 Euclid Av., 44115. Tel. (216) 566-9200.
Menorah Park Center for the Aging 27100 Cedar Rd., 44122.
Montefiore Home, Dave Myers Parkway, 44122.
Mt. Sinai Medical Center, One Mt. Sinai Dr. 44106
Newspaper: "Cleveland Jewish News", 3645 Warrensville Center Rd., Suite 230, 44122.
Places of Jewish interest: The Temple Museum of Religious Art Library, Abba Hillel Silver Archives (Jewish art objects, religious & ceremonial treasures, rare books and manuscripts) University Circle at Silver Park, 441062; the collection of Jewish art & sculpture, Park Synagogue, 3300 Mayfield Rd., 44118; Discovery Place–Jewish Children's Museum, Mayfield; Olyn and Joseph B. Horwitz Collection of Jewish Ceremonial Art Objects, Judaica and Religious Artifacts, Fairmount Temple, 23737 Fairmount Blvd., 44122.
Restaurants: Empire Kosher Kitchen, 2234 Warrensville Center Rd. Tel. 691-0006; Yacov's Restaurant, 13969 Cedar Rd., 44118; Kinneret Kosher Restaurant, 1869 S. Taylor Rd., 44118; Peking Kosher Chinese Restaurant, 1841 S. Taylor Rd., 44118. Academy Party Center, 4182 Mayfield Rd., 44121; Del: Cellar, Hillel Bldg.-CWRU, 11291 Euclid Av., 44106.

COLUMBUS

Syn.: Agudas Achim (O), 2767 E. Broad St., 43209; Ahavas Sholom (O), 2568 E. Broad St., 43209; Cong. Beth Jacob (O), 1223 College Av., 43209. Mikva on premises; House of Tradition (O), 57 E. 14th St., 43201; Tifereth Israel (C), 1354 E. Broad St., 43205; Beth Shalom (R), 3100 E. Broad St., 43209; Beth Tikvah (R), 6121 Olentangy River Rd., 43085; Temple Israel (R), 5419 E. Broad St., 43213.
Leo Yassenoff Jewish Center, 1125 College Av., 43209. Tel. 231-2731.
Jewish Fed., 1175 College Av., 43209. Tel. (614) 237-7686.
Ohio State University B'nai B'rith Hillel Foundation, 46 E. 16th Av., 43201.
Kosher Delicatessen: Martin's Kosher Foods, 3685 E. Broad St., 43213.
Kosher Bakery: Leah's Bakery, 2996 E. Broad St., Columbus, Oh 43209.

DAYTON

Syn.: Shomrei Emunah (O), 1706 Salem Av., 45406; Beth Jacob (Traditional), 7020 N. Main St., 45415; Beth Abraham (C), 1306 Salem Av., 45406; Temple Beth Or (R), 5275 Marshall Rd., 45429; Temple Israel (R), 1821 Emerson Av., 45406.
Mikva: 556 Kenwood Av., 45406.
Jewish Fed. of Greater Dayton, Jesse Philips Bldg., 4501 Denlinger Rd., 45426. Tel. (513) 854-4150. Includes Dayton Jewish Centre, Com. Relations Council and Jewish Family Service.
Jewish Home for Aged: Covenant Hse., 4911 Covenant Hse. Dr., 45426; Apartments for Elderly & Handicapped, Covenant Manor, 4951 Covenant Hse. Dr., 45426.
Weekly Newspaper: "Dayton Jewish Chronicle", 118 Salem Av., 45406.
Bakery: Rinaldo's Bake Shoppe, 910 W. Fairview Av.

LORAIN

Syn.: Agudath B'nai Israel (C), 1715 Meister Rd., 44053.

TOLEDO

Syn.: Cong. Etz Chayim (O), 3853 Woodley Rd., Toledo, Oh 43606; B'nai Israel (C), 2727 Kenwood Blvd., Toledo, Oh 43606; The Temple-Congregation Shomer Emunim, 6453 Sylvania Av., Sylvania, 43560.

YOUNGSTOWN AREA

Syn.: Children of Israel (O), 3970½ Logan Way, 44505. Mikva on premises; Beth Israel Temple Centre (C), 2138 E. Market St., Warren, 44482; Ohev Tzedek-Shaarei Torah (C), 5245 Glenwood Av., 44512; Temple Beth Israel (R), 840 Highland Rd., Sharon, PA 16146; Temple El Emeth (C), 3970 Logan Way, 44505; Rodef Sholom (R), Elm St. & Woodbine Av., 44505.
Youngstown Area Jewish Fed., 505 Gypsy La., 44501. Tel. (216) 746-3251.

OKLAHOMA

OKLAHOMA CITY

Syn.: Emanuel Synagogue (C), 900 N.W. 47th St., 73106; Temple B'nai Israel (R), 4901 N. Pennsylvania Av., 73112.
Jewish Fed. of Greater Oklahoma City, 3022 N.W. Expressway, Suite 116, 73112. Tel. (405) 949-0111.
B'nai B'rith Hillel Foundation, 494 Elm St., Norman.
Bakery: Ingrid's Kitchen, 2309 N.W. 36th St., 73112.

TULSA

Syn.: B'nai Emunah (C), 1719 S. Owasso Av., 74120; Temple Israel (R), 2004 E. 22nd Pl., 74114.
Com. Centre, 2021 E. 71st St. 74136. Tel. (918) 495-1111. Heritage Academy (day school) is also at this address.
Jewish Fed., 2021 E. 71st St., 74136. Tel. (918) 495-1100.
Chabad House, Lubavitch of Oklahoma, 6622 S. Utica Av., Tel. (918) 492-4499/493-7006. Exec. Dir. Rabbi Yehuda Weg. Hospitality for travellers.
The Gershon & Rebecca Fenster Museum of Jewish Art, 1223 E. 17th Pl., 74120, is the only independent Jewish Museum in the South-West. It is well worth a visit.

OREGON

ASHLAND

Temple Emek Shalom-Rogue Valley Jewish Com. (R), 1081 E. Mountain, 97520. Tel. (503) 488-2909.

EUGENE

Syn.: Beth Israel (C), 2550 Portland St., 97405. Tel. (503) 485-7218.

PORTLAND

Syn.: Ahavath Achim (Sephardi, O), 3225 S.W. Barbur Blvd., 97201; Kesser Israel (O), 136 S.W. Meade St., 97201; Shaarie Torah (O), 920 N.W. 25th Av., 97209; Neveh Shalom (C), 2900 S.W. Peaceful Lane, 97201; Beth Israel (R), 1931 N.W. Flanders St., 97209; Chabad, 14355 Scholls Ferry Rd., 97007; Gesher, 10701 SW 25th Av., 97219; Havurah Shalom, 6651 SW Capitol Hwy, 97219.
Mikva: Ritualarium, 1425 S.W. Harrison St., 97201.
Jewish Fed. of Portland, 6651 S.W. Capitol Highway, 97219. Tel. (503) 245-6219.
Mittleman Jewish Com. Centre, (Kosher restaurant), 6651 S.W. Capitol Highway, 97219. Tel. (503) 244-0111.
Kosher meat & foodstuffs obtainable from Albertson's, Shattuck Rd., 97221.

SALEM

Syn.: Beth Shalom, 1795 Broadway NE, 97303.

PENNSYLVANIA

ALLENTOWN

Syn.: Agudas Achim (O), 625 N. Second St., 18102. Tel. (215) 432-4414; Sons of Israel (O), 2715 Tilghman St., 18104. Tel. (215) 433-6089; Beth-El (C), 1702 Hamilton St., 18104. Tel. (215) 435-3521; Keneseth Israel (R), 2227 Chew St., 18104. Tel. (215) 435-9074; Am Haskalah (Reconstructionist), Ott & Walnut Sts., 18104. Tel. (215) 435-6512.
Mikva: 1836 Whitehall St., 18104.
Jewish Fed., 702 N. 22nd. St., 18104. Tel. (215) 821-5500. The Com. Centre and Jewish family service are at the same address. Tel. (215) 435-3571.
Glatt Kosher Restaurant: Com. Centre, 702 N. 22nd St., 18104. Since opening hours vary according to season, it is advisable to Tel. (215) 435-3571.

ALTOONA

Syn.: Agudath Achim (C), 1306 17th St., 16601; Temple Beth Israel (R), 3004 Union Av., 16602.
Com. Centre, 1308 17th St., 16601.

BETHLEHEM

Syn.: Agudath Achim (O), 1555 Linwood St., 18017; Cong. Brith Sholom (C), Macada & Jacksonville Rds., 18017.

BLUE BELL

Syn.: Tiferet Bet Israel (C), 1920 Skippack Pike, 19422. Tel. (215) 275-8797.

EASTON

Syn.: B'nai Abraham (C), 16th & Bushkill Sts., 18042. Established 1888; Covenant of Peace (R), 15th & Northampton Sts., 18042. Established in 1839.
The cemetery in 7th St., 18042, has graves with tombstone inscriptions dating from the early 18th century.

ERIE

Syn.: Brith Sholom Jewish Centre (C), 3207 State St., 16508; Anshe Hesed (R), 10th & Liberty Sts., 16502.
Jewish Com. Council, G. Daniel Baldwin Bldg., 1001 State St., 16501. Tel. (814) 455-4474.

HARRISBURG

Syn.: Kesher Israel (O), 3rd & Schuylkill Sts., 17110; Beth El (C), Front & Wiconisco Sts., 17110; Chisuk Emuna (C), 5th & Division Sts., 17110; Ohev Sholom (R), 2345 N. Front St., 17110.
United Jewish Com. of Greater Harrisburg, 100 Vaughn St., 17110. Tel. (717) 236-9555.
Kosher Self-Service Snack Bar: J.C.E., Front & Vaughn, 17110.
Kosher meat is available at the Uptown Shopping Plaza, 17110.

HAZLETON

Syn.: Agudas Israel (C), 77 N. Pine St., 18201; Beth Israel (R), 98 N. Church St., 18201.
Jewish Com. Council, 99 N. Laurel St., 18201. Tel. (717) 454-3528.

JOHNSTOWN

Syn.: Beth Sholom Cong. (C), 700 Indiana St., 15905.
United Jewish Fed., 700 Indiana St., 15905. Tel. (814) 536-0647.
Grandview Cemetery contains the graves of Jews who died in the famous
Johnstown flood of 1889. Approximately 22 perished.

LANCASTER

Syn.: Degel Israel (O), 1120 Columbia Av., 17603; Beth El (C), 25 N. Lime
St., 17602; Temple Shaarai Shomayim (R), N. Duke & James Sts., 17602.
Jewish Community Center, 2120 Oregon Pike, 17601.
Jewish Fed., 2120 Oregon Pike, 17601. Tel. (717) 569-7352.

LEVITTOWN

Named after its builder, William Levitt, Levittown is one of the largest
planned towns in the U.S.A.
Syns.: Cong. Beth El (C), 21 Penn Valley Rd., Fallsington, 19054. Tel. (215)
945-9500; Temple Shalom (R), Edgeley Rd., off Mill Creek Pkwy. 19057. Tel.
(215) 945-4154.

MCKEESPORT

Syn.: Gemilas Chesed (O), 1400 Summit St., White Oak 15131. Rabbi Irvin
Chinn. Tel. (412) 678-9859; Tree of Life-Sfard (C), Cypress Av., 15131; B'nai
Israel (R), 536 Shaw Av., 15132.

PHILADELPHIA

Thanks are due to Lewis Bokser for the information about Philadelphia.
There is a large Jewish com. in Greater Philadelphia. In the city centre on
Spruce St., between 8th & 9th Sts., opposite the Pennsylvania Hospital, is
Mikveh Israel Cemetery, founded in 1738, which is a national shrine.
Buried there are Haym Salomon, who gave his fortune to help the
Revolutionary War and was never repaid; he was featured on a postage
stamp some years ago; Rebecca Gratz, and Aaron Levy, who founded the
city of Aaronsburg in Pennsylvania.
In the city centre, at Broad & Pine, are the Y.M. & Y.W.H.A., said to be the
second oldest in the country; the Rosenbach Museum, 2010 Delancy St.; the
Jewish Publication Society, 1930 Chestnut St., 19103; the headquarters of
the Fed. of Jewish Agencies and the Allied Jewish Appeal, 226 S. 16th St.,
19102.
The old Mikveh Israel Synagogue (Sephardi), established in 1740, is
located near Independence Hall in Commerce St., between 4th and 5th Sts.
(just north of Market St.). Services have been held there without a break for
250 years. A number of members are Afro-American or Black. Between
1828 & 1972, the cong. had only three ministers, one of them, the Rev. Leon
Elmaleh, serving for 75 years (1897 until 1972). It contains many religious
and personal memorabilia of early Jewish settlers in America. Many of
these pioneers became mayors and governors of the cities and States in
which they settled. There are guided tours of the synagogue for visitors.
Attached to the synagogue is the National Jewish Museum.
At the Balch Institute, 18 S. 7th St., can be found the Philadelphia Jewish
Archives, which collect congregational, organisational, family and personal
records.
Rodeph Shalom, originally Orthodox and now Reform, is the second oldest
synagogue in the city and is at Broad & Mt. Vernon Sts.
The Chapel of the Four Chaplains at the S.E. corner of Broad & Berks Sts.,
on the campus of Temple University, is a memorial to the Rev. Clark V.
Poling, the Rev. George Fox, John P. Washington and Rabbi Alexander D.

Goode, who turned their lifejackets over to sailors who had none when their troopship was sunk in the Second World War.

A complex near the Olney Av. station of the Broad St. Subway, beginning at Old York Rd. and Tabor Rd., and extending south about half a mile, contains the Albert Einstein Medical Centre with its nurses' training school and residences (the Centre is being greatly expanded and new buildings added); the Willowcrest-Bamberger Post-Hospital Care Nursing Home; the York Houses, which are high-rise apartments for retired or semi-retired persons, and the Philadelphia Geriatric Centre with its Home for the Aged. At 7601 Old York Rd., 19141, is Gratz College, a school for Hebrew studies at the high school and advanced levels.

It houses the Annenburg Research Institute for Judaic & Near Eastern Studies (formerly Dropsie University with its 150,000 volume library) which offers post-doctoral courses.

The Samuel Fleisher Memorial (formerly the Graphic Sketch Club) is at 719 Catherine St. It has a museum and sanctuary devoted to all monotheistic religions.

The Uptown Home for the Aged, founded by the late Mrs. David Bokser, is at Bustleton Av. & Glendale.

Many sections of the Free Library, on Parkway, are gifts of Jews, such as the Fleisher Collection, said to be the largest collection of classical and symphonic music in the world, and the Rosenbach Collection of children's books. At the N.W. end of Parkway is the Art Museum, in front of which is the Phillips Fountain, named after Henry M. Phillips, who bequeathed large sums for works of art. A statue of Moses is to be seen in the western part of Fairmount Park.

A sculptured memorial to the six million martyrs of the Holocaust stands at 16th St. & Benjamin Franklin Parkway. A huge sculpture by Jacques Lipshitz can be found in the patio of the Municipal Service Bldg., at 15th St. and John Kennedy Blvd., opposite City Hall.

Synagogues

Beth Zion (C), 18th & Spruce Sts., 19103, is in the city centre. Near by are Kesher Israel (O), 412 Lombard St.; Society Hill (C), 418 Spruce St., 19106; B'nai Abraham (O), 6th & Lombard Sts., 19147; and Meysos Israel (Sephardi), 521 Lombard St., 19147.

On Old York Rd., about a mile above City Line, is Beth Sholom (C), designed by the late Frank Lloyd Wright. Keneseth Israel (R) is immediately above at Old York Rd., & Township Line, 19141, while Adath Jeshurun (C), is at Ashbourne & Old York Rd., 19117.

On the way to Chestnut Hill are Germantown Com. Centre (C), Lincoln Dr. & Ellet St., 19119; Beth Tikvah (C), 1001 Paper Mill Rd., 19118; Temple Sinai (C), Limekiln Park & Dillon Rd., Dresher; and Beth Or (R), Penllyn Pk. & Dager Rd., Spring House. In N.E. Phila. are Beth Uziel (C), Wyoming Av. & Rorer St., 19120; Temple Sholom (C), Large St. & Roosevelt Blvd., 19124; Temple Menorah (C), Tyson & Algard Sts., 19135; Beth Emeth (C). Bustleton & Unruh, 19149; Ahavath Torah (O), 7525 Loretto Av.; B'nai Abraham (C), Willits & Eastview Sts., 19152; Oxford Circle Jewish Com. Centre (C), Algon & Unruh Sts., 19149; Ner Zedek (C), Bustleton & Oakmont Sts., 19152; Aitz Chaim (O), 7601 Summerdale Av.; Beth Ami (C), 9201 Old Bustleton Av., 19115; B'nai Israel-Ohev Zedek (O), 8201 Castor Av., 19152; B'nai Jacob Bershu Tov (O), 1147 Gilham St.; Young Israel (O), 6427 Large St.; Beth Torah (R), 608 Welsh Rd.; Shaare Shamayim (O), 9768 Verree Rd. Hebrew Academy Elementary School is at Old Bustleton Av., below Welsh Rd. Adath Zion (C), Penway & Friendship St. In W. Phila. are Beth T'fillah (C), 7630 Woodbine Av., 19151; Beth Jacob (O), 6801 Larchwood Av.; Beth Hamedrash of Overbrook Park (O), 7505 Brookhaven

Rd.; Lenas Hazedek (O), 2747 Cranston Rd..

Near by, above City Line, are Adath Israel (C), Old Lancaster Rd. & Highland Av., 19118; Lower Merion (O), 123 Old Lancaster Park, Cynwyd; and Beth Hillel (C), Remington Rd., Wynnewood, 19096.

In the suburbs west of the city are Israel of Upper Darby (C), Bywood & Walnut. 19082; Beth El (C), 715 Paxon Hollow Rd., Broomall, 19104; Temple Sholom (R), 55 N. Church Lane, Broomall, 19008; Beth Israel (O), Gayley Ter. & Baker, Media, 19063; B'nai Aaron (C), 560 Mill Rd., Havertown, 19083; Beth Am Israel (C), 1301 Hagys Ford Rd., Penn Valley; Beth Elohim (R), 410 Montgomery Av., Wynnewood, 19096; Kesser Israel (C), 206 N. Church St., West Chester and Brith Achim (R), 700 Moore Rd., King of Prussia; Beth Chaim (C), 350 E. Street Rd., Feasterville, 19047; Oheve Sholom (C), 944 Second St. Pike, Richboro, 18954; Shir Ami (R), 101 Richboro Rd., Newtown, 18940.

Mikvaot: Ahavat Torah, 7525 Loretto Av.; Lower Merion Syn., 123 Old Lancaster Park, Cynwyd; Torah Academy, 742 Argyle Rd., Wynnewood, 19096.

Fed. of Jewish Agencies of Greater Philadelphia, 226 S. 16th St., 19102. Tel. (215) 893-5600.

The London "Jewish Chronicle" is available from the Rev. P. Schwartz, Bar-Mitzvah Training Centre, 6809 Castor Av.

Restaurants: Hillel Hse. of Univ. of Pennsylvania, 202 S. 36th St., serves lunches & dinners during the academic year. Prior booking necessary; The Broad Noodle, Hillel Hse. of Temple Univ., 2014 N. Broad St. Dairy foods. Lunch available during the academic year; Dragon Inn Glatt Kosher Chinese Restaurant, 7628 Castor Av., 19152. European Dairy, 20th & Sansom Sts.; Tel. (215) 742-2575; Golani Pizza & Falafel, 7638 Castor Av., 19152.

Maccabean Restaurant 128 S. 12th St. Pa 19107; Tel. (215) 922-5922. Glatt Kosher.

PITTSBURGH

Thanks are due to Edie B. Naveh, Director of the Pittsburgh Community Relations Committee of the United Jewish Federation, for the following information.

There are about 45,000 Jews in Pittsburgh, a significant number in the Squirrel Hill area (where an Eruv is in operation), which also houses the majority of Jewish institutions. There are smaller coms. in East Liberty, Stanton Heights, Oakland and the South Hills and East and North Hills areas round Pittsburgh.

Syn.: Adath Israel (O), 3257 Ward St., 15213; Adath Jeshurun (O), 5643 E. Liberty Blvd., 15224; Beth Hamedrash Hagodol (O), 1230 Colwell St., 15219; B'nai Emunoh (O), 4315 Murray Av., 15217; B'nai Zion (O), 6404 Forbes Av., 15217; Bohnei Yisroel (O), 6401 Forbes Av., 15217; Kether Torah (O), 5706 Bartlett St., 15217; Kneseth Israel (O), 1112 N. Negley Av., 15206; Machsikei Hadas (O), 814 N. Negley Av., 15206; Poale Zedeck (O), Phillips & Shady Avs., 15217; Shaare Tefillah (O), 5741 Bartlett St., 15217; Shaare Torah (O), 2319 Murray Av., 15217; Shaare Zedeck (O), 5751 Bartlett St., 15217; Torath Chaim (O), 728 N. Negley Av., 15206; Ahavath Achim (C), Lydia & Chestnut Sts., Carnegie, 15106; Beth El of South Hills (C), 1900 Cochran Rd., 15220; Beth Shalom (C), Beacon & Shady Avs., 15217; B'nai Israel (C), 327 N. Negley Av., 15206; New Light (C), 1700 Beechwood Blvd., 15217; Parkway Jewish Centre (C), 300 Princeton Dr., Pittsburgh, 15235; Tree of Life (C), Wilkins & Shady Avs., 15217; Rodef Shalom (R), 4905 5th Av., 15213; Temple David (R), 4415 Northern Pike, Monroeville, 15146; Temple Emanuel (R), 1250 Bower Hill Rd., South Hills, 15243; Temple Sinai (R), 5505 Forbes Av., 15217; Dor Hadash (Rec.), 6401 Forbes Av., 15217.

Organisations

Mikva: 2326 Shady Av., 15217. Tel. (412) 422-7110.

Com. Centre: 5738 Forbes Av., 15217. Tel. (412) 521-8010.

The "Pittsburgh Jewish Chronicle" is at 5600 Baum Blvd. Tel. (412) 687-1000.

Anathan House, 1620 Murray Av., 15217, is the headquarters of the Pittsburgh branch of the National Council of Jewish Women.

Montefiore Hospital, a leading research and teaching hospital and nurses' training school, 3459 5th Av., 15213, has a kosher kitchen. **(K)**

Riverview Centre for Jewish Seniors, provides intermediate and skilled nursing care, Brown's Hill Rd., 15217. Tel. (412) 521-5900.

United Jewish Fed. of Greater Pittsburgh building, 234 McKee Pl., 15213, Tel. (412) 681-8000, Fax (412) 681-8804, houses all administrative offices of the Fed. & the Com. Relations Committee.

Holocaust Center of the United Jewish Federation, 242 McKee Pl., 15213. Tel. (412) 682-7111; serves as a living memorial by providing educational resources, sponsoring community activities, housing archives and cultural materials related to the Holocaust.

Jewish Education Institute, 6401 Forbes Av., 15217. Tel. (412) 521-1100; offers resources in Jewish education to synagogue schools, day schools, and other community organisations.

Bookseller: Pinsker's, 2028 Murray Av., 15217. Tel. (412) 421-3033.

Kosher Restaurants: King David's, 2020 Murray Av., 15217. Tel. (412) 422-3370; Yaacov's, 2109 Murray Av., 15217. Tel. (412) 421-7208.

Kosher Meat, Poultry, etc: Brauner's Emporium, 2023 Murray Av., 15217; Greenberg's Kosher Poultry, 2223 Murray Av.; Koshermart, 2121 Murray Av.; Pastries Unlimited, 4743 Liberty Av., & 2119 Murray Av.; Prime Kosher, 1916 Murray Av. All the above are under rabbinical supervision.

POTTSTOWN

Syn.: Cong. Mercy & Truth (C), 575 N. Keim St., 19464.

READING

Syn.: Shomrei Habrith (O), 2320 Hampden Blvd., 19604; Kesher Zion (C), Eckert & Perkiomen Sts., 19602; Oheb Sholom (R), 13th & Perkiomen Sts., 19604.

Com. Centre, 1700 City Line St., 19604. Tel. (215) 921-0624.

Jewish Fed., 1700 City Line St., 19604. Tel. (215) 921-2766.

SCRANTON

Syn.: Beth Shalom (O), Clay Av. at Vine St., 18510; Cong. Machzikeh Hadas (O), cnr. Monroe and Olive., 18510; Ohev Zedek (O), 1432 Mulberry St., 18510; Temple Israel (C), Gibson St. & Monroe Av., 18510; Temple Hesed (R), Lake Scranton, 18505.

Scranton-Lackawanna Jewish Fed., 601 Jefferson Av., 18510. Tel. (717) 961-2300. The Com. Centre is at the same address. Tel. (717) 346-6595.

Jewish Family Service, 615 Jefferson Av., 18510.

Jewish Home, 1101 Vine St., 18510.

Yeshivath Beth Moshe, 930 Hickory St., 18505.

SHARON

Syn.: Temple Beth Israel (R), 840 Highland Av., 16146.

WALLINGFORD

Syn.: Ohev Shalom (C), 2 Chester Rd., 19086. The syn. vestibule contains 12 stained glass panes (designed & executed by Rose Isaacson) each depicting a Jewish holiday.

Another work in glass by Rose Isaacson is on display in the vestibule. Depicting Jeremiah crying out to God, it is a memorial to the Six Million murdered in the Holocaust.

WILKES-BARRE

Syn.: Ohav Zedek (O), 242 S. Franklin St., 18702; Temple Israel (C), 236 S. River St., 18704; B'nai B'rith (R), 408 Wyoming Av., Kingston, 18704; United Orthodox Syn. (O), 13 S. Welles St., 18702.
Jewish Fed. of Greater Wilkes-Barre & Comm. Center, 60 S. River St., 18702. Tel. (717) 822-4146/(717) 824-4646.

WILLIAMSPORT

Syn.: Ohev Sholom (O & C), Cherry & Belmont Sts., 17701; Beth Ha-Sholom (R), 425 Center St., 17701.

RHODE ISLAND

BARRINGTON

Syn.: Temple Habonim (R), 165 New Meadow Rd., 02806.

BRISTOL

Syn.: United Brothers Syn. (C), 215 High St., 02809.

CRANSTON

Syn.: Temple Torat Yisrael (C), 330 Park Av., 02905; Temple Sinai (R), 30 Hagan Av. 02920.

MIDDLETOWN

Syn.: Temple Shalom (C), 220 Valley Rd., 02840.

NARRAGANSETT

Syn.: Cong. Beth David (C), Kingstown Rd., 02882.

NEWPORT

Syn.: Touro (Sephardi, O), 85 Touro St., 02840. The syn., built in 1763, is one of the finest examples of New England Colonial architecture. It has been declared a national shrine by the U.S. Government. The Jewish cemetery, the oldest in the U.S., dates back to 1677 and was immortalised in Longfellow's poem "The Jewish Cemetery of Newport". Judah Touro is buried there.
Com. Centre: Touro St.

PAWTUCKET

Syn.: Ohawe Shalom, East Av., 02860.

PROVIDENCE

Syn.: Beth Sholom (O), 275 Camp Av., 02906; Cong. Sons of Jacob (O), 24 Douglas Av., 02908; Mishkon Tfiloh (O), 203 Summit Av., 02906; Shaare Zedek (O), 688 Broad St., 02907; Temple Emanu-El (C), 99 Taft Av., 02906; Beth El (R), 70 Orchard Av., 02906.
Jewish Com. Centre of Rhode Island: 401 Elmgrove Av., 02906. Tel. (401) 861-8800. The Com. Centre houses the Rhode Island Holocaust Memorial Museum, the state memorial to the victims of the Holocaust. Many survivors now living in Rhode Island have donated memorabilia & personal mementoes. There is also a garden of remembrance. For further details, contact the Com. Centre.

Jewish Fed. of Rhode Island, 130 Sessions St., 02906. Tel. (401) 421-4111.
The Rhode Island Historical Society in Providence has a vast amount of material regarding Colonial Jews.
Kosher meals are available at Brown University Hillel, 80 Brown St., 02912.

WARWICK

Syn.: Temple Am David (C), 40 Gardiner St., 02888.

WESTERLY

Syn.: Cong. Shaare Zedek (O), Union St., 02891.

WOONSOCKET

Syn.: B'nai Israel (C), 224 Prospect St., 02895.

SOUTH CAROLINA

CHARLESTON

Syn.: B'rith Sholom (O) & Mikvah, 182 Rutledge Av., 29403. Tel. (803) 577-6599; Emanu-El (C), 5 Windsor Dr., 29407. Tel. (803) 571-3264; Beth Elohim (R), 86 Hasell St., 29401. Tel. (803) 723-1090.
Beth Elohim dates from 1749. It is the birthplace of Reform Judaism in the United States, the second oldest syn. bldg. in the country, and the oldest surviving Reform syn. in the world. It has been designated a national historic landmark. A museum is housed in the administration bldg. next door.
The cong.'s cemetery in Coming St. is the largest and oldest in the South, and contains graves of Revolutionary War soldiers. In City Hall Park, there is a plaque honouring Francis Salvador, the first Jew to hold public office in the Colonies and to die in the Revolution.
Sherman House (Old Age House), 1637 Raoul Wallenberg Blvd., 29407. Tel. (803) 763-2242.
Jewish Fed. & Com. Centre, 1645 Raoul Wallenberg Blvd., 29407. Tel. (803) 571-6565.
Addlestone Hebrew Academy (Day School), 1639 Raoul Wallenberg Blvd., 29407. Tel. (803) 571-1105.
Kosher restaurants
Nosh with Josh, 217 Meeting St. 29407. Tel. (803) 577-6674; Circus Donuts, 1091 Savannah Hwy., 29407. Tel. (803) 571-2768; Lash Kosher Meats, 1107 King St., 29403. Tel. (803) 577-6501.

COLUMBIA

Syn.: Beth Shalom (C), 5827 N. Trenholm Rd., 29206; Tree of Life (R), 6719 Trenholm Rd., Cola, 29206. Tel. (803) 787-0580.
Chabad, 4540 N. Trenholm Rd., 29206.
Com. Centre; 4540 Trenholm Rd., 29206.
Columbia Jewish Fed.: 4540 Trenholm Rd., Cola, 29206. Tel. (803) 787-2023.
Delicatessen: Groucho's, Five Points, 29205.

GEORGETOWN

Although there are now very few Jews in Georgetown, and there is no synagogue, there is a very old Jewish cemetery, which is maintained by the city.

MYRTLE BEACH

Syn.: Temple Emanu El (C), 406 65th Av., N., 29577. Tel. (803) 449-5552 or 650-0348. Beth El (O), Hwy 17 N., 50th St., Tel. 449-3140.

Chabad Lubavitch (O), 2803 N. Oak St. Tel. 626-6403.

SOUTH DAKOTA

ABERDEEN
Syn.: B'nai Isaac (C), 202 N. Kline St., 57401. Tel. 225-3404 or 225-7360.

DEADWOOD
The cemetery here contains a number of graves of Jewish pioneers of the Gold Rush days.

RAPID CITY
Syn.: Syn. of the Hills (R), P.O. Box 1392, 57709. Tel. 342-9524.

TENNESSEE

CHATTANOOGA
Syn.: Beth Sholom (O), 20 Pisgah Av., 37411; B'nai Zion (C), 114 McBrien Rd., 37411; Mizpah Cong. (R), 923 McCallie Av., 37403.
Jewish Fed. & Comm. Center: P.O.B. 8947, 37414. Tel. (615) 894-1317. Fax (615) 894-1319.

MEMPHIS
Syn.: Anshei Sephard-Beth El Emeth (O), 120 E. Yates Rd. N., 38117; Baron Hirsch Cong. (O), 369 Winter Oak La., 38119. Mikvah on premises. Baron Hirsch East Educational Centre (O), 5631 Shady Gr. Rd., 38117; Beth Sholom (C), 482 S. Mendenhall Av., 38117; Temple Israel (R), 1376 E. Massey Rd.
Jewish Fed. & Comm. Center, 6560 Poplar Av., Germantown, 38138. Tel. (901) 767-7100/761-0810.
Kosher Delicatessen: Rubenstein's, 4965 Summer Av., 38122. (Under rabbinical supervision. Closed Shabbat).
Kosher Restaurant: M.I. Gottlieb's, 5062 Park Av., 38119. (Under rabbinical supervision. Closed Shabbat).
Kosher Bakeries: Carl's Bakery, 1688 Jackson Av., 38107. (Under rabbinical supervision. Closed Shabbat).

NASHVILLE
Syn.: Sherith Israel (O), 3600 West End Av., 37205.Tel. (615) 292-6614. Mikva on premises; West End Synagogue (C), 3814 West End Av., 37205. Tel. (615) 269-4592. The Temple (R), 5015 Harding Rd., 37205. Tel. (615) 352-7620.
Com. Centre, 801 Percy Warner Blvd., 37205.
Jewish Fed. of Nashville & Middle Tennessee, 801 Percy Warner Blvd., 37205. Tel. (615) 356-6242. Com. Center, 801 Percy Warner Bvd., 37205. Tel. (615) 352 7170 Library/Archives on premises.

TEXAS

AMARILLO
Syn.: Temple B'nai Israel (R), 4316 Albert St., 79106. Tel. (806) 352-7191.

AUSTIN
Syn.: Chabad Hse. (O), 2101 Nueces Av., 78705. Mikva on premises;

Agudas Achim (C), 4300 Bull Creek Rd., 78731; Cong. Beth El (C), 8902 Mesa Dr., 78731; Temple Beth Israel (R), 3901 Shoal Creek Blvd., 78756. Hillel, 2105 San Antonio St., 78705.
Jewish Fed. of Austin, 11713 Jollyville Rd., 78759. Tel. (512) 331-1144.

BEAUMONT
Syn.: Temple Emanuel (R), 1120 Broadway, 77704. Tel. (409) 832-6131.

CORPUS CHRISTI
Syn.: B'nai Israel (C), 3434 Fort Worth Av., 78411; Temple Beth El (R), 4402 Saratoga St., 78413.
Com. Council, 750 Everhart Rd., 78411. Tel. (512) 855-6239.

DALLAS
Syn.: Cong. Beth El Binah, P.O. Box 64460, Dallas, TX 75206; cong. Anshai Emet (C), 1301 Custer Rd., #810, Plano, TX 75075; Cong. Beth Emunah (C), 206B S. Jefferson, Irving, TX 75060; Cong. Beth Torah (C), 720 Lookout, Richardson, TX 75080; Cong. Ner Tamid (R), 4018 Marsh Ridge, Carrollton, TX 75007; Cong. Ohev Shalom (O), 6959 Arapaho #575, Dallas, TX 75248; Cong. Shaare Tefilla (O), 6131 Churchill Way, Dallas, TX 75230; Cong. Shearith Israel (C), 9401 Douglas, Dallas, TX 75225; Cong. Tiferet Israel (T), 10909 Hillcrest, Dallas, TX 75230; Forest Lane Shul (O), 7008 Forest Lane, Dallas, TX 75230; Temple Emanu-El (R), 8500 Hillcrest, Dallas, TX 75225; Temple Shalom (R), 6930 Alpha, Dallas, TX 75240; Young Israel of Dallas (O), 1456 Preston Forest Sq. #145, Dallas, Texas 75230.
Jewish Fed. of Greater Dallas & Comm. Center, 7800 Northaven Rd., Suite A, Dallas, Texas 75230. Tel. (214) 369-3313. The Center houses the Dallas Memorial Center for Holocaust Studies and the Dallas Jewish Historical Society.
Newspaper: *Texas Jewish Post* (weekly), 11333 N. Central Expressway, Dallas, Texas 75230.
(K) Kosher Meat & Delicatessen: Reichman's, 7517 Campbell Rd., Dallas, Texas 75230. Tel. (214) 248-3773. Under supervision of Vaad Hakashrus, which will also give further information about kosher food.
Kashrut Council (Vaad Hakashrus of Dallas, Inc.).
Mikvah: Cong. Tiferet Israel.

EL PASO
Syn.: B'nai Zion (C), 805 Cherry Hill La., 79912. Mikva on premises; Mount Sinai (R), 4408 N. Stanton St. 79902. Chabad House, 6505 Westwind 79912.
Jewish Fed., 405 Wallenberg Dr., 79912. Tel. (915) 584-4437.
Jewish Com Center. 405 Wallenberg Dr 79912 915 584 4437.
Jewish Family and Childrens Service 401 Wallenberg Dr 79912 915 581 3256
El Paso Holocast Museum and Study Center 401 Wallenberg Dr 79912 for information call 484-4437.
Chai Manor Housing for the elderly 406 Wallenberg 79912 833-1588.
Kosher delicatessen, etc: Alex's, 1000 Wyoming St., 79902; Kahn's Bakery & Sweet Shop, 918 N. Oregon St., 79901. Both the foregoing are under rabbinical supervision.

HOUSTON
Syn.: Beth Rambam (O), 11333 Braesridge Blvd., 77071; Chabad Lubavitch Centre (O), 10900 Fondren Rd., 77096. Mikva on premises; United Orthodox Syns. (O), 4221 S. Braeswood Blvd., 77096. Mikva on premises; Young Israel (O), 11523 Bob White St., 77035; Beth Am (C), 1431 Brittmore Rd., 77043; Beth Yeshurun (C), 4525 Beechnut St., 77096; B'rith Shalom (C), 4610 Bellaire Blvd., 77401; Cong. Shaar Hashalom (C), 16020 El Camino

Real, 77062; Beth Israel (R), 5600 N. Braeswood Blvd., 77096; Emanu-El (R), 1500 Sunset Blvd., 77005; Jewish Community North (R), 18519 Klein Church Rd., Spring, 77039; Cong. for Reform Judaism (R), 801 Bering Dr., 77057; Temple Sinai (R), 783 Country Pl., 77079; K'nesseth Israel (Unaffiliated), cnr. Sterling & Commerce Sts., Baytown.
Com. Centre, 5601 S. Braeswood Blvd., 77096.
Jewish Fed. of Greater Houston, 5603 S. Braeswood Blvd., 77096. Tel. (713) 729-7000.
Kosher Restaurants: Com. Centre Snack Bar, 5601 S. Braeswood Blvd., 77096; Simon's Gourmet Kosher Foods, 5411 Braeswood, 7549. Wonderful vegetarian Chinese, 7549 Westheimer. The foregoing are under rabbinical supervision.

SAN ANTONIO

Syn.: Rodfei Sholom (O), 3003 Sholom Dr 78230. Mikva on premises. Rabbi's Tel. (512) 492-4277; Agudas Achim (C), 1201 Donaldson Av., 78228; Beth El (R), 211 Belknap Pl., 78212.
Jewish Fed., 8434 Ahern Dr., 78216. Tel. (512) 341-8234.
Jewish Comm. Center, 103 West Rampart, 78216.
Holocaust Museum, 8434 Ahern Dr., 78216.
There is an exhibit dealing with Texan Jewish history at the Institute of Texan Cultures, Hemisphere Plaza (in the downtown-Riverfront area).
Kosher food & delicatessen available from Delicious Food, 7460 Callaghan Rd., 78229. Tel. (512) 366-1844.

WACO

Syn.: Agudath Jacob (C), 4925 Hillcrest Dr., 76710; Rodef Sholom (R), 1717 N. New Rd., 76707.

UTAH

OGDEN

Cong. Brith Sholem, 2750 Grant Av., Ogden, 84401. Tel. (801) 782-3453.

SALT LAKE CITY

Syn.: Chavurah B'Yachad (Rec.), 509 E. Northmont Way, Salt Lake, 84103. Tel. (801) 364-7060; Kol Ami, 2425 E. Heritage Way, Salt Lake, 84109. Tel. (801) 484-1501.
United Jewish Council & Jewish Welfare Fund, 2416 E. 1700 St. S., 84108. Tel. (801) 581- 0102. The Com. Centre is at the same address (801) 581-0098. There is a Judaica Chair at the University of Utah.

VERMONT

BURLINGTON

Syn.: Ahavath Gerim (O), cnr. Archibald & Hyde Sts., 05401; Ohavi Zedek (C), 188 N. Prospect St., 05401; Temple Sinai (R), 500 Swift St., 05401.

VIRGINIA

ALEXANDRIA

Syn.: Agudas Achim (C), 2908 Valley Dr., 22302; Beth El Hebrew Cong. (R), 3830 Seminary Rd., 22304.

ARLINGTON

Syn.: Arlington-Fairfax Jewish Cong. (C), 2920 Arlington Blvd., Arlington 22204. Tel. (703) 979-4466. Daily Minyan and Shabbat services. Rabbi: Dr. Marvin I. Bash. (Includes the areas known as Crystal City, Roslyn, and Skyline).

CHARLOTTESVILLE

Syn.: Temple Beth Israel (R), 301 E. Jefferson St., 22902. Tel. (804) 295-6382. The Hillel Jewish Center at The University of Virginia, 1824 University Circle, 22903. Tel. (804) 295-4963.

DANVILLE

Syn.: Temple Beth Sholom (R), Sutherlin Av. This bldg. is 95 years old, one of the oldest syns. in the South. Fri. evg. and holiday services.

FAIRFAX

Syn.: Cong. Olam Tikvah (C), 3800 Glenbrook Rd., 22031, two miles from Beltway Exit 6W. Tel. (703) 425-1880.

FALLS CHURCH

Syn.: Temple Rodef Shalom (R), 2100 Westmoreland St., 22043. Tel. 532-2217.

HAMPTON. See Virginia Peninsula.

NEWPORT NEWS. See Virginia Peninsula.

NORFOLK

Syn.: B'nai Israel Cong. (O), 420 Spotswood Av., 23517; Beth El (C), 422 Shirley Av., 23517; Temple Israel (C), 7255 Granby St., 23505; Ohef Sholom (R), Stockley Gdns. at Raleigh Av., 23507.
The Commodore Levy Chapel, Frazier Hall, Bldg. C-7 (inside Gate 2), Norfolk U.S. Navy Station is the U.S. Navy's oldest syn. Services are open to civilians. Inq. to the Jewish Chaplain.
Communal Mikva. Inq. to B'nai Israel.
United Jewish Fed. of Tidewater, 7300 Newport Av., 23505. Tel. (804) 489-8040. This bldg. also houses the Com. Centre.
Kosher Meat: Silver Cleaver, 742D W. 21st St., 23517. Tel. (804) 627-6736.

RICHMOND

The Richmond com. is the sixth oldest in the United States.
Syn.: Keneseth Beth Israel (O), 6300 Patterson Av., 23226; Young Israel-Kol Emes (O), 4811 Patterson Av., 23226. Mikva on premises; Beth El (C), 3330 Grove Av., 23221; Beth Ahabah (R), 1117 W. Franklin St., 23220. The syn. also houses Jewish archives which are of great historical interest; Or Ami (R), 9400 N. Huguenot Rd., 23235; Or Atid (C), 501 Parham Rd., 23229.
Com. Centre, 5403 Monument Av., 23226. Tel. (804) 288-6091.
Jewish Com. Fed., 5403 Monument Av., 23226. Tel. (804) 288-0045.
Places of interest include the cemetery for the Jewish soldiers of the Civil War.
Chabad-Lubavitch of the Virginias, 212 Gaskins Rd., 23233. Tel. (804) 740-2000. Kosher facilities and rooms for Shabbat and holidays.

VIRGINIA BEACH

Syn.: Chabad Lubavitch (O), 533 Gleneagle Dr.; Kehillat Bet Hamidrash (C), 952 Indian Lakes Blvd; Temple Emanuel (C), 25th St. & Baltic Av., 23451.

Note: Alexandria, Arlington, Fairfax, Falls Church and Reston are all part of Greater Washington, D.C.

VIRGINIA PENINSULA

Syn.: Adath Jeshurun (O), 12646 Nettles Dr., Newport News, 23606. Mikva on premises; B'nai Israel (Traditional), 3116 Kecoughtan Rd., Hampton, 23661; Rodef Shalom (C) 318 Whealton Rd., Hampton, 23666; Temple Sinai (R), 11620 Warwick Blvd., Newport News, 23601.

United Jewish Community of the Virginia Peninsula, 2700 Spring Rd., Newport News, 23606. Tel. (804) 930-1422.

Kosher Bakery: Brenner's Warwick Bakery, 240 31st St., Newport News, 23607. Under supervision of Va'ad Hakashrut.

WASHINGTON

SEATTLE

The Jewish com. in the Seattle area numbers some 30,000 (27,000 Ashkenazi & 3,000 Sephardi), and makes up just over one per cent of the total population.

Syn.: Bikur Cholim Machzikay Hadath (O), 5145 S. Morgan St., 98118. Tel. (206) 721-0970; Bikur Holim (Sephardi, O), 6500 52nd Av. S., 98118. Tel. (206) 723-3028; Chabad Hse. (O), 4541 19th Av. N.E., 98105. Tel. (206) 527-1411; Ezra Bessaroth (Sephardi, O), 5217 S. Brandon St., 98118. Tel. (206) 722-5500; Yeshiva Gedola of Greater Seattle (O), 5220 20th Av. N.E., 98105. Tel. (206) 527-1100; Cong. Shaarei Tefilah-Lubavitch (Traditional), 6803 40th St. N.E., 98115. Tel. (206) 523-1323; Emanuel Cong. (Traditional, but with mixed seating), 3412 65th Av. N.E., 98115. Tel. (206) 525-1055; Cong. Beth Shalom (C), 6800 35th Av. N.E., 98115. Tel. (206) 524-0075; Herzl-Ner Tamid (C), 3700 E. Mercer Way, Mercer Island, 98040. Tel. (206) 232-8555; Beth Am (R), 8015 27th Av. N.E., 98115. Tel. (206) 525-0915; B'nai Torah (R), 6195 92nd Av. S.E., Mercer Island, 98040. Tel. (206) 232-7243; Temple de Hirsch-Sinai (R), 1511 E. Pike St., 98122. Tel. (206) 323-8486.

Congregation Tikuah Chadarhah (Gay-Lesbian). Tel. 328-2590. Southland Jewish Center (0) 236-2386. South King County Community Synagogue (Liberal) (206) 722-2822.

Organisations

Va'ad Harabanim, 6500 52nd Av. S., 98118. Inq. concerning kashrut, etc., should be addressed to the Board.

B'nai B'rith Hillel Foundation, University of Washington, 4745 17th Av.

N.E., 98105. Tel. 527-1997. The University library has a Jewish archives section dealing with the Seattle com.

Com. Centre, 3801 E. Mercer Way, Mercer Island, 98040. Tel. (206) 232-7115. A Holocaust memorial with a bronze sculpture by Gizel Berman has been dedicated here. Northend Com. Center. 8606 35th Ave NE (206) 526 8073

Jewish Family Service, 1214 Boylston Av., 98101. Tel. (206) 461-3240.

Jewish Fed. of Greater Seattle, 2031 3rd. Av., 98121. Tel. (206) 443-5400. The Jewish Fed. publishes "The Jewish Transcript", at the same address. The Washington Association of Jewish Communities also shares the same address.

Jewish books and religious articles are obtainable from: B'nai B'rith Hillel Foundation and the following syns.: Beth Am, Beth Shalom, Bikur Cholim Machzikay Hadath, Bikur Holim, Ezra Bessaroth, Herzl-Ner Tamid, Temple de Hirsch-Sinai. (For addresses, see above.)

Kosher hotels: The Va'ad Harabanim supervises the catering at the following hotels: Bellevue Hilton, 100 112th St. N.E., Bellevue, 98004. Tel. (206) 455-3330; Four Seasons Olympic Hotel, 4th & University Sts. Tel. (206) 621-1700; Red Lion Inn, 18740 Pacific Highway S. Tel. (206) 246-8600; Red Lion Inn, Bellevue. Tel. (206) 455-1300; Seattle Hilton, 8th & University Sts. Tel. (206) 624-0500; Seattle Sheraton. Tel. (206) 621-0900; Westin Hotel, 5th & Westlake Sts. Tel. (206) 728-1000. Stouffer Madison, 6th & Madison, Tel (206) 583 0300

The following supply kosher food: Bagel Deli, 340 15th Av. E., Tel. (206) 322-2471 & 1309 N.E. 43rd St. Tel. (206) 634-3770; Brenner Brothers Bakery, 12000 N.E. Redmond Rd., Bellevue. Tel. (206) 454-0600; Great Harvest Bread Co., 5408 Sand Point Way N.E., 98105. Tel. (206) 524-4873; Kosher Delight, 1509 1st Av. Tel. (206) 624-4555; Noah's Grocery, 4700 50th St. S. Tel. (206) 725-4267; Park Deli, 5011 S. Dawson St., Seward Park 98118. Tel. 206-722-NOSH; Varon's Kosher Meats, 3931 M.L. King Way S., 98108. Tel. (206) 723-0240.

SPOKANE

Syn.: Temple Beth Shalom (C), 1322 E. 30th Av., 99203. Tel. (509) 747-3304.

Jewish Com. Council, North 221 Wall, Suite 500, Spokane, Wa 99201. Tel. (509) 838-4261

There are also Jewish communities in other towns in the State: Aberdeen, Bainbridge Island, Bellingham, Edmonds, Fort Lewis, Kent, Pullman, Tacoma and Yakima.

WEST VIRGINIA

HUNTINGTON

Syn.: B'nai Sholom (C & R), 949 10th Av., 25701. Tel. (304) 522-2980.

WISCONSIN

MADISON

Syn.: Chabad Hse (O), 1722 Regent St., 53705; Beth Israel Centre (C), 1406 Mound St., 53711; Beth El (R), 2702 Arbor Dr., 53711.

Madison Jewish Com. Council, 310 N. Midvale Blvd., Suite 325, 53705. Tel. (608) 231-3426.

B'nai B'rith Hillel Foundation, 611 Langdon St., 53703.

MILWAUKEE

Syn.: Agudas Achim (O), 5820 W. Burleigh Av., 53210; Anshai Lebowitz (O), 3100 N. 52nd St., 53216; Beth Jehudah (O), 2700 N. 54th St., 53210; Chabad Hse. (O), 3109 N. Lake Dr., 53211; Lake Park Syn. (O), 3207 Hackett Av., 53211; Anshe-Sfard-Kehillat Torah (O), 6717 N. Green Bay Av., 53209; Temple Menorah (C), 9363 N. 76th Street, 53223Milwaukee Jewish Home Chapel (O), 1414 N. Prospect Av., 53202; Beth El Ner Tamid (C), 2909 W. Mequon Rd., 53092; Beth Israel (C), 6880 N. Green Bay Av., 53209; Cong. Shalom (R), 7630 N. Santa Monica Blvd., 53217; Cong. Sinai (R), 8223 N. Port Washington Rd., 53217; Emanu-El B'ne Jeshurun (R), 2419 E. Kenwood Blvd., 53211; Chabad of North Shore (O), 2233 W. Mequon Rd., Mequon, WI 53092.

Com. Centre: 6255 N. Santa Monica Blvd., 53217.

Milwaukee Assoc. for Jewish Education, 6401 N. Santa Monica Blvd., 53217.

Milwaukee Jewish Council, 1360 N. Prospect Av., 53202. Tel. (414) 276-7920.

Milwaukee Jewish Fed., 1360 N. Prospect Av., 53202. Tel. (414) 271-8338.

Sinai-Samaritan Medical Centre, Sinai Campus, 950 N. 12th St., 53233.

SHEBOYGAN

Syn.: Temple Beth El (T), 1007 North Av., 53083.

WYOMING

CASPER

Syn.: Temple Beth El, 4105 S. Poplar, P.O.B. 3534, Casper, 82602. Tel. (307) 237-2330.

CHEYENNE

Syn.: Mt. Sinai, 2610 Pioneer Av., Cheyenne, 82001. Tel. (307) 634-3052.

GREEN RIVER

Syn.: Congregation Beth Israel, P.O.B. 648, Green River, WY, 82935. Tel. (307) 875-4194.

LARAMIE

Syn.: Laramie J.C.C., P.O.B. 202, Laramie, 82070. Tel. (307) 745-8813.

NATIONAL TOURIST INFORMATION
OFFICES IN LONDON

Australian Tourist Commission, Gemini Hse., 10-18 Putney Hill, SW15 6AA. Tel. 081-780 1424.
Bahamas Tourist Office, Bahamas Hse., 10 Chesterfield St., W1X 8AH. Tel. 071-629 5238.
Belgian Tourist Office, Premier Hse., 2 Gayton Rd., Harrow, Middx., HA1 2XU.Tel. 081-861 3300.
Bermuda Tourism (BCB Ltd.), 1 Battersea Church Rd., London SW11 3LY. Tel. 071-734 8813.
Bulgarian National Tourist Office, 18 Princes St., W1R 7RE. Tel. 071-499 6988.
Canada – Tourism Canada, Canada Hse., Trafalgar Sq., SW1Y 5BJ. Tel. 071-930 8540.
Cyprus Tourism Organisation, 213 Regent St., W1R 8DA. Tel. 071-734 9822.
Czechoslovakia – Cedok (London) Ltd., Czech Travel Bureau, 17-18 Old Bond St., W1X 4RB. Tel. 071-629 6058.
Danish Tourist Board, Tel. 071-734 2637.
Egyptian State Tourist Office, 168 Piccadilly, W1V 9DE. Tel. 071-493 5282.
Finnish Tourist Board, 66 Haymarket, SW1Y 4RF. Tel. 071-839 4048. Fax. 071-321 0696.
French Government Tourist Office, 178 Piccadilly, W1V 0AL. Tel. 071-499 6911 (recorded message). Written inquiries dealt with promptly (but £1 in stamps requested for post & packing for bulky literature).
Gibraltar Information Bureau, Arundel Gt. Court, 179 Strand, WC2R 1EH. Tel. 071-836 0777-8.
Greece – National Tourist Organisation of Greece, 4 Conduit St., W1R 0DJ. Tel. 071-734 5997-9.
Holland – Netherlands Board of Tourism, 25-28 Buckingham Gate, SW1E 6LD. Tel. 071-630 0451.
Hong Kong Tourist Association, 125 Pall Mall, SW1Y 5EA. Tel. 071-930 4775 Fax. 071-930-4777.
India – Government of India Tourist Office, 7 Cork St., W1X 1PB. Tel. 071-437 3677. Fax. 071-494 1048.
Ireland – Irish Tourist Board, 150 New Bond St., W1Y 0AQ. Tel. 071-493 3201.
Israel Government Tourist Office, 18 Gt. Marlborough St., W1V 1AF. Tel. 071-434 3651.
Italian State Tourist Board (ENIT), 1 Princes St., W1R 8AY. Tel. 071-408 1254. Fax. 071-493 6695.
Jamaica Tourist Board, 111 Gloucester Pl., W1H 3PH. Tel. 071-224 0505.
Japan National Tourist Organisation, 167 Regent St., W1R 7FD. Tel. 071-734 9638.
Luxembourg Tourist Office, 122/124 Regent St., W1R 5FE. Tel. 071-434 2800. Fax. 071-734-1205.
Malta National Tourist Office, Mappin House, Suite 300, 4 Winsley St., W1N 7AR. Tel. 071-323 0506. Fax. 071-323 9154.
Mexico Ministry of Tourism Office, 60-61 Trafalgar Sq., 3rd Floor, WC2N 5DS. Tel. 071-734 1058.
Moroccan National Tourist Office, 174 Regent St., W1R 6HB. Tel. 071-437 0073.
Northern Ireland Tourist Board, N. Ireland Business Centre, 11 Berkeley St., W1X 6BU. Tourist inf.: Tel. 0800 282 662.
Norwegian Tourist Board, 5-11 Lower Regent St., SW1Y 4LR. Tel. 071-839 6255.
Portuguese National Tourist Office, 22/25a Sackville St., W1X 1DE. Tel. 071-494 1441. Fax. 071-494 1868. Telex 265653.

Romanian National Tourist Office, 17 Nottingham St., W1M 3RD. Tel. 071-224 3692.

Russia & the former republics, Intourist Travel Ltd., 219 Marsh Wall, E14 9FJ. Tel. 071-538 8600.

Scottish Tourist Board, Tourist Information Centre, 19 Cockspur St., SW1Y 5BL. Tel. 071-930 8661.

South African Tourism Board, 5/6 Alt Grove, London SW19 4DZ. Tel. 081-944 6646.

Spanish National Tourist Office, 57-58 St. James's St., SW1A 1LD. Tel. 071-499 0901.

Swedish Tourist Board, 29-31 Oxford St., W1R 1RE. Tel. 071-437 5816.

Swiss National Tourist Office, Swiss Centre, New Coventry St., W1V 8EE. Tel. 071-734 1921.

Turkish Information Office, 1st Floor, 170-173 Piccadilly, W1V 9DD. Tel. 071-734 8681-2.

United States Travel & Tourism Administration, 24 Grosvenor Square, P.O. Box 1EN, London W1A 1EN. Tel. 071-495 4466. Fax. 071-495 4377. (Please note that we no longer have a walk-in facility.)

Yugoslav National Tourist Office, 143 Regent St., W1R 8AE. Tel. 071-439 0399.

OTHER COUNTRIES

AFGHANISTAN

From a peak of some 40,000 a century ago, Afghanistan's Jewish population has dwindled to about 120 today. Most are of Persian origin. There are some 12 families in Kabul, the capital, and five or six in Herat. All of them, in both cities, are strictly Orthodox. There is one rabbi/shochet in the country. Jewish settlement in Afghanistan goes back much further than the last century. There were Jews in the country 800 years ago, although little is known of their history until about 120 years ago. In recent years, many have emigrated to Israel.

KABUL

The syn. is on the 2nd floor of a building in Charshi Torabazein St.

ALGERIA

There are approximately 200-300 Jews in Algeria today. Most live in Algiers, and there are a few families in Blida, Constantine and Oran. Algiers is the headquarters of the Algerian Consistoire. In 1962, when Algeria became independent, the community numbered 130,000. Of this total almost a quarter – 30,000 – lived in Algiers. By 1968, only some 2,000 Jews remained in the country, and their number has continued to dwindle over the years.

ALGIERS

Association Consistoriale Israélite d'Alger, 6 rue Hassena Ahmed (formerly rue de Suffren). Tel. (213) 262-85-72. Pres.: Roger Said.
Fédération des Communautés Isráelites d'Algérie. Same address & Tel. as above.
Syn.: 6 rue Hassena Ahmed.

BLIDA

Consistoire d'Algérie, 29 rue des Martyrs. Tel. 3492657. Pres.: Roger Said.

ARGENTINA

The Argentine community, which includes about 50,000 Sephardim, is estimated to total about 250,000. About a fifth live in rural areas. It is by far the largest in Latin America. The Ashkenazi majority come from East European stock. Immigration from Russia and other East European countries began in 1889.

Greater Buenos Aires, the capital, has some 160,000 Jews. There are important communities in 11 provincial centres: Rosario (15,000), Cordoba (10,000), Santa Fé (5,000), La Plata (4,000), Bahia Blanca (4,000), Mendoza (4,000), Mar del Plata (4,000), Parana (3,000), Resistencia (2,000), Corrientes (1,500), and Salta (1,500). Altogether there are about 90 Jewish communities in Argentina, including a number of families in the former colonies set up by the Jewish Colonization Association (J.C.A.), who live on the land or from economic activities linked with agriculture. Several of these colonies were in the provinces of Buenos Aires, Santa Fé, La Pampa and Entre Rios.

The three most important Jewish colonies are: Moisesville (where 20 per cent of the total population of 3,000 are Jews) in the province of Santa Fé, Rivera (with a Jewish population of 1,000 – half the total) in La Pampa, and General Roca (1,000 Jews) in Rio Negro, in the south.

BUENOS AIRES

Synagogues & Religious Organisations

The number of synagogues in Buenos Aires, where there is a minyan at least on Friday night and Saturday morning, is nearing fifty (their addresses can be obtained by inquiring from one of the community centres below). A list of the most important synagogues follows.

Congregacion Israelita de la Republica Argentina (the oldest Argentine Synagogue) Libertad 785. Tel. 45-2474/40-8929 Centro).

Asociacion Shuva Israel Paso 557. Tel. 962 6255 (Once).

Ashkenazi

Orthodox: Adat Iereim, Argerich 380; Ahabat Israel, Serrano 69; Anshei Galitzia, Jose Evaristo Uriburu 234; Baron Hirsh, Billinghurst 664. Tel. 86-2624; Bet Jabad Lubavitch, Jean Jaures 361. Tel. 87-5908; Bet Jabad Lubavitch Belgrano, 11 de Septiembre 858. Tel. 772-5324; Bet Rajel, Ecuador 522. Tel. 86-2701; Brit Abraham, Antezana 145. Tel. 855-6567; Etz Jaim, Julian Alvarez 745. Tel. 772-5324; Ezra, Azcuenaga 778; Floresta Norte, Cervantes 1034; Jebrat Mishnaiot, Tucuman 2186; Shomrei Shabat, Sarmiento 2309; Sinagoga Israelita Lituana, Jose Evaristo Uriburu 348. Tel. 952-7968; Tefilat Moshe, Manuel Artigas 5779; Torah Vaaboda, Julian Alvarez 667. Tel. 854-0462; Zijron Le David, Azcuenaga 736. Tel. 953-0200. Beit Jabad Villa Crespo, Serrano 69.

Sephardi

Orthodox: Aderet Eliahu, Ruy Diaz de Guzman 647. Tel. 28-9306; Agudat Dodim, Avellaneda 2874. Tel. 611-0056; Akedat Itzjak, Anchorena 829; Bajurim Tiferet Israel, Helguera 611. Tel. 611-3376; Comunidad Israelita, Camargo 870. Tel. 854-1952 or 0287; Etz Hajaim, Pueyrredon 645; Etz Jaim, Carlos Calvo 1164. Tel. 28-6290; Israelita, Monroe 5640. Tel. 51-6722; Jaike Grimberg, Campana 460. Tel. 69-2347; Jerusalem, Tucuman 2153; Kehal Jaredim, Helguera 270. Tel. 612-0410; Maguen Abraham, Helguera 547; Od Yosef Jai, Tucuman 3326. Tel. 88-2349; Ohel Abraham, Campana 560; Or Misraj, Ciudad de la Paz 2555. Tel. 784-5945; Or Torah, Brandsen 1444. Tel. 21-3426; Shaar Hashamaim, Viamonte 2342; Shaare Tefila, Paso 733. Tel. 962-2865; Shaare Tzion, Helguera 453. Tel. 612-9484; Shalom, Olleros 2876. Tel. 552-2720; Shebet Ajim, Pinzon 1261. Tel. 28-5261; Shuba Israel, Ecuador 627. Tel. 86-0562; Sinagoga Rabino Eliahu Freue, Canalejas 3465; Sinagoga Rabino Shaul Setton Dabbah, Boulogne sur Mer 833; Sinagoga Rabino Zeev Gringberg, Canalejas 3047. Tel. 611-3366; Sinagoga Saban Lavalle 2656; Sucath David, Paso 724. Tel. 962-1091; Yeshurun, Republica de la India 3035. Tel. 802-9310; Yesod Hadat, Lavalle 2449. Tel. 961-1615.

Conservative: Templo La Paz (Chalom) Olleros 2876. Tel. 552-6730.

The following three syns. make no distinction between Ashkenazi & Sephardi – Conservative: Comunidad Bet El, Sucre 3338. Tel. 552-2365; Colegio Wolfson, Comunidad Or-El, Amenabar 2972. Tel. 544-5461. Comundad Jerusalem, 24 de Noviembre 1434. Tel. 93.0012/0907; (P.Patricios); Beit Hilel, Araoz 2854. Tel. 804-2286; (Palermo); Dor Jadash, Murillo 649. Tel. 854-4467; (V. Crespo); Or Jadash, Varela 850. Tel. 612-1171/(Flores); Congregacion Hebrea de San Martin, Tucuman 130 (San Martin). Reform: Templo Emanu-El, Tronador 1455. Tel. 552-4343.

German

Orthodox: Ajdut Yisroel, Moldes 2449. Tel. 783-2831.

Conservative: Nueva Comunidad Israelita, Arcos 2319. Tel. 781-0281.

Progressive: Asociación Religiosa Lamroth Hakol, Caseros 1450 (Florida); Benei Tikva, Vidal 2049. Tel. 795-0380.

All Conservative syns. are affiliated to the World Council of Synagogues; all Reform & Liberal syns. to the World Council for Progressive Judaism, and all except the Orthodox syns. to the Latin American Rabbinical Seminary (see below).
Mikvaot: Bogotá 3015 (Flores); Ecuador 731 (Once); Helguera 270; Larrea 734 (Once); Moldes 2449. (Belgrano); José Hernandez 1750 (Belgrano).
The Orthodox Ashkenazi Chief Rabbi of Argentina is Rabbi Shlomo Benhamu Anidjar. The Central Rabbinate of the Vaad Hakehillot (Orthodox) is at Ecuador 1110. Tel. 961-2944.
Latin American Rabbinical Seminary (Seminario Rabínico Latinoamericano) (Conservative), Dean: D. Feinstein. Rabbinical Director: Rabbi Sergio Spolsky. José Hernandez 1750. Tel. 783-2009 & 783-6175.
High School for Jewish Studies, Ayacucho 632.
Michlalat Madaei Hayahadut, Ayacucho 632.

Representative Organisations
AMIA (Central Ashkenazi community). Pasteur 633. Tel. 953-9777 & 2862. Pres.: Luis Perelmuter. Sec: Morris Azar.
Asociacion Israelita Sefaradi Argentina (AISA), Paso 493. Tel. 952-4707
B'nai B'rith. Office for Latin America: Talcahuano 438, 3rd Floor. Tel. 40-1087. Office for Argentina: Juncal 2573. Tel 80-4625.
DAIA (Political representative body of Argentine Jewry). Pasteur 633, Fifth Floor. Tel. 953-5380 & 5394. Pres.: Dr. Ruben Beraja. Sec.: Edgardo Gorenberg.
ECSA (Central Sephardi body) Larrea 674, Fourth Floor.
Latin American Jewish Congress. Larrea 744, 1030. Tel. 952-9604; Fax 961-4534. Pres.: Benno Milnitzky. Dir.: M. Tenenbaum.
Vaad Hakehillot, Pasteur 633, Second Floor.

Cultural Organisations, Libraries, etc.
Latin American Rabbinical Seminary Library, José Hernandez 1750. Tel. 783-2009. 781-4057.
Museo Judio (Jewish Museum) de Buenos Aires, Libertad 769. Tel. 45-2474.
ORT, Montañeses 2845. Tel. 782-7571.
Sociedad Hebraica Argentino (with library, art gallery, etc.), Sarmiento 2233. Tel. 48-5570.
YIVO Library, Pasteur 633, Third Floor. Tel. 951-6624.

Homes for Aged
Agudat Dodim, Avellaneda 2735.
Hajnasat Orjim, Valentin Gomez 2952.
Kehal Yereim, Argerich 630.
Hogar Adolfo Hirsch, Gaspar Campos 2975. (San Miguel).

Hospital
Hospital Israelita Terrada 1164. Tel. 581-8172.

Sports & other Clubs
C.A.S.A. (Sephardi), Av. Del Libertador General San Martin 77, Vicente Lopez. Tel. 791-8460.
Hacoaj, Estado de Israel 4156. Tel. 88-4270.
Maccabi, Tucuman 3135. Tel. 86-0350.
Sociedad Hebraica, Sarmiento 2233. Tel. 48-5570.

Zionist Organisations
Argentine Zionist Org. & Jewish Agency, Cangallo 2471. Tel. 48-2450. Pres.: Victor Leidenfarb.

B'nei Akiva, Azcuenaga 736.
Keren Hayesod, Valentin Gomez 2950. Tel. 87-0268 & 87-2293.
Instituto Cultural Argentina Israel, Paraguay 1535. Tel. 42-9205 & 44-4995.
Fund for Argentine-Israeli Agricultural Co-operation, Corrientes 2194.
OSFA (Argentine WIZO), Larrea 1225. Tel. 82-6347.
Israel Embassy: Av. de Mayo 701. Tel. 342-1465.

Newspapers
"La Voz Judia", "Nueva Sion", "Die Presse", "Semanario Israelita", "Mundo Israelita".

Booksellers
Agudat Dodim, Bogota 2973. Tel. 613-7900.
Ediciones del Seminario Rabínico Latinoamericano, José Hernandez 1750. Tel. 783-2009.
Editorial Yehuda, Lavalle 2168, Oficina 37.
Kehot Lubavitch Sudamerica, San Luis 3281.
E. Milberg, Lavalle 2223. Tel. 47-1979.
Otzar Hatora, Viamonte 2712. Tel. 865-7208. Fax 962-7931.
Libreria Editorial Sigal. Corrientes 2854. Tel. 8865-7208. Fax 962-7931.
Talitav, Viamonte 2399. Tel. 47-9384.

Kosher Restaurants, etc.
(K) Bar Helueni, Tucuman 2620. Tel. 961-0541;
(K) Confiteria y Pizzeria Kasher Center, Av. Cordoba 2424. Tel. 962-1947.
(K) Gueula (Pizzeria), San Luis 2539. Tel. 962-5249.
(K) Hambra Aranguren 3192. Tel. 613-9828.
(K) Restaurant Maadanim, Nazca 544. Tel. 611-9686.
(K) Restaurant Sucath David, Tucuman 2349. Tel. 952-8878.
Giardino (Vegetarian) Lavalle 835.

Meat & Groceries.
There are 20 kosher butchers' shops supervised by the Central Rabbinate as well as 18 kosher grocery shops & supermarkets.

Other Principal Communal Centres
Avellaneda (Greater Buenos Aires), H. Yrigoyen 987.
Bahia Blanca, Buenos Aires Prov., Las Heras 40; Bet Jabad Lubavitch, O'Higgins 584. Tel. (091) 49-638; Espana 42. Tel. 39040.
Catamarca, Catamarca Prov., Salta 842.
Ceres, Santa Fé Prov., Teodoro Herzl 50.
Cipoletti, Neuquen Prov., Irigoyen 161.
Ciudadela, Buenos Aires Prov., Alianza 310.
Concepción del Uruguay, Entre Rios Prov., Ameghino 132.
Concordia, Entre Rios Prov., Entre Rios 478; Agudat Israel, Andrade 138; Bet Jabad Entre Rios 212. Tel. (045) 211934.
Cordoba, Cordoba Prov., Centro Union Israelita de Cordoba, Alvear 254.
Corrientes, Corrientes Prov., San Martin 1493.
Formosa, Formosa Prov., Rivadavia 1246.
General Roca, Rio Negro Prov., Chacabuco 446.
Jujuy, Jujuy Prov., Belgrano 865.
Lanus, Buenos Aires Prov., Sitio de Montevideo 1021. Tel. 241-0551.
Lomas de Zamora (Greater Buenos Aires), Gorriti 333; Anshei Emuna, Boedo 693. Tel. 243-5480.
Mar Del Plata, Buenos Aires Prov., Sociedad Union Israelita Marplatense,

Espana 1853; Sinagoga Gabriel, Tres de Febrero 2451; Bet Abraham, Falucho 1539.
Kosher Restaurant: **(K)** Sucath David, Bogota 2165. (Summer only).
Mendoza, Mendoza Prov., Av. Espana 1930.
Miramar, Buenos Aires Prov., Calle 27 entre 14 y 16.
Moisesville, Santa Fé Prov.
Parana, Entre Rios Prov., 9 de Julio 391.
La Plata, Buenos Aires Prov., Calle 11 1426.
Posadas, Misiones Prov., Rivadavia 199.
Resistencia, Chaco Prov., Ameghino 355.
Rio Cuarto, Cordoba Prov., Belgrano 462.
La Rioja, La Rioja Prov., 9 de Julio 175.
Rivera, Buenos Aires Prov.
Rosario, Santa Fé Prov., Paraguay 1152; Bet Jabad Lubavitch, Maipu 1428. Tel. (041) 67440; Shebet Ajim, Dorego 1160; Etz Hajaim, Catamarca 2032. Tel. (041) 251-341.
Salta, Salta Prov., Caseros 945.
San Juan, San Juan Prov., Cordoba 939.
San Luis, San Luis Prov., Pedernera 1049.
Santa Fé, Santa Fé Prov., 4 de Enero 2539.
Santiago del Estero, Santiago del Estero Prov., La Plata 146.
Tigre, Buenos Aires Prov., Maraboto 535.
Tucuman, Tucuman Prov., Las Piedras 980; 9 de Julio 625 (Sephardi). Tel. (081) 220734; Bet Obadia (Lubavitch), Lamadrid 752. Tel. (081) 311-257. Las Piedras 980 (Conservative).
Villa Angela, Chaco Prov., Rivadavia 81.
Villaguay, Entre Rios Prov., Balcarce 654.
Zapala, Neuquen Prov., Calle Julio Argentino Roca.
Zarate, Buenos Aires Prov., L. N. Alem 115.

AUSTRALIA

Jews have lived in Australia since 1788. Sixteen known Jews, and possibly others, arrived on the first fleet of convict ships in 1788, although it was not until the 1820s that the first regular, organised worship began. In 1832, the Government recognised the establishment of the congregation in Sydney. It was also in Sydney that the first syn. in Australia was built – in 1844. Jews rose to prominence in political, commercial and cultural life in 19th-century Australia. In more recent times, there have been two Jewish Governors-General, as well as a Jewish Chief Justice and Commander-in-Chief of the armed forces (in the First World War).
However, the country's Jewish population has always been small, never reaching 0.6 per cent of its total population. Only because of waves of immigration at crucial periods has Jewish life remained viable. Today, Australian Jewry totals some 100,000. There are about 40,000 in Melbourne, 35,000 in Sydney, with smaller communities in the federal capital, Canberra, as well as Perth, Brisbane and Adelaide.
General inf. from the Australian Tourist Commission, Gemini Hse., 10-18 Putney Hill, SW15 6AA. Tel. 081-780 1424.
Note: Some information is given about kosher hotels, restaurants, etc., but as these details are liable to change, visitors should consult the ministers of synagogues about accommodation and meals.

AUSTRALIAN CAPITAL TERRITORY

CANBERRA

The A.C.T. Jewish Com. syn. & office are at the National Jewish Memorial

Centre, cnr. Canberra Av. & National Circuit, Forrest, 2603. Tel. 295-1052.
Postal address: P.O. Box 3105, Manuka 2603.
Israel Embassy, 6 Turrana St., Yarralumla, 2600. Tel. 73-1309.

NEW SOUTH WALES

NEWCASTLE
Syn.: 124 Tyrrell St. Pres.: Dr. J. Rosenberg. Sec.: Dr. L. Fredman Tel. 21-5212.

SYDNEY
Synagogues & Religious Organisations
Adath Yisroel, 243 Old South Head Rd.,
Bondi. Tel. 300-9447.
Bankstown & District, 41 Meredith St., Bankstown. Tel. 707-4038.
Central, Bon-Accord Av., Bondi Junction. Tel. 389-5622.
Coogee-Randwick-Clovelly Cong., 121 Brook St., Coogee. Tel. 665-6318.
Cremorne & District, 10b Yeo St., Neutral Bay. Tel. 908-1853.
Great, Elizabeth St. Offices: 166 Castlereagh St. Tel. 267-2477. The War
Memorial Centre built beneath the syn. in the 1950s houses the Rabbi L. A.
Falk Memorial Library, a collection of Judaica and the A. M. Rosenblum
Jewish Museum.
Illawarra, Railway Parade, Allawah. Tel. 587-5643.
Kehillat Masada, Link Rd., St. Ives. Tel. 488-8266.
Kingsford-Maroubra Cong., 635 Anzac Pde., Maroubra. Tel. 344-6095.
Mizrachi, 339 Old South Head Rd.,
Bondi. Tel. 30-2031.
North Shore, 15 Treatts Rd., Lindfield. Tel. 46-3710.
North Shore Temple Emanuel (Liberal), 28 Chatswood Av., Chatswood.
Tel. 419-7011.
Paramatta, 114 Victoria Rd. Tel. 683-5381.
Roscoe St. Syn., 54 Roscoe St., Bondi.
Sephardi, 40 Fletcher St., Woollahra. Tel. 389-3982. Rabbi Marc Sevy 389-
2717.
Shearit Yisrael, 140-146 Darlinghurst Rd., Darlinghurst. Tel. 30-1248.
South Head & District, 666 Old South Head Rd., Rose Bay. Tel. 371-7656.
Strathfield & District, 19 Florence St., Strathfield. Tel. 642-3550.
Western Suburbs, 18 Georgina St., Newtown. Tel. 798-0376.
Temple Emanuel (Liberal), 7 Ocean St., Woollahra. Tel. 328-7833.
Beth Din, 146 Darlinghurst Rd., Darlinghurst. Tel. 361-3914 & 327-7022.
Mikva, 117 Glenayr Av., Bondi. Tel. 30-2509.
Kashrut Authority: Rabbi M. D. Guttnick, POB 206, Bondi 2026. Tel. 369-
4286. Fax 389-7652.

Representative Organisations
B'nai B'rith, 22-38 Yurong St., E. Sydney. Tel. 361-6035. Fax. 331-3131.
National Council of Jewish Women, 111 Queen St., Woollahra. Tel. 363-
5053.
N.S.W. Association of Jewish Ex-Service Men & Women, 146 Darlinghurst
Rd., Darlinghurst. Tel. 389-9859.
N.S.W. Jewish Board of Deputies, 146 Darlinghurst Rd., Darlinghurst, 2010.
Tel. 360-1600. Fax. 331-4712.
Sephardi Federation of Australian Jewry, 40-44 Fletcher St., Woollahra. Tel.
30-3192.

Cultural & Educational Organisations
Australian Jewish Historical Society, 166 Castlereagh St. Tel. 267-2477.

Emanuel School, 20 Stanley St., Randwick. Tel. 398-8388.
Masada College. Primary School, 15a Treats Rd., Lindfield. Tel. 467-2066;
Secondary School, 9-15 Link Rd., St. Ives. Tel. 449-3744.
Moriah War Memorial College, 17 Vivian St., Bellevue Hill. Tel. 327-5834.
Mount Sinai College, 6 Runic Lane, Maroubra. Tel. 349-4877.
New South Wales Board of Jewish Education, 134 Old South Head Rd.,
Bondi Junction. Tel. 369-1551.
Shalom College, University of New South Wales, P.O.B.1, Kensington. Tel.
663-1366. This is a Jewish residential college and the central address of the
Jewish student movement in New South Wales. Accom. for travellers
available on occasion. **(K)** Kitchen and dining facilities. Inq. to Dr. Hilton
Immerman.
Sydney Jewish Museum, 148 Darlinghurst Rd., Darlinghurst. Tel. 360-7999.
Yeshiva College, 32 Flood St., Bondi. Tel. 387-3822.
Yeshiva Girls School, 60 Penkivil St., Bondi. Tel. 387-8811
For inf. about tours of Jewish Sydney, contact Karl Maehrischel. Tel. 328
7604.

Welfare Organisations, Hospitals, etc.
Jewish Community Services (ex-Australian Jewish Welfare Society), 146
Darlinghurst Rd., Darlinghurst. Tel. 331-5184. Fax. 360-5574.
Sir Moses Montefiore Home, 120 High St., Hunters Hill. Tel. 816-1333.
Wolper Jewish Hospital, 8 Trelawney St., Woollahra. Tel. 328-6077.

Sporting & Social Clubs
Hakoah Club, 61-67 Hall St., Bondi. Tel 30-3344.
NSW Maccabi Inc. 140 Darlinghurst Rd., Darlinghurst. Tel. 360-5100. Fax.
332-4207.

Zionist Organisations
N.S.W. State Zionist Council, 146 Darlinghurst Rd., Darlinghurst, 2010. Tel.
360-6300.
WIZO State Council, 53 Edgecliff Rd., Bondi Junction. Tel. 387-3666.
Israel Consulate-General, 37 York St. Tel. 264-7933. Fax. 290-2259.

Newspaper
"Australian Jewish News", 140 Darlinghurst Rd., Darlinghurst, 2010. Tel.
360-5100. Fax 332-4207

Booksellers, etc.
Amzalak Bookstore, 10 Castlefield St., Bondi. Tel. 365-1812.
Avenue Gifts & Jewish Bookshop, 68 Hall St., Bondi. Tel. 30-6412.
Gold's Book & Gift Co., 166 O'Brien St., Bondi, 2026. Tel. 300-0495.
Shalom Gifts, 323 Pacific Highway, Lindfield. Tel. 416-7076.

Guest House
(K) Guest House Restaurant, 31 Penkivil St., Bondi. Tel. 387-2042. Strictly
Orthodox. Meals, Mon. to Thurs. 5-8 p.m., Sun. 12-2 p.m.

Restaurants
(K) Lewis' Continental Kosher Kitchen, 2 Curlewis St., Bondi. Tel. 30-
1833. Take-away kosher food.
(K) Nargila, 169 Glenayr Av., Bondi. Tel. 365-6562.
(K) Savion, 38 Wairoa Av., Bondi. Tel. 306-357.

QUEENSLAND

BRISBANE

Syns.: Brisbane Hebrew Cong., 98 Margaret St. Tel. 229-3412 Sec. 397-1213; Givat Zion (South Brisbane Hebrew Cong.), 43 Bunya St., Greenslopes; Tel. 359-5364; Temple Shalom,13 Koolatah St., Camp Hill, 4152. Tel. 398-8843.

Religious Groups

Brisbane Chevra Kadisha, 242 Kingsford Smith Drive, Hamilton 4007. Tel. 357-8611 (b) or 262-6564 (h). Pres.: Lance Philips.
Chabad House of Queensland, 43 Cedar St., Greenslopes, 4120. Tel. 848-5886 or 018-73-2879. Contact: Ken Thomas.
Queensland Mikvah, 46 Bunya St., Greenslopes, 4120. Tel. 848-5886. Contact: J. Thomas.

Organisations

Queensland Jewish Board of Deputies. Pres.: Laurie Rosenblum, 27 Berkeley St., Holland Park, 4121. Tel. 397-4878. Fax 832-6845. State Zionist Council, 144 Adelaide St., 4000. Tel. 229-4462.
Jewish Communal Centre, 2 Moxom Rd., Burbank, 4156. Tel. 349-9749.
Queensland Jewish Help in Need Society, 87 Ascot Ter., Toowona. Tel. 870-9504.
Brisbane Jewish Women's Guild, 42 Morningview St., Chapel Hill. Tel. 229-3412. Exec. Dir.: 878-2796. Catering service available.
National Council of Jewish Women, 24 Ceratonia St., Sunny Banks Hill, 4109. Tel. 345-9509.
Quennsland Union of Jewish Students, 51 Bunora Av., Ferny Hills, 4055. Tel. 351-2090.
(K) Brumby's Bakery, 408 Milton Rd., Auchenflower 4066. Tel. 371-8744.

GOLD COAST

Syn.: Gold Coast Hebrew Cong., 34 Hamilton Av., Surfers' Paradise, 4215. Tel. (075) 701-851; Temple Shalom, 25 Via Roma, Isle of Capri 4217. Tel. (075) 70-1716.

Organisations

Association of Jewish Organisations, 31, Ranock Av., Benown Waters, 4217. Tel. 97-2222. Maccabi Gold Coast, 108 Pappas Way, Carrara 4211. Tel. 942-261.
Goldstein's Bakery, PO Box 147, Ashmore City, 4214. Tel. 39-3133.

SOUTH AUSTRALIA

ADELAIDE

Syns.: Adelaide Hebrew Cong. (O), 13 Flemington St., Glenside SA 5065. Tel. (08) 338 2922. Mail to: PO Box 320, Glenside SA 5065 and Mikva. Beit Shalom, 39-41 Hackney Rd., Hackney, 5069. Tel. 362-8281.
South Australian Zionist Council & Habonim, 13, Flemington St., 5065. Tel. 379-0144.
National Council of Jewish Women, PO Box 10, Glenside 5089. Tel. 337-2369.
B'nai Brith, 4 Giles St., Dernan Court, 5057. Tel. 337-5767. Friends of the Hebrew University, 218 Brougham Pk., North Adelaide, 5006. Tel. 267-1081.
(K) Kosher products & Judaica available from Kosher Imports, c/o Hebrew Congregation.

TASMANIA

HOBART
Syn.: Argyle St., P.O. B. 128B, 7001. Sec.: Miss A. Rauner. Tel. 28-4097. The synagogue is the oldest in Australia, having been consecrated in July, 1845. Open Sat., 10 a.m. and every second. Fri. in the month at 6.15 p.m. Other days by arrangement.

LAUNCESTON
The syn. in St. John St. is the second oldest in Australia, founded in 1846. Inf. from the Pres., Dr. C. Meyerowitz. Tel. (004) 27-0270. Hon. Tr.: Mrs. B. Sandor, P.O. Box 66, 7250. Tel. 431143. There is also a Chabad Hse. Tel. 34-0705.

VICTORIA

BALLARAT
Syn.: 211 Drummond Street North, 3350. Tel. 32-6330.

GEELONG
Syn.: Yarra St.

MELBOURNE
Synagogues & Religious Organisations
Adass Israel (O), 16-24 Glen Eira Av., Ripponlea, 3182. Tel. 568-3344. Kashrut services, & Mikva.
Bentleigh Progressive, 549 Centre Rd., 3204. Tel. 563-9208.
Bet Hatikva Syn. (I), 233 Nepean Highway, Gardenvale, 3185. Tel. 576-9755.
Brighton (O), 134 Marriage Rd., E. Brighton, 3186. Tel. 592-9179.
Brunswick Talmud Torah, 32 Lord St., E. Brunswick, 3057.
Burwood Hebrew Cong. (O), 38 Harrison Av., 3125. Tel. 808-3120.
Caulfield Hebrew Cong. War Memorial (O) 572 Inkerman Rd., Caulfield, 3161. Tel. 525-9492.
E. Melbourne, 488 Albert St., E. Melbourne, 3002. Tel. 662-1372.
Elwood Talmud Torah Cong. (O), 39 Dickens St., Elwood, 3184. Tel. 531-1547.
Kew (O), 53 Walpole St., Kew, 3101. Tel. 853-9243.
Leo Baeck Centre (L), 33 Harp Rd., E. Kew, 3102. Tel. 819-7160.
Melbourne, cnr. Toorak & St. Kilda Rds., S. Yarra, 3141. Tel. 26-2255.
Mizrachi, 81 Balaclava Rd., Caulfield, 3161. Tel. 527-5680.
Moorabbin & District (O), 960 Nepean Highway, Moorabbin, 3189. Tel. 553-3845.
North-Eastern Jewish War Memorial Centre, 6 High St., Doncaster, 3108. Tel. 857-8084.
St. Kilda (O), Charnwood Gr., St. Kilda, 3182. Tel. 537-1433.
Sassoon Yehuda-Sephardi Syn., 73 Darling Rd., E. Malvern, 3145. Tel. 529-1818.
Sephardic Syn. Cong. Rambam, (O), 90 Hotham St., East St. Kilda 3183. Tel. 527-328.S.
S. Caulfield (O), 47 Leopold St., S. Caulfield, 3162. Tel. 578-5922.
Southern Jewish Com. Centre, 139-141 Marriage Rd., E. Brighton, 3187. Tel. 578-5637.
Southern Liberal Cong., 549 Centre Rd., Bentleigh, 3204. Tel. 557-6933.
Temple Beth Israel (L), 74-82 Alma Rd., St. Kilda, 3182. Tel. 510-1488.
Yeshiva Shule (O), 92 Hotham St., E. St. Kilda, 3183. Tel. 525-9535.

Melbourne Beth Din, Syn. Chambers, 572 Inkerman Rd., N. Caulfield, 3161. Tel. 527-8337.

Association of Rabbis and Ministers of Australia & New Zealand, c/o 12 Charnwood Grove, St. Kilda, 3182. Tel. 537-1433. Fax 525-3759.

Council of Orthodox Synagogues of Victoria, c/o Jetset House, 5 Queens Rd., 3000. Tel. 828-8000.

Rabbinical Council of Victoria, 6 High St., Doncaster, 3180. Tel. 531-1547.

Victorian Union for Progressive Judaism, 74 Alma Rd., St. Kilda, 3182. Tel. 510-1488.

Representative Organisations

Jewish Community Council of Victoria, 219 Balaclava Rd., (Suite 6), Caulfield, 3162. Tel. 523-5566. Fax. 523-0494. Contact: Helen Brustman.

Australasian Union of Jewish Students (Melbourne Branch), 306 Hawthorne Rd., Caulfield.

B'nai B'rith, 99 Hotham St., E. St. Kilda, 3183. Tel. 527-5169 offers a hospitality service to all Jewish visitors to Melbourne. Corr. to 15 Leaburn Av., Caulfield VIC. 3162.

National Council of Jewish Women, 54 Westbury St., Balaclava, 3183. Tel. 527-3299.

Victorian Jewish Board of Deputies, 401 Swanston St., 3000. Tel. 67-5341.

Cultural & Educational Organisations, etc.

Australian Jewish Historical Society, PO Box 255, Camberwell 3124. Tel. 882-2600.

Australian Institute of Jewish Affairs, POB 5402CC, 3001 Tel. 828-8570.

Beth Rivkah Ladies' College, 14-20 Balaclava Rd., E. St. Kilda, 3183. Tel. 527-3768.

Bialik College, 6 Shakespeare Gr., Hawthorne, 3122. Tel. 818-5525, & 429 Auburn Rd., E. Hawthorn, 3123. Tel. 20-7982.

Jewish Holocaust Centre, 29 Mackinnon Rd. Tel. 578-7148.

Jewish Museum of Australia, cnr. Arnold St. & Toorak Rd., S. Yarra, 3141. Tel. 26-1922.

Kadimah Jewish Cultural Centre & National Library, 7 Selwyn St., Elsternwick, 3185. Tel. 523-9817.

Makor Library, 306 Hawthorn Rd., South Caulfield 3162. Tel. (03) 272-5611. Fax (03) 272-5540.

Welfare Organisations

Australian Jewish Welfare & Relief Society, 466 Punt Rd., S. Yarra, 3141. Tel. 26-3727. Fax 867-4789.

Melbourne Hebrew Memorial Hospital, 95-107 High St. Rd., Ashwood, 3147. Tel. 277-1255.

Montefiore Homes for the Aged, 619 St. Kilda Rd., 3004. Tel. 510-8556 (with Synagogue).

Zionist Organisations

Australia-Israel Chamber of Commerce (Victoria Division), 4th Floor, 416 Gore St., Fitzroy. Tel. 41-2153.

Betar, 14 Dickens St., Elwood. Tel. 94-3165.

Bnei Akiva, 81 Balaclava Rd., Caulfield, 3162. Tel. 527-6067.

Habonim, 1 Sinclair St. Elsternwick, 3185. Tel. 528-1256.

Hashomer Hatzair, 214 Inkerman St., E. St. Kilda, 3182. Tel. 534-1091.

State Zionist Council of Victoria, 306 Hawthorn Rd., Caulfield. The following organisations are at the same address: Australia-Israel Publications, J.N.F., Magen David Adom, United Israel Appeal, WIZO, Zionist Fed. of Australia.

Booksellers, etc.
M. & L. Balberyszki, 98 Acland St., St. Kilda.Tel. 534-6003.
Chevrat Serarim Chabad Book Co-op., 92 Hotham St., E. St. Kilda, 3183. Tel. 527-4177.
Gold's Book & Gift Co., 36 William St., Balaclava, 3183. Tel. 527-8775.
Kantors, 350 St. Kilda Rd., St. Kilda, 3182. Tel. 534-4341.
Weekly Newspaper. "Jewish News", 11 Hoddle St., Abbotsford. Tel. 41-7591.

Hotels
(K) Kimberley (luxury accom.) 441 Interman Rd. (P.O.B. 66) Balaclava 3183. Tel. (03) 526 3888. Fax. (03) 525-9686.
(K) St Moritz, 14 The Esplanade, St. Kilda Beach, 3182. Tel. 525-5522.

Restaurants
(K) Bessa Foods, 57 Kooyong Rd., Caulfield, 3162. Tel. 509-2387. Fax 509-2387.
(K) Big K Bakers, 320 Carlisle St., Balaclava, 3183. Tel. 527-4582.
Blusztein's Corner Store, 636 Inkerman St., Caulfield North, 3162. tel. 527-5349.
(K) Cafe Carlisle (Kosher Vegetarian and Pizza), 271 Carlisle St., Balaclava 3183. Tel. 527-8639.
Cohen's, 230-232 Balaclava Rd., Caulfield, 3161. Tel. 500-9434. Fax 509-2909.
(K) Dairy Bell Ice Cream, 60 Belgrave Rd., Malvern East, 3145. Tel. 571-9211. Fax 572-2865.
(K) E & S Delicatessen, 74 Kooyong Rd., Caulfield, 3161. Tel. 576-0804.
Grefen Liquor Store, 144 Chapel St., Balaclava, 3183. Tel. 531-5032.
(K) Glicks Cakes and Bagels, 330a Carlisle St., Balaclava, 3183. Tel. 527-2198.
(K) Haolam Kosher Take-Away and Catering, Shop 5, 320 Carlisle St., Balaclava, 3182. Tel. 527-7255.
(K) Haymishe Cookies, Shop 4, 320 Carlisle St., Balaclava, 3183. Tel. 527-7116.
(K) Kemps Deli, 209 High St., Kew, 3101. Tel. 861-8157.
(K) Kraus, 62 Glen Eira Rd., Elsternwick, 3185. Tel. 523-8463. Fax 523-0595.
(K) Manshari, 219 Carlisle St., Balaclava. Tel. 525-9789.
Milecki's Balaclava Health Food, 227 Carlisle St., Balaclava, 3183. Tel. 527-3350.
Norgen-Vaaz, Chadstone Shopping Centre, 569-0496, 76 Acland St., St. Kilda. Tel. 534-9528.
(K) Old Carlton Deli, 25 Village Av., Doncaster, 3108. Tel. 816-3023.
Rishon Foods Pty. Ltd., 23 Williams St., Balaclava, 3183. Tel. 527-5142.
Rosenstar, 267 Carlisle St., Balaclava, 3182. Tel. 527-5534. Fax 525-9439.
(K) Rutti's Pizza, 241 Carlisle St., Balaclava, 3183. Tel. 525-9939.
(K) Shimon's The Felafel King, 285a Carlisle St., Balaclava, 3183. Tel. 527-9284.
(K) Singer's Cnr Balaclava and Hawthorn Rd., Caulfield 3161. Tel. 528 2544.
(K) The Olive Branch, 441 Inkerman Rd., East St. Kilda. Tel. 526 3865. Proprietor: M. Khoen.
Tempo Beverages, 391 Inkerman St., St. Kilda, 3183. Tel. 527-5021.

Butchers
(K) Balaclava Junction Kosher Butchers, 113 Hawthorn Rd., Caulfield. Tel. 523-8516.

(K) Balaclava Kosher Poultry, 283a Carlisle St., East St. Kilda, 3183. Tel. 527-3284.

(K) Chedva Kosher Butchers, 257 Carlisle St., Balaclava. Tel. 527-3795.

(K) Continental Kosher Butchers, 155 Glenferrie Rd., Malvern, 3144. Tel. 509-9822.

(K) Eatmore Kosher Poultry, 85 Acland St., St. Kilda, 3182. Tel. 534-1145. Fax 534-2931.

(K) Melbourne Kosher Butchers, 251 Inkerman St., East St. Kilda, 3182. Tel. 525-4230.

Ripponlea Fish Supply, 49 Glen Eira Rd., Ripponlea, 3182. Tel. 528-5625.

(K) Smorgasbord Chicken Centre, 253 Carlisle St., Balaclava, 3182. Tel. 525-8252.

Tasmanian Pacific Fish Supply, 29 Glen Eira Rd., Ripponlea, 3182. Tel. 528-3851.

(K) Weislitzer Kosher Butcher Shop, 280 Carlisle St., Balaclava. Tel. 534-5591.

WESTERN AUSTRALIA

PERTH

Synagogues & Religious Organisations

Northern Suburbs Congregation. 4 Vernon St., Noranda, 6062. Rev. Ch. Davidowitz. Tel. 275 5932.

Perth Hebrew Cong., Freedman Rd., Menora. 6050, Tel. 271-0539

Temple David (Liberal), 34 Clifton Cres., Mt. Lawley, 6050. Tel. 271-1485

Chabad House (Lubavitch), 396 Alexander Drive, Dianella 6062. Tel. 275-4912.

Representative Organisation

Council of Western Australian Jewry Inc. Pres.: Doron Ur, J.P., P.O. Box 763, Morley, 6062.

Welfare Organisation

Welfare Society. Pres.: Mr. L. Cohen, 44 Noranda Av., Noranda, 6062.

Zionist Organisations

Jewish National Fund, Jewish Centre, 61 Woodrow Av., Mount Yokine, 6060.

M.D.A. as J.N.F.

National Council of Jewish Women (affiliated I.C.J.W). Mrs. E. Braune, same address as J.N.F.

West Australian Zionist Council & Habonim. Same address as J.N.F.

WIZO. Pres.: Mrs. A. Segler, 51 Armadale Cres., Mt. Lawley, 6050.

Other organisations

Fellowship of Jewish Doctors of W.A. Hon. Sec.: Dr. B. M. Saker, Roy. Perth Hospital. Tel. (09) 224 3094.

Sport. Maccabi (same as J.N.F.)

Students W.A. Jewish students society.

Seniors. Jewish Seniors Club, Mrs. R. Trobe, O.A.M., 1/24 Broomhall Way, Noranda. 6062. Tel. 375-1492

Aged Home. Maurice Zeffert Home, 91 Woodrow Av., Yokine 6060.

AUSTRIA

Nazi Germany's annexation and occupation of Austria in 1938 marked the beginning of the end for an ancient and numerous community. There were some 200,000 Jews in Austria at that time – 180,000 of them in Vienna –

with a documented history going back to 906 C.E., although there were Jewish settlers in the area several hundred years earlier.

As the centuries passed, Austrian Jewry's fortunes waxed and waned, protection alternating with persecution, which reached a peak in 1420, after a charge of ritual murder had been levelled against the Jews. Almost the entire Jewish population of Austria was burnt to death, forcibly baptised or expelled.

Those who remained were harried and hounded for the next 350 years. Then the Empress Maria Theresa decreed another expulsion of the Jews – in 1770. Later in the eighteenth century, Jews reappeared in Austria. They were to live under considerable disabilities until 1867, when they were accorded full rights.

From then onwards, until 1938, the Austrian Jewish community flourished, despite the endemic antisemitism which, as in so many other European countries, was a feature of life in Austria. Between 1938 and 1940 about 120,000 Jews managed to leave. Some 60,000 men, women and children were killed in Nazi death camps. Today, there are about 12,000 Jews in Austria, between 8,000 and 10,000 of them in Vienna.

BADEN

Syn.: Grabengasse 14. Services, Fri evg., Sat morn., Sat. evg. From May to Sept., a **(K)** Kiddush-Shabbat meal is available in a small room adjoining the syn. Bookings must be made by the previous Wed. by telephoning Elieser Th. Schärf, Com. Pres., on (2252) 520043 or 42733.

The Jewish cemetery, containing some 3,000 graves, is at Halsriegelstr. 30. Tel. (2252) 85405.

EDLACH

A memorial to Dr. Theodor Herzl, erected by the Viennese Jewish com., can be seen in the garden of the local sanatorium, where the founder of the Zionist movement died in 1904.

EISENSTADT (Burgenland)

The restored private syn. of Samson Wertheimer, Habsburg court Jew & Chief Rabbi of Hungary (1658-1724) is now part of the Austrian Jewish Museum, which is at Unterbergstr. 6. Tel. 026 821 5145. The museum is open daily except Mon. from 10 a.m. to 5 p.m.

The Eruv Arch, spanning Unterbergstr., is at the end near the Esterhazy Palace. The road chain was used in former times to prevent vehicular traffic on Shabbat and Yomtov.

Old & New Cemeteries. The old cemetery, closed around 1875, contains the grave of R. Meir b. Isak (Mram Asch), d. 1744, which is to this day the scene of pilgrimages, particularly on the anniversary of his death.

Keys of the cemeteries are with the porter of the local hospital, which adjoins the old cemetery.

GRAZ

Com. Centre: Synagogenplatz 1. Tel. 912468. President Consul: Kurt Brühl

INNSBRUCK

Com. Centre: Zollerstr. 1. Tel. 586892. Pres.: Dr. Esther Fritsch.

KOBERSDORF (Burgenland)

The keys of the cemetery on the Lampelberg are with Mr. Piniel, Waldgasse 25 (one of the two houses to the left of the cemetery) & Mr. Grössing, Haydngasse 4. The syn. is being rebuilt.

LINZ
Com. Centre: Bethlehemstr. 26. Tel. 779805. Pres.: Georg Wotzasek.

SALZBURG
Syn. & Mikva: Lasserstr. 8.
Com. Centre: Lasserstr. 8. Tel. 75665. Pres.: Marco Feingold.

SEMMERING
Kosher Boarding Houses: **(K)** Pension Alexander, Hochstr. 87, 2680. Tel. 02664-336. Restaurant on premises; **(K)** Schweizerhof, Südbahnstr. 33, 2680. Breakfast. Tel. 02664-332.

VIENNA
Synagogues & Religious Organisations
The Chief Rabbi of Vienna is Rabbi Paul Chaim Eisenberg. Tel. 53104-17.
Syn.: Seitenstettengasse 4, 1010. Built in 1824-1826 and partly destroyed during the Nazi period, this beautiful syn. was restored by the com. in 1988. Guides to syn. available from Jewish Com. Centre, Seitenstettengasse 2. Tel. 53-1-04. For inf. about guided tours, contact the Com. Offices, Seiteisstetteng 4, Vienna 1010. Tel. 53104-16.
Prayer rooms: Agudas Yisroel, Grünangergasse 1, Vienna 1010. Tel. 512-83-31; Tempelgasse 3, Vienna 1020. Tel. 24-92-62. Rabbi David Grünfeld; Machsike Haddas, Desider Friedmann-Platz, Vienna 1010. Rabbi Chayim Stern. Tel. 2141347; Misrachi, Judenplatz 8, Vienna 1010. Tel. 535-41-53; Ohel Moshe, Lilienbrunngasse 19. Tel. 26-88-64, Vienna 1020. Rabbi Abraham Yonah Schwartz (see also Other Orgs.); Agudas Yeshurun, Riemergasse 9, Vienna 1010; Thora Etz Chayim, Grosse Schiffgasse 8, Vienna 1020. Tel. 2145206; Shomre Haddas, Glasergasse 17, Vienna 1090; Sephardi Centre, Tempelgasse 7, 1020. Rabbi M. Israelov and Rabbi A. Michaelsvili.
Mikvaot: Agudas Yisroel, Tempelgasse 3, Vienna 1020. Tel. 24-92-62; Machsike Haddas, Fleischmarkt 22, Vienna 1010. Tel. 512-52-62.

Cemeteries:
The Vienna central cemetery in the Simmering district, Vienna 1110, has a Jewish section (Gate 5) and there is an older Jewish part at Gate 1. Tel. 76-62-52. Those wishing to visit the Währinger cemetery, Semperstr. 64a, Vienna 1180, and the Floridsdorfer cemetery, Ruthnergasse 28, Vienna 1210, must first obtain a permit from the Com. Centre.
The Rossauer cemetery, Seegasse 9, Vienna 1090, the oldest Jewish cemetery in Vienna, which dates from the 16th century, has been restored, after having been devastated by the Nazis. It is open daily from 8 a.m. to 3 p.m. Access is via the front entrance of the municipal home for the aged at Seegasse 9-11, but a permit must be obtained beforehand from the Com. Centre. Tel. 53104-32.

Youth Organisations
Dachverband der jüdischen Jugend Österreichs, Vienna 1090, Währinger Strasse 24. Tel. 34 54 99; Jewish Students Organisation, Vienna 1090, Währinger Strasse 24. Tel. 34 54 99; Bnei-Akiva, Judenplatz 8, 1010, Tel. 5354153; Hashomer-Hatzair, Vienna 1010, Desider Friedmann-Platz 1 Tel. 5337499.

Other Organisations
B'nai B'rith, Taubstummengasse 17, Vienna 1040. Tel. 65-22-383. Pres.: Prof. Dr. J. Allerhand.

Com. Centre, Seitenstettengasse 4, Vienna 1010. Tel. 53-1-04. Pres.: Paul Grosz.
Documentation Centre of Austrian Resistance Movement, Old City Hall, Wipplingerstr. 8, Vienna 1010. Tel. 534-36-332. Dir.: Dr. Wolfgang Neugebauer.
Documentation Centre of Union of Jewish Victims of the Nazis, Salztorgasse 6, Vienna 1010. Tel. 533-91-31. Dir.: Simon Wiesenthal.
Home for Aged, Bauernfeldgasse 4, Vienna 1190. Tel. 36-16-55.
Jewish Student Assoc., Währingerstr. 24.
Jewish Welcome Service, Stephansplatz 10, Vienna 1010. Tel. 5334324. Dir.: Dr. Leon Zelman.
Mauthausen memorial site. Those wishing to visit the site should contact the Jewish Welcome Service or Tel. 072 38/24 39.
Jewish Museum, 4 Seitenstetteng. 1010. Tel. 535-0431. Open Sunday - Thursday 10.00 a.m.-5 p.m.
Ohel Moshe Hilfs- & Versorgungsverein. Head office: Lilienbrunngasse 19, 1020. Tel. 26-88-64. Com. Rabbi: Rabbi Avraham Yona Schwartz. Tel. 216-3695. Mikva on premises. **(K)** Guest rooms on premises. Up to 7 nights' accom. for Orthodox travellers with free breakfast. Vaad Hakashrut, Karmelitergasse 13, 1020. Tel. 33-73-64.
Sigmund Freud Museum, Berggasse 19, Vienna 1090. Tel. 3191596.
Tourist Inf. Centre, Kärntner Str. 38 Tel. 313 8892. Open daily, 9 a.m. to 7 p.m.

Zionist Organisations and Israel Embassy
Israel Embassy, Anton-Frank-Gasse 20, Vienna 1180. Tel. 470 47 41.
Jewish Agency, Stubenring 4. Tel. 5123636.
Keren Kayemet & Keren Hayesod. Desider Friedmann-Platz 1. Tel. 5127705.
WIZO. Desider Friedmann-Platz 1. Tel. 5127705.
Zionist Fed. of Austria, Desider Friedmann-Platz 1.

Kosher restaurants
Arche Noah (under supervision of Rabbi Chayim Grünfeld, Agudas Yisroel) Vienna 1010, Seitenstettengasse 2/Judengasse. Tel. 533 13 74; **Tuv-Taam** (café, restaurant, pizzeria) Shalom Bernholtz Vienna 1020, Franz-Hochedlinger-Gasse 23. Tel. 216 08 68.

Kosher Butchers
Rebenwurzel (under the supervision of Rabbi Chayim Stern, Machsike Haddas) Vienna 1010 Singerstrasse 24. Tel. 512 13 20; B. Ainhorn (under the supervision of Rabbi Chayim Grünfeld, Agudas Yisroel) Vienna 1020, Grosse Pfarrgasse 6. Tel. 2145621.

Kosher bakery
Engländer (under the supervision of Rabbi Abraham Yonah Schwartz, Ohel Moshe) Vienna 1020, Hollandstrasse 7. Tel. 214 56 17.

Kosher supermarket
Kosher Supermarket and Shutnes Laboratory (under the supervision of Rabbi Abraham Yonah Schwartz, Ohel Moshe) Vienna 1020, Hollandstrasse 10. Tel. 26 96 75.

Books and religious articles
Chabad-Simcha-Center, Vienna 1020, Hollandstrasse 10. Tel. 216 29 24; Bookshop "Chai" Vienna 1020, Lessinggasse 5. Tel. 216 46 21.

BAHAMAS

The Jewish population of these islands, formerly a British colony, is put at round about 85. However, it is estimated that at least 350,000 of the 3 million tourists who visit the Bahamas every year are Jewish. In Nassau, the capital, on New Providence Island, there are a number of Jewish residents. The only active syn. is the Luis Torres Synagogue, E. Sunrise Highway, P.O.B. F.1761, Freeport, Grand Bahama Island (Tel. 373-2008), which has a Jewish population of about 50. Services are held to suit the requirements of those attending. The Pres. of the cong. is Jack Turner. Tel. 373-1041.

Hon. Consul-General of Israel: Ralph D. Seligman. Tel. 32-24130 & 36-24421.

The Jewish cemetery, a walled-off section of the public cemetery, is at the corner of Shirley St. and Lovers' Lane, Nassau.

Most major hotels can make special arrangements with regard to kosher food.

General inf. from Bahamas Tourist Office, Bahamas Hse., 10 Chesterfield St., W1X 8AH. Tel. 071-629 5238.

BARBADOS

A Jewish com. was formed on the island of Barbados by refugees from Brazil after its reconquest by the Portuguese in about 1650. In 1802 all political disabilities of the Jews were removed, although this was not confirmed by Parliament until 1820.

Nevertheless, Barbados was the first British possession to grant full political emancipation to its Jews. The island gained its independence in 1966, remaining a member of the British Commonwealth. A syn. bldg. in Bridgetown, dating from 1833 (although parts are much older, going back to 1654), remains from the days of the original Jewish population. In 1929, the syn. bldg. was sold, because only one Jew still remained on the island, and turned into offices. The syn. and the cemetery in Synagogue Lane which surrounds it and is still in use, are in process of restoration and repair after years of neglect. The restoration of the synagogue is now 90% completed and the original clock and chanuka lamp have been returned from the museum. What is most urgently needed now is the restoration of the tombstones in the adjoining cemetery whose condition has deteriorated. In the 1930s and 1940s Jews returned to Barbados, but of more than 30 European Jewish families on the island in the 1940s, only about 20 remain today.

Services are held Fri. evgs. at 7 p.m. at "True Blue," Rockley New Rd., Christ Church, during the summer, and at the Syn. in winter.

Synagogue Restoration Project, P.O.B. 256, Bridgetown. Tel. (809) 432-0840.

Local inq. to Henry Altman, "Sea Shell," Gibbes Beach, St. Peter. Tel. 422-2664.

BELGIUM

Belgian Jewry, like the communities of other European countries, achieved religious equality nearly 160 years ago – in 1831, when Belgium became a kingdom and religious equality was made part of the fundamental law of the State.

By the late 1930s, there were 100,000 Jews in Belgium, including refugees from Nazi Germany, but their respite from persecution was a short one. When Hitler's armies invaded Belgium in 1940 and swept on to occupy the whole of Western Europe as far as the Spanish border, few Belgian Jews managed to escape to safety. After introducing their racialist legislation,

the Nazis began rounding up the Jews and deported 25,000 of them to concentration camps.
The names of the 23,838 who did not return after the end of the Second World War are engraved on the national monument to the Jewish Martyrs of Belgium. This stands in the Anderlecht district of Brussels.
There are about 40,000 Jews in Belgium today, most of them in Antwerp and Brussels.
General inf. from the Belgian Tourist Office, Premier Hse., 2 Gayton Rd., Harrow, Middx., HA1 2XU. Tel. 081-861 3300.

ANTWERP

Synagogues & Religious Organisations
Machsike Hadass (Israelitische Orthodoxe Gemeente), Jacob Jacobsstr. 22. Tel. 233-55-67.
Rabbinate: Jacob Jacobstr. 22. Tel. 232-00-21. Rabbi Ch. Kreiswirth. Private address: Quinten Matsijslei 35, Tel. 234 31 48 Dayan E. Sternbuch. Tel. 233-71-94; Dayan T. Weiss. Tel. 230-21-63.
Main Syn.: Oostenstr., 43. Annexe: Jacob Jacobsstr. 22.
Shomre Hadass (Israelitische Gemeente), Terliststr. 35. Tel. 232-01-87.
Rabbinate: Terliststr. 35. Tel. 226-05-54. Dayan J. Kohen. Tel. 230-35-81.
Rabbi D. Lieberman, Belgiëlei 194. Tel. 239-18-83.

Other Synagogues
Alexander, Isabellalei 44.
Beth Hamidrash, Oostenstr. 44.
Beth Mordechaj, Van Leriusstr. 54.
Beth Yitshak, Mercatorstr. 56.
Chasidé Alexander, Isabellalei 44.
Chasidé Belz, Van Spangenstr. 6.
Chasidé Bobov, Lange Leemstr. 224.
Chasidé Gur. Antoon Van Dyckstr. 43.
Chasidé Lubawitz, Brialmontlei 48..
Chasidé Satmar, Jacob Jacobsstr. 6.
Chasidé Tsortkow, Van Leriusstr. 37.
Chasidé Wiznitz, Brialmontlei 16-20 & Jacob Jacobsstr. 31-33.
Chug Avrechei Agudath Israel, Breughelstr. 38.
Eisenmann Syn., Oostenstr. 29.
Gitschotel, Marsstr. 50.
Héchal Aharon, Van Leriusstr. 38
Or Schraga, Van Leriusstr. 22.
Sanz Klausenburg, Van Leriusstr. 46.
Bouwmeesterstr. 7. Tel. 237-2661.
Mizrachi, 65 Isabellalei.
Moriyah, Terlistr. 35.
Romi Goldmuntz, Van den Nestlei 1. Tel. 230-13-64.
Sephardi Synagogue, Hoveniersstr. 31. Mikvaot: Machsike Hadass, Steenbokstr. 22. Tel. 239-75-88; Shomre Hadass, Van Diepenbeeckstr. 42. Tel. 239-09-65.

Representative Organisation
B'nai B'rith, Nervierstr.14. Tel. 239-39-11.

Cultural & Educational Organisations, etc.
Plantin-Moretus Museum, Vrijdagmarkt (near Groenplaats). Tel. 233-06-88. Open daily (except Mon.). Contains examples of early Jewish printing, like the famous Polyglot Bible.

Romi Goldmuntz Centre, Nerviersstr. 12. Tel. 239-39-11.

Student and Youth Organisations
Agudath Israel, Lamorinièrestr. 67. Tel. 230-85-13.
Bne Akiva, Consciencestr. 22. Tel. 230-22-19.
Hashomer Hatsair, Lamorinièrestr. 202. Tel. 239-61-01.
Hanoar Hatsioni, Gretry St. 12. Tel. 2813422.

Sport & Miscellaneous Organisations
Antwerp Tourist & Inq. Office, Suikerrui 19. Tel. 232-01-03.
Diamond Exchanges: Beurs voor Diamanthandel, Pelikaanstr. 78;
Diamantclub, Pelikaanstr. 62; Diamantkring, Pelikaanstr. 86; Nieuwe
Kring, Hovenierstr. 2; Vrije Diamanthandel, Pelikaanstr. 70.
Fed. of Jewish Women's Assoc. Mrs. Zucker, Beukenlaan 10b. Tel. 828-38-
76.
Royal Maccabi Sports Club, Pelikaanstr 92, B53 Tel. 226 1708. 10-12. Tel.
239-56-73.

Welfare Organisations, Hospital, etc.
Jewish Welfare Org., Jacob Jacobstr. 2. Tel. 232-38-90.
Home for the Aged and Geriatric Centre. Marialei 6-8. Tel. 218-93-99.
Apfelbaum-Laub Home, Marialei 2-4.

Zionist Organisations
Keren Hayesod, Schupstr. 1. Tel. 232-97-74.
Keren Kayemet, Hoveniersstr. 12. Tel. 231-26-28.
Mizrachi, Isabellalei 65. Tel. 230-21-12.
WIZO, Gretrystr. 53. Tel. 239-05-71.
Zionist Federation, Schupstr. 1. Tel. 232-97-74.

Booksellers
Epstein, Van den Nestlei 7. Tel. 232-75-62; I. Menczer, Simonstr. 40. Tel.
232-30-26; N. Seletsky, Lange Kievitstr. 70. Tel. 232-69-66; Stauber, Van
Leriusstr. 3. Tel. 231-80-31.

Newspapers
"Belgisch Israelitisch Weekblad," Pelikaanstr. 106-108. Tel. 233-70-43.

Restaurants
(K) Blue Lagoon, Lange Herentalsestr. 70.
(K) Dresdner, Simonstr. 10. Tel. 232-54-55.
Falafel Behi, Lange Leemstr. 188 Tel. 218 8211; Lange Herentalstr. 60. Tel.
234-2632.
(K) Gelkop (Diamantkring), Van Leriusstr. 28. Tel. 233-07-
(K) Hoffman, Diamantkring, Hoveniersstr. 2. Tel. 225-2040 & 225-2424.
(K) Jacob, Lange Kievitstr. 49. Tel. 233-11-24.
(K) Sam (Diamantbeurs), Pelikaanstr. 28. Tel. 233-92-89.
(K) Snack Bar Hoffy's, Lange Kievitstr. 52. Tel. 234-35-35.
(K) Snack Bar, Romi Goldmuntz Centre, Nerviersstr. 12. Tel. 239-39-11.

Kosher Meat, Poultry, etc.
Butchers: **(K)** Berkowitz, Isabellalei 9. Tel. 218-51-11. **(K)** Fruchter Simonstr.
22. Tel. 233-18-11; **(K)** Kosher King, Lange Kievitstr. 40. Tel. 233-67-49. and
Isabellalei 7, Tel. 239-41-89 **(K)** Moszkowitz, Lange Kievitstr. 47. Tel. 232-
14-85.
Poulterers: **(K)** Farkas, Lange Kievitstr. 66; Tel. 232-13-85; **(K)** Mandelovics,

Isabellalei 96. Tel. 218-47-79; **(K)** Weingarten, Lange Kievitstr. 124. Tel. 233-28-28.
Bakers: **(K)** Gottesfeld, Mercatorstr. 20. Tel. 230-00-03; **(K)** Grosz, Pelikaanstr. 130. Tel. 233-91-10; **(K)** Kleinblatt, Provinciestr. 206. Tel. 233-75-13 & 226-00-18; **(K)** Steinmetz, Lange Kievitstr. 64. Tel. 234-09-47.
Dairies: **(K)** Herzl & Gold, Korte Kievitstr. 38. Tel. 232-23-65; Stark, Mercatorstr. 24. Tel. 230-25-20; **(K)** Super Discount, Belgielei 104-108. Tel. 239-06-66. Col-Bo, B.U.B.A. Jacob Jacobsstr. 40. 40. Tel. 2341212. Grosz-Modern Terlinststr. 28. Tel. 2324626.

ARLON
Syn.: Rue St. Jean (est. 1863). Sec.: J. C. Jacob, 9 rue des Martyrs.
A monument has been erected in the new Jewish cemetery to the memory of the Jews of Arlon deported and massacred by the Nazis.

BRUSSELS

National Monument to the Jewish Martyrs of Belgium
This monument commemorates the Jews of Belgium who were deported to concentration camps and killed by the Nazis during the Second World War. The names of all 23,838 are engraved on the monument, which has been erected in the Brussels district of Anderlecht, at the corner of rue Emile Carpentier and rue Goujons. The square in which the monument stands has been renamed "Square of the Jewish Martyrs".

Religious Organisations
Consistoire Central Israélite de Belgique. Pres.: Professor A. Georges Schnek. Sec.: 2 Rue Joseph Dupont, 1000. Tel. 512-21-90. Communauté Israélite de Bruxelles. Rabbi Albert Guigui. Tel. 512-43-34 & 512-92-37. Sec.: 2 rue Joseph Dupont. Tel. 512-43-34 & 512-92-37.
Machsike Hadass (Communauté Israélite Orthodoxe de Bruxelles). 67a rue de la Clinique. Tel. 524-14-86. Rabbi Chaikin.

Synagogues
Adath Israel, 126 rue Rogier, Schaerbeek. Tel. 241-16-64.
Ahavat Reim, 73 rue de Thy, St.-Gilles. Sec.: Tel. 648-38-37.
Beth Hamidrash, rue du Chapeau, Anderlecht. Tel. 524-14-86.
Beth Israel, 74 Av. Stalingrad.
Beth Israel, 33 Houzeau de Lehaie, Molenbeek.
Beth Itshak, 115 Av. du Roi, 1060. Tel. 538-33-74 & 520-13-59.
Communauté Israélite de Bruxelles, 32 rue dé la Régence.
Maale, 11 Av. de Messidor. Sec.: 20 Av. Mozart. Tel. 345-92-10.
Or Hahayim, 77 rue P. Decoster, 1190. Tel. 344-23-42.
Machské Hadass (Communauté Israélite Orthodoxe de Bruxelles). Rabbi I. Chaikin. Tel. 522-07-17. Sec.: 67a rue de la Clinique. Tel. 521-12-89.
Syn. & Beth Hamidrash: 67a rue de la Clinique. (Mikva on premises. Tel. 537-14-39.)
Sephard Cong. of Brussels (Communauté) Sepharadite de Bruxelles). Syn. & Sec.: 47 rue du Pavaillon, 1030. Tel. 215-21-38.
Liberal Syn. (Member of World Union for Progressive Judaism), 96 Av. Kersbeek. Tel. 345-59-92. Rabbi Abraham Dahan.
Beth Din (Machsike Hadass). 67a rue de la Clinique. Tel. 522-07-17.

Representative Organisations
B'nai B'rith, 319 Av. Brugmann, 1180 Bruxelles.
Centre Communautaire Laïc Juif, 52 rue Hotel des Monnaies. Tel. 537-82-16. Jewish Restaurant on premises open daily for lunch and Friday eve.

Comité de Coordination des Organisations Juives de Belgique, 68 Av. Ducpétiaux. Tel. 537-16-91.
Fédération Nationale des Anciens Combattants et Résistants Juifs Armés de Belgique, 2 Av. Albert. Tel. 345-69-28.
Union des Anciens Résistants Juifs de Belgique, 148 Chaussée d'Ixells.
Union des Déportés, 68 Av. Ducpétiaux. Tel. 537-16-91.
World Jewish Congress (Belgian Section), 16 Av. de la Toison d'Or. Tel. 512-70-34.

Cultural & Educational Organisations, Schools, etc.
Amis Belges de l'Universite Hebraique de Jerusalem, 319 Ave Brugmann - 1180 Bruxelles.
Athenée Maïmonide, 67 Blvd. Poincaré. Tel. 523-63-36.
Athénée Ganenu, 3 rue Melkriek, 1180. Tel. 376-11-76.
Beth Aviv, 123 Av. Molière, 1180. Tel. 347-37-19.
Beth Chabad, 87 Av. du Roi. Tel. 537-11-58.
Centre National des Hautes Etudes Juives, 17 Ave F. Roosevelt. Tel. 650.33.48.
La Maison de la Culture Juive, 77 rue P. Decoster, 1190. Tel. 343-62-24.
Yeshiva des Etudiants de Bruxelles, 94 rue de la Source, 1060.
Yessodé Hatorah, 67a rue de la Clinique.

Student, Youth & Sports Organisations
Fed. of Jewish Youth, 52 rue Hotel des Monnaies. Tel. 537-82-16.
Jewish Students' Union, 89 Chaussée de Vleurgat. Tel. 648-19-59.
Jewish Youth Centre, 89 Chaussée de Vleurgat. Tel. 648-18-59. (★ restaurant on premises. Open daily from noon to 2.30 p.m. and 6 p.m. to 9 p.m. except Fri. evg. and Sat. afternoon.
Maccabi, 89 Chaussée de Vleurgat. Tel. 648-18-59.

Welfare Organisations, Hospitals, Homes, etc.
Centrale d'Oeuvres Sociales Juives (combined welfare and fund-raising org.), 91 Av. H. Jaspar, 1060. Tel. 538-80-36.
Home for Aged, 31-35 rue de la Glacière. Tel. 537-46-99.
Service Social Juif, 66-68 Av. Ducpétiaux. Tel. 538-81-80.
United Hias Service, 42 rue de Livourne.

Zionist Organisations
Bnei Akiva, 262 rue des Alliés, 1190. Tel. 343-78-13.
Hanoar Hatzioni, 234 Chaussée d'Alsemberg.
Keren Kayemet, Ave Maraix 19A - 1050 Bruxelles. Tel. 513.92.32.
Mizrachi, 2 Av. Rogier. Tel. 215-36-97.
Org. of Gen. Zionists & Independents, 168 Av. du Roi, 1060 Bruxelles.
Pioneer Women, 46 rue de l'Ermitage. Tel. 49-39-19.
Poale Zion, 118 Av. Albert. Tel. 537-42-99.
Union of General Zionists, 11 Av. du Polo.
WIZO, 48 Av. Brugmann. Tel. 343-38-61.
Zionist Fed. of Belgium, 66 Av. Ducpétiaux. Tel. 538-56-29.
Zionist Revisionists, 1 Blvd. de la Révision. Tel. 521-95-50.
Museum 74 Ave de Stalengrad 1000 Bruxelles. Tel. 512-19.63.
Israel Embassy and Consular Section, 40 Av. de l'Observatoire. Tel. 374-90-85 & 373.13.11.

Bookseller
Colbo, 121 rue du Brabant. Tel. 217-26-20
Menorah, Ave J. Voldens, 33-1060 Bruxelles. Tel. 537.50.73.

Newspapers and Periodicals
"Centrale" (monthly), 91 Av. Henri Jaspar. Tel. 538-80-36 & "Kehilatenou" (monthly), 2 rue Joseph Dupont. Tel. 512-35-78. "La Tribune Sioniste" (fortnightly), 68 Av. Ducpétiaux.
"Regards" (fortnightly), 52 rue Hotel des Monnaies. Tel. 538.49.84. Fax. 537.55.65.
(The "Jewish Chronicle" is obtainable from W. H. Smith & Son, 71-75 Blvd. Adolphe Max.)
"APEJ", daily, 27 Rue Ph. Leban - 1040 Bruxelles. Tel. 231-11-74.

Kosher Bakery
(K) Bornstein, 62 rue de Suède, St. Gilles. Tel. 537-16-79.

Kosher Butcher
(K) Lanxner, 37 Av. Jean Volders. Tel. 537-06-08 & 121 rue de Brabant. Tel. 217-26-20.
(K) Yarden, 85 Ave des Sept Bonniers, 1190 Bruxelles. Tel. 744-1729.

CHARLEROI
Com. Centre: 56 rue Pige-au-Croly. Sec.: M. Weinberg, 65 rue van der Velde, 6300 Marchiennes.

GHENT
The com. is a very small one and there is no permanent syn. However, services are held on the High Holy-days. Jacques Bloch, Veldstr. 60, Tel. (091) 25-70-85, the treas. of the com., will be happy to meet Anglo-Jewish visitors.

KNOKKE
Syn.: 28 Van Bunnenlaan. Tel. (050) 61-103-72.
Kosher Restaurant: **Rue du Congo** (Steenmetz).

LIEGE
Syn.: 19 rue L. Fredericq.
Com. Centre: 12 Quai Marcellis.

MONS
Nearby, at **Casteau** the International Chapel of NATO's Supreme Headquarters Allied Powers Europe, includes a small Jewish Community (est. 1951) that holds regular services. Further inf. SHAPE, 7010, Belgium. Tel. 44.58.08 or 44.48.09.

OSTEND
Syn.: 3 Maastrichtplein. Inf.: Kalter. Tel. (059) 70-35-58.

BERMUDA
There is a small but active Jewish community in Bermuda. High Holy-day services are normally held at the U.S. Naval Air Station chapel. There is also a Sabbath service on the first Fri. of each month. Further inf. is available from the Jewish Com. of Bermuda, P.O. Box HM 1793, Hamilton, HM HX.
General inf. from Bermuda Tourism (BCB Ltd.), 6 Burnsall St., SW3 3ST. Tel. 071-734 8813-4.

BOLIVIA
Although there have been Jews in Latin America for many centuries, they are comparative newcomers to Bolivia, which received its first Jewish

immigrants only in 1905. They remained a mere handful until the 1920s, when some Russian Jews made their way to the country. After 1935, German Jewish refugees, began to arrive in Bolivia. Also from Rumania and mostly from Poland. Today some 640 Jews live there, mostly in the capital of La Paz (about 430), Cochabamba (120) and Santa Cruz (85), Tarija and other cities (5).

COCHABAMBA

Syn.: Calle Junin y Calle Colombia, Casilla 349.
Asociación Israelita de Cochabamba, P.O.B. 349 Calle Valdivieso.

LA PAZ

Syns.: Circulo Israelita de Bolivia, Casilla 1545 Calle Landaeta 346, P.O.B. 1545. Services Sat. morn. only. Pres.: Guillermo Wiener.
Comunidad Israelita Synagogue, Calle Canada Strongest 1846, P.O.B. 2198, is affiliated to the Circulo. Fri. evg. services are held. There is a Jewish school at this address. Circulo Israelita, P.O.B. 1545 is the representative body of Bolivian Jewry. All La Paz organisations are affiliated to it.
Two Homes for Aged: Calle Rosendo Gutierrez 307, and Calle Diaz Romero 1765.
Information office for Israeli tourist. Centro Shalom, Calle Canada Stronguest 1846, La Paz Country Club, Quinta J.K.G. Obrajes. Calle 1, esquina calle Hector Ormachea Castilla 1545 - La Paz.

SANTA CRUZ

Centro Cruceño P.O.B. 469.
WIZO, Casilla 3409.

BOSNIA HERCEGOVINA

The state of the Jewish Community remains in doubt in the midst of the civil war amongst the former Yugoslav republics.

SARAJEVO

Syn.: Dobrovoljacka St. 83, by the river bank near Princip Bridge. The head of the Jewish com. will be glad to show the treasures of the Jewish Museum, including priceless Jewish relics of the Spanish Inquisition. Pres.: Ivica Chereshnes. Tel. 272-142; Fax 271-851.
There is an historic Jewish cemetery (Kovacici, Nevesinjska St.) in the town.
On a hill called Vrace, not far from the centre of the town, is a monument to the 7,000 Jews from the area who fell victim to the Nazis.
Jewish Museum: Marshall Tito St. 98. Tel. 535 688.

BRAZIL

Marranos from Portugal and, later, Sephardim from Holland were the first Jews to settle in Brazil about 400 years ago. Their early history was bedevilled by the struggle for power in this vast country between the Portuguese and Dutch, as well as by the Inquisition, which the Portuguese revived when they were on top, and which was abolished when the Dutch gained the upper hand.
Finally, in 1822, Brazil declared her independence of Portugal. Some Marranos reverted to open Judaism when liberty of worship was proclaimed, and in the years that followed, European Jews, mainly Ashkenazim, began to immigrate. Communities grew up in Rio de Janeiro, Recife, Bahia, Sao Paulo and elsewhere and continued to grow, especially after the First World War, in the 1930s and again after the Second World War.

Today, Brazil's Jewish population numbers about 175,000. All save about 25,000 live in Rio and Sao Paulo. The overwhelming majority, some 140,000, are Ashkenazim.

AMAZONAS STATE

MANAUS
Social Centre: Grupo Kadima, Rua Ramos Ferreira 596.

BAHIA STATE

SALVADOR
Syn.: Rua Alvaro Tiberio 60. Com. Centre & Zionist Org. at same address. Tel. 3-4283.

BRASILIA FEDERAL DISTRICT

F Syn. & Com. Centre: ACIB, Entrequadras Norte 305-306 Lote A. Tel. 23-2984.
Embassy of Israel: Av. das Nacoes Sul, Lote 38. Tel. 244-7675, 7875, 5886 & 4886.

MINAS GERAIS STATE

BELO HORIZONTE
Syns.: Avenne Leonardo Malchez 630, Centro.
Mikva: Rua Grande do Norte 477. Tel. 2210690.
Com. Centres & Clubs: Uniao Israelita de Belo Horizonte, Rua Pernambuco 326. Tel. 2246013; Associacao Israelita Brasileira, Rua Rio Grande do Norte 477. Tel. 2210690.
Comunidade Religiosa Israelita Mineira, Rua Rio Grande do Norte 477.

PARA STATE

BELEM
Syns.: Shaar Hashamaim, Rua Alcipreste Manoel Theodoro 842; Eshel Avraham, Travessa Campos Sales 733.
Com. Centre: Travessa Dr. Moraes 37.

PARANA STATE

CURITIBA
Syn.: Francisco Frischman (Orthodox), Rua Cruz Machado 126. Min.: Rabbi David Ben-Hayon.
Com. Centre and S. Guelman School, Rua Nilo Pecanha 664. Tel. 23-3734.

PERNAMBUCO STATE

RECIFE
Syn.: Rua Martins Junior 29.
Com. Centre: Rua da Gloria 215.

RIO DE JANEIRO STATE

CAMPOS
Com. Centre: Rua 13 de Maio 52.

NITEROI
Centro Israelita: Rua Visconde do Uruguai 255, 24030.
Sociedade Hebraica, Rua Alvares de Azevedo 185. Icarai, 24220.

PETROPOLIS
Machane Israel Yeshiva, Rua Duarte da Silveira 1246, 25600. Tel. 42-4952.
Sinagoga Israelita Brasileira, Rua Aureliano Coutinho 48, 25600.

GREATER RIO DE JANEIRO
Synagogues & Religious Organisations
Agudat Israel, Rua Nascimento Silva 109, Ipanema 22421.
Ahavat Shalom, Rua Juvenal Galeno 29.
Associacao Religiosa Israelita (Liberal), Rua General Severiano 170, Botafogo, 22290. Tel. 2269666 & 2379283.
Associacao Religiosa Krasnik, Rua Barano de Uba 201, Estacio, 20260.
Beth Aaron, Rua Gago Coutinho 63, Laranjeiras, 22221.
Beth El, Rua Barata Ribero 489, Copacabana, 22040.
Beth Yaacov, Rua dos Artistas 205.
Chevre Kedishe (Orthodox), Rua Barao de Iguatemi 306. Tel. 248-8716.
Conselho das Congregacoes Sefaraditas, Rua Barata Ribeiro 489. Tel. 2576193.
Grande Templo Israelita, Rua Tenente Possolo 8, Centro, 20230. Tel. 2323656.
Kehilat Moriah (Orthodox), Rua Pompeu Loureiro 48. Tel. 2574299.
Kehilat Yaakov, Rua Capelao Alvares da Silva 15, Copacabana, 22041.
Monte Sinai (Orthodox), Rua Sao Francisco Xavier Tijuca, 20550.
Sidon, Rua Conde Bonfim 521.
Sinagoga Beirutense, Rua Pontes Correia 49, Andarai, 20510.
Sinagoga da Penha, Rua Bulhoes Marcial 7.
Templo Sidon, Av. Rio Branco 156-3110, Centro, 20040.
Templo Uniao Israel, Rua Jose Higino 375 & 381, Tijuca, 20520.
Uniao Israelita Shel Guemilut Hassadim (Orthodox, Sephardi), Rua Rodrigo de Brito 37. Tel. 2264885.
Jewish Cemetery: Av. Presidente Vargas 583/2006, Centro 20071.
Mikva: Rua General Canabarro 454.

Representative Organisations
B'nai B'rith, Largo do Machado 29-418, Catete, 22221.
Bene Herzl (Sephardi), Rua Barata Ribeiro 489.
Federacao Israelita do Rio de Janeiro, Rua Mexico 90-5°, 20031. Tel. 2406278.

Cultural Organisations, Clubs, etc.
Associacao Sholem Aleichem, Rua Sao Clemente 155, Botafogo, 22260. Tel. 2267740.
Biblioteca Bialik, Rua Fernando Osorio 16, Flamengo, 22230. Tel. 205-1946.
Biblioteca Theodor Herzl, Av. Copacabana 807, Salas 1005-6, Copacabana 22050.
Centro de Cultura Yiddish, Av. Copacabana 69010° andar.
Hebraica Club, Rua das Laranjeiras 346, Laranjeiras. 22240. Tel. 2458722.
Instituto Israelita Brasileiro de Cultura e Educacao, Rua das Laranjeiras 405, Laranjeiras, 22240.
Jewish Museum, Rua Mexico 90-1°, Andar.
Monte Sinai Club, Rua Sao Francisco Xavier 104, Tijuca, 20550.
Schools
Bar-Ilan Day School, Rua Pompeu Loureiro 48, Copacabana, 22061. Tel. 2574299.
Colegio Hebreu Brasileiro, Rua Prudente de Moaris 1172, Ipane Ipanema, 22420.
Eliezer Steinbarg School, Rua das Laranjeiras 405, Laranjeiras, 22240.

A. Liessin School, Rua Sao Clemente 275-277, Botafogo, 22260.
Max Nordau School, Rua Prudente de Morais 1172, Ipanema, 22420.
Scholem Aleichem School, Rua Professor Gabizo 211, Tijuca, 20271.
Talmud Torah Herzlia, Rua Ibituruna 37, Maracana, 20271. Tel. 2488450.

Welfare Organisations, Hospitals, etc.
Communal Fund (Funds Comunitario), Rua Mexico 90-1°.
Children's Home: Rua Jose Higino 240. Tel. 2380080, 2586162.
Homes for Aged: Av. Geremario Dantas 278 (Jacarepagua). Office: Rua
Uruguaiana 10. Tel. 252 6887; Rua Santa Alexandrina 464. Tel. 2737045 &
2737196.
Hospital Israelita, Rua Lucio de Mendonca 56, Maracana, 20270. Tel.
2282128.

Zionist Organisations
Naamat-Pioneiras, Rua Fernando Osorio 16, Flamengo, 22230.
United Zionist Org. of Rio, Rua Decio Vilares 258, Copacabana, 22041. Tel.
2562850.
WIZO, Praia do Flamengo 278, Sala 92, Copacabana, 22041.

Restaurant
(K) Shalom, Rua Pompeu Loureiro 48 (Copacabana). Tel. 2574299.

RIO GRANDE DO SUL STATE
ERECHIM
Syn.: Av. Pedro Pinto de Souza 131.

PASSO FUNDO
Syn.: Rua General Osorio 1049.

PELOTAS
Syn.: Rua Santos Dumont 303.

PORTO ALEGRE
(Jewish population about 15,000.)
Syns. & Com. Centres: Centro Israelita Porto Alegrense, Rua Henrique Dias
73. Tel. 219649; Linath Ha-Tzedek, Rua Bento Figueredo 55; Poilisher
Farband, Rua Joao Telles 329; Uniao Israelita Porto Alegrense, Rua Barros
Cassal 750. Tel. 246515. All the foregoing are Orthodox with daily services.
The Centro Hebraico Riograndense (Sephardi), Rua Cel. Machado 1008 has
services on Sabbaths only, as does SIBRA (Liberal), Mariante 772. Tel.
318133.
City Rabbinate: Rua Henrique Dias 73. Tel. 219649. Rabbi Efraim F.
Ginsberg & Rabbi Saul Farber.
Mikva: Rua Francisco Ferrer 170.

Clubs, Organisations, etc.
B'nai B'rith: Rua Joao Telles 508. Tel. 247126.
Club Campestre: Av. Colonel Marcos 1345. Tel. 492235.
Federacao Israelita do Rio Grande do Sul. Same address as B'nai B'rith. Tel.
247126.
Gremio Esportiva Israelita: Av. Protasio Alves 3435. Tel. 318435.
Home for Aged: Lar Dos Velhos. Rua Leopoldo Bettiol 501. C.P. 5043. Tel.
418400.
Organizacao Sionista Unificada, Rua Francisco Ferrer 170. Tel. 312296.
WIZO: Rua Henrique Dias 73. Tel. 219649.

(K) Kosher Butcher: Rua Fernandes Vieira 518. Tel. 250441.

SANTA MARIA
(First Jewish settlement in Brazil, established by Jewish Colonization Assoc.)
Syn.: Trav. Augustura.

SAO PAULO STATE
CAMPINAS
Syn. & Com. Centre: Beth Yacob, Rua Barreto Leme 1203. Tel. 31-4908.

MOGI DAS CRUZES
Jewish Soc.: Rua Dep. Deodato Wertheimer 421. Tel. 469-2505.

SANTO ANDRE
Syn. & Com. Centre: Rua Siqueira Campos 780. Tel. 449-1568.
School, Rua Onze de Junho 172. Tel. 449-1568.

SANTOS
Syn.: Rua Campos Sales 137.
Club: Rua Cons. Neblas 254. Tel. 32-9016.

SAO CAETANO DO SUL
Syn.: Rua Para 61. Tel. 442-3514.

SAO PAULO
Synagogues & Religious Organisations
Beit Chabad, Rabbi Shabsi Alpern, Rua Chabad 54/60. Tel. 852-4794 & 282-1819.
Centro Judaico Religioso de Sao Paulo (Orthodox). Office hours: 9 a.m. to 1 p.m. weekdays. Tel. 220-5642. Rabbi Elyahu B. Valt. Tel. 64-90-54 (home).
Comunidade Israelita Ortodoxa de Sao Paulo, Hitachdut Kehilot Hacharedim, Rua Haddock Lobo 1279. Tel. 282-1562 & 852-9710. This com. has two syns.: Beit
Itzchok, Rua Haddock Lobo 1279. Tel. 881-3804; Adas Yereim, Rua Tocantins 86. Min.: Rabbi M.A. Iliovitz, Rua Haddock Lobo 1091. Tel. 282-1562 & 852-9710.
Comunidade Israelita Sefaradi, Rua da Abolicao 457. Tel. 36-9982. Syn.: Templo do Rito Portugues. Same address & Tel. Min.: Rabbi J. Kadoch.
Comunidade Ortodoxa Israelita e K'hal Machzikei Hadass, Rabbi E. B. Valt. Rua Padre Joao Manuel 727. Tel. 282-6762.
Congregacao Israelita Paulista (Liberal), Rua Antonio Carlos 653. Tel. 256-7811.
Congregacao K'hal Chasidim, Rabbi Joel Beer (Ratzferter Rebbe), Rua Mamore 597. Tel. 220-1735.
Congregacao Mekor Haim (Sephardi), Rua Sao Vicente de Paula 254. Tel. 67-2029. Min.: Rabbi Itzhak Dichi.
Congregacao Monte Sinai (Sephardi), Rua Piaui 624. Tel. 66-5303.
Congregacao Tiferet Lubavitch, Rabbi Jacob Begun, Rua Alagoas 726, Higienopolis. Tel. 66 7783.
Sinagoga Beth Jacob, Rua Artur de Azevedo 1781.
Sinagoga Beth Yacov (Syrian & Lebanese), Rabbi Efraim Laniado, Rua Bela Cintra 801. Tel. 256-3115 & 258-7931.
Sinagoga Centro Israelita (Orthodox), Rua Newton Prado 76. Tel. 220-0185.
Sinagoga e Talmud Torah (Orthodox), Rua Tocantins 296. Tel. 220-0225.
Sinagoga Israelita Bras (Sephardi), Rua Odorico Mendes 174. Tel. 279-3145.

Sinagoga Israelita do Bom Retiro, Rua da Graca 160.
Sinagoga Israelita Paulista (Hungarian), Rua Augusta 259. Tel. 256-5970.
Templo Beth-El (Ashkenazi), Rua Avanhandava 137-Esquina Rua
Martinho Prado 128. Tel. 256-8671 & 256-1246.
Mikvaot: Bom Retiro, Rua Tenente Pena 310; Rua Haddock Lobo 1279. Tel.
881-3804; Rua Padre Joao Manoel 727. Tel. 282-6762; Rua Mamore 597.

Communal Organisations, etc.
B'nai B'rith, Rua Cacapava 105. Tel. 282-5589 & 853-4804.
Com. Centre & Syn.: Rua Teixeira Mendes 54. Tel. 278-8919.
Federacao Israelita do Estado de Sao Paulo, Av. Paulista 726, 2nd Floor.
Tel. 288-6411.
Instituto de Cultura Hebraica, Rua Bela
Cintra 1233. Tel. 881-8185.

Hospitals
Albert Einstein, Rua Albert Einstein. Tel. 240-3322.
Linat Hatzedek, Rua Rodolfo Miranda 287. Tel. 227-8011.

Zionist Organisations
All the Zionist orgs. are at Rua Correa Mello 75. Tel. 221-9233 & 220-4133.
Israel Consulate, Rua Luis Coelho 308, 7th Floor. Tel. 257-2111 & 257-2814.

Booksellers
Oitzer Haseforim, Al. Lorena 1178. Tel. 64-6404.
Weltman's, Rua Ribeiro de Lima 604. Tel. 220-5079.

Newspapers, etc.
"O Hebreu" (Portuguese monthly), Rua Mamoré 570. Tel. 220-1717.
"Resenha Judaica" (Portuguese fortnightly), Rua Antonio Carlos 582. Tel.
258-2066.
"Revista Shalom" (Portuguese monthly), Rua da Graca 201. Tel. 220-0265.

Travel Agencies
Monumento Viagens E Turismo Ltda., Rua Augusta, 2516/111. Tel.
2824499. Fax. 2824707.
Vértice, Rua Sâo Bento 545, 10° And. Tel. 36-6341. Fax 34-6530.

Restaurants
★ **Buffet Mosaico**, Rua Hungria 1000. Tel. 815-6788 & 815-6980.
★ **Buffet Wegh**, Rua Correa de Mello 172, Ap. 14. Tel. 227-7304.
★ **Kineret Lanches**, Rua Correa de Mello 162. Tel. 227-6559.
(K) **Tamar**, Rua Alagos 952. Tel. 67 3192.

Bakery & Catering
★ Mazal Tov, Rua Peixoto Gomide 1724. Tel. 645-208 & 282-0761, & Rua
da Graça 68. Tel. 223-1045.

Butchers
(K) Samuel Gaida, Rua da Consolocao 3297. Tel. 852-4773. Under
supervision of Rabbi M. A. Iliovitz.
(K) Mehadrin, Rua Guarani 206. Tel. 227-9141. Under supervision of Rabbi
M. A. Iliovitz.
(K) Tifereth, Rua Martinico Prado 389. Tel. 825-1042 & 826-8588. Under
supervision of Rabbi Elyahu B. Valt.

SOROCABA
Syn. & Com. Centre: Rua Dom Pedro II 56. Tel. 31-3168.
Cong. HAR-EL (C) 1735 Inglewood Av., V7V 1Y8. Tel. (604) 9228245.

BULGARIA
Bulgarian Jewry dates from the 2nd century C.E. when, after the Byzantine conquest, Greek Jews established a congregation in Serdica (now Sofia). After the establishment of the Bulgarian State in 681, Jewish settlement in the country increased, and during the reign of King Ivan Alexander (1331-1371) the Jewish com. flourished. His Queen was Theodora, a former Jewess whose original name was Sarah.
Rabbi Shalom of Nitra founded the first rabbinical school in Vidin, in 1370. His successor, Rabbi Dosa Ajevani, became famous for his commentary on Rashi. In the middle of the 15th century, Ashkenazi Jews driven out of Bavaria settled in Bulgaria and built a synagogue in Sofia. More than 30,000 Jews, expelled from Spain, arrived at the end of the 15th century, among them Joseph Caro, the codifier of the Shulchan Aruch. By the end of the 16th century Bulgaria's Sephardi Jews had assimilated the Ashkenazi and other groups.
By the beginning of the Second World War in 1939, there were about 50,000 Jews in Bulgaria. Since 1948, about 45,000 have emigrated to Israel; and today's Jewish population is about 5,000, of whom 3,200 live in Sofia. The others are scattered throughout the rest of the country. It is worth noting that few Jews became victims of the Nazis during the German occupation of Bulgaria in the Second World War, even though the Bulgarian Government was allied to Nazi Germany, thanks to the support of the Bulgarian population.
General Inf. from Bulgarian National Tourist Office, 18 Princes St., W1R 7RE. Tel. 071-499 6988.

PLOVDIV
Syn.: Tsar Kalojan St. 15 (in the courtyard of a large flats complex).
Library & House of Culture: Vladimir Zaimov St. 20.

SOFIA
Social & Cultural Org. of Bulgarian Jews: Alexander Stambolisky St. 50. The org. publishes a periodical, "Evreiski Vesti", & a yearbook. It also maintains a museum devoted to "The Rescue of Bulgarian Jews, 1941-1944".
Syn. & Central Jewish Religious Council: Ekzarh Josef St. 16. Pres.: Yosif Levy.
Take the No. 2 tram to the last stop for a large Jewish cemetery.

BURMA
(see Union. of Myanmar)

BYELORUS
BARANOVICHI
Syn.: 39 Svobodnaya St.

BOBRUISK
Syn.: Engels St.

BORISOV
Syn.: Trud St.

BREST
Syn.: Narodnaya St.

GOMEL
Syn.: 13 Sennaya St.

MINSK
Syns.: 22 Kropotkin St. Tel. (017-2) 55-82-70; Kommunisticheskaya St.

MOGHILEV
Syn.: 1 2nd Krutoy La.

ORSHA
Syn.: Nogrin St.

RECHITSA
Syn.: 120 Lunacharsky St.

CANADA
Jews played some part in the British military occupation of Canada and a number settled in Montreal at an early date. But in the ten years following the conquest of Quebec in 1759, there were only ten Jews in Canada. A century later, this figure had grown to 1,250. At the end of the 19th century, large-scale emigration began from Eastern Europe, and many emigrants chose to settle in Canada. Today, the Jewish population is about 305,000. Chief centres are Montreal, Toronto and Vancouver.
General inf. from Tourism Canada, Canada Hse., Trafalgar Sq., SW1Y 5BJ. Tel. 071-930 8540.

ALBERTA
CALGARY
Synagogues
House of Jacob (O), 1613 92nd Av. S.W., T2V 4V7; Beth Tzedec (C), 1325 Glenmore Trail S.W., T2Y 4Y8. Tel. (403) 255-8688; Temple B'nai Tikvah (R), Calgary Jewish Centre, 1607 90th Av. S.W. Tel. (403) 252-1654.
Calgary Rabbinical Council. Tel. (403)-253-8600 Fax (403) 253-7915.
Calgary Jewish Community Council, 1607 90th Av. S.W. Tel. (403) 253-8600. The Com. Centre is at the same address. The Council issues a booklet 'Keeping Kosher in Calgary'.

Kosher Food
(K) **Café Merkaz**, Calgary Jewish Centre, 1607 90th Av. S.W. Sun.-Thurs., 10.00 a.m. to 7.00 p.m.; Fri. 10.00 a.m. to 1.00 p.m. Tel. (403) 255-5311.
(K) **Schaier's Meat & Kosher Deli,** 2515 90th Av. S.W. Tel. (403) 251-2552.
(K) **Wolf's Kosher World & Deli,** 42, 180-94 Av. S.E. Sun.-Thurs 10.00 a.m. to 8.00 p.m., Fri. 10.00 a.m. to 2.00 p.m. Tel. (403) 253-3354

EDMONTON
Syns.: Beth Israel, 10205 119th St., T5K 1Z3. Tel. (403) 482-2470; Beth Shalom, 11916 Jasper Av., T5K 0N9. Tel. (403) 488-6333; Temple Beth Ora (R), 7711 140th St., T5R 0H3. Tel. (403) 486-5648.
For additional inf., contact Howard Bloom, Edmonton Jewish Fed., 7200 156th St. Tel. (403) 487-5120.

Newspaper:
Jewish Star, 7200 156th St. T5R 1X3 Tel. 238-0100.
(K) Kosher restaurant at J. Comm. Center 7200 156th St. Tel. (403) 444-4957.

LETHBRIDGE
Syn.: Beth Israel (O), 914 15th St. S. Tel. (403) 327-8621.

MEDICINE HAT
Syn.: Sons of Abraham (O), 540 5th St. S.E., T1A 1S6. Tel. (403) 526-3880.

BRITISH COLUMBIA

RICHMOND
Syns.: Eitz Chaim (O), 8080 Francis Rd., V6Y 1A4. Tel. (604) 275-0007; Beth Tikvah (C), 9711 Geal Rd., V7E 1R4. Tel. (604) 271-6262.
Orthodox Rabbinical Council of B.C. (604)-275-0042. Fax (604) 277-2225.
Richmond Jewish Day School, P.O. Box. 36523, Richmond V7C 5M4. Tel. (604) 275-3393.

SURREY - WHITE ROCK
Syn: Chabad (O) 210-6950 Nicholson Rd., Delta V4A 127. Tel. 596-9030.

VANCOUVER
Vancouver, has a Jewish population of 30,000. The Jewish presence in B.C. is comparatively recent with the first Jews arriving on the heels of the news of the Cariboo gold rush of 1858. They were followed some thirty-five years later by European Jews escaping from religious and economic persecution. Jews have continued to come to B.C., mainly to Vancouver, from Europe, the Orient, Israel, South America and South Africa forming a sophisticated and international community. Many Jews have moved to Vancouver from eastern Canada and the Prairie Provinces.
Information on many smaller cities in the Province with Jewish communities can be obtained from Shalom Vancouver.

Synagogues
Beth Hamidrash Cong. (S), 3231 Heather St. V5Z 3K4. Tel. (604) 872-4222.
Congregation Beth Israel (C), 4350 Oak St., V6H 2N4 Tel. (604) 731-4161.
Har-El Cong. (C). 1735 Inglewood Av., West Vancouver, B.C., Tel. (604) 922-8245.
Chabad-Lubavitch Centre (O), 5750 Oak St., V6M 2V9. Tel. (604) 266-1313.
Louis Brier Chapel (O), 1055 West.41st Av., V6M 1W9. Tel. (604) 261-9376.
Schara Tzedeck Cong. (O), 3476 Oak St., V6H 2L8. Tel. (604) 736-7607.
Or Shalom (T), 561 West 28th Av., V5Z 2H2. Tel. (604) 872-1614.
Temple Shalom (R), 7190 Oak St., V69 3ZP Tel. (604) 266-7190.

Other Organisations
Shalom Vancouver - Jewish Information, Referral & Welcome Service for newcomers and visitors, 950 West 41st Av. Tel. (604) 266-9111. Publishes a 'Guide to the Jewish Communities of Vancouver and B.C'. Coordinator: Janet Kolof.
Canadian Jewish Congress (Pacific Region), 950 West 41st Av., V5Z 2N7. Tel. (604) 261-8101. Exec. Dir.: Erwin Nest.
Jewish Community Centre of Greater Vancouver. 950 West 41st Av., V5z 2N7. tel. (604) 266-911. Exec. Dir.: Gerry Zipursky.
Jewish Federation of Greater Vancouver. 950 West 41st Av., V5Z 2N7. Tel. (604) 266-8371.
Hillel House/Network, University of British Columbia. Tel. (604) 224-4748 & 224 2512. Exec Dir : Zack Kaye.
Louis Brier Home and Hospital: 1055 West 41st Av. V6M 1W9 Tel. (604) 261-9376. Only Jewish facility of its kind in B.C. Admin: Ken Levitt.

Accommodation
Mrs. Louise Houta, 638 West 17th Av., V5Z 1T8. Tel. (604) 872-3887, can provide accom. close to the syn., transport, shopping, etc.

Kosher Food
Cafe Mercaz. Jewish Community Centre, 950 West 41st Av., V5Z 2N7. Tel. (604) 266-9111.
Leon's Kosher Korner, 3710 Oak St. Tel. (604) 736-6348. Butcher shop, Bakery.
Kosher Food under supervision of Orthodox Rabbinical Council of B.C. Tel. (604) 275-0042. Rabbi Mordechai Feurstein, Rabbinic Administrator Fax (604) 277-2225.
For vegetarian restaurants contact Shalom Vancouver, 950 West 41st Av., Tel. (604) 266-9111.

Newspaper
Jewish Western Bulletin, 3268 Heather St., Vancouver V5Z 3K5. Tel. (604) 879-6575. Fax (604) 879-6573.

VICTORIA
Syn.: Cong. Emanuel (C), 1461 Blanshard St., V8W 2O3. Tel. (604) 382-0615.

MANITOBA

WINNIPEG
Synagogues & Religious Organisations
Ashkenazi Congregation (O), 297 Burrows Av., R2W 1Z7. Tel. (204) 589-1517.
Bnay Abraham (O), 235 Enniskillen Av., R2V 0H6. Tel. (204) 339-9297.
Chavurat Tefila (O), 459 Hartford Av., R2V 0W9. Tel. (204) 338-9451.
Chevra Mishnayes (O), 700 Jefferson Av., R2V 0P6. Tel. (204) 338-8503.
Herzlia-Adas Yeshurun (O), 620 Brock St. at Fleet Av., R3N 0Z4. Tel. (204) 489-6262 or 489-6668.
Lubavitch Centre. (O), 2095 Sinclair St., R2V 3K2. Tel. (204) 339-8737.
Talmud Torah-Beth Jacob (O), 427 Matheson Av., R2W 0E1. Tel. (204) 589-5345.
Beth Israel (C), 1007 Sinclair St., R2V 3J5. Tel. (204) 582-2353.
Rosh Pina (C), 123 Matheson Av. E., R2W 0C3. Tel. (204) 589-6306.
Shaarey Zedek (C), 561 Wellington Cres., R3M 0A6. Tel. (204) 452-3711.
Temple Shalom (R), 1077 Grant Av., R3M 1Y6. Tel. (204) 453-1625.
Mikveh Chabad-Lubavitch, 455 Hartford Av., R2V 0W9. Tel. 338-4761.
Vaad Ha'Ir, 370 Hargrave St., R3B 2K1. Tel. 943-0406. Fax 956-0609. The Vaad Ha'ir will be pleased to give inf. about kashrut.

Representative Organisations
B'nai B'rith Canada, Mid-West Region, 2nd Floor, 370 Hargrave Av., R3B 2K1. Tel. (204) 942-2597.
National Council of Jewish Women, 1588 Main St., R2V 1Y3. Tel. (204) 339-7291.
Winnipeg Jewish Community Council/
Canadian Jewish Congress, 200-370 Hargrave St., R3B 2K1. Tel. (204) 943-0406.
Y.M.H.A. Jewish Com. Centre, 370 Hargrave St., R3B 2K1. Tel. (204) 947-0601.

Cultural & Educational Organisations, etc.

B'nai Brith Jewish Community Camp, c/o YMHA Jewish Community Centre, 370 Hargrave St., R3B 2K1, Tel. (204) 947-0601.

B'nai Brith Youth Organisation (usually referred to in North America as "BBYO". c/o YMHA, 370 Hargrave St., R3B 2K1. Tel. (204) 943-0406, Ext. 251 0r 252.

Camp Massad, #25-370 Hargrave St., R3B 2K1. Tel. (204) 943-2815.

Jewish Historical Society of Western Canada, #404 -365 Hargrave St., R3B 2K3. Tel. (204) 942-8422.

Jewish Public Library, 1725 Main St., R2V 1Z4. Tel. (204) 338-4048.

Jewish Student Assoc. Co-ordinator, c/o Y.M.H.A., 370 Hargrave St., R3B 2K1. Tel. (204) 947-0601.

Joseph Wolinsky Collegiate Institute, 437 Matheson Av., R2W 0E1. Tel. (204) 589-5345.

Sarah Sommer Chai Folk Ensemble, c/o 370 Hargrave St., R3B 2K1, Tel. (204) 956-1765.

Winnipeg Board of Jewish Education, 200-370 Hargrave St., R3B 2K1. Tel. (204) 949-1482.

Winnipeg Jewish Theatre, #504-365 Hargrave St., R3B 2K3. Tel. (204) 943-3222.

YMHA Jewish Community Centre Day Camp (Summers Only), 370 Hargrave St., R3B 2K1. Tel. (204) 947-0601, Ext. 227.

Welfare Organisations, Homes, etc.

Jewish Child & Family Service, 2055 McPhillips St., R2V 3C6. Tel. (204) 338-0358.

Sharon Home for Aged, 146 Magnus Av., R2W 2B4. Tel. (204) 586-9781.

Zionist Organisations

Canadian Zionist Federation, Mid-West Region, 303-365 Hargrave St., R3B 2K3. Tel. (204) 943-6494.

Hadassah-WIZO Council of Winnipeg, 205-309 Hargrave St., R3B 2J8. Tel. (204) 942-8201.

Histadrut-Amal, 1727 Main St., R2V 1Z4. Tel. (204) 339-5755.

J.N.F., 401-365 Hargrave St., R3B 2K3. Tel. (204) 947-0207.

Naamat Council of Jewish Women 1727 Main St., R2V 1Z4. Tel. (204) 334-3637.

State of Israel Bonds, #606-283 Portage Av., R3B 2B5. Tel. (204) 942-2291.

Local Offices of Israeli Universities

Canadian Associates of Ben-Gurion University, #127-167 Lombard Av., R3B 0T6. Tel. (024) 237-7519.

Canadian Friends of the Hebrew University, #1063 - 167 Lombard Av., R3B 0V3. Tel. (204) 942-3085.

Canadian Technion Society, #506 - 365 Hargrave St., R3B 2K3. Tel. (204) 942 2446.

Miscellaneous

B'nai Brith Women of Winnipeg, #207-2211 McPhillips St., R2V 3M5. Tel. 338-8229.

Glendale Country Club, 400 Augier Av. Tel. (204) 832-1306.

Gwen Secter Creative Living Centre, 1588 Main St., R2V 1Y3. Tel. (204) 339-1709.

Winnipeg Women's ORT, 190 Sherbrook St., R3C 2B6. Tel. (204) 786-6789.

Jewish Media

Jewish Post & News, 117 Hutchings St., R2X 2V4. Tel. (204) 694-3332.

Jewish Radio Hour Weekly— Sundays, at 1.30 p.m.
WJCC Presents T.V. show Channel 11, Monthly — Sundays, at 12.00 Noon.
Yiddish TV Hour. Channel 11—Tuesdays, 8.30 p.m. (repeated on Wednesdays, 3.00 p.m.)

Kosher Restaurant
(K) Cafe Shalom, Y.M.H.A. Jewish Com. Centre, 370 Hargrave St., R3B 2K1. Tel. (204) 942-6625.
"Desserts Plus" — 1595 Main St., R2V 1Y2. Tel. (204) 339-1957.
Gwen Secter Creative Living Centre, 1588 Main St., R2v 1Y3. Tel. (204) 339-1709.

Kosher Bakeries
(K) City Bread, 238 Dufferin Av., R2W 2X6. Tel. (204) 586-8409; **(K)** Gunn's, 247 Selkirk Av., R2W 2L5. Tel. (204) 582-2364; **(K)** Miracle Bakery, 1385 Main St., R2W 3T9. Tel. (204) 586-6140. **(K)** Goodies' Bake Shop, 2 Donald St., R3L 0K5. Tel. 489-5526/949-2480. Hearthstone Bakery, 635 Leila Ave., R2V 3N7. Tel. (204) 339-8929.

Kosher Butchers
Acme Produce, 525 Jarvis St. Tel. (204) 589-6454; **(K)** Omnitsky's, 1428 Main St., R2W 3V4. Tel. (204) 586-8271; **(K)** Tuxedo IGA. 1853 Grant Av., Tel. (204) 489-1563.

Kosher Food
Eliyahu's Food Mart, 686 McGregor St., R2V 3E5. Tel. (204) 586-4514.

NEW BRUNSWICK
FREDERICTON
Syn.: Sgoolai Israel (O), Westmoreland St. E3B 3L7. Tel. (506) 454-9698. Mikva on premises.

MONCTON
Syn.: Tiferes Israel (O), 50 Steadman St., E1C 4P4. Tel. (506) 858-0258. Mikva on premises.

SAINT JOHN
Syn.: Shaarei Zedek (C), 76 Carleton St., E2L 2Z4. Tel. (506) 454-9698.
Com. Centre. Tel. (506) 657-1962.
Beth Israel (C), 4350 Oak St., V6H 2N4. Tel. (604) 731-4161. School 731-1313.
Temple Sholom (R), 7190 Oak St., V6P 3Z9. Tel. (604) 266-7190.

NEWFOUNDLAND
ST. JOHN'S
Syn.: Hebrew Congregation of Newfoundland (Beth El) (C), 128 Elizabeth Av., A1B 1S3. Tel. (709) 726-0480. Kosher food available. Inq. to syn.

NOVA SCOTIA
GLACE BAY
Syn.: Sons of Israel (O), 1 Prince St., B1A 3C8. Tel. (902) 849-8605.

HALIFAX
Syns.: Beth Israel (O), 1480 Oxford St., B3H 3Y8. Tel. (902) 422-1301. Mikva

on premises; Shaar Shalom (C), 1981 Oxford St., B3H 4A4. Tel. (902) 423 5848.
Atlantic Jewish Council, 1515 S. Park St., Suite 304, B3J 2L2. Tel. (902) 422-7491. Also at this address: Canadian Jewish Congress; Canadian Zionist Fed.; United Israel Appeal; ORT; Young Judea; B'nai B'rith; Hadassah; Jewish National Fund; Atlantic Provinces Jewish Student Federation; Chabad-Lubavitch.

Newspaper
Shalom, 1515 S. Park St., Suite 304, B3J 2L2. Tel. 422-7491.

SYDNEY
Syn.: Temple Sons of Israel (C), P.O. Box 311, Whitney Av., B1P 6H2. Tel. (902) 564-4650.

YARMOUTH
Syn.: Agudath Achim (C), 42 William St., B5A 1Y3.

ONTARIO
BELLEVILLE
Syn.: Sons of Jacob (C), 211 Victoria Av., K8N 5A2. Tel. (613) 962-1433.

BRANTFORD
Syn.: Beth David (O), 50 Waterloo St., N3T 3R8. Tel. (519) 752-8950.

CHATHAM
Syn.: Children of Jacob (C), 29 Water St. N7M 3H4. Tel. (519) 352-3544.

CORNWALL
Syn.: Beth-El (C), 321 Amelia St., K6H 3P4. Tel. (613) 932-6373.

GUELPH
Syn.: Beth Isaiah (O), 47 Surrey St. W., N1H 3R5. Tel. (519) 822-8487.

HAMILTON
Synagogues
Adas Israel (O), 125 Cline Av. S., L8S 1X2. Tel. (416) 528-0039.
Beth Jacob (C), 375 Aberdeen Av., L8P 2R7. Tel. (416) 522-1351.
Anshe Sholom (R), 215 Cline Av. N., L8S 4A1. Tel. (416) 528-0121.
Communal inq. to Mrs. Clare Mandel. Exec. Dir., Hamilton Jewish Fed., 1030 Lower Lions Club Rd., Ancaster, L9G 3N6. Tel. (416) 648-0605.

Newspaper
Hamilton Jewish News, PO Box 7528, L9G 3N6. Tel. 648-0605.

KINGSTON
Syns.: Beth Israel (O), 116 Centre St., K7L 4E6. Tel. (613) 542-5012.
Temple Iyr Hamelech (R), 331 Union St. W., K7L 2R3.
B'nai B'rith Hillel Foundation, 26 Barrie St. Tel. (613) 542-1120.

KITCHENER
Syn.: Beth Jacob (O), 161 Sterling Av. S., N2G 3N8. Tel. (519) 743-8422.

LONDON
Syns.: Beth Tefilah (O), 1210 Adelaide St. N., N5Y 4T6. Tel. (519) 433-7081.
Mikva on premises; Cong. Or Shalom (C), 534 Huron St., N5Y 4J5. Tel.

(519) 438-3081; Temple Israel (R), 651, Windermere Rd., N5X 2P1. Tel. (519) 858-4400.
Communal inq. to Gerry Enchin, Exec. Dir., Jewish Com. Council, 534 Huron St. Tel. (519) 433-2201.

Newspaper
London Jewish Community News, 536 Huron St., N5Y 4J5. Tel. 673-3310.
Kosher frozen meat, prepared foods & selected groceries available. Inq. to M. Sober, Tel. (519) 438-7486.

MISSISSAUGA
Syn.: Solel Cong. (R), 2399 Folkway Dr., L5L 2M6. Tel. (416) 820-5915.

NIAGARA FALLS
Syn.: B'nai Jacob (C), 5328 Ferry St., L2G 1R7. Tel. (416) 354 3934.

NORTH BAY
Syn.: Sons of Jacob (O), 302 McIntyre St. W., P1B 2Z1. Tel. (705) 474-2170.

OAKVILLE
Syn.: Shaarei-Beth El (C), 186 Morrison Rd., L6L 4J4. Tel. (416) 845-0837.

OSHAWA
Syn.: Beth Zion (O), 144 King St. E., L1H 1B6. Tel. (416) 723-2353.

OTTAWA
Synagogues & Religious Organisations
Adath Shalom Cong. (O), Tel. 613-228-0574.
Beth Shalom (O), 151 Chapel St., K1N 7Y2. Tel. (613) 232-3501.
Beth Shalom West (O), 15 Chartwell Av., Nepean, K2G 4K3. Tel. (613) 723-1800.
Chabad Hse., 64 Templeton St. Tel. (613) 234-6214.
Machzikei Hadas (O), 2310 Virginia Dr., K1N 6S2. Tel. (613) 521-9700.
Young Israel of Ottawa (O), 627 Kirkwood Av., K1Z 5X5. Tel. (613) 722-8394.
Agudath Israel (C), 1400 Coldrey Av., K1Z 7P9. Tel. (613) 728-3501.
Temple Israel (R), 1301 Prince of Wales Dr., K2C 1N2. Tel. (613) 224-1802.

Representative Organisations
B'nai B'rith, Men's Lodges. Inf. from L. Bronstein, 50 Beaver Ridge. Tel. (613) 998-9060. Women's Chapters. Inf. from Mrs. Paul Eisenberger, 392 Piccadilly Av. Tel. (613) 729-1859.
Com. Centre, 151 Chapel St. Tel. (613) 232-7306.
Jewish Social Services Agency. Tel. (613) 235 6000.
Jewish Students' Union. Tel. (613) 232-7306.
Vaad Ha'ir (Jewish Com. Council), 151 Chapel St. Tel. (613) 232-7306. Exec. Dir.: Gerry Koffman and Vaad Hakashruth (Fax (613) 563-4593).
Israel Embassy, Suite 601, 410 Laurier Av. W., K1R 7T3. (613) Tel. 237-6450.

Newspaper
Ottawa Jewish Bulletin & Review, See Vaad Ha'ir above.

Club
Rideau View Golf & Country Club, Pres.: D. Molot, 185 Metcalfe St., Manotick. Tel. (613) 692-4112.

Kosher Meals
From Oct. to June, a **(K)** kosher Sun. evg. meal is available at Young Israel of Ottawa. Address & Tel. above.

Kosher Meat, etc.
(K) United Kosher Meat & Deli Ltd., 378 Richmond Rd. Tel. (613) 722-6556. (Meals & sandwiches available on week-days.)
(K) Kosher bread & other products are available from Rideau Bakery, 384 Rideau St. Tel. (613) 234-1019, & 1666 Bank St. Tel. (613) 737-3355.

OWEN SOUND
Beth Ezekiel (C), 313 11th St. E., N4K 1V1. Tel. (519) 376-8774.

PEMBROKE
Syn.: Beth Israel, 322 William St., K8A 1P3. Tel. (613) 732-7811.

ST. CATHARINES
Syns.: B'nai Israel (C), 190 Church St., L2R 4C4. Tel. (416) 685-6767; Temple Tikvah (R), 83 Church St., P.O.B. 484., L2R 3C7. Tel. (416) 682-4191.
Com. Centre, Newman Memorial Bldg. Tel. MU 5-6767.

SUDBURY
Syn.: Shaar Hashomayim (O), 158 John St., P3E 1P4. Tel. (705) 673-0831.

THORNHILL
Syn.: Beth Avraham Yaakov of Tor (O), 613 Clark Av. W. L4J 3E3. Tel. (416) 886-3810; Chabad Lubavitch Com. Centre (O), 770 Chabad Gate, L4J 3V9. Tel. (416) 731-7000; Chabad Lubavitch of Markham, 135 Holm Cres., L3T 5J4. Tel. (416) 881-2012; B'nai Shalom N. (C), 275 Arnold Av., L4J 1C3. Tel. (416) 731-2797; Shaareh Haim (C), 9711 Bayview Av., L4C 4X7. Tel. (416) 884-3353; Shaar Shalom (C), 2 Simonston Blvd., L3T 4L1. Tel. (416) 889-4975; Temple Har Zion (R), 7360 Bayview Av., L3T 2R7. Tel. (416) 889-2252; Temple Kol Ami (R). Tel. (416) 660-5199.
Bookseller: Israel's The Judaica Centre, 441 Clark Av. W., L4J 6W7. Tel. (616) 881-1010.

THUNDER BAY
Syn.: Shaarey Shomayim (O), 627 Gray St. P7E 2E4. Tel. (416) 622 4867.

TORONTO
Synagogues & Religious Organisations
Orthodox
Agudath Israel, 129 McGilvray Av., M5M 2Y7. (416) 789-5514; Anshei Minsk, 12 St. Andrew's St., M5T 1K6. Tel. (416) 593-9892; Associated Hebrew Schools Chapel, 3630 Bathurst St., M6A 2E3. Tel. (416) 789-7471; Associated Hebrew Schools Chapel, 252 Finch Av. W., M2R 1M9. Tel. (416) 223-4845; Bais Hamedrash N'siv Olam, 2837 Bathurst St., M6B 3A4. Tel. (416) 782-5986; Baycrest Centre Syn., 3560 Bathurst St., M6A 2E1. Tel. (416) 789-5131; Beach Hebrew Institute Syn., 109 Kenilworth Av., M4L 3S4. Tel. (416) 694-7942; Beth Abraham, 55 Ameer Av., M6A 2Z1. Tel. (416) 789-5131; Beth Haminyan, 145 Ava Rd.; Beth Jacob V'Anshe Drildz, 147 Overbrook Pl., Downsview, M3H 4R1. Tel. (416) 638-5955; Beth Knesseth Anshei Stashov, Slipia, 11 Sultana Av., M6A 1S9. Tel. (416) 789-1333; Beth Lida Forest Hill Syn., 22 Gilgorm Rd., M5N 2M5. Tel. (416) 489-2550; Beth Radom Cong., 18 Reiner Rd., Downsview, M3H 2K9. Tel. (41) 636-3451; B'nai Akiva Yeshiva Cong., 159 Almore Av., M3H 2M9. Tel. (416) 630-6772;

Chevra Shass, 3545 Bathurst St., M6A 2C7. Tel. (416) 781-7126; Cong. Bais Moshe, 81 Bannockburn Av., M6M 2M9. Tel. (416) 781-6421; Cong. B'nai Torah, 465 Patricia Av., Willowdale, M2R 2N1. Tel. (416) 226-3700; Chasedei Bobov, 3703 Bathurst St., M6H 2E8. Tel. (416) 789-0971; First Russian Cong., 25 Bellevue Av., M5T 2N5. Tel. (416) 593-9702; JEP/OHR Somayach Centre of Jewish Learning, 2939 Bathurst St., M6B 2B2. Tel. (416) 787-1681; Kehillat Shaarei Torah, 2640 Bayview Av., Willowdale, M2L 1B7. Tel. (416) 229-2600; Keser Torah, 3387 Bathurst St., M6A 2B8; Kielcer Cong., 2941 Bathurst St., M6B 3B2. Tel. (416) 783-0522; King David Cong., 3173A Bathurst St., M6A 2B1. Tel. (416) 782-7075; Kol Yaakov Anshei Emes, 20 Brunswick Av., M5S 2L7. Tel. (416) 488-1865; Kolel Averichim, 515 Coldstream Av., M6B 2K7. Tel. (416) 783-9314; Lincoln Place Nursing Home, 429 Walmer Rd., Tel. (916) 967 6949; Machzikei Hadath Clanton Park, 11 Lowesmoor Av., Downsview, M3H 3H6. Tel. (416) 633-4193; Magen David Sephardic Cong., 10 McAllister Rd., Downsview, M3H 2M9. Tel. (416) 636-0865; Minyan Avreichem, 2919 Bathurst St., M6B 3B1. Tel. (416) 789-4731; Minyan Sepharad, 475 Patricia Av., Willowdale, M2R 2N1. Tel. (416) 226-3145; Mishkan Avraham, 45 Canyon Av., Downsview, M3H 3S4. Tel. (416) 630-772; Moriah, 65 Waterloo Av., Downsview, M3H 3Y1. Tel. (416) 636-9707; Moriah Inst. Cong., 11 Kainona Av., Downsview, M3H 3H4. Tel. (416) 636-6820; Or Haemet Sephardic School, 37 Southbourne Av., Downsview, M3H 1A4. Tel. (416) 635-9881; Petah Tikva Anshe Castilla, 20 Danby Av., Downsview, M3H 2J3. Tel. (416) 636-4719; Shaarei Shomayim Cong., 470 Glencairn Av., M5N 1V8. Tel. (416) 789-3213; Shaare Tefillah Anshei Lubavitch, 3600 Bathurst St., M6A 2C9. Tel. (416) 787-1631; Shaarei Tzedek, Markham St. (at Ulster); Shaarei Zion Assoc. Hebrew, 6100 Leslie St., Willowdale, M2H 3J1. Tel. (416) 491-6121; Shomer Israel Cong., 60 Rockford Rd., Willowdale, M2R 3A7. Tel. (416) 665-4815; Shomrei Shabboth Chevra Mishnayoth, 583 Glengrove Av. W., M6B 2H5. Tel. (416) 782-8849; Tiferet Israel, 756 Sheppard Av. W., Downsview, M3H 2S8. Tel. (416) 635-7435; Torah V'Avodah B'nei Akivah, 296 Wilson Av., Downsview, M3H 1S8. Tel. (416) 630-9266; Torath Emeth Jewish Centre, 1 Viewmount Av., M6B 1T2. Tel. (416) 782-9676; Yavneh Zion, 788 Marlee Av., M6B 3J9. Tel. (416) 781-1611; Yeshiva Limudei Hashem Cong., 517 Glengarry Av., M5M 1G2. Tel. (416) 783-2494; Yeshiva Torath Chaim, 475 Lawrence Av., W., M5M 1C6. Tel. (416) 781-6941; Zichron Shneur, 2801-3 Bathurst St., M6B 3A4. Tel. (416) 781-0136.

Conservative
Adath Israel, 37 Southbourne Av., M3H 1A4. Tel. (416) 635-5340; Adath Sholom, 864 Sheppard Av. W., Downsview, M3H 2T5. Tel. (416) 635-0131; Bernard Betel Centre, 1003 Steeles Av. W., Willowdale M2R 3T6. Tel. (416) 225-2112; Beth David B'nai Israel Beth Am, 55 Yeomans Rd., Downsview, M3H 3J7. Tel. (416) 633-5500; Beth Emeth Bais Yehuda, 100 Elder St., Downsview, M3H 5G7. Tel. (416) 633-3838; Beth Sholom, 1445 Eglinton Av. W., M6C 2E6. Tel. (416) 783-6103; Beth Tikvah, 3080 Bayview Av., Willowdale, M2N 5L3. Tel. (416) 221-3433; Beth Torah, 47 Glenbrook Av., M6B 2L7. Tel. (416) 782-4495; Beth Tzedec, 1700 Bathurst St., M5P 3K3. Tel. (416) 781-3511; Cong. Beth Habonim, 12 Hollaman Rd., M6B 3B8. Tel. (416) 782-5125; Pride of Israel Temple, 59 Lissom Cres., Willowdale, M2R 2P2. Tel. (416) 661-0505.

Reform
Baycrest Terrace Reform Cong., 55 Ameer Av., M6A 2Z1. Tel. (416) 789-5131; Holy Blossom Temple, 1950 Bathurst St., M5P 3K9. Tel. (416) 789-3291; Temple Emanu-El, 120 Old Colony Rd., Willowdale, M2L 2K2. Tel.

(416) 449-3880; Temple Sinai, 210 Wilson Av., M5M 3B1. Tel. (416) 487-4161.

Other

Darchei Noam (Reconstructionist), 4140 Bathurst St., Suite 221, Downsview, M3H 3P3. Tel. (416) 638-4783; First Narayever Egalitarian Minyan (Egalitarian), 187-189 Brunswick Av., M5S 2M4. Tel. (416) 928-0471; Knesseth Israel, 52 Maria St., M6P 1W2. Tel. (416) 967-1019; Lodzer Centre Holocaust Cong., 12 Heaton St., Downsview, M3H 4Y6. Tel. (416) 636-6665.

Representative Organisations

B'nai B'rith, 15 Hove St., Downsview.

Canadian Council of Liberal Congregations, 534 Lawrence Av. W., Suite 305. Tel. (416) 787-9838 & 787-8200. Exec. Dir.: Rabbi Daniel K. Gottlieb.

Canadian Jewish Congress (Ontario Region), 4600 Bathurst St., Willowdale, M2R 3V2. Tel. (416) 635-2883.

National Council of Jewish Women of Canada, 4700 Bathurst St. National Office: 1111 Finch Av. W. Tel. (416) 633-1251.

National Joint Com. Relations Committee, & Canadian Jewish Congress, 4600 Bathurst St., Willowdale, M2R 3V2 Tel. (416) 635-2883. Exec. Dir.: Manuel Prutschi. Also at this address: Jewish Federation of Greater Toronto, Tel. (416) 635-2883. Exec. Dir.: Steven Ain; Rabbinical Vaad Hakashrut, Tel. (416) 635-9550. Exec. Dir.: Rabbi M. Levin; Council of Jewish Feds., Tel. (416) 635-9567. (All enquiries re Kashrut here.)

Canadian Council for Reform Judaism, 1520 Steele's Av. West, Suite 113. Concord L4K 2P7. Tel. (416) 660-4666.

Cultural & Educational Organisations

Board of Jewish Education, 4600 Bathurst St., Willowdale, M2R 3V2. Tel. (416) 633-7770. Exec. Dir.: Rabbi I. Witty.

Holocaust Education & Memorial Centre, 4600 Bathurst St., Willowdale, M2R 3V2. Tel. (416) 635-2883.

Jewish Inf. Service, 4600 Bathurst St., Suite 345, Willowdale, M2R 3V2. Tel. (416) 635-5600.

Jewish Public Library. See entry above.

Oskar Asher Schmidt Museum. Same address as Jewish Inf. Service.

Welfare Organisations, Hospitals, etc.

Jewish Assistance Services, 4600 Bathurst St., Willowdale, M2R 3V2. Exec. Dir.: Dvora Danziger. Tel. (416) 635-1217.

Jewish Family & Child Service, 4600 Bathurst St., Willowdale, M2R 3V2. Tel. (416) 638-7800.

Jewish Home for the Aged, 3560 Bathurst St. Tel. RU 9-5131.

Jewish Immigrant Aid Services, 4600 Bathurst St., Willowdale, M2R 3V2. Tel. (416) 630-6481.

New Mount Sinai Hospital, 600 University Av.

Student & Youth Organisations

B'nai B'rith Hillel Foundation (at the University of Toronto), 604 Spadina Av. Tel. (416) 923-9861.

Jewish Camp Council, 750 Spadina Av. Tel. (416) WA 4-6211.

Jewish Com. Centre, 4588 Bathurst St., Willowdale. Tel. (416) ME 6-1880. Also at 750 Spadina Av. Tel. (416) 924-6211.

York University Jewish Students' Federation, CS 106, Ross Bldg., York University, 4700 Keele St., Downsview. Tel. (416) 667-3647 & 667-3648.

Zionist Organisations

Borochov Centre, 272 Codsell Av., Downsview, M3H 3X2. Tel. (416) 636-4021.
Canadian Zionist Fed., 1110 Finch Av., W., Downsview, M3J 2T2. Tel. (416) 665-7935.
Hadassah, 788 Marlee Av. Tel. (416) 789-4373.
Hapoel Hamizrachi, 296 Wilson Av., Downsview.
Hashomer Hatzair, 181 Cocksfield Av., Downsview.
Jewish National Fund, 4600 Bathurst St., M2R 3V2. Tel. (416) 638-7200.
Labour Zionist Movement & Histadrut Campaign, 272 Codsell Av., Downsview.
Toronto Zionist Council, 788 Marlee Av. Tel. (416) 781-3571.
United Israel Appeal of Canada, 4600 Bathurst St., Willowdale, M2R 3V2. Tel. (416) 636-7655. Exec. Dir.: S. Ain.
United Jewish Appeal. Same address as above. Tel. (416) 635-2883.
Israel Consulate, 180 Bloor St., W., Suite 700. Tel. (416) 961-1126.

Newspaper

Canadian Jewish News, 10 Gateway Blvd., Suite 420, Don Mills, M3C 3A1. Tel. (416) 422-2331. Fax (416) 422-3790.

Booksellers, etc.

Israel's, The Judaica Centre, 973 Eglinton Av. W., M6C 2C4. Tel. (416) 789-2169. Also, 441 Clark Av., Thornhill, Ont. Tel. 881-1010.
Miriam's, 3007 Bathurst St. Tel. (416) 781-8261.
Negev Importing Co. Ltd., 3509 Bathurst St., M6A 2C5. Tel. (416) 781-9356.
Pardes Hebrew Book Shop, 4119 Bathurst St. Tel. (416) 633-7113.
Zucker's Books & Art, 3453 Bathurst St.

Restaurants & Delicatessen

(K) Bagels Galore (dairy, take-out), First Canadian Pl. Tel. (416) 363-4233.
(K) Chopstix, 3426 Bathurst St. Tel. (416) 787-0345.
(K) Marky's Fine Dining, 355 Wilson Av., Downsview, M3H 1T3. Tel. (416) 636-0163.
(K) Kosher Facilities, York University, 4700 Keele St., Downsview. Tel. (416) 667-3550.
(K) Marky's Delicatessen, 280 Wilson Av., Downsview. Tel. (416) 638-1081.
(K) Mati's Fallafel House (dairy products only), 3430 Bathurst St. Tel. (416) 783-9505.

(K) Milk'n Honey (dairy), 3457 Bathurst St., Downsview. Tel. (416) 789-7651

WINDSOR

Syns.: Shaar Hashomayim (O), 115 Giles Blvd. E., N9A 4C1. Tel. (519) 256-3123; Shaarey Zedek (O), 610 Giles Blvd. E., N9A 4E2. Tel. (519) 252-1594; Cong. Beth-Él (R), 2525 Mark Av., N9E 2W2. Tel. (519) 969-2422.
Jewish Com. Council, 1641 Ouellette Av. Ont. N8X 1K9. Exec. Dir.: Allan Juris. Tel. (519) 973-1772.
Windsor Jewish Community Bulletin, Fax (519) 973-1774.

QUEBEC

MONTREAL

Synagogues & Religious Organisations
Orthodox
Adath Israel Poale Zedek Cong., 223 Harrow Cres., Hampstead, H3X 2X7. Tel. (514) 482-4252.
Anshei Ozeroff, 5380 Bourret St., H3X 1J2. Tel. (514) 738-2012.
Beth Hamedrash Hagadol, 4605 Mackenzie St., H3W 1B2. Tel. (514) 733-5356.
Beth Hazichoron, 3910 de Courtrai Av., H3S 1C1. Tel. (514) 733-8007.
Beth Hillel, 6230 Coolbrook Av., H3X 2M8. Tel. (515) 731-8708.
Beth Israel Beth Aaron Cong., 6800 Mackle Rd., Cote St. Luc, H4W 1A4. Tel. (514) 487-1323.
Beth Tikvah, 136 Westpark Blvd., Dollard des Ormeaux, H9A 2K2. Tel. (514) 683-5610.
Beth Zion, 5740 Hudson Av., Cote St. Luc, H4W 2K5. Tel. (514) 489-8411.
Chevra Kadisha, 5237 Clanranald Av., H3X 2S5. Tel. (514) 482-3366.
Chevra Mishnais Jacob Joseph, 715 du Sablon Av., Chomedey, H7W 4H5. Tel. (514) 681-5844.
Chevra Shas Shevet Achim, 5855 Lavoie St., H3W 2K1. Tel. (514) 731-3231.
Chevra Thillim-Pinsker Kinyan Torah, 1904 Van Horne Av., H3S 1N7. Tel. (514) 737-6206.
Cong. Beth Ora, 2600 Badeaux St., Ville St. Laurent, H4M 1M5. Tel. (514) 748-6559.
Shomrim Laboker, 5150 Plamondon Av., H3W 1G1. Tel. (514) 731-6831.
Tifereth Beth David Jerusalem, 6519 Baily Rd., Cote St. Luc, H4V 1A1. Tel. (514) 489-3841.
Young Israel of Chomedey, 1025 Elizabeth Blvd., H7W 3J7. Tel. (514) 681-2571.
Young Israel of Montreal, 6235 Hillsdale Rd., H3S 2M8. Tel. (514) 737-6589.
Young Israel of Val Royal, 2855 Victor Dore, Ville St. Laurent, H3M 1T1. Tel. (514) 334-4610.
Zichron Kedoshim, 5215 Westbury Av., H3W 2W4. Tel. (514) 735-2113.

Orthodox Sephardi
Beth Menouha, Adath Yeshurun, 5855 Lavoie St., H3W 2K1. Tel. (514) 739-7142.
Beth Yossef, 6235 Hillsdale Rd., H3S 2M8. Tel. (514) 737-6589.
Centre Communautaire Juif-YMHA, 5480 Westbury Av., H3W 3G2. Tel. (514) 735-5565.
Communauté Sépharade de Chomedey 4880 Du Souvenier, Chomedey H7W 1C9. Tel. 514-682-2467.

Communauté Sépharade de Laval, 4860 Notre Dame Blvd., Chomedey, H7W 1V4. Tel. (514) 682-6606.
Communauté Sépharade Petah Tikvah, 2650 St. Louis St., Ville St. Laurent, H4M 1P8. Tel. (514) 744-3434.
Em Habanim, 6655 Côte des Neiges, H3S 2B4, Tel. (514) 731-0534.
Hekhal Shalom, 825 Gratton St., Ville St. Laurent, H4M 2G4. Tel. (514) 747-4530.
Kol Yehouda, 6501 Baily Rd., Côte St. Luc, H4V 1A1. Tel. (514) 481-4859.
Maghen David, 4691 Van Horne Av., H3W 1H8. Tel. (514) 731-1960.
Ohel Yaacov, 3541 Van Horne Av., H3S 1R7. Tel. (514) 733-3212.
Or Hahayim, 5700 Einstein Av., Cote St. Luc, H4W 1V3. Tel. (514) 489-1301.
Rabbinat Sépharade du Quebec, 5850 Victoria Av., H3W 2R5. Tel. (514) 738-1004.
Spanish & Portuguese Syn., 4894 St. Kevin Av., H3W 1P2. Tel. (514) 737-3695.

Traditional
Shaar Hashomayim, 450 Kensington Av., Westmount, H3Y 3A2. Tel. (514) 937-9471.

Conservative
Beth El, 1000 Lucerne Rd., Mount Royal, H3R 2H9. Tel. (514) 738-4766.
Shaare Zedek, 5305 Rosedale Av., H4V 2H7. Tel. (514) 484-1122.
Shaare Zion, 5575 Cote St. Luc Rd., H3X 2C9. Tel. (514) 481-7727.

Reform
Temple Emanu-El Beth Shalom, 4100 Sherbrooke St. W., Westmount, H3Z 1A5. Tel. (514) 937-3575.

Reconstructionist
Cong. Dorshei Emet, 18 Cleve Rd., Hampstead, H3X 1A6. Tel. (514) 486-9400.

Representative Organisations
B'nai B'rith, 6900 Decarie Blvd. H3X 2T8 Tel. (514) 733-5377.
Canadian Jewish Congress National Headquarters, Samuel Bronfman Hse., 1590 Dr. Penfield Av., H3G 1C5. Tel. (514) 931-7531. Publishes National Synagogue Directory.
Federation CJA, 5151, ch. de la Côte Ste-Catherine, Montreal H3W 1M6. Tel. (514) 735-3541. Operates Jewish Information & Referral Service (JIRS) (737-2221) and publishes: 'Rendez-vous à Montréal: a guide to Jewish Montreal'.
Jewish Com. Council, 5491 Victoria Av., Suite 117, H3W 2P9. Tel. (514) 739-6363.
National Council of Jewish Women, Room 102, 5775 Victoria Av., H3W 2R4. Tel. (514) 733-7589.

Cultural & Educational Organisations
Jewish Education Council of Montreal, 5151 Chemin de la Côte Ste.-Catherine, H3W 1M6. Tel. (514) 345-2610, will provide full inf. about schools.

Jewish Public Library, 5151 Cote St. Catherine Rd., H3W 1M6. Tel. (514) 345-2627. There are branches in other parts of Montreal.
Saidye Bronfman Centre, 5170 Cote St. Catherine Rd., H3W 1M7. Tel. (514) 739-2301.
Montreal Holocaust Memorial Center, 5151 Cote St., Catherine Rd., H3W 1M6. Tel. (514) 735-2386.

Welfare Organisations, Hospitals, etc.
Federation CJA, 5151 Cote St. Catherine Rd., H3W 1M6. Tel. (514) 735-3541.
Jewish Rehabilitation Hospital, 3205 Alton Goldbloom St., Chomedey, H7V 1R2. Tel. (514) 688-9550. Kosher food.
Jewish Family Services Social Service Centre, 5250 Decarie Blvd. H3X 2H9 Tel. (514) 485-1112.
Jewish General Hospital, 3755 Cote St. Catherine Rd, H3T 1E2. Tel. (514) 340-8222. Kosher food.
Jewish Hospital of Hope, 7745 Sherbrooke St. E., H1L 1A3. Tel. (514) 352-3120.
Jewish Immigrant Aid Services of Canada, 5151 Cote St. Catherine Rd. H3W 1M6. Tel. (514) 342-9351.
Maimonides Hospital & Home for the Aged, 5795 Caldwell, Cote St. Luc. H4W 1W3. Tel. (514) 483-2121.

Student & Youth Organisations
B'nai B'rith Hillel Foundation, 3460 Stanley St. H3A 1R8. Tel. (514) 845-9171.
B'nai B'rith Youth Org., 6333 Decarie Blvd., H3X 2T8. Tel. (514) 733-8221.
Y.M. & Y.W.H.A., 5500 Westbury Av., H3W 2W8. Tel. (514) 737-6551. Kosher cafeteria.
Young Adult Division., 5151 Cote St. Catherine Rd., H3W 1M6. Tel. (514) 345-2637.

Zionist Organisations
Bnei Akiva, 5250, Decarie Blvd., (Suite 550), H3X 2H9. Tel. (514) 486-9526.
Hadassah-WIZO Org., 1310 Greene Av. Westmount, H3Z 2B8. Tel. (514) 937-9431.
Jewish National Fund, 1980 Sherbrooke St. W., Suite 500, H3H 1E8. Tel. (514) 934-0313.
Mizrachi Hapoel-Hamizrachi Org. of Canada, 5250 Decarie Blvd., H3X 2H9. Tel. (514) 483-3660.
Canadian Zionist Fed., 5250 Decarie Blvd., Suite 550, H3X 2H9. Tel. (514) 486-9526.
Kotel, 6414 Victoria Av., H3W 2S6. Tel. (514) 739-4142.
Israel Consulate-General, Suite 2620, 1155 René Lévesque Blvd., West, H3B 4J5. Tel. (514) 393-9372.

Newspaper
Canadian Jewish News, 6900 Decarie Blvd., H3X 2T8. Tel. (514) 735-2612.

Booksellers, etc.
Book Centre Inc., 5006 Queen Mary Rd., H3W 1X2. Tel. (514) 731-2677.
Kotel, 6414 Victoria Av., H3W 2S6. Tel. (514) 739-4142.

Rabbi J. Rodal's Hebrew Book Store & Gift Shop, 5689 Van Horne Av., H3W 1H8. Tel. (514) 733-1876.
Victoria Gift Shop, 5875 Victoria Av. H3W 2R6. Tel. (514) 738-1414.

Restaurants
★ **B.B.Q. McDavid,** 5611 Cotes des Neiges. Tel. (514) 341-1633.
(K) B'nai B'rith Hillel Foundation, 3460 Stanley St. Tel. 845-9171.
(K) Chabad Hse., 3429 Peel St. Tel. (514) 842-6616.
(K) Earnie & Elie's Place, 6900 Decarie Blvd., H3X 2T8. Tel. (514) 344-4444.
(K) El Morocco II, 3450 Drummond St. Tel. (514) 844-6888 & 844-0203.
(K) Foxy's, 5987A Victoria Av. Tel. (514) 739-8777.
Golden Age Cafeteria, 5700 Westbury Av., H3W 3EB. Tel. (514) 739-4731.
★ **Golden Spoon** (Cuiller d'or) 5217 Decarie Blvd. Tel. (514) 481-3431.
(K) Kotel 1422 Stanley St., H3W 3E8. Tel. (514) 739-4731.
★ **L'Elysée Dame,** 70 Notre Dame. Tel. (514) 842-6016.
(K) Odelia Snack Bar, 5897A Victoria Av. Tel. (514) 733-0984.
★ **Pizza Pita,** 5710 Victoria Av. Tel. (514) 731-7482.
(K) Y.M.H.A. Cafeteria, 5500 Westbury Av. Tel. (514) 737-8704.
All the kosher establishments listed here are under the supervision of the Jewish Community Council of Montreal. In addition, the Council supervises some 31 butchers, as well as bakeries, caterers, etc.
Visitors requiring additional inf. about kosher establishments, food, etc., should contact the Exec. Dir., Jewish Community Council (Vaad Ha'ir), Room 117, 5491 Victoria Av. Tel. (514) 739-6363. Fax (514) 739-7024.

QUEBEC CITY
Syn.: Beth Israel Ohev Sholom, 20 Cremazie St. E., G1R 1Y2. Tel. (418) 523-7346.

STE. AGATHE-DES-MONTS
Syn.: House of Israel Cong., 31 Albert St., J8C 1Z6. Tel. (819) 326-4320.
Mount Sinai Hospital, 5690 Cavendish Blvd., Cote St. Luc, Quebec H4W 1S7.

SASKATCHEWAN
MOOSE JAW
Syn.: Moose Jaw Hebrew Com. (C), 937 Henry St., S6H 3H1. Tel. (306) 692-3677.

REGINA
Syn.: Beth Jacob (O), 1640 Victoria Av., S4P 0P7. Tel. (306) 757-8643.

SASKATOON
Syn.: Agudas Israel (C), 715 McKinnon Av., S7H 2G2. Tel. (306) 343-7023.

CANARY ISLANDS
(See Spain)

CHILE

The Jewish population is 22,000, of whom the great majority live in Santiago, the capital, and its environs. There are some Jewish families in Antafugasta, Arica, Chuquicamata, Concepción and Puerto Montt.

ARICA
Sociedad Israelita Dr Herzl, Casilla 501.

CONCEPCIÓN
Communidad Israelita, 111. Religious leader: Americo Grünwald.

IQUIQUE
Comunidad Israelita, Playa Ligade 3263, Playa Brava.

LA SERENA
Com. Centre, Cordovez 652.

RANCAGUA
Comunidad Israelita, Casilla 890

SANTIAGO
Synagoques
Bicur Joilim (Orthodox), Av. Matte 624.
Comunidad Israelita de Santiago (Ashkenazi) Rabbi Eduardo Wainsgortín, Serrano 214-218. Tel. 393872.
Jafets Jayim (Orthodox) (Rabbi Itzhak Shaked), Miguel Claro 196.
Maguen David (Seph), Av. R. Lyon 812.
Maze (Hungarian), Pedro Bannen 0166. Tel. 2742536.
Sociedad Cultural Israelita B'ne Jisroel (German), Portugal 810. Tel. 2265238. (Rabbi Efraim Rosenzweig)
Jabad Lubavitch. Rabbi Menashe Perman, E. Yanez, Gloria 62 (Las Condes). Tel. 228-2240.
Communal Headquarters (Comite Representativo de las Entidades Judias de Chile), Miguel Claro 196. Tel. 2358669.
Homes for Aged: Hogar Israelita de Ancianos Abrahamy Malvina Wainstein, Francisco de Villagra 325, Los Guindos; Cisroco Maipu 525.
Maccabi, Av. las Condes 8361.
WIZO, M. Montt 207.
Zionist Offices: Federacion Sionista de Chile, Merced 136. Tel. 382248.
Israel Embassy, San Sebastian 2812, Casilla 1224. Tel. 2461570.

Restaurants
(K) M. Montt 1273 Av. Miguet Claro 196.
★ Comunidad Israelita de Santiago Tarapaca 870 (2nd floor).

TEMUCO
Comunidad Israelita, General Cruz 355.

VALDIVIA
Com. Centre. Arauco 136 E.

VALPARAISO
Comunidad Israelita, Rabbi Dr. L Cogan. Alvarez 490, Vina del Mar. Tel. 680373.

COLOMBIA
(Jewish population approx. 8,000)

BARANQUILLA
Centro Israelita Filantropico, Carrera 43, No. 85-95, Apartado Aereo 2537. Tel. 342310 & 351197. Tel. 344514. Pres.: Jaime Eisenband.
Comunidad Hebrea Sefaradita, Carrera 55 No. 74-71. Apartado Aereo 51351. Tel. 340054 & 340050. Rabbi Meir Botton. Pres.: Eli Suez.
School: Colegio Hebreo Union, Carrera 43 No. 85-95. Apartado Aereo 3656. Tel. 354369. Pres.: Victor Levy.

BOGOTA
Synagogues
Asociacion Israelita Montefiore (German), Carrera 20 No. 37-54. Tel. 245-5264. Pres.: Abraham Bibliowicz.
Centro Israelita de Bogota (Ashkenazi), Transversal 29, No. 126-31. Tel. 274-9069. Rabbi Alfredo Goldschmidt. Pres.: Dr. Leon Birbragher. **(K)** Kosher meals available by prior arrangement with Rabbi Goldschmidt. Tel. 218-2500.
Congregacion Adath Israel, Carrera 7a, No. 94-20. Tel. 257-1660 & 257-1680. Mikva on premises. Rabbi Alfredo Goldschmidt. Pres.: Benjamin Korc.
Comunidad Hebrea Sefaradi, Calle 79, No. 9-66. Tel. 256-2629 & 249-0372. Mikva on premises. Rabbi Abraham Benchimol. Pres.: David Cohen.
Jabad (Chabad) House, Calle 92, No. 10, Apt. 405. Tel. 36408. Rabbi Joshua Rosenfeld. Calle 92, No. 10-49/400. Tel. 257-4920.
Colegio Colombo Hebreo, Diag. 154 No. 46-65. Apartado Aereo 51775. Tel. 671-1303 & 4991.
Confederacion de Asociacones Judias de Colombia, Transversal 29, No. 126-31. Tel. 274-9069. Pres.: Leon Birbragher.
Union Rabinica Colombiana, (Orthodox). Same address as Confederacion above. Tel. 274-9069 or 218-2500. Ch.: Rabbi Alfredo Goldschmidt.
Jewish Monthly: "Menorah", Apartado Aereo 9081. Dir.: Eliecer Celnik.
Israel Embassy, Calle 35, No. 7-25, Edificio Caxdax. Tel. 245-6603 & 245-6712.

CALI
The Jewish population totals some 2,000.
Centro Israelita de Beneficencia (Sephardi), Calle 44A, Av. 5a Norte Esquina. Apartado Aereo 77. Tel. 686918. Rabbi Shaul Vaknin. Pres.: Albert Levi.
Sociedad Hebrea de Socorros (Ashkenazi), Av. 9a Norte No. 10-15. Tel. 611065 & 611077. Pres.: Moises Bacall.
Union Cultural Israelita (German), Apartado Aereo 5552. Pres.: Julio Westheiner.
Jewish Day School: Colegio Hebreo Jorge Isaacs, Calle 5A No. 38-81. Tel. 361560 & 501232. Tel. 641379 & 641393.

MEDELLIN
Union Israelita de Beneficencia, Carrera 43B No. 15-150, Apartado Aereo 4702. Tel. 668560. Pres.: Dr. Benjamin Rabinowich.
Jewish Day School: Colegio Hebreo Teodoro Herzl, Apartado Aereo 4378. Tel. 366697 & 366717. Pres.: Dr. Arturo Yanovich.

COMMONWEALTH OF INDEPENDENT STATES
(i.e. Remnant of the former U.S.S.R.)
A selection of information provided by the Commission on Jewish

Education in the Republics of the former Soviet Union has been used as a first step in increasing coverage of these areas now that Jewish communal life is beginning to burgeon again.

Note: The break up of the Soviet Union into its separate republics signalled by the resistance to the attempted coup of August 1991 far outruns our capacity to retain contact with appropriate authorities and to give current information under new headings such as Latvia, Georgia etc.

The latest Soviet census, taken in 1989, gives the Jewish population of the U.S.S.R. as 1,450.000 Emigration and Aliyah in the past three years has hastened the lowering of this figure.

In Moscow alone there were estimated to be about 250,000 Jews.

The list of synagogues given below is complete as far as can be ascertained. It must be pointed out, however, that not all the cities and towns where a synagogue is listed are open to tourists, and even where they are, the synagogue is often difficult to find. Intending visitors must check with Intourist which areas may be visited. The Intourist London Office is at 219 Marsh Wall, Isle of Dogs, E14 9FJ. Tel. 071-538 3202.

ALMA-ATA (Kazakhstan)

Syn.: Tashkentskaya St., 1a 480057. Tel. (327-2) 30-68-98.

ANDIZHAN (Uzbekistan)

Syn.: 7 Sovetskaya St.

ASTRAKHAN (Russia)

Syn.: 30 Babushkin St.

BAKU (Azerbaijan)

Syns.: Mountain Jews: Dmitrova St. 39, 370014. Tel. (892-2) 32-88-67; Ashkenazi: Pervomoskaya St., 271. Tel. (892-2) 94-15-71.

BERDICHEV (Zakarpatsky)

Syn.: 8 Sverdlov St., Zhitomir Oblast.

BEREGOVO (Zakarpatsky)

Syn.: 17 Sverdlov St.

BIROBIDJAN (Russia)
Syn.: 9 Chapaev St., Khabarovsk Krai.

BUKHARA (Uzbekistan)
Syn.: 20 Tsentralnaya St.

BUYNAKSK (Daghestan)
Syn.: Narodov Vostoka St.

CHIMKENT (Kazakhstan)
Syn.: Svobody St., 47th La. (Sephardi).

DERBENT (Daghestan)
Syn.: 94 Tagi-Zade St.

DUSHANBE (Tadzhikistan)
Syns.: Bokharan: Nazyina Khikmeta St. 26; Ashkenazi: Proletarsky St.

FRUNZE (Kirghizia)
Syn.: 193 Karpinsky St.

IRKUTSK (Russia)
Syn.: 17 Karl Liebknecht St.

KATTA-KURGAN (Uzbekistan)
Syn.: 1 Karl Marx Alley.

KERMINE (Uzbekistan)
Syn.: 36 Narimanov St.

KLINTSY (Bryansk)
Syn.: 82 Lermontov St.

KOKAND (Uzbekistan)
Syn.: Dekabristov St., Fergan Oblast.

KOROSTEN (Zhitomir)
Syn.: 8 Shchoksa St.

KUBA (Azerbaijan)
Syn.: 46 Kolkhoznaya St.

KUIBYSHEV (Russia)
Syn.: 84 Chapaev St.

KURSK (Russia)
Syn.: 3 Bolshevitskaya St.

MAKHACHKALA (Daghestan)
Syn.: 111 Yermoshkin St.

MALAKHOVKA (Moscow)
Syn.: 2nd Korenyovsky La., Moscow Oblast.

MARGELAN (Uzbekistan)
Syn.: Turtkulskaya St., Fergan Oblast.

MOSCOW (Russia)

Syns.: Central, 8 Arkhipova St., off B. Khmelnitsky Str. Tel. (095) 924-24-24; Mar'ina Roshcha, at 5a Viacheslavsky Lane. Tel. (095) 289-23-25; Chabad Center, Poliakoff Syn., Bolshaya Brennaya 6. Tel. (095) 202-7696. Fax (095) 202-7645. Dir.: Rabbi B. S. Cunin.
Commission on Jewish Education in the Republics of the former Soviet Union, Witsa Lyapidevskogo 10-2-73, 125581. Tel. (095) 455-6224. Dir. Inna Lyakhovitsky.
Jewish Museum at the Poliakoff Synagogue.
(K) Shamir "Hamburger" Restaurant (Parev) (also called "Vege-Burger"), 12 Krasnoprudnaya St., Tel. 007-0950264-9592.

NALCHIK (Russia)

Syn.: 73 Rabochaya St., cnr. Osetinskaya.

NAVOY (Uzbekistan)

Syn.: 36 Narimanov St.

NOVOSIBIRSK (Russia)

Syns.: 23 Luchezarnaya St.; Sad Dzerzhinskov.

ORDZHONIKIDZE (Russia)

Syn.: Revolutsiya St.

PENZA (Russia)

Syn.: 15 Krasnaya St.

PERM (Russia)

Syns.: Pushkin St.; Kuibyshev St.

ROSTOV-ON-DON (Russia)

Syn.: 18 Gazetnaya La.

SACHKHERE

Syns.: 145 Sovetskaya St.; 105 Tsereteli St.

ST. PETERSBURG (Russia)

Syns.: 2 Lermontovsky Prospekt. Tel. (812) 114-11-53. (This is the second street past the Kirov Opera & Ballet Theatre.) Mikva on these premises. Adv. booking req. Tel. 007-812-1138974.
(K) Dining Room at Shamir School on Ligovskiy Prospekt, 161-8. Tel. (812) 116-10-03.
Organisation
St. Petersburg Jewish Assoc., Ryleev St. 29-31, a/b103. Tel. (812) 272-41-13.

SAMARKAND (Uzbekistan)

Syns.: 34 Khudzumskaya St.; 45 Respublikanskaya St.; 5 Denauskaya St.

SARATOV (Russia)

Syns.: Posadskov St.; 2 Kirpichnaya St.

SHAKHRISABZ (Tadzikistan)

Syn.: 23 Bainal Minal St.

SVERDLOVSK (Russia)

Syns.: 18/2 Kirov St.; 14 Kuibyshev St.

TASHKENT (Uzbekistan)

Syns.: Sephardi, 3 Sagban St. Tel. (371-2) 40-07-68; Gorbunova St. 62. Tel. (371)-2) 53-54-47; Ashkenazi, 77 Chempianov St.; 9 Chkalov St.

TULA (Russia)

Syn.: 15 Veresaevskaya St.

CORSICA

(See France)

COSTA RICA

(Jewish population 2,500)

SAN JOSE

Centro Israelita de Costa Rica, Calle 22 y 22. Tel. 225449. Apartado Postal 1473-1000.
Israel Embassy, Calle 2, Avenidas 2 y 4. Tel. 21-60-11 & 21-64-44. Apartado Postal 5147.

CROATIA

(Former constituent republic of Yugoslavia)
It is not known how far the Jewish communities have survived the civil strife accompanying the break up of the Yugoslav Federation.

DUBROVNIK

Syn.: Zudioska St. 3 (St. of the Jews). This is the second oldest synagogue in Europe and is located in a very narrow street off the main street — the Stradun or Placa. The Jewish com. office is in the same building. Zudioska St. is the third turning on the right from the town clock tower.
There are only 7 Jewish men and 10 Jewish women in Dubrovnik. Tourists help to make up a minyan in the syn on Fri. Evg. & high holidays.

RIJEKA

The synagogue in Filipovica St., 9 is well maintained but no regular services are reported. Pres.: Josip Engel.

SPLIT

The syn. at Split is one of the few in Yugoslavia to have survived the wartime occupation. The Jewish com. numbers about 120. Inf. from com. offices, Zidovski prolaz 1. Tel. 45-672. Pres.: Eduard Tauber. There is a Jewish cemetery established in 1578.

ZAGREB

Com. Headquarters, Palmoticeva St. 16, P.O.B. 362. Tel. 434-619. Fax 434-638. Pres.: Nenad Porges. Exec. Vice Pres.: Srdjan Matic.
Before the war Zagreb had 11,000 Jews. Now there are about 1,400. Despite this decimation, there is a very active com. life. The old people are well looked after, in a fine home for the aged built to the order of the Fed. of Jewish Com. in Yugoslavia. Pres.: Alfred Lustig. Bukovacka str. 55. Tel 210-026.
There is an impressive monument in the Mirogoj Cemetery to the Jewish victims of the Second World War. There is a plaque on the spot of the pre-war Central Synagogue in Zagreb in Praska St., 7. where a new community Centre & Synagogue will be built soon.

CUBA

(Population less than 1,000 of whom the majority are in Havana)
Havana has a fine Conservative syn. and modern com. centre at Patronado de la Casa de la Comunidad Hebrea de Cuba, Calle 13 e I, Vedado. Tel. 32-8953. There is also an Orthodox Beth Hamedrash (Hadath Israel) at Calle Picota 52, Habana Vieja. Tel. 61-34-95. The United Hebrew Congregation (Reform), is at Av. de los Presidentes 502. The Jewish cemetery is at Guanabacoa.

CYPRUS

The Jewish population is about 25. There are cemeteries at Margo (near Nicosia) and at Larnaca (disused). The Margo cemetery is in the Turkish-occupied part of the island, and access is barred to residents of the Greek part.
General inf. from Cyprus Tourism Organisation, 213 Regent St., W1R 8DA. Tel. 071-734 9822 & 2593.
Committee of the Jewish Com. of Cyprus. Nicosia: c/o Mr. F. E. Yeshurun, P.O.B. 4784. Tel. 02-427982.
Israel Embassy, 44 Archbishop Makarios Av., Nicosia.

CZECH REPUBLIC

The beautiful buildings of the ancient Jewish quarter of Old Prague are a monument to what was once a great and flourishing Jewish community. The Jews of Prague have been in the Czech capital for close on 1,000 years and elsewhere in Bohemia almost as long. Between the 16th and 18th centuries, Prague Jewry enjoyed its "golden age." One of the largest and most important communities in Europe, the Prague community lived in an extensive and self-contained Jewish quarter (Judenstadt).
Its ancient synagogues, two belonging to the Jewish com. in Prague, the others forming part of the Jewish Museum, its scholars, its Hebrew printing press, its Jewish craft guilds, its communal institutions, lent added lustre to an already illustrious part of the Jewish people.
In 1745, however, the Jews were exiled from Prague and allowed to return only three years later, on payment of exorbitant taxes. Full equality was granted to Prague Jews in 1848, and the ghetto later abolished.
When the Republic of Czechoslovakia was formed in 1918, after the First World War, it became the first country in the world to recognise Jewish nationality. By 1935, there were an estimated 150,000 Jews in Slovakia, 120,000 (including 40,000 refugees from Nazi Germany) in Bohemia and Moravia, and 105,000 in Ruthenia (now part of the Soviet Union).
The German occupation in 1939 spelt the end for the 375,000 Jews of Czechoslovakia. Some managed to emigrate, but many were rounded up by the Nazis and killed in concentration camps. The names of all 77,297 Bohemian and Moravian Jews who died in the camps were engraved on the inside walls of the famous old Pinkas Synagogue in Prague's Jewish quarter. (The syn., now part of the Jewish Museum, is being rebuilt). By 1968, the 25,000 Jews still in Czechoslovakia in 1945, the end of the Second World War, had dwindled to 18,000 or so. According to the Federation of Jewish Communities in the Czech Republic, there are some 12,000 Jews in Czechoslovakia today, of whom 6,000 live in the Czech Republic.
There are eight communities in Bohemia and Moravia in the regional cities of Prague, Plzen, Ustinad Labem, Teplice, Liberec, Brno, Olomouc and Ostrava. There are kosher kitchens in Prague and Košice with supervision including services of a Shochet from Budapest or Vienna.
General inf. from Cedok (London) Ltd., Czech Travel Bureau, 17-18 Old Bond St., W1X 4RB. Tel. 071-629 6058.

BOSKOVICE
Medieval ghetto. Jewish cemetery.

BRNO
Syn.: Skorepka 13 (but reported that the site is under development). Com. Centre: Hybesova 14. Services, Fri. evg. & Sat. morn.

HOLESOV
The 'Schach" Syn., dating from 1560, now a museum, should be visited. It is open in the mornings. At other times, the curator will show visitors round, if contacted. The old cemetery is close by.

KARLOVY VARY (Karlsbad)
Prayer house & Com. Centre, Ceskoslovenské armády 39. Services, Fri. evg. & Sat. morn.

MIKULOV (Nikolsburg)
Only one syn., now being restored, remains of the many which flourished here when the town was the spiritual capital of Moravian Jewry and the seat of the Chief Rabbis of Moravia. The cemetery contains the graves of famous rabbis.

OLOMOUC
Prayer house & Com. Centre, Komenskeho 7.

OSTRAVA
Prayer house & Com. Centre, Revolucni 17.

PLZEN (Pilsen)
(The Great Synagogue is closed now).
Prayer house & Com. Centre: Smetanovy sady 5. Services Fri. evg.

PRAGUE
Syns.: Jubilee Syn., Jerusalemskà 7. Services, Fri. evg. & Sat. morn.; Old-New Syn. (Altneuschul), Cervena ul.7 Tel. 231-09-09.
Federation of Jewish Coms. in the Czech Republic (Federace zidovsk´ych obcí v CR): 110 01, Maislova 18. Prague 1. Dir. Dr. Tomas Kraus. Tel. 231-85-59. Chief Rabbi: Karol Sidon.
(K) Kosher Restaurant, Maislova 18. Mon.-Sat., lunch; Fri. evg., dinner. Tel. 231-89-96.
Jewish Town Hall with Hebrew clock, Maislova 18.
Jewish Museum. Old Jewish Cemetery, the oldest in Europe, containing the graves of such famous rabbis & scholars as Avigdor Karo (died 1439), Yehuda Löw ben Bezalel (1609), David Gans (1613) & David Oppenheim (1736); High Syn. (The Spanish Syn. is empty, closed now). (exhibition of Jewish synagogue hangings, vestments, and other fine decorated fabrics); Pinkas Syn. (memorial to 77,297 victims of Nazi persecution, under 'renovation' since 1968); Maisl Syn. (silver treasures exhibition); Klaus Syn. (Jewish life and Jewish Holy-days);
The New Jewish Cemetery, Prague 1, 3-Žižkov, Nad vodovodem 1. Contains the grave of Franz Kafka.

TEREZIN
There is a new museum in the town Terezín (converted into a ghetto called Theresienstadt by the Nazis) dedicated to the Jews who were deported from there to Auschwitz death camp, There is also a cemetery in which

11,250 individual and 217 mass graves and the crematorium are placed: 34,000 people died in Terezín.

DENMARK

There are 6,000 Jews in Denmark today, nearly all of whom live in Copenhagen. A small community of Polish refugees has been formed in Aarhus.

The Royal Library (8 Christians Brygge, Copenhagen) houses a Jewish collection including the famous "Bibliotheca Simonseniana" and part of the library of the late Professor Lazarus Goldschmidt. The library has a Jewish Department under the direction of Ulf Haxen. In the Liberty Museum there is a special division devoted to the Resistance Movement, and also a section dealing with "The Persecution of the Jews."

General inf. from Danish Tourist Board, Sceptre Hse., 169-173 Regent St., W1R 8PY. Tel. 071-734 2637-8.

COPENHAGEN
Synagogues & Religious Organisations
The Chief Rabbi of Denmark is Rabbi Bent Melchior, 27 Frederiksborggade. 1360 Copenhagen K. Tel. 3313 8282. Rabbi Bent Lexner, 9 Oestbaneg., 2100 K. Tel. 3526 3540.

The main syn., with daily services, is at 12 Krystalgade, 1172K. After Fri. evg. service during the summer, there is a kiddush to which all visitors are invited.

The Machsike Hadass Syn. at 12 Ole Suhrs Gade, 1354K, holds regular daily and Shabbat services. Rabbi B. Steinhaus, Tel. 3332 5618, & Rabbi M. E. Winkler, Tel. 3313 3933. There is a mikva on the premises. Tel. 3393 7662 or 3332 9443. From May to Sept., services are held in the syn. at 6 Granvaenget, Hornbaek, N. Seeland.

Representative Organisations
B'nai B'rith. Pres.: Bent Bograd, Holbergsgade 28A, 1057K. Tel. 318 13948-3332 8847.

Jewish Com. Centre (Det mosaiske Troessamfund): 6 Ny Kongensgade, 1472K. Tel. 3312 8868. Mikva on premises.

Cultural & Welfare Orgs., etc.
Homes for Aged: Meyers Minde, 12 Krystalgade, 1172K. Tel. 3312 5523, & N. J. Fraenckels Stiftelse, 93 Skoleholdervej, 2400NV. Tel. 3134 3168.

Royal Library, 8 Christians Brygge, 1219K. The Royal Library houses a Jewish collection including the famous *Bibliotheca Simonseniana* and part of the library of the late Professor Lazarus Goldschmidt. The library has a Jewish Department under the direction of Ulf Haxen. In the Liberty Museum there is a special division devoted to the Resistance Movement, and also a section dealing with "The Persecution of the Jews."

Student & Youth Organisations, etc.
B'nei Akiva, 6 Ny Kongensgade.

Hakoah Sports Club. Inq. to Ch.: Bjarne Karpantschof, 6 Ny Kongensgade.

Jewish Youth Club, 6 Ny Kongensgade, Inq. to Ch.: Mette Gerschwald, Carl Plougsvej 3, 1913 Frederiksberg C. 31 23 26 95. Tel. 3123 2695.

Zionist Organisations
Keren Kayemet, 6 Ny Kongensgade. Tel. 3313 1776.

WIZO, 6 Ny Kongensgade. Tel. 3311 1965.

Zionist Federation, 6 Ny Kongensgade. Tel. 3312 6271.

Israel Embassy, 4 Lundevangsvej, 2900 Hellerup. Tel. 3162 6288.

Kosher Food
(K) Kosher Butcher: Kosher Delikatesse, 87 Lyngbyvej 2100. Tel. 3318 5777.

HORNBAEK
Syn. Granavenget 8 (open from Shavuoth to after Succoth). Tel. 4220 0731.

Hotel
(K) Villa Strand, Kystvej 12. Tel. 4396 9400 and 4220 0088. (Under the supervision of Rabbi Mikael Guttermann.)

DOMINICAN REPUBLIC
(Jewish population 200)

SANTO DOMINGO
Syn.: Centro Israelita de la Republica Dominicana, Av. Ciudad de Sarasota 21.
Israel Embassy, Av. Pedro Henriquez Urena 80, Apartado Postal 1404. Tel. 686-7359 or 4727.

SOSUA
Felix G. Koch, Tel. (809) 571-2284, welcomes Jewish visitors.

ECUADOR
(Jewish population 1,300)

GUAYAQUIL
Syn. & Com. Centre, cnr. Calle Paradiso & El Bosque. Pres.: Isaac Pienknaeura, Boyaca 1313, P.O.B. 5976.

QUITO
Com. Centre: Asociación Israelita de Quito, 18 de Septiembre 954, Casilla 800-A. Tel. 502733.
Israel Embassy, Av. Eloy Alfaro 969, Casilla 2463. Tel. 547-322 or 548-431.

EGYPT
There are about 270 Jews in Egypt, 150 in Cairo and 120 in Alexandria.
General inf. from Egyptian State Tourist Office, 168 Piccadilly, W1V 9DE. Tel. 071-493 5282.

ALEXANDRIA
Syn.: Eliahu Hanavi, 69 Nebi Daniel St., Ramla Station. Pres. of Com.: Clement R. Setton. Tel. 4923974 & 5974438.

CAIRO
Syns.: Shaarei Hashamayim, 17 Adli Pasha St. Tel. 749025. Dir.: Murad S. Gabbai; Ben-Ezra, 6 Harett il-Sitt Barbara, Miri Girgas (St. George's), Old Cairo. Tel. 847695; Vitali Madjar, 5 Misalla St., Palmyra, Heliopolis; Meir Eraim, 55 No. 13 Street, Maadi. (This is a small American-Israeli cong., which holds occasional services.)
Com. Offices: 13 Sebil el-Khazendar St., Midan el-Geish, Abassiya. Tel. 824613 or 824885. Pres.: Youssef Dana. Tel. 758868. Sec.: Murad Gabbai. Tel. 744850.
Israel Embassy, 6 Ibn Malek St., Gizeh. Tel. 845260, 845205 or 28862.
Israel Government Tourist Office, 6 Ibn Malek St., 4th Floor. Tel. 729734 or 730997.

EL SALVADOR
(Jewish population about 30 families)

SAN SALVADOR
Syn. (Conservative), 23 Blvd. del Hipodromo 626, Colonia San Benito. Fri. evg. services only. Further inf. from Max Starkman. Tel. 237366.
Comunidad Israelita de El Salvador, Aptdo. Postal (06) 182. Pres.: Jean-Claude Kahn, Colonia y Calle Maquilishuat 135. Tel. 981388.
Israel Embassy & Consulate. Colonia Escalon, 85 Av. Norte No. 619. Tel. 238770 or 239221.

ESTONIA
TALLIN
Syn.: 9 Lasteya Str. Tel. (014-2) 55-71-54.
Organisation: Jewish Culture Society, Karu St. 47, 200001.

ETHIOPIA
The Jews of Ethiopia, who sometimes call themselves Beta Israel, and are known as Falashas, represent one of the oldest Jewish communities in the world. As a result of Operation Moses and extensive emigration to Israel in the past few years and now following a further mass exodus to Israel, the community probably numbers fewer than 1,500, when account is taken of casualties from the famine and the hazards of reaching the refugee camps in the Sudan, estimated at between 3,000 and 4,000. This is about a third of the number in 1981, when the World Ort Union was forced to suspend its

aid programme. The Falashas' origin is uncertain, but it is believed that Judaism first reached Ethiopia during the first or second centuries C.E., probably from Egypt, where flourishing Jewish communities existed.

ADDIS ABABA
Com. Centre, P.O. Box 50. Tel. 111725 & 446471.

ASMARA
Syn., Via Hailemariam Mammo 34.

FINLAND
The settlement of Jews in Finland dates from about 1850. The original community consisted mostly of Jewish soldiers in the Russian Army in Finland, so-called Cantonists who decided, after 25 years of military service, to settle there with their families. There are about 1,300 Jews in Finland today, about 1,000 of whom live in Helsinki.
General inf. from Finnish Tourist Board, 66 Haymarket, SW1Y 4RF. Tel. 071-839 4048.

HELSINKI
Syn. (O) & Com. Centre, school, kindergarten & home for aged, Malminkatu 26. Tel. 6921297 & 6941302. Services, Mon.-Fri., 7.45 a.m..; Fri. evg., 7.45 p.m. (summer), 5 p.m. (winter); Shabbat & Sun., 9 a.m.
All orgs., including Hazamir Choir, Jewish War Veterans, Keren Kayemet, Library, Maccabi, WIZO & the Youth Club can be contacted via the above Tel. numbers.
Kosher Butcher: **(K)** Ritus, Uudenmaankatu 28. Tel. 644951. Open Thurs., 9 a.m. to 5 p.m.; Fri., 9 a.m. to 2 p.m.
Kosher meals available at the Com. Centre by prior arrangement from: Avi Machbubi, Tel. 6941296 or 877 9627.
Israel Embassy, Vironkatu 5A. Tel. 1356177.

TURKU
Syn.: Brahenkatu 17. The Sec., Mrs. Anneli Zewi, is always pleased to meet visitors.
Com. Centre, Brahenkatu 17b. Tel. 312557.

FRANCE
The first Jewish settlers in France arrived with the Greek founders of Marseilles about 500 B.C.E. After the destruction of the Second Temple, Jewish exiles established new communities, or reinforced old ones, in the South of France, where they lived on equal terms with their Gentile neighbours. Rabbis who become known for their oratory attracted Christians to the synagogues. But gradually the priesthood inculcated in the masses a hatred of the Jews which, with the coming of the Crusades, vented itself in pogroms. Yet it was during this period that French Jewry achieved its noblest spiritual flowering.
Rashi and Rabenu Tam are the best known of hundreds of brilliant medieval French rabbis and scholars. In 1394 the Jews were banished from the whole of France, save the small area under the jurisdiction of the Popes of Avignon. When Alsace-Lorraine became part of France early in the 17th century, the Jews there were unmolested, and small numbers trickled into the rest of France. Ten years before the French Revolution, the 500 Jews of Paris built their first ritual bath. In 1791 the emancipation of French Jewry was the signal for the ghetto walls to crumble throughout Europe.
During the Second World War, under German occupation, 120,000 Jews were deported or massacred; but the post-war influx from Central and

Eastern Europe and North Africa has increased the Jewish population to
some 700,000.
There are about 380,000 in the Paris area; 85,000 in Marseille; between
30,000 and 35,000 in Lyon; between 25,000 and 30,000 in Nice; between
20,000 and 23,000 in Toulouse; 18,000 in Strasbourg: and about 8,000 each
in Bordeaux and Grenoble.
The Consistoire Central Israélite de France et d'Algérie (17, rue Saint
Georges, 75009 Paris) publishes its 'Annuaire', listing all the communal
organisations of France.

General inf. from the French Government Tourist Office, 178 Piccadilly,
W1V 0AL. Tel. 071-499 6911 (recorded message only) or 071-491 7622 for
urgent messages. Written inquiries dealt with promptly (but 80p. in stamps
requested for post & packing for bulky literature).

AGEN (Lot-et-Garonne)

Syn. & Com. Centre: 52 rue Montesquieu, 47000. Tel. 5366-24-20.

AIX-EN-PROVENCE (Bouches du Rhône)

Syn. & Com. Centre: 3 bis rue de Jérusalem, 13100. Tel. 4226-69-39.
Inf. about kosher butchers from Rabbi H. Harboun.

AIX-LES-BAINS (Savoie)

Syn.: Rue Paul Bonna. 73100. Tel. 7935-28-08. Mikva on premises.
Mikva, Pavillon Salvador, rue du Président Roosevelt, 73100. Tel. 7935-38-
08.
Rest Home: Maison de Retraite du C.O.J.A.S.O.R., Av. de Berlioz, 73100.
School: Tomer Deborah, Chemin de St. Pol, 73100.
Yeshiva: Route de Tresserve, 73100. Tel. 7935-03-17.
Kosher Meat & Provisions, **(K)** Berdah, 29 Av. de Tresserve, 73100. Tel.
7961-44-11.

AJACCIO

(See under Corsica at end of section on France.)

AMIENS (Somme)

Syn. & Com. Centre: 38 rue du Port d'Amont, 8000.

ANGERS (Maine-et-Loire)

Syn.: 12 rue Valdemaine, 49100.

ANNECY (Haute-Savoie)

Syn. & Com. Centre: 18 rue de Narvik, 74000. Tel. 5045-82-22.

ANNEMASSE (Haute Savoie)

Syn.: 13 rue de la Paix, 74100.
Kosher Butcher: **(K)** Yarden, 59 rue de la Libération, 74240 Gaillard. Tel.
5092-64-05.

ANTIBES JUAN-LES-PINS (Alpes-Maritimes)

Syn.: Villa La Monada. Chemin des Sables, 06600. Tel. 9361-59-34.
Kosher Butchers: **(K)** André Sebbah, 28 Av. Maiziers, 06600. Tel. 9334-60-
11; **(K)** Krief, 3 rue Louis-Gallet, 06160. Tel. 9374-73-30.

ARCACHON (Gironde)

Syn.: Cours Desbey. Open July & Aug. only.

AVIGNON (Vaucluse)
Syn.: 2 Place de Jérusalem, 84000. Tel. 9085-21-24.
Com. Centre: 18 rue Guillaume-Puy, 84000. Tel. 9082-64-87.
Mikva: 7 rue des Sept-Baisers, 84140 Montfavet. Tel. 9086-30-30.
Kosher Butcher: **(K)** Chelly, 15 rue Chapeau-Rouge, 84000. Tel. 9082-47-50.
The Conseil Général de Vaucluse, Place Campana, B.P.147, 84008 Avignon
(Tel. 90.86.43.42) publishes a guide to the Jewish sites of the Vaucluse.

BAR-LE-DUC (Meuse)
Syn.: 7 Quai Carnot.

BASTIA
(See under Corsica at end of section on France.)

BAYONNE (Basses-Pyrénées)
Syn. & Com. Centre: 35 rue Maubec, 64100. Tel. 5955-03-95.

BEAUVAIS (Oise)
Syn. & Com. Centre: Rue Jules Isaac, 60000.

BELFORT (Territoire de Belfort)
Syn.: 6 rue de l'As-de-Carreau, 90000. Tel. 8428-55-41.
Com. Centre: 27 rue Strolz, 90000. Tel. 8428-55-41.

BENFELD (Bas-Rhin)
Syn.: 7a rue de la Dîme, 67230.
Com. Centre: 6 rue du Grand Rempart, 67230.

BESANCON (Doubs)
Syn.: 23c Quai de Strasbourg, 25000.
Com. Centre: 10 rue Grosjean, 25000. Tel. 8180-82-82.
Kosher meat, groceries & frozen food: M. Croppet, 18 rue des Granges. Tel.
8183-35-93. Thurs. only.

BEZIERS (Hérault)
Syn. & Com. Centre: 19 Place Pierre-Sémard. Tel. 6728-75-98.

BIARRITZ (Basses-Pyrénées)
Syn.: rue de Russie (cnr. rue Pellot), 64200. Services, Yom Kippur only.

BISCHHEIM-SCHILTIGHEIM (Bas-Rhin)
Syn. & Com. Centre: Place de la Synagogue, 67800 Bischheim. Tel. 8333-02-
87.

BITCHE (Moselle)
Syn.: 28 rue de Sarreguemines, 57230. Services, Rosh Hashana & Yom
Kippur.

BORDEAUX (Gironde)
Syn.: 8 rue du Grand-Rabbin-Joseph-Cohen, 33000. Tel. 5691-79-39.
Com. Centre: 15 Pl. Charles-Gruet, 33000. Tel. 5652-62-69.
Mikva: 213 rue Ste. Catherine, 33000. Tel. 5691-79-39.
Kosher Restaurant: **(K) M. Saada,** 137 Cours Aristide-Briand. Tel. 5692-74-
90.

BOULAY (Moselle)
Syn.: Rue du Pressoir, 57220. Tel. 8779-28-34.

BOULOGNE-SUR-MER (Pas de Calais)
Syn.: 63 rue Charles Butor.

BOURGES (Cher)
Jewish Religious Assoc. (Association Cultuelle Israélite): B. David, 62-66 rue Charlet 18000. Tel. 4824-5301. Services, Yom Kippur only.

BOUZONVILLE (Moselle)
Syn. & Com. Centre: Rue des Bénédictins, 57320.

BREST (Finistère)
Syn. & Com. Centre: 40 rue de la République, 29200. Services, Fri., 7.30 p.m.

CAEN (Calvados)
Syn. & Com. Centre: 46 Av. de la Libération, 14000. Tel. 3143-60-54.
Kosher Butcher: **(K)** M. Lasry, 26 rue de l'Engannerie, 14000. Tel. 3186-16-25. Open Thurs.

CAGNES-SUR-MER (Alpes Maritimes)
Syn.: 5 rue des Capucines, 06800.

CALUIRE ET CUIRE (Rhône)
Syn. & Com. Centre: 107 Av. Fleming, 69300. Services, festivals only.

CANNES (Alpes-Maritimes)
Syn.: Habad Lubavitch, 22, Rue Cdt Vidal (Angle Bd. de Lorraine) 06400, Tel. 9298-6751; 20 Blvd. d'Alsace, 06400. Tel. 9338-16-54.
Com. Centre: 3 rue de Bône, 06400. Tel. as above.
Kosher Hotel: **(K) Hotel Acapulco** (60), 16 Blvd. d'Alsace, 06400. Tel. 9399-16-16. Under the supervision of Rabbi Mordechai Bensoussan, Regional Rabbi of Nice, Côte d'Azur & Corsica.
Kosher Butchers: **(K)** Marcel Benguigui, 17 rue Maréchal-Joffre, 06400. Tel. 9339-57-92; **(K)** J.-Y. Zana, 44 rue Jean-Jaurès, 06400. Tel. 9338-46-59.

CARPENTRAS (Vaucluse)
Services are held on festivals in the ancient syn. in the Place de la Mairie, 84200, classed as a national monument. Built in 1367 and rebuilt in 1741, it is worth a visit. Inq. to Freddy Hadoad. Tel. 9063-10-56.

CAVAILLON (Vaucluse)
The remains of the old syn., built in 1774, are regarded as a French historical monument. Inq. to 23 rue Chabrun.

CHALONS-SUR-MARNE (Marne)
Syn. & Com. Centre: 21 rue Lochet, 51000.

CHALON-SUR-SAONE (Saône-et-Loire)
Syn.: 10 rue Germiny, 71100.

CHAMBERY (Savoie)
Syn. & Com. Centre: 44 rue St.-Réal. Services, Fri. evg., 7 p.m. and festivals.

CHATEAUROUX (Indre)
Inq. to Michel Touati, 3 Allée Emile Zola, Montierchaume, 36130 Déols. Tel. 5426-05-47.

CLERMONT-FERRAND (Puy de Dôme)
Syn. & Com. Centre: 6 rue Blatin. Tel. 7393-36-59.
(K) Kosher meat is available at the Com. Centre on alternate Thurs. Tel. 7860-13-25.

CLOUANGE (Moselle)
Syn.: Rue Jean-Buger, 57120. Services, festivals only.

COLMAR (Haut-Rhin)
Syn.: 3 rue de la Cigogne, 68000. Tel. 8941-38-29. Mikva on premises.
The Chief Rabbi of the Haut-Rhin region is Rabbi Jacky Dreyfus, 1 rue des Jonquilles, 68000. Tel. 8923-13-11.

COMPIEGNE (Oise)
Syn. & Com. Centre: 4 rue du Dr.-Charles-Nicolle, 60200.

CREIL (Oise)
Syn. & Com. Centre: 1 Place de la Synagogue, 60100. Tel. 4425-16-37.

DIEUZE (Moselle)
Syn.: Av. Foch, 57260.

DIJON (Côte d'Or)
Syn. & Com. Centre: 5 rue de la Synagogue. Tel. 8066-46-47. Mikva.
Kosher Butchers: **(K)** Albert Lévy, 25 rue de la Manutention. Tel. 8030-14-42; **(K)** Albert Sultan, 4 petite rue Pouffier. Tel. 8073-31-38.

DUNKERQUE (Nord)
Syn. & Com. Centre: 19 rue Jean-Bart, 59140.

ELBEUF (Seine-Maritime)
Syn.: 29 rue Grémont, 76500. Tel. 3577-09-11.

EPERNAY (Marne)
Syn.: 2 rue Placet, 51200. Services, Yom Kippur only. Tel. 2655-24-44.

EPINAL (Vosges)
Syn.: Rue Charlet, 88000. Tel. 2982-25-23.

ERSTEIN (Bas-Rhin)
Syn.: Rue du Vieux-Marché, 67150. Services, Rosh Hashana & Yom Kippur only.

EVIAN-LES-BAINS (Haute-Savoie)
Syn.: Adjacent to 1 Av. des Grottes, 74500. Tel. 5075-15-63.

FAULQUEMONT-CREHANGE (Moselle)
Syn. & Com. Centre.: Place de l'Hotel de Ville, 57380. Services, festivals & High Holy-days only.

FORBACH (Moselle)
Syn. & Com. Centre.: 98 Av. St.-Rémy, 57600. Tel. 8785-25-57.

FREJUS (Var)
Syn.: Villa Ariane, rue du Progrès, Fréjus-Plage, 83600. Tel. 9452-06-87.
Kosher Restaurant, Delicatessen & Takeaway: **(K) Yarden Food Centre,** Le Capitole, 3 Blvd. d'Alger, 83600. Tel. 9440-15-25.

GRASSE (Alpes-Maritimes)
Syn. & Com. Centre: 82 Route de Nice, 06130. Tel. 9336-05-33 after 7 p.m.
Services, festivals & High Holy-days only. (Reports on existence of this
Centre needed. Ed.)

GRENOBLE (Isère)
Syn. & Com. Centre: 11 rue André-Maginot, 38000. Tel. 7687-02-80. Mikva.
Tel. 7687-02-80.
Consistoire Israélite de Grenoble (CIG), 4 rue des Bains, 38000. Tel.
76461514. Rabbinat: 76476372. **(K)** Restaurant Universitaire. Tel. 76874036.
Radio Kol Hachalom. Tel. 76872122.
(K) Kosher Meals: Inq. to 11 rue André-Maginot.
Kosher Butchers: **(K)** C. Cohen, 19 rue Turenne, 38000. Tel. 7646-48-14; **(K)**
Losky, 32 rue de Stalingrad, 38000. Tel. 7687-04-01; **(K)** Sebbag, 6 rue
Aubert-Dubayet, 38000. Tel. 7646-40-78.

GROSBLIEDERSTROFF (Moselle)
Syn. 6 rue des Fermes, 57520.

HAGONDANGE (Moselle)
Syn.: Rue Henri-Hoffmann, 57300.

HAGUENAU (Bas-Rhin)
Syn.: 3 rue du Grand-Rabbin-Joseph-Bloch, 67500. Tel. 8873-38-30.
Mikva: 7 rue Neuve.

HAYANGE (Moselle)
Syn. & Com. Centre: 43 rue de Verdun, 57700. Tel. 8284-12-84.

HYERES (Var)
Syn.: Chemin de la Ritorte, 83400. Tel. 9465-31-97.

INGWILLER (Bas-Rhin)
Syn.: Cours du Château, 67340.

INSMING (Moselle)
Syn.: Rue de la Synagogue, 57670.

JUAN-LES-PINS. See Antibes.

LA CIOTAT (Bouches du Rhône)
Syn. & Com. Centre: 1 Square de Verdun, 13600. Tel. 4271-93-93.

LA ROCHELLE (Loire)
Syn. & Com. Centre: 40 Cours des Dames, 17000. Tel. 4641-17-66.
For inf. about kosher food, etc., contact Pierre Guedj, 19 rue Bastion
d'Evangile, 17000. Tel. 4667-38-91.

LA SEYNE-SUR-MER (Var)
Syn. & Com. Centre: 5 rue Chevalier-de-la-Barre, 83500. Tel. 9494-40-28.
Kosher Butcher: **(K)** Elie Benhamou, 17 rue Baptistin-Paul, 83500. Tel.
9494-38-60.

LE HAVRE (Seine-Maritime)
Syn. & Com. Centre: 38 rue Victor-Hugo, 76600. Tel. 3521-14-59.

LE MANS (Sarthe)
Syn.: 4-6 Blvd. Paixhans, 72000. Tel. 4386-00-96.

LENS (Pas de Calais)
Syn. & Com. Centre: 87 rue Casimir-Beugnet, 62300.

LIBOURNE (Gironde)
Syn.: 33 rue Lamothe, 33500.

LILLE (Nord)
Syn. & Com. Centre: 5 rue Auguste-Angellier, 59000. Tel. 2030-69-86.
Kosher Butcher: **(K)** Cassab, 16 bis rue Jeanne-d'Arc, 59000. Tel. 2057-33-07.

LIMOGES (Haute-Vienne)
Syn. & Com. Centre: 25-27 rue Pierre-Leroux, 87000. Tel. 5577-47-26.
(K) Kosher meat and food products available from the Com. Centre Thurs. afternoon & Sun. morning, as well as by special request.

LIXHEIM (Moselle)
Syn.: Rue de la Synagogue, 57110.

LORIENT (Morbihan)
Syn.: c/o Mme. Frandji, 18 rue de la Patrie, 56100. Services, festivals & Holy-days only.

LUNEVILLE (Meurthe-et-Moselle)
Syn.: 5 rue Castara, 54300.

LYON (Rhône)
Synagogues & Religious Organisations
Regional Chief Rabbi: Rabbi Richard Wertenschlag, 13 Quai Tilsitt, 69002. Tel. 7837 1343.
Beth Din, 34 rue d'Armenie, 3e. Tel. 78629763. Fax 78950947.
Consistoire Israélite de Lyon. Same address. Tel. 7837-13-43. Fax 783 82657.
Consistoire Israélite Sepharade de Lyon, Yaacov Molho Com. Centre, 317 rue Duguesclin, 69007. Tel. 7858-18-74. FAX. 7858 1749.

Synagogues
Ashkenazi, 13 Quai Tilsitt, 69002. Tel. 7837-13-43. This is the city's main syn.
Benarrous, 3-5 rue St.-Jacques, 69003.
Beth David, 202 rue André Philip, 69003. Tel. 6895-28-65.
Chaare Tsedek (N. African), 18 rue St.-Mathieu, 69008. Tel. 7800-72-50.
Jewish Day School, 40 rue Alexandre Boutin, Villeurbanne, 69100. Tel. 7824-38-91.
Lubavitch, 3 passage Cazenove, 69006. Tel. 7889-08-32.
Mizrahi (N. African), 11 rue Ste.-Catherine, 69001. Tel. 7850-87-13.
Neveh Chalom (Sephardi), 317 rue Duguesclin, 69007. Tel. 7858-18-54.
Orah Haim, 17 rue Albert-Thomas, St.-Fons, 69190. Tel. 7251-50-02.
Patah Eliahu, 3 Impasse Professeur-Beauvisage, 69008. Tel. 7800-37-21.
Rav Hida (N. African), La Sauvegarde, La Duchère, 69009. Tel. 7835-14-44.
Synagogue de la Fraternité (Sephardi), 4 rue Malherbe, Villeurbanne, 69100. Tel. 7884-04-32.
Yeshiva Pinto, 20 bis rue des Mûriers, Villeurbanne, 69100. Tel. 7803-89-14.
12 Chemin de la Batterie, Bron, 69500.

48 rue de la Marne, Bron, 69500. Tel. 7826-95-15.
1 rue de Dublin, Rillieux, 69140. Tel. 7888-50-89.
12 Av. Division Leclerc, Vénissieux, 69200. Tel. 7831-69-60.
6 Av. de la Libération, Meyzieu, 69330. Tel. 7804-17-92.
26 rue Chevreul, Villeurbanne, 69100. Tel. 7884-09-55.
7 rue du Docteur Frappaz, Ville-urbanne, 69100. Tel. 7854-12-32.

Mikvaot
Chaare Tsedek. (as above) Jewish Day School. (as above) Neveh Chalom.
(as above) Orah Haim. (as above) St.-Fons, 17 rue Albert-Thomas, St. Fons,
69190. Tel. 7867-39-78; Synagogue de la Fraternité. (as above) Yeshiva
Pinto.(as above) Rav Hida (as above); Rillieus (as above).

Representative Organisations
B'nai B'rith, 9 Av. Général Leclerc, 69007.
F.S.J.U., 146 Grande-Rue de la Guillotière, 69007. Tel. 7872-88-23.

Youth Organisations
Betar, 13 Quai Tilsitt 69002. Tel. 78 69 1203.
Bnei Akiva, 317 rue Duguesclin, 69007.
Dror, 18 rue du Bâtiment-d'Argent, 69001. Tel. 7827-35-46.
Eclaireurs et Eclaireuses Israélites de France (Jewish Scouts), c/o Alain
Majerowicz, 13 Quai Tilsitt, 69002. Tel. 7850-29-01.
Lubavitch, 3 Passage Cazenove, 69006.

Zionist Organisations
Jewish Agency, 169 Cours Lafayette, 69006. Tel. 7824-39-02.
WIZO, 18 rue du Bât. D'Argent.

Jewish Media
CIV News, 4 rue Malherbe, Villeurbanne, 69100. Tel. 7884-04-32.
Hachaar, 18 rue St. Mathieu, 69008. Tel. 7800-72-50.
La Voix Sépharade, 317 rue Duguesclin, 69007. Tel. 7858-18-74.
Le Bulletin, 13 Quai Tilsitt, 69002. Tel. 7837-13-43.
Radio Judaïca Lyon (R.J.L.), P.O.B. 7063, 69341. Tel. 7803-99-20. FM 94.5.

Jewish Booksellers
Decitre, Place Bellecour, 69002.
F.N.A.C., rue de la Règublique, 69002.
Levi-Its'hak, 3 Passage Cazenove. Tel. 78931617.
Mazal, 46 rue Jean-Claude-Vivant, Villeurbanne, 69100. Tel. 7852-85-94.
Menorah (Ouaknine), 52 rue Montesquieu, 69007. Tel. 7869-09-35.

Kosher Restaurants
(K) Le Grillon d'Or, 20 rue Terme, 69001. Tel. 7827-33-09.
(K) Jardin d'Eden, 3 Rue Jean Jaurès. Tel. 7233-8565.
(K) Lippmann, 4 rue Tony-Tollet, 69002. Tel. 7842-49-82.
(K) L'Orient Express, 140 rue Dedieu, 69100. Tel. 78.68.99.23.
(K) ORT School, 133 rue Marius Berliet, 69008. Tel. 7874-25-05.
(K) Pizzeria Le Pinnochio, 5 rue Alexandre Boulin, Villeurbanne. Tel.
7868-62-95.
(K) Pizzeria Obadia, 2 rue Jubin Villeurbanne. Tel. 7244-33-62.
Details of kosher bakers, butchers, provision merchants, etc. can be
obtained from the Consistoire Israélite, address & Tel. above.

MACON (Saône-et-Loire)
Syn. & Com. Centre: 32 rue des Minimes, 71000.

MARIGNANE (Bouches du Rhône)
Syn. & Com. Centre: 9 rue Pilote-Larbonne, 13700.

MARSEILLE (Bouches du Rhône)
Synagogues & Religious Organisations
Regional Chief Rabbi: Rabbi Jacques Ouaknin. Tel. 9137-49-64.
Consistoire Israélite de Marseille, 117-119 rue Breteuil, 13006. Tel. 9137-71-84.
Main Synagogue (Sephardi), 117 rue Breteuil, 13006. Tel. 9137-49-64.

Other Synagogues
Ashkenazi Syn., 8 Impasse Dragon, 13006.
Bar Yohai, (Sephardi), 171 rue Abbé-de-l'Epée, 13005. Tel. 9142-38-19.
Berith Thora, 24 Chemin du Rove. Tel. 91-60-51-94.
Beth Chalom (Sephardi), 24 rue Montgrand, 13006. Tel. 9133-61-79.
Beth Myriam (Sephardi), 60 Chemin Vallon-de-Toulouse, 13009. Tel. 9175-14-97.
Beth Simha (Sephardi), 31 Av. des Olives, 13013. Tel. 9170-05-45.
Bné Israel (Sephardi), 60 rue Ste.-Sophie. Tel. 9149-84-73.
Chalom Aleikhem, 16 Lotissement Demoiselle, Calas-Cabriès.
Chalom Rav (Sephardi), 8 Impasse Dragon, 13006.
Chevet Ha'him (Sephardi), 18 rue Beaumont, 13001. Tel. 9150-30-07.
Hekhal Chelomo, 91 Chemin du Merlan. Tel. 9102-75-98.
Keter Torah (Sephardi), 44 rue du Tapis-Vert, 13001. Tel. 9190-72-39.
La Source, 104 Blvd. Paul-Claudel, 13009. Tel. 9175-20-98.
Le Collel (Ashkenazi), 43a Chemin Vallon-de-Toulouse, 13009. Tel. 9175-28-64.
Merkaz Netivot Chalom (Sephardi), 27 Blvd. Bonifay, 13004. Tel. 9189-40-62.
Merlan, La Cerisaie, Bâtiment G1, 13014. Tel. 9198-53-92.
Neve Itzhak (Sephardi), 73 rue St.-Ferréol, 13001. Tel. 9133-93-39.
Ohel Yaakov, 20 Chemin Ste.-Marthe, 13014. Tel. 9162-70-42.
Oratoire du Parc Fleuri, 121 Blvd. Paul-Claudel. Tel. 9126-59-32.
Or Hatikva, 35 Av. Paul Sirvent, Plan-de-Cuques, 13380.
Or Torah (Sephardi), 14 rue St.-Dominique, 13001. Tel. 9190-64-30.
Ozer Dalim (Sephardi), 8 Impasse Dragon, 13006. Tel. 9153-33-73.
Tiferet Israel (Sephardi), 205 Blvd. Ste.-Marguerite, 13009. Tel. 9175-63-50.
U.L.I. (Sephardi), 21 rue Martiny, 13008. Tel. 9171-97-46.
Yavneh (Sephardi), 37 Blvd. Barry, 13013. Tel. 9166-13-15.
Yechivah Beth David, 13 Blvd. du Redon, 13009. Tel. 9182-18-89.
Zekhout Avoth, 3 rue Général-Mont-sabert, Logis Neuf, Allauch, 13190. Tel. 9105-00-33.
Com. Centres: Centre Edmond Fleg, 4 Impasse Dragon,13006. Tel. 9137-42-01; Centre La Rose, 31 Av. des Olives, 13013. Tel. 9170-05-45; Centre Tif'eret Israël, 205 Blvd. Sainte.
Mikvaot: Aquarius, 82 Cannebière. Tel. 9147-40-74; Beth Simha La Rose, 31 Av. des Olives, 13013. Tel. 9170-05-45; Lonchamp, 45a rue Consolat, 13001. Tel. 9162-42-61.

Representative Organisation
B'nai B'rith, 41 Cours d'Estienne d'Orves, 13001. Tel. 9133-80-50.

Cultural & Educational Organisations
Assoc. of Cultural & Youth Centres, 67 rue Breteuil, 13006. Tel. 9137-40-57.
Jewish Library, 4 Impasse Dragon, 13006. Tel. 9137-42-01.

Welfare Organisations, Hospitals, etc.
F.S.J.U. (United Jewish Welfare Fund). Representative, H. Zana, 67 rue Breteuil. Tel. 9137-40-57.
C.A.S.I.M. (Marseille Regional Welfare Agency). 61 rue de la Palud, 13006. Tel. 9154-37-36. Dir. H. Zana.
Coopération Féminine. 67 rue Breteuil. Tel. 9181-79-59.
Home for Aged, "Les Oliviers," 24 Impasse des Joncs. Tel. 9173-04-58.

Student & Youth Organisations
Jeunesse Lubavitch, 73 rue St.-Ferréol, 13006. Tel. 9133-80-96.
Jewish Scouts, 6 Impasse Dragon, 13006. Tel. 9153-54-32.
Maccabi-Sports, 2 rue Gustave-Ricard, 13006. Tel. 9133-13-10.
Union des Etudiants Juifs de Marseille, 74 rue Paradis, 13006. Tel. 9177-38-43.

Zionist Organisations
A.U.J.F. (United Jewish Appeal), 173 rue Paradis, 13006. Tel. 9137-03-21.
Jewish Agency Immigration Dept., 95 Cours Pierre-Puget, 13006. Tel. 9133-26-26.
WIZO, 2 Blvd. Théodore Thurner, 13006. Tel. 9148-64-26.
Israel Consulate-General, 454 rue Paradis, 13008. Tel. 9177-39-90.

Jewish Media
L'Arche Provençale (monthly), 67 rue Breteuil, 13006. Tel. 9137-40-57.
Radio Juive de Marseille, P.O.B. 243, 13269 Cédex 8. Tel. 9154-12-12.

Bookseller
Librairie Jasyber, 95 rue St. Pierre, 13005. Tel. 9148-17-37.

Kosher Restaurants
(K) Centre Edmund Fleg, 4 Impasse Dragon, 13006. Tel. 9137-42-63.
(K) Eden-Up, 30 rue Tapis-Vert, 13001. Tel. 9191-47-59.
(K) La Crêpe à Musique, 26 rue Sainte, 13001. Tel. 9133-94-46.
(K) Le Dizengoff, 50 Cours Julien, 13006. Tel. 9148-55-45.
(K) Le Lotus de Nissane, 94 Cours Julien, 13006. Tel. 9142-61-60.
(K) Le Sunset Plazza, 24 rue Pavillon, 13001. Tel. 9133-27-77.
(K) ORT, 23 rue des Forges, 13010. Tel. 9179-61-65.
(K) Presto Pizza Cash, Centre Commercial Résidence Bellevue, entrance rue Gaston Berger, 13010. Tel. 9175-19-00.
(K) Snack Chez Alain, 11 rue Glandevès, 13001. Tel. 9189-41-43.
(K) Snack Erets, rue Rouget-de-Lisle, 13001. Tel. 9154-03-70.
(K) Snack Partouche, 5 rue de l'Arc, 13001. Tel. 9133-26-23.

Kosher Butchers
There are 21 kosher butchers licensed by the Chief Rabbinate in various parts of the city, and they display a sign to that effect. Full details from the Consistoire, 117-119 rue Breteuil, 13006. Tel. 9137-71-84.

MELUN (Seine-et-Marne)
Syn. & Com. Centre: Cnr. rues Branly & Michelet, 77000. Tel. (1) 6452-00-05.

MENTON (Alpes-Maritimes)
Syn. & Com. Centre: Centre Altyner, 106 Cours du Centenaire. Tel. 9335-28-29.

MERLEBACH (Moselle)
Syn. & Com. Centre: 19 rue St.-Nicolas, 57800.

METZ (Moselle)
Chief Rabbi of Moselle, Rabbi Marc-Raphaël Guedj. Tel. 8775-04-44.
Main Syn.: 39 rue du Rabbin-Elie-Bloch. Tel. 8775-04-44 or 8775-14-93. This street was renamed from rue de l'Arsenal, in memory of a youth movement rabbi deported and killed by the Nazis during the Second World War.
Other syns: Yechouroun, 39 & 41 rue du Rabbin-Elie-Bloch; 2 rue Paul Michaux.
Com. Centre: Same address & Tel. as Main Syn.
Mikva: Rue Kellerman.
Kosher Restaurant: **(K) Galil**, 39 rue du Rabbin-Elie-Bloch. Tel. 8775-04-44. Open until noon every weekday.
Kosher sections in supermarkets:
Cali, 3 rue du Rabbin-Elie-Bloch; SUMA, 23 rue de Verdun.
(K) Butcher: Claude Sebbag, 22 rue Mangin, 57000. Tel 87633350.

MONTAUBAN (Tarn-et-Garonne)
Syn. & Com. Centre: 14 rue Ste.-Claire, 82000. Tel. 6303-01-37.

MONTBELIARD
Syn.: Rue de la Synagogue, 25200.

MONTPELLIER (Hérault)
Syns.: Ben-Zakai, 7 rue Général-Laffon, 34000. Tel. 6792-92-07; Mazal Tov, 18 rue Ferdinand-Fabre, 34000. Tel. 6779-09-82.
Com. Centre: 27 rue Ferdinand-Fabre, 34000. Tel. 6779-68-93.
Kosher Butchers: **(K)** Camille Bensoussan, 33 rue de la Valfère, 34000. Tel. 6766-03-22; Gilbert Bensoussan, 41 rue de Lunaret, 34000. Tel. 6772-67-94.

MULHOUSE (Haut-Rhin)
Syn. & Com. Centre: 19 rue de la Synagogue, 68100. Tel. 8966-21-22. Mikva on premises.
Kosher Butcher: **(K)** Ersel, 51 rue d'Illzach, 68100. Tel. 8942-39-61.

NANCY (Meurthe-et-Moselle)
Syn.: 17 Blvd. Joffre, 54000. Tel. 8332-10-67. Chief Rabbi: Rabbi Edmund Schwob.
Com. Centre: 19 Blvd. Joffre, 54000. Tel. 8332-10-67.
The Musée Historique Lorrain, 64 Grand' Rue, has an important collection of sifrei Torah, prayer books & other ritual objects.
Kosher Restaurant: **(K) Restaurant Universitaire,** 19 Blvd. Joffre, 54000. Tel. 8332-10-67. Open weekdays until noon.

NANTES (Loire-Atlantique)
Syn. & Com. Centre: 5 Impasse Copernic, 44000. Tel. 4073-48-92. Mikva on premises.

NICE (Alpes-Maritimes)
The community numbers approx. 30,000
Synagogues & Religious Organisations
Centre Consistorial & Syn.: 22 rue Michelet, 06100. Tel. 9351-89-80. Publishes an annual calendar and guide to Nice and district.
Main Syn.: 7 rue Gustave-Deloye, 06000. Tel. 9392-11-38.

Other Syns. & Com. Centres: 8 rue Marceau, 06000. Tel. 9385 8206; 1 rue Boissy d'Anglas 06000. Tel. 93 80 5896; 9 ave Andre Theuriet. Tel. 9398 47 89. A.C.I. Aschkenaze, 1 rue Blacas, 06000 Tel. 93623868; Cercle des Etudes Juives, Les Oliviers, 31 Av. Henri Barbasse. Tel. 9351-4363.
Rabbinate: Regional Chief Rabbinate of Nice, Côte d'Azur & Corsica: 1 rue Voltaire 06000. Tel. 0195-82-06.
Mikva: 22 rue Michelet. Tel. 9351-89-80.
General Inf., Tourist Welcome Offices – Pavillon d'Accueil, Av. Thiers, 06000. Tel. 9388-69-63 & 9387-35-44. Visitors to Nice will appreciate Chagal's Musée Biblique in the town.

Bookseller
Librairie Tanya, 25 rue Pertinax, 06000. Tel. 9380-21-74.

Kosher Restaurants
(K) Le cheme Chamayime, 22 rue Rossine. Tel. 9388 4701.
(K) Le Gani, 11 rue de Paganini. Tel. 9388 4701.
(K) Roi David Ten Li Hai, 9 rue Clément-Roassal, 06000. Tel. 9387-65-25. Also take-away.
(K) King Georges, 26 rue Pertinax 06000. Tel. 93130799.
A list of kosher butchers & bakers can be had from Chief Rabbi Mordehai Bensoussan, Tel. 9385 82 06.
Groceries etc. Mickael Supermarket, 37 rue Dabray 06000. Tel. 93 88 81 23; K'gel, 11 rue Fricero, 06000. Tel. 93 86 33 01; Nizzard, 26 rue Pertinax 06000 Tel. 93 62 30 77; Mahédrin, 12 rue Trache 06000. Tel. 93 88 06 96.

NIMES (Gard)
Syn.: 40 rue Roussy, 30000. Mikva on premises. Tel. 6629-51-81.
Com. Centre: 5 rue d'Angoulême, 30000. Tel. 6626-19-51.

OBERNAI (Bas-Rhin)
Syn.: Rue de Sélestat, 67210.

ORLEANS (Loiret)
Syn. & Com. Centre: 14 rue Robert-de-Courtenay (to the left of the cathedral), 45000. Kosher meat available every Wed., 4.30 p.m. to 7.30 p.m.
At Pithiviers, near Orléans, there is a monument to the Jewish victims of Nazi persecution.

PARIS
Memorial to the Unknown Jewish Martyr
This stands at the corner of rue Geoffroy l'Asnier and rue Grenier sur l'Eau, Paris 75004, near the Métro Pont-Marie. The memorial, which is

open daily, except Saturdays, from 10 a.m. to 12 noon and from 2 to 5 p.m., is one of the most unusual edifices in Paris. It is divided into two main parts an underground crypt and a four-storey building. The roof of the crypt forms a spacious street-level courtyard, in the middle of which stands a huge bronze cylinder shaped like a crematorium urn. The building contains a library, reading-room and museum devoted to the archives of the Centre de Documentation Juive Contemporaine – which gathers data on Nazi anti-Jewish crimes.

Religious Organisations
The Consistoire Central: Union des Communutés Juives de France, which represents French Jewry in all religious matters, has its headquarters in Paris at 17 rue St. Georges, 75009. Tel. 49 70 8800. Pres.: Jean-Pierre Bansard. The Chief Rabbi of France, Rabbi Joseph Sitruk, can be contacted at 17 rue St. Georges. Exec. Dir.: Léon Masliah.
In addition, Paris Jewry is represented by the Consistoire de Paris, at the same address. Tel. 4285-71-09. Pres.: Benny Cohen. Chief Rabbi of Paris: Rabbi Alain Goldmann.
Communauté Israélite de la Stricte Observance, 10 rue Cadet, 75009. Tel. 4246 3637; Le Conseil Representatif du Judaisme Traditionaliste de France, 23 bis, rue Dufréncy 75016. Tel. 4504 1309; Jeunesse Lubavitch, 8 rue Lamartine 75009 Tel. 4526 8760.

Synagogues

Consistoire de Paris
★Belleville, 120 Blvd. de Belleville, 75020. Tel. 4636-73-72.
★Brit Chalom, 18 rue St.-Lazare, 75009. Tel. 4878-45-32.
★Buffault, 28 rue Buffault, 75009. Tel. 4526-80-87.
Chasseloup-Laubat, 14 rue Chasseloup-Laubat, 75015. Tel. 4273-36-29.
★D. I. Abravanel, 84-86 rue de la Roquette, 75011. Tel. 4700-75-95.
Fleischmann, 18 rue des Ecouffes, 75004. Tel. 4887-97-86.
★Fondary, 13 rue Fondary, 75015. Tel. 4250-25-78.
★Julien Lacroix, 75 rue Julien Lacroix, 75020. Tel. 4358-28-39.
★Montmartre, 13 rue Ste.-Isaure, 75018. Tel. 4264-48-34.
Place des Vosges, 14 Place des Vosges, 75004. Tel. 4887-79-45.
★Rue Lamblardie, 15 rue Lamblardie, 75012. Tel. 4347-36-78.
★Rue Notre-Dame-de-Nazareth, 15 rue Notre-Dame-de-Nazareth, 75003. Tel. 4278-00-30.
★Rue des Saules, 42 rue des Saules, 75018. Tel. 4606-71-39.
★Rue des Tournelles, 21 bis rue des Tournelles, 75004. Tel. 4274-32-80.
★Rue Vauquelin, 9 rue Vauquelin, 75005. Tel. 4707-21-22.
★Rue Vercingétorix, 223 rue Vercingétorix, 75014. Tel. 4545-03-43.
Rue de la Victoire, 44 rue de la Victoire, 75009. Tel. 4285-71-09.
★These synagogues are used by the North African community.

Other Orthodox
18 rue Basfroi, 75011.
32 rue Basfroi, 75011. Tel. 4367-89-20.
45 rue de Belleville, 75019.
Beth El, 3 rue Saulnier, 75009. Tel. 4770-09-23.
24 rue Bourg-Tibourg, 75004.
10 rue Cadet, 75009.
Centre Rambam, Synagogue des Originaires du Maroc, 19-21 rue Galvani, 75017. Tel. 4574-51-81.
17 rue de la Cour-des-Noues, 75020.
11-13 rue Curial, 75019.

15 Cour Debille, 75011.
19 rue Domrémy, 75013.
80 rue Doudeauville, 75018.
5 rue Duc, 75018.
9 rue Guy-Patin, 75010.
9 Av. Hoche, 75008.
1 rue Jadin, 75017.
8 rue Lamartine, 75009.
4 rue Martel, 75010.
25 rue Michel-Leconte, 75003.
31 rue de Montevidéo, 75016. Tel. 4504-66-73.
10 rue Pavée, 75004.
13-15 rue des Petites-Ecuries, 75010.
30 Blvd. du Port-Royal, 75005.
Rachi Synagogue, 6 rue Ambroise-Thomas, 75009. Tel. 4824-86-94.
17 rue des Rosiers, 75004.
25 rue des Rosiers, 75004.
4 rue Saulnier, 75009.
70 Av. Secrétan, 75019.
37 Blvd. de Strasbourg, 75010.
51 Blvd. de Strasbourg, 75010.
29 rue de Thionville, 75019.
37 rue des Trois-Bornes, 75011.
61-65 rue Vergniaud, 75013. Tel. 4588-93-84.
6 bis Villa d'Alésia, 75014.
25 Villa d'Alésia, 75014.

Conservative
Adath Shalom. 22bis, rue des Belles Feuilles 75116. Tel. 4553 8409.

Liberal
24 rue Copernic, 75016. Tel. 727-25-76.
Syn. & Centre, Mouvement Juif Libéral de France, 11 rue Gaston-de-Caillavet. Tel. 4575-38-09.

Mikvaot
176 rue du Temple, nr. Place de la République, 75003. Tel. 4271-89-28; 6 rue Ambroise Thomas, 75009. Tel. 4824-86-94; 50 rue du Faubourg St.-Martin, 07010. Tel. 4206-43-95; 36 rue Basfroi, 75011. Tel. 4367-8920; 31 rue Thionville, 75019. Tel. 4245-74-20; 75 rue Julien Lacroix, 75020. Tel. 4636-30-10.

Representative Organisations
Anti-Defamation League of B'nai B'rith, 4 bis rue de Lota, 75016. Tel. 4553-03-22.
B'nai B'rith, 38 rue de Clichy, 75009. Tel. 4082-91-11.
Conseil Représentatif des Institutions Juives de France (C.R.I.F.), 19 rue de Téhéran, 75008. Tel. 4561-00-70.
World Jewish Congress, 78 Av. des Champs Elysées, 75008. Tel. 4359-94-63.

Cultural & Educational Organisations
Alliance Israélite Universelle, 45 rue La Bruyére, 75009. Tel. 4280-35-00. The Alliance is responsible for the maintenance of 124 schools (with 28,000 pupils) in various parts of the Mediterranean.
Alliance Israélite Universelle Library, 45 rue la Bruyère, 75009. (Tues. and Thurs. 1-5 p.m., Wed. 1-7.30 p.m., closed in Aug.). Tel. 4744-75-84.

Association Culturelle des Israélites Nord Africains, 151 Blvd. Magenta, 75010. Tel. 4525-72-76.
Centre de Documentation Juive Contemporaine, 17 rue Geoffroy l'Asnier, 75004. Tel. 4508-06-04. Daily except Sat. and Sun.
Jewish Art Museum, 42 rue des Saules, 75018. (Open Sun., Tues. & Thurs., 3-6 p.m.) (Métro: Lamarck.)
Library of Federation of Jewish Societies of France, 68 rue de la Folie Méricourt, 75011.
Medem Library (Yiddish), 52 rue René Boulanger, 75010.
ORT, 10 Villa d'Eylau, 75016. Tel. 4553-55-16.
Ozar Hatorah, 2 rue Fléchier 75009, Tel. 48-78-77-14 - Recently opened a new network of schools in Paris and throughout France.
Rabbinical Seminary Library, 9 rue Vauquelin, 75005. Tel. 4707-21-22.

Welfare Organisations
American Jewish Joint Distribution Committee (Office for France), 33 rue de Miromesnil, 75008. Tel. 4268-05-68.
C.A.S.I.P. (Paris Jewish Committee for Social Welfare Action), 60 rue Rodier, 75009. Tel. 4526-16-50.
C.O.J.A.S.O.R. (Jewish Committee for Social Welfare Action and Reconstruction), 6 rue Rembrandt, 75008. Tel. 4359-03-63.
F.S.J.U. (Unified Jewish Social Welfare Fund), 19 rue de Téhéran, 75008. Tel. 4563-17-28.
O.P.E.J. (Operation for the Protection of Jewish Children), 10 rue Théodore Ribot, 75017. Tel. 4622-00-87 and 00-88.
OSE, 9 Passage de la Boule Blanche, 75012. Tel. 4345-60-07.

Student and Youth Organisations
Centre Edmond Fleg, 8 bis rue de l'Eperon, 75006. Students' clubhouse, cultural centre, library. Tel. 4633-43-24.
Centre Rachi (Jewish University Students' Centre), 30 Blvd. du Port Royal, 75005. Tel. 4331-98-20.
Eclaireurs Israélites de France (Jewish Scouts), 27 Av. de Ségur, 75007. Tel. 4786-60-33.
Front des Etudiants Juifs (Jewish Students' Front), 59 Blvd. de Strasbourg, 75010. Tel. 4523-14-89.
Jewish Group Holidays: C.A.E.J., British European Centre for Jewish Youth, 7 rue Marbeuf, 75008. Tel. 4720-81-25; ★Centres Culturels de Vacances et de Loisirs, 19 rue de Téhéran, 75008. Tel. 4563-49-81 (Dept. of F.S.J.U.); A.M.E. Vacances Françaises, 27 Av. de Ségur, 75007. Tel. 4783-63-29.
Jewish Student Hostels: **(K)** Foyer-Logement Merkaz Ohr Joseph, 44-48 Quai de la Marne, 75019. (Métro: Ourcq). Male students only. Tel. 4245-83-37. Restaurant on premises. Pension accom. available for students & visitors all year round except Aug.
(K) Jewish Youth Centre & Com. Centre, 19 Blvd. Poissonnière, 75002. Tel. 4233 64-96. Open for lunch at mid-day on the Sabbath, on presentation of pre-paid tickets. These are available at the centre until 1 p.m. on Fri. Centre closed Aug.
Maccabi, 20 rue Nungesser-et-Coli, 75016. Tel. 4605-35-78.
Union des Etudiants Juifs de France (Jewish Students' Union), 47 rue de Chabrol, 75010. Tel. 4523-45-69.

Zionist Organisations
Betar, 59 Blvd. de Strasbourg, 75010. Tel. 4523-14-89.
Bné Akiva, 78 rue Bichat, 75010. Tel. 4240-40-29.

Fédération des Organisations Sionistes de France, 38 rue Turbigo, 75003. Tel. 4274-00-55.
Israël Hatzeira, 47 rue de Chabrol, 75010. Tel. 4770-97-34.
Jewish Agency, 17 rue Fortuny, 75017. Tel. 4766-03-13.
Keren Hayesod & Aide à Israel, 10 rue d'Aumale, 75009. Tel. 4041-91-50
Keren Kayemeth Leisrael, 110 rue de Rivoli, 75001. Tel. 4041-91-50.
Mizrachi-Hapoel Hamizrachi European Office, 4 rue Martel, 75010. Tel. 4521-62-74.
Siona (Sephardi Zionists), 52 rue Richer, 75009. Tel. 4246-04-39.
WIZO, 24 rue du Mont-Thabor, 75001. Tel. 4260-38-19.
Youth Aliyah, 256 rue Marcadet, 75018. Tel. 4229-39-16.
Zionist Movement of France, 38 rue de Turbigo, 75003. Tel. 4272-70-30.
Israel Embassy & Consulate, 3 rue Rabelais, 75008. Tel. 4256-47-47.

Booksellers, etc.
Bibliophane, 26 rue des Rosiers, 75004. Tel. 4887-82-20.
Diasporama, 20 rue des Rosiers, 75004. Tel. 4278-3050. Fax 4274-3876. Judaica Artefacts, music, etc.
Keren Hasefer, 9 rue Vauquelin, 75005 (by correspondence only). Books, records & educational material.
Libermann (Hebraica, Judaica), 12 rue des Hospitalières Saint-Gervais, 75004. Tel. 4887-32-20. Antiquities, Jewish paintings.
Librairie Allouche, 7 rue des Rosiers, 75004.
Librairie Colbo, 3 rue Richer, 75009. Tel. 4770-21-81.
Librairie L. Kra, 6 Pl. d'Estienne d'Orves, 75009. Tel. 4770-41-85.
Librairie du Progrès, 23 rue des Ecouffes, 75004. Tel. 4272-94-44.
Service Technique pour l'Education, 19 Blvd. Poissonnière, 75002. Tel. 4508-47-56. Open during Aug. Books and records. Inf. for Jewish tourists.

Jewish Newspapers
Actualité Juive 47 Ave Mathuriu Moreau, 75019. Tel. 4206-03-03. Obtainable from most Jewish shops.
Information Juive, Journal des Communautés, 17 rue St. Georges, 75009. Tel. 4285-71-09.
L'Arche (monthly), 14 rue Georges Berger, 75017. Tel. 4763-70-52.
Tribune Juive (weekly), 18 rue Volney, 75002. Tel. 4261-82-07.
Unsere Stime (Yiddish), 20 rue F. Duval, 75004.
Unser Weg (Yiddish), 4 rue Martel, 75010.
Unser Wort (Yiddish), 14 rue du Grand Prieuré, 75011. Tel. 4355-51-99.

Jewish Radio Programme
Radio Communauté Judaïque FM, P.O.B. 124, 75825. Tel. 4763-43-58.

Hotels
(K) Hôtel le Galilée, 8 Ave. de la Soeur Rosalie 75013. Tel. 4354 9387.
(K) Hotel-Restaurant Lebron, 4 rue Lamartine, 75009. Tel. 4878-75-52.
Hotel Concorde St.-Lazare (324), 108 rue St.-Lazare, 75008. Tel. 4294-22-22.
Montalembert, 3 rue de Montalembert, 75007. Tel. 4548-68-11 & 4548-61-59.
P.L.M.-Saint Jacques (812), 17 Blvd. St.-Jacques, 75014. (Métro: St.-Jacques). Tel. 4589-89-80. (K) Kosher kitchen, but catering is for special groups and parties by prior arrangement only at present.

Kashrut
For update information on provisions and establishements consult Cachére Magazine, 10 rue de Platrières, 75020. Tel. 4040 9808. Fax. 40409522.

BRING THE JEWISH WORLD INTO YOUR HOME

NEWSPAPER SALES MANAGER,
JEWISH CHRONICLE,
25 Furnival Street, London EC4A 1JT
Tel: 071-405 9252 Fax: 071-405 9040

Please forward the **JEWISH CHRONICLE** for one year to:

Name ....(TG94)
(Block Letters Please)

Address ....

....

....

I enclose remittance for:

Value ....

Signed ....

Name ....
(Block Letters Please)

Address ....

....

....

Payment can be made by ACCESS, VISA, EUROCARD or MASTERCARD

ANNUAL SUBSCRIPTION RATES: **UK** £45.00. **Europe All-up Service,** (inc. Eire), £65.00. **Other countries** by sea mail (except North America), £60.00. **United States,** Air Freight $84.00. **Canada,** Air Freight C$112.00. Air Mail rates can be obtained on request to the Newspaper Sales Manager.

Kosher Restaurants

The **(K)** restaurant at the Jewish Youth Centre & Com. Centre, 19 Blvd. Poissonnière, 75002 (Métro: Bonne Nouvelle), Tel. 4233-64-96, is open from Mon. to Fri. between 12 noon & 2 p.m., and 7 p.m. & 9 p.m. except during Aug., when the centre is closed. Jewish visitors from Britain are especially welcome and are invited to participate in various activities organised at the Centre. Inq. to the manager.

For updated information regarding restaurants, contact Tel. 4285-05-45.

(K) Fri. night & Sat. afternoon meals under the supervision of the Paris Beth Din are available against payment in advance from Beth El Syn., 3 rue Saulnier, 75009. Tel. 4770-09-23.

(K) Adolphe, 14 rue Richer, 75009. Tel. 4770-91-25.

(K) Auberge Ashkefarade, 2 rue Lamartine, 75009. Tel. 4878-42-83.

(K) Aux Iles Philippines, 17 rue Laplace. Tel. 4633-18-59.

(K) Aux Surprises, 40 bis rue du Faubourg-Poissonnière, 75010. Tel. 4770-55-96, 4770-24-19 or 4246-18-02. (Dairy).

(K) Azar & Fils, 6 rue Geoffroy-Marie, 75009. Tel. 4770-08-38.

(K) Berbèche Burger, 47 rue Richer, 75009. Tel. 4770-81-22.

(K) Brasserie de Tunis, 11 rue Geoffroy-Marie, 75009. Tel. 4824-19-03.

(K) Cash Food, 63 Rue de Vinaigriers, 75010. Tel. 4203-95-75.

(K) Centre Comunautaire, 8 Rue de la 8 Mai 1945 94000. Tel. 4377-01-70.

(K) Centre Edmond Fleg, 8 bis rue de l'Eperon, 75006. Tel. 4633-43-31.

(K) Centre Communautaire, 19 Blvd. Poissonnière, 75002. Tel. 4233-64-96.

(K) Centre Rachi, 30 Blvd. du Port Royal, 75005. Tel. 4331-98-20.

(K) Chalom, 10 rue Richer, 75009. Tel. 4246-77-70.

(K) Chez François, 5 rue Ramponeau, 75020. Tel. 4797-87-28.

(K) Chez Gabin, 92 Blvd. de Belleville, 75020. Tel. 4358-78-14.

(K) Chez Harry (Galil), 24 rue Richer, 75009. Tel. 4824-12-50.

(K) Delices de Maroc, 7 rue Montyon, 75009. Tel. 4022-00-17.

(K) Douer Restaurant, 21 rue Bergère, 18 Cité Bergère, 75009. Tel. 4523-53-22.

(K) Eilat's Food, 8 rue Geoffroy-Marie, 75009. Tel. 4246-39-56.

(K) Elygel, 116 Bld. de Belleville, 75020. Tel. 4797-09-73.

(K) Falafel Meny, 39 rue Richer, 75009. Tel. 4246-03-73.

(K) Gagou, 8 rue de la Grange Bateliere, 75009. Tel. 4770-05-02.

(K) Georges de Tunis, 40 rue Richer, 75009. Tel. 4770-43-77.

(K) Habiba, 3 ter rue des Rosiers, 75004. Tel. 4887-39-73.

(K) Hattab Letun, 8 rue du Passage-St.-Martin, 75010. Tel. 4206-42-77.

(K) Hotel Restaurant Lebron, 4 rue Lamartine, 75009. Tel. 4878-75-52.

(K) King Salomon, 46 rue Richer, 75009. Tel. 4246-31-22. (Dairy).

(K) L'Atikva, 3 Cour des Petites Ecouries, 75010. Tel. 4770-67-07.

(K) La Cave des Amateurs, 48 rue Volta, 75003. Tel. 4277-04-25.

(K) La Grillade, 17 rue Montyon, 75009. Tel. 4824-06-57.

(K) La Halavite, 26 bis rue de l'Ourcq, 75019. Tel. 4034-40-84.

(K) La Palme d'Or, 23 Blvd. des Filles-du-Calvaire, 75011. Tel. 4355-28-77.

(K) La Parnassa, 53 Bld. Montparnasse, 75006. Tel. 4544-97-47.

(K) La Rose Blanche, 10 bis rue Geoffroy-Marie, 75009. Tel. 4523-37-70.

(K) La Tartelière, 231 Blvd. Voltaire, 75011. Tel. 4024-14-75. (Dairy).

(K) La Toasterie, 48 rue Richer, 75009. Tel. 4770-55-96, 4770-24-19 or 4246-18-02.

(K) Le Bambou d'Eilat, 2 rue de Nantes, 75019. Tel. 4209-19-14.

(K) Le Castel, 4 rue Saulnier, 75009. Tel. 4770-44-08.

(K) Le Chalom, 231 Blvd. Voltaire, 75011. Tel. 4348-29-32.

(K) Le Chandelier, 7 rue Dufresnoy, 75016. Tel. 4504-90-50.

(K) Le Cotel, 5 Bld. Henri Poincarre, 95200. Tel. 3992-42-38. (Dairy).

(K) Le Cristal, 11 rue Montyon, 75009. Tel. 4246-21-65.

(K) Le Gros Ventre, 7-9 rue Montyon, 75009. Tel. 4824-25-34.

(K) Le Laguna, 8 rue d'Estienne d'Orves, 94000. Tel. 4207-10-38. (Dairy).
(K)Le Leviatane, rue St. Blaise, 75020. Tel. 4367-87-09.
(K) Le Milki, 56 rue Richer, 75009. Tel. 4770-24-19. (Dairy).
(K) Le Nouveau Magenta, 73 Blvd. Magenta, 75010. Tel. 4824-70-24.
(K) Le Rolls Pizzeria, 126 Blvd. Voltaire, 75011. Tel. 4086-53-46, 56 Av. de la République, 75011. Tel. 4338-63-18. 27 Bld. de Charonne, 75001. Tel. 4009-71-98. 91 av. Secretan 75019. Tel. 4239-50-41.
(K) Le Shalom, 231 Bld. Volaire, 75001. Tel. 4348-29-32.
(K) Le Takei's, 54 rue Richer, 75009. Tel. 4824-96-05. (Parve).
(K) Le Verre à soi, 9 rue de Cléry, 75002 Tel. 42.36.99.50.
(K) Les Ailes, 34 rue Richer, 75009. Tel. 4770-62-53.
(K) Les Jardins de Nazareth, 44 rue ND de Nazareth, 75003. Tel. 4278-98-22.
(K) Les Relais, 69 Bld. de Belleville, 75020. Tel. 4357-83-91.
(K) Les Tables de la Loi, 15 rue St.-Gilles, 75003. Tel. 4804-38-02.
(K) Lotus de Nissane, 39 rue Amelot, 75011. Tel. 4355-80-42.
(K) Lumière de Belleville, 102 Blvd. de Belleville, 75020. Tel. 4797-51-83.
(K) Maxime Chemama, 16 rue de la Comines, 75003. Tel. 4027-07-07.
(K) Mazal Tov, 25 rue des Rosiers, 75004. Tel. 4027-87-40.
(K) Mitsou Yan, 18 Faubourg-Montmartre, 75009. Tel. 4523-02-22.
(K) New Beauregard, 18 rue Beauregard, 75002. Tel. 4236-66-30.
(K) Nini, 24 rue Saussier-Leroy, 75017. Tel. 4622-28-93.
(K) Paparon Follies, 27 rue Richer, 75009. Tel. 4770-81-97.
(K) Paris Texas, 101 Av. Jean-Jaurès, 75019. Tel. 4245-48-61.
(K) Patrick, 11 rue Montyon, 75009, Tel. 4770-21-20.
(K) Resto Flash, 10 rue Lucien Sampaix, 75010. Tel. 4245-03-30.
(K) Snack Quick Delight, 24 rue Richer, 75009. Tel. 4523-05-12.
(K) Tibi, 128 Blvd. de Clichy, 75018. Tel. 4522-96-99.
(K) Yahalom, 24 rue des Rosiers, 75004. Tel. 42.77.12.35.
(K) Yris Cash Pates, 10 rue Saulnier, 75009. Tel. 4824-99-64.

Kosher Butchers & Bakers & Patisseries
A full list of authorised butchers & bakers and patisseries can be had from the Association Consistoriale Israélite de Paris, 17 rue Saint-Georges, 75009. Tel. 4285-71-09.

PARIS SUBURBS
Alfortville
Syn.: 1 rue Blanche. Tel. 4378-86-43.

Antony
Syn.: 49 Av. Léon-Blum. Tel. 4666-19-17.

Argenteuil
Syn.: 23 rue de l'Asperge.

Armentières/Lizy-sur-Ourcq
Syn.: Château de Vignois.

Asnières
Syn.: 73 bis rue des Bas. Tel. 4793-32-55.

Athis-Mons
Syn.: 55 rue des Coquelicots. Tel. 6938-14-29.

Aubervilliers
Syns.: 34 rue du Goulet (Ashkenazi); 150 rue de la Goutte-d'Or (Sephardi); 29 rue des Ecoles (Sephardi).

Aulnay-sous-Bois
Syns.: 3 rue Clermont-Tonnerre (Ashkenazi); 80 rue Maximilien-Robespierre (Sephardi). Tel. 4869-66-93.

Bagnolet
Syn.: 15-17 rue D.-Vienot. Tel. 4364-10-10.

Bobigny
Syn.: 11 rue Mathurin-Renaud. Tel. 4832-68-66.

Bois Colombes
Syn.: 14 Impasse Doussineaux.

Boissy-St Leger
Syn.: Galerie le Boecien.

Bondy
Syn.: 28 Av. de la Villageoise. Tel. 4847-50-70.

Boulogne-Billancourt
Syn.: 11 rue des Abondances. Tel. 4603-90-63.

Brunoy
Syn.: Av. du Petit-Château.

Cachan
Syn.: 4 bis rue des Peupliers. Tel. 4665-7279.

Champigny-sur-Marne
Syn.: 25 Av. du Général-de-Gaulle. Tel. 4885-72-29.

Charenton
Syn.: 42 ter, rue des Bordeaux.

Châtillon-sous-Bagneux
Syn.: 10 rue de Malakoff.

Chelles
Syn.: 14 rue des Anémones. Tel. 6008-14-84.

Chevilly-Larue
Syn.: 10 rue de l'Adjudant-Chef-de-Ricbourg. Tel. 4687-88-58.

Choisy-le-Roi/Orly
Syn.: 28 Av. de Newburn. Tel. 4853- 48-27.

Clichy-sous-Bois
Syn.: 21 Allée Veuve-Lindet.

Clichy-sur-Seine
Syn.: 12 rue de Belfort. Tel. 4739- 02-43.

Colombes
Syn.: 34 Av. Henri-Barbusse. Tel. 4781-67-65.

Créteil
Syn. & Com. Centre: Rue de 8-Mai-1945, 94000. Tel. 4377-01-70. **(K)** Kosher meals available. There is also a syn. in Pl. Jean-Giraudoux.

Dourdan-Etampes
Syn.: 3 route Danvers Morigny. Tel. 6459-19-91.

Drancy
Syn.: 8 Blvd.-St.-Simon.

Elancourt
Syn.: Centre Administratif des Sept-Mares.

Enghien-les-Bains
Syn.: 47 rue de Malleville. Tel. 4412-42-34.

Epinay-sous-Sénart
Syn.: Centre Commercial Principal, 1 Av. Victor-Hugo.

Epinay-sur-Seine
Syn.: 41 rue de Paris; 7 allee Berthier. Tel. 4822-83-67.

Ermont
Syn.: 36 rue de Stalingrad. Tel. 3415- 92-14.

Evry
Syn.: Allée du Pourquoi-Pas.

Fontainebleau
Syn.: 38 rue du Parc. Tel. 6422-28-92.

Fontenay-aux-Roses
Syn.: 17 Av. Paul-Langevin. Tel. 4660-75-95.

Fontenay-sous-Bois
Syn. & Com. Centre: 5 rue Jean-Pierre-Timbaud. Tel. 4876-52-33. There is also a syn at 79 Blvd. de Verdun.

Garges-les-Gonesse
Syns.: 14 rue Baptiste-Corot. Tel. 3986-75-64. 6 rue Defat et 4 rue Toulouse-Lautrec.

Gonesse
Syn.: Neve chalom, 40 rue de la Liberte.

Issy-les-Moulineaux
Syn.: 72 Blvd. Galliéni. Tel. 4558-25-76.

Ivry-sur-Seine
Syn.: 11 rue Ferdinand-Roussel. Tel. 4658-12-70.

La Celle-St.-Cloud
Syn.: 8 Allée Centrale.

La Courneuve
Syn.: 13 rue Saint-Just. Tel. 4836-75-59.

Lagny
Syn.: 21 rue de la Ferme Toray.

La Varenne-St. Hilaire
Syns.: 10 bis Av. du Château. Tel. 4889-73-87; 30 rue St. Hilaire. Tel. 4633-43-31.

Le Blanc-Mesnil
Syn.: 63-65 Av. Maxime-Gorki. Tel. 4865-58-98.

Le Chesnay
Syn. & Com. Centre: 9 rue de Versailles.

Le Kremlin-Bicêtre
Syn.: 41-45 rue J.-F.-Kennedy. Tel. 4672-73-64.

Le Perreux-Nogent
Syn.: 165 bis Av. du Général-de-Gaulle.

Le Pré-St.-Gervais
Syn.: 7 Av. du Belvedere.

Le Raincy
Syn. & Com. Centre: 19 Allée Chatrian. Tel. 4302-06-11.

Les Lilas
Syn.: 14 rue de la Croix-de-l'Epinette. Tel. 4845-39-59.

Les Ulis
Syn.: Résidence Chantereine. B.P.52. Tel. 6907-44-35.

Levallois-Perret
Syn.: 92 rue Marius-Aufan.

Le Vésinet
Syn.: 29 rue Henri-Cloppet. Tel. 3053-10-45.

Livry-Gargan
Syn.: 25 Av. Gallieni.

Longjumeau
Syn: Residence les Yvelines-Bat B2. Tel. 6448-70-08.

Maisons-Alfort
Syn.: 68 rue Victor Hugo. Tel. 4378-03-18.

Massy
Syn.: Allée Marcel-Cerdan. Tel. 6920-94-21.

Maurepas
Syn.: 4 Av. de Béarn. Tel. 3050-45-84.

Meaux
Syn.: 11 rue Paul-Barennes. Tel. 6434-76-58.

Meudon-la-Forêt-Clamart
Syn.: Rue de la Synagogue, Meudon-la-Forêt. Tel. 4632-64-82.

Montigay-Les-Cormeilles
Syn.: 2 allee de Bretagne.

Montmorency
Syn.: 9 rue de Pointoise.

Montreuil
Syn.: 179 bis rue de Paris.

Montrouge
Syn.: 90 rue Gabriel-Péri. Tel. 4253-50-26.

Nanterre
Syn.: 9-11 rue Maurice-Thorez.

Neuilly-sur-Seine
Syn. & Com. Centre: 12 rue Ancelle. Tel. 4624-49-15; and 19 Bld. de la Saussaye.

Noisy-le-Sec
Syn.: 2 rue de la Sierre Feuillere.

Pantin
Syn.: 68 rue Jules-Aufret. Tel. 4844-39-14.

Poissy
Syn.: 12 rue Laurence-Caroline.

Puteaux
Syn.: 24 bis rue Roque-de-Fillol. Tel. 4776-21-25.

Ris-Orangis
Syn.: 1 rue Jean-Moulin, angle rue du Temple. Tel. 6943-07-83.

Roissy-en-Brie
Syn.: 2 rue Paul-Cézanne, 77680.

Rosny-sous-Bois
Syn.: 62-64 rue Lavoisier. Tel. 4854-04-11.

Rueil-Malmaison
Syn.: 6 rue René-Cassin. Tel. 4708-32-62.

St.-Brice
Syn.: 17 Av. du Général-de-Gaulle.

St.-Denis
Syn.: 51 Blvd. Marcel-Sembat. Tel. 4820-30-87.

St.-Germain-en-Laye
Syn.: 6 Impasse St.-Léger. Tel. 3973-13-47.

St. Mater-des-Fosses
Syn.: 84 Bld du General Giraud. Tel. 4886-05-50.

St.-Ouen
Syn.: 10 rue Mariton.

St.-Ouen-l'Aumône
Syn.: 9 rue de Chennevières. Tel. 3037-71-41.

Sarcelles
Syns.: 74 Av. Paul Valéry, 95200. Tel. 4990-20-51; 24 rue Henri-Prost. Kosher Restaurants: **(K) Fast Food**, 13 Av. Edouard-Branly, 95200. Tel. 3419-12-02; Le Cotel, Bld. Henri Poincarre 95200.

Sartrouville
Syn.: 1 rue de Stalingrad. Tel. 39-15-22-57.

Savigny-sur-Orge
Syn.: 1 Av. de l'Armée-Leclerc. Tel. 6944-38-83.

Sevran
Syn.: 10 Av. de Livry. Tel. 43-85-36-36.

Stains
Syn.: Square Lamartine, Clos St.-Lazare. Tel. 4821-04-12.

Suresnes
Syn. & Com. Centre: 42 rue du Docteur-Bembinger.

Torcy
Syn.: 1 rue de l'Orangerie.

Trappes
Syn.: 7 rue du Port-Royal. BP. 93.

Vanves
Syn.: 1 rue Falret.

Verneuil
Syn.: Le Parc Noir, Allée des Tamaris, Bâtiment C.

Vigneux
Syn.: 2 rue Henri-Charon. Tel. 6903-45-53.

Villejuif
Syn.: 106 Av. de Gournay. Tel. 4680-46-06.

Villemomble
Syn.: 16 Av. Morice.

Villeneuve-la-Garenne
Syn.: 42-44 rue du Fond-de-la-Noue. Tel. 4794-89-98.

Villepinte
Syn.: 8 rue des Tilleuls.

Villiers-le-Bel
Syn.: 1 rue Léon-Blum. Tel. 3994-30-49.

Villiers-sur-Marne
Syn.: 20 rue Léon-Dauer. Tel. 4930- 25-80.

Vincennes
Syn.: 30 rue Céline-Robert (Ashkenazi & Sephardi). Tel. 4328-82-83.

Vitry-sur-Seine
Syn.: 133-135 av. Rouget de L'Isle. Tel. 9680-76-64 or 4573-06-58 (P.M.).

Yerres
Syn.: 16 rue de Coucy. Tel. 6046-89-77.

PAU (Pyrénées Atlantiques)
Syn. & Com. Centre: 8 rue des Trois-Frères-Bernadac, 64000. Tel. 5962-37-85. Mikva on premises.

PERIGUEUX (Pyrénées Atlantiques)
Syn. & Com. Centre: 13 rue Paul-Louis-Courrier, 24000. Tel. 5353-99-12.

PERPIGNAN (Pyrénées Orientales)
Syn.: 54 rue Arago, 66000.
Kosher butcher: (K) Gilbert Sabbah, 3 rue P.-Rameil, 66000. Tel. 6835-41-23. There are two monuments of importance in the cemetery of Haut Vernet at Perpignan and in the com. cemetery of Rivesaltes, near the camp from which thousands of Jews were deported to Auschwitz.

PHALSBOURG (Moselle)
Syn.: 16 rue Alexandre-Weill, 57370.

POITIERS
Syn. & Com. Centre: 1 rue Guynemer, 86000.

REIMS (Marne)
Syn. & Com. Centre: 49 rue Clovis, 51100. Tel. 2647-68-47.
There is a war memorial in the Blvd. Général Leclerc with an urn containing ashes from a number of Nazi death camps.

RENNES (Ille-et-Villaine)
Syn.: 23 rue de la Marbaudais, 35000.

ROANNE (Loire)
Syn. & Com. Centre: 9 rue Beaulieu, 42300. Tel. 7771-51-56.

ROUEN (Seine-Maritime)
Syn. & Com. Centre: 55 rue des Bons-Enfants, 76100. Tel. 3571-01-44. The

Jewish Youth Club can provide board-residence for student travellers and holiday-makers.

ST. AVOLD (Moselle)
Syn.: Pl. du Marché, 57500. The American military cemetery here contains the graves of many Jewish soldiers who fell in the Second World War.

ST. DENIS
(See under Réunion at end of section on France.)

ST.-DIE (Vosges)
Syn.: Rue de l'Evêché, 88100. Services, festivals & Holy-days only.

ST.-ETIENNE (Loire)
Syn. & Com. Centre: 34 rue d'Arcole, 42000. Tel. 7733-56-31.

ST.-FONS
Syn. & Religious Assoc. (Association Cultuelle): 17 Av. Albert-Thomas, 69190. Tel. 7867-39-78. Mikva.

ST.-LAURENT DU VAR
Syn. & Com. Centre: Villa "Le Petit Clos", 35 Av. des Oliviers, 06700.

ST.-LOUIS (Haut-Rhin)
Syns.: Rue de la Synagogue, 68300; 3 rue de l'Industrie, 68300.
Com. Centre: 19 rue du Temple, 68300.

ST.-QUENTIN (Aisne)
Syn. & Com. Centre: 11 ter Blvd. Henri-Martin. Tel. 2308-30-72.

SARREBOURG (Moselle)
Syn.: 12 rue du Sauvage.

SARREGUEMINES (Moselle)
Syn.: Rue Georges-V, 57200. Mikva on premises. Tel. 8795-09-52.

SAVERNE (Bas-Rhin)
Syn.: Rue du 19 Novembre, 67700.

SEDAN-CHARLEVILLE (Ardennes)
Syn.: 6 Av. de Verdun, 08200.

SELESTAT (Bas-Rhin)
Syn. & Com. Centre: 4 rue Ste.-Barbe, 67600.

SENS (Yonne)
Syn. & Com. Centre: 14 rue de la Grande-Juiverie, 89100. Tel. 8695-16-65.

SETE (Hérault)
Syn. & Com. Centre: 4 Quai Mas-Coulet, 34200. Tel. 6780-10-90.

STRASBOURG (Bas-Rhin)
Consistoire Israélite du Bas-Rhin, 46a rue du Vieux-Marché-aux-Vins, 67000. Tel. 8832-76-57. Fax 8875 7320.
Regional Chief Rabbi: Rabbi René Gutman, 5 rue du Général-de-Castelnau, 67000. Tel. 8832-38-97.

Synagogues & Religious Organisations
There are in all more than 15 syns. in Strasbourg; the following are amongst the largest and oldest.

Ashkenazi
Adath Israël, 2 rue St. Pierre-le-Jeune, 67000.
Ets Haïm, 28a rue Kageneck, 67000. Mikva on premises.
Synagogue de la Paix & Com. Centre: 1a rue du Grand-Rabbin-René-Hirschler, 67000. Tel. 8835-61-35.

Sephardi
1a rue du Grand-Rabbin-René-Hirschler, 67000.
Mikva: 1a rue du Grand-Rabbin-René-Hirschler, 67000. Tel. 8836-43-68.

Booksellers
Librairie Hebraïque Tannenbaum, André Fraenckel successeur, 19 rue du Maréchal-Foch, 67000. Tel. 36-38-39; Librairie Shné-Or, 15 rue de Bitche, 67000. Tel. 8837-32-37.

Jewish Newspaper
Unir (monthly), 1a rue du Grand-Rabbin-René-Hirschler, 67000.

Restaurants
(K) Le King, 28 rue Sellénick, 67000. Tel. 8852 1771
(K) Lévy, 4 rue Strauss-Durkheim, 67000. Tel. 88356821.
(K) Restaurant Universitaire, 11 rue Sellénick, 67000. Tel. 8825-67-97.

Kosher Food
Meat: **(K)** Buchinger, 63 Faubourg de Piérre, 67000. Tel. 8832-85-03 & 13 rue Wimpheling, Tel. 8861 0698; David, 20 rue Sellénick, 67000. Tel. 8836-75-01. Groceries: **(K)** Cacher Centre, 12 Blvd. Poincaré. Tel. 8832-25-55; **(K)** Franc Prix, 31 Faubourg de Saverne, 67000, Tel. 8832-04-40 & 13 rue du Général-Rapp, Tel. 8836-16-51; **(K)** Yarden, 3 rue Finkmatt. Tel. 8822-49-76. Patisserie: **(K)** Meyer, 9 rue de la Nuée-Bleue. Tel. 8832 7379.

TARBES (Hautes-Pyrénées)
Syn. & Com. Centre: Cité Rothschild, 6 rue du Pradeau, 65000.

THIONVILLE (Moselle)
Syn. & Com. Centre: 31 Av. Clémenceau, 57100. Tel. 8254-47-89.

TOUL (Merthe-et-Moselle)
Syn.: Rue de la Halle, 54200.

TOULON (Var)
Syn. & Com. Centre: Av. Lazare Carnot, 83050. Tel. 9492-61-05. Mikva. Kosher Butchers: **(K)** Abecassis, 8 rue Vincent-Courdouan, 83000. Tel. 9492-39-86; **(K)** Fennech, 15 Av. Colbert, 83000. Tel. 9492-70-39.

TOULOUSE (Haute-Garonne)
Regional Chief Rabbi: Rabbi Georges Haik, 17 rue Calvet, 31500.
Synagogues
Adat Yechouroun (Ashkenazi), 3 rue Jules-Chalande, 31000.
2 rue Palaprat, 31000. Tel. 6162-90-41 (Sephardi).
14 rue du Rempart-St.-Etienne, 31000. Tel. 6121-69-56.
Chaaré Emeth, 35 rue Rembrandt, 31000. Tel. 6140-03-88.
Mikva, 15 rue Francisque Sarcey, 31000. Tel. 6121-20-32.

Com. Centre: 14 rue du Rempart-St.-Etienne, 31000. Tel. 6123-36-54.
Kosher Restaurants: **(K) Le Barbecue**, 15 rue des Blanchers, 31000. Tel. 6121-67-66; **(K) Com. Centre**, 14 rue du Rempart-St.-Etienne, 31000. Tel. 6123-36-54. (Students only).
Kosher Butchers: **(K)** Amsellem, 6 rue de la Colombette, 31000. Tel. 6162-97-55; **(K)** Benichou, 7 rue des Châlets, 31000. Tel. 6163-77-39; **(K)** Cacherout Diffusion, 37 Blvd. Carnot, 31000. Tel. 6123-07-59; **(K)** Carmel, 1 rue Denfert-Rochereau, 31000. Tel. 6162-32-74; **(K)** Ghnassia, 397 Route de St.-Simon, 31000. Tel. 6142-05-81; **(K)** Lasry, 8 rue Matabiau, 31000. Tel. 6162-65-28; **(K)** Mikael's 42 rue Merly, 31000. Tel. 6162-91-62; **(K)** Otgergoust, 21 Pl. Victor Hugo, 31000. Tel. 6121-95-36; **(K)** Superette "Le Carmel", 9 Av. de Toulouse, L'Union, 31240. Tel. 6109-58-09.

TOURS (Indre-et-Loire)
Syn.: 37 rue Parmentier, 37000. Tel. 4705-56-95.
Com. Centre: 6 rue Chalmel, 37000.

TROYES (Champagne-Ardennes)
Syn. & Com. Centre: 5 rue Brunneval.
Mikva: 1 rue Brunneval, Tel. 2573-34-44.
A memorial statue of Rashi was unveiled at the Troyes cemetery in 1990.

VALENCE (Drôme)
Syn. & Com. Centre: 1 Place du Colombier, 26000. Tel. 7543-34-43.

VALENCIENNES (Nord)
Syn. & Com. Centre: 36 rue de l'Intendance, 59300. Tel. 2729-11-07.

VENISSIEUX (Rhône)
Syn. & Com. Centre: 12 Av. de la Division-Leclerc, 69200. Tel. 7870-69-85.

VERDUN (Meuse)
Syn.: Impasse des Jacobins, 55100.

VERSAILLES (Yvelines)
Syn.: 10 rue Albert-Joly, 78000.
Com. Centre: 39 rue de Versailles, Hagège. 78150 Le Chesnay. Tel. 3954-05-65. Mikva.

VICHY (Allier)
Syn.: 2 bis rue du Maréchal Foch, 03200.

VITRY-LE-FRANCOIS (Marne)
Syn.: rue du Mouton, 51300. Services Yom Kippur only.

VITTEL (Vosges)
Syn.: Rue Croix-Pierrot, 88800.

WASSELONNE (Haut-Rhin)
Syn.: Rue des Bains, 67310.

CORSICA
(Jewish population 150-200)

AJACCIO

There are between 10 and 15 families in the town. Inq. to Jo Michel Reis, La Grande Corniche, Route des Sanguinaires. Tel. 9521-57-52.

BASTIA

This port town has a Jewish population of 25-35 families.
Syn.: 3 rue du Castagno, 20200. Services, Sat. morn. & festivals.
Com. Pres.: Jacques Ninio, 13 Blvd. Paoli, 20200. Tel. 9531-50-16.

MARTINIQUE

FORT-DE-FRANCE

Syn. & Com. Centre: Maison Grambin, Plateau Fofo, Voie 1, 97200. Pres.: André Gabay, 43 Orée du Parc Mongéralde, 97200.

REUNION

An island département of France in the Indian Ocean, with a Jewish population of about 50, mostly Sephardim. High Holy-day services and communal seder held at Communauté Juive de la Réunion, 8 rue de l'Est, St. Denis, 97400. Further inf. from Georges Hening, 32 rue Jules Aubert, 97400 St. Denis. Tel. (19-262) 21-60-60.

TAHITI

(French Polynesia)

PAPEETE

A.C.I.S.P.O. (Jewish Religious Assoc.): B.P. 50041 à Piare. Pres.: Sauveur

GEORGIA

AKHALTSIKHE

Syn.; 109 Guramishvili St.

BATUMI

Syn.: 6 9th March St.

GORI

Syn.: Chelyuskin St.

KULASHI

Syn.: 170 Stalin St.

ONNI

Syn.: Baazova St.

POTI

Syns.: 23 Ninoshivili,; Tskhakaya St.

SUKHUMI

Syn.: 56 Karl Marx St.

SURAMI

Syn.: Internatsionalnaya St.

TBILISI

Syn.: 45-47 Leselidze St. There is an Ashkenazi syn. near by, at 65 Kozhevenny La. The lane is unmarked, but there is a small drinking

fountain on the corner at the entrance to the lane. It is advisable to ask for directions at the Sephardi syn. in Leselidze St.
Organisation: Jews of Georgia Assoc., Tsaritsy Tamari St. 8., 380012. Tel. (883-2) 34-10-57.

TSHKINVALI
Syn.: Isapov St.

TSKHAKAYA
Syn.: Mir St.

VANI
Syn.: 4 Kaikavadze St.

GERMANY
Even the Nazis, with their extermination policy, failed to sever completely Jewish connections with Germany, which go back uninterruptedly to Roman times, although official Jewish communities are of more recent date. In West Berlin, for instance, the community celebrated its 300th anniversary in 1971.
Hitler was the latest and most virulent persecutor of German Jewry, but though he came nearest of all to wiping out the country's Jews, he did not succeed in obliterating their incalculable contribution over the centuries to German and world culture, the sciences, the economy and other fields of human endeavour.
When the Nazis gained power in 1933, more than half a million Jews lived in Germany, 160,000 in Berlin. Today there are only some 40,000 registered members of the German community, including some 9,400 in Berlin, 5,300 in Frankfurt & 4,100 in Munich and recent immigrants from Russia.
Buildings, monuments and relics of all kinds abound in Germany today, perpetuating the memory of a great and numerous community reduced to a pale shadow of its former self.

AACHEN
Rep. Organisation: Bundesverband Jüdischer Studenten in Deutschland Oppenhoffallee 50. Tel. (0241) 75998.

ALSENZ
The restored 18th-century syn. in this small village is at Kirchberg 1.

AMBERG
Com. Centre: Salzgasse 5. Tel. (09621) 1-31-40.

ANDERNACH
This Rhine Valley town contains an early 14th-century mikva. Key obtainable from tourist office.

AUGSBURG
Com. Centre: Halderstr. 8. Tel. (0821) 51-79-85. There is a Jewish museum in the restored Liberal syn. See also Ichenhausen below.

BAD KREUZNACH
Com. Centre: Gymnasialstr. 11. Tel. (0671) 2-69-91.

BAD NAUHEIM
Syn. (Sabbaths only) & Com. Centre: Karlstr. 34. Tel. (06032) 56-05. Min.: Rabbi Wald.

(K) Kosher meals can be obtained at Club Shalom, in the Syn. & Com. Centre bldg., entrance from Friedensstr. Under the supervision of Rabbi Wald. Tel. (06032) 3-11-57;
Kosher Hotel: **(K) Accadia**, Lindenstr. 15/Frankfurterstr. 22. Tel. (06032) 3-90-68.
Deutscher Koordinierungs Rat der Gesellschaften für Christlich — Jüdische Zusammenarbeit, Otto-Weiß-Str. 2. Tel. (06032) 91-11-0.

BADEN-BADEN
Syn & Community Centre: Werder Str. 2, Tel. 07221-39 1021.

BAMBERG
Com. Centre: Willy-Lessing-Str. 7. Tel. (0951) 2-32-67.

BAYREUTH
Com. Centre: Münzgasse 2. Tel. (0921) 6-54-07.

BERLIN
Synagogues & Religious Organisations
Pestalozzistr. 14 (Liberal),.1000 Berlin 12. Tel. (030) 313-84-11. Min.: Rabbi Ernst Stein.
Dernburgstr. 26. 1000 Berlin 19. Tel. (030) 321-20-56.
Fränkelufer 10-12. 1000 Berlin 36. Tel. (030) 614-51-31.
Joachimstaler Str. 13. 1000 Berlin 15. Tel. (030) 88-42-030. Mins.: Rabbi David Weisz, M.A., Wielandstr. 33. Tel. (030) 881-23-90, & Rabbi Ernst M. Stein, Joachimstaler Str. 13. Tel. (030) 884-20-321.
Adass Jisroel (est 1869) 40 Tucholsky St., 0-1040 Berlin Mitte. Tel. 281 3135.
Com. Centre: This has been built on the site of a famous syn. destroyed by the Nazis – Fasanenstr. 79-80 (off the Kurfürstendamm). Tel. (030) 88-42-030.
Rykestr. 53, 1055. Tel. 448-52-98.
Neue Synagogue Berlin – Centrum Judaicum, Oranienburger-Str. 28, 1040. Tel. 280-12-50 or 280-12-51. Dir.: Dr. Hermann Simon.
Cemeteries: Heerstr. am Scholzplatz, Berlin-Charlottenburg. Tel. (030) 304-32-34; 2 Wittlicher St, 0-1120 Berlin-Weissensee. Cemeteries: Herbert-Baum-Str. 45, 1120 Berlin-Weissensee. Tel. (0372) 365-33-30; Adass Yisroel, Wittlicher Strasse (Falkenberger Chaussee), 1120 Berlin-Weissensee; Schönhauserallee 23, 1058 Berlin-Prenzlauer Berg.

Representative & Student Orgs.
B'nai B'rith Leo Baeck Lodge, Com. Centre, Fasanenstr. 79-80. Tel. (030) 883-53-17; Janusz Korczak Lodge, Passauerstr. 4. Tel. (030) 213-96-26; Raoul Wallenberg Lodge, Kurfürstendamm 48-49. Tel. (030) 881-36-58.
Jüdischer Kulturverein Berlin e. V. Monbijouplatz 4, 1020 Berlin. Tel. (030) 208 93 17. Contact: Dr. Irene Runge.
Jüdische Studentenvereinigung in Berlin, Fasanenstr. 79-80, Berlin 12. Tel. (030) 883-17-96.
Makkabi (Jüdischer Turn- und Sportverband), Joachimstaler Str. 13. Tel. (030) 883-17-80. Secretariat: Passauer-Str. 4. Tel. (030) 213-88-89.
Zentralrat der Juden in Deutschland. Office Berlin Oranienburger Str. 31, 1040. Tel. (030) 238 6606.

Homes, Hospitals, etc.
Homes: Altenheim, Iranische Str. 3, Berlin 65. Tel. (030) 492-30-61; Heinrich-Stahl-Wohnheim, Baseler Str. 11, Berlin 45. Tel. (030) 833-27-94; Leo-Baeck-Wohnheim, Herbartstr. 26, Berlin 19. Tel. (030) 321-20-56; Pflegeheim, Iranische Str. 2, Berlin 65. Tel. (030) 492-42-90; Dernburgstr. 36,

Berlin 19. Tel. (030) 321-20-56. Home for Aged: Wilhelm-Wolf-Str. 30-38, 1110 Berlin-Niederschönhausen. Tel. 482-47-37.
Hospital: Iranische Str. 2-4, Berlin 65. Tel. (030) 492-30-61.

Zionist Organisations
Jewish Agency, Joachimstaler Str. 13. Tel. (030) 881-94-25.
Jewish National Fund, Joachimstaler Str. 13. Tel. (030) 883-43-60.
State of Israel Bonds, Kurfürstendamm 61. Tel. (030) 883-40-91.
United Israel Appeal-Keren Hayesod, Joachimstaler Str. 13, 1000 Berlin 15. Tel. (030) 883-52-73.
WIZO, Föderation Deutschland Joachimsthaler Str. 13, 1000 Berlin 12.
Zionist Org. Regional Office, Joachimstaler Str. 13. Tel. (030) 881-77-97.

Library, Bookshop & Newspapers
Literaturhandlung, Joachimstaler-Str. 13, D-10719 Berlin. Tel. 030/88 24 250. Fax. 030 88 54 713.
Jewish Library, Oranienburger Str. 28. Tel. 280-12-29.
There is a branch office of the Allgemeine jüdische Wochenzeitung (weekly) at Oranienburger Str. 31, 1040 Berlin (East) 030/238-66-06 & 282 87-42.
The Jüdischer Kulturverein publishes its Jüdische Korrespondenz monthly in German and Russian.

Restaurants, etc.
Cafe Oren Oranienburger Str. 28, 1040 Berlin. Tel. (030) 282-82-28/2801 201.
(K) Com. Centre, Fasanenstr. 79-80, Berlin 12. Tel. (030) 884-20-339. Open only for lunch.
(K) Beth Café, Tucholskystrasse 40, 1040 Berlin-Mitte. Tel. 281-31-35.
(K) Kolbo, Auguststr. 77/78, 1040 Berlin. Tel. (030) 281-3135.
★ **Schalom Snack Bar**, Wielandstr. 43. Tel. (030) 312-11-31.

BIELEFELD
Com. Centre, Stapenhorststr. 35. Tel. (0521) 12-30-83.

BONN/BAD GODESBERG
Syn. & Com. Centre: Tempelstr. 2-4, cnr. Adenauer Allee. Tel. (0228) 21-35-60.

Representative Organisation
Zentralrat der Juden in Deutschland (Central Council of Jews in Germany).
Secretariat, Rüngsdorfer Str. 6. Tel. (0228) 35-70-23.
Israel Embassy, Simrockallee 2. Tel. (0228) 82-31.
Jewish Community Fund of N.W. Germany, Rungsdorfer Str. 6, 5300 Bonn 2.

Newspaper
Allgemeine jüdische Wochenzeitung (weekly), Rüngsdorfer Str. 6. Tel. (0228) 35-10-21.

BRAUNSCHWEIG
Com. Centre: Steinstr. 4. Tel. (0531) 4-55-36.

BREMEN
Syn. & Com. Centre: Schwachhauser Heerstr. 117. Tel. (0421) 498-51-04.
Min.: Rabbi Dr. B. Z. Barslai.

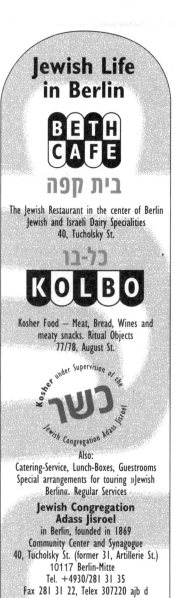

CHEMNITZ
Com. Centre: Stollberger Str. 28. Tel. 3-28-62.

COBLENZ
Com. Centre: Schlachthof Str. 5. Tel. (0261) 4-22-23.

COLOGNE
Syn. & Com. Centre: Roonstr. 50. Tel. (0221) 23-56-26 & 23-56-27. Daily services. There are a youth centre, Jewish museum & library at the same address.
Germania Judaica, Kölner Bibliothek zur Geschichte des Judentums, Josef-Haubrich-Hof 1, 5000, Tel. 0221-232349.

(K) Kosher meals are available at the Com. Centre.
Home for Aged, Cologne-Sülz, Berrenratherstr. 480.
WIZO: Franzstr. 12. Tel. (0221) 40-47-14 & 72-82-84.
Hotel: Leonet (80), Rubensstr. 33. Tel. (0221) 23-60-16.

DARMSTADT
Com. Centre: Wilhelm-Glässing-Str. 26. Tel. (06151) 2 88 97.

DORTMUND
Syn. & Com. Office: Prinz-Friedrich-Karl-Str. 9. Tel. (0231) 52-84-97. Min.: Rabbi Dov Barsilay. Tel. (0231) 52-84-96. (There is a home for the aged at the same address.)
Landesverband der Jüdischen Kultusgemeinden von Westfalen, Prinz-Friedrich-Karl-Str. 12. Tel. (0231) 52-84-95.

DRESDEN
Syn.: Fiedlerstr. 3. Tel. 69-33-17.
Com. Centre: Bautzner Strasse. 20. Tel. 57 86 91.
Representative Organisation: Landesverband der Jüdischen Gemeinden von Sachsen, Thüringen, Bautzner Str. 20, 8060 Dresden. Tel. 578691.
A memorial to the six million Jews killed in the Holocaust stands on the site of the Dresden Synagogue, burnt down by the Nazis in November, 1938.

DUISBURG
Salomon Ludwig Steinheim-Institut für deutsch-jüdische Geschichte (Institute of German-Jewish History, affiliated to Duisburg University), Geibelstr. 41. Tel. (0203) 37-00-71.

DÜSSELDORF
Synagogue
Syn. & Com. Office: Zietenstr. 50. Tel. (0211) 48-03-13.

Representative & Youth Orgs.
B'nai B'rith, Kasernenstr. 23. Tel. (0211) 32-99-11 & 32-48-48.
Landesverband der Jüdischen Gemeinden von Nordrhein, Mauerstr. 41. Tel. (0211) 44-68-09.
Youth & Student Centre, Mauerstr. 41. Tel. (0211) 48-03-14.

Home for Aged
Nelly Sachs Home for the Aged, Nelly-Sachs-Str. 5. Tel. (0211) 43-42-45.

Zionist Organisations
Jewish National Fund, Kaiserstr. 28. Tel. (0211) 49-40-08.

WIZO, Zietenstr. 63. Tel. (0211) 48-36-86.

Hotel
Gildors Hotel (under Israeli ownership), Collenbachstr. 51. Tel. (0211) 48-80-05.

ERFURT
Com. Centre: Juri-Gagarin-Ring 16. Tel. 2-49-64.

ESSEN
Com. Centre: Sedanstr. 46. Tel. (0201) 27-34-13.

ESSINGEN
Largest cemetery in the Palatinate, where Anne Frank's ancestors are buried, 16th c. Key at the Mayor's office.

FRANKFURT-ON-MAIN
Synagogues & Religious Organisations
Altkönigstr. 27 (Beth Hamidrash West End). Tel. (069) 72-38-05.
Baumweg 5-7. Tel. (069) 43-93-81 & 49-9-07-58.
Freiherr-vom-Stein-Str. 30 (Westend Syn.). Tel. (069) 72-62-63. This is the city's main syn.
Röderbergweg 29 (Beth Hamidrash). Tel. (069) 61-59-14.
Com. Centre: Westendstr. 43. Tel. (069) 74-07-21. The com. produces a monthly magazine, "Jüdische Gemeinde-Zeitung Frankfurt".
The **(K)** com. restaurant, the **König David,** is at the Youth Centre, Savignystr. 66, which see for details.
Cemeteries: Eckenheimer Landstr. 238, Tel. (069) 56-18-26; Old Cemetery: Rat-Beil-Str. Tel. (069) 55-73-59 for appointment; Battonstr. Key obtainable from Com. Centre.
Mikva: Westend Syn.

Representative Organisations
B'nai B'rith, Liebigstr. 24. Tel. (069) 72-41-37-9.
Landesverband der Jüdischen Gemeinden in Hessen, Hebelstr. 6. Tel. (069) 44-40-49.
Verband jüdischer Akademiker in Deutschland e.V., Im Trierschen Hof 17, Tel. 29 35 17.
Verband Jüdischer Heimatvertriebener und Flüchtlinge in der Bundesrepublik Deutschland, Friedrichstr. 27. Tel. (069) 72-55-30.
World Jewish Congress, Hebelstr. 17. Tel. (069) 55-77-73.

Welfare & Miscellaneous Orgs.
Central Welfare Org. of Jews in Germany. Headquarters: Hebelstr. 6. Tel. (069) 43-02-06 & 43-02-08.
Homes for Aged: Bornheimer Landwehr 79b. Tel. (069) 43-96-02; Budgestiftung, Wilhelmshöher Str. 279. Tel. (069) 47-87-10.
Jewish Museum, Untermainkai 14-15. Tel. (069) 212-350-00. Sun., Tues. & Thurs., 10 a.m. to 5 p.m.; Wed., 10 a.m. to 8 p.m.; Fri. 10 a.m. to 3 p.m. Closed Mon.
Jewish Restitution Successor Org., Telemannstr, 18. Tel. (069) 714170.
Jüdisches Lehrhaus, c/o R. Karafiat, Lange Str. 28. Tel. (069) 28-85-41.
ORT Germany, Hebelstr. 6. Tel. (069) 44-90-81.
Youth Centre & Students' Assoc., Savignystr. 66. Tel. (069) 75-13-22. The com. restaurant, the **(K)** König David, Tel. (069) 75-23-41, is open Sun., Tues., Wed. & Thurs. from noon to 3 p.m. & 6 p.m. to 9 p.m., & Fri. from

after the evening service until 11 p.m. Closed Mon. It is also closed for the whole of August.

Zionist Organisations
Jewish Agency, Hebelstr. 6. Tel. (069) 49-07-87.
Jewish National Fund. Head Office, Feldbergstr. 5. Tel. (069) 72-05-21.
Makkabi, Westendstr. 43. Tel. (069) 75-19-20.
State of Israel Bonds, Hebelstr. 6. Tel. (069) 49-04-70.
United Israel Appeal-Keren Hayesod. Head Office: Friedrichstr. 27. Tel. (069) 72-90-62.
WIZO, Westendstr. 43. Tel. (069) 75-22-36.
WIZO Aviv, Friedrichstr. 29. Tel. (069) 72-12-01.
Youth Aliyah, Hebelstr. 6. Tel. (069) 4-98-01-51.
Zionist Org. in Germany, Hebelstr. 6. Tel. (069) 4-98-02-51.
Zionist Youth in Germany, Falkensteiner-Str. 1. Tel. (069) 55-69-63.

Hotels
Hotel Excelsior & Monopol (200), Mannheimer Str. 7-13, 6000, 1. Tel. (069) 25-60-80.
Luxor Hotel, Am Allerheiligentor 2-4. Tel. (069) 29-30-67/69. This hotel, which is under Jewish management, is within walking distance of the Freiherr-vom-Stein-Str. syn.
Kosher Food: **(K)** Aviv Butchery & Deli, Hanauer Landstr. 50. Tel. (069) 43-15-39; Joseph Rosenfeld Butchery, Liebigstr. 17. Tel. (069) 72-18-65. Kosher bread is obtainable from Donath Werner, Raimundstr. 21. Tel. (069) 52-62-02.

FREIBURG
Com. Centre: Nussmannstr. 14. Tel. (0761) 38-30-96.

FRIEDBERG/HESSEN
The mikva, built in 1260, is at Judengasse 20. The town council has issued a special explanatory leaflet about it, and it is now scheduled as an historical monument of medieval architecture.

FULDA
Com. Centre; von Schildeckstr. 13. Tel. (0661) 7-02-52.

FÜRTH
There is a beautifully restored syn. at Julienstr. 2, as well as a mikva.
Com. Centre: Blumenstr. 31. Tel. (0911) 77-08-79.

GELSENKIRCHEN
Com. Centre: Von-der-Recke-Str. 9. Tel. (0209) 2-31-43 & 20-66-28.

GIESSEN
Com. Centre: Nordanlage 7. Tel. (0641) 3-11-62.

HAGEN
Com. Centre: Potthofstr. 16. Tel. (02371) 1-32-89.
Hotel: Central, Dahlenkampstr. 2. Tel. (02371) 2-32-58.

HALLE/SAALE
Com. Centre: Grosse Märkerstr. 13. Tel. 2-69-63.

HAMBURG
Syn.: Hohe Weide 34. Tel. (040) 49-29-04.

Com. Centre: Schäferkampsallee 27. Tel. (040) 44-09-44/46.
B'nai B'rith. Joseph Carlebach Lodge: c/o Franz Fischer, Am Hehsel 35.
Tel. (040) 5-38-16-88.
Home for Aged: Schäferkampsallee 27. Tel. (040) 44-09-44 & 44-09-46.
WIZO: Dürerstr. 2. Tel. (040) 8-99-26-83.

HANOVER
Syn. & Com. Centre: Haeckelstr. 10. Tel. (0511) 81-0472. Min.: Rabbi Henry
G. Brandt. Tel. (0511) 81-67-30.
Home for Aged: Haeckelstr. 6. Tel. (0511) 81-57-50.
Landesverband der Jüdischen Gemeinden von Niedersachsen, Haeckelstr.
10. Tel. (0511) 81-27-62.
Vegetarian Restaurant: **Schmelz**, Karmaschst. 16, 4th Floor.

HEIDELBERG
Com. Centre: Sophienstr. 9. Tel. (06221) 2-08-20.
Bundesverband jüdischer Studenten in Deutschland, Landfriedstr. 12, Tel.
18-22-01.
Hochschule für Jüdische Studien (College for Jewish Studies), Friedrichstr.
9. Tel. (06221) 2-25-76. Daily minyan Mon. to Fri. during term-time Apr. 15
to Jul. 15 & Oct. 15 to Feb. 15. **(K)** Kosher meals available (by arrangement
& in advance) Mon.-Fri. at college restaurant, Theaterstr., 100 yds. from
college. Zentralarchiv zur Erforschung der Geschichte der Juden in
Deutschland. Dir: Dr. Peter Honigmann, Bienen Str. 5, 6900 Heidelberg.

HERFORD
Com. Centre: Keplerweg 11. Tel. (05221) 20-39.

HOF/SAALE
Com. Centre: Am Wiesengrund 20. Tel. (09281) 532-49.

ICHENHAUSEN
Museum of Jewish history in the fine baroque syn. Not far from Augsburg.

KAISERSLAUTERN
Com. Centre: Basteigasse 4. Tel. (0631) 6-97-20.

KARLSRUHE
Com. Centre: Knielinger Allee 11. Tel. (0721) 7-20-36.
Oberrat der Israeliten Badens, Knielinger Allee 11. Tel. (0721) 7-20-35.
Landesrabbiner von Baden, Benjamin D. Soussan, c/o Israelitische
Gemeinde Freiburg Nuß mannstr. 14. Freiburg. Tel. 0761/392-43

KASSEL
Com. Centre: Bremer Str. 9. Tel. (0561) 1-29-60.

KONSTANZ
Com. Centre: Sigismundstr. 19. Tel. (07531) 2-30-77.

KREFELD
Com. Centre. Wiedstr. 17b. Tel. (02151) 2-06-48.

LEIPZIG
Com. Centre: Löhrstr. 10. Tel. 29-10-28.

LÜBECK
Com. Centre: An der Mauer 136. Tel. (0451) 7-66-50.

MAGDEBURG

Com. Centre: Gröperstr. 1a. Tel. 5-26-65.
Representative Organisations: Landesverband de Jüdischen Gemeinden von Sachsen-Anhalt, Brandenburg, Mecklenburg-Vorpommern, Gröper Str. 1a Magdeburg. Tel. 55-2665.

MAINZ

Com. Centre: Forsterstr. 2. Tel. (06131) 61-39-90.
The key to the twelfth-century Jewish cemetery can be obtained at the "new" Jewish cemetery, which is at Untere Zahlbacherstr. 11.

MANNHEIM

Com. Centre: F 3-4. Tel. (0621) 15-39-74.

MARBURG/LAHN

Com. Centre: Unterer Eichweg 17. Tel. (06421) 3-28-81.

MINDEN

Com. Centre: Kampstr. 6. Tel. (0571) 2-34-37.

MÖNCHENGLADBACH-RHEYDT

Com. Centre: Albertusstr. 54. Tel. (02161) 2-38-79.

MÜLHEIM/RUHR-OBERHAUSEN

Com. Centre: Kampstr. 7, Mülheim. Tel. (0208) 3-51-91.

MUNICH

There is a Jewish memorial at the site of the infamous Nazi concentration camp at Dachau, some 10 miles from Munich. There are trains every half-hour from Munich main railway station (Hauptbahnhof). From Dachau Station take the bus going to "Dachau Ost".
At the corner of Maxburgstr. and Herzog-Maxstr. is a monument marking the destruction of Munich's synagogues by the Nazis on November 10, 1938. As can be seen from the list below, some have since been rebuilt.
The Israeli sportsmen murdered by Arab terrorists at the 1972 Olympic Games are commemorated by a memorial at Connollystrasse 31.

Synagogues

Possartstr. 15. Mikva on premises.
Reichenbachstr. 27. Mikva on premises.
Schulstrasse 30. Fri. evenings and Sabbath mornings only.
Schwabing Syn., Georgenstr. 71. Fri. evg. and Sabbath morn. only.
Rabbiner: Itzchak Ehrenberg, Reichenberg Str. 27.

Miscellaneous Organisations

Jüdisches Museum München, Maximilian Str. 36.
B'nai B'rith, Georgenstr. 71. Tel. (089) 2-71-27-74 & 2-71-82-98.
Com. Centre: Reichenbachstr. 27. Tel. (089) 2-01-49-60.
Home for Aged: Kaulbachstr. 65. Tel. (089) 34-75-90.
WIZO: Reichenbachstr. 27. Tel. (089) 2-01-50-91.
Landesverband der Israelitischen Kultusgemeinden in Bayern, Effnerstr. 68. Tel. (089) 98-94-42 & 99-94-43.
Literaturhandlung, Fürstenstr. 17 D-80333 München. Tel. 089/280 01 35 Fax 089/28 16 01.
United Israel Appeal-Keren Hayesod, Reichenbachstr. 27/lll. Tel. (089) 2-01-55-20.

Youth Centre & Union of Jewish Students in Bavaria, Prinzregentenstr. 91. Tel. (089) 47-10-67.
(K) Restaurant run by the com., Reichenbachstr. 27/1. Tel. (089) 2-01-45-65.

MÜNSTER
Com. Centre: Klosterstr. 8-9. Tel. (0251) 4-49-09.

NEUSTADT/RHEINPFALZ
Com. Centre & Home for Aged. Ludwigstr. 20. Tel. (06321) 26-52.

NUREMBERG
Com. Centre & Home for Jewish Aged, Johann-Priem-Str. 20. Tel. (0911) 5-62-50.

ODENBACH
There is a syn. with baroque paintings in this small village near Bad Kreuznach. Inf. from Bernard Kukatzki, Tel. (06235) 3332; H. Dittrich, Tel. (06753) 2745.

OFFENBACH
Com. Centre: Kaiserstr. 109. Tel. (0611) 81-48-74. David Binzer, Seligenstädter Strasse 153a, Tel. (0611) 89-21-28 or 89-20-72, will be pleased to meet Jewish visitors.

OSNABRÜCK
Com. Centre: In der Barlage 41. Tel. (0541) 5-75-75.

PADERBORN
Com. Centre: Pipinstr. 32. Tel. (05251) 2-25-96.
Potsdam Com. Centre: Heinrich-Mann- Allee 103, Hans 16, Tel. 87-20-18.

POTSDAM
Comm. Centre: Heinrich-Mann-Allee 103, Haus 16, Tel. 872018.

RECKLINGHAUSEN (including Bochum & Herne)
Com. Centre: Am Polizeipräsidium 3. Tel. (02361) 1-51-31.

REGENSBURG
Com. Centre: Am Brixener Hof 2. Tel. (0941) 5-70-93 or 2-18-19.

RÜLZHEIM
The key to the early 19th-century syn. in this village near Karlsruhe is obtainable from the town hall.

SAARBRÜCKEN
Com. Centre: Lortzing Str. 8. Tel. (0681) 3-51-52.

SCHWERIN/MECKLENBURG
Com. Centre: Schlachterstr. 3-5. Tel. 81 29 97.

SPEYER
This town contains the oldest (11th century) mikva in W. Germany, Judenbadgasse. To visit it, obtain the key from the desk at the Hotel Trutzpfuff, in Webergasse, just round the corner, or contact Professor Stein at the Historical Museum.

There are some early 19th-century village syns. in the wine-growing region of the Palatinate. For inf., contact B. Kukatzki, Tel. (06235) 3332.

STRAUBING

Com. Centre: Wittelsbacherstr. 2. Tel. (09421) 13-87.

STUTTGART

Com. Centre & Israelitische Religionsgemeinschaft Württembergs: Hospitalstr. 36. Tel. (0711) 29-56-65. Min.: Rabbi Joel Berger.
A ★ kosher restaurant (closed Mon.) is attached to the Com. Centre.

SULZBURG

There is a beautifully restored early 19th-century syn. here, some 20 miles from Freiburg. Keys obtainable from Mayor's office.

TRIER

Com. Centre, Kaiserstr. 25. Tel. (0651) 4-05-30 & 3-32-95.

WACHENHEIM

A large 16th c. Cemetery Key available form the Town Hall.

WEIDEN

Com. Centre: Ringstr. 17. Tel. (0961) 3-27-94.

WIESBADEN

Syn.: Friedrichstr. 33. Tel. (06121) 30-18-70 & 30-12-82. Inq. about kosher meals to Communal Offices, Friedrichstr. 33. Tel. (06121) 30-18-70.

WORMS

The original Rashi Synagogue here, built in the eleventh century and the oldest Jewish place of worship in Europe, was destroyed by the Nazis in 1938. After the Second World War it was reconstructed and was reconsecrated in 1961. The bldg. also contains a 12th-century mikva & a Jewish museum. There is also an ancient Jewish cemetery.

WUPPERTAL

Com. Centre: Friedrich-Ebert-Str. 73. Tel. (0202) 30-02-33.

WÜRZBURG

Syn. & Com. Centre: Valentin-Becker-Str. 11. Tel. (0931) 5-11-90.
There is a mikva (for appointment Tel. (0931) 5-11-90) at the same address.
Home for Aged, Valentin-Becker-Str. 11.
★ Kosher meals can be obtained at the Com. Centre, where there are also guest rooms for tourists.
There are old Jewish cemeteries in Würzburg, Heidingsfeld and Hochberg.

GIBRALTAR

Gibraltar Jewry numbers about 600. Sephardi Jews settled there soon after the British occupation in 1704, coming from Italy, North Africa and, later, from England. The Shaar Hashamayim Synagogue was built in the middle of the eighteenth century. Gibraltar Jews are known for their hospitality.
The old Jewish cemetery is well worth a visit. It contains the graves of many saintly men, including that of the revered Rev. R. H. M. Benaim.
General inf. from Gibraltar Information Bureau, Arundel Gt. Court, 179 The Strand, WC2R 1EH. Tel. 071-836 0777-8.

Synagogues & Religious Organisations
Abudarham, 20 Parliament Lane. Tel. 77789.
Nefusot Yehuda, 65 Line Wall Rd. Tel. 74208.
Shaar Hashamayim, 47-49 Engineer Lane. Tel. 78069.
Etz Hayim, Irish Town. Tel. 75955
Mikva: 10 Bomb Hse. Lane. Inf. from Hon. Treas., Mrs. Luna Garson, 1 Baker's Passage. Tel. 78316, or Hon. Sec., Mrs. Orovida Hassan, 77 Irish Town. Tel. 77658.
Managing Board of Jewish Com. President: Mr. D. Benaim. Sec.: Mrs. Esther Benady, 10 Bomb Hse. Lane. Tel. 72606. Fax 40487.
Jewish Social & Cultural Club. Hon. Sec.: S. Attias, 10 Bomb Hse. Lane. Tel. 72606. **(K)** Leanse Restaurant.
There is a Kosher restaurant in the Jewish Club which opens daily from 10 a.m. to 11 p.m., except Saturdays, but arrangements can be made with this restaurant owner for Shabat meals.
WIZO. Pres.: Mrs. Luna Garson, 1 Baker's Passage. Tel. 77316. Hon. Sec.: Miss Vera Bentubo, 281 Main St. Tel. 78531.
Israel Consulate, 3 City Mill Lane. Tel. 75955 & 75956. Consul: Moses Benaim, 1 Baker's Passage. Tel. 77244.
Recommended Jewish shops: M. I. Abudarham, Cornwall's Lane (wines & all other kosher products); J. Attias (tailor & outfitter), 6 St George's Lane; Benamor & Co., 133 Main St.; Cohen & Massias Ltd., 52, 142 & 143 Main St., (jewellery & watches); A. Edery (kosher meat, wines & all other products), 26 John Mackintosh Sq.; Ladies wear, 10 John Mackintosh Sq.; S. M. Seruya Ltd., 165 Main St.; Teo (men's outfitters), 138 Main St.; Cohen's Camera Centre, 207 Main St.
There are no kosher hotels in Gibraltar, but the Holiday Inn and Rock Hotel will provide vegetarian or fish diets.

GREECE
There have been Jewish coms. in Greece since the days of antiquity. Before the Second World War, 76,500 Jews lived in Greece (56,000 in Salonika). Today there are barely 5,000, of whom 2,900 live in Athens, 1,200 in Salonika, 375 in Larissa, 166 in Volos, and the remainder in a number of other towns throughout Greece.
General inf. from National Tourist Org. of Greece, 4 Conduit St., W1R 0DJ. Tel. 071-734 5997-9.

ATHENS
Syn.: Beth Shalom (Sephardi), 5 Odos Melidoni. Min.: Rabbi Yaacov Arrar. Tel. 3252-773.
Central Board of the Jewish Coms. of Greece, 2 Sourmeli St. Tel. 8839-951/2/3. Pres.: Joseph Lovinger.
Jewish Com. of Athens, 8 Odos Melidoni. Tel. 3252-875.
Jewish Youth Centre, 9 Vissarionis St. & Sina St. Tel. 3637-092. Visiting Jewish young people welcomed.
Jewish Museum, 36 Amalias Av. Tel. 323-1577. Open 9 a.m. to 1 p.m. Sun. to Fri.
Keren Kayemet (known locally as Ethnikon Evraikon Kefalaion), 2 Nikis St. Tel. 3227-598. Pres.: Daniel S. Alhanati.
B'nai B'rith, 15 Paparigopoulou.
Israeli Diplomatic Representation, 1 Marathonodromon, Palaion Psychichon. Tel. 6719-530. Central Consular Section. Tel. 6719-530.

CHALKIS (Halkis)
Said to be the oldest Jewish com. in Europe, with an uninterrupted history of more than twenty-two centuries. Jews have lived in Chalkis since 200

B.C.E. Until the last century the com. was called "Koutsouk Safed" because of its strict religious devotion.

There is a syn. in Kotsou St. which has been rebuilt and renewed many times on its original foundations. Tombstone inscriptions in the cemetery go back more than fifteen centuries.

Additional inf. from the Pres. of the com., Leon Levy. Tel. 21630.

By the main bridge linking Chalkis and the mainland, there is a commemorative bust of Colonel Mordecai Frizis, the first Greek officer to be killed during the Second World War. He was a leading member of the community.

CORFU

There is an ancient syn. and cemetery here on Velissariou St. The Pres. of the com. is Armando Aaron. Tel. 38802. Moise Soussis, c/o the King Alkinos Hotel, will be pleased to meet Jewish visitors. (Tel. 39300).

JOANNINA

There is an an ancient syn. here, together with a Com. Centre. Inf. from the Pres. of the com., Moise Eliasaf. Tel. 29429.

LARISSA

Syn. & Com. Centre, 27 Kentavron St. Tel. 226-396. Pres.: Michael Levi.

Jewish Martyrs' Sq. is a memorial to the Jews of the city murdered by the Nazis.

RHODES (Dodecanese Islands)

The syn., built in 1731, is at 1 Simmiou St., in the old Jewish district. Visitors desiring to see round it should contact the caretaker, Lucia Sulan. Tel. 29406.

Com. Office: 5 Polydorou St. Pres.: M. Soriano. Tel. 22364.

SALONIKA (Thessaloniki)

A memorial to the 50,000 Jews who were deported from the city during the Second World War and murdered in the gas chambers of Auschwitz stands in the centre of the cemetery built after the war in the suburb of Stavroupolis. The old cemetery was destroyed in 1943 on the orders of the Nazis.

Syn.: Yad le Zikaron, 24 Vassileos Irakliou St. Min.: Rev. Mois Halegua. Office: 24 Odos Tsimiski.

Anglo-Jewish visitors are invited to visit the Jewish Centre at 24 Odos Tsimiski, Tel. 275-701, where the offices of the community are situated. The Israelite Fraternity House is at the same address. Tel. 221-030. Pres.: Rafael Molho.

The Centre for Historical Studies of Salonika Jews is at the same address as the syn. Tel. 031-223231.

TRIKKALA

Syn.: Odos Diacou. Pres.: Ovadia Sabah. Tel. 27534.

VERRIA

Syn. in the ancient Jewish quarter.

VOLOS

Inq. to Mr. Raphael Frezis, Com. Pres., 20 Pavlou Mela St. Tel. 25640.

Small Jewish coms. are to be found in Cavala & Carditsa. In Hania, the former capital of the island of Crete, there is an old synagogue in the former Jewish quarter, at 20 Parodos Kondulaki.

GUATEMALA

There are approximately 850 Jews in Guatemala.

GUATEMALA CITY

Syns.: Maguen David (Sephardi), 7a Av. 3-80, Zona 2. Tel. (5022) 20932; Centro Hebreo (Ashkenazi), 7a Av. 13-51, Zona 9. Tel. (5022) 367643. A new com. centre is due to open in 1993.

 Zionist Org. of Guatemala, 7a Av. 13-51, Zona 9, P.O.B. 105. Tel. (5022) 363975.

Israel Embassy, 13 Av. 14-07, Zona 10. Tel. (5022) 371305.

HAITI

There are 44 Jews in Haiti, all of them living in Port au Prince, the capital. Religious services are held at the home of the Honorary Consul.

Jacques Bigio, of the Versailles Department Store in Port au Prince, Tel. 23-0638, is always pleased to see Anglo-Jewish visitors.

Honorary Consul, (Israel). Mr. Gilbert Bigio.

HOLLAND

There were some Jews in Holland during the Middle Ages, but Dutch Jewish history effectively began with the settlement of Marranos in Amsterdam at the end of the 16th century. Dutch Jewry was given freedom of worship early in the 17th century and was formally emancipated in 1796. Holland was the first country in the modern world to admit Jews to Parliament (1797).

In 1940 there were approximately 140,000 Jews in the country, but as the result of the Nazi occupation, not more than 30,000 remain, of whom more than half live in the Amsterdam area, where there is much of Jewish interest to be seen.

General inf. from Netherlands Board of Tourism, 25-28 Buckingham Gate, SW1E 6LD. Tel. 071-630 0451.

AMERSFOORT

Syn.: Drieringensteeg 2. Min.: Rabbi J. S. Jacobs. Tel. 033-726204. Rabbi S. Evers. Tel. 033-720943.

AMSTERDAM/AMSTELVEEN

Synagogues & Religious Organisations

Ashkenazi Chief Rabbinate of Holland. P: M.Just.Sec.: E. M. Maarsen, van der Boechorststr. 26, 1081 BT. Tel. 020-6443868.

Ashkenazi Rabbinate of Amsterdam. Rabbis L-B. van de Kamp, F. Lewis, I. Vorst. Same address & Tel. as above.

Ashkenazi Syns.: Gerard Doustr. 238, Jacob Obrechtplein; Kehilat Jaakow (E. European), Gerrit v. d. Veenstr. 26; Lekstr. 61; van der Boechorststr. 26 (Buitenveldert); Nieuwe Kerkstraat 149 (E.European) (for information Tel. 6766400). Straat van Messina 10, Amstelveen.

Portuguese (Sephardi) Syn. & Com. Centre: Mr. Visserplein 3. Tel. 020-6245351. The Cong. has launched an appeal to cover essential restoration work — 'Adopt a tile' at NGL50.

Liberal Syn.: Jacob Soetendorpstr. 8. Tel. 020-6423562. Min.: Rabbi David Lilienthal. Tel. 020-6412580.

Mikvaot: Heinzestr. 3. Tel. 020-6763155 or 6620178 (Ashkenazi); Mr. Visserplein 3. Tel. 020-6245351 (Sephardi).

Ashkenazi Com. Offices, van der Boechorststr. 26. Tel. 020-6460046.

Com. Centre: van der Boechorststr. 26. Tel. 020-6440180.

Representative Organisations
Nederlands Israëlitisch Kerkgenootschap (Fed. of Dutch Jewish Congs.), van der Boechorststr. 26. Tel. 020-6449968. Pres.: Dr. E. M. Wikler. Rabbis M. Just & R. Evers.
Verbond Liberaal Religieuze Joden in Nederland (Fed. of Dutch Liberal Congs.), Jacob Soetendorpstr. 8. Tel. 020-6423562.

Cultural Organisations
Anne Frank Foundation, Prinsengracht 263-265. Tel. 020-6264533.
Jad Achat, van de Boechorststr. 26. Tel. 020-6461905.

Welfare Organisations
(K) Beth Shalom Home for Aged, Kastelenstraat 82 (Buitenveldert). Tel. 020-6611516.
(K) CIZ General Hospital, Laan van de Helende Meesters 8, Amstelveen. Tel. 020-65474711.
Joods Maatschapelijk Werk (Jewish Welfare Office), de Lairessestr. 145-147. Tel. 020-6730629.

Student and Youth Organisations
Ijar Student & Youth Org., de Lairessestr. 13. Tel. 020-6768226.
Maccabi. Sec.: E. M. Menko, Str. v. Sicilie 24, 1183 GN Amstelveen. T. 020-6478970.
Sjoeche Youth Society, P.O.B. 71797, 1008 DG. Tel. 020-6446659.

Zionist Organisations
Bnei Akiva, Amstelveenseweg 665. Tel. 020-6463872.
Ichud Haboniem, Landskroon 5. Tel. 644 1406.
Keren Kayemet, Bronckhorststr 16. Tel. 020-6736750.
Keren Hayesod Joh. Vermeerstr. 24. Tel. 020-6719123.
Federatie Nederlandse Zionisten (Federation of Dutch Zionists), Joh. Vermeerstr. 24. Tel. 020-6719126.
WIZO, Joh. Siegertstr. 8. Tel. 020-6944269.
Zijon, Joh. Vermeerstr. 24. Tel. 020-6719126.

Places of Interest
The Portuguese Syn., which has been completely restored, Mr. Visserplein 3, is open from May to Sept., Sun., 10 a.m.-1 p.m., Mon. to Fri., 10 a.m.-12 noon & 1 p.m.-4 p.m.; Livraria Montezinos & Ets Haim Library, Mr. Visserplein 3 (open Sun. 9 a.m.-1 p.m.); the Jewish Historical Museum (housed in a complex of 3 former syns.), Jonas Daniel Meijerplein 2-4. Tel. 020-6269945. Open daily, 11 a.m.-5 p.m.; the monument in the Meijerplein to the dock workers of Amsterdam, who went on strike in protest against the Nazi deportation of the Jews; the monument to the Jewish Resistance, Zwanenburgwal (next to the new Town Hall); the monument in the Weesperstraat to those who helped the Jews during the Second World War Nazi occupation; the Hollandse Schouwburg, Plantage, Middenlaan 20, a one-time theatre used as a collecting point for Jews deported by the Nazis in 1942 and 1943, and converted into an annexe of the Historical Museum; Anne Frank House, the original hiding place of Anne Frank, where she wrote her Diary. Several exhibitions. Prinsengracht 263, near Westermarkt. Tel. 020-6264533. Open weekdays from 9 a.m.-5 p.m. Suns. & holidays, 10 a.m.-5 p.m.; Biblioteca Rosenthaliana (a fine collection of Judaica and Hebraica), in the university library. Singel 423; the Resistance Museum (housed in the Lekstr. Syn. bldg.), Lekstr. 61; the Portuguese cemetery, Ouderkerk-on-the-Amstel, 10 miles south-east of Amsterdam (Manasseh ben Israel is buried here).

Booksellers, etc.
Joachimsthal's Boekhandel Europaplein 85, 1078 GZ. Tel. 020-66640017.
Samech Books, Gunterstein 69. Tel. 020-6421424.

Newspaper
Nieuw Israëlietisch Weekblad, Rapenburgerstr. 109. Tel. 020-6235584 &
6237763.

Hotels
Hotel Arsenal, Frans van Mierisstr. 97. Tel. 020-6792209. Pre-packed
kosher breakfasts available for guests.
Hotel Doria, Damstraat 3, 101252. Tel. 020-6388826.
Hotel Golden Tulip, Barbizon Centre, Stadhouderskade 7. Tel. 020-
6851351. **(K)** Kosher food for groups.
Okura, Ferdinand Bolsstr. 333. Tel. 6787111. **(K)** Kosher food for groups.

Kosher Meals
(K) Kosher meals are available Mon. to Thurs. from 5.45 p.m. to 7.15 p.m.
at Students' Mensa, Meschibat Nefesh, de Lairessestr. 13 (near
Concertgebouw). Tel. 020-6767622. Under supervision of Amsterdam
Rabbinate. No accom. is available. Trams 3, 12, 16; buses 26, 65, 66; **(K)**
Kosher meals available Fri. night & Shabbat. Kosher meals, sandwiches &
lunch boxes delivered to hotels, & Shabbat meals available from Marcus
Ritueel. See kosher butchers below.

Kosher Food
(K) Bakeries: Lipar Neuhaus, Scheldestr. 55. Tel. 020-6794764; Theeboom,

Bolestein, 45-47. Tel. 020-6427003; Tweede Sweelinckstr. 5. Tel. 020-6627086; Maasstraat 16. Tel. 020-6624827.
Kosher Butchers: **(K)** Marcus Ritueel, Ferd. Bolstr. 44. Tel. 020-6719881. **(K)** Meyer, Scheldestr. 63. Tel. 020-6640036
(K) Restaurant: Hatikwa (Dairy), Kastelenstraat. 80, 1083. Tel. 020 642 24299.
(K) Sandwiches, etc.: S. Meyer, Scheldestr. 45, 1078 GG. Tel. 020-6731313; Mouwes Koshere Delicatessen, Kastelenstraat 261, 1082. Tel. 020-6610180.
(K) Mrs. B. Hertzberger, Plantage Westermanlaan 9. Tel. 020-623 4684. 5 minutes from Portuguese Syn. Friday night and Shabbat meals only. Reservation in advance. Also lunchboxes for groups.
(K) Choclatery Bonbon Jeannette, Europaplein 87. Tel. 020-6649638.

For inf. about syns., services & kosher food outside Amsterdam, Rotterdam & The Hague, contact Chief Rabbinate of Holland, Tel. 020-6443868.

ARNHEM

Syn. & Com. Centre: Pastoorstr. 17a. Tel. 085-425154.
Liberal Cong. Inq. to Secretary. Tel. 08811-63152.
Home for Aged: "Beth Zikna," Beekstr. 40. Tel. 085-433788, where arrangements can be made for **(K)** kosher food.

BUSSUM

Syn. & Com. Centre: Kromme Englaan 1a. Tel. 02159-14882.
Home for Aged: **(K)** Het Gooi, Ceintuurbaan 281. Tel. 02159-12241.

DELFT

Hillel House, Beth Studentiem, Jewish students' centre at the Technical University, Koornmarkt 9. Tel. 015-120300.
(K) Mensa, open Mon-Thurs 18.00 p.m. by previous arrangement.

EINDHOVEN

Syn.: H. Casimirstr. 23. Tel. 040-511253.
Inq. to Sec. Tel. 040-415598.

ENSCHEDE

Syn. & Com. Centre: Prinsestr. 16. Tel. 053-323479 or 353336.
Liberal Cong. Inq. to Sec., Tel. 053-324908. Syn. at Haaksbergen.

GRONINGEN

Syn. & Com. Centre: Folkingestr 2. Tel. 050 123151 or 129516.

HAARLEM

Syn. & Com. Centre: Kenaupark 7. Tel. 023-326899. Min.: Rev. A. M. Goldberg. Tel. 023-242051. Mikva on premises.

HILVERSUM

Syn. & Com. Centre: Laanstr. 30. Inq. to Sec. Tel. 035-212044.
Inter-Provincial Chief Rabbinate: Laanstraat 30. Tel. 035-239238. Rabbis J. S. Jacobs, S. Evers, A. L. Heintz.

LEIDEN

Syn. & Com. Centre: Levendaal 16. Tel. 071-125793.
Jewish Students' Centre, Levendaal 8. Tel. 071-130382.

ROTTERDAM

Syn. & Com. Centre: A. B. N. Davidsplein 4. Tel. 010-4669765. Mikva on premises.
Liberal Syn.: Molenhoek Hillegersberg. Inq. to Sec. Tel. 010-4613211.
Kosher Butcher: **(K)** Piket, Walen-burgerweg 97. Tel. 010-4672856 Wed. only. Kosher groceries available Wed. & Thurs. p.m.

THE HAGUE & SCHEVENINGEN

Syns.: Syn. & Com. Centre: Corn. Houtmanstr. 11 & Bezuidenhoutseweg, The Hague. Tel. 070-3473201. Mikva on premises; Scheveningen Harstenhoekweg 44, Scheveningen Min: Rabbi P. A. Meijers. Tel. 070-3824472. Contact: Rabbi P. A. Meijers or P. M. Jacobs. Tel. 070-385 1436 for catering under supervision of the Rabbinate.
Liberal Syn., Prinsessegracht 26, The Hague, Min.: Rabbi A. Soetendorp. Tel. 070-3656893.
Spinoza House, in Paviljoensgracht, is of special interest, as is the 18th-century Portuguese Syn. in the Prinsessegracht, which is now used by the Liberal cong.
B'nai B'rith Nederland, P.O.B. 96842, 2509 JE. Tel. 070-3247350.
CIDI, Israel Inf. & Documentation Centre, P.O.B. 11646, 2502 AP. Tel. 070-3646862 or 3645533.
Israel Embassy, Buitenhof 47. Tel. 070-3647850.
(K) Jacobs Kosjere Delicatessen, Haverkamp 220. Tel. 070-347-4980.

UTRECHT

Syn. & Com. Centre: Springweg 164. Min.: Rabbi A. L. Heintz. Tel. 030-314742.
Kosher Bakery: **(K)** De Tarwebol, Zadelstr. 19. Tel. 030-314887.
(K) Delicatessen Milk & Honey, Poorstr. 93. Tel. 030-733114.

HONDURAS

(Most of the estimated 200 Jews in Honduras are Ashkenazi.)

SAN PEDRO SULA

Com. Sec.: Mauricio Weizenblut. Tel. 530157. Services Fri. & Sat. at syn. & com. centre.

TEGUCIGALPA

Com. Pres.: Helmut Seidel. Tel. 31-5908. Services usually held in private homes.
Israel Embassy & Consulate, Palmira Bldg., 5th Floor. Tel. 32-4232 or 32-5176.

HONG KONG

(Jewish population about 600 families)
The Hong Kong com. dates from about 1857. The syn. was built in 1901.
General inf. from Hong Kong Tourist Assoc., 125 Pall Mall, SW1Y 5EA. Tel. 071-930 4775.
Ohel Leah Syn. and Mikvah, 70 Robinson Rd. Tel. (5) 594872. Hon. Pres.: Lord Kadoorie, O.B.E. Min.: Rabbi Shmuel Lopin.
Fri. night, Sat. & weekday services are held at the syn. For further inf., Tel. 801 5442 or 801 5274 (Rabbi) Fax (852) 877-917. Sat. & weekday morn. services are held at the Hilton Hotel. Further inf. from Rabbi Mordechal Avtzon (Lubavitch). Tel. 523 9770.
The Jewish Club, 4th floor, 33 Queens Rd. (Melbourne Plaza), Central. Tel. (852) 8015440.

(K) 2 Kosher Restaurants (under Mashgiach supervision), Library, Health Club. Temporary membership for travellers.

Israel Consulate-General, Admiralty Centre, Tower II, Room 701, 18 Harcourt Rd. Tel. 529 6091.

Hotels: Hilton Tel. 233111; Hyatt, 19 Chatham Rd., Kowloon. Tel. 366 23 21; Mandarin; Peninsula (350), Kowloon. Tel. (3) 666251; Regent, Salisbury Rd., Tsimshatsui. Tel. (3) 7211211; Sheraton. Tel. (3) 691111.

Pre-packed kosher food available on request at all the main hotels, or contact Jewish Club.

HUNGARY

The Jewish population of Hungary is about 100,000, of whom some 80,000 live in the capital, Budapest, and the rest mainly in rural areas. (In 1930 the city had a Jewish population of 230,000 – the second largest in Europe). It is probable that Jews lived in this part of Europe in Roman times. The governing body of Hungarian Jewry is the Central Board of Hungarian Jews.

BUDAPEST

Central Board of Hungarian Jews (Magyar Izraeliták Országos Képviselete), VII, Sip utca 12. Tel. 122-64-78. Dir.: Gusztav Zoltai.

The Central Rabbinical Council (Conservative) is at VII, sip utca 12. Tel. 1421-180. Its Pres., Rabbi Alfred Schöner, is Chief Rabbi of Hungary.

The Orthodox Central Synagogue is at VII, Kazinczy utca 27. Pres.: Herman Fixler. Tel. 1-324-331. (K) Kosher milk & cheese are available here three mornings a week. There are, in addition, 29 other syns. and prayer houses. Details from the Central Board of Hungarian Jews.

Heroes Syn., VII Wesselényi u. 5.
The Dohány St. Synagogue, VII, Dohány utca 4-6, was built in 1859, and is
the main Conservative synagogue. It is the second largest in the world. In
its grounds lie buried the Hungarian Jewish victims of the Nazis. There is
also a commemorative plaque to Hanna Senesh, the Jewish girl parachutist
who was captured and tortured before being shot by the Nazis. In the
synagogue itself is a plaque commemorating Theodor Herzl, the founder of
Zionism.
There are 20 other syns. in the city.
A Gothic syn. dating from the 14th century has been uncovered in
Budapest, in Tancsincs Mihaly utca, on the site of the medieval walled
town of Budavár, where the Jewish com. lived in the Middle Ages.
Mikva, VII, Kazinczy utca 16.
Jewish Museum, VII, Dohány utca 2. Tel. 142-8949. Dir.: Dr. Ilona
Benoschofsky. Open in summer only.
Rabbinical Seminary, Central Archive & Jewish Library, VII, József körut
27. Tel. 1-342-121. Princ.: Dr. Joseph Schweitzer.
There is a statue to Raoul Wallenberg, the Swedish diplomat in Budapest
who saved hundreds of thousands of Hungarian Jews from the Nazis
towards the end of the Second World War, at II, Szilagyi Erzsebet Fasor.
The Holocaust Memorial was inaugurated in 1990. It stands at the corner of
Rumbach Sebestyén and Wesselényi Streets in the grounds of the former
Great Synagogue.
Talmud Torah, VII, Sip utca 12.
Cemeteries: Chevra, X Gránátos u. 12; Farkasréti, XII Erdi u. 9; Kereperi,
VIII Solgótarjani u.; Obudei, III Külsö Bécsi u.369; Rakoskeresztúri u.6.
Jewish Elementary and High School VII Wesseleny U. 44.
Charité Hospital & Nursing Home, XIV, Amerikai ut 53. Superintendent:
Dr. András Losonci. Tel. 2-515-518
Ujpest Home for Aged, IV, Berzeviczy G. utca 8. Tel. 1-293-627.
Fortnightly Newspaper, "Uj Elet, (New Life)" produced by the Central
Board.
Kosher Restaurants: **(K) Hannah**, VII, Dob utca 35. Tel. 1-421-072; **(K)**
Shalom, VII, Klauzal ter 1-2. Tel. 1-413-396 or 1-221-464.
(K) Central Kitchen & Food Distribution, IX, Pava utca 9-11.
There are 12 kosher butchers' shops in Hungary. Inf. from the Central
Board. There is also a **(K)** kosher bakery at Dob utca 28.
Tours of Jewish sites are provided by Kultours, 31c Tanács Krt; Tel. (36-1)
122-6527.

SOPRON

The 13th-century syn. & mikva here have been restored and were reopened in June, 1976. They are closed on Tues. There is a Jewish Museum
at Uj utca 11.
There are also Jewish communities in Debrecen, Miskolc, Pecs and Szeged,
Szombathely and other cities. The beautiful Szeged Syn. has recently been
restored.

INDIA

Indian Jewry comprises: (1) The Bene Israel, who form about 92 per cent,
with the Bombay region as their main centre; (2) the Jews of Cochin &
neighbourhood, on the Malabar Coast; (3) Jews from Iraq, as well as Iran,
Bokhara & Afghanistan, who first arrived as a small handful of people
some 200 years ago.
There are altogether about 5,500 Jews in India, of whom some 4,350 live in
Bombay.
The Bene Israel, according to tradition, arrived in India before the Christian

era. The Bene Israel now have more than 20 syns. in India (19 Sephardi and one Liberal). A monument has been erected in the village of Navgaon where they landed.

Jews from Iraq first arrived in about 1796, escaping persecution. They are to be found chiefly in Bombay, Poona and Calcutta. They have two syns. in Bombay, one in Poona, and three in Calcutta. Among the more illustrious of their members were the Sassoon, Ezra and Kadoorie families, who established a large number of mills and other business enterprises.

The Jews of Cochin, on the Malabar Coast, arrived as traders about the first century & have records dating as far back as the eighth century. There are only about 200 Jews in the State of Kerala today, the rest having emigrated to Israel and other countries.

General inf. from Government of India Tourist Office, 7 Cork St., W1X 2AB. Tel. 071-437 3677-8.

AHMEDABAD

Syn.: Magen Abraham, Bukhara Mohalla, opp. Parsi Agiari.

BOMBAY

Syns.: Beth El Syn., Mirchi Galli, Mahatma Gandhi Rd., Panvel, 410206; Beth El Syn., Rewdanda, Allibag Tehsil, Raigad; Beth Ha-Elohim Syn., Penn; Etz Haeem Prayer Hall, 2nd Lane, Umerkhadi 400009; Gate of Mercy (Shaar Harahamim), 254 Samuel St., Nr Masjid Railway Station, 400003. Tel. 52-20-50. This is the oldest Bene Israel syn. in India, established in 1796 & known as the Samaji Hasaji Syn. or Juni Masjid until 1896 when its name was changed to Shaar Harahamim; Hessed-El Syn., Poynad, Alibag Tehsil; Knesseth Eliahu Syn., Forbes St., Fort, 400001; Kurla Bene Israel Prayer Hall, 275 S.G. Barve Rd. (Pipe Rd.) Kurla, W. Bombay, 400070; Magen Aboth Syn., Alibag; Magen David Syn., opp. Richardson & Cruddas, Byculla, 400008; Magen Hassidim Syn., 8 Mohammed Shahid Marg (formerly Moreland Rd.), Agripada, 400011; Rodef Shalom Syn., Sussex Rd., Byculla, 400027; Shaare Rason Syn., 90 Tantanpura St., 3rd Rd., Don Tad, Israel Mohalla, Khadak, 400009; Shaar Hashamaim Syn., Tembi Naka, opp. Civil Hospital, Thane, 400601; Shahar Hatephilla Syn., Mhasla; Tifereth Israel Syn., 92 K.K. Marg, Jacob Circle, 400011.

The following organisations exist in Bombay: Bene Israel Stree Mandal (Women's Org.). Pres.: Miss Lily Sampson. Sec.: Mrs. Milka Joseph; Bikur Holim, Indu House, Ballard Estate. Sec.: Moses N. J. Sultoon; B'nai B'rith Lodge of India, 2626. Pres.: Basil David. Sec.: Tobias Aaron; Bombay Zionist Assoc. Pres.: E. M. Jacob. Tel. 52-20-50. Sec.: Moses Talegawkar; Central Jewish Board, P.O.B. 539. Pres.: Benjamin Solomon. Hon. Sec.: S. Abraham; Council of Indian Jewry, c/o Jewish Club. Pres.: Professor Nissim Ezekiel. Exec. Ch.: Sec.: Daniel Jacob; Jewish Club, Jeroo Bldg., 137 Mahatma Gandhi Rd. Ch.: Miss S. Kelly. Sec.: E. Mashal. Kosher food available; Jewish Relief Assoc., c/o Feil & Co., Gresham Hse., Sir P. M. Rd. Ch.: Sec. G. Solomon; Jewish Women's League. Pres.: Mrs. M. Sopher. Sec.: Mrs. N. Ezra.

Israel Consulate, 50 Kailash, G. Deshmukh Marg, 26. Tel. 3862793.

Jewish Travel Agent: Tov Tours & Travels (India), B-9, New Empire Premises, Kondivita St., 400 059. Tel. 6300750. Tours of Jewish India.

CALCUTTA

Syns.: Bethel Syn., 26/1 Pollack St.; Magen David Syn., 109a Peplabi Rash, Bihari Bose Rd. (formerly Canning St.), 1; Neveh Shalome Syn., 9 Jackson Lane, 1.

General inq. to Sec., Jewish Assoc. of Calcutta, 1 & 2 Old Court House Corner. Tel. 22-4861.

COCHIN

Syns.: Chennamangalam, Jew St., Chennamangalam. Built in 1614 & restored in 1916, this syn. has been declared an historical monument by the Govt. of India. A few yards away is a small concrete pillar into which is inset the tombstone of Sara Bat-Israel, dated 5336 (1576); Paradesi, Jew Town, Mattancherry, Cochin 2, the only Cochin syn. still functioning. Built 1568.
Inq. to S. S. Koder, Princess St., Fort, Cochin. Tel. 24288 & 24988.

NEW DELHI

Syn. Judah Hyam Synagogue, 2 Humayun Rd. Inq. to Pres., Jewish Welfare Assoc., 74 Babar Rd. Tel. 371 4252, or J. M. Benjamin, Vice-Pres., J.W.A., A/7 Nirman Vihar Patparganj, Delhi 110092. Tel. 2243136. The Judah Hyam Synagogue Annexe houses a library and centre for Jewish & inter-faith studies.
Diplomatic relations with Israel have recently been established.

PUNE

Syns.: Ohel David Syn., Synagogue St., Poona Camp (Cantonment), Pune, 411001; Succath Shelomo Syn., 93 Rasta Peth, Pune 411011. Inq. to Hon. Sec. David Soloman, 247/1 Rasta Peth, Trupti Apt., Pune 411011. Also: Dr. S. B. David, 9 Bund Garden Rd., Pune 411001.

IRAN

There have never been any reliable statistics on the number of Jews living in Iran. Today, there are an estimated 28,000. Most live in Tehran. The Tomb of Daniel is near Ahavaz (Shoush) and that of Mordechai and Esther is venerated at Hamadan.

ISFAHAN

The main syn. is in Shah Abbas St., and there are also some 20 syns. in the old Jewish quarter – called the Mahalleh – near the Friday Mosque.

TEHRAN

The three central syns. are the Haim, in Gavamossaltaneh St., the Iraqi, in Anatole France St., and the Meshedi in Kakh Shomali Av., opposite the Abrishami School.
There are numerous old syns. in what was once the Jewish quarter of Tehran and is still known as the Mahalleh (off Sirus Av.).

IRISH REPUBLIC

A Sephardi community was established in Dublin in the middle of the seventeenth century. In 1918 the office of Chief Rabbi of Eire was established, the first incumbent being Rabbi Isaac Herzog (who became Chief Rabbi of Israel, and died in 1959). Other holders of the office have included Lord Immanuel Jakobovits. The Jewish population is about 1,500, most of whom live in Dublin.
General inf. from Irish Tourist Board, 150-151 New Bond St., W1Y 0AQ. Tel. 071-493 3201.

CORK

In the seventeenth and eighteenth centuries there was a settlement in Cork of Sephardi Jews. Their burial ground has been identified in legal documents – it was a few hundred yards from the present syn. This cong. came into being in the latter part of the nineteenth century, in the days of the exodus from Tsarist Russia. There is a Jewish cemetery in Cork.

Syn.: 10 South Ter. Services: Sabbath morn. 10.30 a.m. and all Holy-days. Pres.: F. Rosehill. Tel. 870413.

DUBLIN
Synagogues & Religious Organisations
Chief Rabbi of Ireland: Vacant. Office: Stratford Schools, 1 Zion Rd., 6. Tel. 923751.
Communal Min.: Cantor Alwyn Shulman.
Syn.: Adelaide Rd.
The Jewish Home, "Denmark Hill", Leinster Rd. West, 6. Services are held daily, Fr. evg. at start of Sabbath and Sabbath morn.
Machzikei Hadass, 77 Terenure Rd. North.
Terenure, Rathfarnham Rd.
Progressive Synagogue, 7 Leicester Av. 6. Tel. 973955. Hon Sec.: Mrs. J. Finkel. Tel. 907605. Services are held on Fri. evg. at 8.15 p.m., first Sabbath in the month and Sabbath morn. at 10.30 a.m.
Board of Shechita, 1 Zion Rd., 6.
Cemeteries: Aughavannagh Rd., Tel. Dolphin's Barn 540806. Dolphin's Barn, Dublin, 8. Inq. to caretaker. The old Jewish cemetery at Ballybough (Tel. Ballybough: 369756), may be visited on application to the caretaker. There is a Progressive cemetery at Woodtown, Co. Dublin.

Cultural & Educational Organisations, Schools, etc.
Com. Centre, 1 Zion Rd., 6. Tel. 923751.
Irish Jewish Museum, 3-4 Walworth Rd., 8. Inf. from Dr. G. Tolkin. Tel. 283 2703: Museum Tel. 53 1797.
Stratford Schools, 1 Zion Rd., 6. Tel. 922315.
Talmud Torah, Com. Centre, 1 Zion Rd., 6. Tel. 922315.

Welfare Organisations, Homes, etc.
Board of Guardians. Sec.: Mrs. J. Steinberg. Tel. 908413.
The Jewish Home, "Denmark Hill", Leinster Rd. West, 6. Tel. 972004.

Student & Youth Organisations
Students' Union: Inf. from Comm. Centre.

Zionist Organisations
J.I.A., J.N.F., Zionist Org. of Ireland, are all at Stratford Schools, 1 Zion Rd., 6. Tel. 922318.

Sport & Miscellaneous Organisations
Edmondstown Golf Club, Edmonstown, Rathfarnham, 14. Tel. 931082.
Jewish Medical Society. Inf. from Dr. E. Eppel, 202 Kimmage Rd. W., 12. Tel. 902427.
Jewish Representative Council of Ireland, 1 Zion Rd., 6. Tel. 967351.
Maccabi Assoc., Clubhouse & Sports Ground, Kimmage Rd. West. Tel. 555490.
(K) Kosher meals by arrangement with the Jewish Home.

Booksellers
Barry's Bookshop, Barry Gross, 137 Butterfield Av., Dublin 14. Fax/Tel. 353-1-934211.

Kosher Suppliers
Butchers: **(K)** Suissa's, 31 Lower Clanbrassil St. Suissa. Tel. 540249.; **(K)** B. Erlich, 35 Lower Clanbrassil St. Tel. 542252.
Baker: **(K)** Bretzel 1a Lennox St. Tel. 752724.

ITALY

The Jewish com. of Italy, whose history goes back to very early times, increased considerably at the time of the Dispersion in 70 C.E. During the Middle Ages and the Renaissance there were newcomers from Spain and Germany. Rich syns. as well as rabbinical schools, yeshivot and printing houses were set up and gained wide renown.

A decline of Italian Judaism began during the last century: assimilation, concentration in big towns and emigration reduced many once-flourishing centres. During the first years of fascism Italian Jews did not suffer, but after 1938 – under Nazi pressure – racial laws were introduced and, during the German occupation from 1943 to 1945, nearly 12,000 Jews, especially from Rome, were murdered or banished.

There are 35,000 Jews in Italy today, the most important coms. being in Rome (15,000), Milan (9,500), and Turin (1,285), followed by Florence, Trieste and Venice.

Inf. on Italian Jewry, its monuments and history may be obtained from Unione Comunità Ebraiche Italiane (Union of Italian Jewish Communities), Lungotevere Sanzio 9, Rome. Tel. 580-36-67 & 580-36-70. Pres.: Mrs. Tullia Zevi.

General & hotel inf. from Italian State Tourist Office (ENIT), 1 Princes St., W1R 8AY. Tel. 071-408 1254.

ANCONA

Syn. & Mikva, Via Astagno. Rabbi Cesare Tagliacozzo, Via S. Marcellino 11. Tel. 55-654.
Com. Offices, Via Fanti 2 bis. Tel. 202638. Pres.: C. Calderolli.

ASTI

Syn., Via Ottolenghi 8.
Museum. V. Ottolenghi 8. Tel. 0141-53281 or 0141-54271.
Cemetery. Via Martiri Israelitici.

BOLOGNA

Syn., Via Mario Finzi. Rabbi A. Someck.
Com. Offices, Via Gombruti 9. Tel. 232-066. Com. Pres.: Bianca Finzi.
Kosher Restaurant: **(K) Eshel Israel,** Via Gombruti 9. Tel. 340-936. Under supervision of Rabbi G. H. Garelik of Milan.

CASALE MONFERRATO

Syn. & Com. Offices, Vicolo Salomone Olper 44. Com Pres.: Dr. Giorgio Ottolenghi. Tel. 0142-71807.
The synagogue, built in 1500 and rebuilt in 1866, also contains a Jewish museum.
Casale-Monferrato is on the Turin-Milan road, and can be reached by turning off it about 13 miles beyond Chivasso.

FERRARA

Syn., Via Mazzini 95. Min.: Rabbi Luciano Caro. Tel. 0532-47004.
Mikva, Via Mazzini 95.
Cemetery, Via delle Vigne 2.
Com. Offices, Via Mazzini 95. Com. Pres.: Celestina Ottolenghi. Tel. 0532-751337.

FLORENCE (Firenze)

Syn., Via Luigi Carlo Farini 4. Tel. 245-252. Min.: Rabbi Umberto Sciunnach, Via L. C. Farini 2a. Tel. 244-711.

Mikva, Via L. C. Farini 4. Tel. 245-252 or 055-2476110.
Com. Offices, Via L. C. Farini 4. Tel. 245-252. Pres.: Carlo Lopes Pegna.
Jewish Museum, Via L. C. Farini 4. Tel. 245-252. There is a communal religious & artistic souvenir shop on the premises.
Nathan Cassuto School (Kindergarten, Primary & Secondary), Via L. C. Farini 4. Tel. 245-252.
B'nai B'rith, Via L. C. Farini 4.
Home for Aged, Via Carducci 11. Tel. 241-210.
Cemeteries: Viale Ludovico Ariosto 14 & Via di Caciolle 13. Tel. 416-723.
Kosher Butcher, **(K)** Bruno Bigazzi, Mercato Coperto di S. Ambrogio. Tel. 248-0740.
Kosher Poultry, **(K)** Giovannino, Via Macci 106. Tel. 666-534.

GENOA

Syn., Via Bertora 6. Tel. 891-513 & 892-637. Rabbi Giuseppe Momigliano. Pres.: Vito Sciunnach. Services every evg. & Shabbat morn.
Com. Offices, Via Bertora 6.
R. Pacifici School, Via Maragliano 3-4. Tel. 591-402 & 280-726.
Kosher Butcher: **(K)** Firpo, Corso Torino 2r. Tel. 587-658.

GORIZIA (Gradica)

Syn., Via Ascoli 13. Tel. (3831) 896-290.
Cemeteries: Goricia-Valdiroze (dates back to 1371). Gradisca-Via del Campi 15. Contact: Tel. 0481-3831.

ISCHIA

Hotel: Grand Hotel Punta Molino. Tel. (081) 99 15 44.

LEGHORN (Livorno)

Syn., Piazza Benamozegh 0586-24290. Min.: Rabbi Dr. Isidoro Kahn. Office, Via Mical 21. Tel. 810-265 & 28-722.
Mikvah: Signore Kahn. Tel. 882-584.
Bnei Akiva, Via Mameli 88.
Com. Pres.: Paola Jarach Bedarida.
Kosher Butcher: **(K)** Corucci, Mercato Centrale. Tel. 884596.

MANTUA (Mantova)

Syn. & Com. Offices, Via G. Govi 11. Tel. 321490. Com. Pres.: S. Vivanti.
Cemetery: Via Legnano.

MERANO

Syn. & Com. Offices, Via Schiller 14. Tel. 23-127. Pres.: Federico Steinhaus.

MILAN

The Chief Rabbi is Rabbi Dr. Giuseppe Laras. Office: Via Eupili 6. Tel. 345-2096 or 5512029. Pres.: Giorgio Sacerdoti.

Synagogues & Religious Organisations
Beth Shelomo, Corso di Porta Romana 63.
Central Synagogue, Via Guastalla 19. Tel. 5512101. Mikva on premises.
Home for Aged, Via Jommelli 18. Tel. 230-504. Services on Sabbaths and festivals.
New Home for Aged, Via Leone XIII 1. Tel. 436-331. Services on Sabbaths and festivals. Mikva on premises.
New Synagogue, Via Eupili 8. Services on Sabbaths and festivals. (also community Offices).

Ohel Yacob, Via Benvenuto Cellini 2 (Rabbi G. H. Garelik – Lubavitch). Tel. 708-877. (Cafeteria).
Orthodox Sephardi Synagogue, Via Guastalla 19 (Rabbi Y. Haddad).
Persian Synagogues: Angelo Donati Beth Hamidrash, Via Sally Mayer 4-6. Mikva on premises; Via Tuberose 14. Tel. 415-1660.

Representative Organisations
B'nai B'rith, Via Eupili 8.
Com. Offices, Via Eupili 6. Tel. 389-031. Com. Pres.: Giorgio Sacerdoti.

Welfare Organisations, Homes, etc.
Home for Aged, Via Jommelli 18. Tel. 230-504. Pres.: Eugenio Mortara.
New Home for Aged, Via Leone XIII 1. Tel. 4982604. (Kosher meals by arrangement).
OSE, Via Leone XIII 1.
Welfare Committee, Via Guastalla 19. Tel. 791-851.

Zionist Organisations
A.D.E.I.-WIZO, Piazza della Repubblica 6. Tel. 659-8102.
Keren Hayesod, Via Caminadella 2. Tel. 863-290.
Keren Kayemet, Via Eupili 6. Tel. 342-455.
Youth Aliyah, Corso Independenza 12. Tel. 738-9308.
Zionist Federation of Italy, Via Caminadella 2. Tel. 864-186.
Israel Consulate-General, Corso Europa 12. Tel. 705-509 & 705-477.

Miscellaneous Organisations
Contemporary Jewish Documentation Centre, Via Eupili 6. Tel. 316-338.
Italian Maccabi Federation, Via Paolo da Cannobis 9. Tel. 877-785 & 877-786.
Jewish Youth Assoc. (C.G.E.) Club, Via Sant' Antonio 4. Tel. 866-932.
Kosher Distributor Via della Branda 2. Tel. 588248.

Kosher Restaurants
(K) Eshel Israel, Via Benvenuto Cellini 2. Tel. 545-9877. 1 p.m. to 2.30 p.m. & 7 to 9 p.m.
(K) Da Mosè, Via Mosé Bianchi 103. Tel. 481-4035.

Kosher Butchers
(K) Levi, Via Soncino 3.
(K) S. Malki, Via Caterina da Forli 58. Tel. 407-2788.

MILANO-MARITTIMA
Kosher Hotel: **(K) Hotel Liberty,** Traversa 14. Tel. 991-281. Under supervision of Rabbi G. H. Garelik. Summer only.

MODENA
Syn. & Com. Offices, Piazza Mazzini 26. Tel. 223-978. Rabbi Dr. R. Lattes.
Kosher Butcher: **(K)** Macelleria Duomo, Mercato Coperto (Covered Market), Stand 25. Tel. 217-269.

NAPLES (Napoli)
Syn. & Com. Offices, Via Cappella Vecchia 31. Tel. 416-386.

OSTIA ANTICA
Here can be found the partially restored excavated remains of a fourth century C.E. synagogue built on the site of another one which stood there 300 years earlier. This is the oldest synagogue site in Europe.

Ostia Antica is about 40 minutes by train from Rome (Termini or Pyramid Stations). To reach the synagogue, cross the footbridge on leaving the station. The entrance to the excavations is straight ahead.

PADUA (Padova)
Syn. & Com. Centre, Via S. Martino e Solferino 9. Tel. 875-1106. Min.: Rabbi A. Viterbo.
Mikva. Viterbo 8719501.
There are two ancient cemeteries, one near San Leonards and the other in Via Codalunga (near Bastione della Gatta). Isaac Ben Yehuda Abrabanel, Minister of Finance for King Alphonse V of Portugal is buried here.

PARMA
Syn. & Com. Offices, Vicolo Cervi 4.

PERUGIA
Syn., P. della Republica 77 or contact. S. Pacifico. Tel 075-21250.

PISA
Syn. & Com. Offices, Via Palestro 24. Tel. 27-269. Services are held on festivals and Holy-days. During the week the resident beadle will be glad to show visitors round the syn., which is famed for its beauty. It is very near the Teatro Verdi.

RICCIONE
In the summer, **(K)** kosher food (supervised by Rabbi S. Sacerdoti of Ferrara) is obtainable at the Vienna Touring Hotel.
The Hotel **Nevada.** Tel. 601245 provides vegetarian food and particularly welcomes Jewish guests.

ROME
Synagogues & Religious Organisations
The Chief Rabbi of Rome is Rabbi Dr. E. Toaff, Via Catalana 1.
Lungotevere Cenci 9 (Orthodox Italian service). Tel. 687-5051/2/3.
Via Balbo 33 (Orthodox Ashkenazi service).
Via Balbo 33 (Orthodox Italian service). Tel. 475-9881.
Via Catalana (Orthodox Sephardi service). This is in the basement of the main syn. at Lungotevere Cenci 9.
Mikvaot: Lungotevere Cenci 9 and Via Balbo 33.
The Italian Rabbinical Council's headquarters is at Lungotevere Sanzio 9. Tel. 580-3667 & 580-3670.
Beth Din, Lungotevere Cenci. Tel. 687-5051/2/3.

Representative Organisations
B'nai B'rith, Lungotevere Sanzio 14. Tel. 812-3608 & 812-3655.
Rome Communal Offices: Lungotevere Cenci 9. Tel. 687-5051/2/3. Pres.: G. Saban.
Union of Italian Jewish Communities, Lungotevere Sanzio 9. Tel. 580-3667 & 580-3670. Pres.: Mrs. Tullia Zevi.
World Jewish Congress, Italian Section, Piazza Scanderbeg 85. Tel. 675-033.

Cultural & Educational Organisations, Schools, etc.
A. Sacerdoti School, Lungotevere Sanzio 14. Tel. 658-8007.
Dario Ascarelli School, Lungotevere Sanzio 12. Tel. 580-3662.
Davide Almagià Seminary, Lungotevere Sanzio 14. Tel. 589-4809.
Italian Rabbinical College, Lungotevere Sanzio 14. Tel. 580-9196.
Jewish Cultural Centre, Via del Tempio 4. Tel. 687-5051/2/3.

Kindergarten, Lungotevere Sanzio 14. Tel. 580-3668.
ORT Schools: Via San Francesco di Sales 4-6. Tel. 655-504; Viale Trastevere 60. Tel. 480-6274.
Vittorio Polacco Elementary School, Lungotevere Sanzio 12. Tel. 580-3668.

Welfare Organisations, Hospitals, etc.

American Jewish Joint Distribution Committee, Via Messina 15. Tel. 861-741.
HIAS, Viale Regina Margherita 269. Tel. 844-1041.
Hospital & Convalescent Home, Via della Borgata della Magliana. Tel. 523-2634.
Orphanage, Arco de' Tolomei 1. Tel. 580-0539.
OSE, Viale Trastevere 60. Tel. 581-6486.
Welfare Committee, Viale Trastevere 60. Tel. 581-6486.
Museum, etc.
The Jewish Museum, in the main syn. bldg. at Lungotevere Cenci 9, contains a permanent exhibition covering the 2,000-year history of the Italian Jewish community.
Another link with this long history is the Rome Ghetto almost adjoining. It can be reached by taking buses 44, 56, 60 or 75, near the neighbouring Ponte Garibaldi. It is a maze of narrow alleys dating from Imperial Roman times, within which, until 1847, all Roman Jews were confined under curfew.
A striking monument has been erected to the memory of 335 Jewish and Christian citizens of Rome who were massacred in 1944 by the Nazis. Named Fosse Ardentine, it lies just outside the Porta San Paolo, a few yards from the main syn.
Jewish Guides: G. Palombo, Via val Maggia 7. Tel. 810-3716 & 993-2074; Ruben E. Popper, 12 Via dei Levii. Tel. (afternoons only) 761-0901.

Zionist Organisations

Bnei Akiva, Com. Centre, Lungotevere Cenci. Tel. 687-5051/2/3.
Hashomer Hatzair, Lungotevere Sanzio 14.
Jewish Agency, Corso Vittorio Emanuele 173. Tel. 654-5290 & 655-953.
Keren Hayesod, Corso Vittorio Emanuele 173. Tel. 656-8564.
Keren Kayemet Leisrael, Via A. Gramsci 42a. Tel. 360-08-56.
Israel Embassy, Via Michele Mercati 12. Tel. 3021541.

Newspaper

"Shalom", Monthly, Lungotevere Cenci 9.

Hotels & Restaurants

(K) **Da Lisa,** Via Foscolo 16-18. Tel. 730-027.
(K) **Meeting Meal Quick Restaurant,** Via Portico d'Ottavia 7B/8. Tel. 686-1349.
(K) **Uno,** Via Portico d'Ottavia 1/E. Tel. 6547937.
★ **Pensione Carmel,** Via Goffredo Mameli 11. Tel. 580-9921. Prop.: Maria Bahbout.
Marini Strand Hotel, Via del Tritone 17, 00187. Tel. 672-061. Under Jewish management.
Hotel Viminale, Via Cesare Balbo 31. Next door to syns.

Kosher Food

Makolet, Piazza Armellini 6. Tel. 856-862 & 475-5274.
(K) Tavola Calva, via Livorno 10, Piazza Bologna. Tel. (06) 44292025.

Kosher Butchers
(K) Massari, Piazza Bologna 11. Tel. 429-120.
(K) Sion Ben David, Via Filippo Turati 110. Tel. 73-33-58.
(K) Terracina, Via Portico d'Ottavia 1b. Tel. 654-1364.

Bakery
Limentani Settimio, Via Portico d'Ottavia 1.

SENIGALLIA
Syn., Via dei Commercianti.

SIENA
Syn., Vicolo delle Scotte 14. The com. has issued a brochure in English, giving the history of the syn., which dates back to medieval times. Services are held on the Sabbath and High Holy-days. Further inf. from Dr. Enzo Franco. Tel. 284-647 & 287-590.
Kosher Butcher: Tel. 281-056.

SPEZIA
Syn., Via 20 Settembre 165.
Talmud Torah, Via 20 Settembre 200.
Inq. to Alberto Funaro, Via R. Migliari 32. Tel. 28-504.
Zionist Office: Via 20 Settembre 68.

TRIESTE
Syns., Via Donizetti 2 (Ashkenazi & Sephardi). Min.: Rabbi Grassici, Via del Monte 1. Tel. 631898.
Com. Offices, Via San Francesco 19. Tel. 768-171. Pres.: D. Misau, Via Segantiu 14. Tel. 302-480.

TURIN (Torino)
Syn., and Mikvah, Via S. Pio V 12. Min.: Rabbi Roberto Colombo.
Com. Offices: Via S. Pio V 12. Tel. 669-2387.
Bookseller: Libreria Luxemburg, 7 Via C. Battisti, 10123. Tel. (011) 532-007.

URBINO
Syn., Via Stretta.

VENICE
Synagogues & Religious Organisations
In summer, Sabbath services are held in the Schola Spagnola, Ghetto Vecchio. In winter all services are held in the Schola Levantina. There are five syns. (as well as a Jewish museum) in the ghetto.
To reach the ghetto, start out from the railway stn. Facing it and then turning right, go along the Fondamento dei Scalzi, which almost immediately becomes the Lista di Spagna. Continue to the Campo S. Geremia and then, where the street narrows, along the Salizada S. Geremia. You will then come to a bridge. Cross it, and then turn left along the canal for about 75 yards until you see a chemist's shop – Farmacia. Immediately after it you will find the narrow entrance to the ghetto.
To reach the ghetto from the Grand Canal, alight at the San Marcuola landing stage. Walk away from the canal past the church, until you reach the Rio Terra S. Leonardo, a broad shopping thoroughfare. You will then see yellow street signs in Italian and Hebrew directing you to the syns. in the ghetto.
Mikva: Jewish Rest Home, Ghetto Nuovo 2874. Tel. 715-118.
Com. Offices: Ghetto Vecchio 1188a. Tel. 715-012. Pres.: Roberto Bassi.

Jewish Museum, Schola Tedesca, Ghetto Nuovo.
Cemeteries: Via Cipro 70 & Riviera San Nicolo 2, Lido, at the corner of Via Cipro.
(K) Kosher meals can occasionally be had in the Jewish Rest Home, Ghetto Nuovo 2874. Tel. 716-002. Very early booking is advised.
Hotels: **Buon Pesce,** S. Nicolo 50. Tel. 760-533. Open Apr. to Oct.; Danieli. Tel. 26-480; Europa & Regina. Tel. 700-477.
Jewish articles & religious appurtenances are available from Mordehai Fusetti, Ghetto Vecchio 1219. Tel. 714-024. Glass figures of Jewish interest are blown at Toso Gianni, Ghetto Nuovo 2884 & are also available from David's, Ghetto Nuovo 2880.

VERCELLI

Syn., Via Foa 70.
Com. Offices, Via Oldoni 20. Pres.: Dario Colombo.

VERONA

Syn., Via Portici 3. Min.: Rabbi Dr. C. Piattelli.
Com. Centre, Via Portici 3. Tel. 800-7112. Pres.: Carlo Rimini.

VIAREGGIO

Com. inq. to Giulio Arieti, Via Bertini 53. Tel. 51-327.
Cemetery: Via Marco Polo.
Kosher Meat: Available during the summer from **(K)** Macelleria Filli Satucci, Piazza del Mercato Nuovo. Tel. 42-691.

SARDINIA

There is no Sardinian Jewish community today, but the island is of more than passing Jewish interest. In 19 C.E. the Emperor Tiberius exiled Jews to Sardinia. There was a synagogue at Cagliari, the island's capital, at least as early as 599, for in that year a convert led a riot against it. Sardinia eventually came under Aragonese rule, and when the edict of expulsion of the Jews from Spain was issued in 1492, the Jews of the island had to leave. Since then there has been no community there.

SICILY

Although there are very few Jews in Sicily today, there is a long and varied history of Jewish settlement on the island stretching back to at least the sixth century C.E. and possibly – according to some scholars – to the first or second centuries.
By the late Middle Ages, the community numbered 40,000. In 1282, Sicily passed under Spanish rule. A century or so later, there was a wave of massacres of Jews, and another in 1474. These culminated in the introduction of the Inquisition in 1479, and the expulsion of the Jews in 1492.

JAMAICA

Jewish settlement in Jamaica, composed in the first instance of fugitives from the Inquisition, goes back to before the period of the British occupation in the mid-seventeenth century. In the eighteenth century there was also a small Ashkenazi influx from England. Jewish disabilities on the island were abolished in 1831.
There were formerly syns. at Port Royal, Spanish Town and Montego Bay. The only one now existing is at Kingston, where the Ashkenazi and Sephardi coms. were combined in 1921. This city contains the majority of the island's 350 Jews.

General inf. from Jamaica Tourist Board, 111 Gloucester Pl., W1H 3PH. Tel. 071-224 0505.

Syn.: Shaare Shalom, Duke & Charles Sts., Kingston (semi-R). Services, Fri. 5.30 p.m. (May to Oct.) & 5 p.m. (Nov. to April). Sabbath 10 a.m; festivals, 9 a.m. all year round. Sec.: Ernest H. de Souza, J.P., 2a King's Dr., Kingston, 6. Tel. 92-77948.

JAPAN

Taking into account businessmen, students, and other professionals with their families in Japan for 3-5 years the Jewish population can easily run to a couple of thousands at any given time. Exact data on permanent residents are not available and there are very few long-time residents who make Japan their permanent domicile. Conservative estimate: about 600 individuals.

Generel inf. from Japan National Tourist Organisation, 167 Regent St, W1R 7FD. Tel. 01-734 9638-9.

KOBE

There have been Jews in Kobe for more than a century. Today's Jewish population numbers some 30 families.

During the Second World War, Kobe's two synagogues were destroyed. The Ohel Shelomoh Synagogue (Orthodox) and community centre 12/12 Kitano-cho 4-chome, Ikuta-ku (P.O.B. 639). Tel. (078) 221 7236. M3H 3S4. Tel. (416). There is a mikva on the premises. Sec.: Bruce M. Benson. Tel. (078) 222 3950.

NAGASAKI

There are no Jews living in Nagasaki. The old Jewish cemetery is located at Sakamoto Gaijin Bochi. The site of the first syn. in Japan is Umegasaki Machi.

OKINAWA

While there is no native Jewish com. on Okinawa, there are normally 200-300 Jews serving with the U.S. military on the island. Regular services are conducted by the Jewish chaplain at Camp Smedley D. Butler, and visitors are welcomed.

TOKYO

There are 160 Jewish family members of the Jewish Com. of Japan, Jewish Com. Centre, 8-8 Hiroo, 3-Chome, Shibuya-ku, 150. Tel. 3400-2559 Fax (03) 3400-1827. Pres.: F. Harris. Beth David Syn. is in the Com. Centre premises. Services held Fri. evg., 7.00 p.m.; Shabbat morn., 9.30 a.m., and on High Holy-days & festivals. Rabbi James Lebeau. Kosher meals available Advance notification requested.

Israel Embassy, 3 Niban-cho Chiyodaku. Tel. 3264-0911.

YOKOHAMA

Inf. concerning the Jewish cemetery here may be obtained from the Jewish Community of Japan, in Tokyo.

YOKOSUKA

There is a Jewish chaplain at the United States naval base here, and some religious services at the base are open to visitors. Further inf. can be obtained by telephoning (0468) 26-1911, Ext. 6773. Yokosuka is about 13/4 hours' journey south of Tokyo.

KENYA

Jewish settlement in what was British East Africa dates from the beginning of this century. In 1903, when the British Government offered Zionists a territory in Kenya for Jewish settlement, there were already a number of Jews in the capital, Nairobi.

The "Uganda Plan," as the offer became known, did not materialise, yet shortly afterwards more Jews settled in the territory. In 1907 the Nairobi Hebrew Congregation was formed, and the foundation-stone for the first synagogue was laid in 1912.

The community was small until 1933, when new immigration started, especially from Central Europe. Today, there are some 500 Jews in the country, including about 400 Israelis. Nearly all live in Nairobi.

NAIROBI

Syn., cnr. University Way & Uhuru Highway. PO Box 40990. Tel. 222770.
Rosh Kehilla: Dr. David Silverstein. Sec.: Arnie Gordon.
Com. Centre: Vermont Memorial Hall. Open Mon.-Fri. 9.00am-12.00pm. (J. Moran or M. Raifman). Services Fri. evg. 6.30pm. Sat. morning 8.00am. All Festivals. Kosher chickens and meat available.

LATVIA
DAUGAVPILS

Syn.: Gogol Str.; Suvorov Str.
Jewish Community, Saules Str., 47. Fax 8 254 24658.

LIEPAJA

Jewish Community, Kungu St. 21. Tel. 25336

REZHITSA

Syn.: Kaleru Str.

RIGA

Syn.: 6/8 Peitavas Str. Tel. 371-2-210827. Fax 371-2-224549.
Organisations: Jewish Culture Society, Skolas 6, Loek, 226050. Tel. (013-2) 28-95-80. Fax 70 132 289573.
Shamir-M, Dubina Fonds Jewish Community Center, 7 Sporta Str., Riga LV-1001. Tel. 371-2-334012. Fax 371-2-334382.

LITHUANIA

There are approximately 5,000 Jews in the newly restored Lithuanian Republic, 4,000 of whom live in Vilnius.

DRUSKININKAI

Jewish Community, 9/15 Sporto Str. Tel. 54-590.

KAUNAS

Syn.: 11 Ozheshkienes Str.
Jewish Community, 26 B Gedimino Str. Tel. 203-717.

KLAIPEDA

Jewish Community, 3 Ziedu Skersqatvis. Tel. 93-758.

PANEVEZYS

Jewish Community, 6/22 Sodu Str., Panevezys 5300. Tel. 68-848.

SHIAULIAI
Jewish Community, 24 Vyshinskio. Tel.26-795.

VILNIUS
Main Syn. and matzah bakery: 39 Pylimo Str. Tel. 370-2-612 523.
Zalman Rejzen Foundation Supporting Jewish Culture, Education, and Science in Lithuania, 4 Pylimo, 1st (British) floor. Tel. 370-2-612 695. P.O. Box 1075, Vilnius 2001.
Jewish Publishing House "YAD – Yerushalayim de'Lita Publishers", 4 Pylimo, 2nd (Br.) floor, P.O. Box 1075, Vilnius 2001. Tel./fax 370-2-615 758.
WIZO branch in Vilnius, 4 Pylimo, Vilnius 2001. Tel. 611 736.
Jewish Community of Lithuania, 4 Pylimo, Vilnius 2001. Ground floor. Tel. 370-2-613 003. Fax 370-2-615 758.
Centre of Yidish Culture and Musik "Folkszinger", 4 Pylimo, Vilnius 2001, 2nd floor. Tel. 370-2-227 074 or 412 541.
The Israel Centre of Cultures and Art in Lithuania, 4 Pylimo, Vilnius 2001. 2nd floor. Tel. 370-2-611 736 or 652 139.
Jewish Community of Vilnius, 4 Pylimo, Vilnius 2001. Tel./fax 370-2-632 951.
State Jewish Museum, 4 Pylimo, Vilnius 2001. 1st floor. Tel. 370-2-632 951.

LUXEMBOURG
There are today about 1,200 Jews in Luxembourg, the majority in Luxembourg City.
General inf. from Luxembourg National Tourist & Trade Office, 36-37 Piccadilly, W1V 9PA. Tel. 071-434 2800.

ESCH-SUR-ALZETTE
Syn.: 52 rue du Canal. Pres.: Robert Wolf, 42 rue du X Septembre. minyan: Friday Evening.

LUXEMBOURG CITY
Syn.: 45 Av. Monterey. Tel. 452914.
Chief Rabbi emer.: Rabbi Dr. Emmanuel Bulz, 2 rue Marguerite de Brabant. Tel. 442569.
Chief Rabbi: Joseph Sayagh, 15 Bld. Grande Duchesse Charlotte. Tel. 452366
Cantor: Michel Heyman, 15 Bld. Grande Duchesse Charlotte.
B'nai B'rith: Yves Steinitz, 15 Rue de la Fonderie. Tel. 496362.
Jewish Council. Ch.: Guy Aach, 18 rue des Dahlias. Tel. 452458.
WIZO. Mrs. Irmy Meyer, 46 rue du X Septembre. Tel. 452455.

MADEIRA
See under Portugal.

MAJORCA
See under Spain.

MALAWI
LILONGWE
Israel Embassy, P.O. Box 30319. Tel. 731333 & 731789.

MALAYSIA
There are now only three Jewish families in the Malaysian island State of Penang (Pulau Pinang), all resident in the capital of Georgetown. The syn.

at 28 Jalan Nagore is closed. There is a cemetery in Jalan Yahudi (Jewish Street).

MALTA

There have been a few Jews in Malta since the Roman period. In the Middle Ages, in addition to the community on Malta itself, there was also one on the nearby island of Gozo, but with the expulsion of the Jews from Sicily in 1492, they both came to an end. From 1492 and thoughout the period of the Knights of St. John (which began in 1530) there were no practising Jews, apart from slaves. A new community originating from North Africa arose at the end of the eighteenth century. There are about 30 Jewish families in Malta today, both Sephardim and Ashkenazim.

General inf. from Malta National Tourist Office, Suite 207, College Hse., Wrights La., W8 5SH. Tel. 071-938 2668.

There is a small Synagogue in Valletta (182 St. Ursula St.) where a morning service is normally held on the first Shabbat of every month and the first days of the main festivals. Sec., Tr. Stanley L. Davis, O.B.E., "Melita", Triq Patri Guze Delia, Balzan BZN 07, Malta. Tel. 445924, will gladly give information on request. Pres. is George Tayar, Triq ic-Cawl, Kappara. Tel. 338663.

MEXICO

Marrano Jews went to Mexico with the Spaniards at the beginning of the sixteenth century. Sixty years ago the country had about a thousand Jews, most of them coming from the U.S.A., and others from England and Germany. Today's Jewish population is about 50,000. Those in Mexico City (about 40,000) include Ashkenazim and Sephardim. General inf. from Mexico Ministry of Tourism Office, 7 Cork St., W1X 1PB. Tel. 071-734 1058-9.

CUERNAVACA

Kosher Hotel (Syn. attached) **(K)** The Eishel, Madero 404. Tel. 2-05-16 & 2-01-79.

GUADALAJARA

Comunidad Israelita de Guadalajara, Juan Palomary Arias 651. Tel. (36) 416-463.

MEXICO CITY

The community is increasingly moving out of the city towards the suburbs of Tecamachalco and communal organisation is highly developed.

Synagogues & Religious Organisations

Agudas Achim, Montes de Oca 32, Condesa
Beth Itzhak (O), Eujenio Sue 20, Polence.
Bircas Shumel, Plinio 311, Polanco. Tel. 280-2769.
Cuernavaca, Prolongación Antinea Lote 2, Delicias.
Maguen David (Sephardi), Benaard Shaw 110, Polanco.
Nidche Israel, Acapulco 70, Condesa. Tel. 211-0501 or 211-0934. There is a **(K)** kosher restaurant on the first floor of the syn. building.
Ramat Shalom, Fuente del Pescador 35, Tecamachalco. Tel. 251-3854.
Sephardi Synagogue, Monterey 359. Tel. 564-11-97 & 564-13-67.
Bet El (C), Horacio 1722, Polanco. Tel. 545 3967. Or Damesek, Seneca 343. Tel. 280-6281.
Kolel Aram Zoba, Sofocles 346, Col. Polanco. Tel. 280 2669/4866/8789.
Organizacion T.O.V., Fuente de Concordia 73, Col. Tecamachalco. Tel. 389 8756/66, 2946486. Fax 5899101.

Misrash Latora, Cerrada de Los Morales 8, Col. Polanco. Tel. 202 1254/8617.
Shaare Shalom, AV. de Los Bosques 53, Tecamachalco. Tel. 2510973.
Shuba Israel, Edgar Alan Poe 43, Col. Polanco. Tel. 545 8061/280 0136. Mikve for men in premises.
Kolel Maor Abraham, Lafontaine 344, Col. Polanco. Tel. 545 2482.
Bet Midrash Tecamachalco, Fuente de Marcela 23, Col. Tecamachalco. Tel. 251 8454. Mikve for men in premises.
Eliahu Fasja, Fuente de Templanza 13, Col. Tecamachal Co. Tel. 294 9388.
Jajam Elfasi (only Shabath services), Fuente Del Pescador 168, Col. Tecamachalco.
Alianza Monte Sinai, Alejandro Dumas 139, Col. Polanco. Tel. 5314932, 5458691.
Monte Sinai, Fuente de Sulpicio, Tecamachalco.
Beth Israel Community Centre (C) – English-speaking – Virreyes 1140, Lomas. Tel. 520-85-15.
Comunidad Monte Sinai, Tennyson 134, Polanco. Tel. 280-9956.
Mikvaot: Banos Campeche 58. Tel. 574-22-04; Platón 413. Tel. 520-9569; Av. de los Bosques 53, Tecamachalco. Tel. 589-55-30.

Representative Organisations
Central Jewish Committee, Cofre de Perote 115, Lomas, Barrilaco 11010. Mexico, D.F. Tel. (525) 540-7376. International Affairs Director: Susy Norten. Fax 540-3050.
Tribuna Israelita, Cofre de Perste 115 (as previous). Dr. Dina siegel. Tel. (525) 520-9393.
B'nai B'rith, Cofre de Perote 115, Lomas, Barrilaco. Mexico, D.F.
Consejo Mexicano de Mujeres Israelitas, Acapulco 70-60. piso Roma Norte Tel. 211-2733.
Federación Femenina A.C., Luis G. Urbina 58, Polanco Chapultepec. Tel. 280-6874.
Na'amat, Damas Pioneras, A.C., Vicente Suárez 67, Hipódromo Condesa. Tel. 286-5589.

Cultural & Educational Organisations, etc.
Alianza Monte Sinai: Tennyson 134, Tel. 545-8691.
Colegio Hesreo Maguen David; Antiguo Camino a Tecamachalco no. 370; Tel. 570-0935.
Colegio Hebreo Tarbut, Loma del Parque 116, Vista Hermosa. Tel. 259-4259.
Colegio Israelita, Segundo Retorno del Recuerdo 44, Col. Vista Hermosa, Cuajimalpa. Tel. 570-3262.
Colegio Monte Sinai, Avenue Parque de Chapultepec 56, Naucalpan de Juarez. Tel. 576-06-21.
Colegio Sefaradi, Progreso 23, Col. Florida Insurgentes. Tel. 524-50-68.
Cultural Centre, Culiacan 71. Tel. 564-52-37.
Federación Mexicana de Estudiantes Universitarios Judíos, Calderón de la Barca 18, Polanco. Tel. 280-0534.
Jewish Sports Centre (Centro Deportivo), Av Manuel Avrila Camacho 620, Lomas de Sotelo, D.F.
Nuevo Colegio Israelita, Prolongación Manuel Avila Camacho 30. Tel. 557-5564.
OSE Medical Centre, Mexicali 86, First Floor. Tel. 286-57-52 or 286-52-54.
Yeshiva de México, Anatol France 13. Tel. 520-1219.
Yeshiva Keter Torah; Lago Meru 55. Tel. 531-0973.
Yiddish-Hebrew Teachers' Seminary, Acapulco 70. Tel. 211-09-71.
Zionist Organisations

Bnei Akiva, 191 Av. Amsterdam.

J.N.F. & Zionist Offices, Acapulco 70, Third Floor, Condesa, D.F. Tel. 211-12-22 & 211-27-25.

WIZO Organización Femenina, Monte Blanco 1285, Lomas de Chapultepec. Tel. 540-5861.

Israel Embassy, Sierra Madre 215. Tel. 540-63-40.

Newspapers & Periodicals, etc.

CDI (Spanish weekly), Centro Deportivo, nr. Plaza de Toros of Cuatro Caminos. Tel. 557-30-00.

Di Shtime (Yiddish, weekly). Pedro Moreno 149. Tel. 546-17-20.

Foro de Vida Judia en el Mundo (Spanish monthly), Aviacion Commercial 16, C.P. 15700. Tel. 571-11-14.

Imagen David, Revista, Maguen David; La Fontaine 229. Tel. 203-9964.

Jerusalem de Mexico (Bookshop), Anatore France 359, Local C, Polanco. Tel. 5312269.

Kesher (Spanish monthly), Ap. Postal 41-969, Lomas de Chapultepec. Tel. 203-0517.

La Voz de la Kehila (Spanish monthly), Acapulco 70, Second Floor. Tel. 211-05-01.

Kosher Restaurants

Aladinos; Ingenieros Militares 255; 395-2949. Mac David; Torcualto Tasso 152; 250-8977.

(K) Macabim, 5 de Febrero 36. Tel. 709-1446.

Tanqueria Piny; Ejercito Nacional y Emerson; 250-5168. Kosher Taco; Cofre de Perote 244, 540-0521.

(K) Ramat Shalom, Fuente del Pescador 35. Tel. 251-3854.

(K) Sabre Kosher, San Jerónimo 726. Tel. 709-3368.

(K) Shalom, Acapulco 70, First Floor. Tel. (905) 211-19-90. This kosher (dairy only) restaurant is above the Nidche Israel Syn. Under the supervision of Rabbi Abraham I. Bartfeld.

(K) Wendys, Homero & Sofocles, Col. Polanco. Tel. 395-3083.

Kosher Food

Casa Amiga, Horacio 1719, Col. Polanco. Tel. 540-1455.

(K) Super Teca Kosher, Acuezunco 15, San Miguel. Tel. (905) 589-98-23, 98-60 or 32-25.

MONTERREY

Centro Israelita de Monterrey, Canada 207, Nuevo León. Tel. (83) 461-728.

TIJUANA

Syn., Centro Social Israelita de Baja California, Av. 16 Septembre 18. Tel. 86-26-92 or 86-26-93. Rabbi David Weicman. For details of services at Syn. Maguen David at the Centre & of kosher food, contact Rabbi Weicman. Tel. 86-24-33.

MOLDOVA
CISINAU

Syn.: Yakimovsky per. 8, 277000. Tel. (042-2) 22-12-15.

TELENESHTY

Syn.: 4 28th June St.

MONACO
MONTE CARLO
Syn. & Com. Centre: 15 Av. de la Costa (opp. Balmoral Hotel), MC 98000.
Tel. 9330-16-46. Services, Fri. evg. 6.30 p.m., Sat. morn. 8.45 a.m. & 5.30
p.m. Min.: Rabbi Isaac Amsellem, 4 Blvd. de Belgique. Tel. 9330-04-76.

MOROCCO
There is a legend that King Solomon sent emissaries to Morocco to raise
funds among Israelites living there towards the building of the Temple in
Jerusalem, but it is more likely that the first Jewish settlements in Morocco
were established by Jewish slaves who accompanied the Phoenicians there
in the 3rd century B.C.E. Hebrew grave markers and the ruins of a
synagogue have also been found at the Roman colony of Volubilis.
Today's Jewish community is said to have been founded when a hundred
Jewish families, fleeing from Roman persecution in Tripolitania during the
first century C.E., sought refuge in the High Atlas. Eventually, the
neighbouring Berber tribes converted to Judaism, even establishing Jewish
kingdoms, it is said. More Jews went to Morocco with the Expulsion from
Spain in 1492.
At its peak in the 1950s the Moroccan Jewish community numbered some
300,000. Today, it has dwindled through emigration to about 8,000.
General inf. from Moroccan National Tourist Office, 174 Regent St., W1R
6HB. Tel. 071-437 0073.

AGADIR
Syn.: Av. Moulay Abdallah, cnr. rue de la Foire. Mikva on premises.
Com. Offices, Imm. La Paternelle Av. Hassan II. Pres.: Simon Levy.

CASABLANCA
Synagogues & Religious Organisations
There are 25 active syns., of which the principal ones are: Benisty, 13 rue
Ferhat Achad; Bennaroche, 24 rue Lusitania; Em Habanim, 14 rue
Lusitania; Hazan, rue Roger Farache; Ne'im Zemiroth, 29 rue Jean-Jacques
Rousseau; Temple Beth El, rue Verlet Hanus.
Mikvaot: 32 rue Officier de Paix Thomas. Tel. 2766-88; 116 rue Galilée; 84
rue des Anglais.
Com. Offices, 1 rue Adrienne Lecouvreur. Tel. 2269-52 & 2228-61.
Council of Moroccan Jewish Communities, same address.

Welfare Organisations
American Joint Distribution Com., 3 rue Rouget de Lisle. Tel. 2747-17 &
2795-63.
Jewish Com. Social Service, 1 rue Adrienne Lecouvreur. Tel. 2769-52.
OSE (medical), 203 Blvd. Ziraoui. Tel. 2678-91.
Jewish Home for Aged, rue Verlet Hanus.
Kosher Restaurants: **(K)** Bon Délice, 261 Blvd. Ziraoui opp. Lycée Lyautey;
(K) La Truffe Blanche, 57 rue Taher Sebti. Tel. 2772-63.

EL JADIDA
Com. Offices: P.O. Box 59. Pres.: Simon Bensimon.

ESSAOUIRA (formerly Mogador)
Syn.: 2 rue Ziri Ben Atyah. Com. Offices: 29 rue des Syaghines. Pres.:
Meyer Cohen.
Meyer Cohen & Simon Look will receive visitors. Inq. to 22 or 29 rue
Syaghine. Tel. 22-70.

FEZ

Syns.: Beth El, rue de Beyrouth; Sadoun, ruelle 1, Blvd. Mohammed V.
Talmud Torah: rue Dominique Bouchery. Mikva on premises.
Com. Offices: rue Dominique Bouchery. Kosher Restaurant on the premises.
Mrs. Danielle Mamane, La Boutique, Hotel Palais Jamai, will be pleased to assist Jewish visitors.

KENITRA

Syn.: rue de Lyon. Min.: Rabbi Yahia Bennaroche.
Mikva: 58 rue Salah Eddine.
Com. Offices: 58 rue Sallah Eddine. Pres.: Rabbi Yahia Ben-Harroch.

MARRAKESH

Syns.: Attias, rue Saka; Bitton, rue de Touareg; Haim Abitbol, Av. Mohammed Zerktouni; Lazama, rue Talmud Torah.
Mikva: Villa Oliviery, Blvd. Zerktouni (Gueliz).
Com. Offices: P.O.Box 515. Pres.: Henri Cadosh, P.O. Box 515. Tel. 222-65.

MEKNES

Com. Centre & Syn.: 5 rue de Ghana. Tel. 219-68 or 225-49. Mikva on premises. Mr. Benamram will help tourists if telephoned 24 hours in advance at either of the above numbers.

OUJDA

Com. Offices: Texaco Maroc, 36 Blvd. Hassan Loukili. Pres.: Henri Amsellem.

RABAT

Syn.: 3 rue Moulay Ismail. Mikva on premises.
Com. Offices: 9 rue Moulay Ismail. Tel. 245-04. Pres.: Albert Derhy.

SAFI

Syns.: Mursiand, rue du R'bat; Beth El, rue du R'bat.
Com. Offices: 1 rue Boussouni. Pres.: J. Cabessa.

TANGIER

Syns.: Shaar Raphael, 27 Blvd. Pasteur. Mikva on premises. Tel. 231-304; Temple Nahon, rue Moses Nahon.
There are a number of other syns. in the old part of the town in rue des Synagogues, off rue Siaghines.
Com. Centre, 1 rue de la Liberté. Tel. 316-33 or 210-24. Pres.: Abraham Azancot.
Nursing Homes: Benchimol, 78 rue Haim Benchimol; Laredo Sabbah, 98 rue Bourakia.
Hotels: El Minzah (100), 85 rue de la Liberté. Tel. 358-85; La Grande Villa de France, rue de Belgique; Les Almohades (150), Av. des F.A.R.; Rambrant, Av. Pasteur. Tel. 378-70/71; Rif, Av. d'Espagne. Mr. A. Serfati will be glad to help visitors.

TETUAN

Syns.: Benoualid, in the old Mellah; Pintada, in the old Mellah; Yagdil Torah, adj. Com. Centre.
Com. Offices: 16 rue Moulay Abbas. Pres.: José Bendelac.

UNION OF MYANMAR (BURMA)

(Jewish population about 16)

RANGOON

Syn.: Musmeah Yeshua, 85 26th St.
Sec. of Com.: Jack Samuel. Tel. 75062.
Embassy of Israel: 49 Prome Rd. Tel. 22290 or 22291.

NAMIBIA

Some Jewish settlers came to this territory before the First World War, when it was a German colony. The cemetery at Swakopmund dates from those times. In 1910 a congregation was established at Keetmanshoop. It had a synagogue and cemetery at one time, but is no longer in existence.
In the 1920s and 1930s there were never more than 100 Jewish families in various centres in Namibia. Today, the figure stands at only 11 families. Efforts are made to arrange services for the High Holy-days.

WINDHOEK

Syn., Corner Tal & Post Sts.
Schools: Jewish Kindergarten; Talmud Torah.
The Sam Cohen Communal Hall is in Louis Botha Av.

NETHERLANDS ANTILLES

ARUBA

There is a syn. in Oranjestad in Adrian Laclé Blvd. Tel. 23272. Services Fri., 8 p.m.

CURAÇAO

Jews first settled on the island in 1651. The Jewish population numbers about 450 today.
Among the items of interest are the famous old sand-floored building of the Mikvé Israel-Emanuel Synagogue in Willemstad and the ancient Jewish cemetery in Blenheim. Both institutions are the oldest of their kind in the Western Hemisphere.
The cong., founded in 1651, is in its fourth building, which dates from 1732. In addition to the syn., the building, at the corner of Columbusstr. & Hanchi di Snoa, also houses a Jewish historical museum.
The Temple Emanuel building (1864) in the Hendrikplein is not in use for worship, but is a tourist attraction. Both buildings are in the centre of Willemstad.
Syns.: United Netherlands Portuguese Cong. "Mikvé Israel-Emanuel". (Sephardi, Reconstructionist), P.O. Box 322. Tel. 611067. Min.: Rabbi Aaron L. Peller. Pres.: Rene D. L. Maduro. Sabbath and Holy-day services, Fri. at 6.30 p.m. (second Fri. in month, family service), Sat. at 10 a.m.; Congregation Shaarei Tsedek (Orthodox, Ashkenazi) is at Leiliweg 1a, P.O.B. 498. Tel. 375738. Pres.: Paul H. Moron. Tel. 378505/617333. Services, Fri. at 6.45 p.m., Sat. at 7 a.m.
Community Hebrew School, Gladiolenweg 2. Tel. 75554.
Israel Consulate: Dr. P. Ackerman, Blauwduifweg 5, P.O.B. 3058, Willemstad. Tel. 377068. Fax 370707.
Travel inf. from S. E. L. Maduro & Sons, Inc., Emancipatie Blvd. 19. Tel. 76900.
There is no kosher restaurant in Curaçao, but kosher food is available at some out-of-town supermarkets.

NEW ZEALAND

There were Jews among the settlers in New Zealand even before the establishment of British sovereignty in 1840. David Nathan founded the Auckland Jewish com., and Abraham Hort the Wellington com. in the early 1840s. The first Mayor of Auckland, under the Municipal Corporations Act, and also the second, were Jews. Among important positions occupied by Jews have been those of Administrator, Prime Minister, and Chief Justice.

New Zealand's Jews number about 5,000. The majority live in Auckland and Wellington provinces.

Immigrants should apply for inf. to the Sec., Auckland Hebrew Cong., P.O.B. 68-224, Auckland, Auckland Jewish Council, P.O.B. 4315, Auckland, or the Jewish Com. Centre in Wellington, the capital.

AUCKLAND

Auckland Hebrew Cong., Grey's Av., Box 68224. Sec.: Mrs. L. Scher. Tel. 373-2908. Fax. (09) 303-2147, Rabbi: R. Genende.

Liberal Cong. (Temple Shalom), 180 Manukau Rd., Epsom 3. Tel. 524 4139. Rabbi: David Goldberg; Sec.: Mrs. H. Levin.

Auckland Jewish Council & Auckland Zionist Society, P.O.B. 4315. Tel. 309-9444. Fax. 373-2283.

B'nai B'rith. Lodge Pres.: Stephen Scher, Chapter Pres.: Veronica Meltzer.

Chevra Kadisha: Sec.: G. Resnick. Tel. 520 0801.

Syn. Women's Guild. Mrs. B. Joshua. Tel. 373-2908.

Council of Jewish Women: Pres.: Mrs. Lesley Eisig, 3 Holly Way, Sunnyhills, Pakuranga. Tel. 480-9819.

Kadimah College, Box 68224, Newton. Tel. 3733 072.

WIZO: Mrs. J. Lardner-Rivlin. Tel. (Off.) 373-072.

Zionist Fed. of New Zealand, P.O.B. 4315. Tel. 309-9444. Affiliated orgs.: B'nei Akiva, Friends of the Hebrew University, Habonim, Dror, J.N.F., WIZO, Youth Aliyah.

Restaurant: L'Haim, 39 Elliott St. Tel. 377-3263.

Shelleys Catering services provide Kosher meals for all New Zealand Flights. Tel. 649 603299.

CHRISTCHURCH

Syn., 406 Durham St. Tel. 657412. Rev. J. Leverton. Tel. 265543.

Council of Jewish Women. Pres.: Mrs. Grace Hollander, 13 Abberley Cres. Tel. 3558961.

New Zealand Jewish Council. Regional Ch.: S. A. Goldsmith. Tel. 3588769.

Zionist Soc. Sec.: D. Baruch, 3A Denman St. Tel. 266458.

DUNEDIN

Syn., Corner George & Dundas Sts.

All com. inq. to E. M. Friedlander. Tel. 775-487.

Council of Jewish Women: Anat Or, 162 Highcliff Rd. Tel. 454-2419.

WELLINGTON

Syn., Wellington Jewish Com. Centre, 80 Webb St. Fax. & Tel. 3845-081. Sec. Mrs. E. Gianoutses. The centre contains the Beth El Syn. (Orthodox) of Wellington Hebrew Cong. (Min.: Rabbi L. Brown) & the Wellington Jewish Social Club, a Mikva and Kosher Co-op.

Temple Sinai (Liberal), 147 Ghuznee St. Tel. 3850-720. Fax 385 4138.

B'nai B'rith. Sec.: R. Wiseman. Tel. 3859-519 (office), 4759-251 (home).

Council of Jewish Women. Pres.: Mrs. Shirley Payes, 11 Parnell St., Lower Hutt. Tel. 567-1679. Sec.: Mrs. N. Walker. Tel. 476-7625. Fax 801 6966.

Home for Aged, Rata St., Naenea, Lower Hutt. Tel. 567-8633.
Union of Jewish Women. Sec.: Mrs. N. Walker, 17 Eagle St., 5. Tel. 4767-625.
WIZO. National Pres.: Mrs. Doris Lewis, 4 Lethenty Way, 5. Tel. 4767-296.
Youth Aliyah.
Zionist Soc. of New Zealand. Jewish Com. Centre, Webb St. Tel. 3844-229.
Fax. 384-6542.
The monthly "New Zealand Jewish Chronicle" is edited by J. Clearwater.
Tel. 385-0720.
Zionist Soc. of New Zealand, Wellington Jewish Com. Centre, Webb St.
Tel. 384 4229. Fax 384 6542.
Israel Embassy, DP Tower, 111 The Terrace. Tel. 472-2368. Fax 499-0632.
(There is no kosher restaurant in Wellington. Visitors who want kosher meals & kosher food should contact the Jewish Com. Centre Syn., Webb Street. Tel. 384-5081.)

NORWAY

Norway's Jewish com. is one of Europe's youngest and smallest. Jews first arrived in the country in 1851, but it was not until 1881 that comparatively large-scale Jewish immigration began. By the beginning of the Second World War, in 1939, there were 1,500 Jews in Norway.
The war and the Nazis reduced Norwegian Jewry by more than half. In 1947 the Government invited 500 D.P.s to settle in the country. The Jewish population is now about 1,600, of whom about 900 live in Oslo.
General inf. from Norwegian Tourist Board, 5-11 Lower Regent St., SW1Y 4LX. Tel. 071-839 6255.

OSLO

Syn., & Com. Centre: Bergstien 13-15, 0172. Tel. 292612. Min.: Rabbi Michael Melchior, Bergstien 13. Tel. 2269 2612. Pres.: Kai Feinberg, P.O. Box 740, 0105. Tel. 2230-2925.
There is a Jewish war memorial in Ostre Gravlund Cemetery.
B'nai B'rith. Pres.: Narve Bermann, Ths. Heftyesgt. 42B, 0264. Tel. 2255-1654. Ken Harris. Trollhaug 24, 1370 Asker Tel. 787934.
Wizo. Mrs. Anne Sender. Gamlelinja 33 C. Holmlia. 1254 Oslo 12. Tel. 22610551.
Israel Embassy, Drammensveien 82c, 2. Tel. 22447924.
There are no kosher hotels or restaurants in Oslo but there is a **(K)** kosher food centre at Waldemar Thranes gt. 360171 Oslo 1. Tel. 22609166. Open 16-19 Tues.-Thurs., 12-14 Fri. Closed Sat. Under supervision of Rabbi Michael Melchior.

TRONDHEIM

Syn. & Com. Centre, Ark. Christiesgt. 1. Pres.: Jacob Komissar.

PANAMA

(Jewish population 6,000)

COLON

Com. Centre, Apartado 513.

PANAMA CANAL AREA

Inq. to Chaplain, 193rd Infantry Brigade, Fort Amador. Tel. 82-3610 or 82-3771.

PANAMA CITY

Inq. to. P.O.Box 6629, Panama 5. Fax (507) 286796.

Chief Rabbi: Rabbi Sion Levy, Calle 44-40, Bella Vista, 85 Apartado 6222, Panama, 5. Tel. 274212.
Syns.: Sociedad Israelita Shevet Ahim (Orthodox, Sephardi), Calle 44-27. Tel. 255990 & 259590. Daily services. Mikva on premises; Beneficiencia Israelita Beth El (Ashkenazi), Calle 58E, Urb. Obarrio. Tel. 233383. Mikva on premises. Koll Sherit Israel (Reform), Av. 5 34-16. Tel. 254100.
Jewish Centre, Calle 50 Final. **(K)** Restaurant open daily for lunch & supper. Closed Sat. Tel. 26-0455.
Israel Embassy, Edificio Grobman, Calle, Manuel Maria Icaza, 5th Floor. Tel. 64-8257.
Kosher Food & Meat: Comisariato Kosher, Calle F, El Cangrejo, Plaza Einstein. Tel. 365254 or 365253, Calle San Sebastian, Paitilla.
(K) Shalom Kosher, Plaza Bal Harbour, Paitilla. Tel. 64-4411.
(K) Danny's Pizza, Urb. Marbella Centro Comercial La Florida. Tel. 644951.
(K) Bakery: Pita Pan, Centro Bal Harbor. Tel. 642786.
(K) Coma Pan, Centro Comercial La Florida. Tel. 638363.

PARAGUAY
(Jewish population 1,200)

ASUNCION

Syn., General Diaz, 657.
Com. Centre (Consejo Representativo Israelita de Paraguay – Jewish Representative Council of Paraguay), General Diaz 657, P.O.B. 756. Tel. 41744. Sec.-General: Rolf Kemper.
Israel Embassy, Juan O'Leary y General Diaz, Edificio Lider II-3er. Piso, P.O. Box 1212. Tel. 95097.

PERU
(Jewish population 5,500)

LIMA

Syn. & Com. Centre, Husares de Junin 163, Jesus Maria. Tel. 241-412 & 244-797.
Centro Social y Cultural Sharon, Av. 2 de Mayo 1815, San Isidro. Tel. 40-0290.
Sociedad de Beneficencia de 1870, Jose Galvez 282, Miraflores.
Sociedad de Beneficencia Israelita Sefaradi, Enrique Villar 581. Tel. 717-230.
Israel Embassy, Natalio Sanchez 125-6to. piso, Lima. Tel. 321 005.

PHILIPPINES REPUBLIC
(Jewish population 150)

MANILA

Syn., & Com. Centre, Jewish Assoc. of the Philippines, H.V. de la Costa St., cnr. Tordesillas St., Salcedo Village (close to Mandarin Hotel), Makati, Metro Manila, 1200. Tel. 815-0265 & 815-0263. Services, Fri., 6.30 p.m.; Sat., 9 a.m. Mikva available. Kosher requirements by arrangement.
Israel Embassy, Fifth Floor, Room 538, Philippines Savings Bank Bldg., 6813 Ayala Av., Makati, Metro Manila. Tel. 88-53-20. Postal address: P.O.B. 374, Makati, Metro Manila, 1299.

POLAND

Jews settled in Poland in the ninth century, coming from Germany, Bohemia and Russia. The first documentary evidence of Polish Jews is dated 1185, and there is also evidence on coins: Jews were in charge of Polish coinage in the twelfth century, and coins bore Hebrew inscriptions. The Kalisz Statutes of 1264, granted by Duke Boleslaw the Pious, were a charter of Jewish rights. Casimir the Great, the last Polish king of the Piast dynasty (1303-1370), was a protector of the Jews and was, according to legend, married secretly to a Jewess, Esther.

There was persecution under the first Jagiellon kings, and anti-Jewish decrees were issued by the Church in 1420. The granting of rights and privileges (resulting in eras of Jewish freedom and prosperity) alternated in Polish history with the withdrawal of such rights and consequent periods of persecution and, sometimes, expulsion.

Jewish learning flourished from the sixteenth century onwards. Mystic Chasidism, based on the Cabbala, had its wonder-rabbis. Famous Talmudic scholars, codifiers of the ritual, and other eminent men of learning were produced by Polish Jewry.

Of the 3,500,000 Jews in Poland in 1939, about three million were exterminated by Hitler. Many put up a heroic fight, like those of the Warsaw Ghetto in 1943. Fewer than half a million fled to the West and to the Soviet Union.

After the Second World War there were several waves of emigration, the last of which was in 1968. Today's ageing Jewish population numbers an estimated 6,000.

Syns. and Social Cultural Societies (TSZK) are known to exist in the following towns:

Biala, Bielsko, Bytom, Czestochowa, Dzierzoniów, Gliwice, Katowice, Legnica, Lublin, Milejczyce, Sosnowiec, Swidnica, Szczecin, Tarnów, Tykocin, Walbrzych, Wloclawek, Wroclaw, Zamosc, Zary k/Zag, Zgorzelec.

Foreign tourists are advised to address all their queries and requests to the Foreign Tourists' Office, Krakowskie Przedmiescie St., Warwaw 13. Tel. 26-16-68.

BIELSKO-BIALA
Elzbieta Wajs, Ul Mickiewicza 26, 43-300. Tel. 224 38.

BYTOM
(Not available). Ul Smolenia 4, 41902. Tel. 81 3510.

CRACOW
There is a monument in ul. Jerozolimska to the victims of the Nazi death camps. The site of the Auschwitz (Oswiecim) death camp is about 40 miles from Cracow. A Jewish pavilion was inaugurated at the Auschwitz Museum in 1978.

Synagogues
The famous Remuh Synagogue and cemetery, which date from the 15th & 16th centuries, are at ul. Szeroka 40. A number of famous rabbis are buried there. Both the Remuh and the Temple (which dates from 1844) at ul. Miodowa 24 hold services on Sabbaths & Holy-days. There is also a mikva at ul. Miodowa 24. For appointments & inf. Tel. 620-64.

The Old Syn. (14th century), ul. Szeroka 2, is one of the oldest syn. buildings in Europe. It has been restored and serves as a Jewish Museum, which is part of Cracow History Museum. The Kuppa Syn. (1595), ul. Miodowa, is now a factory. The Poper Syn. (1620), ul. Szeroka, now serves as a non-Jewish young men's club. The High Syn. (1620), ul. Jozefa, is an architect's home. The Izzaka Syn., ul. Izzak, is an artist's studio. Cemetery, ul. Miodowa 55. Tel. 545-66.

Religious Org.: Zwiazek Wyznania Mojzeszowego, ul. Skawinska 2. Tel. 66-23-47.
Mr. Jakubowicz, Ul Skawinska 2, 31-006 Tel. 662347.
Secular Org.: Towarzystwo Spoleczno-Kulturalne Zydow (Social and Cultural Assoc. of Jews).
Jewish Club: T. S. K. Z. Kraków imienia Mordchaja Gebirtiga, ul. Slawkowska 30. Tel. 22-98-41.

GLIWICE

Mr. Farber. Ul Dolnych Walow 9, 44-100. Tel. 31 47 97.

KATOWICE

Felix Lipman, Ul Mlynska 13, 40-09 8. Tel. 53 7742.

LEGNICA

Mr. Blado, Ul Chojnowska 37, 59-220. Tel. 22730.

LODZ

Jewish Cong., Zachodnia, 78. Tel. 335-156.
Jewish Chd, Sec. Oleg Grinsztajn. Tel. 331-221, 336-825.

LUBLIN

Dr. Weiss. Ul Lubartowska 10, 20-080. Tel. 22353.

SZCZECIN

(No contact) Ul. Niemcewicza 2, 71-553. Tel. 221905.

WALBRZYCH

Not available. Ul Mickiewicza 18, 55-300. Tel. Not available.

WARSAW

The Gesia cemetery should be visited. A pilgrimage should also be made to Treblinka, a village situated half-way between Warsaw and Bialystok, about two hours' journey north-east of Warsaw. In 1942-43 it was the site of one of the most infamous extermination camps set up by the Nazis in Europe. About 750,000 Jews, including about 300,000 from the Warsaw Ghetto, perished there. The Ghetto Fighters' Memorial is near Mila Street, in a park bounded by Zamenhof and Anielewicz Streets. At the corner of Mila St. & Dubois is a small monument with an inscription in Polish, Hebrew & Yiddish.
Religious Org.: Zwiazek Religijny Wyznania Mojzeszowego, ul. Krajowej Rady Narodowej 6. Tel. 20-43-24.
Syn. & Vaad Hakehilla, 6 Twarda St., Tel. 204324. Rabbi M. Joskowicz.
Secular Org.: Zarzad Glowny Towarzystwa Spoleczno-Kulturalnego Zydow w Polsce (Main Board of the Cultural & Social Assoc. of Polish Jews), Plac Grzybowski 12. Tel. 200-556.
The Jewish Historical institute, Alega Swierczewskiego 79. Tel. 27-15-30, has a remarkable collection of Judaica. It includes a library of documents on the story of the Warsaw Ghetto and the Ghetto Uprising, and a large collection of manuscripts stolen by the Germans from all over Europe.
(K) Restaurant: **Menora,** Plac Grzybowski, 2.
(V) Ekologia Restaurant, Rynek 13, Nowy Miasto.

WROCKLAW

Ul. Pawla Wlodkowica 9 50072. Wrocklaw. Tel. 36401. Pres.: Moses Finklesztajn.

PORTUGAL

Portugal has one of the smallest Jewish communities in Europe (about 700), mostly concentrated in and around Lisbon.

Communal life largely revolves round the Jewish Centre, which, since it was established in 1948 in Lisbon's finest residential quarter, has acted as a strong unifying influence between Sephardim and Ashkenazim. The community maintains a shechita board.

General inf. from Portuguese National Tourist Office, New Bond St. Hse., 1-5 New Bond St., W1Y 0NP. Tel. 071-493 3873.

FARO

The Jews of the Algarve have recently arranged for the restoration of the cemetery of Faro (1838-1932). Details from Ralf Pinto, rua Infante dom Henrique, 12 3° B, 8500 Portimao.

LISBON

Main Syn., Rua Alexandre Herculano 59. Tel. 3881592. Min.: Rabbi Abraham Assor. Services on Fri. evg. & Sat. morning.

Communal Offices, Rua Alexandre Herculano 59. Tel. 658604.

Jewish Club and Centre, Rua Rosa Araujo 10. Tel. 572041.

Israel Embassy, Rua Antonio Enes 16-4°. Tel. 570251, 570145, 570374 & 570478.

Kosher meals are obtainable if prior notice is given, from **(K)** Mrs. R. Assor, Rua Rodrigo da Fonseca 38.1°D. Tel. 3860396. She can also supply delicatessen.

For **(K)** kosher meat contact the communal offices.

OPORTO

Syn., Rua Guerra Junqueiro 340.

PONTA DELGADA

Capital of the island of Sao Miguel, in the Azores, a group of Atlantic islands owned by Portugal. Syn., Rua do Brum 16.

TOMAR

The ancient syn. in Rua de Joaquim Jacinto (built 1492-1497) has been reopened as a museum. A Marrano, Luis Vasco, is the custodian and guide. Tomar is north of Lisbon, near Fatima.

MADEIRA

During the war most Gibraltar Jews were evacuated to Madeira, but only a few Jews live there now. There is no organised community.

General information can be obtained from the Portuguese National Tourist Office in London, and in Madeira from Tourismo da Madeira, Av. Arriaga, Funchal.

Vegetarian and fish meals can be had at the Hotel Madeira Palácio (260), P.O. Box 614, Tel. 30001; the Madeira-Sheraton Hotel (292), Largo Antonio Nobre, Tel. 31031; Reid's Hotel and the Savoy Hotel, all in Funchal.

PUERTO RICO

(Jewish population 4,000)

SAN JUAN-SANTURCE

Syns.: Com. Centre-Shaare Zedeck Synagogue (Conservative), 903 Ponce de Leon Av., Santurce, 00907. Tel. 724-4157. Min.: Rabbi Alejandro B. Felch. Temple Beth Shalom (Reform), San Jorge Av. & Loiza St., Santurce.

Some major hotels provide kosher style meals in the winter season. Frozen kosher poultry and delicatessen are available at some Pueblo supermarkets.

ROMANIA

There have been Jews in the territory that is now Romania since Roman times. The country's Jewish population today is some 18,000, of whom about 10,000 live in Bucharest. There are 82 functioning synagogues, 6 of them in Bucharest, including two at the two homes for the aged. There are Talmud Torah classes in 24 communities throughout the country.

General inf. from Romanian National Tourist Office, 17 Nottingham St., W1M 3RD. Tel. 071-224 3692.

ARAD

Syns.: Orthodox, 12 Cozia St.; Neolog, 10 Tribunul Dobra St.
Mikva, 16 Cozia St.
Talmud Torah: 10 Tribunul Dobra St.
Com. Office: 10 Tribunul Dobra St. Tel. 966-16-097.
Home for Aged: 22 7 Noiembrie St.
(K) Restaurant: 22 7 Noiembrie St.

BACAU

Syns.: Cerealistilor, 29 Stefan cel Mare St.; Avram A. Rosen Syn., 31 V. Alecsandri St.
Talmud Torah: 11 Alexandru cel Bun St.
Com. Office: 11 Alexandru cel Bun St. Tel. 931-34-714.
(K) Restaurant: 11 Alexandru cel Bun St.

BOTOSANI

Syns.: Great, 1a Marchian St.; Yiddish, Gh. Dimitrov St.; Mare, 18 Muzicantilor St.
Mikva, 67 7 Aprilie St.
Talmud Torah, 69 7 Aprilie St.
Com. Office, 220 Calea Nationala. Tel. 985-14-6-59.
(K) Restaurant, 69 7 Aprilie St. Tel. 985-15-9-17.

BRASOV

Syn.: 27 Poarta Scheilor St.
Talmud Torah, 27 Poarta Scheilor St.
Com. Office, 27 Poarta Scheilor St. Tel. 921-43-5-32.
(K) Restaurant, 27 Poarta Scheilor St. Tel. 921-44-4-40.

BUCHAREST

Chief Rabbi of Romania: Rabbi Dr. D. M. Rosen. Tel. 13-25-38.
Fed. of Romanian Jewish Coms, Strada Sf. Vineri 9. Tel. 13-17-82 or 14-30-08. Pres.: Th. Blumenfeld.
The Fed. publishes a bi-monthly, "Revista Cultului Mozaic" in Romanian, Yiddish, Hebrew & English, with a circulation of 10,000. It is at 24 Popa Rusu St. Tel. 11-80-80.
Jewish Com. of Bucharest, Strada Sf. Vineri 9. Tel. 15-74-41.
Principal Synagogues
Choral Temple,Strada Sf. Vineri 9. Tel. 14-72-57. Talmud Torah on premises.
Credinta (Faith), 48 Vasile Toneanu St.
Great Syn. (Sephardi), 9-11 Vasile Adamache St. Tel. 15-08-46.
Ieshua Tova, 9 Nikos Beloiannis St. (near the Lido and Ambassador Hotels). Tel. 59-56-75.

Mikva, 5 Negustori St.

Homes for Aged
Amalia & Chief Rabbi Dr. Moses Home, 105 Jimbolia St.
Martin Balus Home, 55 Ripiceni St.
Both homes have a prayer hall.

Cultural Organisations
Museum of the Jewish Community in Romania, 3 Mamoulari St. Tel. 15-09-50. Open Sun. morn. & Wed.
Romanian Jewish History Research Centre, 3 Mamoulari St. Tel. 15-08-37.
Jewish State Theatre. Tel. 20-45-30.
Embassy of Israel: 6 Burghelea St. Tel. 13-26-34/5/6.
(K) Restaurant operated by the Jewish com., 18 Popa Soare St. Tel. 22-03-98.

CLUJ NAPOCA
Syns.: Beth Hamidrash Ohel Moshe, 16 David Francisc St.; Gah Hevra, 13 Croitilor St.; Templul Deportatilor, 21 Horea St.
Mikva, 16 David Francisc St.
Talmud Torah, 16 David Francisc St.
Com. Office, 25 Tipografilor St. Tel. 951-16-6-77.
(K) Restaurant, 5-7 Paris St. Tel. 951-11-0-26.

CONSTANTA
Syns.: Great Temple, 2 C.A. Rosetti St.; Small, 3 Sarmisagetuza St.
Talmud Torah, 3 Sarmisagetuza St.
Com. Office: 3 Sarmisagetuza St. Tel. 916-11-5-98.

DOROHOI
Syns.: Beth Solomon, 2 Piata Unirii St.; Great, 4 Piata Unirii St.; Rabinsohn, 14 Republicii St.
Talmud Torah, 14-18, Dumitru Furtuna St.
Com. Office, 14-18 Dumitru Furtuna St. Tel. 986-13-4-24.
Home for Aged: 95 Spiru Haret St. Tel. 986-11-7-97.
(K) Restaurant: 14-18 Dumitru Furtuna St.

GALATI
Syn.: Meseriasilor, 9-11 Dornei St.
Talmud Torah, 7 Dornei St.
Com. Office: 9-11 Dornei St. Tel. 934-13-6-62.
(K) Restaurant, 7 Dornei St.

IASI (JASSY)
Syns.: Great, 7 Sinagogii St.; Schor, 5 Sf. Constantin St.
Mikva, 15 Elena Doamna St.
Talmud Torah, 15 Elena Doamna St.
Com. Office: 15 Elena Doamna St. Tel. 981-14-4-14.
(K) Restaurant, 15 Elena Doamna St. Tel. 981-14-4-14.

ORADEA
Syns.: Great, 4 Mihai Viteazu St.; Neolog, 22 Independentei St.; Sas Hevra, 4 Mihai Viteazu St.
Mikva, 5 Mihai Viteazu St.
Talmud Torah, 4 Mihai Viteazu St.
Com. Office: 4 Mihai Viteazu St. Tel. 991-34-8-43.
(K) Restaurant: 5 Mihai Viteazu St. Tel. 991-31-3-83.

PIATRA NEAMT

Syns.: Leipziger, 12 Meteorului St.; Old Baal Shem Tov, 12 Meteorolui St. Historical Monument.
Talmud Torah, 7 V.I. Lenin St.
Com. Office, 7 V.I. Lenin St. Tel. 936-23-8-15.

RADAUTI

Syns.: Chesed Sel Emeth, 2 Toplita St.; Great, 11 Mai St.; Vijnitzer, 49 Libertatii St.
Com. Office: 11 Aleea Primaverii, Block 14, Apt. 1. Tel. 989-61-3-33.

SATU MARE

Syn.: Great, 4 Decebal St.
Com. Office: 4 Decebal St. Tel. 997-11-7-28.

SIGHET

Syn.: Great, 8 Viseului St.
Talmud Torah, 8 Viseului St.
Com. Office, 10 Viseului St. Tel. 995-11-6-52.
There is a memorial to the Jewish victims of Nazism in Gh. Doja St.

SUCAEVA

Syn.: Gah Chavre, 14 I.C. Frimu St.
Talmud Torah, 8 Armeneasca St.
Com. Office, 8 Armeneasca St. Tel. 987-13-0-84.

TIMISOARA

Syns.: Cetate, 6 Marasesti St.; Fabric, 2 Splaiul Coloniei; Iosefini, 53 Resita St.
Mikva, 55 Resitei St.
Talmud Torah, 5 Gh. Lazar St.
Com. Office, 5 Gh. Lazar St. Tel. 961-32-8-13.
Home for Aged, 2 Splaiul Coloniei St. Tel. 961-3-63-48.
(K) Restaurant, 10 Marasesti St. Tel. 961-32-8-13.

TIRGU MURES

Syn.: 21 Scolii St.
Talmud Torah, 10 Brailei St.
Com. Office, 10 Brailei St. Tel. 954-15-0-01.

VATRA DORNEI

Syns.: Great, 54 M. Eminescu St; Vijnitzer, 14 6 Martie St.
Com. Office, 54 M Eminescu St. Tel. 988-71-9-57.

SENEGAL
DAKAR

M. Clement Politis, 13 rue San Diniéry (P.O.B. 449). Tel. 23-27-84 or 23-51-74, will be pleased to receive overseas visitors.

SINGAPORE

The Jewish community of Singapore, numbering about 240, dates from 1840. The street in which Jewish divine service was first held in a house is now known as Synagogue Street. The first building to be erected as a synagogue was Maghain Aboth, opened in 1878. This was rebuilt and enlarged in 1925. Another synagogue, Chesed-El, was built in 1905. The community is mainly Sephardi.

The affairs of the community are managed by the annually elected Jewish Welfare Board, Robinson Rd., P.O. Box 474. Pres.: Mr. Jacob Ballas. Syns.: Chesed-El, 2 Oxley Rise, S-0923. Tel. 7328832. Services Mon. only; Maghain Aboth, Waterloo St. Tel. 3360692. Daily & Sabbath services held at Maghain Aboth Syn.
Talmud Torah: Sir Manasseh Meyer's Hebrew School, 71 Oxley Rise, S-0923. Tel. 7379746.
Israel Embassy, 58 Dalvey Road, Singapore 1025. Tel: 2350966.

SLOVAK REPUBLIC
BRATISLAVA (Pressburg)
Syn.: Heydukova 11-13.
Mikva: Žamocka 13. Tel. 312642. **(K)** Kosher food is obtainable here, also. (Open for lunch only).
Union of Jewish Comm. in Slovakia. Kozia 21/II, 81447. Ch.: Prof. Pavel Trausner. Exec.: Fero Alexander. Tel. 427-312167. Fax 427 311106.
The underground mausoleum contains the graves of 18 famous rabbis. The key is available from the Com. Offices.

GALANTA
Syn.: Partizanska 907. Daily services are held at the syn. There is also a mikva.

KOSICE (Kaschau)
Syns.: Puskinova ul. 3; Beth Hamidrash, Zvonarska ul. 5.
Com. Centre: Zvonarska ul. 5. Tel. 21047.
(K) Kosher Restaurant: Zvonarska ul. 5.

PIESTANY
Syn.: Hviezdoslavova 59. Shabbat and festival services.
Old Cemetery: Janosikova ul. 606.

TRNAVA
Syn.: Kapitulska ul. 7.
Monument to Deportees: in the courtyard of the former syn., at Halenarska ul. 32.

SLOVENIA
Judovska Skupnost Slovenije (Jewish Community of Slovenia), Judovska Obćina Ljubljana (Jewish Community of Ljubljana), P.O. Box 569, 61101 Ljubljana, Slovenia.
The newly independent Republic of Slovenia has a tiny Jewish community of 58 members. There is no synagogue and no kosher restaurant. The nearest synagogue is in Trieste, Italy. Services are being held also at the Jewish community office in Zagreb, Croatia. Appointments with Exec. Cttee. members of the Jewish community of Ljubljana by writing only.
The Jewish community of Ljubljana is taking care of Jewish cemeteries in Ljubljana, Lendava, Lendva, Murska Sobota and Rožna dolina/Nova Gorica/. There are monuments to victims of fascism at the Ljubljana and Lendava cemeteries. The Rožna dolina/Nova Gorica/ cemetery is protected as a historic monument. The old synagogue in Maribor, 1429, is currently being renovated by the municipality of Maribor as a historic monument.

SOUTH AFRICA
The Jewish community began as an organised body in Cape Town in 1841, although individual Jews had settled there much earlier. The organisation

of religious life varies with the density of the Jewish population (which totals about 114,000). In all, there are about 200 organised communities, most of which have their own synagogues.

The major supermarket chains — Pick and Pay, and Checkers — stock a large range of kosher items.

General inf. from South African Tourism Board, 5-6 Altgrove, Wimbledon SW19. Tel. 081-944 6646.

CAPE PROVINCE

CAPE TOWN
Synagogues & Religious Organisations
Arthur's Rd., 31 Arthur's Rd., Sea Point. Tel. 434-8680.
Bellville, P.O. Box 41, Bellville. Tel. 948-1169.
Camps Bay, Chilworth Rd., Camps Bay. Tel. 438-8082.
Cape Town Hebrew Cong., 84 Hatfield St., Gardens. Tel. 45-1405.
Chabad Centre, 6 Holmfirth Rd., Seapoint. Tel. 434-3740.
Claremont, Grove Av., Claremont. Tel. 61-9007.
Constantia, Herzlia School Hall, Kendal Rd., Lower Constantia. Tel. 75-2520.
Green and Sea Point Hebrew Cong., Marais Rd., Sea Point. Tel. 439-7545.
Milnerton, Jewish Guild, de Grendel Rd., Milnerton. Tel. 52-4285.
Muizenberg, Camp Rd., Muizenberg. Min.: Rabbi G. Rockman. Tel. 88-1488.
Rondebosch, Stuart Rd., Rondebosch. Tel. 61-3507.
Sephardi Hebrew Cong., Weizmann Hall, Regent Rd., Sea Point. Tel. 439-1962.
Somerset West, Church St., Somerset West. Tel. 26-419.
Stellenbosch, Van Ryneveld St., Stellenbosch. Tel. 7-1809.
Temple Israel (Reform), Upper Portswood Rd., Green Point. Tel. 434-9721.
Temple Israel (Reform), Salisbury Rd., Wynberg. Tel. 797-3362.
Tygerberg, Hopkins St., Parow. Tel. 92-3541.
United Orthodox Hebrew Cong., 12 Schoonder St., Gardens. Tel. 45-2239.
Wynberg Hebrew Cong., cnr. Piers & Mortimer Rds., Wynberg. Tel. 797-5029.
Beth Din, 191 Buitenkant St. Tel. 461-6310. Inf. about **(K)** kosher food available from the Beth Din.
Union of Orthodox Syns. of South Africa, Cape Council, 191 Buitenkant St. Tel. 461-6310.
Mikva: Arthur's Rd., Sea Point. Tel. 434-3148.

Representative Organisation
S. African Jewish Board of Deputies' Cape Council, 3rd Floor, Leeusig Hse., 4 Leeuwen St. 8001. Tel. 23-2420.

Cultural & Educational Organisations, Schools, etc.
Cape Board of Jewish Education, Ground Floor, Leeusig Hse., 4 Leeuwen St. Tel. 23-1825.
Jacob Gitlin Library, Ground Floor, Leeusig Hse., 4 Leeuwen St. Tel. 24-5020.
Jewish Museum, 84 Hatfield St., Gardens. Curatrix-Secretary: Mrs L. Robinson. Tel. 45-1546. Sun. 10 a.m. to 12.30 p.m., Tues. and Thurs. 2 p.m. to 5 p.m., & by appointment. Closed on Jewish and Public holidays.
United Herzlia Schools: Herzlia Primary School, Southern Suburbs, Kendal Rd., Constantia. Tel. 434-9551; Herzlia Primary School, Clairwood Av., Highlands Estate. Tel. 45-2148; Herzlia Weizmann Primary School, 40 Kloof Rd., Sea Point. Tel. 44-9551; Herzlia Milnerton, de Grendel Rd.,

Milnerton. Tel. 52-2220; Herzlia Middle School, Mynor Av., Highlands Estate. Tel. 45-3131; Herzlia High School, Highlands Áv., Highlands Estate. Tel. 461-1035.

Miscellaneous Organisations
Cape Jewish Board of Guardians, 4th Floor, Leeusig House, 4 Leewen St. Tel. 23-3783.
Cape Jewish Seniors Org. 3 Bellevue Rd., Sea Point. Tel. 434-9691.
Union of Jewish Women of South Africa (Cape Town Branch), 7 Albany Rd., Sea Point. Tel. 434-9555/6.
Western Province Zionist Council, Leeusig Hse., 4 Leeuwen St. Tel. 24-5020. Also at this address: Betar, Bnei Akiva, Bnoth Zion, Habonim, Israel United Appeal, Jewish National Fund, Maccabi, Magen David Adom, Mizrachi Federation, ORT, Poalei Zion, Revisionist Zionists, S. African Union of Jewish Students, Union of General Zionists, United Zionist Assoc.

Sports & Country Clubs
Glen Country Club, Victoria Rd., Clifton. Tel. 438-1512.
Keurboom Sports Club, Av. de Mist, Rondebosch. Tel. 61-4521.
King David Country Club, Pallotti St., Philippi. Tel. 934-0365.
Delicatessen
(K) Dee's Deli, 359a Main Rd., Sea Point. Tel. 439-1632.

Kosher Restaurant
(K) Belmont Kosher Restaurant, 3 Holmfirth Rd., Sea Point. Tel. 434-0829.

Hotels
(K) Cape Sun, Strand St. Tel. 23-8844.
(K) Belmont Kosher Hotel, Holmfirth Rd., Sea Point. Tel. 439-1155.
Mount Nelson, P.O.B. 2608. Tel. 28-1000.

EAST LONDON
Syn.: Shar Hashomayim (Orthodox), 56 Park Av., P.O.B. 1043. Inq. to Rabbi Y. Shalpid. Tel. 0431-22071.

KIMBERLEY
Synagogues
Beth Hamedrash, Baronial St. Tel. 5652.
Communal Hall, Voortrekker St.
Griqualand West Hebrew Cong., P.O. Box 68, 8300.

OUDTSHOORN
Syn.: Baron von Rheede St. Communal Hall, P.O.B. 362, 6620. Tel. 2969. There is a Jewish section in the C.P. Nel Museum.

PAARL
Syn.: New Breda St. Communal Hall & Talmud Torah attached. Tel. 24087.

PORT ELIZABETH
Syns.: Port Elizabeth Hebrew Cong. United Syn., Glendinningvale. Tel. 331332; Summerstrand, Brighton Dr. Tel. 531-651. Temple Israel (Progressive), Upper Dickens St. Tel. 336642.
Wedgwood Park (Jewish) Country Club. Town office, 404 Southern Life Bldg., Main St. Tel. 72-1212.

NATAL

DURBAN

Synagogues, etc.

Great (Orthodox), cnr. Essenwood Rd. & Silverton Rd., P.O.B., Musgrave Rd., 4062. Tel. 21-5177.

Temple David (Progressive), 369 Ridge Rd. Tel. 28-6105.

Com. Centre, Durban Jewish Club, 44 Old Fort Rd., P.O.B. 10797. Marine Parade 4056. Tel. 37-2581. **(K)** Sylvias. Tel. 324650.

Council of Natal Jewry, Tel. 37-2581, & Natal Zionist Council, Tel. 37-507, both at 44 Old Fort Rd.

ORANGE FREE STATE

BLOEMFONTEIN

O.F.S. & Northern Cape Zionist Council, Com. Centre, 2 Fairview (P.O.B. 564). Tel. 30-4161 & 30-4170.

United Hebrew institutions, Com. Centre. Tel. 30-3801.

TRANSVAAL

BENONI

United Hebrew Institutions, 32 Park St. Tel. 845-2850.

BOKSBURG

United Hebrew Institutions, 11 Heidelberg Rd., Parkdene. Tel. 52-6721.

BRAKPAN

United Hebrew Institutions, 664 Voortrekker Rd. Tel. 55-8245.

EDENVALE

Com. Centre, cnr. 3rd St. & 6th Av. Tel. 53-9897.

GERMISTON

United Hebrew Institutions, President St. Tel. 825-2202.

GLEN HAZEL

Beth Harer (Glen Hazel Area Hebrew Congregation, Mikva and Yeshiva College). Tel. 640-5061. Corr. P.O.B. 28836, Sandringham 2131.

JOHANNESBURG

Synagogues & Religious Organisations

Union of Orthodox Syns. of South Africa, Goldberg Centre, 24 Raleigh St., Yeoville. The Beth Din is at the same address & Tel., as is the UOSSA Women's Guilds org.

The Kashrut Dept., issues an annual kosher guide for the whole country.

Orthodox

Adath Jeshurun, P.O.B. 5128. Tel. 648-6300. Mikva, 41 Hunter St., Yeoville. Tel. 648-6300.

Berea, Tudhope Av. Tel. 642-3825.

Beth Hamedrash Hagadol, Morningside, Sandton. Tel. 883-2747.

Chasidim Cong., Harrow Rd., Yeoville. Tel. 648-7406.

Cyrildene Observatory Hebrew Cong., 32 Aida Av., Cyrildene. Tel. 616-3312.

Emmarentia, 129 Barry Hertzog Av. Tel. 646-6138.

Etz Chayim Cong., 20 Barnato St., Berea. Tel. 642-4548.

Great, Wolmarans St., Joubert Pk. Tel. 724-8581.
Jeppestown Hebrew Cong., P.O.B. 115, Jeppe. Tel. 614-2822.
Kensington Hebrew Cong. Tel. 622-3543.
North-Eastern Hebrew Cong., Orchards. Tel. 640-3101.
Northern Suburbs Hebrew Cong., 5 Kenneth Rd., Bramley. Tel. 786-0437.
Orange Grove Hebrew Cong. 7, 9th St. Tel. 640-3149.
Oxford, 20 North Av., Riviera. Tel. 646-6020.
Parkview-Greenside, Chester Rd. Tel. 788-5036.
Poswohl Shul (National Monument), Mooi St. Tel. 337-6972 (morns. only).
Randburg Hebrew Cong., 94 Blairgowrie Dr., Blairgowrie. Tel. 789-2827.
South-Eastern Hebrew Cong., 198 Prairie St., Rosettenville. Tel. 26-4652.
Sydenham-Highlands North Hebrew Cong., 24 Main Rd., Rouxville. Tel. 640-5021.
Valley-Observatory Hebrew Cong., 11 The Curve, Observatory, P.O.B. 4951. Tel. 648-9900.
Yeoville, Hunter St. & Kenmere Rd. Tel. 648-1210.
Beth Din, Goldberg Centre, 24 Raleigh St., Yeoville. Dayan: Rabbi M. A. Kurtstag.
Mikva: Goldberg Centre, 24 Raleigh St., Yeoville. Tel. 648-9136.

Progressive
Temple David, Middle Rd., Morningside, Sandton. Tel. 783-7117.
Temple Emanuel, 38 Oxford Rd., Parktown. Tel. 646-6170.
Temple Israel, Cnr. Paul Nel & Claim Sts., Hillbrow. Tel. 484-3003 or 642-1514.
Temple Shalom, 357 Louis Botha Av., Highlands North. Tel. 640-3182.
The Southern African Union for Progressive Judaism, 357 Louis Botha Av., Highlands North. Tel. 640-6614.

Representative Organisations
B'nai Brith Sheffield House, 29 Kruis St. P.O.B. 7065. Tel. 331-0331.
Jewish Ex-Service League. P.O.B. 5254. Tel. 337-6972 (morns. only).
South African Jewish Board of Deputies. P.O.B. 87557, Houghton, 2041. Tel. 486-1434. Fax 646-4940.
South African Yiddish Cultural Fed. 253 Bree St. Tel. 23-3815.
Union of Jewish Women. Tel. 331-0331.
United Sisterhood. 38 Oxford Rd., Parktown. Tel. 646-2409.

Cultural Organisations
Jewish Library, 4th Floor, Sheffield Hse., Corner Main & Kruis Sts. Mon.-Fri. 9 a.m. to 4 p.m. Tel. 331-0331.

Welfare Organisations
"Arcadia", S.A. Jewish Children's Home, 22 Oxford Rd., Parktown. Tel. 646-6177.
Chabad House, 33 Harley St., Yeoville. Tel. 648-1133.
Jewish Family & Com. Council. Tel. 648-9124.
Witwatersrand Hebrew Benevolent Assoc., 176 Shakespeare Hse. Tel. 838-1283.
Sandringham Gdns. (Home for Aged), George Av., Sandringham. Tel. 640-5187.

Student & Youth Organisations
South African Union of Jewish Students, Students' Union, Witwatersrand University, 1 Jan Smuts Av., Braamfontein. Tel. 716-3062.
Hillel House, 22 Muller St., Yeoville. Tel. 648-1175. **(K)** Restaurant open to public.

Zionist Organisations
South African Zionist Federation, Zionist Centre (and library), 84 De Villiers St., cnr. Banket St., P.O.B. 18. Tel. 337-3000. Other Zionist organisations are also at this address.
South African Zionist Revisionist Org., 100 Plein St., P.O.B. 4474. Tel. 29-3924.

Miscellaneous
Jewish Guild, Rivonia Rd., Morningside. Tel. 783-7109.

Booksellers
Judaica Booksellers, Shop 3, Yeoville Blvd., Kenmere Rd. Tel. 648-7003.
Kollel Bookshop, 22 Muller St., cnr. Grafton Rd., Yeoville. Tel. 648-2707.
L. Rubin, 442 Louis Botha Av., Rouxville. Tel. 640-7615/6.

Media
"Dorem Afrike" (quarterly), 253 Bree St. Tel. 23-3815.
"Tradition", 24 Raleigh St., Yeoville.
"Jewish Affairs" (quarterly magazine of the S.A. Jewish Board of Deputies), Sheffield Hse., Kruis St.
"The Herald Times", P.O.B. 31015, Braamfontein. Tel. 887-6500.
"Zionist Record", P.O.B. 150.
"The Jewish Sound", Swazi Radio, Atkinson Hse., Eloff St. Tel. 331-0444. Sun. 7 p.m. to 8 p.m. on 1,400 kHz & 49 and 60 metres. Presenter: Rabbi Yossy Goldman.

Restaurants
Courtleigh Hotel, Tel. 648-1140.
(K) Kamfie's Bakery and Fast Food, 434 Louis Botha Av, Highlands N. Tel 640-5065/6.
(K) Feigel's Kosher Delicattessen, 53 Raleigh St., Yeoville. Tel. 648-3123. (Closed Shabbat and Yom Tov.)
(K) Hillel House, 22 Muller St., Yeoville. Tel. 648-9601.
★ King David Pizzeria and Coffee Bar (Milchik only) Gallaghers Corner, Cnr. Louise Botha St. and 9th St. Orange Grove. Tel. 728-3040.
(K) Kosher meals can be obtained at the Johannesburg Zionist Assoc. Luncheon Club. Inq. to Zionist Assoc. Tel. 337-3000, Ext. 214.
(K) King Saul Masada, 45 Raleigh St., Yeoville. Tel. 648-6908.
(K) Rib and Steakhouse, 15 Kingswood Rd., Glenhazel. Tel. 887-0853.
(K) Wachenheimer's Nashesei, 54 Beit St., Doornfontein. Tel. 402-4500.
N.B. The Capri Hotel, Carlton Hotel and Transvaal Hotel all have Kosher facilities (prior arrangement only).

KEMPTON PARK
United Hebrew Institutions, Casuarina St. Tel. 970-1697. (Reported no longer active).

KRUGERSDORP
United Hebrew Institutions, Cilliers St. Monument. Tel. 954-1367.

PRETORIA
Synagogues
Adath Israel, 441 Sibelius St., Lukasrand. Tel. 343-2257.
Pretoria United Hebrew Cong. Great Synagogue, 717 Pretorius St. Arcadia. Tel. 344-3019.
Temple Menorah (Progressive), 315 Bronkhorst St., New Muckleneuk, P.O.B. 1497. Tel. 46-7296.

Menorah Nursery School, 310 Lange St., New Muckleneuk. Tel. 46-7298.
Sammy Marks Museum. Swartkoppies Hall. Tel. 83-3239. Info.: Pretoria
Council of BOD. Tel. 344-2372.
Jewish Accommodation for Fellow Aged (JAFFA), 42 Mackie St., Baileys
Muckleneuk, 0181. Tel. 346-2006.
Israel Embassy & Consulate-General, 3rd Floor, Dashing Centre, 339 Hilda
St., Hatfield. Tel. 421-22227.

RANDFONTEIN

United Hebrew Institutions, Maugham Rd. Tel. 693-2542.

SPRINGS

United Hebrew Institutions, First Av. Tel. 56-2583.

SOUTH KOREA

There are about 100 families in the Capital, Seoul, including U.S. military
personnel and their families.
Religious services are held at the South Post Chapel, building 3702,
Yongsan Military Reservation, on Fri. evg. at 7.30 p.m. Further inf. from
Jewish Chaplain's office. Tel. 7917-4335, Rabbi Dennis Beck-Berman or 793-
2728, Larry Resenberg. Civilians welcome to participate in all Jewish
activities, inc. kosher le-Pesach sedarim, meals and services.

SPAIN

There are about 12,000 Jews in Spain: 3,000 in Barcelona, 3,500 in Madrid,
1,500 in Malaga, 800 in Ceuta (North Africa), 950 in Melilla (North Africa),
and the rest in Alicante, Benidorm, Seville, Valencia and the Balearic and
Canary Islands. Newcomers continue to arrive, especially from Morocco
and South America. Small communities existed in Seville, Barcelona and
Madrid before the Second World War, founded by Sephardim from
Morocco, Turkey and Greece, and by Ashkenazim from Eastern and
Central Europe.
Today, Spanish Jewry is flourishing, consolidating its communal
organisations, and expanding its synagogues and newly created day
schools. The various coms. have enjoyed full official recognition as
religious associations since June, 1967.
General inf. from Spanish National Tourist Office, 57-58 St. James's St.,
SW1A 1LD. Tel. 071-499 0901.

ALICANTE

Com. Pres.: Ralph Cohen. Tel. 229-360. Syn.: Ramón y Cajal 9.

AVILA

The Mosen Rubi Church, cnr. Calle Bracamonte and Calle Lopez Nunez,
was originally a syn., built in 1462.

BARCELONA

The ancient community of the city lived in the area of the Calle el Call. The
cemetery was in Montjuich (Mountain of the Jews). Most of the tombstones
are in the Provincial Archaeological Museum.
Syn.: Calle Porvenir 24. Tel. 200-61-48 & 200-85-13 – the first syn. to be built
in Spain since the Inquisition, nearly 500 years ago. The building comprises
two separate syns., the Sephardi, in the lower part, and the Ashkenazi
above it. Services in the Ashkenazi syn. are held only on Rosh Hashana &

Yom Kippur, but there is a daily service in the Sephardi syn. The com. headquarters is above the Ashkenazi syn.
Min.: Rabbi Salomon Bensabat.
Com. Headquarters & Mikva: Calle de l'Avenir 24. Tel. 200-61-48 & 200-85-13. Pres.: Simon Emergui.
Jewish Travel Agency: Viajes Moravia, Consejo de Ciento 380. Tel. 246-03-00.
Vegetarian Restaurant: Calle Canuda 41. Closed during Aug.

BEMBIBRE
The syn. here was converted into a church.

BESALU
The Juderia is by the River Fluviá. A mikva was recently discovered there.

BURGOS
The Juderia (old Jewish quarter) was in the area of the Calle Fernan Gonzalez.

CACERES
Part of the Juderia still exists. The San Antonio Church on the outskirts of the town is a 13-century former syn.

CEUTA (N. Africa)
Inq. to Calle Sargento Coriat 8. Pres.: Menahem Gabizon.

CORDOBA
The ancient syn. (declared a national monument) is at Calle de los Judios 20. Near by, a statue of Maimonides has been erected in the Plazuela de Maimonides. The entrance to the ancient Juderia is near the Almodovar Gate.

EL ESCORIAL
The library of the San Lorenzo Monastery contains a magnificent collection of medieval Hebrew Bibles and illuminated manuscripts. On the walls of the Patio of Kings, in the Palace of Philip II, are sculpted effigies of the six Kings of Judah.

ESTELLA
The Santa Maria de Jus Castillo Church was once a syn.

GERONA
The Juderia is in the north-west of the town. There is a Jewish museum, the Isaac el Cec Centre, at Sant Llorenc S.N. Tel. 216761.

GRANADA
The Juderia ran from the Corral del Carlon to Torres Bermejas.

HERVAS
This village in the Gredos Mountains, 150 miles west of Madrid, has a well-preserved Juderia, declared a national monument. Its main street has been renamed Calle de la Amistad Judeo Cristiana.

MADRID
The capital's first syn. since the Expulsion of the Jews in 1492 was opened in Dec., 1968, in Calle Balmes 3. The bldg. also houses the Com. Centre, as well as a mikva, library, classrooms, an assembly hall and the offices of the

Com. Centre. Tel. 445-9843 & 445-9835. Nearest underground station: Metro Iglesias.

Min.: Rabbi Yudah Benasuly Tuati.

Com. Pres.: Jacques Laredo.

Lubavitch Syn.: Chabad Hse., Calle Jordan 9, Apt. 4 Dcha., 28010. Tel. 445-96-29. Min.: Rabbi Y. Goldstein.

The com. maintains a Jewish school, Colegio Estrella Toledano, in the suburb of Moraleja.

(K) Kosher meals are available at the Com. Centre at Calle Balmes 3. Tel. 446-43-32.

Federación de Comunidades Israelitas d'Espana, Calle Balmes 9. Sec.-General: Samuel Toledano. Tel. 253-06-07.

Of special interest to Jewish visitors to Madrid are the following:

Arias-Montano Institute, Calle del Duque de Medinaceli 4 (in front of Palace Hotel & American Express). Library with more than 16,000 volumes about Sephardi history.

Museo Arquelogico (National Archaeological Museum), Calle de Serrano 13. See casts of Hebrew inscriptions from medieval bldgs.

Calle de la Fé (Street of the Faith) facing San Lorenzo Church, is the ancient Jewish quarter.

Israeli Embassy: Velazquez 150, 7th Floor, 28002. Tel. 411-13-57.

Travel Agency: Viajes Transit, Fernando el Catolico 12 & Vallehermoso 40. Tel. 447-7916.

Jewish religious articles and Spanish handicrafts are obtainable from Sefarad Handicrafts, Jose Antonio Av. 54. Tel. 248-2577 & 247-6142.

MALAGA

Syn. and Com. Centre: Calle Duquesa de Parcent 8. Tel. 21-40-41. Services daily, 8 a.m., Fri. evg. 8.30 p.m., Sat. morn. 9 a.m. Min.: Rabbi Joseph Cohen.

Pres.: Elias Levy.

There is a statue of the 11th-century Hebrew poet, Shlomo lbn-Gabirol, a native of Malaga, in the gardens of Alcazaba Castle, in the heart of the city.

MARBELLA

Syn.: Beth El, 21 Calle Jazmines, Urbanizacion El Real, about 2 miles from the town centre to the east. Tel. 77-40-74, 77-07-57 or 82-49-83. Services, Fri. evg. 6.30 p.m.; Shabbat morn. & all festivals, 10 a.m. Pres.: Victor Ohayon. Mikva on premises.

Com. Centre, 7 Calle Pablo Casals in the town centre.

MELILLA (N. Africa)

Of the 14 syns. in Melilla nine are in the Barrio Poligono. They are open on festivals and the High Holy-days only. The remaining five, which are open all year round, are: Yamin Benarroch, Calle Lopez Moreno 8; Isaac Benarroch, Calle Marina 7; Jacob Almoznino, Calle Luis de Sotomayor 4; Salama, Calle Alfonso XII 6; Solinquinos, Calle O'Donnell 13.

Inq. to: Calle General Mola 19. Pres.: David Waknin.

MONTBLANC

The Jewish quarter was in the Santa Clara district, where the church was once a syn.

SANTIAGO DE COMPOSTELA

The cathedral has 24 statues of Biblical prophets framed in the so-called "Holy Door".

SEGOVIA

The Alcazar contains the 16th-century "Tower of the Jews".
Calle de la Juderia Vieja and Calle de la Juderia Nueva are the sites of the medieval Jewish quarters, where the medieval former syn. now houses the Corpus Christi Convent.

SEVILLE

Syn.: Calle del Peral 10. Services Fri. evg.
Pres.: Simon Hassan. Tel. 27-55-17.
The old syn., now the Los Venerables Sacerdotes, is in the Barrio de Santa Cruz. Seville Cathedral preserves in its treasures two keys to the city presented to Ferdinand III by the Jews.
The Columbus Archives (Archives of the Indies), 3 Queipo de Llano Av., preserve the account books of Luis de Santangel, financier to King Ferdinand and Queen Isabella.
Arco & Torreon of the Juderia, in the old Calle de la Juderia, was the gate connecting the Alcazar and the Jewish quarter.
There is a Jewish cemetery in part of the city's Christian burial ground in the Macarena district.

TARAZONA

The Juderia is near the bishop's palace.

TARRAGONA

Tarragona Cathedral, Calle de Escribanias Viejas, has in its cloister a seventh-century stone inscribed in Latin and Hebrew. Some very old coins are preserved in the Provincial Archaeological Museum. The gate to the medieval Juderia still stands at the entrance to Calle de Talavera.

TOLEDO

Though it now has no established community, Toledo is the historical centre of Spanish Judaism. Well worth a visit are two ancient former syns. One is the El Transito (in Calle de Samuel Levi), founded by Samuel Levi, the treasurer of King Pedro I, in the 14th century. It has been turned by the Spanish Government into a museum of Sephardi culture. The other, now the Church of Santa Maria la Blanca, is the oldest Jewish monument in Toledo, having been built in the 13th century. It stands in a quiet garden in what was once the heart of the Juderia, not far from the edge of the Tagus River. Also of interest is the house of Samuel Levi, in which El Greco, the famous painter, lived. The house is now a museum of his works.
Plaza de la Juderia, half-way between El Transito and Santa Maria la Blanca, was part of the city's two ancient Jewish quarters, where many houses and streets are still much as they were 500 years ago.

TORREMOLINOS

Syn.: Beth Minzi, Calle Skal La Roca 13, a small street at the seaward end of the San Miguel pedestrian precinct. Tel. 383952 (Hon. Sec.). Sephardi/Ashkenazi services held on Sabbath at 10.30 a.m.

TORTOSA

The Museum of Santo Domingo Convent preserves the sixth-century gravestone of "Meliosa, daughter of Judah of blessed memory".

TUDELA

The remains of the Juderia are near the cathedral. There is a memorial stone to the great Jewish traveller, Benjamin of Tudela.

VALENCIA

Syn.: Calle Asturias 7-4°. Services: Fri. evg. & festivals. Office: Av. Professor Waksman 9. Tel. 33-99-01. Pres.: Samuel Serfaty. Tel. 334.34.16.

VITORIA

The monument on the Campo de Judizmendi commemorates the ancient Jewish cemetery.

ZARAGOZA

This city was once a very important Jewish centre. A mikva has been discovered in the basement of a modern building at 126-132 Calle del Coso.

CANARY ISLANDS

GRAN CANARY

Syn.: Calle Leon y Castillo 238, 1st. Fl.
Pres.: Solomon Zrihen, Calle Nestor de la Torre 34. Tel. 24-84-97.

TENERIFE

There are 12 Jewish families in the island capital of Santa Cruz. An official Jewish community was formed in the town in 1972 – Comunidad Israelita de Tenerife. Pres.: Pinhas Abecassis. Tel. 24-72-96 & 24-72-46.
Jacques Benchetrit, Général Mola, 3, Santa Cruz 38006. Tel. 274157 welcomes Jewish visitors.

MAJORCA

Palma Cathedral contains some interesting Jewish relics, including a candelabrum with 365 lights, which was originally in a syn. In the "Tesoro" room are two unique silver maces over 6 feet long converted from Torah "rimonim". The Santa Clara Church stands on the site of another pre-Inquisition syn. The Montezion Church was, in the 14th century, the Great Syn. of this capital. In Calle San Miguel is the Church of San Miguel, which also stands on the site of a former syn. It is not far from the Calle de la Plateria, once a part of the Palma Ghetto.
Majorca's Jewish population today numbers about 300, although fewer than 100 are registered with the com. Founded in 1971, it was the first Jewish com. to be officially recognised since 1435. The Pres. is Joe Segal, 22-36-55. The Jewish cemetery is at Santa Eugenia, some 12 miles from Palma. The com. now has a syn., dedicated in June, 1987. It is in Calle Monseñor Palmer, and services are held on Fri. & the High Holy-days. A communal Seder is also held.

SRI LANKA

There are only 3 Jewish permanent residents in the country, but there is a somewhat larger transient Jewish population, many of them Israelis.

SURINAM

There are about 225 Jews in Surinam.

PARAMARIBO

Syns.: Sedek Ve Shalom, (Sephardi), Herenstr. 20; Neveh Shalom, (Ashkenazi), Keizerstr. 82. Services are held every Shabbat in each synagogue alternatively. Contact Pres: R. Fernandes, Commewijnestraat 21. Tel. 498324. Fax 471154.
Zorg en Hoop. Tel. 98324 for info.
Mailing address. Jewish Community, P.O.B. 1834, Paramaribo. Tel. 11998.
Mikveh facilities and Kosher bread available.

SWEDEN

In 1775 the first Jew was granted the right to live in Sweden – Aaron Isaac, of Germany, who founded the Stockholm cong. In 1782 Jews were admitted to Gothenburg and Norrköping, and the com. in Kariskrona was founded not long afterwards. After Sweden's Jews were emancipated in 1870, coms. were founded in Malmö and several other towns. There are some 16,000 Jews in Sweden. About half of them are former victims of the Nazis, and some 2,000 settled in Sweden from Poland after 1968.
General inf. from Swedish National Tourist Office, 3 Cork St., W1X 1HA. Tel. 071-437 5816.

GOTHENBURG

Syn.: Storgatan 5 (Orthodox). Östra Larmgatan 12 (Conservative, organ used). Tel. (031) 17-72-45.
Jewish Com. Centre and Com. Office: Östra Larmgatan 12. Tel. (031) 17-72-45.
Jewish Youth Org., Östra Larmgatan 12. Tel. (031) 11-18-07.
Kosher Food, Dr. Allardsgatan 4. Tel. (031) 82-13-08.

HELSINGBORG

Jewish Centre: Springpostgränden 4.

LUND

Syn.: Winstrupsgatan 1. Tel. (046) 14-80-52. Services on festivals and High Holy-days only.
Com. Centre & Students' Club (Jusil), same address & Tel. as above.
Institute for Jewish Culture, same address & Tel. as above.

MALMÖ

Syn.: Föreningsgatan (cnr. Betaniaplan), Orthodox.
Jewish Com. Centre with old-age home & com. office: Kamrergatan 11. Tel. 11-84-60 & 11-88-60.
Mikva: Kamrergatan 11. Tel. 11-88-60.
Jewish Youth Club, Kamrergatan 11. Tel. 11-84-60.
B'nei Akiva, same address as above.
B'nai B'rith club rooms, Kamrergatan 11.
Wizo, same address as above.
Kosher meat, etc.: Kosher Centre, Carl Herslowsgatan 7. Tel. 23-55-15.

STOCKHOLM

Synagogues
Adas Jeshurun (Orthodox), Riddergatan 5, Tel. 6618282.
Adas Jisroel (Orthodox), St. Paulsgatan 13. Tel. (08) 44-19-95. Rabbi Aron Katz. Tel. 6795160.
Great Synagogue (Conservative, organ used), Wahrendorffsgatan 3b. Min.: Rabbi Morton H. Narrowe, Tortstenssonsgatan 4. Tel. (08) 663-95-24. Services Mon., Thur., Fri. evg. & Sat. morn. Open to tourists Mon.-Fri., 10 a.m. & 2 p.m.

Representative Organisations
Com. Centre, Judaica House, Nybrogatan 19. Tel. (08) 663-65-66 & (08) 662-66-86. Special (K) tourist menu available Mon.-Fri., noon to 2 p.m. Prepared (K) food by arrangement. During school term time (end Aug. to mid-Dec. & mid-Jan. to end May), (K) meals can be obtained at the Scholl lunch room on the premises, & (K) snacks at the cafeteria between 5.30 &

9.30 p.m. All food is under the supervision of Rabbi Aron Katz. There is a mikva on the premises, as well as a book & gift shop.
Com. Offices, Wahrendorffsgatan 3. Tel. (08) 679 51 60. Also on premises: library & Raoul Wallenberg Room, named after the Swedish diplomat who saved scores of thousands of Hungarian Jews from the Nazis, was arrested by the Russians in Budapest in 1945 and disappeared.

Cultural Organisations, Schools, etc.
Hillel Kindergarten & Day School, Judaica House, Nybrogatan 19. Tel. (08) 662-16-11 (day school), (08) 667-88-94 (kindergarten).
Yiddish Assoc.: Nybrogatan 19. Tel. (08) 663-45-58.
Jewish Museum, Hälsingegatan 2. Tel. (08) 31 01 43.

Student & Youth Organisations
Jewish Students' Club, Judaica House, Nybrogatan 19. Tel. (08) 660-62-63.
Open house for tourists, Wed. 7 to 9.30 p.m., from June to August.
Jewish Youth Org., same address. Tel. (08) 661-72-71.

Zionist Organisations
Bnei Akiva, Judaica House, Nybrogatan 19. Tel. (08) 663-65-75.
Habonim, same address as above. Tel. (08) 660-56-90.
Keren Kayemet, same address as above. Tel. (08) 661-86-86.
Keren Hayesod, same address as above. Tel. (08) 667-67-70.
Maccabi, same address as above. Tel. 660184.
Solidarity Committee for Israel, same address as above. Tel. (08) 661 50 98.
WIZO, same address as above. Tel. (08) 661-39-91.
Zionist Federation of Sweden, same address as above. Tel. (08) 662-60-98.
Israel Embassy, Torstenssonsgatan 4. Tel. (08) 661-33-09 & (08) 663-04-35.

Travel Agencies
Ritchie Travel, Fleminggatan 33. Tel. (08) 652 52 52. Fax. (08) 650 36 00; Sabra Tours, P.O. Box 45119. Tel. (08) 662 6969. Fax 6672444.

Jewish Periodical
Judisk Krönika, P.O.B. 7427, 10391. Tel. (08) 6795160.
Menorah, P.O. Box 5053, 102 42 Stockholm. Tel. (08) 667 67 70. Fax. (08) 663 76 76.

Kosher Food & Supplies
(K) Jewish items are available at the Com. Centre shop: Menorah, Nybrogatan 19, 11439.
Frozen Kosher Meat from the U.S. can be bought at the Konsum, Sibyllegatan 8. Tel. (08) 667 47 30.
SAS, Scandinavian Airlines, serve kosher meals on all flights leaving Swedish airports for abroad, if advance notice of this requirement is given to SAS offices in Sweden or to a Swedish travel agency. Only new crockery and cutlery are used.
There are no kosher restaurants in Stockholm, but (K) lunches are served at 1 Trappa Upp, P.O. Box 5053, 10242. Tel. 6610930 under supervision of Rabbi Aaron Katz, and at the Com. Centre during the summer. (K) Dinners can be arranged at the Com. Centre for groups.

UPPSALA
Jewish Students' Club, Dalgatan 15. Tel. (08) 12-54-53.

SWITZERLAND
The Jews were expelled from Switzerland in the 15th century, and it was

not until the beginning of the 17th century that they were permitted to settle in Lengnau and Endingen. Both villages have old syns. In 1856 immigration increased, chiefly from Germany, Alsace, and Eastern Europe. The Jewish population, 3,150 in 1850, is now about 17,600. Zurich, Basle and Geneva have the largest communities.

General inf. from Swiss National Tourist Office, Swiss Centre, New Coventry St., W1V 8EE. Tel. 071-734 1921.

Swissair 1, Swiss Court, London W1V 4BJ, publish an annual 'Jewish city guide of Switzerland'.

AROSA

Kosher Hotel: **(K) Levin's Hotel Metropol.** Open July & Aug., Dec.-Apr. Tel. (081) 31-21-21. Mikva on premises and own Kosher bakery. Fax 01/291 1919

BADEN

Syn.: Parkstrasse 17. Services on Fri. evg., 18.30 (winter), 19.30 (summer), Sabbath morn. (8.45 a.m.) and all festivals. Pres.: Dr. Josef Bollag, Schartenfelsstr. 47, 5400. Tel. (042) 33-44-88 (office), (056) 21-51-28 (home). Kosher meals available at Schweizerhof and Verenahof hotels and others.

BASLE

In 1897 the first Zionist Congress was held in Basle, in the Musiksaal of the Stadt-Casino, in the Steinenberg-Barfusserplatz, and this important event is commemorated by a plaque in German & Hebrew.

Orthodox Syns.: Leimenstr. 24. 4051. Tel. (061) 272-98-50. Rabbi Dr. I. M. Levinger; Leimenstr. 45. 4051. Tel. (061) 271-60-24; Ahornstr. 14. Rabbi B.-Z. Snyders, Rudolfstr. 28. Tel. (061) 302-53-91.

Com. Centre & Hebrew Day Sch.: Leimenstr. 24, 4051. Tel. (061) 272-98-50.

Jewish Museum, Kornhausgasse 8, 4051. Tel. (061) 261-95-14. Open Sun., 10 a.m. to 12 noon & 2 to 5 p.m.; Mon. & Wed., 2 to 5 p.m.

B'nai B'rith. Inq. to Dr. J. Kertesz, Ob. Wenkenstr. 96, 4125 Riehen. Tel. (061) 676010.

Old Age Home: La Charmille, Inzlingerstr. 235, 4125 Riehen. Tel. (061) 67-00-57.

Union of Jewish Students. Inq. to Barbara Lévy, Offenburgerstr. 61, 4057. Tel. (061) 6930935.

Weekly Newspaper: "Jüdische Rundschau-Maccabi", Leonhardstr. 37. 4051. Tel. (061) 272-85-89.

Hebrew Bookshop & Gifts. Victor Goldschmidt, Mostackerstr. 17. 4051. Tel. (061) 272-65-65.

Kosher Restaurant: **(K) Topas,** Leimenstr. 24. 4051. Tel. (061) 271-87-00 (under the supervision of local rabbinical authority). Lunch and dinner available daily except Sat. night & Wed.

Kosher Butchers: **(K)** Genossenschaftsmetzgerei, Friedrichstr. 26. Tel. (061) 301-34-93. **(K)** H. Hess, Leimenstr. 41. 4051. Tel. (061) 272-88-35.

BERNE

Syn. & Com. Centre: Kapellenstr. 2. Tel. (031) 381-49-92. Min.: Rabbi Marcel Marcus, Sulgenrain 28, 3007.

Com. Pres.: L. O. Zwillenberg, Holligenstr 93, 3008. Tel. (031) 371 1905.

WIZO: Mrs. Edith Bino. Ahornweg, 50. 3028, Spiegel bei Bern, and Mrs. Brigitte Halpern, Hofmeisterstr. 7. 3006.

Israel Embassy: Alpenstr. 32. 3006. Tel. (031) 351-10-42. Consul Sect.: (031) 352-62-15.

BIEL-BIENNE

Syn., Rüschlistr. 3. Pres.: Vital Epelbaum, Bahnhofstr. 30, 2502. Tel. (032) 220262. Fax (032) 236074.

BREMGARTEN/AARGAU

Inq. to Com Pres., Werner Meyer-Moses, Ringstr 37, 5620 Bremgarten. Tel. (057) 33-66-26.

LA CHAUX-DE-FONDS

Syn. & Com. Headquarters: 63 rue du Parc. Spiritual leader: M. Margulies, 50 rue du Chapeau-Râblé, 2300.
Inq. to Com. Sec.: Laurent Sobel, 9 Rue du Chalet, 2300. Tel. (039) 28 02 19.

DAVOS

Syn. and Mikva: Etania Rest Home, Richtstattweg 3, 7270. Tel. (081) 46-54-04. Fax (081) 46 25 92. **(K)** Kosher meals available. Open all year except Nov. and May.
A range of **(K)** kosher items is available at Co-op Shopping Centre, Davos-Dorf.

ENDINGEN

Inq. to Com. Pres.: J. Bloch, Buckstr. 2, 5304. Tel. (056) 52-15-46, who can also arrange for visits to the old syns. & cemetery.

ENGELBERG

Hotel. **(K)** Marguerite. Tel. (041) 94-25-22. Open Dec.-Apr. & May-Oct. Under supervision of Agudas Achim, Zurich. Mikva on premises.
Kosher items can be obtained at the Rhyner-Fresch and Co-op stores.

FRIBOURG

Syn.: 9 Av. de Rome, 1700. Tel. (037) 23-13-70. Chazan, Claude Layani, 135 Fort St. Jacques, 1752 Villars-sur-Glâne. Tel. (037) 24-85-04 (home), (037) 25-13-12 (office).
Com. Pres.: Dr. Claude Nordmann, P.O.B. 170, 1701. Tel. (037) 31-29-20.
Société des Dames Israélites. Pres.: Hortense Bollag, 22 Beaumont, 1700. Tel. (037) 24-16-45.
WIZO: Mrs. M. P. Goutenmacher, ch. des Eaux Vives 21, 1752 Villars-sur-Glâne. Tel. (037) 24 10 37.

GENEVA

Chief Rabbi: Rabbi Dr. Alexandre Safran.
Communauté Israélite de Genève, Rabbi of Cig: Chief Rabbi David Messas, 10 rue St Léger, 1205. Tel. (022) 310-46-86. Fax (022) 3117356.

Synagogues

The Geneva Syn. (Ashkenazi), Place de la Synagogue; Hekhal Haness (Sephardi), 54 ter route de Malagnou. Tel. (022) 736-96-32. Mikva on premises; Liberal (French-speaking), 12 Quai du Seujet. Tel. (022) 732-32-45; Machsike Hadass (O), 2 Place des Eaux Vives. Tel. (022) 346-08-92.
Com. Centre: 10 rue St Léger.

Representative Organisation

World Jewish Congress, 1 rue Varembé, 1202. Tel. (022) 734-13-25.

Welfare Organisations

American Jewish Joint Distribution Com. Overseas Headquarters, 75 rue de Lyon, 1211. Tel. (022) 344-90-00.

Hias, 75 rue de Lyon, 1211. Tel. (022) 345-93-50.

Home for Aged: "Les Marroniers," 15 rue Cavour. Tel. (022) 344-87-60.

ORT, 1 rue de Varembé. Tel. (022) 734-14-34.

Zionist Organisation

WIZO. Mme. Ruth Rappaport, 14 Chemin Diodati, 1223 Cologny. Tel. (022) 736 65 73; Mme. Blanka Waechter, 36 Av. de l'Ermitage, 1224 Chêne-Bougeries. Tel. (022) 349 50 44; Mme Gabriella Lévy, 15 Chemin Rieu, 1208. Tel. (022) 347 32 85.

Clubs

Jewish students at 10 rue St Léger. Tel. (022) 310 4686.

Club Maccabi, 54 ter Route de Malagnou. Tel. (022) 736-90-15.

Kosher Food

Kosher Restaurant: **(K)** Le Jardin Rose, 10 rue St Léger. Tel. (022) 3104686.

(K) Kosher meals are available at home for aged (see above), if ordered in advance – for Shabbat, before 9.30 a.m. on Fri.

Kosher Butchers: **(K)** Bitton Maghensa, 21 rue Montchoisy. Tel. (022) 736-31-68; **(K)** Cash-Express, 5 ave Théodore Weber. Tel. (022) 735 0100.

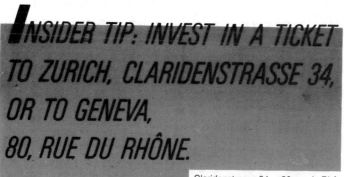

GRINDELWALD

Hotel: **(K)** Wagner-Kahn's Hotel Silberhorn. Tel. (036) 53-28-22. Fax. (036) 53 4822 Mikva on premises. Open mid-December until after Succot.

KREUZLINGEN

Oratory: Hafenstr. 42. Inf. from Ludwig Kiefe, Redingstr. 2. Tel. (072) 72-30-32.

WIZO. Inf. from Mme. Erica Marx, Langhaldenstr 6a, 8280. Tel. (072) 75-44-35.

LAUSANNE

Syn.: 1 Av. Juste-Olivier (cnr. Av. J. Olivier/Av. Florimont). Tel. (021) 320-99-11. Mikva: 1 Av. Juste-Olivier (corner Av. J. Olivier/Av. Florimont). Tel. (021) 729-98-20. Rabbi S. Morali, Beau-Séjour 28. Tel. (021) 320-54-94. P.—Werner Fink. Tel. (021) 729-65-76

Com. offices: 3, Av. Georgette. Tel. (021) 312-67-33. Com. Center and Restaurant of the Com. Center: 3 Av. Georgette. Tel. (021) 312-67-31. (serves just lunch from 12.00-2.00 p.m.). Bnai Brith: P.—Jak Er-Kohen. Tel. (021) 323-47-27.

WIZO. Inq. to Mrs. M. Guttmann. Tel. (021) 323-56-02 or Mrs. N. Schwed. Tel. (021) 617-90-90.

Union of Jewish Students: Case postale 250, 1009 Pully.

Kosher food available from Kolbo Shalom, 7 Av. Juste-Olivier. Tel. (021) 312-12-65.

LENGNAU AARGAU

(K) Home for Aged. Tel. (056) 51-12-03. Visits to old syns. & cemetery can be arranged.

LUCERNE

Syn.: Bruchstr. 51. Rabbi B. Pels, Berglistr. 22c. Tel. (041) 22-30-54. Inf. from Cantor M. Eisemann, B.A., Sälistr. 11, Tel. (041) 22-35-30, who also sells Jewish books, & Pres.: Hugo Benjamin, Bundesplatz 1, 6000. Tel. (041) 23-98-10.

Mikva: Bruchstr. 51. Tel. (041) 45-47-50.

WIZO. Inq. to Maya Bollag, Rütiweidhalde 3, 6033 Buchrain.

There is a Yeshiva at Kriens, near Lucerne (Rosh Yeshiva, Rabbi I. Kopelman). Tel. (041) 45-26-85.

Beth Jacob Seminary, Schlossweg 1. Tel. (041) 42-24-79. Princ.: Rabbi J. Ehrentreu, Bruchstr. 26. Tel. (041) 23-32-84.

Pre-packed kosher meals are available from the restaurant of the Drei Könige Hotel, Bruchstr. 35.

(K) Kosher Butcher, Bruchstr. 26. Tel. 22-25-60. Open morns. only.

LUGANO

Syn.: Via Maderno 11, Tel. (091) 23-56-98, has a mikva attached. Mikva appointments: Frau Neuman, Tel. (091) 235309. The minister is Rabbi B. Z. Rabinowitz, 5 Via Marco da Carona. Tel. (091) 23-61-34. The Pres. of the cong. is D. Heller, Via Beltramina 15. Tel. (091) 51-35-31.

WIZO. Inq. to Mme. Fritzi Esther Spitzer, Via Berna 2, 6900. Tel. (091) 23-36-86.

Kosher food obtainable from H. Pollach, via Olgiati 1. Tel. (091) 22 9955.

Kosher Hotel

(K) Hotel Dan (34), Via Domenico Fontana 1. Under supervision of Rabbi B. Z. Rabbinowitz. Tel. (091) 54-10-61. Open all year round.

ST. GALLEN

Syn.: Frongartenstr. 18. Rabbi H. Schmelzer, Dierauerstr. 2. Tel. (071) 23-59-23.

Com. Headquarters, Frongartenstr. 16. Tel. (071) 22-71-55. Com. Pres.: Dr. Roland Richter, Merkurstr. 4, 9000. Tel. (071) 22-16-14.

ST. MORITZ

(K) Bermann's Hotel Edelweiss, 7500 St. Moritz-Bad. Tel. (082) 3-55-33 or (01) 491-4595. Fax (082) 38 740 Open July-Aug. & Dec. until after Pesach. Mikva on premises.

SOLOTHURN

Inq. to Robert Dreyfus, Postfach 347, 4502. Tel. (065) 23-23-23.

VEVEY

Syn. & **(K)** Home for Aged: Les Berges du Léman, 3 Blvd. Plumhof. Tel. (021) 923-53-54. **(K)** Kosher meals available for tourists.

WINTERTHUR

Syn.: Rosenstr. 5 (Blaukreuzhaus).
Com. Pres.: Silvain Wyler, Möttelistr. 37, 8400. Tel. (052) 232-81-36 (home); (052) 232-44-02 (off.).

YVERDON

Com. Pres.: Laurent Ashenden, Chemin du Fontenay 18, 1400 Yverdon-les-Bains. Tel. (024) 21-64-77.

ZUG

(K) Restaurant Glashof, Baarerstr. 41, 6301. Tel. 042 221-24-8.

ZURICH

Synagogues & Religious Organisations

Orthodox: Agudas Achim, Erikastr. 8; Tel. (01) 463-57-98. Mikva: Tel. (01) 463-79-25. Bet Chabad, Manessestr. 198; Rabbi M. Rosenfeld. Tel. (01) 281 14 79; Israelitische Cultusgemeinde, Löwenstr. 10 (Sec., Lavaterstr. 33, 8002. Tel. (01) 201-16-59); Israelitische Religions-gesellschaft, Freigutstr. 37, 8002. Mikva: Tel. (01) 20121-80 or 201-73-06. (Sec., Manessestr 10. Tel. (01) 241 80 57); Hugo-Mendel-Stiftung, Billeterstr. 10; Minyan Sikna, Sallenbachstr. 40; Minyan Wollishofen, Etzelstr. 6. Tel. (01) 202-45-07 or (01) 482 87 51.

Liberal Cong.: Or Chadasch, Fortunagasse 13, 8001. Tel. (01) 221-11-53.

There is a Jewish prayer room in Terminal B at Zurich airport.

Representative Organisations

B'nai B'rith. Pres.: Dr. Paul Wildman. Tel. (01) 201-16-03.

Federation of Swiss Jewish Communities, Gotthardstr. 65, 8002. Tel. (01) 201-55-83.

Union of Jewish Students. For inf., contact Lavaterstr. 33, 8002. Tel. (01) 202-66-84.

Welfare Organisation

Swiss Jewish Welfare Fed., Gerechtigkeitsgasse 14, 8002. Tel. (01) 201-58-50.

Zionist Organisations

Keren Hajessod, Tel. (01) 461 6868;

Keren Kajemet Leisrael, Tel. (01) 211 5885.

Swiss Zionist Fed., (Schweizerischer Zionistenverband), Schrennengasse 37, 8003. Tel. (01) 462-04-07.

WIZO. For inf., contact Martine Barth, Zellerstr. 57, 8039. Tel. (01) 482-83-69 (home) or (01) 202-58-47 (office).

Miscellaneous Organisations

Borsalino, Jewish Discothèque & Meeting Place, Lavaterstr. 33.

Jewish Ski Club. For inf., contact Dr. David Reinisch, Postfach 285, 8027. Tel. (01) 4611125.

Maccabi Switzerland. Inq. to Dr. M. Engelmayer, Rossbergstr. 41. Tel. (01) 202-01-14 (01) 202-81-40 (off.).

Newspaper

"Israelitisches Wochenblatt" (weekly), Florastr. 14, 8008. Tel. (01) 383-70-94.

Die Judische Zeitung (weekly) Posttach 1012, 8039. Tel. (01) 201-46-17.

Jewish Bookshops: Victor Goldschmidt, Seestr. 41, 8002. Tel. (01) 202-50-44. (This is also a gift shop); Morasha, Manessestr 10. Tel. (01) 291 01 29.

Hotel

Ascot, Tessinerplatz 9, 8002. Tel. (01) 201-18-00.

Kosher Restaurant

(K) Schalom Café-Restaurant, Lavaterstr. 33 (near Enge Station). Tel. (01) 201-14-76.

(K) Restaurant Fein and Schein (dairy), also 'take away fleishig' Schontalstr. 14. Tel. (01) 241-30-40.

Kosher Food

(K) Metzgerei Adass, Löwenstr. 12. Tel. (01) 211-52-10; Taam-Metzgerei, Aemtlerstr. 8. Tel. (01) 463-90-94.

Kosher Grocer & Provision Merchants: **(K)** Aron Herzberg, Zwinglistr. 17. Tel. (01) 242-78-75. **(K)** Chaimson, Zentralstr. 10. Kosher food is also available in the grocery dept. of the Jelmoli dept. store in Bahnhofstr., near the main railway station, as well as at Pick & Pay, cnr. Lavaterstr./General Wille-Strasse.

Kosher Bakery: **(K)** Ruben Bollag's Kosher Bakery, Waffenplatzstr. 5. Tel. (01) 202-30-45; Brauerstr. 110, cnr. Hohlstr. & Feldstr. Tel. (01) 242-87-00. In addition to chalot, bread, cakes, etc., fresh & tinned kosher food is also available. Under supervision of Rabbi Daniel Levy.

Boxes of **(K)** kosher food can be purchased at Zurich airport by passengers in transit.

Miscellaneous

Israeli Arts & Crafts available from Menorah, Löwenstrasse 3 (entrance, Sihlstrasse), 8001. Tel. 211-84-34.

TAIWAN

There are more than 35 families in Taiwan, most of them living in the capital, Taipei.

TAIPEI

Taiwan Jewish Com., Com. Centre: No. 1, Lane 61, Teh Hsing E. Rd, Shihlin, Taipei. Pres.: Don Shapiro. Tel. 873-3843; Fax 886-2-3964022. Sec.: Jacques Bijo. Services are held on most Fri. evg. at 7.30 p.m. Visitors to check in advance. All Holy-days and major festivals are celebrated.

The com. holds brunches & Kabbalat Shabbat dinners several times a month. Only kosher dairy food is served at the Com. Centre. Inq. to: Don Shapiro, Tel. 396-0159 (o); 873-3843(h). Fax 396-4022, or Mrs. F. Chitayat. Tel. 861-6303.

Shabbat & festival services (Orthodox), are held at the Ritz Hotel, 41 Min Chuan E. Rd. Tel. (886-2) 597-1234. Further inf. from Rabbi Dr. E. F. Einhorn. Tel. (886-2) 591-3565

There are no kosher restaurants in Taipei, but Y.Y.'s Steakhouse has a separate kitchen & dining room, where ★ kosher meat meals are served on separate crockery, with separate cutlery. No milk products are available in this section. Chungshan N. Rd., Section 3, cnr. Teh Huei St.

THAILAND

The Jewish community of Thailand numbers about 250. Only a handful are Thai nationals, and they are of European and Asian origin.

BANGKOK

Syns.: Even Chen Syn, (O), Welcome Palace Hotel, 30 Naret Rd. Tel. 237-7920; Syn., club and kosher restaurant under supervision of Rabbi M. Dahan. Daily morn. & evg. minyan. Regular Fri. evg. & Shabbat morn., afternoon & evg. services. Light kosher meal after services. Further inf.: Yehuda Abraham. Tel. 233-5466 (office). Rony Avram. Tel. 237-1697 (office), Motti ben David. Tel. 234-0606 (office), Salim Eubani. Tel. 234-5893 (office), 318-1577 (home). Beth Elisheva Syn., 121 Soi Sai, Nam Tip 2 (Soi 22), Sukhumvit Rd. Tel. 258-2195.

The Jewish Assoc. of Thailand, Com. Centre, Beth Elisheva Syn. Bldg., address above. Tel. 258-2195. Pres.: Michael Gerson. Tel. 252-7209 252-2809 (h).

Israel Embassy, 31 Soi Lang Suan, off Ploenchit Rd. Tel. 252-3131/3.

TUNISIA

The Jewish population of Tunisia is approximately 2,000, most of whom live in Tunis. There are also some small communities, mainly in Jerba, Sfax, Sousse and Nabeul.

JERBA

There are Jews in two villages on this small island off the Tunisian coast. There is also a magnificent synagogue, El Ghriba, many hundreds of years old, in the village of Er-Riadh (Hara Sghira).

SFAX

Syn.: Azriah, 71 rue Habib Mazoun (near the Town Hall).

TUNIS

Chief Rabbi: Rabbi Haim Madar, 26 rue de Palestine. Tel. 282-406 & 283-540.

Syns.: Grande Synagogue, 43 Av. de la Liberté; Beth Yacob, 3 rue Eve. Nohelle. Tel. 348964.
Com. Offices: 15 rue du Cap Vert. Tel. 282-469 & 287-153.
Lubavitch Yeshiva. Rabbi Nison Pinson, 73 rue de Palestine. Tel. 791-429.
American Joint Distribution Com.: 101 Av. de la Liberté. Tel. 282-835 & 283-208. Local rep.: Gilles Maarek.

TURKEY

After the Expulsion of the Jews from Spain in 1492, at a time when Jews were not tolerated in most of the Christian countries of Western Europe, what was then the Ottoman (Turkish) Empire was their principal land of refuge. Last year (1992) they celebrated the 500th anniversary of the establishment of the community. Under the national constitution, their civil rights were reconfirmed. In recent years, many Jews have emigrated to Israel, Western Europe and the United States, and Turkey's Jewish population today numbers about 27,000, of whom 24,500 live in Istanbul.
General inf. from Turkish Tourist Office, 1st Floor, 170-173 Piccadilly, W1V 9DD. Tel. 071-734 8681-2.

ANKARA

Syn.: Birlik Sokak, Samanpazari. Tel. 11-62-00. This syn. is not easy to find. Off Anafartalar Caddesi in Samanpazari, there is a stairway down at the right of the T. C. Ziraat Bankasi.
The syn. is several buildings along the street on the left, behind a wall. Services every morn. Sabbath morn. services begin at 7 or 7.30 a.m. depending on the time of year.
Israel Legation, Vali Dr. Resit Caddesi, Farabi Sok, No. 43 Cankaya. Tel. 126-39-04 & 126-39-07.

BURSA

Syn.: Gerush Syn., Kurucesme Caddesi. Min.: Rabbi Uriel Arezo. Tel. 368636. Pres.: Ezra Ventura. Tel. 361584. Services, Fri. evg., Shabbat morn. & festivals. The syn. is in the old Jewish quarter. There are 180 Jews in the town.

ISTANBUL

Chief Rabbinate: Rabbi David Asseo, Yemenici Sokak, 23 Beyoglu. Tel. 144-8794 & 144-1980.

Synagogues
Ashkenazi Cong., 37 Yuksek Kaldirim. Tel. 252-2157.
Italian Cong., 29 Okcu Musa Caddesi, Galata. Tel. 244-7784.
Neve Shalom, 67 Buyuk Hendek Caddesi, near the Galata Tower (Galata Kulesi). Tel. 244-1576.
Sisli Syn., 4 Efe St., Osman Bey. Tel. 240-6599.
The syn. at the summer resort of Buyukada Island is open from June to Sept. inclusive, as well as for the High Holy-days.
Com. Centre: Buyuk Hendek, Sokak. No. 61, Galata. Tel. 244-1576.
There are also some 12 Jewish institutions in Istanbul, including a hospital, home for the aged, summer camp for children, a high school, a primary school & religion classes, as well as 4 Jewish clubs. In addition, there are several old synagogues in the Balat and Haskoy areas which are worth a visit.
The Chief Rabbinate can supply inf. about a kosher restaurant and kosher butchers.
Israel Consulate-General, Vali Konagi Caddessi, 73, Kat 4, Nisantasi. Tel. 246-4125.

Weekly: "Salom" (Turkish & Ladino). Tel. 247-3082.

IZMIR

This community, numbering 2,400, is the second largest in Turkey Its institutions include a Jewish School, a hospital and a club.
Syns.: Beth Israel, 265 Karatas St., Kanamursil District, nr. the Asansor (Lift); Bikur Holim, Esrefpasa Caddesi.
Jewish Com. Council: Azizler Sokak 920/44, Güzelyurt. Tel. 123708.
Kosher Meat: Tel. 148395, Tues. & Thurs., or inquire at syn.

UKRAINE

BERSHAD
Syn.: 25 Narodnaya Str.

CHERNIGOV
Syn.: 34 Kommunisticheskaya Str.

CHERNOVTSY
Syn.: 24 Lukyana Kobylitsa Str.

KHARKOV
Syn.: 48 Kryatkovskaya Str.

KIEV
Syn.: 29 Shchekovichnaya St. Tel. (044) 416-13-83; Reform Cong., 7 Nemanskaya St. Tel. (044) 295-65-39.

KREMENCHUG
Syn.: 50 Sverdlov Str.

ODESSA
Syn.: 3 Lesnaya St. There is also a small syn. and matzah bakery at Gazovy La., Moskovskaya St.

ZHITOMIR
Syn.: 59 Bazarnaya Str.

URUGUAY

Jewish population about 35,000, mostly living in Montevideo.

MONTEVIDEO
The central body of Uruguayan Jewry is the Comite Central Israelita, whose offices are at Rio Negro 1308, Piso 5, Esc. 9. Tel. 916057, 90-6562.
In addition, there are four separate Montevideo Kehillot, each with its own syn.:
Comunidad Israelita de Uruguay (Ashkenazi), Canelones 1084, Piso 1. Tel. 92-5750; Comunidad Israelita Hungara, Durazno 972. Tel. 90-8456; Comunidad Israelita Sefaradi, Buenos Aires 234. Tel. 96-1136, 95-4751; Nueva Congregacion Israelita (Central European), Rio Branco 1168. Tel. 90-0969, 91-1709.
Other syns.: Adat Israel, Democracia 2370; Anshei Jeshurun, Durazno 972; Bet Aharon, Harishona, Inca 2287; Vaad Ha'ir, Canelones 828; Templo Sefaradi de Pocitos L. Franzini 888; Soc. Israelite Adat Yeshurun-Alarcon 1396.
Centro Lubavitch, Av. Brasil 2704. Tel. 79-3444. Dir.: Rabbi Eliezer Shemtov.

ORT: Cuareim 1457. Tel. 983281.
Sports Club: Hebraica-Maccabi, Camacua 623. Tel. 96-1246, 96-1249.
Young Zionist Fed., Cipriano Payan 3030.
Zionist Org. of Uruguay, Hector G. Ruiz 1278, Piso 4. Tel. 983482.
Israel Embassy, Bulevar Artigas 1585-89. Tel. 404164, 404165 & 404166.
Jewish Newspaper: "Semanario Hebreo" (Spanish-language weekly),
Soriano 875/201. Tel. 92-5311. Editor J. Jerozolimski, who also directs a
daily Yiddish radio programme.
Restaurant: **La Vegetariana (Vegetarian),** San Jose 1056 and Avda. Brasil
3086.

VENEZUELA

The Jewish com. of Venezuela now numbers between 20,000 and 23,000,
about 90 per cent of whom live in Caracas, the capital, with the rest mainly
in the oil centre of Maracaibo. The earliest important Jewish settlement in
Venezuela was in the coastal town of Coro, where probably the oldest
Jewish cemetery still in use in South America is situated.
While the Coro communtiy was made up of Sephardim from nearby
Curaçao, the community in Venezuela today is about equally divided
between Sephardim and Ashkenazim.

CARACAS

There are seven syns. in Caracas, three Askhenazi and four Sephardi. The
Ashkenazi syns. are:
Great Syn. of Caracas (Gran Rabinato de Caracas). Av. Francisco Javier
Ustáriz, San Bernardino. Tel. 51-18-69. Rabbi Tzvi Laufer.
Shomrei Shabbat Assoc. Syn., Av. Anauco, San Bernardino. Tel. 51-71-97.
Min.: Rabbi Meyer Rosenbaum. Mikva.
Union Israelita de Caracas Syn. & Centre, Av. Marques del Toro, San
Bernardino. Tel. 51-52-53. Min.: Rabbi Pinhas Brener. Mikva on premises.
This is the syn. of the Ashkenazi kehilla. If notified in advance, the Union
Israelita office can arrange **(K)** kosher lunches. There is also a meat snack
bar open in the evening. Sabbath observers may wish to stay at the Hotel
Avila, which is next door to the synagogue, or the Aventura, which is a
short walk away.
The Union building also houses the C.A.I.V., the representative org. of
Venezuelan Jewry, WIZO, the Anti-Defamation League and the offices of
the newspaper, "Nuevo Mundo Israelita".
The Sephardi syns. are:
Shaare Shalom, Av. Bogota, Quinta Julieta, Los Caobos. Min.: Rabbi Isaac
Sananes.
Bet El, Av. Cajigal, San Bernardino. Tel. 52-20-08.
Keter Tora, Av. Lopez Mendez, San Bernardino.
Tiferet Yisrael, Av. Maripérez, Los Caobos. Tel. 781-19-42. Rabbi I. Cohen.
Mikva on premises.
Chabad-Lubavitch Centre, Apartado 5454, 1010A. Tel. 52-38-87.
Yeshiva Guedola de Venezuela, Quinta Lore, Av. Washington, 8, San
Bernardino. Tel. 51-41-67. There is a branch at 12a Avenida, Quinta Mi
Reina, Los Palos Grandes, ALtamira, Caracas 1062. Tel. 33 68 86.
B'nai B'rith Centre & Hillel Hse., 9na Transversal entre 7a Av. Avila,
Altamira. Tel. 32-65-96.
Kabbalat Shabbat services (Conservative) are held on the first Fri. of every
month at 8.30 p.m. Details of this and other events of interest to Anglo-
Jewish visitors are given in the "Daily Journal" (in English), which is sold
at all major hotels.
Zionist Fed., Bet-Am Bldg., Ave Washington, San Bernardino. Tel. 51-48-
52. All major Zionist orgs. are housed here.

Bakeries: Le Notre, Avenida Andres Bello, Tel. 782 4448 Pasteleria Kasher, Avenida Los Proceres, Tel. 515086. Take Away: Mini Market, Avenida Los Caobas, Tel. 7817204.

Israel Embassy & Consulate, Centro Empresarial Miranda, Av. Miranda esq. Los Ruices, Los Ruices. Tel. 2394110.

Bookshop: Libreria Cultural Maimonides, Av. Cristobal Mendoza, San Bernardino. Tel. 516356.

MARACAIBO

Syn. & Com. Centre: Associación Israelita de Maracaibo, Calle 74 No. 13-26. Tel. 70333.

Jewish School: Colegio Bilu. Address as above.

PORLAMAR

Or Meir Syn. (and Mikva) Margarita Island. Rabbi Y. El-Harrar.

VIRGIN ISLANDS (West Indies)

ST. THOMAS

There have been Jews in the Virgin Islands since the 18th century, and they played an important part in the life of the islands under Danish rule. The Virgin Islands have been American territory since 1917. Today the community numbers about 450, of whom some 125 families are affiliated to the Hebrew congregation of St. Thomas.

Inq. to Rabbi Bradd Boxman, St. Thomas Syn., P.O.B. 266, Charlotte Amalie, V.I., 00804, U.S.A. Tel. 809-774-4312. The syn. was built in 1833.

YUGOSLAVIA

(The rump of the Federal Republic of Yugoslavia at present comprises only Serbia and Montenegro. Bosnia Hercegovina, Croatia, Slovenia and Macedonia are separate republics).

Today the Jews of former Yugoslavia are estimated at no more than 6,500, organised in 25 coms. In 1941 there were about 75,000 organised in 112 coms.

General inf. from Yugoslav National Tourist Office, 143 Regent St., W1R 8AE. Tel. 071-439 0399.

BELGRADE (Beograd)

The Belgrade com. before the war numbered about 11,000. Today it numbers about 1,400.

The headquarters of the Fed. of Jewish Coms. in Yugoslavia is in 7 Juli St. 71a/lll, 11001. P.O.B. 841. Tel. 624-359 & 621-837. Fax 626-674. Pres.: David Albahari. Sec.: Miroslav Grinvald. Office of the local com. in the same bldg. on the second floor. Tel. 624-289. Pres.: Brane Popović. There is also a Jewish historical museum in 7 Juli St. 71a/l. Tel. 622-634 It is open daily from 10 a.m. to 12 noon except Mon. The syn. is at Birjuzova St. 19. (Services held on Friday evenings & Jewish holidays) In the Jewish cemetery there are monuments to fallen fighters and martyrs of fascism, and fallen Jewish soldiers in the Serbian army in the 1st World War. In 1990 a new monument to Jews killed in Serbia was erected by the Danube, in the pre-war Jewish quarter Dorcol.

NOVI SAD

Com. Offices, JNA St. 35. Tel. 613-882. Pres.: Vladimir Rotbart. Synagogue no longer open, it's reported to be extremely beautiful but is currently being converted to a concert hall! In the Jewish cemetery there is a monument to the Jews who fell in the war and the victims of fascism.

SKOPJE (Macedonia)

Since the earthquake disaster of 1963 there have been about 90 Jews in the town. The com. offices are at Borka Talevski St. 24. Tel. 237-543. Pres.: David Sadikario.

SUBOTICA

Com. offices. Dimitrija Tucovica St 13, Tel. 28-483. Pres.: Mirko Vajcenfeld.

ZAMBIA

(Jewish population 40)

MIDLANDS

Syn.: Lusaka Hebrew Cong., Chachacha Rd., Lusaka. Ch.: M. C. Galaun, P.O.B. 30299, Lusaka. Tel. 229190.

ZIMBABWE

(Jewish population approx. 977, of whom 606 live in Harare, 353 in Bulawayo, and about 18 in other centres.) The first cong. was founded in Bulawayo in 1894 & the second in Salisbury (now Harare) a year later.

BULAWAYO

Syn.: Bulawayo Hebrew Cong., Jason Moyo St. P.O.B. 337. Tel. 60829.
Central African Zionist Organisation, No. 9 Jewish Communal Centre, 41 Jason Moyo St., P.O.B. 1162. Tel. 67383-4.

HARARE

Syns.: Harare Hebrew Cong., Milton Park Jewish Centre, Lezard Av., P.O.B. 342. Tel. 727576 (office); Sephardi Cong., Josiah Chinamano Av., P.O.B. 1051. Tel. 722899 (office); Progressive Jewish Cong., P.O.B. 828. Tel. 726434 (office).
Com. Centre: Lezard Av. Tel. 727576.
Central African Jewish Board of Deputies, P.O.B. 342. Tel. 723647.
Central African Zionist Organisation, P.O.B. 1954. Tel. 702506-7.
Union of Jewish Women, P.O.B. 2518.

VEGETARIAN ORGANISATIONS

Extensive information in this section has been compiled with the aid of the Vegetarian Society of the U.K. Ltd., Parkdale, Dunham Rd., Altrincham, Ches. WA14 4QG. Tel. 061-928 0793, whose Vegetarian Travel Guide has been invaluable (edited by Jane Bowler at £4.50 + £1.50 p&p). The Society's magazine gives up to date information on hotels, restaurants etc. More detailed inf. is available from the Society. (Please send a large stamped addressed envelope – 2 x 18p. stamps.) Intending visitors should always inquire first whether accom. is available and not just assume that it is.

There is also a **Jewish Vegetarian & Natural Health Society** affiliated to the international Vegetarian Union. All inq. to the Sec., International H.Q., Bet Teva, 853-855 Finchley Rd., London NW11 8LX. Tel. 01-455 0692.

★ Dining room open Sun. 12 noon to 3 p.m. & 6 p.m. to 10 p.m., & Mon.-Thurs. 6 p.m. to 10 p.m.

A selection of restaurants, B&B and hotels has been included throughout the U.K. section.

OTHER COUNTRIES

The Vegetarian Travel Guide has an extensive section on facilities for vegetarians overseas and lists vegetarian restaurants in a large number of countries. It recommends "the Vegetarian Passport" compiled by the Dutch Vegetarian Society (De Nederlandse Vegetariesbond, Larensweg 26, 1221 CM Hilversum) as a very comprehensive book which should help you to get by almost anywhere in the world.

The following is a list of national vegetarian societies.

ARGENTINA

Argentinian Vegetarian Society, Sarmiento 1371, Piso No. 705, 1041 Buenos Aires.

AUSTRALIA

The Australian Vegetarian Society, P.O.B. 65, Paddington NSW 2021. Tel. 02349-4485.
The Jewish Vegetarian Society, 6/3 Ocean Rd, Bondi, NSW 2062.

AUSTRIA

Ôsterreichische Vegetarier Union, Leechgassen 2, A-8010, Graz.

BELGIUM

Association Internationale des Vegetariens de Langue Française, 25 Avenue Chazal, 1030 Brussels. Tel. 733-6288.
Vegetariersbond van Belgie, Rozenlaan 11, 2232 Schilde. Tel. 03353-6485.

CANADA

Vegetarian Awareness Network (Vegenet). Tel. 800-3288343.

CZECH REPUBLIC

Czech Vegetarian Society, c/o Peter Pribus, Kubelikova 17, Cz 13000 Prague.

DENMARK

Vegetarence Omsorgs and Statteforening, Riskar 14, Smørumndre, 2765 Måløv Smørumneøre.
Dansk Vegetar and Rakostforening, NY Vestergårdsvej 6, 3500 Vaerløse. Tel. 42-48-0267.

FRANCE
Alliance Vegetarienne (ALLVEG), Alvignac 46500 Gramat. Tel. 8533-63-33

GERMANY
Vegetarier-Bund Deutschlands, e.V. Bloemenstrasse 3, D-3000 Hannover. Tel. 0511-42-46-47.

HONG KONG
Hong Kong Vegetarians and Friends, 16 Green Villas, Takuling San Tsuen, Clearwater Bay, 190104 Kowloon. Tel. 3-719-0104.

INDIA
The Indian Vegetarian Congress, National HQ, 1 Eldams Rd, 600018 Madras. Tel. 450-364.
The 1992 World Vegetarian Congress is to be held in India.

IRELAND
The Vegetarian Society of Ireland, 31 Pembroke Rd, Ballsbridge, Dublin 4. Tel. 983-489.

ISRAEL
Israeli Vegetarian Society, Leventin 2, P.O.B. 2352, 61022 Tel Aviv.

ITALY
Associazione Vegetariana Italiana, Dott Via XXV Aprile 41, 20026 Novate Milanese, Milan.

JAMAICA
Vegetarian Society of Jamaica Ltd, c/o 36 Calypso Crescent, Caribbean Terrace, WI Kingston.

JAPAN
Japanese Vegetarian Union, c/o Japan Medical Centre, 718 Dalsen, 410-21 Nirayama. Tel. 5597-85849.

NEW ZEALAND
New Zealand Vegetarian Society Inc., Box 77-034, Auckland 3.

NORWAY
Norges Vegetariske Landsforbund, Munkedamsveien 3B, 0161 Oslo 1. Tel. 02782-258.

PORTUGAL
Associacao Vegetariana Portuguesa, Sede Provisoria, Rua do Salitre 136. Lisbon 1.

SINGAPORE
Food Reform Vegetarian Information Service, Blk 508 West, Coast Drive No. 6-257, 0512 Singapore.

SOUTH AFRICA
Vegetarian Society of South Africa, P.O.B. 23567, Joubert Park, 2044 Johannesburg. Tel. 642-7471.

SPAIN
Federacion Naturists Vegetariana Española, P.O.B. 5326, 08080 Barcelona. Tel. 93-215-6088.

SRI LANKA
Sri Lanka Vegetarian Society, 17 Beach Rd, Kotuwegoda, Matara.

SWEDEN
Svenska Vegetariska Foreningen, Radmansgarten 88, 113 29 Stockholm. Tel. 324929.

SWITZERLAND
Arbeitskreis fur Lebenserneuerung, Schwarzenbachweg 16, CH-8049 Zurich. Tel. 01-341-88-47.

THAILAND
Thai Vegetarian Society, Sannak Poo Sawan 270, Soi 65, Petchkasem Rd, Khet, Pasicharoen 10160, Bangkok.

USA
North American Vegetarian Society (NAVS), P.O.B. 72, Dolgeville, 13329.
Vegetarian Awareness Network (Vegenet), P.O.B. 76390. Tel. 202-347-8343 and 800-872-8343.
International Jewish Vegetarian Society, P.O.B. 144, Hurleyville, New York 12747.

HOLIDAY CAMPS
GREAT BRITAIN

Bnei Akiva. Head Office: 2 Halleswelle Rd., NW11 0DJ. Tel. 081-209 1319. Leeds Youth Centre: Palestrant Hse., Street Lane Gdns., Street Lane, LS17. Tel. 0532 688290 or 695347. Manchester Youth Centre: 72 Singleton Rd., Salford, M7 0LU. Tel. 061-740 1621. **(K)** Winter & summer camps. Contact the camps director, Jonny Ross for further details.

Camp Aguda, Stamford Hill, N16 5DN. Tel. 081-800 6688 & 081-800 0338. **(K)** Camps arranged in two sections for boys: Pirchim (9-15), and Zeirim (15 upwards), in England & on the Continent. Branch office: 35a Northumberland St., Salford, M7, Lancs.

(K) Ezra Youth Movement, a Alba Gdns., NW11 9NR. Tel. 081-458 5372. Junior camp, 8-13, in England. Separate intermediate camps for boys & girls, 14-18, in England, Europe & Israel.

Habonim-Dror Camps. 523 Finchley Rd., NW3 7BD. Tel. 071-435 9033. Fax: 071-431 4503. Camps for ages 9-22 in Britain, France, Holland & Israel over summer & winter holidays. Year scheme in Israel for post-'A' level students.

Hanoar Hatzioni (Zionist Youth Movement). ★ Head Office: 31 Tetherdown, Muswell Hill, N10 1ND. Tel. 081-883 1022-3. Annual summer & winter camps in England. Age groups, 7-17. Holidays in Israel. Age group, 15½+. Jewish educational seminars monthly, weekly activities.

Kibbutz Representatives. 1A Accommodation Rd., NW11 8ED. Tel. 081-458 9235; Kibbutz Ulpan & working programmes all year round. Summer schemes.

Mizrachi-Hapoel Hamizrachi. Gen. Sec.: Simon Kritz. **(K)** Family holiday schemes, tours to Israel, seminars. 2b Golders Green Rd., NW11 8LH. Tel. 081-455 2243/4.

Union of Jewish Students. B'nai B'rith-Hillel Hse., 1-2 Endsleigh St., WC1H 0DS. Tel. 071-380 0111. Fax 071-383 0390. Seminars & week-end schools for students. Summer holiday schemes in Israel.

ABROAD

CAEJ British European Centre for Jewish Youth, rue Marbeuf, 75008 Paris, France. Tel. 472-08-125. Winter sports & holidays with Jewish families in Paris and the U.S.A. Also, kosher hotel in French Alps, under supervision of the Beth Din.

★ **CCVL Centres Culturels de Vacances et de Loisirs**, w rue de Téhéran, 75008 Paris, France. Tel. 331-4563 4981. Fax 331-4562 1612. Group holidays for children & teenagers, Feb., Mar., Apr., Jul., Aug. Kosher. Sporting, cultural & Jewish activities. Also for families, Passover & summer.

Merkos L'Inyonei Chinuch: Via Carlo Poerio 35, 20129 – Milan, Italy. Pres.: Rav G. M. Garelik. Tel. 02-225213. Hebrew Day School, Yeshiva & High Sch., Kindergarten, Talmud Torah, Tel. 02-5392010; Chabad House Via Fratelli Bronzetti 18. Tel. 02-713682. Lubavitch Youth Org. Tel. 02-7610531. Summer and winter camps for boys & girls aged 7-13 and summer Yeshiva for boys in Pieve Di Camaiore. Tel. 0584-981266 or 02-7610531. Publications Tel. 02-225213. Chabad House in Venice, (Ghetto). Kosher food available. Tel. 041-716214.

OSE-Italia: **(K)** Viale Trastevere 60, Rome. Tel. 581-6486. Camps, during July & Aug. at Caletta, nr. Leghorn (for children 6-13) and Goria de Veleso, Como (Colonia Enzo Sereni), for children 5-12.

BOOKSELLERS

The booksellers listed below specialise in Jewish books. Many also supply religious requisites.

GREATER LONDON

J. Aisenthal, 11 Ashbourne Pde., Finchley Rd., NW11. Tel. 081-455 0501.

Blue and White Shop, 6 Beehive La., Gants Hill, Ilford, Essex, IG1 3RD. Tel. 081-518 1982.

Carmel Gifts, 62 Edgware Way, Edgware, Middx. Tel. 081-958 7632. Fax 081-958 6226.

R. Golub & Co. Ltd., 305 Eastern Av., Gants Hill, Ilford, Essex, IG2 6NT. Tel. 081-550 6751.

Aubrey Goldstein, 7 Windsor Court, Chase Side, N14 5HT. Tel. 081-886 4075.

Dillons The Bookstore, 82 Gower St., WC1E 6EG. Tel. 071-636 1577.

Hebrew Book & Gift Centre, 18 Cazenove Rd., N16 6BD. Tel. 071-254 3963 (day) & 081-802 4567 (evg.).

B. Hirschler, 62 Portland Av., N16 6EA, & 71 Dunsmure Rd., N16 5PT. Tel. 081-800 6395. Also maps, ceremonial art, etc.

J. Hochhauser, 61 Lordship Pk., N16 5UP. Tel. 081-800 8804.

Jerusalem the Golden, 146a Golders Green Rd., NW11 8HE. Tel. 081-455 4960 or 458 7011. Fax: 081-203-7808.

Jewish Books & Gifts (Sandra E. Breger), Rosecroft Walk, Pinner, Middx., HA5 1LJ. Tel: 081-866 6236.

Jewish Chronicle Bookshop, 25 Furnival St., EC4A 1JT. Tel. 071-405 9252.

Jewish Memorial Council, Books Dept., 2nd Floor, Woburn Hse., Upper Woburn Pl., WC1H 0EP. Tel. 071-387 3081.

J. T. Books, 13 Sentinel Sq., Brent St., NW4 2EL. Tel. 081-203 6350. Fax: 081-203-6712.

Kuperard (London) Ltd., No. 9 Hampstead West, 224 Iverson Rd., NW6 2HL. Tel. 071-372 4722. Fax: 071-372 4599. (Also distributors and direct mail).

Manor House Bookshop and J. T. Books (Rare out of print Judaica), 80 East End Rd., N3 2SY. Tel. 081-349 9484.

Menorah Book Centre, 16 Russell Parade, Golders Green Rd., NW11. Tel. 081-458 828.

Muswell Hill Bookshop, 72 Fortis Green Rd., N10 3HN. Tel. 081-444 7588.

George & Vera Nador, 63 Cranbourne Rd., Northwood, Middx., HA6 1JZ. Tel. 0923-821152. Rare Hebraica, Judaica, maps. By appointment only.

M. Rogosnitzky, 20 The Drive, NW11 9SR. Tel. 081-455 7645 or 4112.

Selfridges Departmental Store, Jewish Section of Book Dept., Oxford St., W1A 1AB. Tel. 071-629 1234.

S. Simpson, 1a Granville Rd., N. Finchley, N12 0HJ. Tel. 081-445 6723.

Stamford Hill Stationers, 153 Clapton Common, E5 9AE. Tel. 081-802 5222.

Swiss Cottage Books, 4 Canfield Gdns., NW6 3BS. Tel. 071-625 4632.

W. H. Smith, Brent Cross Shopping Centre, NW4. Tel. 081-202 4226.

Waterstone's Booksellers Ltd., 68 Hampstead High St., NW3 1QP. Tel. 071-794 1098.

REGIONS
BIRMINGHAM

Lubavitch Bookshop, 95 Willows Rd., B12 9QF. Tel. 021-440 6673. Fax 021-446 4199.

GATESHEAD

J. Lehmann, 20 Cambridge Ter., NE8 1RP. Tel. 091-490 1692.

GLASGOW

J. & E. Levingstone, 47 & 55 Sinclair Dr., G42 9PT. Tel. 041-649 2962.

LEICESTER

Bookshop: Com. Centre, Highfield St., LE2 0NQ. Inq.: J. Markham, 74 Wakerley Rd., LE5 6AQ. Tel. 0533 737620.

LIVERPOOL

Book & Gift Centre, Jewish Youth & Community Centre, Dunbabin Rd., L15 6XL. Sun. only, 11 a.m. to 1 p.m.

MANCHESTER & SALFORD

J. Goldberg, 11 Parkside Av., Salford, M7 0HB. Tel. 061-740 0732.
Hasefer, 18 Merrybower Rd., Salford, M7 0HE. Tel. 061-740-3013
B. Horwitz, (Wholesale & retail Judaica), 20 King Edward Bldgs., Bury Old Rd., M8. Tel. 061-740 5897, & 2 Kings Rd., Prestwich. Tel. 061-773 4956.
Jewish Book Centre (Terence Noyek), 25 Ashbourne Gr., Salford, M7 0DB. Tel. 061-792 1253.

OXFORD

B. H. Blackwell Ltd., 48-51 Broad St., OX1 3BQ. Tel. 0865 792792, has a Jewish book section.

SOUTHEND

Dorothy Young, 21 Colchester Rd., SS2 6HW. Tel. 0702 331218 for appointment.

M

N

O

ADVERTISERS' INDEX

BANKS

BOOKSELLERS AND PUBLISHERS

HOTELS AND GUEST HOUSES

MISCELLANEOUS

RESTAURANTS & DELICATESSEN

TRAVEL AGENTS

Readers' Comments

In the interests of making *The Jewish Travel Guide* as up-to-date and, thus, as useful as possible, the Editor would welcome readers' comments and/or current information about any of the establishments listed in this edition.

Please write giving the name and address of the establishment as listed, together with your comments or relevant up-to-date details to:

> The Editor
> The Jewish Travel Guide
> Vallentine Mitchell & Co. Ltd.
> 11 Gainsborough Road
> London E11 1RS